THE SOCIAL ENVIRONMENT
A PRIMER ON WORLD CIVICS

THIRTEENTH EDITION

Germán Muñoz
Paul S. George
Phyllis Baker
David M. Shaheen
Michael Lenaghan
Víctor Vázquez-Hernández

Workbook By: Magdalena Rivera-Lamarre

Learning Solutions

New York   Boston   San Francisco
London   Toronto   Sydney   Tokyo   Singapore   Madrid
Mexico City   Munich   Paris   Cape Town   Hong Kong   Montreal

Pearson Learning Solutions, 501 Boylston Street, Suite 900, Boston, MA 02116
A Pearson Education Company
www.pearsoned.com

Printed in the United States of America

5 6 7 8 9 10 V092 15 14 13 12

000200010270593890

CY/JG

ISBN 10: 0-558-86463-5
ISBN 13: 978-0-558-86463-7

Table of Contents

Preface

The Social Environment was originally written with the college student in mind, utilizing Miami-Dade College's core course "The Individual and the Social Environment" as a model for the development, content, and organization of the material. This course was wisely designed by the college to give all students, regardless of their academic majors and levels of achievement, basic knowledge on culture, government, economics, and international affairs, to instill in them a life-long love of learning and inquiry, and to prepare them to better exercise the rights and duties of citizenship. We now believe that third and fourth-year college students also need exposure to the content of this book.

The Social Environment is a comprehensive, critical, multicultural and global approach to the study of the individual in his or her relationship to the social environment. The book is an academic response to the forces of globalization which are changing both the social environment and the ways in which it is interpreted and understood. The highlights of the book include the following: introduces students to the social sciences as analytical tools within the context of the wider field of knowledge; applies social science concepts in a multicultural framework; balances content on American society with information on other national groups; and ends with a review of major current events from a geopolitical perspective to keep students and faculty up-to-date on political and economic issues worldwide. **This is the only introductory social science textbook with an annually revised, updated section on global current affairs.**

We are convinced that our textbook, **The Social Environment,** will help faculty and students achieve their respective goals of teaching and learning. First, its chapters address the competencies, or content objectives, which students must master to successfully complete the course, as specified by the College-wide Core Course Review Committee. Second, the authors of the Social Environment have been teaching this class since its inception, and actually collaborated in creating the competencies for the course. As a result, they are well-informed about the academic needs of M-DC students, as well as of college students in general. And third, the five writers, all of whom have doctorates either in history, anthropology, sociology and political science have extensive expertise in introducing and explaining social science concepts within a liberal arts, multidisciplinary, and multicultural framework which encourages critical thinking. **The Social Environment** represents the academic work of seven scholars teaching in the largest college in the United States which hosts students from over eighty countries, a truly global institution. Some of us also teach at such institutions as Florida Atlantic University, Florida International University, St. John Vianney College Seminary, and Universidad Hayek.

We recognize Professor Magdalena Rivera-Lamarre who has made valuable suggestions and who is responsible for the development of our workbook. We are also grateful to the following people for the support they have always given to our academic activities: Dr. Eduardo J. Padron, District President of Miami-Dade College; our social science colleagues throughout the eight campuses of MDC; and our secretaries Anabel Farinas, Rosa Padron, Yusimi Sijo, Debbie Yi, Natalie Echavarria, Samuel Lopez, Elisa Melendez, and Beverly Ozores.

—Phyllis Baker, Ph.D
Paul George, Ph.D
Michael Lenagha, Ph.D
Germán Muñoz, Ph.D
David M. Shaheen, Ph.D
Víctor Vázquez-Hernández Ph.D

CHAPTER ONE

Core Principles

Thinking Critically, Multiculturally, and Globally

Phyllis Baker

Welcome to the study of the *Social Environment*. This is a course full of adventure, exploration, and opportunities for intellectual development and overall personal growth. The revolution in communications and information of the latter part of the 1900s and early 2000s, more powerful than prior revolutions in agriculture and industry, has brought us greater awareness of our social and cultural diversity, and greater recognition of the growing interconnectedness of all human beings. Modern scholars have traveled to every continent and discovered the remarkable diversity in the ways humans organize their societies to survive natural disasters, food scarcities, political conflicts, loneliness, and alienation. They have also found behind these apparent social differences many similar types of behaviors, which reflect our common human nature, fears, desires, and hopes.

As technology grows in sophistication and the world shrinks in space and time, we should be able to better learn from each other and about each other. This knowledge can be both terrifying and promising. It is terrifying because in our search for understanding, we become aware of so many global problems: population explosions in many poor countries which cannot feed their people, and population implosions in developed countries which will find it harder to pay for the retirements of future generations; ethnic, political, and civil unrest throughout the world; the potential for biological, chemical, and nuclear disasters; the killing of the weak among us by the powerful over us; the spreading of viruses worldwide; and the irresponsible use of human and natural resources, among others.

Yet, there is also much that is promising. Wisdom, charity, and courage are also part of the human equation. We can also act harmoniously to address many of these common problems. The important question is whether as the planet becomes smaller and the population larger we can coexist and live peacefully and effectively together. The answer will depend on whether as we learn more about each other, people will also be willing to wisely respect each other's differences and to search for enlightened ways to satisfy everyone's basic human needs.

Our book the *Social Environment* is an introduction to the cultural, social, political, and economic concerns which affect all of us. We hope it will stimulate greater understanding about human social interaction. The academic disciplines used to achieve this goal include philosophy, history, anthropology, sociology, economics, political science, geography, and international relations. However, we do not just want to expose you to a vast amount of information to enhance your sense of culture. Neither do we want you to behave in a particular political or social way after you have finished reading the book. What we really want is for you to learn how to think critically, multiculturally, and globally. This type of thinking resulting from a life-long effort at intellectual improvement gives one a better chance to understand the truth in a particular social situation. There is no better way to achieve this than through the interaction in class when students, teachers, and authors participate in discussions in constructive ways.

Critical Thinking

Critical thinking is the ability to conceptualize and synthesize information in the most careful, exact, logical, and analytical manner. This book is on thinking about the social environment. The process of critical thinking involves various mental modalities: **recall**—memorization of what was said, done, read, or experienced; **similarity**—searching for likeness, common denominators, bonds and connections between things and events; **differences**—observing points of departures, how ideas, experiences, events and people are not alike, and what makes them unique; **cause and effect**—making educated predictions as a result of tracing an effect back to its cause; **generalization**—narrowing down, isolating, and predicting possible outcomes of an event or situation; **substantiation**—stating what ideas or facts support an assumption; and **synthesis**—blending and evaluating the best information available at the time.

The following intellectual tasks exemplify the many mental operations the mind performs when engaged in critical thinking. You will be performing some of these functions as you read the book and do some of the assignments in the workbook: **analyze**—break into separate parts and discuss, examine, or interpret each part; **compare**—examine two or more things. Identify similarities and differences; **contrast**—show differences. Set in opposition; **criticize**—make judgments. Evaluate comparative worth; **define**—give the meaning of whatever you are studying; **describe**—give a detailed account. Make a picture with words. List characteristics, qualities, and parts; **discuss**—consider and debate or argue the pros and cons of an issue. Write about any conflict. Compare and contrast; **enumerate**—list several ideas, aspects, events, things, qualities, reasons, etc.; **evaluate**—give your opinion or cite the opinion of an expert. Include evidence to support the evaluation; **illustrate**—give concrete examples. Explain clearly by using comparisons or examples; **interpret**—comment upon, give examples, describe relationships. Explain the meaning. Describe, then evaluate; **outline**—describe main ideas, characteristics, or events; **prove**—support with facts; **state**—explain precisely; **summarize**—give a brief,

condensed account, include conclusions, avoid unnecessary details; and **trace**—show the order of events or progress of a subject or event.

When you perform all these mental operations, you will be maximizing your capacity to think critically. Critical thinking implies a deep level of thought, evaluation, reasoning, and decision-making. **It requires humility, flexibility, patience, courage, and open-mindedness.** Humility is essential for you to listen to what others have to say and teach you. Flexibility is necessary for changing your mind when you are wrong and for pursuing other paths. Patience is crucial for there are many truths for which we are not yet ready. However, with hard work and some good fortune we will be receptive to them one day. Courage is important for asking unpopular questions and accepting controversial results. Open-mindedness is required to be open to new ideas and inspiration. Rigid, proud thinkers have great difficulty understanding what is real. They tend to exclude valuable information in their intellectual processing. We must realize that often we allow our perceptions and judgments to be distorted by our individual experiences, emotions, and prejudices, as well as by the cultural premises we use.

Multiculturalism

A second motive of our book is to help you to think multiculturally. True, there are many definitions of multiculturalism, some mostly applicable to the area of the academic curriculum, others to the political question of how societies should treat their diverse populations. **For us, multiculturalism is an intellectual method of understanding reality by studying one's subject matter from a wide range of points of view, including those premises, values, attitudes, and beliefs used by other cultures to explain their existence and to organize their lives.** This multicultural approach to knowledge is crucial not necessarily because one needs to respect and like every other culture, or enhance the self-esteem of a wide variety of people by looking at the world the way they do.

Intellectual multiculturalism is necessary because for one to be truly educated and have a chance to understand the social environment, it is essential to get as complete a picture as possible of whatever topic is under study. The scholar must be attentive to a wide variety of facts and to as many world-views as possible to fully understand human beings and their interaction with each other. This is what we mean by intellectual and methodological multiculturalism. It is a means of understanding reality rather than a tool of political ideology to change or reform the world. We want to increase your understanding of the social environment. How you act afterwards is your own private matter.

Multiculturalism as an educational movement became popular during the 1970s. Its original focus was to include in the American educational curriculum the works and experiences on non-European people. ***Academic multiculturalism* in this context is an educational program recognizing past and present cultural diversity in U.S. society and promoting the equality of all cultural traditions.** This attempt to widen the canon of the great books required to be read at school is wise since not only did the traditional curriculum neglect the life experiences of non-Western individuals, but it also underrepresented certain aspects of the Western experience itself.

Therefore widening the scope of the curriculum is a good idea. The difficult part is determining which topics or books should be included in the curriculum for there is not enough time to cover every subject equally. This is a political decision for each community to make. Unfortunately, some critics of the traditional and limited list of great works of the Western world, instead of widening the educational offerings by including classics from other cultures, actually want to eliminate from the curriculum the canon of the Western books. This exclusion is a mistake for it does not help students broaden their minds by learning about a wide range of human perspectives.

Political Multiculturalism refers to a society in which different racial and ethnic groups maintain their distinctive cultures, yet live together in mutual harmony, tolerance, and respect. This type of political multiculturalism believes that society should highlight the cultural differences of its diverse members to enrich itself. Critics of this form of multiculturalism respond that society should stress the common cultural elements to avoid conflicts and divisiveness, and to ensure that people do not evaluate ideas according to the race, sex, ethnicity, or religion of those who present them.

Both educational and political multiculturalism are issues which require judicious critical thought so they can be discussed productively. Each community will have to reach some sort of compromise on these matters. Our book does not take a position on them. However, we do encourage you to develop intellectual multiculturalism so that your analysis of any topic has a mastery built on the calm absorption of perspectives and facts that transcend the cultural divide.

Globalization

Our third major goal is to make you think globally. **Globalization is a worldwide process by which people, markets, corporations, and countries are being integrated to an unprecedented degree in a way that is enabling them to reach around the world farther, faster, deeper, and cheaper.** It will probably overcome in importance the agricultural revolutions of 8000 B.C., and the industrial revolutions of the 1700s and 1800s. The effects of globalization are just beginning to be felt. You can be sure that every human institution will be touched by them just like these two prior revolutions destroyed and created societies and their cultures. The symbol of this earth-shaking event is the World Wide Web that opens up a universe of information and unites many, both physically and in cyberspace.

Globalization is made possible by the rise in international trade, investment, and banking, and by the astounding improvements in transportation and communications during the 1900s. At the core of it is the revolution in information made possible by the invention of the microchip and computer technology. They increase dramatically human possibilities in gathering, classifying, evaluating, interpreting, and communicating information beyond territorial and national limits. Globalization will be very favorable in some areas and to some people, and will be very devastating in other areas and to other people. Society should try to minimize its unintended negative consequences, particularly its effects on those most hurt by it. However, it cannot be stopped. It is our purpose to help you understand it and deal with it.

The oil crises of 1973 and 1979 which raised the price of oil over 400% brought a new level of awareness and respect for international market forces. It taught us how a decision made or a problem experienced in one part of the world can have tremendous implications for those in other parts of the world. Many countries went bankrupt by the actions of a few. As a result, there is an ever-growing realization that many problems are not restrained by international borders. A devaluation in the Brazilian currency makes it harder for Brazilians to buy dollars and visit Miami or Disney World in Orlando. Many in Miami and Orlando then will lose their jobs, which are very dependent on tourism. The Asian Crisis of 1997 and 1998 scared many international investors who then proceeded to take their investment out of Russia and Latin America, creating crises in those two regions.

Critics of globalization fear that less industrialized and capitalized societies and economies may experience several negative by-products from market globalization. They fear mounting inequalities and exploitation due to the fact that less capitalized societies cannot compete fairly with the more affluent societies. They fear that this produces a win/lose scenario where the rich become richer, and the poor become poorer. Or they believe that the increased alienation of culture may also be a result. In order to raise more capital, less affluent societies are encouraged to grow and produce less of what is desired locally to accommodate those who are able to purchase the most from far away. In many cases, the local people begin to embrace those products (many of which they can't afford) and traditions of the more economically affluent societies. This could cause abandonment or alienation from the cultural practices previously honored and respected. This sets off the cycle and process of deculturalization or the stripping away of culture. Another concern is about the over usage of resources. In order to earn sufficient capital, the less affluent societies are encouraged to use more and more of their vital and valuable natural resources such as water, top soil, trees, and grain to accommodate, ever-expanding markets. This over usage is done primarily to export products to the more economically prosperous societies. This produces a dwindling natural resource level for the people in the poorer local communities.

On the other hand, supporters of globalization believe that this process will force societies to be more productive to compete in the global market place. The need to compete effectively will pressure them to be more open and honest about their political and economic transactions for otherwise they will not attract and retain foreign investment. Globalization will also tend to free some groups, women for example, from some of the customs which keep them from education and the job market. All human resources will then be more appreciated. Destruction of environmental resources is always a possibility, but as countries become more prosperous and modernized hopefully they will learn to protect them by using them more efficiently.

We do not take a political position on globalization, except to say that societies should promote the development of all their human resources, which means, among other things, that they should compassionately but also wisely address the needs of those who do not fare well in the process of globalization. Where we take a position is in affirming the necessity of the reader to think globally, to understand that the world is interconnected, and actions in one place can have reactions in another. In the social environment, events do not tend to take place in isolation.

CHAPTER TWO

The Human Struggle for Knowledge, Understanding and Wisdom:

The Humanities, the Natural Sciences, and the Social Sciences

Germán Muñoz

Ignorance and Knowledge

Imagine yourself setting camp by the Nile River in Egypt or by the Yellow River in China. It is 8000 B.C. After eating the remains of a dead animal, your tribe goes to sleep by the banks of the river. Suddenly a flood drowns everyone. Or picture yourself part of a victorious warrior group in Babylonia around 1753 B.C. celebrating your success by engaging in sexual orgies with prostitutes who give you venereal diseases which will gradually destroy your mental faculties and kill you. Or see yourself as a Taino, an Amerindian, rowing peacefully through the Caribbean Basin in the 1300s A.D. and welcoming a group of Carib Indians who, taking advantage of your friendliness, knock you unconscious and eat you alive. Or think of yourself as a young Maya virgin in Guatemala in the 1400s who is pushed off a cliff 500 feet to her death as a sacrifice to the Gods for the sake of rain.

Or conceive yourself as an Inca in the Andes region of South America in the 1540s, who comes too close to a Spaniard with the flu or with smallpox or some other disease and within days dies together with the entire village as you lack immunological resistance to these diseases or medicines which can help you survive. Or visualize yourself as a young African in the 1600s captured by Arab,

European, or even African slave hunters, who then proceed to ship you across the Atlantic or send you across Africa to the Middle East where you will live as an enslaved animal. You never see your family again. Or form an idea of yourself as a woman in the American Southwest in the 1700s whose major purpose in life as is defined by the society is procreating and who dies in childbirth delivering her thirteenth child. Or finally, see yourself as one of the over 150 million people murdered in the 1900s by radical ideologies which despised you because of your nationality, religion, social class, political identification, race, or ideology.

All these cases have one thing in common. You are a victim of your own ignorance or that of others. In this world, the consequences of ignorance can be deadly. It could be ignorance of the rhythms of the seasons and of the waters, of venereal diseases, of human treachery and cruelty, of the consequences of viruses and bacteria, of technologies of self-defense useful for physical security or for the attainment of basic human needs, and of the inherent, universal dignity of every human being. Ignorance is associated with starvation, genocide, murder, wars, oppression, lower quality of life, and a short life expectancy. Ignorance about the physical world, about our inner selves, and about the motivation and behavior of others is part of the human condition. It undermined the survival and well-being of primitive humans. It is still having devastating effects today.

Fortunately, we seem to be "wired" for acquiring knowledge. Much of the knowledge we are constantly seeking is of a practical nature, that is, it is designed to make or do things, and to achieve some mastery over the forces of the physical world. This **practical knowledge** has allowed humans to make remarkable things throughout history: wheels, snow shoes, clothes, fire, bows and arrows, canoes, ships, houses, roads, bridges, canals, agriculture, metals, machines, and many other things.

All of these products have been made to increase our security, leisure, and personal and social well-being. Humans have also used their practical knowledge to perform incredible feats: survived dramatic climate changes, crossed deserts, climbed gigantic mountains, navigated oceans, spread throughout every continent, travelled to the moon, created civilizations, learned to live in cities, and manipulated nature enough to achieve impressive growth in population.

Another type of knowledge is of a theoretical or speculative nature, that is, it is an expression of our human curiosity, of our distinctively human desire to understand for the sake of understanding, for the sake of its own pleasure, without any immediate practical use. This passion to know and to understand can be seen clearly in the young child who is always asking questions about the wonders of the world because everything seems fantastic or awesome. Out of this disinterested curiosity will come **theoretical knowledge** and the impulse leading to scientific endeavors.

Unfortunately, often "knowledge" is not enough. **Knowledge** is just the remembering of previously learned material. It must be followed by **comprehension,** which could be defined as the ability to grasp the meaning of the material, and to interpret it or predict its consequences and effects. In comprehension, one begins to understand what is known. Comprehension needs to be followed by **application,** which refers to the ability to use learned material in new and concrete situations. This should be followed by **analysis,** which is the ability to break down what has been learned into its component parts so that its organizational structure can be understood. **Synthesis** follows analysis and it refers to the ability to put parts together to form a new whole, to see things in an entirely new way.

However, knowledge is not enough if its accumulation and the technology it has brought into existence has not increased the security humans always crave. True, the increase in knowledge has satisfied numerous human needs and wants. The proof of this is the vast increase in population since the 1800s. Overall, population growth is a sign of progress, of successful dominion over nature. Yet, the 20th Century, the most technologically and materially advanced century ever, was the most devastating in genocides, oppression, wars and environmental disasters. This is the great paradox—humans can impressively control nature, but they do not seem to control effectively their most intimate, selfish, and aggressive impulses. The social environment is witness to this tragedy.

The Mental Powers of Human Knowing

Humans are by nature seekers of knowledge. Their inborn curiosity and remarkable mental powers continually move them to find the truth about things. Truth is that which corresponds with what is, with reality. The acquisition of knowledge, difficult and even impossible at times, is made possible through the senses and the intellect. All human knowledge has its starting point in sensation. **The external senses—seeing, hearing, tasting, smelling, and touching are the channels through which things outside come into the person.**

Outside stimuli cause modification of the sense organs producing sensation nerve impulses which go to the brain where further physiological changes take place. The different aspects of things brought in by the external senses are then coordinated by a faculty called **the unifying sense,** which helps create a perception—a sense cognition of an individual object in space. A perception is made up of several sensations projected into space and linked to images of past experiences.

This unifying sense also stores in the **memory** the information coming from the senses. Another power which deals with sense information is the **imagination.** It brings back into consciousness the image of concrete individual things not present to the senses but which were at one time made available by them. The image produced by the imagination is a recall of a previous perception, or a reordering of previous sense impressions in a totally new way. The **estimative power,** a kind of inborn wisdom alerts the organism to what is harmful or useful.

These four, the unifying sense, the memory, the imagination, and the estimative power are called internal senses. There is no visible organ by which they operate, as in the case of the external senses. However, they do have a physical basis in certain areas of the brain. Although they do not have any visually observable organs, one can infer their existence because of the mental operations they perform. All of these, the external and the internal senses, are called **sense powers** because they deal with the particular, individual aspects of things. Perceptions, memories, and images are not in themselves ideas, but they are the materials out of which the intellect will create ideas.

Sensations, perceptions, memories, images and other internal sense materials are examples of sense knowledge. Humans share these powers with the higher animals. However, there are activities which only humans can perform, and which imply the presence of higher mental faculties: the ability to invent and use a language based on arbitrary symbols to communicate; self-awareness; reflection on their knowledge, and distinguishing among various degrees of certitude ("only man knows that he

A bust of the philosopher Plato. Courtesy of FPG/Taxi/Getty Images.

knows"); awareness of human origins, destiny, and death; religion and the speculation about superior beings in another dimension beyond human life; awareness of time and history; conscious appreciation of the beautiful, and involvement in techniques to create and appreciate beauty; creativity in technology, mathematics, literature, morality and ethics; and degrees of freedom from instincts and natural tendencies.

These differences between what animals and humans can do are so radical that it makes no sense to refer to the human person as just a "naked ape" as the materialists do. This is to confuse the different levels of visible existence: mineral, plant, animal and human. At the lowest level is the mineral. Minerals are found at the level of plants, animals and humans but one does not refer to these as minerals. For instance, plants have cells, nutrition, growth and reproduction which minerals do not have. One also finds plant-like features in animals but we do not call animals plants for animals have active locomotion, senses, imagination, and intelligence which plants do not have. Animals have a higher existence than minerals and plants. In the same manner, there are animal characteristics in humans but they should not be called animals for humans have additional powers like self-awareness, abstract intelligence, and intellectual reasoning which animals do not have. Humans are a higher form of existence which incorporates the mineral, the plant and the animal worlds, but go beyond them.

There is in human knowing more than just the presence of sense knowledge, of knowing only the characteristics of individual objects. While all human knowledge begins with the senses, it is not completed until it engages the intellect. There is nothing in the intellect which was not first in the senses, except the intellect itself. **This intellectual knowing in the human includes the powers of conception, judgment, and abstract reasoning.** These mental operations help distinguish humans from the higher animals.

The first act of the intellect is conception by which the mind generates concepts. A concept is an act by which the mind grasps or becomes aware of an object without affirming or denying it. It allows the person to become aware of the essence of a thing, of what makes it what it is. Without the intellect, a person could not affirm what is common or different about two or more things. For example, the senses might expose a person to a particular tree which might have four feet and red leaves, and to another with one hundred feet and no leaves. However, it is the intellect which associates the two to the general, abstract idea "tree," so that the person can then understand what the two things are, and what they have in common. **The concept provides the mind with general ideas.** Concepts such as justice, beauty, and goodness do not refer to a particular thing provided by the senses. They are general, abstract ideas generated by the intellect to understand what things are. The ability to produce concepts allows humans to understand and discuss things which are far removed from sense information: God, black holes in space, mathematics, and cosmogonical theories about the origin of the universe such as the "Big Bang."

The second cognitive operation of the intellect is the judgment by which a person affirms or denies something of something. In the act of judging, the mind unites two or more concepts and affirms or denies that this is the way they are found in the world of things outside the mind—or whatever the appropriate realm of existence may be, such as the realm of legend, logic, grammar, mathematics, and so on. This implies a return to sense knowledge to ensure the concept or concepts are real. For example, cows do not fly. This is a judgment.

The third operation of the mind after conception and judgment is reasoning through which arguments are made in support or in opposition to specific positions. This could take the form of inductive or deductive reasoning.

Humans are superbly fitted with powers useful for the pursuit of knowledge—sensations, perceptions, memorization, imagination, conception, judgment, and reasoning. Yet, the presence of error, of distortion, of deception is always a possibility. This is why one of the major struggles of the human race is the search for ways to acquire either certain knowledge, which cannot be further improved or modified, or at least knowledge which has behind it the best possible evidence as support, even though it might be later changed as new evidence is acquired. A description of this search is the theme of this chapter.

Philosophy

All definitions of philosophy are disputable. However, **philosophy** could be seen as a form of inquiry, a process of analysis, criticism, interpretation, and speculation about the mysteries of existence and reality. **It is rational, critical thinking of a systematic kind about the conduct of life, the general nature of the universe, and the justification of belief.** Philosophy is thinking about thinking, as well as systematic thinking about the world, oneself, and others. It rises out of human wonder, curiosity, and the

An engraving of Aristotle. Courtesy of Galleria Spada/Alinari/Art Resource, NY.

desire to know and understand. Philosophy originated in religious questions concerning the nature and purpose of life and death, and the relationship of humanity to superhuman powers or a divine creator. Every society, including atheist ones which do not believe in a personal deity, have some form of religious beliefs from which come world views to interpret reality and to establish systems of ethics for personal conduct.

Originally, people relied on magic, superstitions, some forms of religion, tradition, and authority to understand reality. Some ancient Greek philosophers considered these as unreliable and sought answers by thinking and by studying nature. At first, philosophy meant the desire for wisdom (philo = desire and sophia = wisdom). Wisdom at that time meant the cultivation of learning in general. This was the meaning given by the **pre-Socratic** philosophers starting in 585 B.C. These thinkers sought to identify the fundamental substances of nature out of which everything else was derived. They did not believe gods or supernatural forces caused natural events, and therefore, searched for natural explanations for natural phenomena. These pre-Socratics formed the tradition of philosophy for those who followed them. They distinguished between rational explanations and mythical, poetic, and religious arguments. The **Sophists,** one of a class of Greek teachers of rhetoric, philosophy, and "successful" living, challenged conventional moral assumptions in the 400s B.C. and stimulated reflections on ethics, particularly by Socrates.

Later, philosophy became identified with wisdom itself. With **Socrates** (469 B.C.), philosophy turned its attention from the physical world toward the study of human beings. Socrates was particularly interested in virtue, those moral habits such as prudence, temperance, courage, justice, and others, to achieve happiness. He exposed unexamined, mere claims to knowledge and wisdom, and tried to replace vague opinions with precise and clear ideas. Socrates did this by seeking definitions of abstract concepts such as knowledge, virtue, justice, wisdom, etc., through a question and answer method **(dialectic)** which continually asked those who claimed to know such questions as "what do you mean?" and "what do you know?" This dialectical or "socratic" method was an artful use of proper questions so that with the aid of clear examples, he could make those conversing with him to arrive at the proper conclusions on their own, and thus to think for themselves instead of accepting conclusions on the authority of others. Every answer to a question led to further questions until the meaning of the concept was clear.

Socrates' great pupil, Plato (428 to 348 B.C.), distinguished a mere opinion (doxa), one which is not supported by rational explanation but is just a prejudice, from a justified opinion (episteme). With this distinction between a mere opinion and a justified or rationally-supported one, Plato started his philosophy. For him, philosophy was not anymore the love of wisdom, nor knowing itself, but that type of knowing which is the result of an intentional and methodological search for truth. Philosophy became a dialectical conversation through which one criticizes answers given to previous questions to achieve a more precise understanding. **The result was that philosophy became a rational, reflective knowing acquired through a dialectical method.** Wisdom now included intellectual inquiry, the understanding and the practice of morality, and the type of cultivated, enlightened opinion and attitudes which lead to happiness.

Aristotle (384 to 322 B.C.), Plato's pupil, continued this meaning of philosophy, but included in it the totality of human understanding acquired by rational inquiry. He divided philosophy into three parts: **Logic,** the study of the means of obtaining knowledge and how humans learn; **Physics,** the knowledge of things in general, including the human psyche; and **Ethics,** the knowledge of human activities including politics, art, etc., and all human qualities which are not part of nature. This definition of philosophy as the totality of human understanding acquired through rational inquiry lasted until the Middle Ages (900 A.D. to 1500s) when the specific knowledge and beliefs about God became known as **Theology,** and separated from philosophy as a separate discipline. Human knowledge divided into two parts: theology, the knowledge about God; and philosophy—human knowledge about things of nature and of human beings. These contributions made Aristotle the most influential thinker in classical and medieval times.

This is the way philosophy remained until the modern era in the late 1600s. Sir Isaac Newton still used this view of philosophy in 1687 when he published *Mathematical Principles of Natural Philosophy.* **Until the 1700s, no distinction was made between science and philosophy.** However, at this time other disciplines in addition to theology began separating from philosophy. They began to develop different methods, languages, objects of study and specialization. By the 1700s, no one mind could absorb all human thought, and so philosophy ceased to include all human knowledge. **After theology, mathematics was the first to develop as a distinct discipline apart from philosophy.**

From natural philosophy came anatomy, botany, microbiology, physiology, zoology, geology, meteorology, oceanography, astronomy, chemistry, and physics. They became known as the **Natural Sciences,** though later they would split into the Life Sciences and the Physical Sciences. After Newton, the development of separate disciplines from the broad category of Natural Science began. From social philosophy, or the study of humans and society, came anthropology, economics, geography, history, political science, psychology, and sociology. They became known as the **Social Sciences.** Art, architecture, sculpture, dance, drama, music, speech, languages, literature, philosophy, and the study of religion became known as the **Humanities.**

These particular sciences have narrowed significantly that portion of reality they want to observe and measure. Their attention is with only one aspect of reality. **In contrast, philosophy is the discipline which considers** an object from a universal and comprehensive point of view. It takes the broad view of things, looking into the nature of things, and searching for a few unifying principles on which to build a worldview. There are still some areas of knowledge which are mentioned as being part of the traditional field of philosophy.

Metaphysics (beyond the physical) is the study of the fundamental nature of reality, existence, and the essence of things. It deals with what is real. **Epistemology** aims to determine the nature, basis, and extent of human knowledge, and explores the various ways of knowing, the nature of truth, and the relationship between knowledge and belief. **Logic** is the study of the principles and methods of reasoning. It explores how we distinguish between good reasoning and unsound reasoning. **Ethics** examines human conduct, character, and values, and studies the nature of right and wrong, the distinction between good and evil, the nature of justice, of a good society, and of one's responsibilities and obligations.

Aesthetics deals with creation and principles of art and beauty. It involves both works of art created by human beings and the beauty found in nature. The **Philosophy of Language** studies what language is, the relationship between language and thought, and between language and the world, as well as questions about the nature of meaning and of definitions. **Philosophical Psychology** explores the nature of the mental and such terms as intention, desire, belief, emotion, soul, pleasure, pain and others, and how these mental states affect action. The **Philosophy of Religion** deals with such questions as "Is religious language meaningful?," "Can God's existence be proven or disproven?," "Is religious faith unreasonable?," and "How do we decide between theism, atheism, and agnosticism?"

The Humanities

The Humanities are branches of learning that deal with human thought and culture, excluding the sciences. They are a distinct kind of knowledge which is humanistic, concerned with human values and expressions of the human spirit. **The Humanities are a field of study concerned primarily with the human expression of spiritual and aesthetic values through literature, music, art, religion, and philosophy and which attempt to discover the meaning of life.**

The National Endowment for the Humanities includes among the humanities the study of language, linguistics, literature, history, jurisprudence, philosophy, archeology, criticism, theory and practice of the arts, and those aspects of the social sciences which have humanistic content and employ humanistic methods. This list is greater than the courses usually taught in the Humanities departments of universities. Sometimes these subjects can be taught in a way which is not humanistic. Subjects which are not typically seen as humanities—such as natural sciences, can be taught humanistically when their philosophy or their history are studied, that is, when the method used is concerned with human values. Thus, the history of scientific research would be a topic which, though it deals with natural science, it is part of the humanities, for it deals with human achievement.

The term humanities derived from the doctrine of humanitas that **Cicero** (106 to 43 B.C.) developed in account of the special education of an ideal orator. The term humanities was later identified by Aulus Gellius (100s A.D.) with the **Greek Paideia—the general and liberal education used in preparing a free man for manhood and citizenship.** Later Greek and Roman rhetoricians considered humanities the basic program of classical education. Turned to Christian ends by St. Augustine and other Church Fathers, it became the basic education of the Christian Middle Ages. Thus humanitas was originally identified with a program of liberal arts which included mathematical and linguistic arts, as well as some science, history, and philosophy.

The term humanitas disappeared during the Middle Ages but was revived in the 1400s by Italian Humanists who claimed to devote themselves to, and teach the humane disciplines, in contrast to divine or theological studies. **The humanist program of study included grammar, rhetoric, poetry, history, and moral philosophy, studied in the language and literature of the ancient Greeks and Romans.** The emphasis was often in imitating the language and models of the ancient classics.

According to time and place, different studies have been included among the humanities. **Nevertheless, they all agree on a program of more "humane letters," in training the person to be skilled and raised to the peak of human potential in all that is most distinctively human.**

Since the 1800s, the humanities have been more commonly contrasted to the natural sciences. Instead of trying to reach general laws like the sciences, they are concerned with what is individual and with its unique value. They are interested with human actions and works. These are fundamentally different from natural phenomena and call for a different analysis. Human activity is different for it is the result of human purpose, of an inner dimension which purely physical objects do not have. Humans are not only the product of nature, but also of culture, of drives and choices which cannot be known without an understanding and comprehension of purpose and meaning.

The main tradition of the humanities is as an educational program of general and liberal arts education. This is an education which is nonvocational and non-professional, aimed at the maturation of the individual as a person and a citizen, and not as a worker in a specialized field. It is concerned with preserving and developing the arts and skills that find expression in great objects, problems and values of human interest. Language, literature, great books, history, philosophy, and theology are within its range, subjects beyond any one college or university department.

Science

Until the 1700s, no distinction was made between science and philosophy. **Today, it is common to refer to science as a broad field of knowledge that deals with observed facts and the relationships among those facts, and which explores the workings of the world. Science is both a method for obtaining information and a body of systematically arranged knowledge that attempts to discover and explain relationships among observable natural phenomena.** Science comes from the Latin word scientia which means knowledge. Aristotle invented the idea of a science and of separate sciences, each having distinct principles and dealing with different subject matters. The beginnings of "scientific" endeavors precede Aristotle as mathematics and astronomy were used by the Egyptians before 3000 B.C. They collected anatomical and physiological information to embalm the dead, engaged in surgery, and used geometry to construct the pyramids. The Egyptians were concerned with practical knowledge, to do and to build things.

The Greeks or Hellenes were the first to begin a systematic separation of scientific ideas from superstition and mere opinions. Hippocrates, for example, in 400 B.C., was the first to consider medicine as a science apart from religion, and taught that diseases have natural causes. Aristotle showed the need for classifying knowledge and recognized the importance of observation. He developed deductive logic as a means of reaching conclusions once one has established certain premises. Deduction applies to the process by which one starts with a general premise that is accepted as true, applies it to a particular case and arrives at a conclusion which is true if the starting principle was true as in "All animals die; this is an animal; therefore it will die." The Greeks were the first to separate mathematics from purely practical uses and to develop systematic methods of reasoning to prove the truth of mathematical statements.

For Aristotle, whose thought dominated from the classical period to the Late Middle Ages (300s B.C. to 1500s A.D.), science was a type of theoretical knowledge. In theoretical knowledge, humans desire to know the object of study for the sake of knowing and for the beauty of understanding it. The human mind seeks to possess, to grasp the object for itself with no concern for its immediate practical use in making or doing things. Knowledge is its own delight.

Science goes beyond common sense by reflecting on one's knowledge and discovering why it is so. According to **Aristotle,** science, whether mathematical, philosophical, natural, or social, seeks to know the causes of a particular

Galileo Galilei, 1624. Courtesy of Ottavio Mario Leoni/Bridgeman Art Library/Getty Images.

reality. It is a certain knowledge obtained through the understanding of causes. **A cause is that which occasions, determines, produces, or conditions an effect.** It is the necessary antecedent of an effect. Science deals with causality, which is the act of causing. To bring something to be is the meaning of causing. An effect is what comes into being. Cause is what brings it into being.

Aristotle identified four types of causes necessary for the understanding of any particular thing, or of any change taking place in nature or as the result of human action. First, is the efficient cause, that by which something is made. It is the maker of a thing, which, in any process of change, acts upon a changeable object or exerts an influence upon it that results in that changeable object becoming different in a certain respect. **Second, is the material cause, out of which something is made.**

Third, is the formal cause which makes a thing the kind of thing it is. The essence of a thing is what it truly is. And fourth, is the final cause, for the sake of which something is made—the purpose of a thing. For Aristotle, everything moves according to its nature, a nature which is determined by its end. All things point toward an end in nature. He saw that the primary object in knowledge is to know the formal cause, to identify what something is. Once it is known, one can then work back to the efficient cause and ahead to the final cause. **Thus, scientific knowledge was thought to occur when one knows the causes of an object.**

For all its greatness, the Greek approach to science had serious limitations. **They never used mathematics to analyze the physics of motion and other constantly changing properties of nature. Also, they did not test their observations systematically with experiments.** Instead they relied on "common sense" observations. The Romans made few contributions to theoretical science. These very practical people were more concerned with building an empire, laws, institutions of government, and works of engineering and architecture. They mostly accepted the scientific knowledge of the Greeks.

During most of the Middle Ages (900s to 1500s), there was insignificant scientific investigation in Europe. The Arabs did preserve much of the knowledge of the Greeks and made some original contributions. Yet, the Arabs did not use experimental methods or develop the instruments of applied mathematical techniques that were necessary to the development of modern science. **During the 1000s, a major event in Europe was the introduction of the Hindu/Arabic number system which stimulated the development of mathematics and its application in busi-**

ness. Classical and Arabic works were made accessible to Europeans and stimulated academic debate.

Although the Middle Ages are not popularly known for their scientific splendor, it was then that the foundations of modern science were built. Abelard of Bath in the 1130s displayed an understanding of the need for direct observation of nature free from theological assumptions. Another major influence in the development of modern science derived from the Catholic Franciscan order which began to praise the beauty of nature. The Franciscan friars trusted nature and were willing to be guided by experience. It was one of them, **Robert Grosseteste** (1253), who first fully expressed the idea that all physical science should be based on mathematics which could express the laws governing nature. He also emphasized the utility of observation and experimentation to arrive at conclusions about the physical universe.

The most famous of Grosseteste's pupils was **Roger Bacon** (1292), who was the first to speak of experimental science, and who promoted scientific technology and the understanding of the scientific method. Bacon established the principles of the **inductive method,** of reaching conclusions based on acquired observations. He explained the role of experience and experiment in confirming or refuting speculative hypotheses. However, many of the medieval scholars kept relying more on observation and intellectual speculation than on systematic, controlled experimentation.

The acceleration of scientific inquiry in Europe began in 1543 with the publication of two books: **Nicolaus Copernicus'** (Poland) *On the Revolution of Heavenly Spheres,* which challenged Ptolemy's view that the earth was the center of the universe; and **Andreas Vesaluis'** (Belgium) *On the Structure of the Human Body,* which presented precise anatomical knowledge replacing those of the Greek Galen and of the Arab Avicenna. **Tycho Brahe** (1546 to 1601) of Denmark observed the motions of the planets more precisely than anyone before, and thus helped the German **Johannes Kepler** in 1609 to use intricate calculations to show that the heliocentric theory (the sun as the center) could explain the movements of the planets if they orbited the sun in an elliptical instead of a circular path.

Scholars in the late 1500s and early 1600s realized the importance of experimentation and mathematics to scientific advance. It was this realization which helped bring about a revolution in science. This early modern science was still motivated by the Aristotelian ideal of searching for truth and certitude, but it placed more faith in mathematical insight than in the search for causes in the traditional Aristotelian mode.

Galileo Galilei of Italy has often been called the founder of modern experimental science. He questioned Aristotelian philosophy and scientific thought. In his *Dialogue Concerning the Two Chief World Systems* (1632), he compared the Aristotelian-Ptolemaic with the Copernican system and showed how the latter better explained the known facts. Then in his *Discourse on Two New Sciences* (1638), Galileo provided mathematical proof of his new theory of motion. Galileo insisted—he was a pious Catholic—that his views were consistent with traditional Catholic doctrine, but some officials of the Church, Robert Bellarmine in particular, disagreed with some of his ideas and suggested that they be taught as hypotheses instead of as facts.

Galileo developed the law of falling bodies which says that all objects fall at the same speed regardless of their mass. His theory of motion was consistent with a moving Earth while Aristotle's theory assumed a static Earth. Galileo also stated the law of the pendulum which says that pendulums of equal length swing at the same rate whether their arcs are large or small. He was responsible for the first effective use of the **telescope** and developed the hydrostatic balance, an instrument used to find the specific gravity of objects by weighing them in water.

Regardless of his role as the founder of modern experimental science, which some historians question, Galileo's real contribution was the way he approached scientific problems. He reduced them to very simple terms on the basis of everyday experience and common sense logic. Then Galileo analyzed them and resolved them according to simple mathematical descriptions. The application of this technique to the analysis of physics, particularly the physics of motion, led to the development of modern mathematical physics.

Isaac Newton of England used the findings of others to develop a unified view of the forces of the universe. In his *Principia* (1687), he formulated a law of universal gravitation and showed that objects both on the earth and on the heavenly bodies obey this law. **The goal of these physical sciences was the analysis of all natural phenomena by means of induction which relies on observation and experimentation to discover the laws operative in nature, and to establish an orderly system that can offer an intelligent explanation of nature.** Greater precision would be obtained to the extent that the results could be expressed mathematically. In time, the application of this scientific method beyond the area of physics led to significant achievements in biology, chemistry, and evolutionary theory.

No one person could master all the information being generated. The sciences began to separate, each developing its own range of subject matter, vocabulary, and methodologies. Four major groups developed, though the boundaries between them have become less clear with the development of interdisciplinary fields. The first group consists of **Mathematics and Logic,** which are essential tools in almost all scientific study. **Mathematics permit exact statements and numerical predictions.** Mathematics includes arithmetic, algebra, calculus, geometry, probability, and statistics.

Logic is the basis for all scientific reasoning. Scientific reasoning depends on deductive logic which is reasoning from known scientific principles or rules to draw conclusions relating to a specific question. It also relies on inductive logic which requires a scientist to make repeated observations of an experiment or an event from which then a general conclusion could be derived.

A second group of sciences are the Physical Sciences, which examine the nature of the universe and study the structure and properties of non-living matter, from tiny atoms to vast galaxies. They include astronomy, physics, chemistry, geology, and meteorology.

A third group of sciences are the Life Sciences or Biological Sciences, which deal primarily with the growth and function of living organisms. Its two major fields are Botany which deals with plants and Zoology with animals. These can be subdivided to include anatomy, physiology, genetics, molecular biology, paleontology, taxonomy, sociobiology, ecology, bacteriology, ornithology, and marine biology.

The Social Sciences

The fourth group of "sciences" are the *Social Sciences* which deal with individuals, groups, and institutions that make up human society, and which attempt a systematic study of the various aspects of the social relationship of humans. They are disciplines that study the various aspects of human behavior and the institutions which mold it.

The Rise of the Social Sciences

While some of the ideas discussed in the social sciences go back to the ancient Greeks with their initial determination to study all things in the spirit of

dispassionate and rational inquiry, the social sciences as such, do not precede the 1800s as distinct and recognized disciplines of thought. During the Middle Ages many ideas were available on the nature of the state, the economy, religion, morality and human beings; yet these social concerns were intimately related to medieval theology and philosophy. **There was in pre-modern times little pragmatic and empirical approach to the study of man and society.**

When the influence of Catholic philosophical and theological scholasticism began to decline, two new movements rose which inhibited an empirical approach to the study of society: **the Renaissance** (1350s to 1500s), which brought an emphasis in Greek classics and commentary on Plato and Aristotle, and which mainly promoted the humanities; and the **Cartesianism** of Rene Descartes in the 1600s, with its non-empirical emphasis on logic as the right approach to the understanding of the physical and of the social worlds. These two great influences retarded the development of the social sciences. In addition, many of the social thinkers of the 1700s, in particular, were concerned with political reform or with revolution rather than with rigorous, analytical study of society based on acquisition of "the facts."

Yet, in the 1600s and 1700s, there were several factors which prepared the way for the social sciences: rising awareness of the multiplicity and variety of human experience as Europeans traveled to all parts of the world, and as ethnocentrism and parochialism decreased among educated, well-traveled people; spreading sense of the social or cultural character of human behavior in society in its purely historical or conventional rather than biological basis. Therefore, a science of society, would not be a mere extension of biology or physics, but a distinctive discipline with its own subject matter; and the borrowing from the physical and biological sciences of **the concept of structure** which was applied to the analysis of the state, but which others would later use in their study of the human psyche or mind, and of civil society.

Another major concept which became significant in the 1700s was **the idea of developmental change.** This one had started with the ancient Greeks. What thinkers said was that the present is an outgrowth of the past, the result of a line of development caused by conditions and causes immanent in human society. This led to the idea—long before Darwin's theory of evolution—of social speciation, the emergence of one institution from another in time, and of the whole differentiation of function and structure that goes with this emergence. These ideas were used by the philosophes who spread the ideas of the "Enlightenment" to attack the existing order of government and society in Western Europe, for these thinkers had a vision of what was the ideal society. The status quo was seen by them as an obstacle preventing its realization. **These pre-social scientists were more concerned with what ought to be than with what is and why it is. They were still in the tradition of social philosophy rather than of the social sciences.**

However, the fundamental ideas, themes, and problems of the social sciences in the 1800s were above everything else responses to the problems of disorder, change, and instability which were created in European society by the Industrial revolution which began in England after the 1760s and by the French Revolution of 1789. These two events undermined the old order based on kinship, land, social class, religion, local community, and monarchy. The principles of status, authority, and wealth were upset. Social philosophers considered these two revolutions as earth-shaking. The social sciences arose in part from their efforts to understand these events.

New Themes for the Social Sciences

New themes or concerns in social thought emerged in the 1800s which served as the content of the social sciences. One was the **increase in population** due to the industrial revolution and the resulting increase in food production and transportation and to the decrease in the death rate. Many thinkers speculated about the potential consequences of the rise in population. A second concern was the **condition of urban labor,** which seemed to be getting worse in the 1800s, even though in fact it was better off than the lifestyle of the rural masses at earlier times. Economics, for example, became known as the "dismal science" because early economists could see little likelihood that the condition of labor could improve under capitalism.

A third theme of the new social sciences was that of the **transformation of property.** More property was now in industrial form as factories, business houses, and workshops which multiplied under capitalism. There were in addition to tangible or hard property (land, machines, and money) intangible kinds of property such as shares of stock, negotiable equities, and bonds. This led to the growth and power of financial interests, to speculation, to a widening economic and social distance between the capitalists and the masses, to the concentration of property in few hands, and to the economic domination of politics and culture. **Some conservatives (Edmund Burke), liberals (J. S. Mill) and radical socialists (Karl Marx) saw these developments with worry, and they would write conflicting interpretations about these economic, political, and social conditions.**

A fourth issue of the social sciences early on was **urbanization,** as the number of cities and towns grew. Many writers wrote about the bad side of cities—broken families, atomization of human relationships, disrupted values, and social alienation. They criticized the factory system as masses of workers left home and families to work long hours in the factories.

A fifth concern was **technology.** As the spread of mechanization in the factories and in agriculture accelerated, many writers wrote about the possible conflict between humans and nature, between man and man, and even between man and God. There was a fear in some circles that the specialization of work, made possible by technology, could degrade the human mind and spirit. **In the 1800s, the opposition to technology on moral, psychological and aesthetic grounds made its appearance on Western thought.**

A sixth theme was the **growth of the political masses** as the right to vote was expanded to cover the middle classes, then the workers, and then women. Some saw the potential power of the masses as a threat to individual freedom and cultural diversity, for they feared that the uneducated majority would destroy or undermine anything it could not understand or possess.

All these themes, concerns or ideas became tied to new ideologies which addressed the forces unleashed by the Industrial Revolution and the French Revolution. For example, on the whole, liberals welcomed these two revolutions which were democratic, capitalist, industrial, and individualist. Conservatives, in general, distrusted democracy and industrialism as they preferred tradition, authority, and civility. The radicals, in turn, were antagonistic to capitalism, though they accepted technology; some were not democratic while others accepted democracy as a tool to destroy all authority which did not emerge from the people or from their particular political group. Most early social thinkers got caught up in these ideological currents and became involved in partisan struggles rather than in more objective empirical research.

There were three other powerful intellectual tendencies which influenced the social sciences. One was Positivism, a reverence for science as a positive, enlightened form of knowledge superior to magic, religion, philosophy, and the humanities. Auguste Comte was a major representative of the idea of the scientific treatment of social behavior. He believed "sociology" would do for man, the social being, exactly what biology had already done for man, the biological animal. As a result, in the 1800s the distinction between philosophy and science became an overwhelming one.

A second influence was **Humanitarianism,** closely related to the idea of a science of society. In this view, the purpose of social science was thought to be the welfare of society and the improvement of its moral and social condition through the institutionalization of compassion and the extension of welfare from the family and the village to society at large. Many middle class individuals engaged in the betterment of society through social projects: relief of the poor, improvement of slums, improvement of literacy, assistance to the insane, visitation of those in prison, and abolition of slavery. And a third influence was **Evolution** with its concern that the social sciences study development as well as structure.

The Quasi-Sciences

There is no absolute agreement as to which disciplines are social sciences. Most often seven are mentioned: anthropology, economics, geography, history, political science, psychology, and sociology. Portions of these social sciences are not strictly sciences but knowledges which try to apply the methods of the natural sciences to realities and areas of investigation which lie in great part outside the scope of the natural sciences. They have modeled themselves on mathematical physics in order to partake of its scientific stature, but often it is not possible to make sciences out of these social knowledges by the mere insertion of numbers.

Free human acts can never become totally predictable in any absolute fashion, no matter how eager ardent proponents are to make a science out of such bodies of knowledge. Social scientists in order to apply the methods and techniques of the natural sciences have to concentrate only on those areas which can be directly observed and measured. As a result, many important areas of human reality are abandoned, for example, the immaterial operations of the human mind in psychology, or the whole area of Existential and Philosophical Psychology. Those areas of the social sciences which can be subjected to strict scientific study, Physiological and Experimental Psychology, for example, could actually be considered as part of the natural sciences.

The fact that sociology, psychology, economics, and other social sciences are often not "scientific" in the strict sense, and do not have a method on which they can rely completely, does not mean that they do not do valuable and necessary work. Nevertheless, their contribution is often of a different order. **Good social "scientists" are often not so much scientists as they are sages. They are professionals with prudential wisdom. But they are not always scientists for their judgments do not carry the necessity of physical law.** They are not always right. They may be half wrong. They may be completely wrong. Social scientists do not study such simple things as points, lines, angles, numbers, electrons, molecules, or even cells as mathematicians and natural scientists do. They study the most complex and unpredictable existent yet known—human beings. Therefore, the judgments and recommendations of social scientists should not always rigorously determine human action.

Anthropology

Anthropology is the scientific study of humanity and of human culture. It is strictly defined as the science of man, but in practice it is concerned overwhelmingly with "primitive" humans. Anthropology studies the strategies for living that are learned and shared by people as members of a social group, the characteristics that humans share as members of one species—homo sapien sapiens, the diverse ways that they live in different environments, and the material and immaterial creations of social groups ranging from goods to values to beliefs.

Anthropological research is comparative and cross-cultural as diverse groups are analyzed to determine their similarities and differences. Anthropology stresses an insider view of society to understand the world view of a people. **The two major divisions of anthropology are Social and Cultural Anthropology on one hand, and Physical Anthropology on the other.** Social Anthropology deals with social relationships in human groups: marriage, family life, authority, conflict, age, sex, impact of the environment, and the economy. Cultural Anthropology is the study of human culture: artwork, houses, tools, music, religions, symbols, and values. Physical Anthropology—not a social science, is the study of the biological characteristics of human beings. In Europe, anthropology usually means physical anthropology.

Cultural Anthropology can be divided into three disciplines: **Ethnography,** or the study of the culture of a single group; **Ethnology,** or the comparative study of two or more cultures or parts of cultures (this began with the 19th Century search for origins and developmental stages of cultures with an emphasis on marriage, kinship, and religious institutions); and **Archeology,** the ethnography and ethnology of extinct cultures.

Economics

Economics is the study of how society meets its needs for goods and services and how they are distributed. It analyzes the utilization and allocation of available resources among competing uses. Goods and services are everything that can be bought and sold. Production means the processing and making of goods and services, and distribution means the way these are divided among people. Every society has to address what shall be produced, how goods and services shall be produced, who shall receive them, and how fast the economy should grow since scarcity is a basic condition of any economy. **Microeconomics** deals with the small segment of the economy such as households, firms, or industries. **Macroeconomics** deals with large aggregates such as national output, national income, national savings, and national investment.

Geography

Geography is the study of the location and distribution of living things and of the earth features among which they live. Geographers treat four main questions: location of people, animals, vegetation, and things; spatial relations that places, earth features, and groups of people have with one another because of their locations; regional characteristics; and the forces that change the earth. **The two major divisions of the field of geography are Physical Geography and Human Geography. Physical Geography** includes the following disciplines: *Geomorphology*—the study of land forms such as plains, hills, mountains, and plateaus; *Climatology*—the patterns of climates; *Biogeography*—plant geography and zoogeography; *Oceanography*—the study of ocean currents, waves, and tides; and *Soil Geography.*

On the other hand, **Human Geography** includes: **Cultural Geography**—the location of and spread of beliefs, customs, and other cultural traits; **Population Geography**—the patterns of population and reasons for changes; **Social Geography**—the relations of groups with one another; **Urban Geography**—the nature of cities and urban areas; **Economic Geography**—the location and distribution of economic activities such as mining, manufacturing, and agriculture; **Political Geography**—the way in which people in different places make decisions or gain and use power within a political system; and **Historical Geography**—how places looked in the past. Unlike history, the underlying principle of geography is not time but space, and its focus is not so much social as terrestrial.

Geographers use specialized research methods to study earth features and human activities: field study (direct observations), mapping, interviewing and sampling, quantitative methods with the aid of computers to simplify complex information and to present it in a form that is more easily understood, and the use of scientific instruments like remote-sensing devices (aerial and satellite cameras, infrared heat-sensitive film, and radar).

History

History is the memory of the past experience of humankind as it has been preserved, largely in written records. It is the result of historians' work in reconstructing events from the original written traces into a narrative. The existence of written records separates the historic era from prehistoric times, known only through archeology.

The study of history has been regarded either as a branch of the humanities or as a social science. History belongs to both. It deals with all the categories of experience treated separately in the social sciences. The distinctiveness of history lies on its emphasis on the **chronological dimension,** the interrelation of the various aspects of social experience with emphasis on multifactor explanation, and the special regard for the uniqueness and the particular events, individuals, and institutions that have had social significance.

In contrast to other social scientists who seek to develop general laws by examining patterns of behavior that recur through time, historians study primarily the condition or events of a particular time. **Historians seldom attempt to develop general laws, though they may use social science theory to help explain conditions.** Those who try to elaborate general laws of history and to identify the meaning of history are really venturing into the world of philosophy.

While history is tied to the social sciences in its attempts to establish objective truths about humans and society, the historian's work of synthesis and interpretation involves an imagination and creativity more akin to the humanities. Also, the historical narrative is a form of literature, and much of the content of historical study has to do with man's humanistic experience in intellectual and cultural pursuits.

Historical research begins with **primary source records:** documents in archives, eyewitness reports and collections, diaries and letters, newspapers and other publications. The historian begins to classify and question the available data to develop a pattern of events and their significance to create the historical narrative. This direct historical research results in the production of **secondary sources:** articles, monographs, or specialized books. Afterward, the historical information may be reworked for its utility to the reader in **tertiary sources:** textbooks, encyclopedia articles, or popularized accounts.

The process of material selection, facilitated by the use of bibliographic aids and secondary works, must be followed by a stage of evaluation by checking the sources for plausibility and consistency (**internal criticism**), and by comparing them with other evidence on the same topic (**external criticism**). This critical method is essential to expose forgeries, detect errors in manuscripts, deliberate bias and deception, errors of memory and perception, and incompleteness in the historical record. The historian must then develop a conceptual scheme around which the facts are to be organized with an appropriate logical sequence of topics and points. The synthesis can be highly subjective and can be conditioned by time, place, the framework of the author, and the quality of the sources. Nevertheless, accuracy is a definite possibility of the historian's craft.

Political Science

Political Science is the systematic study of political life including politics and government. Politics is the making of decisions by public rather than private or personal means. Government refers to the institutions through which public decisions are made and carried out. **Ultimately, political science deals with power as it tries to understand who gets what, when, and how in the dynamic interaction of people and their governments.**

Traditionally, political science has been divided into various fields of study: **Political Theory and Philosophy,** a study of the opinions and supportive arguments given on such topics as the justification, legitimacy, and purpose of government, individual rights and obligations, freedom, equality, justice, and many others; **Comparative Government,** a comparison of how different societies organize their governments; **International Relations,** an analysis of diplomacy, international law and organization, and other factors which affect the contacts among nations and states; **Government and Politics; Public Administration,** a study of the budget, management, policies, and structure of public institutions, both governmental and independent; **Political Behavior,** a description of the way people respond to certain political conditions; and **Policy Studies,** an analysis of political issues affecting society and how they can be addressed.

Psychology

Psychology is the scientific study of mental processes and behavior. It observes and records how people and animals relate to one another and to the environment. Psychology is related to biology in its study of abilities, needs, and activities of humans and animals and the working of the nervous system. It is related to anthropology and sociology in its investigations of the attitudes and relationships of human beings in a social setting. **Psychology, unlike the other social sciences, concentrates primarily on individual behavior, particularly the beliefs and feelings that influence human actions.**

Psychologists rely on three basic methods: naturalistic observation, systematic assessment, and experimentation. Naturalistic observation involves the watching of the behavior of humans and animals in their natural environment. This usually does not produce knowledge of general laws, but is a good exploratory technique to gain insights and ideas for later testing.

Systematic assessment is used to examine people's thoughts, feelings, and personality characteristics. One type of assessment is the **case study,** a collection of detailed information about an individual's past and present life. Later, different case studies can be compared in the search for general laws to explain behavior. A second type of assessment is the **survey,** or public opinion poll, as measurement of individuals' attitudes and activities after asking questions of people themselves. A third form of assessment is the **standardized tests,** an examination for which average levels of performance have been established and which have shown consistent results.

Experimentation helps psychologists discover or confirm cause-and-effect relationships in behavior. Usually, they divide the subject being tested into two groups: the **experimental group** and the **control group.** For the experimental one, the psychologists keep all variables constant except one condition or stimulus which they want to change to observe its impact on the behavior of the subjects. Nothing is done to those in the control group. Thus, any difference in the behavior of the two groups is assumed to have been caused by the changed stimulus or independent variable.

Sociology

Sociology is the study of individuals, groups, and institutions that make up human society. It is a branch of the science of human behavior that seeks to discover the causes and effects that arise in social relations among persons and in the intercommunications and interactions among persons and groups. **Sociology places attention on the collective aspects of human behavior.**

Sociologists have certain major interests. One is population characteristics. **Demography** studies the size, composition, and distribution of human populations. **Human Ecology** deals mainly with the structure of urban environments and patterns of settlement and growth. A second important interest of sociologists is social behavior such as attitude change, conformity, leadership, morale, and social interaction. A third concern is for social institutions (organized relationships among people to perform a specific function) such as families, school, churches, armies, and others. A fourth subject area is that of cultural influences such as arts, customs, languages, knowledge and religious beliefs. And fifth is the area of social change brought about by fashions, inventions, revolutions and wars, among others.

Modern sociology is divided into several branches: **Criminology** (criminal behavior and causes of crimes); **Demography** (human populations); **Deviance** (behavior which departs from the normal); **Human Ecology** (urban environments); **Political Sociology** (struggle for power); **Social Psychology** (individual social behavior and relationships); **Sociolinguistics** (the use of language); **Sociology of Education** (transmission of culture); **Sociology of Knowledge** (society's knowledge and myths); **Sociology of Law** (relationship of law to social patterns); and **Urban Sociology** (problems of cities).

Sociology shares with psychology the subfield of social psychology even though psychology has traditionally centered its attention on the individual and his mental mechanisms. It is also close to social anthropology. The two subjects used to be taught in some universities until the 1920s, with anthropologists concentrating on the sociology of preliterate people. Now anthropologists are studying aspects of modern society. Sociology also has ties to political science and economics. The methods of sociology are similar to those of psychology and the other social sciences: field observations, surveys or public opinion polls, and controlled experiments to test hypotheses.

The Cultural Foundations of the Scientific Method

While many non-Western groups before the ancient Greeks had developed an impressive body of knowledge, practicality and not theoretical knowledge or science fueled their understanding. The torque in shaduf, a simple lifting machine of the ancient Egyptians, the magnetic compass, rockets, and the Great Wall built by the Chinese, the blowguns of the Amazon tribes, and the aerodynamic boomerangs of the Australian aborigines are all examples of inventions by non-Western peoples. However, their knowledge was of a practical nature. They were not able to proceed to a theoretical understanding of the behavior of things, of the causes of physical objects and their behavior, and of the underlying forces which connect all physical reality. Their explanations took the form of myths and legends involving heroes, deities, and other assorted characters from folklores.

The first steps in the development of a scientific attitude were taken by the Hellenes or ancient Greeks. The scientific method would take centuries to mature as other Europeans would also collaborate in grounding it on several philosophical premises. One was the belief of several ancient Greek philosophers that the physical world runs according to specific **natural laws** which give nature an underlying order and uniformity. The universe in their view is lawful and purposeful. A second assumption was the belief, sometimes called **rationalism,** that the human intellect can understand these natural laws through a process of observation and reasoning. These two ideas are in contrast to those of some cultures which deny the possibility of understanding intellectually the physical or the social world, or which believe that the universe is simply too chaotic for human understanding.

These two ideas might be the greatest contributions of the ancient Greeks. They would lead to the beginning of science. The Catholic Church would adapt them and argue that the natural law is the creation of God, and that the human intellect is God's gift since they view humans as created in the image and likeness of God.

A painting of Saint Thomas Aquinas, 1633. Courtesy of Erich Lessing/Art Resource, NY.

Before the 1200s, most philosophers saw the world as eternal and uncreated. Then in the 1200s the Catholic Church, under leadership of people like Thomas Aquinas, argued dogmatically that God created the universe from nothingness at a specific time. **This view made God the First Cause, the First Mover from Whom came secondary effects and causes. This dynamic view of creation would lead to the scientific belief in laws of motion which would later be developed fully by Isaac Newton. The theology of creation by God led to the science of motion.**

A third idea behind the scientific method is **moderate skepticism,** which states that things are not always what they seem to be. This is an assertion which recognizes the tentative nature of our understanding of phenomena at any given time. Our object knowledge can change as science becomes more accurate in its investigations. Inaccurate observations, overgeneralizations about the significance of our own anecdotal experience, bias on the basis of the human desire to see what one wants to see, and the complexity of existence itself, are all obstacles in the search for truth. One must be very cautious when interpreting the facts gathered through observation or deduced from reasoning.

A fourth cultural ingredient behind the scientific method is **openness,** which includes a willingness to share information with one's peers, a recognition of failure so that new paths can be pursued, and a commitment to objectivity in research as one attempts to be impartial and rational rather than biased and emotional. A fifth assumption of the scientific method is **amorality,** that is, science is concerned with what is, as opposed with what ought to be, thus separating science from morality, ethics, and ideology. And a sixth assumption is **mathematical expression,** that is, that as much as possible the results of scientific reasoning be quantified and expressed mathematically.

Thus behind the scientific method or methods there is a scientific attitude grounded on the belief in a natural order, which can be understood, though cautiously, skeptically, and with an openness to experience and to criticism. This attitude, as it developed in Europe, challenged traditional problem-solving styles based on appeals to the supernatural, to human authority, or one's own knowledge.

Traditional appeals to the supernatural to acquire knowledge have to be rejected. There sometimes are requests for guidance from the gods, or are magical attempts to control the deities for the deliverance of gifts. This rejection of appeals to the supernatural has to occur, not because religion and science are necessarily in opposition, but because the scientific method can only deal with observable and physically reproducible realities. Appeals to human authority, to kings, gurus, priests, sorcerers, shamans, and others as sources of knowledge also has to be abandoned if their understanding is based on superstitions, customs, or hearsay.

Their authority has to be questioned and even attacked, not necessarily because of who they were as authority figures, but because of the way in which they acquire knowledge. In fact, this new scientific attitude grounded on empirical observation and reasoning and on a healthy skepticism and openness, means that the conclusions of scientists also must be rejected if they are the result of prejudice and error. "Scientists" can be as dogmatic, close-minded, and wrong as anyone else. Finally, appeals to one's own knowledge and expertise have to be rejected if they are based on just mere opinion, hunches, or hearsay.

Once scientists had developed a new attitude about the study of physical reality, this became associated with three goals: **verifiability,** to prove the truth or falsehood of statements by testing them enough times to establish confidence in the results; **systematic inquiring,** to sort out and organize bits of information into coherent patterns; and **generality,** to move from specific levels of explanation to broader levels so that one can predict the workings of similar phenomena in the future.

The Scientific Method

The aims of science are description and explanation. Description is a simple account of the observable features or qualities of individual things, acts, or events for example, an eclipse of the sun. Explanation is an attempt to account for the facts, to show why they are what they are, answering how things come about, what causes them, and what laws determine their occurrence. **All scientific explanation involves some law or laws which provide the "principle of explanation."** This is the ultimate aim of science—explanation through the formulation of explanatory laws.

The scientific method is a set of rules developed over the last centuries to ensure that empirical research will lead to valid theories. If properly applied, these rules will lessen the chance of arriving at false conclusions or of accepting generalizations not supported by the evidence.

The scientific method is a very general and flexible set of rules. For this reason, it does not have just one sequential order, but can instead be described in various ways. Usually the first step is the **selection of an area of study.** This allows scientists to concentrate only on matters relevant to the problem. For example, we might be interested in the relationship between nutrition and good student performance in exams. Every other type of information is then excluded.

Once we have selected the area of study and the problem to be investigated, the second step in the scientific method is **observation** and **measurement.** At this point, scientists usually research the existing knowledge on the relation between nutrition and good student examination to see if previous researchers have formulated laws or general propositions regarding this topic. They also make general observations and measurements of the behaviors in question before they subject it to experimentation.

Although scientific observation starts with noticing qualitative distinctions or differences, its ultimate aim is to obtain precise quantitative data, for the aim of science is accuracy and predictability. As a result, it is important to count and to measure so that the laws of arithmetic can be applied to generate general laws. Afterwards, we can take the third step in the scientific method which is the **formulation of a specific researchable hypothesis** within the framework of a more general explanatory theory or general proposition. For instance, we can assert that a nutritional plan based on large amounts of protein juice is helpful in increasing the alertness and exam success of college freshmen.

A hypothesis is an anticipated explanation, essentially a guess—though perhaps an informed one based on previous observation and measurement. The researchers want to determine if there is a cause-effect relationship between two variables such that one causes the other. Following the formulation of a working hypothesis, the fourth step in the scientific method is the **construction of a research design, experimentation,** or techniques for measuring the data relevant to the hypothesis of the study.

The fifth step is that of **data collection** as we observe and record the information intended to test the hypothesis. This part is closely related to the sixth step of the scientific method which is the **classification and organization** of the data after it is gathered so that it can yield maximum usefulness. For example, we could use fifty college freshmen in the experimental group and fifty other students in the control group. Their respective performance in the exam must be collected, classified and organized. One must then determine if there is a significant improvement in the score of the individuals in the experiment group, and if such difference can be explained by the presence of the protein juice Pamurontal. This task is made easier with the use of computer programs which measure correlations or relationships between two or more variables.

The seventh and final step is the **conclusion** which consists of an evaluation of the hypothesis based on the data, and an attempt to generalize from the result of the study. If the hypothesis is not correct, one then has to research for another general proposition or hypothesis. If in fact, high protein juice does improve test performance, one must try to integrate such findings to other data on the qualities of high protein foods to further increase our understanding of the role of nutrition and behavior.

What has made great scientific advancements possible has been the supplementing of simple or ordinary observation with systematic and controlled observation or experimentation. **Experimentation differs from simple or mere observation in that it involves a deliberate disturbance of the normal course of events.** An experiment is a research design that exposes subjects to a specially constructed situation. By systematically recording

subjects' reactions, the scientists can assess the effects of several different variables. Thus the experiment seeks to specify cause and effect relationships between two variables under carefully controlled conditions.

As mentioned earlier, an experiment could be designed to determine if the high protein juice Pamurontal prevents social science students from falling asleep in class and perform better during exams. The scientists can select an **experimental group** of subjects who are exposed to the juice and are observed for changes in behavior. The juice Pamurontal in this experiment is the **independent variable** which in science refers to the factor that the researchers manipulate because they believe it will affect the dependent variable, which in this case is student alertness in class and performance in the freshmen exam. In science, the **dependent variable** is a factor that changes in response to changes in the independent variable.

The experiment will not be complete without a **control group,** whose subjects are not exposed to the independent variable, giving the experimenter a basis for comparison with subjects who are. The control group could be given a drink that looks like juice but it is really mostly water. It is important that both groups be as similar as possible in such characteristics as sex, age, race, weight, social class, etc., to ensure that the experiment is testing only the relationship between the independent variable (Pamurontal, in this case) and the dependent variable (student alertness and exam performance in this particular experiment).

Experiments can be devised for many purposes: to determine what is the case as with "exploratory" experiments pursuing new realms of inquiry; to check on chance observation which seems unusual or unexpected; to re-check generally accepted general "facts" which often turn out to be false; to discover laws governing certain events or conditions; to test a newly conceived hypothesis developed to explain some facts; and to decide between rival hypotheses.

During the process of induction, there is a transition from the individual cases observed, or from propositions pertaining to some cases, to universal statements or assertions pertaining to all cases. On the basis of the conclusions reached by the researcher, one can either support or reject the original hypothesis. The induction process can be assisted by the employment of statistical methods. The discovery of statistical regularities, when tied to careful analysis of the data and procedures involved, can be important. When properly interpreted, statistical correlations and regularities may disclose significant laws of nature.

A scientific theory may be replaced by a new theory if the new one gives a better account of the same facts or explains a number of facts which the old theory could not explain. Comprehensiveness and accuracy of interpretation are the two main criteria of scientific theories.

In place of controlled experimentation, social scientists can also use sample surveys which ask people questions to systematically gather standardized information about the behavior, opinions, attitudes, values, beliefs, and other characteristics. The sample must accurately reflect the population by having the same distribution of characteristics as the general population. The questions must be asked in a neutral, objective manner. The use of modern computers makes it possible to identify relationships between many different variables for large populations. These relationships are usually **correlations** which refer to variables which vary together. However, correlations are not necessarily **cause-effect relationships,** in which one variable causes the other to happen.

A third tool used by social scientists, in addition to experimentation and sample surveys, is the observational study. This is an intensive examination of one unit—person, event, gang, ghetto, religious cult, etc., first-hand in a natural setting. The objective is to learn all one can about the particular subject. If the researchers simply watch without getting involved in the activity itself, the study is called **detached observation.** When they participate in the group or community being studied, then it is called **participant observation.**

Limitations of Science

These three social science research methods have improved our knowledge about human nature and behavior, the development of society and how it affects its members, the variety of human responses to the physical and social environment and other concerns. At their best, they have reduced the incidence of prejudice, superstition, and errors. Yet, they are not always reliable. Regarding experimentation, not everyone or every situation can be tested, labs are often too artificial so that their results do not represent real life situations, natural conditions cannot always be controlled, experimenters can mistakenly influence the results, and not all aspects of the human condition can be subject to empirical examinations because of ethical or methodological restraints.

Sample surveys are often designed unscientifically, the respondents unreliably selected, and the questions prejudicially asked so that the subjects are pressured or influenced to answer in a particular way. In addition, people do not always respond truthfully to the questions. The problem with observational studies is that their results are often based on only one case which makes it difficult to generalize to other cases. Moreover, scientists sometimes fall prey to certain biases about the nature of science, in the view of its critics.

The first prejudice is Physicalism or Materialism which is the doctrine that everything is physical or material. Physicalists believe that the real world contains nothing but matter and energy, and that objects have only physical properties such as spatio-temporal positions, mass, size, shape, motion, hardness, electrical charge, magnetism, and gravity. They believe that the properties of larger objects are determined by those of their physical parts. **Physicalism is also the thesis that whatever exists or occurs can be completely described in the vocabulary of physics so that all psychological relations, for example, can be explained in physical terms.**

This position is criticized by those who believe in God, in an immortal human soul, in a special creation and other realities which cannot be reduced to physical terms. Since the scientific method can only deal with empirical, physical, observable events, it can neither support nor reject the assertion that there might be a spiritual or non-material world. Scientists can neither prove nor disprove the existence of God. Therefore, physicalism is not science, but is instead a philosophical argument.

A major reason why physics (as well as mathematics) is so comprehensive and scientifically accurate is that it deals with very simple and inanimate objects: protons, electrons, atoms, etc. The same cannot be said, for example, of the social sciences whose main subject is man, a being capable of consciousness, self-awareness, insight, conscious motivation, free choices, and logical reasoning, and whose mental world is pregnant with non-physical facts. **The idea of reductionism, of reducing higher-order mental powers to the actions of inanimate elementary particles, confuses two different levels of existence.**

The second error of modern science, according to its critics, is Scientism, an attitude holding that science constitutes the only valid knowledge and is alone capable of solving all human problems. Scientism asserts that truth can be arrived at solely through such techniques as observation of phenomena, description, classification, explanation, and verification, and hence it regards philosophy and religion as purely subjective in character. This view is rejected by those who believe that love, God, affectivity, beauty, personality, and a host of other realities are by their very nature inaccessible to empirical methods. Scientism, by restricting valid knowledge to the level of science only, overgeneralizes the scientific method and overrestricts reality to the confines of matter alone.

Scientific methods can be fine if used properly, but there are other methods which can be useful, even to science itself, but which are not dependent on **scientific methodology.** These include logical analysis, dialectical/Socratic clarification of meaning and of the cognitive situation as a whole, the analysis of categories and their interrelations, the quest for philosophical first premises of the whole of human existence (metaphysics), and ethical and moral reflections. **Thus, there is a whole range of human experience not susceptible to the application of scientific methods, but which can enhance understanding, wisdom, happiness, and even science itself by supporting it with analysis, synthesis, and other cognitive operations.**

Sources

Books

Adler, Mortimer J. (1990) *Intellect: Mind Over Matter.* New York: Macmillan Publishing Company.

Brugger, Walter, and Baker, Kenneth. (1972) *Philosophical Dictionary.* Spokane: Gonzaga University Press.

Forsthoegel, Paulimus F., S.J. (1994) *Religious Faith Meets Modern Science.* New York: Alba House.

Morente, Manuel Garcia. (1997) *Lecciones Preliminarias de Filosofía.* Ciudad Mexico: Editorial Porrua, S.A.

Sullivan, Daniel J. (1992) *An Introduction to Philosophy: The Perennial Principles of the Classical* *Realist Tradition.* Rockford: Tan Books and Publishers, Inc.

Tarnas, Richard. (1991) *The Passion of the Western Mind. Understanding the Ideas that Have Shaped Our World View.* New York: Ballantine Books.

Van Doren, Charles. (1991) *A History of Knowledge. Past, Present, and Future.* New York: Ballantine Books.

Vernaux, Roger. (1981) *Epistemología General o Crítica del Conocimiento.* Barcelona: Editorial Herder.

Zulke, Frank. (1991) *Through the Eyes of Social Science.* Prospect Heights: Waveland Press.

CHAPTER THREE

Tribes, Empires, States, and Nations

A Brief Introduction to World History

Germán Muñoz

States, Nations, Nation-States, and Nationalism

States or countries are today the basic building blocs of international political organization and functioning, but each is a unique assemblage of territory, people, and institutions. A **state** is a political community occupying a definite territory, having an organized government and possessing internal and external sovereignty. Recognition of a state's claim to independence by other states, enabling it to enter into international engagements, is important to their establishment. At their best, states maintain law and order, promote economic well-being, contend with the governments of other states, and assure security against external threats. However, states differ in the amount of territory actually controlled by their governments, the area of the state actually settled and productive, the population size, the degree of centralization of government decision-making and authority, and whether they are nation-states or multinational states.

Although the majority of states have highly centralized governments which tightly control all parts of the country, many function more as a collection of self-governing units than as totally unified entities. Such states are organized on a **federal principle,** with their central governments having direct responsibility for a limited number of activities—mainly transportation, communications, and foreign affairs, and state governments enjoying other responsibilities. Canada, the United States, and Switzerland are examples of these. In contrast, a **unitary state** is a centralized government in which local or subdivisional governments exercise only those powers given to them by the central government. The United Kingdom and France are examples of the unitary form.

It is useful for analyzing world politics to distinguish between states, as sovereign or independent units of political organization with permanent borders and a stable population, and nations as sizable groups of people psychologically united by common bonds of geography, religion, language, race, custom, and tradition, and by shared experiences and common political aspirations. In between the two one can perhaps identify the **ethnic group,** whose members share common cultural norms, values, identities and patterns of behavior and identify themselves and are identified by others as a distinct group. In some cases, the ethnic group slowly dissolves as its members assimilate into the dominant society. In others,

---

*Note: This brief and incomplete introduction of history for beginners is best read with the assistance of the maps in the chapter. Professors often assign this chapter for a take home examination. Many people have their own calendar to record their existence. The Western world is now in the year 2010 after the birth of Jesus Christ (A.D.). Years before his birth are listed as B.C. The Jews are in the year 5771, the Muslims are in the year 1439, and the Chinese are in the year 4706. Some scholars use 2010 ACE (after the common era) instead of A.D. 2010. The student is welcome to use any of these calendars. Our book will use 2010.

the ethnic group retains its cultural identity by living in concentrated geographical areas. However, in both cases they are different from nations in that they do not aspire to political independence.

Although national identity is the key dynamic force in the world's political geography, state organization is the medium through which it operates. States are the basic building blocks of international affairs, at least since the 1648 Peace of Westphalia. Yet, underlying the state is the presence of the national group.

Defining the concept of **"nation"** is a difficult task since each national group exhibits unique qualities. In almost all cases—the multilingual Swiss are one of the exemptions—nations rest upon a common language. However, in some cases language might not be the first thing which binds the individuals of a nation together. **Among elements shared in common by members of a nation are tradition, myths, group perceptions of history, religious beliefs, symbols, past-times and other shared elements which lead to communications efficiency, or iconography.** An important part of iconography is a sense of **homeland.** Most nations have a spatial dimension, a land seen as a nation's own. Usually the group constitutes at least a local majority of the population in that region. **Those groups which have a distinctive language and tradition, but which lack a territorial base do not easily fit into the classification of a nation. This is the case with the Gypsies.**

The Kurds of Southwest Asia are an example of a nation seeking independence. The Kurds are a rugged people of Islamic faith who are much like the Iranians in race and language. Approximately six million Kurds live in what they call Kurdistan, a part of western Asia ruled by Turkey, Iran, Iraq and Syria. These governments will not permit the creation of an independent Kurdistan and so the Kurds do not have yet their own country. Sometimes a nation can lose its country as it happened to the Poles in the late 1700s when Poland was partitioned by Austria, Prussia, and Russia. However, the Polish nation survived the extinction of their country or state, and after World War I the state was recreated.

It is also possible to have a nation which seeks to have self-government or some political autonomy within the confines of another country. This is the case of the Catalans of Spain whose region of Catalonia elected its own parliament in 1980. While the relations of the Kurds to the Turks, Iranians, Iraquis, and Syrians have been violence-ridden, those of the Catalans to the rest of Spain are now economically dynamic and politically stable.

The greatest share of individuals in the developed states of the world are members of national groups. They take their national identity as a matter of fact, easily distinguishing between people with whom they can easily communicate and identify from those who are **"foreigners."** When their national identities are challenged by other groups, they can quickly affirm nationalist values, passionately looking for the defense of the interests of their nations. For example, most Lebanese, Jordanians, Saudi-Arabians, Kuwaitis, and Syrians might see themselves as Arabs, but when there are conflicts among them, they revert to their national identity as Lebanese, Jordanians, etc.

The hallmark of modern nations is their quest for the political recognition of their distinctive identities. This is almost always reflected, at least since the 1600s, in a pursuit of a nation-state of their own. There might be a few nations, like the Montenegrins of Yugoslavia, who appear satisfied with local self-ruling autonomy within a larger state controlled by others. There are groups without a common political agenda, though they are becoming fewer. **Perhaps, it is better to designate them as peoples rather than as nations.** They exist, and struggle for physical survival. They might be unaware of their distinctiveness, and unconcerned about the possibility of creating an independent state for themselves. Examples are the Balinese of Indonesia and many of the tribal groups of Africa. Some countries, particularly African ones, which were created by the Europeans arbitrarily by uniting different groups of people with diverse languages and religions, have experienced difficulty building a common national identity. These countries seem to represent a different category called the **"non-nation state."**

The Evolution of Nations

Humans are social by nature. They cling to one another in a variety of ways, and tend to identify themselves as members of particular groups to which they give allegiance. At times, their loyalty is either to the **family**, or to the **clan**, which is a group of families claiming descent from a particular male of female, or to the **tribe** which could be made up of various clans living in close proximity. The loyalty could also be given to **city-states** made up of several tribes, or to an **empire**, or a **country**. Additional sources of identity could be **religious groups**, **race**, or **gender**. A recent type of identity has been the **nation**. All these social groupings have given humans a sense of security, psychological identity, and meaning. They have also served to justify discriminating against or killing those outside the group.

Although states can be traced back to at least Egypt in Africa (3100 B.C.), and Akkad in Mesopotamia (2721 B.C.), nations are essentially a product of the past three centuries. Before the French Revolution of 1789, most states could be viewed as the personal property of their rulers. The population had little meaningful participation in government, apart from paying taxes and often providing military service. During the early modern period in Europe from the 1500s to the 1700s, even military service was limited since many wars were actually fought by mercenaries. The majority was mostly concerned with physical survival. Social isolation was common. Any broader association of individuals was through a common religion chosen by the king. Different languages might be spoken within the state.

It was principally the land-holding aristocracy and mercantile entrepreneurs who identified themselves with the continuance of the state. They mostly fought each other in numerous wars in Europe from the 1500s to the 1700s. For the vast majority of people, the concept of "England" or "France," or "Spain", etc., was a remote abstraction. While one could argue that modern France and England were the original nation-states, and that their history goes back to their *Hundred Years War* of 1337 to 1453, only a small percentage of the population was involved in this struggle.

However, the progressive development of the commercial, agricultural and industrial revolutions led to upheavals and dislocation throughout European societies. Urbanization increased as more people moved into the cities looking for employment. Individuals from different places came together, sharing new ideas and perspectives. More people received an education. **As individuals began to lose traditional attachments, nationalism began to grow.** While nationalism, as the desire of a nation to have its own independence, is widespread today, once it did not even exist. **People have not always had a sense of nationhood.**

Loyalty to local nobles and religious leaders began to weaken in the late Middle Ages (1500s), and allegiance to kings grew stronger. By the 1700s, England, France, and Spain were becoming **nation-states.** Nation-states are countries in which particular national group constitutes the majority of the population. Japanese, for example, constitute the vast majority in Japan, and Han Chinese the majority in China. Both countries are thus nation-states. **However, nationalism**

was also a result of a change in beliefs. In France, the ideas of **Jean-Jacques Rousseau** stressed the value of the unity of the masses, bound together in pursuit of a common purpose, and affirmed that the laws of a country should come from the people and not from the monarch. **He regarded loyalty to la patrie (the fatherland) almost an article of religious faith. These concepts began to replace traditional religion as the cement holding society together.**

The French Revolution in 1789 and Napoleon Bonaparte's leadership of France introduced measures now identified with nationalism: universal military draft; emotional appeals to flag and country; hero glorification; and the establishment of a system of public education grounded in the national language and dedicated to the spreading of revolutionary doctrines. This intellectual climate led to a program of French expansion and conquest of Europe. French nationalists soon pressed to expel from France the Alsatians who spoke a Germanic language. In turn, people conquered by the French soon developed anti-French (nationalistic) feelings and worked to remove the French and French things and culture.

Different types of nationalism have existed. In the United States, nationalism was behind the ideology of **Manifest Destiny** by which many Americans believed it was their destiny to expand westward to the Pacific and both north and south into Canada and Mexico. In Central Europe, liberal nationalism stressing freedom for national groups, living within larger empires, motivated the Italians and the Germans to fuse their many tiny states into a united Italy and Germany. On the other hand, in the Balkans national groups sought to create small nation states out of the huge Austro-Hungarian, Ottoman, and Russian empires. **Thus nationalism has been used both to unite people to create a larger group or to break up a larger state into smaller units and states.**

During the 1930s, Adolf Hitler of Germany and Benito Mussolini of Italy, promoted **integral nationalism,** the belief that a certain nationality is superior to all the others. **Integral nationalism is an intolerant, ethnocentric form of nationalism that glorifies the state as the highest focus of individual loyalties.** Integral, or totalitarian nationalism aggressively concentrates on the security of the state, the increase of its power vis-a-vis other states, and on the pursuit of national policies motivated by narrow self-interest.

The shift from liberal to integral nationalism in Europe began by the end of the 1800s under the impact of industrial trade, imperial and military rivalries, and as a result of increases in popular pressures for the state to protect the economic and social interests of the masses against foreign competition. It was also stimulated by Darwinian theories about the survival of the fittest. After World War II, nationalism led many African and Asian colonies to demand independence. By the 1970s, over eighty states had become self-governing, and nationalism was used to create national unity since many of these new countries lacked the long history of shared experiences which had led to nationalism in Europe. In the 1990s, nationalism led to the break up of the Soviet Union, Yugoslavia, and Czechoslovakia as national groups wanted to create their own nation-states.

The Agricultural Revolution

No one knows where, when, or how humans originated. **A case could be made for the proposition that the first humans left Africa around 90,000 B.C.,** and then began to spread throughout the world within the following timetable, which could be updated with new findings: Middle East (90,000 B.C.); India and Southeast Asia (60,000 B.C.); Europe (40,000 B.C.); New Guinea and Australia (38,000 B.C.); Central Asia, Northern China, and Siberia (33,000 B.C.); Japan (28,000 B.C.); Alaska (13,000 B.C.); Central America, South America and Chile (11,000 to 9000 B.C.); the Pacific Islands (2000 B.C.); Hawaii (AD 600); and New Zealand (AD 1000).

Obviously, migrations are for humans as natural as breathing. As the last Ice Age ended circa 12,000 B.C., much of the ice melted, and this made the water level of the oceans rise, flooding much of the land surface, and isolating many of the people of the earth. For example, the land bridge from Siberia in Asia to Alaska in the Americas disappeared under the Bering Sea, and many land routes in Southeast Asia were flooded. The isolation among groups and their physical adjustments to different environments might explain much of human migration and ensuing racial differentiation.

Humans responded to the end of the Ice Age and to the consequent shortage of land and big animals by putting less reliance on big game and more on relatively stationary food sources such as fish, shell fish, elk, deer, wild ox, pigs and wild plants. They also invented bows and arrows, stone axes with handles, skis, sleds, canoes, and fishhooks. **The domestication of plants and animals allowed humans to produce food instead of merely collecting it. Humans reacted to major climatological changes by becoming more innovative.**

One of the major revolutions in history was the development of agriculture which is the art or science of cultivating the soil, including the production of crops and the raising of livestock. People took the first steps towards agriculture about 9000 B.C., when they discovered that plants can be grown from seeds, and when they learned that certain animals could be tamed and then raised in captivity. These two discoveries marked the beginning of domestication and made agriculture possible.

Agriculture seems to have developed simultaneously after 8000 B.C. in several world regions, including the upland plateau from Anatolia to Iran, in Mesoamerica, and in the Andes region of South America. *Wheat* and *barley* grew in the Near East and spread to India and Europe, *millet* grew in China; *rice* and *yams* developed in Southeast Asia; and *maize* (corn) in Central America and Peru. Later, other plants such as figs, dates, and olives were grown in the Mediterranean region. In the tropics, humans grew roots and tubers, and in the Western Hemisphere squashes, potatoes, peppers, and tomatoes.

Aside from cultivation, societies also domesticated animals starting with dogs, sheep, goats, and pigs. Others followed: reindeer in northwest Eurasia; geese, cattle and pigs in southern Europe; donkeys, camels, goats and sheep in the Middle East; horses in the south-western steppes of Eurasia; yaks in the Himalayas; zebus, chickens, pigs, and waterbuffalo in Southeastern Asia; and the llama in the Andes. Domestication of plants, and animals, and agriculture allowed more people to live in one place and for the populations of Europe and Asia to increase significantly between 8000 and 4000 B.C., since there was more food available. **Population increase led to the creation of the first villages and cities, beginning probably with Catal Huyuk in Iraq or Jericho in the West Bank of the Jordan River.**

City life produced social class distinctions and stratification based on military might, intellectual know-how, or productivity. For the first time in history, some people did not have to work. This leisure allowed the elite to create many inventions. The accumulation of property and of people in one place led to more formal social arrangements for security and for government services. Agriculture also changed human relationship to the cosmos, especially to the earth, plants, and animals. New forms of religious expression also developed based on the type of agriculture practiced in a given region. Eight major groups—each with a distinctive complex of religious beliefs and activities could be distinguished according to the type of agriculture practiced: Euroasiatic cereal culture; Meso-American maize culture; the tuber culture of Melanesia; the tuber culture of the Amazon Valley; the sub-Arctic reindeer culture; the northeast Asian horse pastoralist culture; the African cattle culture complex; and the camel culture of the Semites.

Civilizations

The period from 4000 to 2500 B.C. in the Near East is often called the Age of Copper to distinguish it from the pre-historical Stone Age. **Instead of stone tools, humans invented metallurgy, the smelting of mineral ores.** Copper was first, to be followed by gold and silver. This was the period of the first civilizations, of urban life and the culture of people at an advanced state of social development. The first probably took place in Sumer, a region settled before 3500 B.C. in the lower part of Mesopotamia (now lower Iraq) though Egyptian civilization is often mentioned as being the oldest. These **Sumerians** are credited with the following inventions: cuneiform writing, the first legal system, based on the principle of "an eye for an eye," money, weights and measures, metallurgy, multiplication and division, the plow, the wheel, and sailing ships. The invention of writing led to the beginning of history as people began to record their commercial transactions and achievements.

Following the creation of Sumerian civilization, another group called **Semites** came into Mesopotamia and captured the region militarily and demographically. They absorbed Sumerian culture and would later make their own important contributions such as the alphabet, the idea of one god (monotheism), and the spreading of the three religions of Judaism, Christianity, and Islam. **The Semites probably originated as nomads in the Arabian peninsula, and around 3000 B.C. were attracted by the prosperity of Sumer.** Semitic languages are generally divided into three categories: northeast semitic (Akkadian); northwest semitic (**Hebrew,** Aramaic, and Eblaite); and southern semitic (**Arabic,** South Arabian, and Ethiopic). Arabic and Hebrew are the main Semitic spoken languages today.

The major Semitic groups in Mesopotamia were the **Akkadians** (2370 to 2200 B.C.), who created the first state in the region, uniting by force, all the many city-states, and who organized the first professional armies in history; the **Babylonians** (1900–1686 B.C.), whose government regulated all economic activities, developed a sophisticated tax system, codified all the laws under their

leader Hammurabi, and developed the foundation of modern algebra; the **Assyrians** (1000–612 B.C.), who were totally dedicated to war and were the best fighting machine ever assembled in the Near East with their iron swords, metal helmets, breast plates, shields, battering rams and siege engines; and the **Chaldeans** (612–539 B.C.), who created the seven-day week. Most Semites live today in Ethiopia, Iraq, Israel, Jordan, Lebanon, Saudi-Arabia, Syria, Turkey, and North Africa.

The largest language family belongs to the **Indo-Europeans** whose descendants today make up 50% of the world's population. The speakers of the parent Indo-European language probably lived in the area north of the Black Sea. From there they migrated from 5000 to 900 B.C. in every direction, changing the language along the way. The earliest language of record is Hittite, followed by Greek and Sanskrit. The Indo-Europeans are the people behind most nations of Europe. The original language evolved into **Albanian, Armenian, Balto-Slavic** (Bulgarian, Czech, Latvian, Lithuanian, Polish, Russian, Serbo-Croatian, Slovenian, Slovak, and Ukranian), **Celtic** (Breton, Irish, Scots, and Welsh), **Germanic** (Dutch, English, German, Scandinavian-Danish, Icelandic, Norwegian and Swedish), **Greek, Indo-Iranian** (Bengali, Farsi, Hindi, Pashto, and Urdu), and **Romance** (French, Italian, Portuguese, Romanian and Spanish).

The Africans

Africa was probably the home of the first humans. The first groups leaving the continent might have done so around 90,000 B.C. However, humans also spread throughout Africa and with time there was an evolution which created distinct characteristics among groups. The Western Blacks developed in the forest and bush country of West Africa, particularly in what is now Nigeria, Cameroon, and Niger. They would be isolated there until they began a massive migration westward, eastward, and southward, beginning around 500 B.C. Eventually they would spread throughout most of Africa south of the Sahara. A second group of Africans are the **Nilo-Saharans,** also black, but with thinner bodies and faces than the Western Blacks. They developed in the middle third of the Nile Valley, south of Egypt.

A third group of Africans are the **Pigmies** who came from the rain forests of the Zaire Basin or Congo. They are small, averaging four feet, six inches, with brown to black skin, broad noses, and scanty hair. A fourth group native to Africa are the **San or Bushmen,** who developed in eastern and southern Africa before being pressured by the Bantu Blacks into the Namib and Kalahari deserts of southwest Africa. They tend to have yellowish rather than black or brown skin and average five feet, two inches in height.

White races predominate north of the Sahara. They are related to the Semites of Arabia and to Caucasian groups from the Mediterranean, and are loosely grouped together by linguists under the name **Hamites.** They are subdivided into three groups: the **Berbers** of Morocco, Algeria, and Tunisia; the **Egyptians** of Northeast Africa; and the **Cushitic** group which is much darker than the Berbers or the Egyptians because of their interaction in this region with Black populations. In the Sudan, in the Sahara, and in the east African highlands, as well as in the nearby coastal areas, there has been mixing of Black and non-Black groups.

The Egyptians

It was among the Mediterranean and Hamitic people, later to be mingled with Nilo-Saharans, that Egypt, the first state in history, was organized by King Menes in 3100 B.C. It was preceded by migrations which created independent city-states, which by 4200 B.C., had developed the first solar calendar with 12 months of thirty days each, and created complex irrigation systems to trap and hold the floodwaters of the Nile. The Old Kingdom which extended from 3100 to 2200 B.C., produced impressive accomplishments: independent states with a sophisticated bureaucracy; a currency; public education for scribes; and the skills of addition, subtraction, and division.

The Middle Kingdom which extended from 2050 to 1350 B.C., was an era of great cultural splendor. **There were three superpowers in the world at this time: the Egyptians, the Babylonians, and the Hittites, an Indo-European group in what today is Turkey, a people who invented the smelting of iron.** The Pharaoh extended his power to the south, conquering the region called Cush (Nubia) in 2000 B.C., extending the southern border of Egypt from the first Cataract of the Nile to the fourth cataract, by the threshold of the Sub-Saharan world.

This extension into Black Africa was halted when in 1780 B.C., the **Hyskos** of Asia, with their use of horses, war chariots, and the long-range bow, easily defeated the Egyptians and ruled them until 1576 B.C. However, as the Egyptians learned the new technology of war, they defeated the Hyskos in 1576 B.C., and chased them into Canaan (Palestine). **They then entered the Age of Empire (1575 to 1087), creating a militarist society which conquered the Phoenicians, the Assyrians, the Syrians, and the Hittites. Egypt's empire now extended from the Nile to Mesopotamia, making it the only superpower.**

Yet, prosperity weakened the Egyptian elite and the overall society. Egypt, by 1200 B.C. was forced to retreat to the Nile, never again to regain its imperial hegemony. In fact, they themselves would be conquered by the following groups: **Libyans** (935 to 730 B.C.), **Nubians** from the south (751 to 656), **Assyrians** (670 to 662), **Persians** (525 to 404), **Macedonians** (333 to 30), and by the **Romans** in 30 B.C. Finally, in the AD 660s they were conquered by the Arab **Muslims.**

The Negro Kingdoms of Africa

In addition to the Hamitic and Nilo-Saharan kingdoms of northeast Africa, there would also be impressive Black kingdoms in West Africa and later in Central and South Africa: Ghana (300 to 1076); Benin (1170 to 1900); Oyo (1200 to 1800); Kanen-Bornu (1250–1836); Congo (1400 to 1700); Songhai (1464 to 1591); Monomotapa (1500 to 1620); Dahomey (1600 to 1894); and Ashanti (1695 to 1901). Part of the collapse of the greatest Negro empires of the Sudan-Ghana, Mali, and Songhai, can be explained by the Muslim invasions which decimated their population, ruined their agriculture, and disrupted their trade. The Muslims also practiced slavery.

Ghana, founded about 300, became one of the first kingdoms of Western Africa and reached its height around 1000. It covered parts of what is now Mali and Mauritania. During the 1200s, the **Mali Empire** replaced Ghana as the most powerful state in the West. It included parts of what are now Gambia, Guinea, Senegal, Mali and Mauritania. Then it was replaced by the **Songhai Empire** that went from the Atlantic Ocean to what is now Central Nigeria. East between Mali and Songhai lay Kanen which lasted until the 1800s. There were prosperous city-state in the southeast with Islamic influence like Mogadiscio, Mombasa and Sofala. They spoke Swahili and had a blend of local Black African and Islamic traditions. Many kingdoms grew in the forests and grasslands of central and southern Africa. The Kongo, Luba and Changamire Empire all developed in the 1400s.

Indigenous African Civilizations to 1901

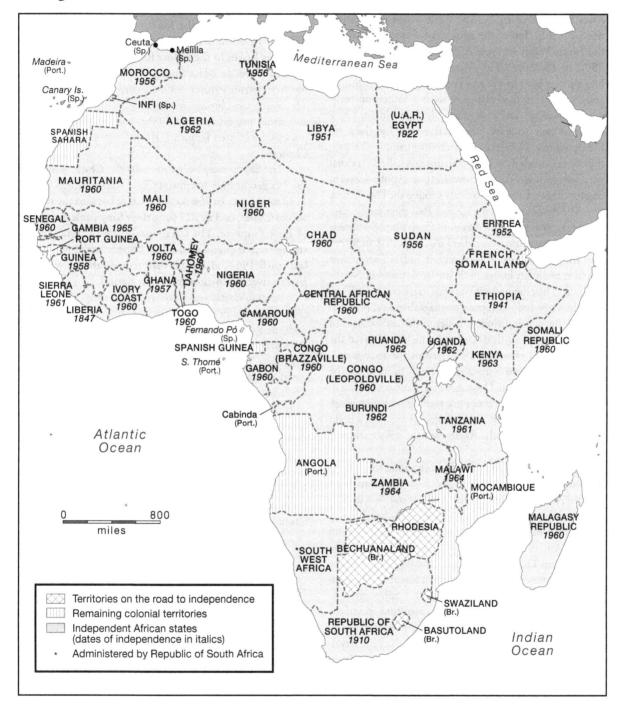

Legend:

- ◇ Territories on the road to independence
- ▥ Remaining colonial territories
- ▦ Independent African states
  (dates of independence in italics)
- * Administered by Republic of South Africa

The Hindus of South Asia

After Sumer and Egypt, the third world civilization was probably that of the agricultural communities of the Indus Valley in present day Pakistan/India, from 2500 to 1500 B.C. The cities at Mohenho Daro and Harappa equaled in size and complexity those of Sumer and Egypt. They had elaborate sewers, sanitation techniques, drainage, and a language called Dravidian. These cities seemed to have been influenced by those in Mesopotamia. However, between 2000 and 1500 B.C., they were invaded by **Indo-Europeans** called **Aryans**, who used bronze swords, arrowheads, and spoke-wheeled chariots drawn by horses to easily subdue the Dravidians.

The Aryans crossed the **Khyber Pass** through the high mountains dividing South Asia from Central and Southwest Asia. The Dravidians were either killed, captured, or forced into the Deccan region of southern India. The Aryans would create many kingdoms in the fertile plains of Northern India. Their descendants continue to govern India. They brought a new Indo-European language, Sanskrit, new religious forms which included deities of the sky in contrast to the Dravidian earth deities and which influenced the development of **Hinduism.** The Aryans also used a caste system of five major castes and outcastes to segregate the population. They would later make substantial advances in mathematics, medicine, chemistry, textile production, imaginative literature, and mysticism. Some nationalistic Hindu historians believe that the Aryans were actually natives of India itself.

India would be invaded by numerous foreigners: **Macedonians** from Greece in 326 B.C.; **Sajthians** from Central Asia in 120 A.D. **Huns** from Central Asia in 450; **Muslims** from Arabia in 700s, creating the long-drawn out conflict between Hindus and Muslims; **Tatars** from Central Asia in 1398; **Muslims** again in 1527; and the **British** from 1757 to 1947. When the British gave India its independence in 1947, the region was split: Pakistan for the Muslims and India for the Hindus, although some Muslims were left behind in India, resulting in serious conflicts between the two groups, particularly in the region of Kashmir. Fortunately for India, the Himalayan Mountains on its north prevented the Chinese from invading the region. The mountains also kept out the Siberian cold from north Asia, but gave India the monsoon rains so important for its survival.

The Chinese

Modern Chinese are descendants of Mongoloid people who have always lived in China. Mongoloids are a major racial stock native to Asia and include people of northern and eastern Asia, Malaysians, Eskimos, and Amerindians. **Chinese civilization, the fourth oldest after the civilization in Sumer, Egypt, and in the Indus Valley, probably began in the Yellow River of northern China around 1800 B.C.** The **Shang Dynasty** controlled the northern territory through a loose confederation of clans. The Shang used bronze weapons, horse-drawn chariots, and could put an army of 5,000 into battle. They also possessed a written language, the forerunner of modern Chinese.

The Shang were overthrown by the **Chou**, a much tougher people from northwest China who governed from 1122 to 256 B.C. **In 256 B.C., the Ch'in became the masters of China, and in 221 B.C., their king took the title of First Emperor. The Ch'in established China's first strong central government. This imperial system would last until 1911, although different dynasties would govern over a two-thousand year period.**

Several dynasties have ruled China: the **Han** (202 B.C.), which extended trade with Central Asia and with the Roman Empire through the **Silk Road;** the **Sui** (581 to 618); the **Tang** (625 to 907) which opened trade with Syria, Persia, Central Asia, and South Asia; the **Song** (960), which developed coal and iron industries, and put China economically ahead of other regions; the **Mongols**, who conquered China in 1260 and made it part of the Mongol Empire extending from the Pacific Ocean to Eastern Europe. **This was the first time the Chinese had been conquered by foreigners; the Ming, who drove the Mongols out by 1368, and who after 1450, isolated China from the rest of the world, leading to its decline;** and the **Manchus,** who in 1644 invaded China from its northeast and ruled until 1911.

Despite changes in dynasties, occasional disruption by outside groups, and the short terms of ruling factions, China has managed to persist and maintain control over essentially the same territory for some 2,000 years. One reason for its long-term cohesiveness has been a powerful and effective central political apparatus that prevented fragmentation. A second reason was a common written language for the scholars, government functionaries and the wealthy landed gentry who controlled the political system. A third key integrating element was the Confucian tradition which emphasized stability, discouraging any fundamental change in the existing order of social, economic, and political relations. China excelled in political organization, scholarship, and the arts, while producing such revolutionary technical inventions as printing, explosive powder, and the mariner's compass.

Pre-Columbian Civilizations in Central and South America, 1200 B.C.–1542 A.D.

Toltec, 900–1200 A.D.	Maya, 100–1542 A.D.	Chimú, 1000–1471 A.D.
Aztec, 1325–1521 A.D.	Zapotec & Mixtec, 300–1524 A.D.	Chavín, 1000–500 B.C.
Teotihuacan, 100 B.C.–750 A.D.	Chibcha, 1200–1538 A.D.	Tiahuanaco, 600–1000 A.D.
Olmec, 1200–100 B.C.	Mochica, 1000 A.D.	Inca, 1200–1535 A.D.

Courtesy of maps.com.

American Civilizations

The Amerindians had spread throughout most of the hemisphere by 12,000 B.C. and by 6000 B.C. had reached the southern tip of South America. They were the first to grow, cacao, corn, kidney and lima beans, peanuts, potatoes, squash tobacco, and tomatoes. The first civilization might have been the **Olmec** in eastern Mexico from about 1200 to 100 B.C. The **Maya** civilization of southern Mexico and Central America reached its peak between 250 A.D. and 900. They produced significant architecture, painting, pottery and sculpture, and had great knowledge of astronomy and writing.

The **Toltec** controlled Central Mexico from about 900 to 1200, but were displaced by the **Aztec** between the 1300s to the early 1500s when they were conquered by the **Spaniards.** These two civilizations constructed large pyramids and cities. The **Incas** ruled a large empire along the west coast of South America during the 1200s and early 1500s. They were superb architects and farmers, and had a centralized empire with a system of roads through the Andes Mountains to connect their cities. The Incas cut terraces into steep hillsides and irrigated them. There were no major urban civilizations in North America though the Iroquois tribe was on the verge of it when the English and the Spanish arrived.

The Hellenes, Persians, and Macedonians

The Hellenes or Ancient Greeks are often considered among the most intellectually brilliant people for their many contributions: **rationalism** or the belief that the human mind can reason and understand reality; **humanism** or the exaltation of human achievement; **democracy; philosophy; theoretical science; literature; medicine; secularization** or the creation in society of a non-religious sector; and **individualism** or an emphasis on the worth, freedom, and development of the individual.

The first wave of Hellenes entered the peninsula around 2000 B.C., and settled in the Peloponnesus, and 400 years later in the mainland at Athens and Thebes. These Hellenes were nomadic Indo-European tribes. After learning from the **Minoans**, who had created the first civilization in the Aegean area, and creating a Helladic Civilization in Mycenea, the Achaean Greeks captured Crete in 1450 B.C. When Minoan civilization was destroyed in 1400 B.C., the Achaeans or Myceneans began a 200-year domination throughout the Aegean Sea which ended around 1200 B.C., when more barbaric Greek tribes (of Indo-Europeans) entered the region.

Much later, in the 750s B.C., due to overpopulation, there was significant migration of Greeks throughout the Aegean and the Mediterranean. **Such important cities as Istanbul, Lisbon, Marseille, Naples, Odessa, and Syracuse were initially Greek colonies.**

The Hellenes were unable to create a large politically unified state although they did make the transition from tribal identification to city-states. They did cooperate among each other—Athens, Sparta, Thebes, Corinth, Megara, Argos and others—to defeat the **Persians.**

The Persians might have originated in Southern Russia about 900 B.C., settled along the eastern shore of the Persian Gulf along what today is Iran, and entered history in the 500s. They called their land the "land of the Arxans" from which the name Iran comes. The Persians made contributions in road-building, irrigation systems, use of coins as money and in religion with such concepts as the dualism between good and evil, Satan, a final judgment, and the resurrection of the body. In 529 B.C., they conquered Egypt and extended their empire from the Nile to the border of India making it the largest up to that time.

When the Persians began to extend their influence into what today is Turkey, they came in conflict with the Hellenes. **From 493 to 479 B.C., Hellenes and Persians fought. The united Greeks, particularly the Athenians and Spartans, defeated the Persians at Salamis (478 B.C.) and at Plataea (479 B.C.) and won the war. This defeat began the decline of Persia and its expulsion from Europe.** The **Persian Wars** marked a great turning in world history. If the Persians had won, they might have conquered Europe, and Persian culture might have become the basis of European civilization, spreading its religious dualism in the form of the religion of Zoroastrianism, preaching the divinity of the rulers, and creating oriental despotism in government. Following this victory against the Persians, the Hellenes failed to unite as a country. In fact, they began to fight as Athens and Sparta and their allies started the **Peloponnesian War** of 431 to 404. Sparta made a military alliance with Persia, its old enemy, built a navy with Persian support, destroyed Athens' maritime trade, and won the war.

From 404 B.C., the Greek city-states of Sparta, Athens, Thebes, Corinth and Argos, among others, would shift alliances to preserve their security. This was an early example of a balance of power system in which peace and security is sought through an equilibrium between rival blocs. However, they never united to form one state. Philip II of Macedonia took advantage

Greek Colonies, c. 550 B.C.

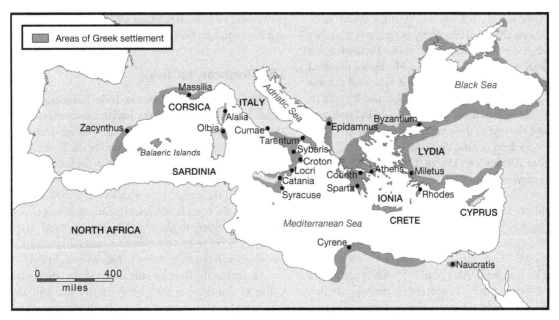

Courtesy of maps.com.

The Persian Empire, 500 B.C.

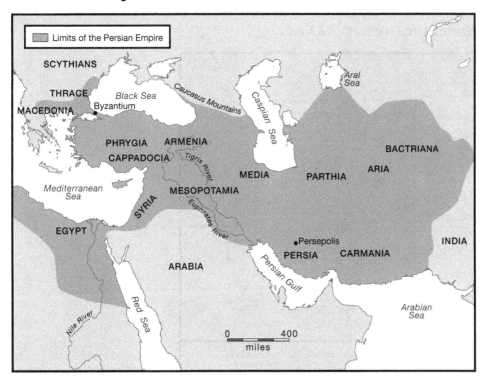

Courtesy of maps.com.

of this Greek weakness to defeat a combined Greek army at **Chaeronea** in 338 B.C. The Macedonians were distantly related to the Hellenes and lived northward from them. He gave them full autonomy, asking only that they supply their quota of troops and taxes. **Following his victory against the Greeks, his son, Alexander, defeated the Persian army at Issus, conquered Tyre, and the rest of Asia Minor, Palestine, Phoenicia, and Egypt. In 331 B.C., he defeated the Persians in Babylonia and conquered the rest of their empire.** However, his troops refused to go deep beyond the borders of India.

Under Alexander (336 to 323 B.C.), Greek culture was carried to the Near East and it mingled with the native cultures of the region to create Hellenistic (Greek-like) civilization. The city-state gave way to centralized monarchy. Loyalty was transferred from the city-state to the culture of Greece, bypassing formal political jurisdictions. Many cities were built and Greeks were assigned to run them. As a result of holding the entire Near East—from Greece to India to North Africa to Persia—into a unified civilization, this Hellenistic era prepared the way for the cultural, economic, and political universality of the Roman Empire which would later absorb it. When Alexander died in 323 B.C., his empire was divided among his generals: the **Seleucid Empire**—

Mesopotamia, Persia, Syria, and eastern Asia Minor; the **Ptolemaic Empire**—Egypt, Palestine, and Phoenicia (Lebanon); and the **Kingdom of Macedonia**—Greece and the Ionian city-states of West Asia Minor.

The Romans/Latins

The Latin (Italic) people were an Indo-European group which might have entered the Italian peninsula around 1500 B.C. From 800 to 600 B.C., they were influenced by the Greek city-states in the south, and by the Etruscans in the north who had also been impacted by the Greeks. However, in 509 B.C., the Romans expelled the Etruscan kings and replaced their monarchy with an oligarchy—though they called it a republic—whose leading members elected consuls to the Senate to represent their interests. Much of the history of Rome to 133 B.C. would consist of the efforts of the other social classes in Rome to gain more rights.

Gradually, the Romans conquered all the cities in the Italian Peninsula, and then between 264 and 146 B.C. defeated the Carthagenians of North Africa, which brought Sicily and Spain into the Roman empire. Rome would defeat Macedonia in 167 B.C., North Africa in 42 B.C., and Egypt in 31 B.C. Then from 9 to 7 B.C., Rome initiated the conquest of Germanic territories and reached

Empire of Alexander the Great, c. 323 B.C.

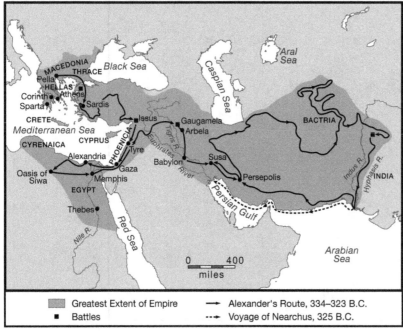

Courtesy of maps.com.

Greek Colonies, c. 550 B.C.

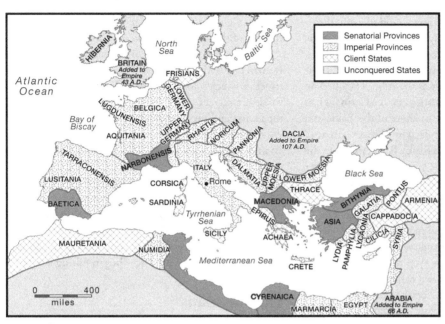

Courtesy of maps.com.

the **Middle Danube River,** which would eventually form the traditional European boundary of the Roman Empire. The Romans considered this territory to the west of Greece as Western Europe. They viewed the Greeks as easterners or orientals. The Roman expansion brought a **Pax Romana** (Roman Peace) to the Mediterranean world since, with some exceptions, the era from 31 B.C. to 180 A.D. was one of peace. This peace was maintained by a Roman fleet which protected the Mediterranean from pirates, and an army of 300,000 which protected the borders.

However, the empire became too large and in 284 A.D., the emperor Diocletian divided it into eastern and western halves, each ruled by its own emperor. The dividing line between East and West came right between what later became Serbia and Croatia, creating significant cultural differences in the Balkans. However, this division did not save the centralized government of the Western empire, saddled with heavy taxation, agricultural disasters, military over-extension, oppressive governments, technological stagnation, moral corruption, and other burdensome conditions.

The gigantic size of their empire and the need to keep it unified forced the Romans to develop their genius in the areas of engineering, and architecture, building magnificent roads, walls, baths, basilicas, amphitheatres, and aqueducts. **They excelled in the area of law and administration.** At their best, they experimented with separation of powers between the executive and legislative branches, awarding citizenship to conquered people, assuming people innocent until proven guilty, preaching equality before the law, creating checks and balances in their constitution, awarding autonomy to the diverse groups within the empire, and codifying all the types of laws so that they would be publicly known. **Rome was a great intermediary, the bridge over which passed many contributions of the ancient Near East, and especially Greece, to form the basis of Western civilization.** They replaced the anarchy of the Hellenistic Age with law and order, and embraced the cultural legacy of the conquered Hellenes, mostly Stoicism. As Rome expanded, the legacy was spread westward throughout most of Europe. The Romans also made important contributions to this heritage. From the Latin language of the Romans came French, Italian, Portuguese, Romanian, and Spanish.

The Germanic People

Barbaric Germanic tribes swept over the Western Roman Empire from 376 to 476 and created additional stress which helped to modify it. It became decentralized. The eastern portion remained as the Byzantine Empire and lasted until 1453, when it was defeated by the Muslim Ottoman Turks.

The Germans originated along the Baltic coast of northeastern Europe. In reality, a very long time would pass before these Germanic tribes would identify themselves as Germans. Their only loyalty was to the tribe. With the exception of manufactured swords and shields, they had no industry and conducted little trade. Their highest political organization was the tribe. They had no territorial state. Before the Christian era, the Germans had moved from **Scandinavia** to the shore of the Baltic and to the mouth of the River Vistula. **The "West Germans" then moved to the east of the Rhine River, pushing the Celts to the west. The Celts, who had an impressive civilization eventually migrated into what is today Ireland, Scotland, and other northeast European regions.** The "East Germans" moved south around 150 miles to the Carpathian Mountains and to the lands north of the Black Sea. However, this Germanic world was disrupted by the expansion westward of the even more barbaric Huns from Asia who had been repelled earlier by the Chinese. **The Huns' then pushed the Germans into the Roman Empire raising their own living standards but weakening an already struggling Roman Empire.**

By the 400s, several major Germanic tribes had penetrated the Western Empire: the **Franks** by the lower Rhine River; the **Alemanni** on the upper Rhine; the **Jutes, Angles,** and **Saxons** along the North Sea and later into England; the **Burgundians** on the Main; the **Vandals** on the Upper Oder, and later into Spain and North Africa; the **Lombards** between the Oder and Vistula rivers, and later into northern Italy; the **Visigoths,** west of the Dneister River, and later into Spain; and the **Ostrogoths,** to the east of the Dneister, and later into Rome itself.

This great movement of people did not destroy Roman civilization, but only the centralized government structure which ruled from Rome. Many of the "Germans" would actually serve in Romanized institutions. Aside from the Franks and the Anglo-Saxons, the German kingdoms did not survive long. The Germans, though, would make an impact on future European history with their technological inclinations, their love of liberty, their fertility, and their fierce fighting spirit. **Also, these migrations of the 300s to 500s prepared the coming of European medieval civilization. Roman civilization had been more Mediterranean than European. At this point, power shifts north of the Alps and a new civilization—Romano-Germanic-Catholic—began taking shape.**

The Christians

Following the death of Jesus Christ in the 20s, his followers continued worshipping in the temple at Jerusalem and began preaching about his divinity, death, and resurrection. Gradually they would be persecuted by other Jewish groups and established a separate identity. The missionary work of Peter and Paul would take the Christian message to the Gentiles, or non Jews, and

Barbarian Penetration of Europe, c. 476 A.D.

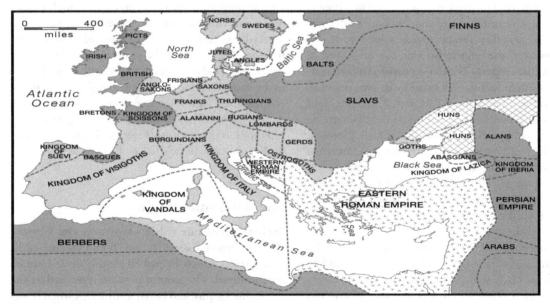

Courtesy of maps.com.

spread the teachings of Jesus throughout the Mediterranean world of the Roman empire. Periodically, the Romans, especially Nero and Diocletian, persecuted and murdered Christians. The Christians were led by bishops in different cities but eventually the bishop of Rome (the Pope) became the most influential. In 312 Rome extended tolerance to the Christians and in the 380s Christianity became the official religion of the empire. It then spread throughout all its territories.

When the centralized Western Roman empire officially collapsed in 476 and the population was threatened by waves of Germans, Muslims, Vikings, and Magyars for 400 years, the Roman Catholic Church became the major institution of the Western European world. It ran schools, orphanages, hospitals, and many local governments through its many parishes. The Church survived making alliances with some of the Romanized Germans, especially the Franks, against other Germans, such as the Lombards.

It made several major contributions during the very difficult years of the Dark Ages (700s to 900s): negotiated truces in the violent countryside by developing rules of order; transmitted technical knowledge and information on many subjects; preserved part of the classical legacy of Greece and Rome; improved the quality of grains and fruits; founded the universities in Europe; performed engineering feats such as opening roads, rebuilding bridges, repairing Roman aqueducts, digging artesian wells, and constructing seawalls, canals, and dikes; introduced water-powered machines; created demand for building trades by building cathedrals; and passed along the Bible to future generations of Christians. The Church was the principal creator of Medieval Western Civilization as it fused the contributions of the Romans with those of the Germanic tribes and of the Catholics. The most important institutions of the Church were the Papacy and the monasteries.

As a result of its many successes, the Catholic Church became the dominant cultural and material institution of the medieval world. The unity of the Christian world however, was shattered in 1054 when the Orthodox Church in Constantinople refused to follow the leadership of the Bishop of Rome, and in 1517 when the Catholic priest Martin Luther rejected the authority of the Roman Catholic Church. Another split in the Christian world occurred in the 1530s when King Henry VIII of England broke away from Rome when the Pope refused to grant him a marriage annulment.

Arabs and Muslims

The religion of Islam was founded by Mohammed in Arabia between 610 and 632. **Islam began with the Arabs, a Semitic group who can be traced as far back as 3000 B.C. on the Arabian Peninsula.** Their major institutions were the clan and the tribe, and their religion was a mixture of animism and polytheism. By 611, Mohammed was preaching monotheism. However, he had to flee his religious enemies in Mecca in 622 and go to Medina where he became the military, political, and religious leader of Islam by 624. Mohammed returned to Mecca in 630, and established his power over the entire region.

It was Islam, with its monotheistic faith in Allah and its belief in Mohammed as the greatest prophet, as well as the promise of paradise in heaven and loot on earth, which united the many poverty-stricken **Bedouin** nomadic Arab tribes. They were then encouraged to fight (Jihad) to defeat the infidel (non-believers), and expand the lands under Allah. As the Muslims expanded, they killed, taxed or forcefully converted those who opposed them.

Many Greco-Roman-Christian-Jewish areas fell before the Islamic onslaught: Syria (633 to 635); Jerusalem and Palestine (638), Persia (637 to 642), and Spain (711). And so, within 100 years, Muslims had built an Islamic empire spreading from northern Spain to the Middle East, engulfing the entire Persian Empire, and reaching the Indus River in the East. They spread far from their original lands. These wars were not defensive but offensive. They threatened Western Europe but were defeated by Charles Martel, a Frank, in 732 at the **Battle of Tours**, (Poitiers). Otherwise, Europe might have become Muslim. Three groups of Muslims almost succeeded in conquering Europe: the Moors in the 700s, the Mongols in the 1200s, and the Turks in the 1500s and 1600s.

Part of the Muslim success occurred because the two major powers in the 600s, the Byzantine Empire and the Persian Empire, had weakened each other by their long wars. Bubonic plagues had spread throughout the Mediterranean after 542, creating demographic havoc. In addition, there was much discontent with the old Greek and Roman rulers in the Near East and Africa. Also, the Muslims allowed the Hellenized Christians and Persians to run the local governments since the Arabs did not possess the skill to govern large territories.

In 661, the political capital of Islam was moved from Medina to Damascus where a politically centralized Arab kingdom was created. In 750 the capital was moved to

Moslem Empire, 750 A.D.

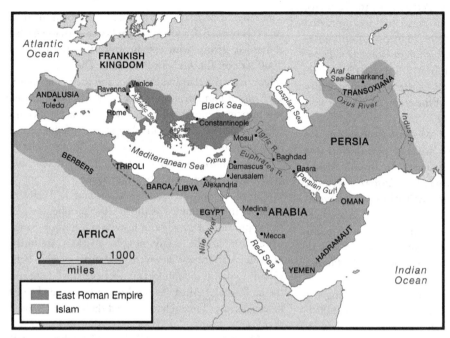

Courtesy of maps.com.

The Empire of Charlemagne, 814 A.D.

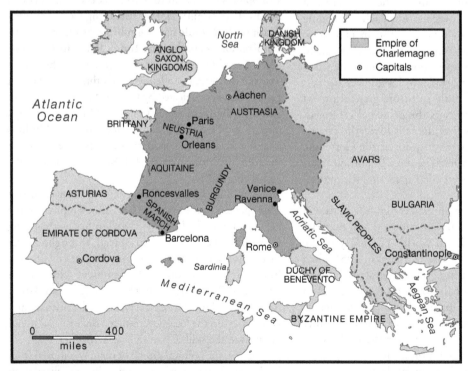

Courtesy of maps.com.

Baghdad where **non-Arab Muslims** were first allowed to high political positions. However, at this time the Islamic empire began to disintegrate into regional units. **Islamic civilization benefiting from various non-Arab sources between the 800s and 1200s surpassed that of Europe, but then began to decline as the Muslims lost the control of the Mediterranean to the Christians during the Christian Crusades of 1095 to 1270.**

The Crusades began in response to the decision by the Islamic Seljuk Turks not to allow Christians to visit the religious places in the Holy Land. The Fatimid leader in Egypt also gave orders to destroy Christian places in the Holy Land. The Christians decided then to recapture Jerusalem and adjacent places from the Muslims. The Crusades blended the Christian spirit of sacrifice with the Germanic martial vigor and zeal. Their goal was not conversion of the Muslims but the opening of the Holy Land to Christians. The Crusades occurred only after Muslims had conducted over 470 years of Jihad wars against Christians and others. The Crusaders failed to retain their early gains but weakened the Muslim hold over the Mediterranean Sea. Their eventual loss of the Mediterranean made the Muslims turn inward and eastward.

The Turks

The Turks are a Turkic-speaking people who came out of Central Asia and include such groups as Tatars, Kirgiz, and others who live in the Balkans, Siberia, and Mongolia, and who speak twenty-five closely related languages. Their ancestors were the Huns who controlled Central Asia during the 300 and 400s, and other nomadic people. In the 1000s, the Seljuk Turks seized Persia, Iraq, and later Asia Minor. **The Ottoman Turks appeared in Asia Minor (Turkey) during the late 1200s. They defeated the Arabs but converted to their religion of Islam as had earlier Turks.**

By the 1500s, the Ottomans had conquered the rest of the Byzantine Empire and built an empire which included much of the Middle East, southeastern Europe, and northern Africa. The only areas outside their control were Turkestan, Morocco, and Shiite Muslim Persia. Mongol and Turkish mercenaries founded the Mogul Empire in 1526, which dominated most of India. Also in 1526, the Turks defeated Christian Hungary at the **Battle of Mohacs. However, after the loss of the Seige of Vienna on September 11th and 12th of 1683,** the Ottoman Empire began to decline.

The collapse of the Turks could have resulted from their failure to acquire modern technology, and to their lack of access of maritime routes since Morocco blocked them from the Atlantic Ocean, Persia blocked them from the Arabian/Persian Gulf, and geographical obstacles prevented them from reaching the Indian Ocean through the Red Sea. Part of the Turkish legacy has been the religion of Islam in Bosnia and in Albania and in other regions of the Balkans, and hatred of Muslims in Serbia which the Turks defeated in the 1300s. The presence of the Turks in Southeastern Europe also prevented the Austrian and the Spanish Catholic Hapsburgs from defeating the Protestant movement in the 1500 and 1600s in the territory of the Germans.

The Mongols

The great event in Asia during the 1200s was the Mongol-Turkish conquest of the traditional eastern trade routes, beginning with Genghis Khan in 1206. Under Genghis, nomadic tribes of east-central Asia were united into a single people. His leadership, and that of his successors, allowed the Mongols to establish an empire which included virtually all of Asia and Russia except northern Siberia and the two southern peninsulas of India and Arabia. **It was the greatest land empire in history.** Invading Poland and Hungary, two Mongol armies almost simultaneously annihilated the Polish and German knights at Liegnitz and the Hungarians at Mohi in 1241. **Since the Mongols became Islamic, their invasion of Europe became the second massive attempt of Muslims to conquer Europe. On the other hand, it can be argued that they were not yet Islamic in 1241.** At one point, Khan had thought of converting to Catholicism.

The Mongols were ready to conquer Vienna and Venice when the expansion stopped due to the order given to all the Mongolian chieftains throughout the empire to return and choose a new Khagan since Genghis Khan had died earlier in 1227. **This order in 1241, saved Europe from complete subjugation. By 1260, the empire broke down into four components: Persia or Iran; China; Turkestan; and the Golden Horde, which was the part that absorbed Russia.**

The small number of Mongols and the crudity of their nomadic culture meant that they contributed little to the more developed lands they conquered. Their terrible cruelty and widespread destruction created great hatred against them from peasant people. Yet, the Mongolian conquests had great positive potential. The unification of China, Inner Asia, and much of Southwest Asia, (from Afghanistan to Yemen to Turkey) and Russia, fostered the growth of regional trade. The impact of Chinese

Mongol Empires of Eurasia, 1227–1405

Courtesy of maps.com.

culture on Russia, Iran, and Iraq were considerable. **Commodities and ideas such as gun-powder, paper money, printing, porcelain, medical knowledge, and art motifs reached Europe from the east through the Mongols and the Muslims. These products would stimulate Europeans later to look for ways to reach China to trade. This search would lead to the European discovery of the New World. The Mongols also might have been transmitted diseases and the plague which decimated from 33 to 50% of the European population in 1348–1349.**

The Slavs

The Slavs originated around 3000 B.C. in a region which is now the Northwestern Ukraine and Southeastern Poland. From 200 to 500, they migrated to other parts of Europe, in part due to the western movement of the Huns. Some settled in Western Russia and Eastern and Central Europe. Others went into the Balkans. The Eastern Slavs are the White Russians or Ukrainians. The Western Slavs include the Czechs, the Slovaks, the Poles and the Wends of East Germany. The Southern Slavs include the Bulgarians, the Croats, the Macedonians, the Serbs, and the Slovenes.

The Russians

The Russians are Great Slavs who originated in the 500s AD by the upper reaches of the Dniester, Dnieper, Neiuman, and Dvina rivers, and from there spread into the Baltic Sea, the Ural Mountains, and the Black Sea. The first Russian states were **Kiev** by the Dnieper and **Novgorod** which commanded East-West trade. Kiev was involved in commerce from Constantinople in the Byzantine Empire to the Baltic Sea. However, Kiev was vulnerable for it was located where the northern forests ended and gave way to the steppes, home to fiery nomads on horses. **In 1237, the Mongols from the east destroyed it. The Mongols made the Russian cities part of their empire.**

The Russians withdrew into the forests and paid annual tribute to the Mongols. Gradually, the city of **Moscow,** deep in the forest zone, away from the nomads, and blessed by an inland river system, became the major Russian city. Ivan the Great (1462 to 1502), expanded eastward and northward, annexed Novgorod, and pushed to the Arctic Ocean and to the Ural Mountains. Ivan the Terrible (1533 to 1584), conquered the Tatars of Kazan and Astrakhan between 1552 and 1554, and obtained control of the Volga River. **By 1547, Ivan the Terrible** had complete control over Russia and then moved into western Siberia and the Caspian Sea.

The Europeans

Medieval European civilization had its beginning in northern France in the 800 to 900s, bringing together elements of Greek, Roman, German, and especially Catholic culture. **This most dynamic civilization in history would begin to expand worldwide once the Europeans managed to overcome, by force and by religious conversion, the violent invasion** of the Muslims from the south in 711, of the Vikings from the north in the late 700s and 800s, and from the Magyars to the east. It was in the 900s when the Europeans began to raise themselves gradually from the devastating physical collapse of the Dark Ages. Centuries would pass before the recovery was completed.

While in the 1500s, Europe stood at the same level of power as India, China, Japan, and Turkey, within one hundred years, Europeans would leave the rest of the world behind economically, militarily, and politically. By 1914, Europeans would control over 85% of the world land mass, and Europe would be the first region in history to lift the majority of its people above the level of starvation.

European society, particularly after the 1500s, would be characterized by an increasing expansion in the following areas: international trade motivated by profit and Christianization; urbanization or growth of large cities; mechanization as machines began to replace animal and human labor; economic specialization as people began to concentrate on doing only a few economic tasks; capitalization as businesses grew larger; secularization, as non-religious activities grew in education, science, and the arts; colonization; statization, as more territories became independent states with governments demanding greater loyalty from their people; bureaucratization, as governmental positions became filled by professional bureaucrats; liberalization, as more people gradually participated in the political process of the emerging countries; and individualization as, increasingly, individuals pursued personal choices rather than what was expected of them for being members of a particular social class or religious group.

All of these characteristics are often collectively known as modernization. Clearly, Europe, particularly its northwestern portion, was the first region of the world to become modern. The spread of these characteristics worldwide are referred also as **Westernization,** since it was in the West, that is, in Europe, where most of them first arose. The **discovery of the Americas** by the Spaniards in 1492 and the **development of the scientific attitude** by Western people are two of major events in world history.

This European dynamism was probably made possible because in contrast to China, India, Turkey, and other regions, including the Maya, Inca, and Aztec empires, no centralized, highly-bureaucratic and collectivist power ever controlled the entire European region. Instead, European history was characterized by the emergence of several states each willing to fight to preserve its sovereignty or independence. This competition among the states encouraged technological breakthroughs and guaranteed the presence of a variety of institutions to address the local needs of Europeans. The political battle between the Holy Roman Emperor and the Pope of the Catholic Church during the Middle Ages weakened both institutions and allowed other states like England and France to grow stronger. The Church was greatly responsible for the limitation in the power of secular governments during the "Middle Ages." Now in the modern period this power would grow. Their global commercial reach also allowed the Europeans to learn from many other peoples and to utilize and process their resources.

The states of Europe took centuries to develop and consolidate. Until the 1700s, most of the states of Europe were simply loosely-held relationships among nobles, kings, and peasants. It took some time for the central power to extend the government laws, taxes, courts, and other institutions throughout their entire domain. Even the soldiers were often groups of mercenaries who could switch allegiances overnight. **Wars before the 1660s were often not between countries but between families and aristocratic groups.** The alliance between kings and the merchant classes against the nobility would gradually strengthen certain national monarchies.

The Hapsburgs

The **House of Hapsburg** was one of Europe's most famous royal families. They originated in Switzerland before the 1020s, but in 1276 conquered Austria and moved their home. For over 300 years, Hapsburgs were the emperors of the **Holy Roman Empire,** a loosely-held, and German-based empire in Western and Central Europe, including Italian territories. It lasted from 962 to 1806. The family had Spanish and Austrian branches which would eventually go their separate ways. The

Hapsburgs of the 1500s controlled the wealth of the following places: Castile, Aragon, Burgundy, Austria, many Italian city-states, the Low Countries of Holland, Belgium, and Luxembourg, and much of the Americas. **One dream of the Hapsburgs was the medieval ideal going back to Charlemagne (800) of uniting all "European" territories under one government and one faith, the Roman Catholic Church.**

Naturally, the Hapsburgs had lots of enemies on all sides. One was the French **House of Valois.** The Valois wanted to establish the Pyrenees Mountains as the natural borders between France and Spain. They also wanted to weaken the Spanish Hapsburg hold over the Italian Peninsula, and annex Burgundy and the Low countries to France. **Therefore, French power could expand only as Hapsburg power declined. Another enemy of the Hapsburgs were the Ottoman Turks on the southern part of Europe. In 1521, the Turks conquered Belgrade, subdued Serbia, and advanced into Hungary. This Turkish and Muslim threat made the Hapsburgs spend lots of resources protecting the southern flank.**

A third enemy of the Hapsburgs was the League of Schmalkaden, made up of Protestant rulers of Northern Europe who used the religious conflict between Martin Luther and the Roman Catholic Church in 1517 to promote their own states. France, though a Catholic country, helped the Protestant Germans and the Muslim Turks against the Catholic Hapsburgs. French opposition prevented the Catholic Hapsburgs from defeating the Protestants of Northern Europe. **The Protestant Rebellion** against the Roman Catholic Church split Christianity in the West, stimulated German nationalism, encouraged industrial capitalism and banking, promoted religious individualism and secularism, and stimulated political absolutism.

The Thirty Years War and The Peace of Westphalia

Starting in the 1500s, many people gradually began identifying more with their secular rulers than with their social class or their religion. This shift accelerated after the **Thirty Years' War** of 1618 to 1648. This was the first European continental war in modern history. It was at once a religious struggle between Protestants and Catholics, and also an attempt by the various German princes to free themselves of the restrictions and burdens of the Holy Roman Empire led by a Catholic Hapsburg emperor. Furthermore, it was a war between Spain and

France, and a struggle by Denmark and Sweden to increase their power in the Baltic. Religious and political issues were combined. It was not a purely religious war.

The war ended with the **Peace of Westphalia of 1648.** Switzerland and Holland were recognized as fully independent countries. **The Holy Roman emperor was not to make any laws, raise taxes, or armies in the empire without the consent of the three hundred rulers of the German states. Thus, Germany could not be unified under Hapsburg rule.** In addition, since the war was fought mostly in Germanic lands, the territory was devastated demographically and physically and it would take 223 years before all the small German states would be united under one German state. Spain lost all prestige. France was the big winner.

Most importantly, the Thirty Years War marked the beginning of dynastic wars and the modern European system of fully sovereign and independent states whose many alliances transcended religious affiliations. The Peace of Westphalia acknowledged that countries were the legitimate players in the international system, each seeking its own interests and entering alliances to promote its security. It recognized the right of states to exist and deal with one another as legal entities. This system of shifting alliances to maintain a balance of power would include such countries as Spain, Portugal, Holland, France, England, Russia, Austria and Prussia, among others. The Hapsburg ideal of a united Europe would have to wait until the 2000s.

The European Inter-State System

After the Peace of Westphalia of 1648, the people of Europe increasingly identified with their particular countries more than they did with their families, clans, feudal overlords, or religions. While these countries had many particular foreign policy objectives in the short-run, each state would have certain goals which remained consistent for centuries.

From the 1500s to the 2000s different countries alternated as dominant world power: Spain in the 1500s, France from 1661 to 1815, England from 1815 to 1914, Germany in the European continent from 1871 to 1945, Russia from 1945 to 1991, and the United States throughout the 1900s. Major confrontations involved the Spaniards versus the English and the French in the 1500s and 1600s, the French versus the British between 1661 and 1815 in Europe, North America and India, the Austrians versus the Turks in the 1500s and

Holy Roman Empire, c. 970 A.D.

Courtesy of maps.com.

The Hapsburg Empire Under Charles V, 1557

Courtesy of maps.com.

versus the Prussians in the 1860s, the Germans versus the French in Europe in 1871, 1914 and 1939, and the United States versus Japan between 1941 and 1945, and versus Russia globally between 1945 and 1991.

Portugal

The first goal of Portugal was to expel the Muslims from its territory. They had invaded Iberia in 711. Portugal began the European voyages of discovery in the 1440s, which led it to explore West Africa, sail around South Africa, and reach India in 1497 and China in 1513. It had colonies in Africa and in Asia. Portugal also reached and claimed Brazil. However, Portugal declined in the 1500s, and from 1580 to 1640 it was actually forcibly annexed by Spain. **Therefore, Portugal's long term objectives would be to regain some of its lost colonies, and to gain freedom from Spain. It would find a valuable ally in England in its struggles first against Spain and later against France.**

Spain

Spain was able to defeat the Muslims in the 1490s after 781 years of struggle against a people who had invaded its territory. **This explains in part why at the moment of the great European discovery of the New World in 1492, Spain had great military leaders and conquerors, but had a rather weak commercial class.** The expulsion of the Jews in 1492 did not help Spain economically either. Spain sought a passage to China and India which would bypass the Muslim-controlled areas of the Middle East. However, instead of going around Africa like the Portuguese, Christopher Columbus sailed west and reached the West Indies. Spanish conquerors followed the explorers after 1519 and defeated the Mexicans (Aztecs) in 1521 and the Incas in 1534. Much of the wealth of the defeated Amerindians was taken to Spain. Nevertheless, it did not help the Spaniards much since the gold and the silver brought into the country created inflation and the rise in prices inhibited the development of industry by

The Voyages of Vasco Da Gama and Ferdinand Magellan

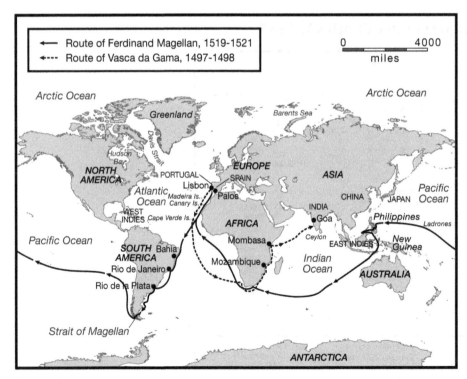

Courtesy of maps.com.

The African Slave Trade, 15th–19th Centuries

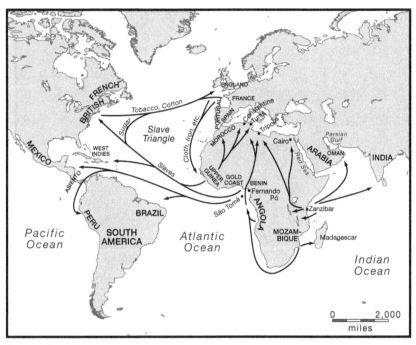

Courtesy of maps.com.

The African Slave Trade, 15th–19th Centuries

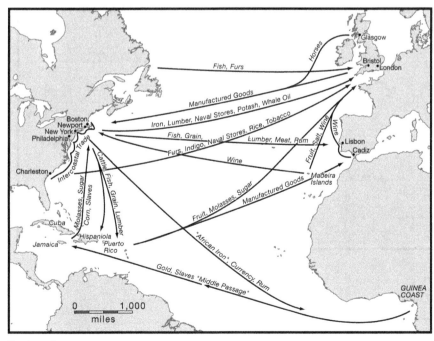

Courtesy of maps.com.

Europe in 1648

Courtesy of maps.com.

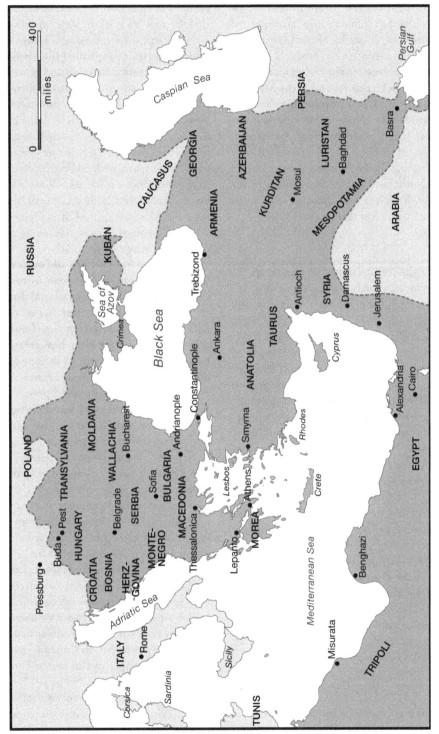

Ottoman Empire, 1680

Courtesy of maps.com.

making it noncompetitive. The wealth from the New World actually was used to stimulate manufacturing and finance in the Protestant countries of northern Europe where Spain bought its manufactured products.

Spain's major interests were the defeat of the Protestants in German territories and of the Muslims in Southeast Europe, and the preservation of its control over the Spanish Netherlands and its empire in the Americas. Yet, it began to decline after the Spanish Armada was defeated in 1588 by the English when it tried to invade England. By 1648, it had also lost its part of the Low Countries and had suffered losses in the Thirty Years War. It then concentrated in keeping its American colonies. Spain lost them all by 1898.

Holland

Holland, part of the Netherlands, was blessed with a favorable geographic location by the ancient trade routes running north to south from Bergen to Gibraltar, and east to west from the Gulf of Finland to Britain. It began to grow rich as a carrier of many goods. Holland developed a merchant marine which in the 1600s began to challenge Portugal in the East and in Brazil. **Its commercial success, coupled with the great immigration of Protestant skilled artisans escaping from Catholic Europe, led to growth in manufacturing and a favorable trade surplus which then stimulated banking.**

The 1600s were Holland's Golden Century. However, it declined in the 1700s due to French and British discrimination against the Dutch merchant marine, wars with Britain from 1652 to 1674 over mercantile disputes, and wars with France from 1697 to 1713 over Louis XIV's territorial ambitions. In addition, the Dutch were unable to match the demographic, agricultural, and commercial assets of the English and the French. **The long-term objective of the Dutch was to deny any major power control of the Low Countries (Holland, Belgium, and Luxembourg).** It joined several alliances to fight Spain, France, and later Germany. Holland also sought to retain its commercial properties in the East Indies by what today is Indonesia.

France

France became the major power in Europe after the Peace of Westphalia of 1648. Earlier, from 1624 to 1642, **Cardinal Richelieu,** the French First Minister, brought about a revolution in the conduct of diplomacy by promoting two new ideas—*raison d'etat,* and balance of power. The first, **raison d'etat,** or reason of state, means that the well-being of the state justifies whatever means are used to further its power. **Thus, the idea of the national interest supplanted the Medieval notion of a universal morality. Religion and morality became secondary to the survival and strengthening of the state.** The second idea, **balance of power,** replaced the concept of a universal monarchy with the belief that if each state pursued its own interest making alliances as it saw fit, this would contribute to the well being of all the countries, for no country would be able to expand extensively since other states would make alliances against it. Richelieu, a secularized Catholic Cardinal, supported Protestants and Muslims against Catholic countries because he was thinking first of France. He also increased the power of the monarchy over the nobility.

The reign of Louis XIV of France (1661 to 1715), started a new era in European history. For the first time, the control of international diplomacy passed to the monarchs, and they began to exert greater authority over their territories. Louis XIV and the monarchs who came after him created the classical balance of power system in Europe in which five or more countries—England, France, Spain, Austria, Prussia and others—pursued power, glory, war and security by entering and terminating alliances with other powers. This system was characterized by the following traits: frequent wars; cautious defensive military tactics; rapid and constant changes in diplomatic alliances; a general unwillingness or inability to seek total victory over an enemy; disinterest in the domestic affairs of other states; alliances made without regard to tradition, religion, or loyalty; subsidies from richer to poorer states; continuous peace negotiations; and a general willingness to compromise on issues.

In general, France pursued certain long-term goals: to control the Low Countries of Belgium, Holland and Luxembourg; to defeat the Austrian Hapsburgs; to extend France westward to the Rhine River; to keep the Germans disunited; to defeat England in the continent, in Canada, in the Ohio Valley, in the Mississippi, and in India. During the time of **Napoleon Bonaparte,** 1799 to 1815, France also tried to conquer the entire European continent and govern Spain, Portugal, the Low Countries, and parts of German territories. Napoleon's continental expansion, although welcomed in some places at first, because of the French Revolution (1789) ideals of liberty, equality and fraternity, stimulated **nationalism** in the Italian

Peninsula and in the German territories. Napoleon's invasion of Spain and Russia and Portugal were disasters from which France never recovered. France's constant expansion from 1661 to 1815 was usually repelled by a coalition of countries which included England, Spain, Austria, and others.

England

England became known as Great Britain in the early 1700s when it absorbed Scotland and Wales, and as the United Kingdom of Great Britain and Northern Ireland in the 1900s. **Its major goal was to cooperate with other states to keep the Low Countries away from the control first of the Hapsburgs, then of France, and later of Germany.** This is a crucial area which can be used by its enemies to attack England. **Another goal from the 1660s to the 1800s, was to keep France from becoming a dominant power in Europe, North America and in India. Still another long-term goal of Great Britain from the 1800s to the 1940s, consisted in keeping Russia from controlling Central Asia and from defeating Turkey, which could have given Russia access to the Mediterranean.** England also needed to keep the Iberian peninsula free of French domination in order to keep the Mediterranean open to English commerce. In pursuit of these goals, England built the best navy and a naval tradition, created an empire, spread British institutions around the world, and encouraged domestic economic growth.

Great Britain was able to defeat France in their long, world-wide struggle between 1661 and 1815 due to several factors: better geographical position as England only had to protect its eastern side, and it is almost an island difficult to invade; fewer enemies; a powerful navy to protect its global assets; superior economy and technology; a larger business and industrial class; and less debt. Great Britain was the greatest world power in history from 1800 to 1914. **The British Empire** dominated in the area of culture, investment, industry, and naval affairs.

Russia

Russia's immediate concern in the 1500s was to defeat the Tatars and other Turkic people. Russia then had to defeat Poland, Lithuania, and Sweden, the greatest northern power of the 1600s. This was accomplished by the early 1700s. **Afterwards, Russia's ambitions were several: gain access to the Baltic to acquire ports useful in the winter; reach the Black Sea to enter the**

Mediterranean and the Middle East; and spread to the Pacific, Central Asia, and the Balkans. By 1796, Russia, Prussia and Austria had divided Poland among themselves. Russia was very active in Asia. In 1850 it won the Kazakh steppes and acquired lands north of the Amur River by the Chinese border. In 1864, it took the Caucasus (Armenia, Azerbaijan, and Georgia), and between 1865 and 1876, it conquered Turkestan in Central Asia. **Russia was the most expansionist of all the European powers, and this worried Great Britain whose territories in India were close to Central Asia.**

Austria

The Austrians are Germans in Central Europe. One of their major weaknesses was their location, being surrounded by many enemies. At first, their major goal was the defeat of France, the Protestants, and the Turks, and to keep these out of the Holy Roman Empire. They, with the support of the Poles, probably saved Europe from the Muslims in September 11–12, 1683. Later, their objective became one of uniting all the Germans of the Holy Roman Empire in a Hapsburg state. After being defeated in 1866 by Prussia, another German state, the Austrians decided to expand into the Balkans. This would lead to a confrontation with Serbia and Russia in the 1910s and caused World War I.

The Congress of Vienna of 1815. One of the earliest examples of multilateral, **summit diplomacy** took place in 1815 when the leaders of Austria, Russia, Great Britain and France, under the leadership of Austrian Prince **Von Metternich**, met to redraw the European balance of power after the final defeat of Napoleon. The Metternich system saved Europe from another continental war for 100 years. Since France had been the major expansionist power from 1661 to 1815, the Congress decided to enact the following measures to contain it in the future: Holland and Belgium were united as the **Kingdom of the Netherlands; Prussia** received most of the left bank of the Rhine; **Austria** received lands in northern Italy, and was made the strongest German state; **Piedmont and Sardinia** were restored in Italy (by 1870 they would unite Italy); Bavaria, Bade, and Wurtenberg were strengthened to prevent France from going east into Germany; and the **German Confederation** of 39 states united the previous 300 German states. **As a result, France could not expand because it was surrounded by countries. It was also forced to return all the territories Napoleon had conquered from 1800 to 1815.**

Colonial Possessions in Latin America in the last Quarter of the 18th Century

NORTH AMERICA

VICEROYALTY OF NEW SPAIN

UNITED STATES

Atlantic Ocean

FLORIDA

BAHAMAS (BR.)

MEXICO

CUBA

WEST INDIES (BR.)

Caribbean Sea

CENTRAL AMERICA

GUIANA

Bogotá

VICEROYALTY OF NEW GRANADA

PORTUGAL

Pacific Ocean

VICEROYALTY OF BRAZIL

Lima

SOUTH AMERICA

VICEROYALTY OF PERU

Bahia

VICEROYALTY OF LA PLATA

Rio de Janeiro

Buenos Aires

0   1,000
miles

PATAGONIA (unclaimed)

Colonial Empires
Portuguese
French
Spanish
British
Dutch

Cape Horn

Courtesy of maps.com.

North America, 1783

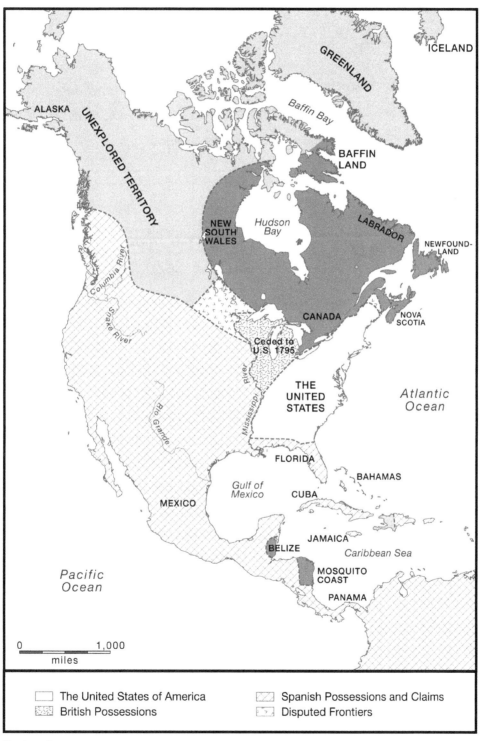

Courtesy of maps.com.

Latin American Independence, First Half of the 19th Century

Courtesy of maps.com.

Metternich also convinced Russia and Austria to fight liberal and democratic forces in their respective countries instead of fighting each other in the Balkans. **However, tensions between the two grew when Austria refused to support Russia in the Crimean War of 1856,** when the latter tried to get control of Constantinople (Istanbul), a strategic spot between the Black Sea and the Mediterranean. In this war, Russia was opposed by Great Britain, France, Turkey, and Sardinia. Russian nationalists would not forgive Austria for this "betrayal."

An event that also affected politics in the Balkans was the creation of the **Austro-Hungarian Empire** in 1867 by the Germans of Austria and the Magyars of Hungary. This empire had control of the following groups: Slovenes, Croats, Bosnians, Serbs, Poles, Czechs and Slovaks, most of whom were Slavs like the Russians. These groups were caught up in the nationalist ideology of the French Revolution and demanded to have their own states.

Germany

Germany did not become a state until 1871. Since the beginning of the Holy Roman Empire in the 900s, the Germans were divided into about 300 states. Napoleon did away with many of these in 1806, and formally ended the Holy Roman Empire. However, it would be **Otto Von Bismarck** (1815 to 1890) of Prussia, one of the German principalities, who would be responsible for the unification of Germany by defeating Denmark in 1864, Austria in 1866, and France in 1871. Prussia thus became the major German state and main force in the new Germany. The German Confederation was absorbed into the new state. **By defeating France and taking Alsace-Lorraine, Germany became the most powerful state in continental Europe, upset the balance of power in the region, and planted the seeds for World War I.**

Once Germany had defeated France, and upset the balance of power in the region, Bismarck's major foreign policy objective was to ensure that France did not enter into an alliance with states which could surround and threaten Germany. Therefore, he created an alliance with Austria and Russia so that neither country would ally with France. Bismarck's major difficulty was that both Austria and Russia were competing in the Balkans. When German leaders, after Bismarck, were not successful in keeping Austria and Russia from bickering over the Balkans, Germany chose to support Austria's claims. This made Russia seek the support of France

against Germany and Austria. Related to the creation of Germany was the birth of Italy from 1866 to 1870.

Western Revolutions

The material development of Western Civilization has been enhanced by numerous revolutions, which are fundamental changes in either the intellectual, political, economic, or social conditions of a society. Since the 1300 and 1400s, the speed of change has accelerated dramatically in Western societies. The Enlightenment, liberalism, industrialization, and socialism have been among the most revolutionary movements.

The Enlightenment is the name given by its supporters to a cultural transformation starting in the 1680s and continuing throughout the 1700s, which placed faith in the possibility and desirability of change and in the conviction that human reason could comprehend the process of nature and society and manipulate them to create a better world. They believed that the rational order that the scientific revolution had discovered in the physical world should also exist in human societies. These thinkers assumed that reason provided them with the means to conduct a radical critique of all traditional beliefs and institutions and that this critique would inspire innovation and improvement. Many of these ideas about enlightenment reform were spread through the emerging print culture by such supporters (philosophes) as Voltaire, Montesquieu, Diderot, Rousseau, Smith, and Hume. While some of the philosophes like Voltaire and Rousseau sought the rejection of most of the Western tradition, others like Montesquieu wanted to preserve what was best in it. Not everyone believes the Enlightenment was a bright, positive force in history. In some places it would lead to discrimination against religion and to increased warfare.

Liberalism

Another revolutionary movement which transformed the West was Liberalism. While there have been different types of liberalisms, its inspiration has remained the same: hostility to concentration of power in cultural, economic, and political institutions that threaten the freedom of the individual, a willingness to examine institutions in the light of new needs, and a dislike of sudden changes. Different forms of liberalism usually disagree on how much power should be given to the government. Yet, they

Africa, 1965

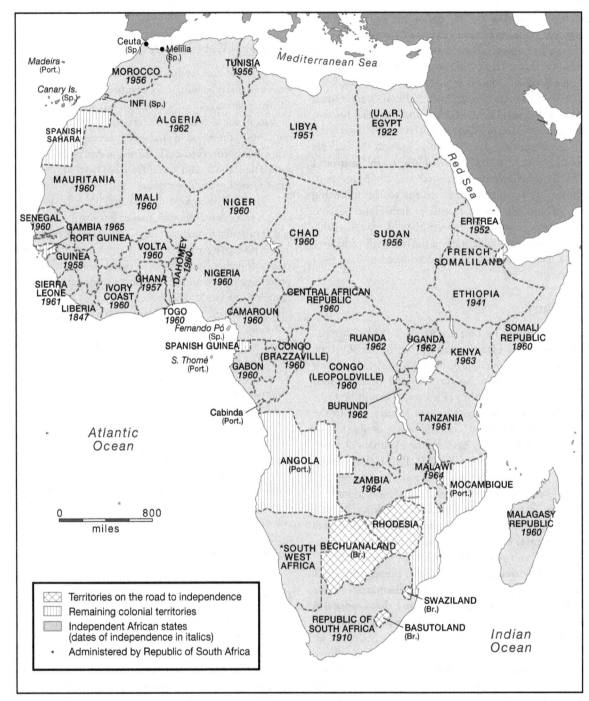

Courtesy of maps.com.

Europe in 1915

Courtesy of maps.com.

support significant political and economic freedom for the individual. **Liberal principles influenced the English Civil War of 1642, the English Declaration of Rights of 1688, the U.S. Declaration of Independence in 1776, the French Revolution of 1789, and its Declaration of the Rights of Man and of the Citizen.** These principles have also spread world-wide in the 1900s, though they have been opposed by fascist and communist ideologies and governments. Unfortunately, the French Revolution which originally advocated liberty, equality, and fraternity, by 1791 had unleashed civil war, persecution of Catholics and other dissidents, and dictatorship, leading to approximately 500,000 deaths.

The Industrial Revolution

In the 1780s, there was a breakthrough in productivity in Great Britain as a mechanical factory system was created which produced goods in vast quantities. The steam engine used heat energy to furnish driving power for machines, ending the age-old dependency on animal, wind, and water power. Coal provided the power to drive the steam engine which would revolutionize the textile industry and industrialization in general. This revolution stimulated population growth, urbanization, prosperity, consumerism, military technology, wars, and imperialism. Industrialization then spread to continental Europe and gradually worldwide.

Socialism

Socialism is a doctrine which advocates economic collectivism through governmental or industrial group ownership of the means of production and distribution of goods. Modern socialism was most of all a reaction to the unregulated capitalism of the late 1700s and 1800s, which had enlarged the freedoms of the industrialists and middle classes, but had not yet extended protection to the lower middle class and the poor. The two major branches of socialism in the 1880s were Communitarian Socialism, which was generally in favor of gradual reforms in small jurisdictions, and **Marxism** which advocated the violent elimination of the capitalist class. Later, there developed in the industrial societies a form of socialism

Europe, 1920

Courtesy of maps.com.

Indian Tribes in America Prior to European Colonization

Courtesy of maps.com.

which is democratic and which seeks greater equality through taxation and spending policies.

The New Western Imperialism

A new wave of Western **imperialism** began in 1870. The old imperialism, except in the Americas, was willing to engage in trade activities with natives of different regions without interfering with their local institutions. This new imperialism imposed European economic, political and cultural institutions over large parts of Africa and Asia. There were many reasons for the new imperialistic wave. The decline of the Ottoman Empire in the 1800s brought many political changes in North Africa which threatened British interests in Egypt. As a result, the British invaded Egypt in 1882 and later Sudan to protect the Suez Canal. However, the French did not want the British to upset the balance of power, so they took most of West Africa.

Six European states had divided Africa among themselves by the Berlin Conference of 1885. Only Liberia and Ethiopia remained as independent African states. Also stimulating the partition of Africa were geographers exploring Africa, whose books about the great

beauty and wealth of the continent excited the imagination of Europeans, Christian missionaries who wanted to propagate the faith and who called on their respective governments for assistance whenever they ran into physical difficulties, private entrepreneurs who manipulated their governments into supporting their exploitation of minerals in the hinterlands, and commercial competitors for raw materials and investments. In Asia, the principal colonial powers were Great Britain, which went into India, China, and Brunei; France, which penetrated the Indo-China Peninsula, (Vietnam, Laos and Cambodia); Japan, which conquered Korea; and the Netherlands, which was established in Indonesia. The major events in East Asia were the collapse of the Chinese Empire founded in 221 B.C., and the industrialization and rise of Japan as the dominant Asian power.

World War I

World War I was one of the most important events in the global affairs of the 1900s. It lasted four years and three months, involved thirty states, ended four empires, gave rise to the first communist country, killed 8.5 million soldiers and ten million civilians, and had a direct cost of $180 billion, and an indirect cost of $151.6 billion. **World War I undermined Europe's global political and economic leadership, and began the slow emancipation process of the colonials living under the European empires in Africa and Asia.** It involved the United States in 1917 and also saw the participation of Japan. These two countries would outstrip most countries in economic and political power in the post-World War I years.

The war had various causes. **One was the conflict between Austria and Serbia over the territory of Bosnia-Herzegovina.** In 1908, Austria annexed it. This upset the balance of power in the Balkans. For the first time, Germany was willing to go to war to back Austria and demanded full Serbian and Russian recognition of the annexation of Bosnia-Herzegovina by Austria. Germany failed to moderate Austria's ambitions in the Balkans. Meanwhile, Russian nationalists wanted Russia to support Serbian aspirations in Bosnia against Austria.

Another conflict was between Great Britain and Germany. Great Britain felt threatened by Germany, which already had the biggest army, but now also wanted to have a navy as large as Great Britain's. In addition, Germany sought to construct a railroad from Germany to Turkey and to Baghdad. This presented a danger to the British Suez Canal and to its Central Asian routes to India. In addition, Germany's products were competing with and beating British commerce worldwide. As a result of these intense Anglo-German confrontations, England in 1906 made a military alliance with France, its long-term rival in Europe, and in 1907 it created an Anglo-Russian Entente. **This meant that there were two competing forces in European diplomacy: the Triple Entente of Russia, Great Britain, and France, and the German-Austrian Alliance.** Instead of a flexible balance of power system in which states entered and left alliances upon convenience, now there were two inflexible alliances waiting for a spark to ignite them.

United States Expansion, 1783–1898

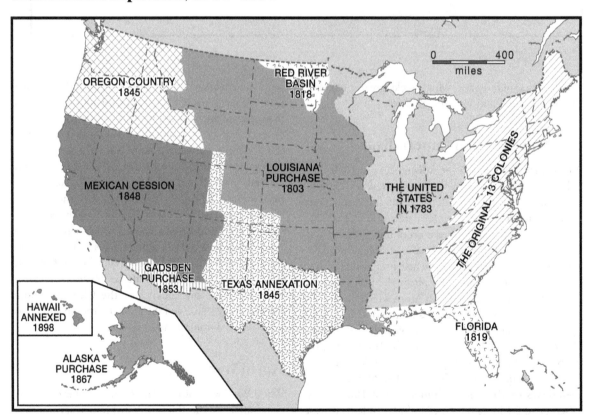

Courtesy of maps.com.

A third cause of World War I was nationalism. Many people had national aspirations. France wanted to recover the province of Alsace and most of Lorraine from Germany. Serbia wanted the provinces of Bosnia and Herzegovina to be controlled by Slavs and not by Austrians. Italy wanted the Terentino region and Trieste from Austria-Hungary. Czechs, Italians, Poles, Slovenes, Croats, Serbs, and Slovaks wanted freedom from Austria-Hungary. Estonians, Finns, Latvians, Poles, and others wanted independence from Russia. Also, Bulgarians, Greeks, Rumanians, Serbs, Armenians, and Macedonians resented Turkish misrule. As the new Balkan sates of Serbia, Greece, Romania, and Bulgaria gained strength, they sought more territory, and this desire created tensions between Austria on one hand, and Serbia and Russia on the other.

There were other causes of World War I, but the immediate one was the assassination on June 28, 1914, of Francis Ferdinand, the heir to the Austro-Hungarian throne, and his wife, by someone with ties to Serbia. By August 14, 1914, all alliances and secret commitments became activated and the war was on. Countries which had no significant bilateral conflicts such as Germany and Russia, and Great Britain and Germany went to war against each other to support their allies.

World War I destroyed the German, Russian, Ottoman (aligned with Germany and Austria), and Austro-Hungarian empires. Among the major territorial changes from the war, the following stand out: France received **Alsace-Lorraine** from Germany; **Poland,** which had been extinguished in the 1790s by Austria, Russia, and Prussia, was recreated with lands from Germany, Russia, and Austria-Hungary; **Czechoslovakia** was created from Austria-Hungary by uniting the Czechs and the Slovaks; **Austria**, and **Hungary** became smaller independent states; **Yugoslavia** was created from the union of Slovenia, Croatia, Bosnia-Hezergovina, Macedonia, Serbia, and Montenegro; and **Lithuania, Estonia,** and **Latvia** became independent of Russia. There were other changes due to the war: Bulgaria lost her outlet to the Aegean Sea; Arabia became independent; Syria and Lebanon became League of Nations mandates, entrusted to France, while Palestine-Trans Jordan and Iraq were entrusted to Great Britain; and Armenia became independent.

These were changes brought about by the Paris Peace Conference of 1919 to 1922 which brought together only the winners of the war. (Russia did not attend because it had become communist during the war), and which for the first time in the history of diplomacy, forced the loser, Germany in this case, to indemnify the civilian population of the victors. The main player at the Peace of Paris was the United States.

The Americans

The most decisive event in world affairs in the late 1800s and early 1900s was the rise of the United States. It had the world's highest income, the most productive manufacturing sectors, and the third largest navy. Wisely, since 1796, the United States had followed a policy of unilateralism avoiding permanent political and military alliances with Europeans. The United States concentrated in expanding westward which placed it in conflict with numerous Amerindian tribes whose level of social and technological sophistication was no match for the European-Americans. Only the Iroquois had been able to create a federation of tribes in North America when the Europeans came.

By the 1800s, the Americans had reached the Mississippi, and in 1830, the India Removal Act moved most Amerindians west of the Mississippi. The Americans then moved into the Plains, the area between the Mississippi River and the Rocky Mountains. In 1890 at the Battle of Wounded Knee in South Dakota, the last major fight between the Americans and the Plains Amerindians took place. The Sioux were defeated. Earlier in the 1830s and 1840s, the United States had defeated Mexico and deprived it of one-third of its territory, including Texas, New Mexico, and California, where gold had been discovered.

Once the United States reached the Pacific, it continued acquiring territory: Alaska in 1867; the Midway Islands in 1867; Hawaii in 1898; Guam in 1898; the Philippines in 1898; Puerto Rico in 1898; Wake Island in 1899; American Samoa in 1899, the Panama Canal Zone in 1903; the Virgin Islands in 1916; the Northern Mariana Islands in 1947; and the Marshall and Caroline Islands in 1947. In the early 1900s, the United States replaced Great Britain as the major financial and political influence in the Caribbean Basin. As the American economy became an integrated national one, and as the U.S. government acquired more fiscal powers and spending responsibilities, Americans began identifying less with their particular states and more with their national identity, particularly after the victorious experience in World War I during 1917 and 1918. American prestige grew as they controlled the Paris Peace Conference and proposed the formation of the **League of Nations** to prevent wars. Americans became the source of financial credit for European reconstruction after World War I.

The Japanese

Japan is separated from the Asian mainland by 115 miles. The Japanese are mostly a Mongoloid people who migrated before the Christian era from Northeast Asia, although the original settlers were the Caucasoid Ainus. Other groups were Malayan and Polynesian immigrants who came from the south. The Japanese were isolated until the AD 400s From 1603 to 1867, Japan was led by the Tokugawa Shogunate, a feudal aristocracy headed by shoguns. The Dutch were the only Westerners allowed to trade with the Japanese. This isolationism ended when the United States in 1853 began forcing Japan to open up ports to Western countries.

After 1867, the Meiji reforms began to modernize Japan to increase its national power and to prevent Western penetration. The Meiji standardized education, built a conscript army, created a small navy, and promoted heavy industry in mining, steel and shipbuilding. **By 1914, Japan was the only non-European country to industrialize.** In addition, Japan began to acquire new territories: the Kurile Islands from Russia in 1875; the Bonior Islands in 1876; the Ryukyu Islands in 1879; Taiwan from China in 1895; and Korea and Southern Sakhalim Islands from Russia in 1905. **By defeating China in 1895 and Russia in 1905, Japan became the leading Asian power.**

World War II

World War II began on September 1, 1939, and ended in August 1945. It cost the lives of fifty-five million soldiers and civilians and $1.2 trillion in property damages. The Allies included Belgium, China, France, India, Poland, Russia (after 1941), the United Kingdom of Great Britain and Northern Ireland, and the United States. The Axis powers included Austria, Bulgaria, Finland, Germany, Hungary, Italy, and Japan.

In a sense, the Second World War was the result of the failure to resolve the causes of World War I. Germany was treated very harshly, losing Alsace-Lorraine, her overseas empire, and part of East Prussia to Poland. Italy did not receive the European and African territories promised by Allies in World War I, and was humiliated at the Paris (Versailles) Peace Conference.

Furthermore, Japan felt it had not received concessions worthy of her military involvement in World War I. **The immediate causes of the war were Germany's takeover of Austria and Czechoslovakia in 1938 and Poland in 1939, Italy's invasion of Ethiopia in 1935, and Japan's expansion into Machuria, China, and Southeast Asia between 1931 and 1941, and the bombing of Pearl Harbor on December 7, 1941.**

However, there were other reasons: **the Great Depression of the 1930s,** a result of World War I, caused **massive unemployment in Europe as well as world wide;** the replacement of the liberal, open, world economy of the period before 1914 with an economy characterized by high tariffs and vicious **protectionism;** the rise in Germany, Italy, Japan, and Russia of **"Fascist" dictators** promising their poverty-stricken and anxious populations prosperity through a philosophy of **imperialism** and **"survival of the fittest;"** England's failure to support France with a military alliance to contain Germany in the continent; the United States' failure to be an active participant in the international system during the post-World War I years; **and the desire of both Russia and Germany to partition Poland between themselves.**

World War II was made possible when Russia's Communist leaders and Germany's Nazis made a secret non-aggression pact in 1939. This allowed Hitler to attack Western Europe without worrying about his eastern front, while Russia moved to acquire parts of Poland and of the Baltic states. Later, in 1942, once he had defeated France and the Low Countries, Hitler turned against Russia. Then, in 1942, the United States, the United Kingdom, and Russia established a wartime alliance against Germany.

The war in Europe ended on May 8, 1945, and the war in Japan on September 2, 1945. World War II completely finished Europe's dominance in global affairs and accelerated the independence of the colonials within the European empires of Africa and Asia. By destroying Germany and dividing it between the communist Russians on one hand, and the democratic states of the United States, France, and the United Kingdom, on the other hand, Central Europe was not strong enough to prevent the spread of communism into Eastern Europe and the Balkans. **World War II also destroyed the multinational balance of power and led to the rise of a bipolar international system with only two super powers: the United States and the Soviet Union, or Russia.**

Asian Independence Since 1945

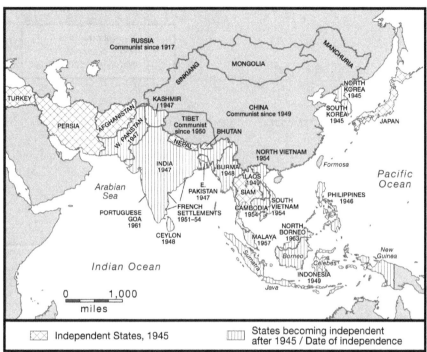

Courtesy of maps.com.

The End of the Empires

Ninety-six countries with about 33% of the world's population won their independence between 1944 and 1985. The Asian colonies did this within a decade, and the African ones within two decades after World War II. There were various reasons for this colonial revolution: weakening of the colonial powers during the war; growth of democratic, anti-imperialistic sentiments within the European powers themselves; decline of Western prestige after the Japanese easily swept the British out of Malaya and Burma, the French from Indochina, the Dutch from Indonesia and the Americans out of the Philippines; Japanese encouragement of the idea of "Asia for the Asians" as they were leaving the region defeated, and their supplying of weapons to local nationalist like Ho Chi Minh's Vietminh in Indochina and Sukarno's Putera in Indonesia; the rise to leadership in the colonial territories of Western-educated individuals such as Gandhi, Nehru, Sukarno, Nkrumah, Azikwe and Bourguiba; the participation of many colonials in both Allied and Japanese armies and labor battalions; and the effect on the colonial populations of Allied ideals of freedom and self-determination.

India and Pakistan's independence were the most important single events of the colonial revolution. India itself was partitioned in 1947 into Pakistan, which became an independent Muslim state, and India, which became a majority Hindu country.

The Cold War

The Cold War is the name given to the bipolar conflict between the United States and the Soviet Union, and their respective allies between 1945 and 1991. The major cause of the breakdown of the wartime alliance between the United States and Russia was Stalin's insistence upon expanding Russian power into Eastern Europe, the eastern Mediterranean, and Southeast Asia. Complicating this **East-West conflict** was the process of decolonization (**North-South conflict**), by which the peoples of Asia and Africa emancipated themselves from the European empires and sought economic assistance and preferential treatment from the developed countries. Commanding

Eastern and Western Europe, c. 1955

Courtesy of maps.com.

crucial raw materials and strategic locations, the emerging countries of Asia and Africa became valuable in the East-West struggle. The tensions were heightened by the presence of nuclear weapons.

The origins of the Cold War are found in the conflicts over the partition of Germany, by the Americans, the British, the French and the Russians after World War II, in the creation of a new bipolar balance of power at the war's end, in the gradual "communization" or "collectivization" of Eastern European states such as Albania (1946), Bulgaria (1946), Yugoslavia (1946), Poland (1947), Romania (1947) Czechoslovakia (1948), and Hungary (1949), and their conversion into a Russian or Soviet sphere of influence. Other factors were the West's fear of communist subversion in France and Italy, Soviet pressures on Turkey, communist-led revolutions in Greece, Malaya and the Philippines, and the resurgence of the Communist-Kuomintang struggle in China. The roots of the Cold War are also found in the development of an active anti-communist philosophy and policy in the United States and in the West, and in the building of alliances and counteralliances that created a pervasive atmosphere of fear and suspicion between wartime allies.

It was understood by the Western allies that the Soviets would not allow threatening alliances close to their borders, but the United States hoped that some of the governments of Eastern Europe would have some degree of pluralism or diversity in ideology and interests. The United Kingdom's Churchill and the Soviet Union's Stalin had even discussed the following power-sharing ratios: Romania (90% Soviet), Bulgaria (80% Soviet), Hungary (50% Soviet), Yugoslavia (50% Soviet), Greece (90% British), and large Soviet interests in Poland and Czechoslovakia.

However, the Soviets moved in their Red Army and prevented non-communist participation in East European elections. Europe became divided into democratic and capitalist Europe, and communist, Russian-controlled Eastern Europe. Reflecting on these events, Winston Churchill announced on March 5, 1946, that "an iron curtain had fallen over Eastern Europe." The American policy began to toughen up in the spring of 1946 when Stalin demanded the evacuation of Azerbaijan. The Russians were supporting guerrillas in Greece from bases in Yugoslavia and Bulgaria. Territorial demands were being made against Turkey and requests were made for Soviet bases in the Straits.

After 1945, the United States began to construct a policy of **internationalism** which is the practice of national involvement in cooperative interstate efforts to solve common security, political economic and social problems. Washington pursued internationalism to contain Russia, international communism, and promote the financial and socio-economic conditions necessary for material prosperity and peace.

The United States tried to contain the Russian expansion in Eastern and Central Europe with three policies which became part of its containment plan: the **Truman Doctrine,** which gave aid to any country fighting communism, particularly in the Mediterranean area; the **Marshall Plan,** which extended to Western Europe over $15 billion in economic aid from 1948 to 1952; and the **North Atlantic Treaty Organization (NATO),** in 1949, which for the first time in U.S. history committed American troops to the defense of other countries. The Russians developed their own military alliance called the **Warsaw Pact.**

When communist North Korea invaded South Korea in 1950, the United States responded by globalizing its containment policy, increasing its defense budget, establishing over fifty military alliances, beefing up its troops in Europe, organizing covert operations in numerous places, and ensuring that its military capabilities surpassed those of the Soviet Union. It would be directly involved fighting communists in Korea from 1950 to 1953, and in Vietnam from 1963 to 1973.

The Russians, on the other hand, began to support political movements and countries outside Europe, starting with Egypt in 1956 and then others such as Cuba, Vietnam, Syria, Ethiopia, etc. **Russian leader Nikita Khrushchev returned to Lenin's idea of penetrating the developing countries to deny the capitalist** countries valuable raw materials, markets and investments and to encircle the capitalists with communist countries. **The United States responded to the Russian challenge by supporting other developing countries.** The result was a significant number of regional conflicts. The Russians themselves would become directly involved in fighting in Afghanistan. However, during the Cold War, the Russians and the Americans fought only through **proxies,** that is, through their respective allies.

The Cold War ended in 1991 when the Soviet Union (Russia) ceased to be a communist state. Russia simply could not compete economically and technologically with the United States and its democratic capitalist allies. The highly-centralized and bureaucratic Russian state inhibited economic competition, technological innovation, the free flow of ideas, free enterprise, and the most basic human rights, all of which are crucial for engaging physical, social, and human capital in their most productive ways.

In addition, the U.S. Reagan administration's strategy of financing opposition to Russia in Afghanistan, Poland, Angola, Nicaragua, Mozambique, Central Asia, and in other places, as well as its efforts to bring down the world prices of oil and gold, which then lowered Russian revenues, and its decision to start an arms race, including in space weaponry (Stars Wars), all accelerated Russia's economic stress. This convinced the new leader of the Soviet Union, Mikhail Gorbachev, that Russia needed substantial changes, including **glasnost** or openness or freedom of expression, and **perestroika,** or greater efficiency in economic production, even adopting some capitalist management techniques. He wanted to reform Russian communism, but his policies actually undermined communism itself by allowing its opponents freedom of expression. Gorbachev then withdrew Russian troops from Eastern Europe and appealed for Western financial and technical aid for Russia.

The Post-Cold War International System

It is too soon to describe the major characteristics of the Post-Cold War international system. Yet, there are some matters and areas which merit attention: the presence of only one military superpower—the United States; the formation of broader, integrated, and exclusive economic markets and unions like NAFTA, MERCOSUR, the European Union and Euroland; the rise of violent nationalist movements in the Balkans, Central Asia, and South Asia, and other areas; the growth of terrorist movements, particularly those associated with so-called Islamic fundamentalism in Southwest Asia, in North Africa, and in other places; the rise of China as a regional superpower threatening the economic expansion and relatively peaceful co-existence among the countries of Southeast Asia and East Asia; the political and economic disintegration of several countries in Tropical Africa; the potentially devastating deterioration of ecological resources needed to sustain the people of many countries during the 21st Century; the constructive and destructive presence of capital funds which enter and exit individual countries looking for higher return on investments, often destabilizing the government and the economies of states, but valuable as a source of capital; the proliferation of illegal drug networks in the developing world which undermine law and order in their countries as they satisfy the demand for drugs in the developed world; the increasing use of the United Nations as a peacemaking or peacekeeping institution; the struggle in the developing world and in the former communist world between those who seek a more democratic, more market-oriented, and open societies and those who want more authoritarian, protectionist, and closed societies; and the polarization of Russia into competing factions, including former communists, organized crime, liberals, neo-Nazis, and others. The "Fundamentalist" Islamic attack against the United States on September 11, 2001, has led to a worldwide confrontation between the U.S., NATO and its allies against terrorist countries and movements everywhere. This has become a new type of World War. If the Cold War could be considered World War III, then the war against global Islamic terrorism could be titled World War IV.

Sources

I. Books

Greer, Thomas G. (1982) *A Brief History of the Western World*. New York: Harcourt Brace Jovanovich Publishers.

Kaiser, David. (1990) *Politics and War: European Conflict from Philip to Hitler*. Cambridge: Harvard University Press.

Kennedy, Paul. (1989) *The Rise and Fall of the Great Powers*. New York: Vintage Brooks.

Kennedy, Paul. (1993) *Preparing for the Twenty First Century*. New York: Vintage Books.

Kissinger, Henry. (1994) *Diplomacy*. New York: Simon and Schuster.

Moynahan, Daniel Patrick. (1994) *Pandemonium: Ethnicity in International Politics*. New York: Oxford University Press.

Muñoz, German. (1997) *Background Lessons on Global Affairs*. New York: American Heritage Custom Publishing Group.

Papp, Daniel S. (1991) *Contemporary International Relations*. New York: MacMillan Publishing Company.

Pfaff, William. (1993) *The Wrath of Nations*. New York: Simon & Schuster.

Poulsen, Thomas M. (1995) *Nations and States: A Geographic Background to World Affairs*. Englewood Cliffs, Prentice-Hall.

Stavrianos, L.S. Global Rift. (1981) *The Third World Comes of Age*. New York: William Morrow and Company.

Stavrianos, L.S. (1995) *A Global History*. Englewood Cliffs, Prentice Hall.

Wallbank, T. Walter, et. al. (1992) *Civilization, Past and Present*. New York MacMillan Publishing Company.

Willis, F. Roy. (1982) *World Civilization*, Toronto: D.C., Heath Company.

CHAPTER FOUR

Conceptualizations of the Family: Race, Ethnicity and Immigration

Víctor Vázquez-Hernández

The family is the most important social institution and agent of **socialization,** which is a lifelong process through which people learn the values, norms, beliefs, attitudes and roles of their culture. It helps in the development of a sense of self and of a sense of community. The family is considered a crucial institution both by those who want to preserve it to achieve proper human nurturing and social stability, and by those who believe there should be greater social experimentation and individual expression.

Sociologists and anthropologists define a family as a group of people who identify themselves as being related to one another, usually by blood, marriage, or adoption, and who share intimate relationships and dependency. The meaning of "family" can be socially constructed within a particular culture or subculture. There are variations within family structures. While "family" may be defined in terms of kinship based on blood or marriage, this need not be the case in some subcultures.

Likewise, the notion of "marriage" is culturally constructed and open to change. **Sociologists often define marriage as a culturally approved relationship, usually between two individuals, that provides for a degree of economic cooperation, intimacy, and sexual activity.** They may be legally certified by the government, as they are in industrial societies, or they may be legitimized by religious organizations, kinship groups, or simply by the norms of the culture. Societies determine what is legal in different ways. The

norm is to make the passage from singlehood to marriage with some ritual. What marriage does is to legitimize a union.

More than likely, the family stands among the oldest social institutions in history. From the beginning of human life on earth, even before nomadic tribes settled into permanently established communities, thousands of years ago, individuals gathered in groups of families for protection and security.

All cultures recognize the family as the most integral part of society and one of the driving forces behind cultural change. The family, as a unit, has been affected by the kinds of social, political and economic changes that take place in society throughout history. With more or less degree of difficulty, families adapt to and survive changes in their immediate social environment.

Types of Families

The typical family of industrialized and post-industrialized societies, such as the United States and Japan, is the nuclear family type. **The nuclear family is a social group consisting of one or two parents and their dependent children.** The number of children in a nuclear family depends on a series of variables largely determined by culture, religious values, and the socio-economic status of the family. In Japanese society, for example, the average nuclear family consists of parents and, at the most, two children. The Japanese have limited space and resources to house and feed large numbers of people.

In many societies, and in some subcultures in the United States and throughout the industrialized world, people live in **extended families which are social groups consisting of one or more parents, children, and other kin, often spanning several generations.** In addition to the basic nuclear family unit, an extended family might also include grandparents, aunts, uncles, cousins, or other close relatives. Most Northern European and North American families are nuclear, while extended families are more common in Eastern and Southern Europe, Africa, Asia, and Latin America. They are found in more than one-half of the world.

Extended families provide for adequate economic and emotional support in a kind of environment that is often hostile to the continuity of a family structure based on a single nuclear arrangement. There is a clearer division of labor. Even the child-rearing function of the family is a shared responsibility. There are cultural variations in who takes responsibility for child-rearing. Traditionally, the role of parent in Western European societies is assumed by the biological parents. However, this is only one of many variations in the world. The native cultures of French Polynesia, for example, have only one word for community and family, and the task of bringing up children is largely the responsibility of the total community of families.

The nuclear family includes only two generations. Therefore, it is a transitorial social phenomenon that normally disintegrates when the children leave the household or the parents die. Conversely, the extended family is more likely to perpetuate itself as a social entity. It does not disintegrate as easily simply because younger members do not have as many options to become economically independent outside the family structure. Extended family units are more likely to preserve traditional family values.

In addition to differences in size, families vary also according to cultural norms governing the number of wives or husbands a person may have. In other words, families can differ according to the particular marriage arrangement allowed by the society. **The two basic cultural patterns are monogamy, in which a person may have only one spouse at a time, and polygamy, in which a person may have more than one spouse at a time. There are two types of polygamy—polygyny, in which a man may have multiple wives, and polyandry, in which a woman may have multiple husbands.**

An American nuclear family. Courtesy of Brain Stablyk/Stone/Getty Images.

Polygamy could be the oldest form of marriage, although there is some doubt since it is known that some very primitive hunting and gathering societies did practice monogamy. The ancient societies of Asia, Africa and the Near East practiced polygyny. The Bible, one of the foundations of the Judeo-Christian religious tradition, mentions polygamy (polygyny) as a sign of class and distinction. Kings David and Solomon and their wives are two of many examples of polygamous relationships mentioned in the Bible. In the Ottoman Empire, the sultans or rulers kept large households of wives called **harems,** sometimes including more than 300 in number. In America, the Mormons who settled in Utah in 1847 practiced polygyny until it was declared illegal in 1890.

Although monogamy is common in industrial societies, polygyny is apparently the rule in many pre-industrial societies. Perhaps in pre-industrial societies warfare often decimated the male population, creating a "surplus" of women who necessarily had to share a smaller number of males if they hoped to have heterosexual relations and bear children. Regardless of the reason for polygyny, today few men actually practice it, even when it is legal. Polyandry has not been practiced by many societies. Less than one percent of world societies engage in it.

Cultural norms and value systems are important in determining the line of descent or **lineage** of the family. Lineage is very important because it promotes membership in a particular kinship group. It allocates power and authority within the family and gives legitimacy to its siblings. Normally, lineage is traced through one of the two sexes. **Patrilineal societies** trace family descent through the male; whereas, **matrilineal,** through females. Most western societies have bilateral descent.

In most cases, lines of descent are associated with the way in which power and authority are allocated in the family structure. If the husband-father is the one in control of the exercise of power and authority, the group is called **patriarchal.** If it is the wife-mother, it is **matriarchal.** A classic example of a patriarchal-patrilineal society is ancient Roman society. In Rome, the father had absolute control of the family and exercised unchecked power and authority over his wife, children and property. The concept of patriarchal family structure and patterns of familial relationships of Rome were extended to the concept of state, and after the collapse of the Republic, to the person of the emperor in the form of "Emperor Worship."

Never to the extreme of Roman society, most modern western societies are basically patriarchal. In the more egalitarian societies, such as the United States, particularly in the aftermath of the Civil Rights Movement of the 1960s and early '70s, and the Women's Movement, when traditional roles of influence and authority of the woman in the family changed, the patriarchal nature of the American family has undergone definite changes. Today, decision-making processes within the American family are a commonly shared experience, sometimes even extended to and including the children.

Another interesting classification of the family includes a category of family based on geographical location. Married couples who are expected to live in a household located near the husband's relatives are **patrilocal.** Those who choose a site near the mother's are **matrilocal.** If the household is separated, autonomous and independent from both, it is then called **neolocal.**

Traditionally, societies all over the world have imposed certain limitations or restrictions on marriages among their members. **Incest,** or sexual intercourse between family members who are socially defined as closely related, is one of those traditional restrictions or **taboos.** A taboo is a strongly held norm whose violation is forbidden, highly offensive, and even unthinkable. Nevertheless, throughout history we have examples of societies, such as Ancient Egypt, where incest was practiced by the pharaoh and members of the imperial families, yet it was a taboo for the rest of the population. Mother-son and father-daughter intercourse has been condemned everywhere as incestuous; brother-sister marriage, although allowed in some places and circumstances, has also generally been prohibited. **The main significance of the incest taboo is that it prevents inbreeding and the isolation of families. If families must go outside to find new sexual partners, alliances among families are made and a larger society becomes possible.**

Types of Marriages

Generally speaking there are two types of marriages: those that are arranged and those based on personal choice. **Arranged marriages are those in which negotiations for selecting a mate or mates are handled by a third party or parties.** This means that immediate families or their respective designates make the choice. This process of selection of mates is normally done while the future partners are still children or adolescents, and sometimes it is done before birth. It is a very convenient and logical way of establishing economic and/or political alliances.

Arranged marriages are practices continued today in many parts of the world such as India, and to some extent Japan, as well as in many traditional societies in Africa and Latin America. It is also seen in Muslim societies. Romantic love, as we understand it in the Western world, is not a consideration for the establishment of a new family in these types of societies. It does not mean, however, that the new family will be dysfunctional, or that the marriage will be an unhappy one. Arranged marriages were also practiced amongst the members of aristocratic and royal families of Europe well until the beginning of the XX century.

Personal-choice marriages are the ones in which the process of selection of mates is carried out through personal choice without the direct intervention of the families. It is the typical union of a man and a woman based on love or on other conditions, and not dictated by economic or political interests. Personal choice marriages are the most common form of establishing families in modern and post-industrialized and highly urbanized societies.

Exogamous marriages are those in which one of the future partners, normally the male, goes outside his kin group or tribe in search of his or her mate. It means that partners come from different social groups. "Outside" the group may mean a different geographical location, race or ethnic group (inter-racial/ethnic marriages), religion, age group, socio-economic background or any possible combination of the above classifications.

Endogamous marriages are those unions involving mates who come from the same kinship group, social category, or other social group. While this is especially likely to be the case of pre-industrial societies, it is frequently true of post-industrial societies as well. Spouses typically have similar educational attainment, share the same beliefs and values, adhere to the same religion, and often even lived close to each other and attended the same schools. Such choices reflect the importance of cultural norms and values in shaping people's perceptions of what constitutes an "appropriate" partner.

Non-Traditional Families

A "family" of friends, single-parent and single-sex families have increased in number in some parts of the post-industrial world. In societies such as the United States, where factors such as a geographical mobility, urbanization and aging affect the stability of nuclear families, a family of friends or fictive kin serves as valuable support system for the individual. In the absence of parents, a mate or children, a circle of friends fulfill the functions of a traditional family structure.

Homosexual and lesbian households have also experienced significant attitudinal changes on the part of society as a whole. While still a taboo in most societies, homosexual and lesbian unions are more openly accepted and respected in some parts of America and other Western societies. Recognition of single-sex relationships have also been advanced by the campaigning and lobbying efforts of homosexual and lesbian organizations in the American Congress since the 1960s.

The number of individuals opting for alternatives outside the traditional family structure is more evident amongst singles than in any other social group, particularly in America and Europe. They choose to live alone, with or without children (biological or adopted), or as unmarried parents in single-family units or households. Both the Civil Rights and Women's Liberation Movement of the 1960s and 1970s have contributed to the incorporation of women in the professional sector of the market and have contributed to the rise of single parenthood. To these factors we must also add the existing high rate of divorce, a world-wide phenomena with profound impact on the family.

Fundamental Functions of the Family in Society: Two Views

Functionalist sociologists look at families in terms of the functions they perform for the larger society. These include **biological reproduction,** which societies need to perpetuate themselves; the **nurturance and socialization of children;** and the **support of those** who are relatively **helpless,** including children, the infirm, and the very elderly. The family also serves to provide **emotional support** for its members and serves to locate or place its children in the society's stratification system as they find jobs. **The functionalists tend to view the family in terms of its contributions to social stability.**

On the other hand, Conflict-theory sociologists argue that families serve to reproduce societal inequality among its members, particularly between men and women. They believe that the family serves to reproduce the relations of authority that exist in the wider society, centered around the authority of the father. Thus the family is seen as perpetuating divisions that exist within the larger society. Yet, conflict theory, in focusing on the oppressive aspects of family relationships, tends to overlook its important positive functions. Since the family serves as microcosm of the larger society, it is a place where social change can also begin. Conflict-theory is actually a way of analyzing social reality which emphasizes the struggles among groups of people, often to the exclusion of the cooperation among such groups, or of individuals within such groups. Conflicts dealing with race, gender and ethnicity and social class are its principal concerns.

The American Family in Perspective

First of all, in a multicultural, multiracial/ethnic society such as ours, there are many "families." However, the American family as a historical cultural entity has been a major contributing factor to the social, political and economic evolution of the American people.

Since the arrival of the first Europeans to American shores during the first half of the XVII century, the family became the center of gravity of colonial society. Whatever their national or religious background, American colonials regarded the family as the basic social and economic institution. No other American colonial experience best typifies this attitude towards the family than the Puritans' own experience in New England.

Early Puritan laws required all people, including singles and the elderly, to live in a household. Although this requirement only lasted for thirty years, the "loner," or single man was looked upon with great suspicion. Often, he was labeled a vagabond or person without a family.

It was therefore the family, and not the individual, that was empowered with political identity in colonial society. Voting qualifications then only recognized the head of a property-owning household as the legitimate voter, regardless of the number of adults living in the home. Similarly, property laws were designed to perpetuate the social and economic status of the family.

Virtually every human activity that took place in the cities, farms and plantations of the American colonies was a family-related activity. Unfortunately for future generations of free African-Americans, slaves were not allowed to legitimize their relationships and establish contracted marriages like everybody else. Similarly, members of the same family could be sold, at any given time and without warning, to different plantations, sometimes in other states. Nevertheless, it was the family that provided the slave communities of the American plantation system with the kinds of survival skills and support systems that enabled African-Americans to survive the horrors of the institution of slavery.

"Going West," largely a post-independence phenomenon, was also a family enterprise. The new generation of men, women and children who gradually carved a country that extended from the Atlantic to the Pacific Ocean

Most marriages are endogamic. Above, a traditional Jewish wedding. Courtesy of R union des Muses Nationaux/Art Resource, NY.

continued to build upon an existing colonial family tradition of struggle and survival. Life in the American frontier, despite all of its challenges and shortcomings, centered around the family.

Perspectives on Critical Changes in the American Family

The family, like any other social institution, is in a constant state of change and adaptation to new historical circumstances and challenges. The American family in particular has undergone a series of transformations that date back to the first colonial settlements in their struggle for survival in the New World. One can also mention the dramatic changes and transformations suffered by Native-American families of North America as a result of their initial encounter with the invading people of Europe, a subject that together with the plight of the African-American and Latino families has often been overlooked by social scientists.

Historically, the crisis that the urban-based American family is undergoing at present can be traced back to the last couple decades of the nineteenth century when American society began to feel, in full force, the impact of rapid industrialization. The dramatic shift from a predominantly rural to a highly urbanized society that followed the American Civil War (1861–1865) was immediately felt in the traditional patterns of human interaction in the family.

As an increasing number of women and children abandoned the household to join the rank and file of the American working force, the family unit was socially and emotionally impacted, in many cases, beyond repair. A rise in prostitution, alcoholism and child abuse did not help, particularly among working class families. With the exception of the assistance provided by the efforts of private individuals and religious institutions such as Jane Addams' *Hull House* in Chicago (a model for women copied throughout the nation) and the Salvation Army, there was virtually no meaningful government legislation to regulate labor and provide for assistance to the family.

The first half of the twentieth century was not much better. Although some legislation was passed before the New Deal to curtail abuses such as child labor, the urban American family continued to experience the effects of industrialization and the population dislocation that resulted in massive urban migration and unmanaged overcrowding in major American cities. Two world wars further contributed to the fragmentation of the traditional family system as a larger number of men were sent to the front and middle class women were forced out of their homes and into the labor force of an ever-growing war economy.

Long overdue social and economic reforms followed the decade of the 1950s and into the 1970s placing the American family in the forefront of American society and legislation. The Civil Rights Movement and President Lyndon B. Johnson's "Great Society" saw to it that the American family would no longer be ignored in the complex political process that followed the unstable decade of the 1960s. Family problems and the importance of the family in the overall social and economic spectrum of the post-Civil Rights national scheme became the focus of attention of social psychologists and other social scientists.

Recently, the rapid integration of American women into the professional and working sectors of society, a decline in religious values and growing cynicism toward institutionalized religion, and the destructive forces of the "drug culture" that plagues and affect virtually every household in America without distinction of socio-economic background, have had and continue to have a disruptive impact on the American family. An alarming rate of divorce accompanied by changing attitudes towards institutionalized marriage and the family have resulted in a serious threat to the core of the American "way of life" and to the stability of the family as a pivotal social institution. This phenomenon is understood by government, religious and educational institutions throughout the nation and millions of dollars are spent annually to help the American family survive this new crisis.

Controlling for factors such as low income, children growing up in **single-parent households** are at a greater risk for experiencing a variety of behavioral problems, including extremes of hyperactivity and withdrawal, lack of attentiveness in the classrooms, difficulty in deferring gratification, impaired academic achievement, school misbehavior, absenteeism, dropping out, involvement in socially alienated peer groups, and the so-called teenage syndrome of behaviors that tend to hang together—smoking, drinking, early and frequent sexual experiences, pregnancies, and in the more extreme cases, abortions, drug use, suicide, vandalism, violence and criminal activity. Many children of single parent households do grow into healthy and productive adults. Yet, it is statistically clear that these children have a greater chance for developmental difficulties than do those of two-parent families.

When teachers were asked in a 1940 national survey to identify the main problems in their schools, they identified such difficulties as talking out of turn, chewing gum, making noise, running in the halls, cutting in line, dress code violations and littering. When teachers were asked by the same survey in 1990 to name their main concerns, they cited drug abuse, alcohol abuse, pregnancies, suicide, rape, robbery, and assault. Today, (2008) teachers might add a lack of personal involvement to these concerns.

When analyzing these social changes, conservatives, as well as some liberal traditionalists, assert that America's social decline is directly related to the deterioration of family life. They acknowledge the impact of industrialization and religious unbelief in America, and the cultural shifts these have forced on the culture, which seems now relatively more concerned with self-expression than with self-control, more with individualism and pleasure-seeking than with concern for others, and more with personal choice than with personal responsibility.

They point out that it was in the 1960s and 1970s that, for the first time in this country's history, there was a direct intellectual, social and political attack on the legitimacy of the traditional family. It came from feminists, social scientists, utopians, and the social welfare sector. For conservatives, this attack against the family is in harmony with the thought of other radicals in Western Civilization—Plato's *Republic;* Hobbes' *Leviathan;* Rousseau's *Social Contract;* Marx's *Communist Manifesto;* and B.F. Skinner's *Walden II,* among others. They all sought to undermine the family to create a new society where only the best would rule, or where the government would be the dominant social institution, or where people would have no restrictions to their desires for pleasure.

Conservatives, furthermore believe that the corruption of society, that is, the creation of a society where it is hard to be good, to be faithful, truthful, and moral, depends on the destruction of the family. The family is where people ideally learn about unselfish love, of being loved for who you are, not for what you do. However, they believe that the destruction of the family itself proceeds from the elimination of marriage which is based on fidelity, and in a sense of obligation to be faithful to each other. Fidelity is the glue which holds marriages together. This fidelity in turn is destroyed, according to conservatives, by the new philosophy of sexual liberation which in some of its manifestations encourages irresponsible, selfish and unfaithful sex. In this view, as government and academia redefine the meaning of marriage to include cohabiting couples, unwed mothers and every other social grouping, marriage, fidelity and parental responsibility vanish. The Sexual Liberation has brought much pain in the form of divorce, unloved children, teenage suicide and pregnancy, abortion, sexually trans-

mitted diseases, and higher medical and insurance costs, among other things.

Conservatives believe that government programs, the media and the entertainment industry also promote the deterioration of the family. Government programs which award funds to unwed mothers and to single-parent families, among others, instead of to struggling two-parent families, undermine family formation. The funding of public day-care programs, but not of mothers or relatives who want to stay home to raise their children, also weakens the family. Biased social scientists who do not inform the public that prolonged day care has been associated with poorer work and study skills, heightened aggression, weakened maternal bonding, sickness, permissiveness, and separation anxiety and depression, according to conservatives, do not allow the population to make intelligent choices about child care for their own kids. Conservatives criticize the media and the entertainment industry for popularizing and legitimizing deviant behavior. They tend to portray or cover what is sensational, different, exciting, forbidden, provocative, but do not give sufficient and fair coverage to those traditional forms of socialization which contribute to the development of emotionally stable individuals.

Furthermore, conservatives point out that a whole industry of school psychologists, counselors, social workers as well as other government employees in the social services areas benefit as the family deteriorates and the state assumes the functions that the family used to exercise. The state also benefits as it receives the votes of the unmarried and the divorced who receive more state services such as subsidies for rent, welfare, day care, and longer hospitalization. As Americans lose attachments to the family, they increase their dependence on the government. Those who live off the government gain as their budgets are increased at the expense of the taxpayers.

There are many who disagree with this conservative interpretation of the crisis of the family and believe that American social life is simply evolving in new directions, adjusting to post-modern forms of life in ways that afford exciting, intellectual, therapeutic and political opportunities. Some actually relish the current crises over the family for according to them, it permits new experimental, alternative social arrangements so that the family can be refined to accommodate legitimate and diverse life styles. In the 1960s and 1970s, feminists often accused the family of being a repressive, patriarchal institution whose conditions were analogous to slavery and rape. Undoubtedly, many were responding to many real abuses committed within the traditional family. Today most of these critics of the traditional family are no longer working for its demise, but hope that in the American experience there might be greater personal choice for forming the arrangement each person desires.

Race, Ethnicity, Immigration and the American Family

Traditionally, much of the social science research has centered around the white family. This attitude, in part explained by the fact that most researchers in the field have been whites, has changed in the last thirty years. Increasingly, more family researchers are of different racial or ethnic backgrounds. They are focusing on serious scholarly research regarding both differences and similarities in American families of various ethnic and racial origins.

A race, a highly misused and misunderstood term, is a "group of individuals sharing the same or similar genetic, biological and physical characteristics." Ethnicity, on the other hand, is a culturally related term. An ethnic group is a group of individuals who share a common cultural heritage. Therefore, there are whites, blacks, and even Asian Hispanics, for example, who may choose to perceive and identify themselves as Afro-Caribbean, Spanish-American, or other.

Today, in fact, there is a serious argument among Latinos in the United States regarding their own ethnicity. Mexicans, Puerto Ricans, and Cubans, the three largest Latino groups in the country, often resent having their own ethnic identity grouped under one single term, i.e. Hispanic. The same argument is beginning to surface among African minorities from the West Indies who prefer to be identified by their own national origins rather than as African-Americans.

Given the importance that race and ethnicity have on the dynamics of the American family and the various processes of socialization of their children, and politics, some cases in American ethnicity and family lifestyle will now be presented.

Ethnic Family Variations

The Latino Family in the U.S.

The presence of "Hispanos" in North America dates to the late 1500s and early 1600s as Spain penetrated into the West and Southwest, claiming all the land to the margins of the Mississippi River, as well as taking Florida and moving West. More recently, Hispanics have come from Spain directly and from South, Central, and Caribbean America.

Mexican-Americans

Mexicans lived throughout California and the Southwest and were a dominant group composed of land-owners, farmers, and entrepreneurs. In the 1830s and '40s, the United States expanded westward and took one third of Mexico's territory. Many of the Mexicans became wage laborers, though some land-owners or **hacendados** survived. However, their political and social status declined significantly. Overnight Mexicans who had lived for generations in the Southwest found themselves in a new country. These Mexicans did not cross the border; the border crossed them. Americans associated them with other Mexicans who began migrating from Mexico in the 1900s.

The family continues to be the most important institution among Mexican-Americans. The extended family has been instrumental in the process of socialization and acculturation although sometimes individuals, to help their families, forgo economic opportunities that could improve their long-term adaptation in the dominant American culture. For example, driven by the economic necessity of having all members of the family cooperate for its survival, many young Mexican-Americans drop out of school at an early age to find work.

Perhaps the single most consistent aspect of Mexican-American culture is familism which is a very strong sentiment toward family cohesiveness and family membership. In some Mexican communities in the United States, individuals maintain strong ties to their communities of origin in Mexico through family ties and other institutions such as the **campadrazgo.** This is a system established through the baptism of a child with parents choosing **padrinos** or godparents, from family members or very close friends. This is a very effective way of networking to assist the family get housing, jobs, and thus adapt to the host culture.

The changing role of women in the United States is also impacting the Mexican-American family. Although the extended family is still the preferred one, the nuclear family model is growing among second and third generation Mexican-Americans in the United States. This is particularly true in light of the rapid entrance of women into the labor and professional markets of the United States. The immediate result has been changes in sex roles and division of labor in the urban, middle-class family structure. The same is also true of Puerto Ricans, Cubans, Nicaraguans, and other Latino groups. Yet, the Mexican male continues to play a major role in the decision-making process of the Mexican-American family. As a community, Mexican-Americans have organized themselves to fit into American society. The League of United Latin American Citizens (LULAC) and the National Council of La Raza are but two examples. Both have organized campaigns around civil rights.

Puerto Ricans

Next to Mexican-Americans, Puerto Ricans are the second largest Latino group in the United States. Puerto Rican migration to the United States began in the early 1900s as a result of the deteriorating economic and social conditions following the Cuban-Spanish-American War of 1898. American labor recruiters began contracting Puerto Rican workers to come to the U.S. The first 5,000 laborers were sent to work in farms in Hawaii. Changes in the traditional sugar, tobacco, and coffee plantations, resulting in part from the American takeover of Puerto Rico created high unemployment in the island. The majority of the migrants went to the city of New York. By the end of the 1980s, close to one million and a half had left Puerto Rico to reside permanently in the United States. More than 800,000 of them chose New York City.

Beset by unemployment and poor education, some Puerto Ricans arrived in the United States with low skills and little or no education. Of all groups of Latinos, Puerto Ricans have been, and to a large extent continue to be, among the most socio-economically disadvantaged. **Therefore, poverty in a hostile environment has underlined the process of survival of many Puerto Rican American families.** This is particularly true of the single-parent (mother) type of household. One of the major problems affecting the stability of the family is poor housing which leads to fragmentation, physical and emotional abuse, and domestic violence.

The extended family concept, even when members are separated from the household, is still very much a common denominator in the Puerto Rican family structure. In many cases, women have become the sole provider in the family, as men are either unemployed or choose to abandon the home. Religion, as is the case with other Latino groups, has played an important role in the survival and adaptation of the Puerto Ricans. While the majority of marriages are Catholic, in South Florida there has been an increase in Hispanic Evangelicals and other Protestant churches, a trend which coincides with an influx of very poor Central American immigrants.

Puerto Ricans in the U.S. have also confronted exclusion and discrimination by fighting back with their own civil rights organizations such as the National Congress for Puerto Rican Rights (NCPRR). After the industrialization program of the 1950s in Puerto Rico (Operation Bootstrap) 100,000s of Puerto Ricans left the island. In the U.S. they concentrated in industrial centers like Chicago, New York and Philadelphia, where Puerto Rican women in particular found jobs in the garment district. This meant that both mothers and fathers worked outside of the home and in many cases, grandparents, aunts or others were hired to care for children. This gave a distinctly working-class nature to most Puerto Rican families. More recently, with a growing amount of 2nd and 3rd generation Puerto Ricans completing college a growing and significant white-collar and middle class has emerged among stateside Puerto Ricans.

Cubans

In addition to the Spanish contributions to the formation of the Cuban national character, West Africa had a highly significant role in the molding of Cuban values and attitudes. The labor demands created by the sugar plantations led to massive importation of African slaves. After the decline of the slave trade following the enactment of the Emancipation Law of 1880, the demand for cheap labor was met by the importation of indentured servants from China, the arrival of a few thousand Indians from Mexico's Yucatán Peninsula, and the continued Spanish immigration, largely from northern Spain and the Canary Islands. After the Blacks, the Chinese came to constitute Cuba's most important ethnic minority in the 1900's.

The Communist revolution in 1959 dramatically changed the social, political, and economic fabric of Cuban society. The Cuban family found itself in massive socio-economic and political conflict. Family members became identified with the various political factions, and as a result, some families were cemented together by their common political beliefs, whereas others were torn apart by divergent loyalties.

The families that arrived in the United States seeking refuge from communism are representatives of both of these phenomena. Some families transplanted themselves to America with their entire extended family network intact, with a strong sense of achievement and success in having protected the family network. Others, on the other hand, felt wounded by the fragmentation brought about by the political schism.

The family plays a pivotal role in determining Cuban patterns of immigration to the United States. In the earliest stages, parents of children, adolescents, and young adults left the island in an effort to secure freedom for their offspring, as well as to protect the integrity of the nuclear family, which was under siege by the Marxist-Leninist regime. Subsequent stages through the 1960s and 1970s were driven by family reunification efforts.

Post-1980 immigration patterns have once again affected the stability of the Cuban family structure both in Cuba and the United States. **The "Mariel Boatlift"** of 1980 caused profound changes in the family, as over 125,000 refugees left their families behind. Many men and women found new partners and established new households in their host country. Others waited and in due time brought their partners and children to the United States to start a new life together.

Even more dramatic than the Mariel Boatlift, the latest migration after 1994 of **balseros** or "raft people" has left thousands of individuals without a family base in their new country. Some families managed to make the crossing together, but the majority of balseros had to leave at least two members of their nuclear family behind in Cuba. Thousands have lost their loved ones at sea in the crossing from Cuba to Florida.

The generational differences generated by different circumstances surrounding the various migration waves from both early post-revolutionary Cubans, who basically adhered to more traditional family values, and those who have been more exposed to communism's totalitarian and atheist value system are significant to family role-modeling in the United States. In spite of this phenomenon, Cuban-Americans from all generational backgrounds continue to exhibit strong family values when compared to their American counterparts. The family tradition in Cuba, although non-existent when measured by North American standards, continues to exist. In fact, it could be argued that the non-traditional Cuban family of today has expanded to include, out of economic necessity and political survival, an extended family of neighbors, close friends and kin leaving outside Cuba.

The traditional Cuban family had already begun its transition from extended to nuclear family prior to the massive migration that began in 1959. The nuclear family is tightly knit but allows for the inclusion of relatives and padrinos ("godparents") within the nuclear family structure. Cubans have a strong preference for lineal or hierarchical family relations and thus, conventionally at least, parents expect respect from their children, and husbands expect the same from their wives.

The economic success of the Cuban American immigration is widely recognized. What is not widely acknowledged, however, is the role that the family has played in this development. Whereas women in pre-Castro Cuba were not fully integrated into the labor market, Cuban women who arrived in the United States were, in many instances, the first to be employed and thereby became contributors to the families' economic well-being. As the wife's resource contribution to the family became greater through her employment, her power to make decisions also increased while that of the husband declined. **As a result, the traditional, patriarchal family structure of Cuban Americans began to change and brought about a disruption of family functioning, particularly during the 1970s.** The younger families are usually comprised of husband and wife teams that grew up in the United States and thus are less likely to find the greater equality in decision making among the spouses disruptive. **As a result, young Cuban-American families are less male-dominated today, and the roles of husbands and wives are less segregated than in the traditional Latin American family that typified Cuba before 1959, and still characterizes much of Latin American society.**

Other Latinos

In addition to Mexicans, Puerto Ricans, Cubans, there are other Latino groups in the United States: Dominicans, Brazilians, Central Americans, Colombians, Venezuelans, and many others. Beginning with the April Revolution in the Dominican Republic in 1965 and the guerrilla wars in Colombia, Nicaragua, Guatemala and El Salvador in the 1960s and 70s, immigrants from these countries have flooded into the U.S. More recently political developments in Venezuela have prompted an increase in the émigré community from that country as well. For all, the family is of paramount importance. **Other cultural characteristics of Hispanic families include a closeness among women, family members of all ages, a high degree of respect for elders, friendship patterns that make men as well as women friends of the entire family rather than just the husband or wife, and a wide**

Excerpts taken and edited from: Robert Staples, "The Black American Family." In Charles H. Mindel, Robert W. Harbenstein and Roosevelt Wright, Jr., *Ethnic Families in America: Patterns and Variations*. Third Edition (New York: Elsevier Science Publishing Co., 1988).

community of social support for family members. Yet, changes that are affecting all American families such as divorce, illegitimacy, and violence have affected them despite strong cultural values emphasizing the importance of family ties.

The African-American Family

As the United States' largest visible minority, the Black, or African-American population has been the subject of extensive study by behavioral scientists. Its family life has been of particular concern because of the unique character of this group, as a result of a history that is uncharacteristic of other ethnic groups. **There are four cultural traits of blacks that distinguish them from other immigrants to the United States: (1) Blacks came from a region with norms and values that were dissimilar to the American way of life; (2) they were from many different tribes, each with its own language, culture, and traditions; (3) in the beginning, they came without women; and, most importantly, (4) they came in bondage as slaves.**

Until relatively recently, almost all studies of Black family life have concentrated on the lower-income strata of the group, ignoring middle-class families and even stable, poor black families. Moreover, the deviation of Black families from middle-class norms often has resulted in them being defined as dysfunctional. Such labels ignore the possibility that although a group's family forms may not fit into the normative model, it may instead have its own functional organization that meets the needs of the group.

Historical Background

Preslavery Period

There are several historical periods of interest in the evaluation of black family life in the United States. One era is the precolonial period of the African continent from which the African-American population originated. **The basis of African family life was the kinship group which was bound together by blood ties, common interests, and mutual functions.** Within each village, there were elaborate legal codes and court systems that regulated the marital and family behavior of individual members.

The Slave Family

In attempting to accurately describe the family life of slaves, one must sift through a conflicting array of opinions on the subject. Reliable empirical facts are few, and speculation has been rampant in the absence of data. Certain aspects of the slave's family life are undisputed. Slaves were not allowed to enter into binding contractual relationships. Because marriage is basically a legal relationship that imposes obligations on both parties and exacts penalties for the violation of those obligations, there was no legal basis for any marriage between two individuals in bondage. **Slave marriages were regulated at the discretion of the slaveowners. As a result, some marriages were initiated by slaveowners and just as easily dissolved.**

Hence, there were numerous cases in which the slaveowner ordered slave women to marry men of his choosing after they reached the age of puberty. The slave owners preferred marriages between slaves on the same plantation, because the primary reason for slave unions was the breeding of children who would become future slaves. Yet, many slaves who were allowed to get married preferred women from a neighboring plantation. This allowed them to avoid witnessing the many assaults on slave women that occurred. Sometimes the matter was resolved by the sale of one of the slaves to the other owner.

Historians are divided on the question of how many slave families were involuntarily separated from each other by their owners. Despite the slaveholder's commitment to keeping the slave families intact, the intervening events of a slaveholder's death, his bankruptcy, or lack of capital made the forceable sale of some slave's spouse or child inevitable. In instances where the slave-master was indifferent to the fate of slave families, he would still keep them together simply to enforce plantation discipline. A married slave who was concerned about his wife and children, it was believed, was less inclined to rebel or escape than would an unmarried slave.

This does not mean that the slave family had a great deal of stability. Although there are examples of some slave families living together for 40 years or more, the majority of slave unions were dissolved by personal choice, death, or the sale of one partner by the master. Although individual families may not have remained together for long periods of time, the institution of the family was an important asset in the perilous era of slavery. Despite the prevalent theories about the destruction of the family under slavery, it was one of the most important survival institutions for African people held in bondage.

In the slave quarters, Black families did exist as functioning institutions and as models for others. The slave narratives provide us with some indication of the importance of family relations under slavery. It

was in the family that the slave received affection, companionship, love, and empathy with his sufferings under this peculiar institution. Through the family, he learned how to avoid punishment, cooperate with his fellow slaves, and retain some semblance of his self-esteem. The socialization of the slave children was another important function for the slave parents. They could cushion the shock of bondage for them, inculcate in them values different than those the masters attempted to teach them, and represent another frame of reference, for their self-esteem besides the master. Probably close to 80% of the children lived within intact slave families.

Much has been written about the elimination of the male's traditional functions under the slave system. It is true that he was often relegated to working in the fields and siring children rather than providing economic maintenance or physical protection for his family, but the father's role was not as insignificant as presumed. It was the male slave's inability to protect his wife from the physical and sexual abuse of the master that most pained him. As a matter of survival, few tried, because the consequences were often fatal.

One aspect of Black family life frequently ignored during the slave era is the free Black family. This group, which numbered about one-half million, was primarily composed of the descendents of the original Black indentured servants and the mulatto offspring of slaveholders. For this minority of Black families, the assimilation and acculturation process was, relatively, less difficult. They imitated the white world as closely as possible. Because they had opportunities for education, owning property, and skilled occupations, their family life was quite stable.

After Emancipation

There has been a prevailing notion that the experience of slavery weakened the value of marriage as an institution among black Americans. Yet, the slaves married in record numbers when the right to the freedom to marry was created by governmental decree. A legal marriage was a status symbol, and weddings were events of great gaiety. The typical household was a simple nuclear family headed by an adult male. **Further evidence that Black people were successful in forming a dual-parent family structure is the data that show that 90 percent of all Black children were born within a marriage by the year 1917.** Children were of special value to the freed slaves, whose memories were fresh with the history of their offspring being sold away.

It was during the late nineteenth century that the strong role of Black women emerged. Men preferred their wives to remain at home, because a working woman was considered a mark of slavery. However, during the period, which has been described as the most explicitly racist era of American history, Black men found it very difficult to obtain jobs and, in some instances, found work only as strikebreakers. Thus, the official organ of the African Methodist Episcopal church exhorted Black families to teach their daughters not to avoid work, because many of them would marry men that would not make on the average more than 75 cents per day. In 1900, approximately 41 percent of Black women were in the labor force, compared with 16 percent of White women.

What was important, then, was not whether the husband or wife worked, but the family's will to survive in an era when Blacks were systematically deprived of adequate educational and work opportunities. Despite these obstacles, Black families achieved a level of stability based on role integration. Men shared equally in the rearing of children; women participated in the defense of the family. A system in which the family disintegrates because of the loss of one member would be in opposition to the traditional principles of unity that defined the African family. These principles were to be tested during the period of the great Black migration from the rural areas of the South to the cities of the North.

The rise of Black illegitimately born children and female-headed households are concomitants of Twentieth century urban ghettos. **Drastic increases in these phenomena strongly indicate that the condition of many lower-class Black families is in part a function of the economic contingencies of industrial America, and a shift to deindustrialization of cities. Unlike the European immigrants before them, Blacks were disadvantaged by the hard lines of northern segregation along racial lines.** Furthermore, families in cities are more vulnerable to disruptions from the traumatizing experiences of urbanization, the reduction of family functions, and the loss of extended family supports.

In the transition from Africa to the American continent, there can be no doubt that African culture was not retained in any pure form. Blacks lacked the autonomy to maintain their cultural traditions under the severe pressures to take on American standards of behavior. Yet, there are surviving Africanisms that are reflected in Black speech patterns, aesthetics, folklore, and religion. They have preserved aspects of their old culture that have a direct relevance to their new lives. Out of the common experiences they have shared, a new culture has been forged that is uniquely Black American. The elements of that culture are still to be found in their family life.

Since the 1960's, there has been a disintegration of much of the Black nuclear family, especially in large cities. Changes in the Black family structure are in tune with the changes in American families. A number of social forces account for the increase in the number of single adult, out-of-wedlock births, divorces, and single-parent households. As many women have become economically and psychologically independent of men, they have chosen to remain single or leave marriages they regard as not satisfying their needs. Many have affirmed this independence with the support of government assistance or with their own employment. Simultaneously, the growing independence of women and the sexual revolution of the 1960s and 1970s allowed many men to flee from the responsibility attendant to the husband and father roles.

Although these sociocultural forces have an impact on the marriage and family patterns of many Americans, they are more pronounced among Blacks because of one critical etiological agent: the institutional decimation of Black males. As an Urban League report concluded, "the attrition of Black males... from conception through adulthood finally results in an insufficient number of men who are willing and able to provide support for women and children in family setting." Thus, many Black women are denied a real choice between monogamous marriage or single life. Most do choose to bear and raise children because that is deemed better than being single, childless, and locked into dead-end, low paying jobs. Although many would prefer a monogamous marriage, that is no longer possible for the majority of Black women. **The same forces that drive many Black men out of social institutions also propel them out of the family.**

Those forces have their genesis in the educational system. Black women are more educated than Black men at all levels except the doctoral level. This, again, is in the overall direction of change in American society. White men have also been losing ground to White women in educational achievements. The reasons for the ascendency of women in the school system are unclear. Some speculate that because teachers are disproportionately female, the behaviors tolerated and most encouraged are those that are more natural for girls. The higher educational level of Black women endows them with educational credentials and skills that make them more competitive in the job market. The changing nature of the economy has placed women at an

advantage. While the industrial sector has been declining, the service and high-technology sectors of the economy have been expanding. **Black women are more highly concentrated in the expanding sector of the economy whereas Black men are overrepresented in the shrinking industrial jobs.**

One consequence of the aforementioned factors is the attrition of Black men in the labor force. As a rule, unemployed males are not good marriage prospects. Along with the number of Black males not gainfully employed is the imbalance in the sex ratio, especially in the marriageable age ranges (18–35 years). They give rise to higher rates of single adults, divorce, out-of-wedlock births, and female-headed households in different historical epochs and across different societies.

The implications of this problem extend beyond the family. A majority of black children live in one-parent households today, and the median income available to those families is well below poverty level. Although many children rise out of poor families to become successful adults, the odds are against them. **What is positive however, is the steady growth of a Black middle class, growing African-American involvement in the political system, and swelling numbers of Black youths availing themselves of educational opportunities at top-flight schools at every level.**

The Haitian Family
By Professor Liz Trentanelli

"Deye mon, gen mon." Behind the mountains there are more mountains. This Creole proverb explains that behind the story there is always another story. To understand the Haitian-American family, one needs to know a little about Haiti's colorful, turbulent history.

History between Haiti and the United States has been marked by controversy, distrust, and fear. Although Haiti is regarded as the world's first independent "Black" republic and the second independent nation in this hemisphere, it has been looked down upon by its larger neighbor to the north. Haiti gained its independence following the war with France between 1791–1803 and its slave history is similar to that of the southeastern U.S. African slaves were brought to many Caribbean islands following the near-decimation of native American Indians such as the Taino, Arawok, and Carib. In Saint Domingo, as Haiti was called then, slaves worked sugar, coffee and indigo plantations. Shortly after the U.S.

fought its war for independence, the French overthrew their monarchy; neither revolution led to liberty of slaves. Therefore, Haitian slaves took matters into their own hands. The U.S. did not formally recognize the island nation until after our own Civil War when the government sought to deport newly freed Blacks to Africa or Haiti.

As in the U.S., African slaves brought their cultural traditions, languages, values and beliefs. Slaves in Haiti were compelled to camouflage the native language and religious rituals brought from West African nations. The Creole language consists of African words and concepts as well as French words, although some have different meanings in Creole lore. Furthermore, the development of voodoo, similar to the Afro-Cuban religion Santeria, was a backlash against French colonial tyranny. True voodoo is based on African "animism" and ancestor worship. It is "holistic"—in other words the whole person and the whole of existence is incorporated into "voodoo": worship, medicine, moral codes, death, and philosophy. The slaves continued to practice their native rituals under the "cloak" of Catholicism, forced on them by the French slave masters.

As in the U.S., slaves had no legal rights or protections, with the exception of biracial, or Mulatto people who were granted some privileges. Many acquired property and wealth. Some even became money lenders to Whites. This unique position led to a split between African slaves and the mixed race people. Slaves thought the Mulattos should have used their power to end their combined plight, while the Mulattos sought to separate themselves from their darker-skinned relatives. This chasm continues to exist today.

Haitian culture is largely misunderstood in the U.S.; this phenomenon continues to threaten assimilation efforts. Unless they lived in Port-au-Prince, most Haitians came from a rural, agrarian, almost feudalistic society. Though the media depicts only the abject poverty and violence among Haitians, many other dimensions of the national psyche are stronger. They are generous people who like to smile and readily greet strangers on the street.

Decades of authoritarian dictatorships created a repressive atmosphere. Ton Ton Macoutes, a paramilitary "enforcement" squad, quelled any dissent. This and the lack of acceptance upon arriving in the U.S. have taught Haitians to appear passive and quiet when pur-

suing their interests. More is known today about Haitian culture through the music of performers. Typical entertainment might include dancing the merengue, salsa and listening to Haitian "compas" and "roots music". One type of Haitian art, the "primitive" style painting in bright colors, is world-renowned, but Haitian artists express their spirituality and political outrage through other media as well. Many of these artists were forced to leave Haiti due to political reprisals. Most Haitians are Catholic–some figures indicate about 90%. In Haiti the Church was usually the safest sanctuary, physically as well as spiritually.

Typically, Haitian men and women share in household management although many jobs are divided according to gender roles. In fact, in Haiti the "market women" often serve as the financial backbone of the family, selling at market produce they grow in gardens at home. Haitians don't easily accept charity without giving something in return. They believe a thing must not be worth too much if it is free.

Throughout Haitian history poor government record keeping and high costs resulted in a limited number of "legally" recognized marriages. Nevertheless this did not squelch the desire to marry anyway; in the U.S. we refer to this type of union as 'common law'. Haitian parents tend to be strong disciplinarians, expecting obedience from children. Children are taught to respect elders; they greet all strangers to the household, especially the adults, individually with a handshake. A more permissive American culture threatens to weaken that bond between Haitian-American parents and children.

Parents in Haiti aspire to send their children to school, a hardship due to the lack of publicly funded schools and the costs of private education. Parents will often sacrifice other necessities in order to pay these expenses. Therefore, upon their arrival in the U.S. Haitian families place a high priority on their children's education. Children who attended school in Haiti tended to develop good vocabularies; many students speak 3 or 4 languages. Creole, largely regarded as the national language, is spoken in most homes. French was until recently the official language of the government and is spoken in many homes. Although for many an English language deficit temporarily slows their progress in American schools, many others studied English and / or Spanish before migrating here.

Inevitably there has been some family separation due to exile. Very seldom were entire families able to migrate together—many individuals came to escape immediate threat of persecution; some couples and entire families attempted to migrate but some of those were returned to Haiti; many died in the Florida Straits. Some found new partners, others work multiple jobs to save money so they can bring their children here; most send money back to other family members in need—it is expected of those who leave.

Compared to refugees from around the world, Haitians have been among the least welcomed in the U.S. Proportionately fewer have been granted political asylum than refugees of other nationalities and races. Until very recently they have been subjected to more strenuous tests of credibility, inconsistent application of screening procedures, unusually long detentions, few interpreters, quicker deportations and repatriations. In the early 1980's the U.S. government identified travel in Haiti or contact with a Haitian as risk factors for contracting the AIDS virus (the government later retracted this assertion but the stigma remains).

If they are successful in their political asylum applications, Haitians take on numerous jobs and may temporarily live two or three families to a home. Unskilled Haitians work for hourly wages in stores and restaurants; many Haitians work while attending college. A Haitian-American middle class has emerged advancing into professions such as law, medicine, teaching, social work, etc. Business opportunities are sometimes undermined by a banking practice known as "redlining" of supposedly unprofitable neighborhoods. While most Haitian-Americans remain in South Florida, significant numbers can be found in New York, Boston and Montreal, Canada.

It is wise not to assume that Haitians and other Caribbean islanders are automatically embraced by the African American society. Despite similar slave history and cultural traits of African origin, they have experienced freedom at different times and in different ways. English, French or Spanish colonial influences were somewhat varied. American culture in general is different from that of the Caribbean islands and the various African nations; furthermore, there exists a desire among many Americans, regardless of race, to blame immigrants for economic and social problems or to limit immigration altogether.

Although they are often subject to same stereotypes that plague African-Americans, they are not integrated into that society. Haitians have had to endure multiple negative stereotypes.

The lack of a strong middle class and stable government in Haiti has left many Haitian-Americans without previous experience that might make assimilation here easier. Haitians in the diaspora learned lessons in democracy from the U.S. and many have returned to help rebuild their country since the coup d'etat of 1991–94 ended. For many other families, the birth of children here and many years spent here building lives and careers indicate a continued presence. Haitian-Americans proudly become naturalized citizens and attempt to assimilate like others before them.

Asian-American Families

Over 12 million Americans can trace their origins to more than a dozen Asian countries with highly diverse cultures. Chinese and Filipino Americans constitute the largest group of Asian Americans, although significant numbers originated in Japan, Korea, Vietnam, Laos, and Cambodia as well. **In general, Asian American families emphasize male authority and traditional gender roles. There is a strong sense of respect for the cultural heritage, commitment to family loyalty, respect for elders, and mutual self-help. Also, there is an intense felt obligation to succeed.**

American-Indian Families

American Indians are highly diverse. There are close to 500 nations although 50 percent of Native Americans come from just nine of these. Their families tend to be extended, often including uncles, aunts, grandparents, and others. Child rearing tends to be permissive, with children stimulated to be internally self-sufficient instead of externally motivated. **There is an emphasis on the group over the individual, stressing harmony in relationships**. The migration of American Indian families from reservations to urban areas has led to increased assimilation and acculturation, with urban Indian families often resembling those of the dominant culture.

Population of the United States by Race and Hispanic/Latino Origin, Census 2000 and July 1, 2005

Race and Hispanic/Latino Origin	July 1, 2005 Population	Percent of Population	Census 2000 Population	Percent of Population
Total Population	296,410,404	100%	281,421,906	100%
Single race				
White	237,854,954	80.2%	211,460,626	75.1
Black or African American	37,909,341	12.8	34,658,190	12.3
American Indian and Alaska				
Native	2,863,001	1	2,475,956	0.9
Asian	12,687,472	4.3	10,242,998	3.6
Native Hawaiian and other				
Pacific Islander	516,612	0.2	398,835	0.1
Two or more races	4,579,024	1.5	6,826,228	2.4
Some other race	n.a.	n.a.	15,359,073	5.5
Hispanic or latino	42,687,224	14.4	35,305,818	12.5

Source: U.S.Census, national Population Estimates

2006 American Community Survey

Hispanic or Latino race	
Total Population	299,398,485
Hispanic or Latino (of any race)	44,252,278
Mexican	28,339,354
Puerto Rican	3,987,354
Cuban	1,520,276
Other Hispanic or Latino	10,404,701

Source: ACS Demographic and Housing Estimates, U.S. Census Bureau

References

Applebaum, Richard P., and Chambers, William J. (1995) *Sociology*. New York: Harper Collins.

Burgess, Ernest, Harvey J. Locke, and Mary M. Thomes. (1963) *The Family*. New York: American Book, (3rd edition).

Cavan, Ruth S. *The American Family*. New York: Thomas Y. Crowell, (1969) (4th edition).

Christensen, Bryce J. (1990) *Utopia Against the Family: The Problems and Politics of the American Family*. San Francisco: Ignatius Press.

Collins, Randall. (1988) *Sociology of Marriage and the Family. Gender, Love, and Property*. Chicago: Nelson-Hall.

Ember, M., and Ember, C.R. (1983) *Marriage, Family, and Kinship: Comparative Studies of Social Organization*. New Haven, CT: HRAF Press.

Faber, Bernard. (1964) *Family Organization and Interaction*. San Francisco, CA: Chandler.

Fox, R. (1983) *Kinship and Marriage: An Anthropological Perspective*. Cambridge University Press.

Goode, William J. (1982) *The Family*. Englewood Cliffs, NJ: Prentice Hall.

Kanello, Nicolas. (1994) *Reference Library of Hispanic America*, Vol. 1 Educational Guidance Service.

Kephart, William M. (1972) *The Family, Society, and the Individual*. Boston: Houghton Mifflin, (3rd edition).

Levinson, D., and Malone, M.J., (Eds). (1980) *Toward Explaining Human Culture: A Critical Review of the Findings of Worldwide Cross-Cultural Research*. New Haven, CT: HRAF Press.

Michael, Robert T., et.al. (1994) *Sex in America: A Definite Survey*. Boston: Little, Brown and Co.,

Pasternak, B. (1976) *Introduction to Kinship and Social Organization*. Englewood Cliffs, NJ: Prentice Hall.

Rabb, T.K. and Rotberg, R.I. (1973) *The Family in History*. New York: Harper and Row.

Reiss, Ira. (1971) *The Family System in America*. New York: Holt, Reinhart and Winston.

Staples, Robert. (1988) "The Black American Family." In Mindel, Charles H., Robert H. Harbenstein and Roosevelt Wright, Jr. *Ethnic Families in America*. New York, NY: Elsevier Science Publishing Co., Inc. (3rd edition). pp. 303–325.

Stephens, William N., (1963) *The Family in Cross-Cultural Perspective*. New York: Holt, Rinehart and Winston.

Szapocznik, Jose and Roberto Hernandez. (1988) "The Cuban American Family." In Mindel, Charles H., Robert H. Habenstein and Roosevelt Wright, Jr. *Ethnic Families in America*. New York, NY: Elsevier Science Publishing Co., Inc. (3rd edition). pp. 160–173.

Whalen, Carmen T. and Víctor Vázquez-Hernández. *The Puerto Rican Diaspora: Historical Perspectives* (Philadelphia: Temple University Press, 2005).

CHAPTER FIVE

The Economy

David M. Shaheen

Economics is a social science discipline that is involved, to a great extent, with decisions that human beings make in regard to how they allocate and manage resources that are scarce. **Scarcity** refers to goods and services that, when they are not in an unlimited quantity, have attained a certain value based on the demand for them in relation to their supply. Economists attempt to study the relationships between the consumption, planning, and production choices that people, governments, and businesses must make on a daily basis. With scarcity as a guiding force, societies and individuals have to make decisions about how resources are distributed, which ones are produced, and it what quantities. In this light, economists define **resources** into different types, calling some **natural resources,** where raw materials are utilized in their natural state or turned into finished goods. Economists categorize other resources as **human resources,** where the number of laborers is related to the demand for their work, turning the labor they provide into a commodity with real value. Additionally, economists define **capital resources** as real or financial possessions held by companies, investors, or governments that can be reinvested, loaned to customers, or held as assets. Such resources can include land, machines, financial holdings, and credit.

In this chapter the reader will be able to take the broad economics definitions presented above and apply them to real examples as to how the economy works in practice.

One will do this by looking at different types of economic systems that outline the evolution of economics as a social science discipline since the 18th century. The reader will also be introduced to economic indicators and concepts that measure the strengths and weaknesses of modern economies—as well as the factors that shape economic growth and development. Contemplating these issues and concepts should assist the reader in understanding contemporary economic issues.

Types of Economic Systems

Peoples in various cultures have historically used different economic systems. In societies where a mutually agreeable medium of exchange, or **money,** could not be implemented, exchanges of goods and services have been done by **barter**—which involves the trading of goods and services. In more complex systems, where people do use money to exchange goods and services with little or no government intervention, such systems are called **market economies.** When governments make decisions to plan production and consumption in an economy while minimizing private economic choices, such systems are called **command economies.** In the real world, most modern governments make decisions that directly impact the economy. This leaves most economic decisions to private groups and individuals, creating **mixed economies.** Thus, neither command nor market models exist in the contemporary world in pure forms. The United States does generally use a market system—but it does so with some government involvement. For example, the U.S. government provides social security pensions to its citizens and mandates minimum wage laws as part of its economic culture. By doing so, it is in fact practicing a mixed economy, because people can still privately save more for retirement and employers can pay higher wages if they choose. Similarly in command economies, like the one that existed in the former Soviet Union where the government set price and wage levels, Soviet governments could rarely prevent illicit private markets from flourishing in their midst. Thus, economic models are purely academic constructs that show tendencies of a country toward a particular form of economic organization. Market and command systems are rarely pure in practice.

The History of Economic Systems and the Growth of Capitalism

Before the Industrial Revolution accelerated the growth of urban societies in the late 18th and 19th centuries, most people lived in agricultural communities and relied upon traditional techniques to plant and harvest. Land was generally the barometer of wealth and social status as owners of largest estates dominated the economic, political, and social world of Western Europe through the 18th century. For most people who were not of noble birth, farming was based largely on **subsistence,** where small farmers who owned land harvested just enough crops on their holdings to feed themselves and—if they were lucky enough—to sell small crop surpluses in their local communities. Small yields, coupled with the fact that little innovation and agricultural improvement occurred in these rural communities before the 17th century, kept economies locally based. These factors made trade in national and international markets not much of a possibility. In this world, lack of food was always a main issue in the mind of the peasant—where poverty and hunger were often exacerbated by famine.

In response to this environment, England was able to find a way out of the traditional economy based on subsistence agriculture by creating an **Agricultural Revolution** in the late 17th and 18th centuries. Pressures created by population growth stimulated technological and agricultural change. Bigger harvests would feed the national population and help wealthy exporters take advantage of the rising demand for food in a Europe also experiencing population increases. The technological changes involved crop rotation methods where nitrogen bearing feed crops, like turnips, would be rotated into the soil in alternate growing seasons. This method was promoted by the English agriculturalist Charles Townshend in the 1730s. Townshend proposed that turnips would oxygenate the soil, allowing farmers to plant seeds on land usually left uncultivated to rest the soil. Thus, if all land was under cultivation instead of leaving some fields uncultivated, more food would be produced. Furthermore, the scientific breeding of animals increased the availability of (and lower the prices of) meat and dairy products. New planting techniques promoted by Jethro Tull, another English agriculturalist in the early 18th century, included the use of manure to fertilize the soil and the use of a mechanical seed drill to create perfect planting rows to maximize grain production. Additionally, the English Parliament sanctioned the enclosures of common public lands in the 18th century, selling the lands to private holders to put more land under private cultivation. Collectively, these changes in agricultural practices led to increasing yields among English farmers who increased their landholdings and adopted innovative methods.

English farmers who practiced the new techniques amassed significant financial capital. The accumulation of income would later be used as capital, which in this context is money used to invest in economic opportunities with the goal of making more money. These capital investments financed industrial innovations, road building, and canal construction—helping develop increasingly efficient internal markets in England. The improvements in transportation led to lowered costs for goods, as shipping costs fell. In short, the availability of investment capital financed new ideas and innovations. The people that actually put their money into financing them—in order to achieve future returns on their investments—were called **capitalists.**

The revolutionary changes in English agriculture created economic changes that helped facilitate industrialization. New inventions like the steam engine and the railroad were financed by the new capitalist class that had accumulated wealth from agricultural surpluses and then profited from them through expansion of production and access to new markets.

Mercantilism and its Critics

The rise of national states in Europe, with France and Spain being prime examples in the Late Middle Ages and the early modern era, was characterized by trends toward administrative centralization and the goal of developing cultural and linguistic uniformity. The process of state building was usually accompanied by government control over economic policy. This type of policy was called **mercantilism,** where monarchies emphasized using government laws to set and profit from national economic policy. The overarching goal of mercantilists was to create a **favorable balance of trade** for the nation, where goods exported to other nations would exceed imported products. This scenario would allow for more gold and silver to remain in the home country, expanding national wealth and raising the likelihood of increased royal tax revenues. Mercantilists favored using high **tariffs** (taxes on imported goods) to promoted local manufacturing. They also favored the power of the state to grant **monopolies** (the exclusive right of one entity to be a seller in a particular economic sector) to certain business enterprises. Mercantilists reasoned that granting a monopoly to a specific company would encourage investors to put their capital in a business because it would be protected from competition. Without this exclusive right of a business to operate in the economy, mercantilists reasoned that capitalists might find investments too risky.

In the 18th century, resistance to mercantile policies developed—primarily in France and England—toward government control of national economic policy. This was in part inspired by **Enlightenment** thought popular among European elites of the mid to late 18th century. The Enlightenment worldview fostered a questioning spirit toward accepted standards of social organization and encouraged the reevaluation of preexisting knowledge. Economic issues were not immune to this questioning spirit. In 18th century France the **Physiocrats,** led by Francois Quesnay, challenged mercantilism and the high tariff policies of the French monarchy. To create national revenue in place of tariffs, Quesnay favored a single tax on land. Once the government had the revenue from the tax, the Physiocrats suggested that monarchs should allow for a system of **laissez-faire** to operate, where market forces of supply and demand would determine the actual prices of goods and wages without government intervention. In economic terms, **supply** refers to the amount of a good or service available in the market. **Demand** refers to the quantity of a good or service which people desire. The point at which supply and demand interact determines the market price of a good or service. For the Physiocrats, the supply and demand relationship would determine

Adam Smith. Courtesy of Archives Charmet/Bridgeman Art Library.

natural prices in the absence of government intervention. This laissez-faire approach, they reasoned, would allow economies to function more efficiently—as free markets would stabilize prices for goods and services at levels that reflected a natural price.

The challenge presented to mercantilism by the laissez-faire ideas of the Physiocrats was most clearly articulated by the 18th century Scottish writer and professor **Adam Smith.** Smith was, and continues to be, considered by most to be the father of economics—giving birth to its identity as a discipline. Being an integral part of the Enlightenment movement that exuded skepticism toward social institutions, Smith believed that mercantilism was retarding economic growth. In his 1776 work titled ***An Inquiry into the Nature and Causes of the Wealth of Nations***, Smith outlined the reasons he believed government should stay out of the economic realm. He thought that monopolies and tariffs stunted economic development because they limited competition. His core idea was rooted in the view that human beings are self interested by nature and hope to maximize their material wealth. Smith portrayed this self interested human condition as neither good nor bad, but a part of nature. Consequently *The Wealth of Nations* examines how people actually behave in the economic realm in regard to their self interest, instead of how societies thought they *should* behave—which represented a pre-Enlightenment worldview of 16th century Europe.

Since Smith's assumption of a self interested human nature was at the root of his economic analysis, he believed that it was the role of government to channel human self interest into the common good. If governments would allow human beings to channel that self interest into commerce, society would be the direct beneficiary because businesses competing with one another would provide for falling consumer prices. To create the freedom of the markets necessary to allow competition to flourish, Smith called for the end of monopolies and tariffs. If mercantilism was removed as the guiding principle of economic life, businesses and industries would compete against one another in a **free market**—where prices of goods and services would be determined by supply and demand relationships.

Smith called the price setting mechanism of markets for products and labor the **invisible hand.** Like the Physiocrats, he insisted that laissez-faire economic policies would also make prices fall and fuel economic growth because consumer saving would allow people to spend their excess income on other goods and services. Rational self interest would stimulate new inventors to create products for the market, as they would see profit opportunities. Smith reasoned this process would accelerate because demand would rise as consumers had extra income. Businesses then, in essence, would be competing for consumer income.

In a related way, Smith thought free trade policies should replace tariffs. In the absence of government taxes on foreign producers, Smith argued that increased international competition in the form of imports would further lower consumer prices. By 1850 England did increasingly adopt Smith's policies, and prices continued to fall for most goods in the 19th century due to these policy changes and mechanization, where lower prices for items were attained by mass production. But the free trade environment Smith described was not without its own problems. Smith pointed out in *The Wealth of*

Nations that competition in the marketplace would force companies to be both more efficient and create better and more innovative products. If they did not, Smith reasoned, they would not survive in a competitive marketplace.

In the competitive environment of 19th century industrialization in Europe and the United States, business failures did occur frequently. Big companies with large cash reserves could endure economic losses that destroyed smaller businesses. The surviving companies would buy out bankrupt competitors or merge with them—which limited price competition. Ironically then, the competitive laissez-faire environment created conditions that would lead to the formation of business monopolies—the opposite of what Smith had intended.

The Marxian Critique of Laissez-Faire Capitalism

The successes of English agricultural reforms and the ensuing Industrial Revolution allowed for the development of capitalism in England. Yet there were contradictions inherent in free market capitalism—such as the tendency of the free market system to allow for monopoly development. Nineteenth century market capitalism allowed for **economic concentration** to occur. Concentration of industry is a condition where government allows large businesses (usually corporations in the modern economy) to dominate their economic sectors. The argument against this development is part of the critique of *The Wealth of Nations* by the German political economist and proponent of Communism, **Karl Marx.** Marx's writings were voluminous, but his most integrated and readable assessment of capitalism as an economic system was *The Communist Manifesto*—penned in 1848 with his collaborator and confidante **Frederick Engels.** Written when Marx was a young man, the short work demonstrated what Marx thought was the scientific basis as to why capitalism would fail—points he would later expand in his 1867 work translated into English as *Capital.* A key belief of Marx was that Smith's ideas on the ability to sustain competitive markets in a laissez-faire system were pure fantasy. Marx believed this because in his view all capitalists were interested in destroying their competition to achieve monopoly status in their economic sectors. Furthermore, Marx argued that the destruction of small companies in a competitive environment created **maldistribution of wealth,** where a small group of people

Karl Marx. Courtesy of Bettmann/Corbis Images.

enriched by the capitalist system controlled the largest share of a nation's wealth. If this trend in wealth inequality continued in successive economic cycles, where recessions would create unemployment and business failures, Marx believed that armies of unemployed and underemployed would develop. After forming a consciousness of themselves as an exploited class, they would foster a revolutionary movement that would bring down the market system.

The description of Marxian theories presented in this chapter is abbreviated to narrow the focus of his ideas to those that were critical of the economic doctrines of Adam Smith. Marx believed that he had discovered scientific mechanisms that explained why capitalism would fail. He felt that the process of industrialization in the 19th century, the exploitative conditions it created, and the wealth accrued unequally to a developing class of capitalists were necessary to historical development. But Marx also believed that capitalism created its own problems that would eventually destroy it, where socialism would be the next stage in historical development.

How would capitalism fail—according to the Marxian critique? Marx tied this proposition, in part, to the concept of **overproduction,** where supplies of a produced good outstrip the demand for them. When unsold inventories caused falling profits, the situation could

cause economic destruction for small companies. Laying off company workers would create social and economic suffering, abetting the chances of political revolution. Furthermore, the scarcity of goods for all workers in the early years of industrialization had created and accentuated class division. As the poor could not afford to buy many of the products created in the industrialization period of the early to mid 19th century, the unequal allocation of goods created for Marx the utmost of absurdities—overproduction.

Yet Marx had to grapple with the question of why 19th century poverty and unemployment were any different from the suffering created by economic downturns of earlier centuries. He explained the difference as being based upon industrial capitalism as a new development in 19th century, where repetitive economic recessions and new labor saving technology created urban unemployment of significant intensity. The new economic and social classes (capitalists) created by industrial capitalism would be directly challenged by workers who developed a greater sense of themselves as an exploited class—as workers no longer in control of their own labor, but rather as cogs in a vast industrial machine.

Marx failed to explain precisely what he thought would occur when capitalism collapsed. Yet his analysis remains important today for students of economics because it probes into questions of how capitalism works. Capitalism, of course, did not fail and the system operates today in most nations of the world. But the laissez-faire version promoted by Adam Smith, and operating in the industrial world of England in 1850 with minimal government intervention, did not endure. That kind of laissez-faire economy was replaced in most industrialized nations, by the end of the 19th century, with systems where governments intervened in their national economies to address the worst abuses of capitalism. By the beginning of the twentieth century, English and American governments had enacted child labor laws, enacted legislation to break up monopolies, and levied taxes on corporate wealth. Consequently, government intervention in the workings of the economy through the granting of subsidies to industrial and agricultural concerns—and the implementation of social welfare legislation—would make nearly all industrialized nations mixed economies in their economic structure. As discussed previously, these systems are directly defined by having national economic life shaped by both government intervention and market mechanisms. In the United States the system is called **regulated capitalism,** where government intervention in the economy since the 1930s has been commonplace—but prices and production decisions are largely left up to the market.

Keynesian Economics and the Great Depression

The Great Depression of the 1930s led people to increasingly question if free market systems could endure. The Russian Revolution of October 1917 and the subsequent institution of state economic planning in the Soviet Union were admired by leftists worldwide. Many saw in **communism,** a system where the state centrally directs, distributes, owns, and controls resources and the modes of production, as the best system for governments to solve economic problems such as unemployment and economic growth. **Fascism,** defined in part as a system where the state directs the economy but allows for government regulated private enterprises to exist and profit, was attractive to those who looked to Nazi Germany and Mussolini's Italy for inspiration. Economic conditions in 1933, where the United States saw unemployment rates as high as 25% and Germany endured a jobless population of 40%, made

Lord Maynard Keynes. Courtesy of George Skadding/Time Life Pictures/Getty.

communism and fascism attractive alternatives to segments of those populations.

The causes of the worldwide economic depression that affected the United States in the 1930s are multifarious. Economists disagree as to its origins and accelerators, but the decline of international trade, high tariff policies, underconsumption by consumers with little disposable income, an increasing maldistribution of wealth, unsold factory inventories, and a tightening of the availability of credit to banks are all given as reasons for the economic catastrophe of the 1930s. Exacerbating the economic problems, private investors in the U.S. refused to pump money into an economy where consumer demand for products appeared minimal.

In this environment, the United States government under Franklin Delano Roosevelt in 1933 began to adopt the policy recommendations of the English economist **John Maynard Keynes.** Keynes believed that governments should use their powers over **fiscal policy,** where governments control taxing and spending, to shape the economic conditions of a nation. The U.S. policies and programs that Roosevelt advocated increased public spending to promote economic growth. The policies took the lead from Keynesian thinking and they were collectively called the **New Deal.** Opposing these views of government intervention in the market economy were the economists classically reared in the thought of Adam Smith and laissez-faire, who believed economic depressions, bankruptcies, and unemployment were the necessary adjustments of markets to get supply and demand back in balance. The laissez-faire proponents thought economic downturns were natural and necessary occurrences—eliminating weak companies from the market in a Darwinian struggle for economic survival. Consequently, classical economists before Keynes believed that the government role in an economic crisis should be restrained with little intervention in the domestic economy. Conversely, Keynes believed that governments should intervene when an economy goes into **recession**—to increase spending and lower tax rates. Recessions are downturns in economic activity that generally lead to increased unemployment, a drop in consumer spending, and deflated prices. During recessions, Keynes thought that governments should increase spending and lower taxes. But such spending to address recessions traditionally lead to budget **deficits** in each fiscal year, where the government spends more than it receives in revenue. The accumulation of these deficits in each government fiscal year would lead to a large **national debt.** To solve this problem and return to a balanced budget, Keynes believed that governments would need to raise taxes and cut spending when economic prosperity returned during an economic **recovery**—where prices would rise, unemployment would lessen, and consumer spending would rebound.

Whereas Keynes championed government spending in recessions and intervention in the workings of the market, classical economic doctrine held that governments should maintain **balanced budgets,** where a government maintains fiscal responsibility by not spending more money than it creates in revenues.

The New Deal policies in the U.S. during the Great Depression of the 1930s had mixed results and created tremendous controversy. Critics noted that the Depression was only effectively ended by America's entry into the Second World War, where **full employment** (a term generally meaning that each person that wants employment has a job) was reached by the economic demands created by the war effort. Yet, New Deal planners that adopted Keynesian thinking had cut unemployment from approximately 25% in 1933 when Roosevelt has taken office, to 14% early in the President's second term. Yet, Roosevelt's Republican critics like Senator Robert Taft of Ohio, as a supporter of classical economic thinking, believed that Roosevelt was threatening liberty by bringing the nation toward socialism by supporting government economic intervention. Conversely on the political left, American Socialist Party leaders like Norman Thomas—who desired an end to free market capitalism—believed that the New Deal reforms had actually saved the system! New Deal policies, in this view, had aborted a possible move toward socialism in the U.S. by restoring faith in the market economy during the deepest economic crisis in American history.

The Command Economy Alternative to Market-Based Approaches

The systematization of economic thought in the 19th century owes much to Adam Smith's analysis of capitalism and his proposals for enhancing economic development in *The Wealth of Nations*. In the 19th century, the term **classical economics** came to be associated with economists like Alfred Marshall in England that sought to refine and build upon Smith's legacy. But because of the Marxian critique and the ideas of Keynes, classical theories that favored market based economies operating with minimal government intervention faced significant

challenges. One of the most pressing that emerged was from the Soviet Union in the 1930s, where a state-controlled approach to economic management was adopted. The communist dictator of that nation in the 1930s, Joseph Stalin, favored the use of a command economy to foster Soviet industrialization. This form of planned economy is in operation when government makes production, investment, and allocation decisions in the economic life of a nation. The planned economy presented a radical alternative to free market capitalism. The system assumes that government direction of economic life is the optimal solution to problems of unemployment and economic crisis.

In its most pure form, governments using a command system seek to control consumer prices, determine wage levels, workplace rules and conditions, and decide what goods would be produced. This government manipulation of economic life requires **central planning,** where economists in government agencies make decisions affecting the supply of goods and services. The planning decisions represent attempts to organize the economic life of individuals and organizations to suit the needs of the state. Command systems affect consumer choice because planning agencies not only decide what consumer goods are produced, but also their quantities for distribution and the prices of each good or service. Consequently, planned economies act as the complete opposite of market systems—where production and consumption processes are determined by private individuals and producers.

As stated earlier in the chapter, the Soviet Union represents the best available historical example of the command economy model. The Soviet system from 1928, when Stalin solidified his control over the **Communist Party** to the fall of the Soviet Union in 1991, clearly represented all elements of a command system in action. V.I. Lenin's death in 1924, as the leader of the **Bolsheviks** who seized power in Russia in October 1917, led to a power struggle among communists to see which person would emerge as leader of the Soviet Union. Stalin consolidated power by 1928, through the use of political terror against enemies of the communist state, administrative support for his leadership, and assassination of party rivals. Under his regime, the Communist Party controlled economic planning, placing emphasis upon using what national resources were available to promote rapid industrialization. Because Communists favored a more equitable system of resource allocation than the Czarist regime before them, and the Soviet state remained largely unindustrialized into the early 1920s, Soviet central planners were forced to use a system of **rationing** to distribute goods. A rationing system distributes consumer goods in limited quantities for each family, allowing the state to conserve resources.

In the Soviet Union under Stalin in the 1930s, conservation of food was rigorously enforced so that most of the harvests could be reserved for international export. The cash received from foreign nations for food shipments was channeled into public investment in heavy industry. Stalin aimed to use agriculture to finance rapid industrialization. Peasants or workers were expected to survive on slim rations from the state to preserve food surpluses for export. Those that protested often disappeared, as victims of the totalitarian communist regime. To speed the industrialization process along in the 1930s, the Stalinist regime forced **agricultural collectivization** of peasant land to facilitate his export goals. In this process, private farms were nationalized by the state to take food from countless millions of Soviet citizens, many of whom would die of starvation. This was done to give the state absolute control over agriculture on collective farms. As a result, the government could sell more food abroad for cash to finance the Soviet industrial drive. As with the individuals that protested any of Stalin's policies, those opposing collectivization were brutally repressed.

Historians debate the human cost of agricultural collectivization and the political terror that was closely linked to that process. All documented historical research shows that deaths attributable to collectivization under the Stalinist regime number in the millions. Yet, it cannot be denied that significant rates of economic growth were achieved as a result of Stalin's industrial drive. Industrialization was achieved as a revolution led from above, using policies put forth by central planners. The Soviet government's central planning agency, **Gosplan,** set production targets known as **five-year plans**—which determined what goods would be produced and the prices charged for each item. The emphasis was traditionally to concentrate on heavy industry at the expense of consumer items.

The Soviet Union experienced high rates of economic growth in the 1930s during the first of the five year plans. But growth rates slowed significantly by the 1970s—as the intensity of industrial growth could not be sustained. The drop in Soviet economic expansion can be explained, in part, by using the economic principle of **diminishing marginal product,** where output at such a high level could not be maintained because the room for continuous growth is minimized. Furthermore, the effectiveness of a command system is stunted by the necessity of **coercion,** which can be defined as the need for, or the threat of, negative reinforcement to compel a person to fulfill an action. Command systems rely upon fear to get people to accept wages, rationing, and work conditions. The Stalinists relied upon fear to motivate factory managers to meet quotas for five year plans. The system included few positive incentives beyond that of social recognition for workers as heroes of socialist labor. Lack of incentives led to problems with quality control and production stagnation, as workers lost their fervor in the idea of a utopian future—with communism increasingly viewed by the 1970s as a failed ideology. This situation provides a direct contrast with the market model, where economic success is rewarded with material gain. Adam Smith's view that markets allow self interest to flourish through commerce, channeled competition into the common good through job creation and lowered consumer prices—creating economic growth.

In the Soviet system, economic rewards were discouraged as antithetical to communism because they fostered wealth inequalities, where Soviet citizens would be recast into diverging economic classes based on the possession of material goods. Consequently, coercion was the real motivating factor for individuals in the workplace—especially once disillusionment set in about the communist worldview. Coercion remained the only way to motivate workers to accomplish tasks, where workers would do just enough not to be punished.

The Soviet Union ceased to exist at the end of 1991. By 1992, each Soviet republic had gained sovereignty. Some chose to ally in the temporary Confederation of Independent States. The Soviet Union disintegrated due to a variety of factors. When Mikhail Gorbachev became the Soviet leader in 1985, he attempted to reform the Soviet system by introducing political and economic changes called *Glasnost* and *Perestroika*. *Glasnost* argued for increasing openness in the Soviet political system for free speech to flourish and *Perestroika* aimed to introduce more market incentives into the command system. The reformist ethos led many to desire an even greater liberalization of society. Concurrently, nationalists demanded freedom for the various Soviet Republics. Others were more interested in obtaining more consumer goods, desiring that Soviet planners lessen the concentration on armaments and heavy industry. Some pushed for religious freedom to be instituted in each republic—from Muslim Kazakhstan to Catholic Ukraine, and an end to Communist Party domination over government policy. Predictably, the Red Army leaders became uneasy with the rapid pace of Gorbachev's reforms and attempted to remove him from power in the summer of 1991. The army coup ultimately failed, but by the end of that year the Soviet Union ceased to exist—as citizens demanded sovereignty for the republics and an end to over seventy years of communist rule. The rising expectations of the Soviet populace had brought the Soviet command system to its knees.

Ultimately, Gorbachev was unable to hold together a diverse Union of breakaway republics without resorting to the kind of violence Stalin used when the Soviet Union was threatened with separatism and internal dissent. Francis Fukuyama has implied that the fall of the Soviet Union helped signal the end of ideological confrontation in world politics between capitalism and communism, ushering in a new age of democratization and the spread of global capitalism. Accordingly, while the Soviet Union teetered on the brink of collapse in the 1980s, the world's most populous communist nation—the **Peoples Republic of China**—began to liberalize its economy. With **Deng Xiaoping** as their leader, China began the transition from a rigid command economy structure toward an economy in the twenty-first century where private production, more open markets, and foreign investments are increasingly welcomed. This process sheds light on the fact that by 1992, for a growing number of mainland Chinese and citizens of other nations throughout the communist world, the fall of the Soviet Union represented the failure of command systems to sustain economic growth. In effect, they failed to provide a legitimate economic alternative to the emerging ideological consensus concerning the effectiveness of market economies to promote economic development.

Monetary Policy and the U.S. Federal Reserve System

As was developed earlier in this chapter, Keynes and the New Dealers believed that aggressive fiscal policies would allow governments to effectively make markets work better by limiting the severity of recessions.

Government spending policies, in their view, could abort the worst phases of the economic cycle. Government could then lower spending during economic recoveries to pare down the accumulated national debt. But other economists believe that **monetary policy,** where the government makes decisions concerning the nation's money supply, is more effective in stimulating economic growth. The importance of monetary policy as an economic tool has been most clearly developed by the American economist **Milton Friedman.** He believes that government central banks can affect economic growth by either slowing or accelerating the supply of money available to lending institutions. In the United States, the **Federal Reserve System** has fulfilled this function since its creation in 1913. The **Fed,** as the system is commonly called, effectively controls the national money supply by determining the rate of interest it charges private banks to borrow money. This rate of interest in called the **discount rate.** By increasing that rate, the Fed assists in combating **inflation**—or the rise in consumer prices. This is because when the Fed raises the discount rate, that action discourages borrowing—as higher discount rates usually result in higher interest rates that consumers pay for private bank loans. Conversely, if the Fed wants to combat **deflation** (a drop in consumer prices), a lack of consumer spending, or a recession, it can increase the supply of money available to creditors by lowering the discount rate.

The Federal Reserve also can increase or decrease the national money supply by determining **reserve requirements,** which detail the amount of money assets banks and financial institutions must keep on hand instead of issued as outstanding loans. The greater the reserve requirement, or money that banks cannot lend out, the smaller the money supply is in the nation. Alternately, the lower the reserve requirement is, the more money financial institutions can loan out to stimulate economic growth and consumer spending.

Additionally, the Fed is involved in **open market operations,** where the central bank buys and sells **government bonds** (loans to the government with a fixed redemption date) issued by the U.S. Treasury. In using this mechanism, the Fed can sell bonds to take currency out of circulation—which can have the effect of lessening inflation. Conversely, when the Fed buys bonds, it gives consumers and institutions back money with interest earnings. They can then spend the money in the economy.

Economists that believe that central banking policies are the greatest tool in which to shape the health of a market system are called **monetarists.** Milton Friedman is acknowledged as a leader of this school of thought. In his 1963 book co-authored with Anna Schwartz, *A Monetary History of the United States, 1867–1960,* Friedman blamed the severity of the Great Depression of the 1930s on the Federal Reserve System's contraction of the nation's money supply—as it had raised discount rates in 1928 and 1932. Friedman and the monetarists also believe that the Keynesian policy of combating recessions through government taxing and spending is largely irrelevant to the creation of economic growth. Rather they think it is the supply of money and interest rates that most influence economic expansion and contraction.

Factors Shaping Economic Growth

The debate between the Monetarists and Keynesians continues to rage into the 21st century as to what factors allow market economies to sustain economic growth in the modem world. Added to this debate, Marxian economists like Paul Baran and Paul Sweezy in their 1966 book *Monopoly Capitalism*, believed that industrial capitalism would stagnate due to economic concentration—partly because they thought ideas for new products would run dry. Countering their assertion, the 20th century economist **Joseph Schumpeter** in his 1942 work, *Capitalism, Socialism, and Democracy,* argued that capitalism would continue to recreate itself with new products and processes. Innovations would continue to foster new demand for products and services, but Schumpeter thought economic suffering would occur as industries selling obsolescent products and services would slowly go out of business. A modern example of this for the late Schumpeter would be the typewriter repairman being replaced by the computer salesman. Schumpeter called this process **creative destruction,** which implies how capitalism should be seen as an evolutionary system.

Whereas Schumpeter focused on innovation and demand for new products in his thinking on creative destruction, the late 19th century American economist **Thorstein Veblen,** in his 1899 book *The Theory of the Leisure Class,* developed the concept of **conspicuous consumption.** This theory held that consumers spend money on goods and services to display their social status. For Veblen, displays of wealth were significant economic

forces because the spending of the financial elites on material items also influenced what others would buy. Consequently, products and services are demanded because of their social value, leading consumers to purchase things to appear as part of a higher social class.

Veblen's concept of conspicuous consumption demonstrates that people will buy goods or services not because they are inexpensive, but because a higher priced item may infer the higher social status of a purchaser. Buying a higher priced item demonstrates the ability of a consumer to purchase expensive items, where the purchase and display acts as a form of domination over others unable to buy such products. Ultimately in his analysis, Veblen showed how the social world drove economic choice, as seemingly irrational forces motivated buyers to purchase goods. This social environment helped capitalism create an artificial demand for status related products that spurred economic growth. These circumstances assist the efforts of the advertising industry, where status anxieties and consumer identities allowed advertisers to manipulate consumers into purchasing goods and services that are not absolutely needed.

Veblen's idea on consumption being dictated by social forces makes it difficult for economists to gauge living standards. Without considering those social and cultural factors that shape spending and saving habits, economists attempt to use quantifiable numbers to determine a **poverty line**—which is defined by government agencies as a level of income necessary for people or families to buy what is required to survive. But these definitions, created by agencies like the U.S. Social Security Administration, tell very little about how people actually *use* the money they receive. As Veblen's analysis shows, social pressures are significant in determining how individuals spend money and gauge their own economic success. For example, a person that earned more money in a particular year than they ever had before may consider themselves economically deprived if people they associate with are earning more. This concept is labeled **relative deprivation** by economists. In part, relative deprivation is fueled in the United States by growing maldistribution of wealth, where the wealth of the top twenty percent of American households has been increasing since 1980 at the expense of the poorest segment of American society. For example, U.S. Census Bureau studies show that aggregate income for the bottom twenty percent of American families have seen their income decline from 5.3% in 1980 to 4.1% in 2003. Conversely, the wealthiest fifth of the American population in aggregate income saw their income rise from 41.1% to 47.6% in the same period.

Economic Indicators

The effects of increasing maldistribution of wealth on the national economy can only be measured indirectly through using other methods to study economic growth. In this vein, each of the terms highlighted in this section are indicators that assist economists in determining the strengths and weaknesses of national, global, and regional economies—helping them measure the outlook for economic growth or recession. The **Consumer Price Index (CPI)** measures the prices of a group of goods and services purchased by people living in urban areas. A more detailed study of prices is called the **Core CPI.** This indicator excludes products from the index where prices change rapidly and often—such as gasoline and food. Economists use CPI studies to gauge rates of inflation or price declines, which tell them much about the health of an economy.

High levels of price inflation can become a particularly onerous economic problem. The term **inflation** can be narrowly defined as the increase in prices and money wages. Wage increases can instigate further consumer price increases, as business react with higher prices. Inflation particularly hurts people on fixed incomes, as they usually are forced to lower their spending on consumer goods and services when they become unaffordable. Inflation also hurt creditors, since fixed term loans become increasingly risky. This is because fixed rate investments are eroded by future inflated prices. An example of this would be when a bank loans money to a borrower at a low rate of interest. If between the time the loan is made and paid off the inflation rate is 100%, the creditor has lost significantly because the value of the money loaned has eroded due to inflation.

A high level of **unemployment** is perhaps the most glaring of economic indicators that measure the strength and weakness of an economy. People without work have little to no power to promote economic growth as their spending power is minimized. Countries or regions with high unemployment rates often face the danger of price deflation in the overall economy. This is because, in an environment of price deflation, businesses lower prices because of lack of demand—since fewer people can afford to purchase their products and services. Widespread unemployment will likely result, as companies that cannot profit when selling merchandise below cost must lay people off.

The new unemployed can no longer patronize other businesses, causing ripple effects throughout the economy.

Another economic indicator frequently used is **per capita income.** To figure this statistic for a nation, one must divide the total national income by the sum of the national population. A hypothetical example would be when national income is 100 million dollars and the national population is 100 persons, per capita income would be one million dollars. This indicator can also be used for measuring state and local economies in the same manner.

When per capita income is used as an indicator with the nation as the level of analysis, it allows economists to determine the wealth of countries in comparison with other nations—or to measure national income growth from year to year. At the state level, per capita income can determine the richest and poorest states in the United States. Yet, care must be taken when using per capita income as an economic indicator. This is because income is often skewed erratically in a specific population. An example would be the state of Connecticut, where sizeable minorities of residents are Wall Street bankers. There income, when factored into a per capita income for Connecticut, makes Connecticut residents appear to have higher incomes than most in the state actually do.

A measure of wealth used extensively by economists is **Gross Domestic Product (GDP).** This statistic has been used since the early 1990s by the U.S. government to measure the market value of all goods and services produced in a country in a specific year. By doing so, GDP tells the actual size of an economy. It measures all items produced in a country, whether by domestic or foreign companies. This is important because, with multinational companies involved in different countries, GDP can monitor economic activity that takes place in a single nation—whether companies are foreign or domestically owned. The measure can also tell of the size of a nation's economy compared to the GDP of other nations.

GDP is directly related to another economic indicator called the **rate of economic growth.** Also known as the growth rate, this statistic measures the rate of increase of GDP factoring in inflation rates in a defined period. This statistic is normally compiled annually. A clear example of this measurement would be a GDP that increases at six percent with an inflation rate at four percent. This example would put the actual rate of economic growth at two percent. The rate of economic growth is an especially important statistic because, in a nation with a rapidly growing population, small growth rates in the economy may not allow for enough economic opportunities for those seeking work, leading to unemployment and potential social and political unrest.

Overproduction and underproduction are problems that reveal a significant amount of information about the strengths and weaknesses of an economy. Overproduction occurs when factories produce more goods that are consumed in the market. When this happens, prices fall for products that have been overproduced, as demand for those items is less than the overstock created. Factories that have gluts of unsold inventories often must limit future production and layoff workers. This can create a major rise in regional unemployment which, as discussed earlier in the chapter, can affect other parts of a local economy as unemployed people often have little choice but to cut consumer spending. Conversely, underproduction occurs when producers create fewer goods than are demanded by the market. This scenario can limit economic growth by lessening potential sales, as producers can't get enough goods to the market to meet demand. Underproduction can also create price inflation in that product sector, as demand for a product being greater than its supply usually leads to higher market prices.

Price inflation in one area of the economy can also affect spending patterns of consumers in other ways. If rising gasoline prices cut into the disposable income (the total amount of personal income available for spending—subtracting government taxes) of consumers, it can lessen their spending on other items—potentially leading to contraction of an economy. Lack of disposable income among the general population can also have a deleterious effect on economic growth. If the distribution of wealth is unbalanced among the population, where a small group of the wealthiest people in a nation control most of a nation's income, the lack of a sizeable middle class with purchasing power can cause an economy to stagnate.

There are other economic measures that are subtle and only indirectly viewed as economic indicators. A health care issue on the surface, the number of years a person is expected to live from birth—or life expectancy—reveals much about national economies. In a nation where infant mortality is low, disease prevention efforts are well funded by government, and quality medical care is available to most of the population, life expectancy will likely be high. In nations where unemployment is high and the government spends little

on health care, lower life expectancies care be expected. Examples of these scenarios can be seen by looking at the United Nations Human Development Index for 2005. The data available for 2003 shows, for example, that life expectancy at birth for citizens in a wealthy industrialized country like Canada was eighty years of age. The high number for Canada in the UN study can be compared with citizens in a nation encumbered by extreme poverty and political instability like Haiti. In this nation, life expectancy at birth in 2003 was just under fifty-two years of age. As such, access to health care can be an effective indicator in helping to measure national economic conditions.

Factors contributing to Economic Development in Market Economies

In addition to studying economic indicators to measure development, economists generally agree that certain dynamics are crucial in facilitating economic growth. Among those factors are the availability of investment capital, plentiful human and natural resources, entrepreneurship, innovation, growth oriented government policies, and the development of stable economic and political institutions. Each of these concepts will be addressed here in greater detail, specifically in relation to the economic history of the United States in the 19th and 20th centuries.

In the U.S. and elsewhere, human capital refers to workers that have been trained to fulfill certain functions that are essential to the productivity and success of industries and businesses. These laborers have training and work experiences that make them valuable assets to their firms. Companies often pay fixed costs to train workers or provide higher wages to obtain workers already trained. Once they are trained for employment duties, workers contribute to the value of an organization. Construction companies need civil engineers to implement their plans and airlines need pilots to skillfully fly their airplanes. In terms of innovation, software developers are instrumental for computer firms as human capital since they create the next generation of programs.

In the United States, skilled workers have traditionally been plentiful—in part because of the historical emphasis placed on education in American society. Though the leaders of the 17th century Massachusetts Bay Colony of New England stressed literacy of common folk primarily for the purpose of Bible reading, a literate society allowed for the development of an urban commercial society to flourish—a society poised to embrace industrialization and international trading relationships. After the American Revolution, the Ordinance of 1785 was passed by U.S. lawmakers under the Articles of Confederation government. It outlined how the U.S. would sell western lands to the public. The law provided for the revenues from the sale of one section of land in each township to be used to create public schools. Skipping forward to the American Civil War period, the Republican Congress passed the Morrill Act of 1862—giving public lands to state governments to sell. Proceeds from the sales went to finance the creation of colleges and universities that would be dedicated to the agricultural and mechanical disciplines. During the Cold War, the Soviet Union put the first satellite into space orbit in 1957. The Soviets followed this success in 1961 by putting the first man, Yuri Gagarin, into space. The United States, fearful of falling behind their Cold War rival in technology, increased federal support for math and science education. As these examples demonstrate, education has historically been an important aspect of American life since the 17th century. Providing for a literate and skilled workforce has traditionally aided in the process of fostering economic development.

A plentiful labor supply is also important to economic development. A scarcity of workers can lead to businesses having to pay higher wages—which cuts into business profits, limits the availability of investment capital, and can discourage the hiring of additional workers. As a nation where immigration is a constant, the United States has consistently possessed a supply of workers, both skilled and unskilled, that has been capable of fulfilling the needs of the labor market.

The availability of natural resources is also significant for facilitating economic growth. Natural Resources, as mentioned earlier in this chapter, are economic goods that are provided by nature. They can be unfinished goods that are processed into exploitable resources—such as wood that can be turned into kitchen cabinets, or crude oil refined into gasoline. Or they can be unprocessed resources like corn that can be sold directly to consumers from the stalk.

Farm products do stimulate economic activity but, arguably, the most important function of food industries is the creation of agricultural self sufficiency. When a society can count on food being available at a reasonable price, it minimizes social unrest, allows workers to spend less income on a food budget, and productive capacities can be concentrated on the development of industrial and service sectors of an economy.

The scarcity of natural resources or their depletion can have detrimental effects on a national economy. Shortages of supplies can lead to price inflation, which can choke consumer spending. The depletion of renewable resources, such as trees that are clear-cut in forests, can cause environmental degradation. Barren land is rarely a tourist attraction. In a country like Costa Rica with its rich rain forests, depletion of their forests would have a negative economic impact on an economy that relies upon those resources for tourist dollars. Using another example, deforestation has indirectly led to deaths in Haiti. Deforestation in that nation has allowed for massive flooding to occur periodically when torrential rains have fallen. This is because soil erosion prevents the land from absorbing the sheer volume of rainwater. Consequently, the economic impact of natural disasters can be so large as to be nearly incalculable.

The potential for economic growth can be associated with the amount of **financial capital** available in an economy. Broadly defined, capital can be defined as assets, both physical and financial, that can be utilized to create more income. An example of physical capital is an ATM machine. It provides banking services to customers by dispensing cash on accounts—while paying for itself by providing efficient service and limiting the need of a company to hire additional bank tellers. The long term profit accrued to the banking institution is significant, based on savings in labor costs and that the 24 hour banking function helps attract customers. Financial capital, on the other hand, is valuable because of its **liquidity,** where assets are readily available as monies to loan or to settle outstanding obligations. This form of capital is essential to promote economic growth in market economies because it provides funding for new ideas and innovations, which allows for the production of new goods and the facilitation of services to consumers.

The importance of financial capital in economic development can be understood by viewing the massive industrial growth of the United States in the late 19th century. As American railroad expansion required significant financial backing, states subsidized some of the building while a significant amount of capital was provided by English financiers. Loans and land grants were necessary for railroad companies to have the area and materials to lay the track necessary for railroad lines to stretch across the continent. The financiers, of course, received generous rates of return on their investments. But their capital was needed since the U.S.—prior to the late 19th century—was still a nation with a small investor class with little capital available for grand financial ventures. Thus, in market economies, the necessity of capital requires the existence of a class of financiers. These people derive a large segment of their wealth from using their financial and physical capital to turn a profit. New inventions of the late 20th century, such as the computer mouse or wireless internet services, needed financial backing to put these products in a form for the general public to demand and utilize. **Entrepreneurs,** which are people that are able to see what the needs of a particular market are and figure out how to provide the service or product for a cost, are also directly encouraged by capitalists. Without the investment assistance of capitalists, entrepreneurs would have less financial support in which to exploit an opportunity.

Government policies and political processes relating to economic development can significantly affect the economic growth opportunities of a nation. For an economy to function efficiently, government stability is essential. Constantly shifting political priorities on taxes and economic regulation can create economic uncertainties. Unstable political situations act to limit financial investment to regions like sub-Saharan Africa, where long-term government stability in the exception rather that the rule. Likewise, limited investment is a prime cause of economic stagnation throughout the underdeveloped world, where civil war and social unrest deter capital outlays. When nations establish and its citizens respect the **rule of law,** where political legitimacy is conferred when people agree to support rule making institutions, it can encourage direct foreign investment.

Building legitimate political institutions is a significant first step for developing nations to promote economic growth. Once this happens, the policies that governments introduce can either facilitate or hinder economic growth. Central banks that control a country's money supply, like the Federal Reserve System of the United States, can provide for financial stability by injecting more money into economies during recessions. Alternately, they can slow the availability of credit to banks to halt inflationary pressures and over-speculation during financial prosperity.

One method that has been used historically to encourage economic growth is to practice the laissez-faire approach that was favored by Adam Smith. Laissez-faire, as discussed earlier in the chapter, refers to the government's policy of letting the economy run itself according to natural laws of supply and demand—where prices would be determined by the market.

The laissez-faire philosophy of promoting economic development was generally adopted by U.S. policymakers in America's industrial take-off period of the late 19th century. Between 1865 and 1900, the U.S. went from being a predominantly agricultural country to becoming the largest global volume producer of industrial goods. As we have seen, this economic environment encouraged monopoly formation. The U.S. government attempted to address the problem of monopolies that were hindering free competition in the market system—the Sherman Anti-Trust Act of 1890 being a good example. But the congressional legislation was ineffective in separating concentrated industrial sectors such as sugar, oil, and railroads through the early 1900s. It was not until the early 20th century that American Presidents like Theodore Roosevelt and Woodrow Wilson had some success at the national level in addressing what they thought was the need for more effective laws to combat monopoly formation.

The United States in the late 19th century experienced social problems that were indirect results of the federal government's hands-off policies—such as the lack of consumer protection. The laissez-faire mentality that protected producers, at the expense of workplace and consumer safety, was institutionalized in the law courts through the theory of **freedom to contract.** It assumed consumers and workers were free agents—that all wage structures and product prices were negotiated as market relationships. This philosophy encouraged judges to limit the liability of companies for damages incurred by consumers using defective products or laborers hurt in industrial accidents. The basis for this thinking was developed early in the 19th century by the U.S. Supreme Court in the 1817 case, *Laidlaw v. Organ,* which held that individuals could not sue or recover damages against a merchant that unknowingly sold defective goods. Such rulings intended to prevent litigation that could create financial risk to developing industries and their investors. In this light, legal interference in the public domain by courts represented an infringement upon laissez-faire doctrine. The legal historian Morton J. Horwitz argued in a 1977 book, *The Transformation of American Law, 1780–1860,* that U.S. law was indirectly subsidizing the costs of economic expansion for corporations and businesses by not intervening in American society to protect consumers and laborers. The freedom to contract philosophy, in this view, had made courts formal instruments that directly supported economic growth.

In economic terms, limited liability rulings encouraged investment by finance capitalists. The same reasoning led to the development of the **corporation.** Since the late 19th century in the United States, corporations have been viewed by courts as organizations involved in economic activities that can be sued and pay taxes like individuals—but the entity is distinct in the eyes of the law from the actual individuals that manage its affairs. Thus, individual assets can't be attached to judgments against a corporation by federal courts. For example, if a person invests in Microsoft Corporation and the company is sued in court, only the amount the individual invested could be lost—not their personal assets outside of the investment. This reasoning was institutionalized by the 1886 U.S. Supreme Court ruling, *Santa Clara County vs. Southern Pacific Railroad Company*, where corporations were guaranteed the same rights to due process of law as individuals. This meant, in effect, that corporations and their investors were given legal protection in the federal courts.

The U.S. government, since the early years of the Republic, has encouraged innovation and invention by protecting the exclusive legal rights of inventions—for a finite number of years—to the individuals and entities that created them. This type of legal protection is called a **patent.** A United States government agency, the U.S. Patent Office, has regulated and governed this process since 1790. It seeks to reward inventors whose innovations have social benefits that can accrue to society. Patents encourage new inventions when people know they can profit from securing exclusive rights to a new idea or product. Thus, patents are believed to encourage an individual's self interest to flourish, where the ideas they develop can benefit the community while rewarding the inventor.

Ultimately, patent laws, U.S. government policies in regard to the 19th century market economy, the development of corporations, 19th century federal government support of the laissez-faire ideology, limiting the liability of businesses in federal courts, and the creation of patent protections—all of these factors have traditionally helped stimulate economic growth. These actions, though they demonstrate how severely limited the government's role was in protecting consumers, workers, and the environment, did assist in facilitating America's development into the world's foremost industrial power by the early 20th century.

While the U.S. government in the 19th century consciously promoted growth by limiting its involvement in the domestic economy, American policy toward international trade in that century was dominated by the tariff issue. As described earlier, Tariffs are rates of taxes on goods imported into a country. In the early American republic, supporters of American industrialization like Alexander Hamilton—the first U.S. Secretary of the Treasury—argued that high tariffs would encourage Americans to buy American made goods. This was because the duties would make foreign goods much more expensive. High tariff supporters reasoned that making foreign goods more expensive would also stimulate domestic production in trades where there were few American manufacturers. Today, tariff policies continue to be used by countries to protect domestic markets—especially where politicians believe that national interests and the health of local industries are at stake. When these policies are utilized by governments today, they are labeled as **protectionism.** For example, When France keeps American wheat out of their nation by imposing high tariffs on imported American grain, the action becomes an indirect subsidy to french wheat farmers because competition against their product is lessened. In economies with nascent, start-up industries, tariffs may benefit small companies by protecting them from fierce international competitors until they are strong enough to compete in a free trade environment against foreign competition.

Each of the factors described above are significant forces that contribute to economic growth in economies that are market oriented. In command economies where government planning organizations control, own, or direct the productive capacities of a nation, governments have to promote development. In the United States, where the modern economy is described as regulated capitalism, some functions in support of a pro-growth economic policy are facilitated by government while others are left to market forces.

References

Bernanke, Ben (2000) *Essays on the Great Depression.* Princeton: Princeton University Press.

Baran, Paul and Paul M. Sweezy. (1966). *Monopoly capital; an essay on the American economic and social order.* New York: Monthly Review Press.

Cassidy, John. (April 3, 2006). *"Relatively deprived; how poor is poor?"* The New Yorker, 82, (7): 42–47.

Freidman, Milton and Anna Jacobsen Schwartz. (1963) *A monetary history of the United States, 1867–1960.* Princeton, Princeton University Press.

Fukuyama, Francis. (1992) *The end of history and the last man.* New York: Free Press.

Gordon, John Steele. (2004) *An empire of wealth; the epic history of American economic power.* New York: Harper Collins.

Heilbroner, Robert. (1999) *The worldly philosophers: the lives, times, and ideas of the great economic thinkers.* New York: Simon & Shuster.

Horwitz, Morton J. (1977) *The transformation of American law, 1780–1860.* Cambridge, MA: Harvard University Press.

Keynes, John Maynard. (1997) *The general theory of employment, interest, and money.* Amherst, NY: Prometheus Books.

Marx, Karl and Frederick Engels. (1998) *The communist manifesto; a modern edition.* New York: Verso.

Schumpeter, Joseph. (1976) *Capitalism, socialism ad democracy.* New York: Harper & Row.

Smith, Adam. (2000) *An inquiry into the nature and causes of the wealth of nations.* New York: Random House.

United Nations Development Programme. *Human development report* 2005. (Ed.) Kevin Watkins, http://hdr.undp.org/reports/global/2005

United States Census Bureau. (2006) *Statistical abstract of the United States; The National Data Book.* (125th Edition). Washington: U.S. Department of Commerce, Economics and Statistics Administration.

Veblen, Thorstein. (1965) *The theory of the leisure class.* New York: A.M. Kelley.

CHAPTER SIX

The American Political Economy

Michael J. Lenaghan

So you have a job and career, earn your income, interest and dividends, pay your mortgage, consumption bills, and your public taxes and fees (federal income taxes, state intangible taxes, local sales and property taxes, airport, park and tollbooth fees, Social Security and Medicare contribution). You enjoy a life in the "home of the brave and the land of the free." What else do you need to know to watch out for your self, loved ones, and neighbors when it comes to current and future economic "quality of life" issues?

Illness, accident, unemployment, a better job opportunity, home purchase, car acquisition, education and training requirements, retirement investments, family growth, and other matters may require your active engagement, or protection of personal and family wealth (savings, stocks, bonds, mutual funds, promissory notes, real estate investment trusts, co-ownership contracts, intellectual property rights—patents, copyrights, and trade marks). You really ought to be in a position to have fundamental information, insights, analytical skills, and creative strategies to maximize opportunities, minimize risks, and optimize the ways you can "connect the dots" on behalf of your self and loved ones.

A basic knowledge of economics and a strong sense of how the political economy functions in our representative, federal democracy are essential elements by which to exercise basic citizenship and promote personal material well-being in our complex, interactive, interdependent national life in a global community. **Economics** is the social science discipline wherein we study how individual households and communities persist and evolve using limited or scarce resources. The **political economy** is the study of the political influence of households, business, and government interacting in the conduct of individual, corporate and public growth, development, diminution and transformation through the use of limited resources and unlimited wants in a society.

The Mixed, Regulated American Economy

The United States of America provides a political economy best described as a mixed, regulated—neither a solely command nor singularly market driven—economy. A **"command economy"** provides central control, direction, evaluation, and accountability to a series of relationships that are most productive when least inhibited by non-consumers. It is most insensitive to consumer needs or wants. A **"market economy"** offers unfettered possibilities for the aggregation of expertise, organization, resources, marketing and sales, with least protections for uneducated, naive consumers or otherwise vulnerable consumers, thereby leaving open avenues of deception, unaccountability and corruption. Extreme command and market economies have both led to wide consumer abuses, corruption, inefficiencies that favor irrationally powerful forces and insensitivity to human and civil rights.

Individual political rights are held in higher regard than property rights within the U.S. Constitution. However, the protection, promotion, and promulgation of property rights are crucial to the very vitality, stability, growth and enormous productivity of the national economy year after year. Therefore, the United States of America has

The American Political Economy Major Indicators (2010)	
Population	307 million
Population Growth	0.977%
Nationality	American
Government	Federal Republic
Economy	Market-Oriented
Infant Mortality	6.22 out of 1,000
Life Expectancy	78 years
Net Migration Rate	4.32 migrants/ 1,000 pop.
Literacy	99%
Poverty	15%
Gross Domestic Product	$14.4 trillion
GDP Per Capita	$46,900
Federal Revenues	$1.914 trillion
Federal Spending	$3.615 trillion
Federal Deficit	$1.701 trillion
Federal Debt	$13 trillion
Imports Balance	$1.445 trillion
Exports Balance	$994.7 billion
Total Trade Balance	$450.3 billion
Inflation	2.39%
Unemployment	9.6%
GDP by Sector	Agriculture: 1.2% Industry: 21.9% Services: 76.9%
Labor Force	154.1 million
Labor Force by Occupation	37.3% managerial, professional, and technical 24.2% sales and office 22.6% manufacturing, extraction, crafts, and transportation 0.7% farming, forestry, fishing 17.6% other services

evolved a political economy in which civil and human rights, a national social contract, and national interests that supersede property rights, and profits under specified circumstances, all lead to a mixed, **regulated economy.**

In some instances, the government is the sole provider or sole licensor of goods and services (atomic and military, toxic and biologic, for example) in the national defense or other national interest with governmental oversight and periodic review and revision of status. In other instances, consumer demand is the sole determinant of goods and services, such as electronic products, foods, clothing, automotive products, cultural, sports and entertainment attendance, and publications. In other cases, government, business, and consumers interact to create demand for office products, the internet, computers, cellulars and more.

However, in all cases, regulations, rules and procedures for producing, marketing, distributing, using and disposing of almost all consumer goods from any source by any end user are generated, applied and enforced by government to promote the common good and insure the public welfare—the social contract exists to protect individual human and civil rights over property rights. The United States has a mixed, regulated economy by consent of the governed in our representative, federal democracy. Our national economy exists in a political framework that reflects the values, beliefs and practices of our constitution and the priorities of our elected officials on behalf of the American people.

Households

Households—yours and mine—are at the center of our economy wherein thousands of decisions to act, defer action, or not to act, daily determine the nature, content and consumption patterns by which our material well-being is measured. Economics define households as groups of individuals living together and making joint decisions. Ultimately, individual and household consumers are at the heart of an economy. Households exist for the wealth, well-being, social progress, comfort, convenience, and pursuit of happiness of their membership, who may or may not generate excessive revenue and material goods in the process. Quality of life indicators range from the highly intangible to the fundamentally monetarily measurable. The household in the United States seldom exists on its own apart from religious, cultural, social, nonprofit, governmental, and corporate "safety nets" and assistance arrangements beyond the traditional nuclear and extended family structure.

Essentially, each of us is in part an economic being: you create wealth by work that produces goods and services that are valued and funded by salaries or purchases

Overall Budget Trends

- In 2008, Washington will spend $2,931 billion, raise $2,521 billion, and run a $410 billion budget deficit.
- Tax revenues strongly correlate with economic growth. Economic growth pushed real 2004–07 tax revenues up 25 percent—the fastest growth in 40 years. A slowing economy and tax rebates may reduce 2008 revenues.
- Spending will increase 7.4 percent (4.5 percent after inflation) in 2008 and has risen 57 percent (30 percent after inflation) overall since 2001.
- The $410 billion budget deficit represents 2.9 percent of the GDP. More importantly, the public-debt-to-GDP ratio stands at 38 percent, which is actually below the post-World War II average and below the level at any point in the 1990s.

U.S. Federal Budget: Summary of Receipts, Outlays, and Surpluses or Deficits (–):								
(in millions of dollars)								
	Total			On-Budget			Off-Budget		
Year	Receipts	Outlays	Surplus or Deficit (–)	Receipts	Outlays	Surplus or Deficit (–)	Receipts	Outlays	Surplus or Deficit (–)
1930	4,058	3,320	738	4,058	3,320	738	...	...	...
1940	6,548	9,468	–2,920	5,998	9,482	–3,484	550	–14	564
1945	45,159	92,712	–47,553	43,849	92,569	–48,720	1,310	143	1,167
1950	39,443	42,562	–3,119	37,336	42,038	–4,702	2,106	524	1,583
1960	92,492	92,191	301	81,851	81,341	510	10,641	10,850	–209
1980	517,112	590,941	–73,830	403,903	477,044	–73,141	113,209	113,898	–689
2000	2,025,198	1,788,957	236,241	1,544,614	1,458,192	86,422	480,584	330,765	149,819
2010 estimate	2,165,119	3,720,701	–1,555,582	1,529,936	3,163,742	–1,633,806	635,183	556,959	78,224
2013 estimate	3,188,115	3,915,443	–727,328	2,422,390	3,285,517	–863,127	765,725	629,926	135,799

Note: Budget figures prior to 1933 are based on the "Administrative Budget" concepts rather than the "Unified Budget."

Where Is All the Money Going?

Defense and homeland security are responsible for just 40 percent of all new spending since 2001. Lawmakers also enacted:

- The 2001 No Child Left Behind Act, which is responsible for much of the 58 percent inflation-adjusted increase in education spending from 2001 through 2008;
- A 2002 farm bill that pushed annual farm spending to double the levels of the 1990s;
- A 2003 Medicare drug entitlement estimated to cost $783 billion over the next decade and trillions in the following decades;
- The 2005 highway bill, which, at $286 billion over six years, is the most expensive highway bill ever; and
- Large expansions of outlays for the refundable Earned Income Tax Credit and Child Tax Credit.

Lawmakers have done little to balance new spending with savings elsewhere in the budget.

Note that this new spending came at a time when net interest payments remained relatively steady due to low interest rates. Interest payments will rise if interest rates increase.

The national debt is $13.4 trillion!
U.S. Treasury Department report to Congress: U.S. debt to rise to $19.6 trillion by 2015.

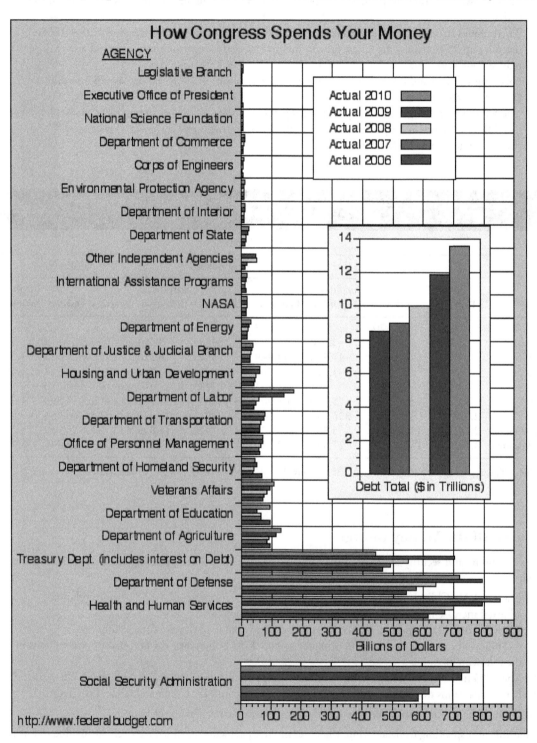

How Congress Spends Your Money

http://www.federalbudget.com

US Federal Deficit as Percent of GDP

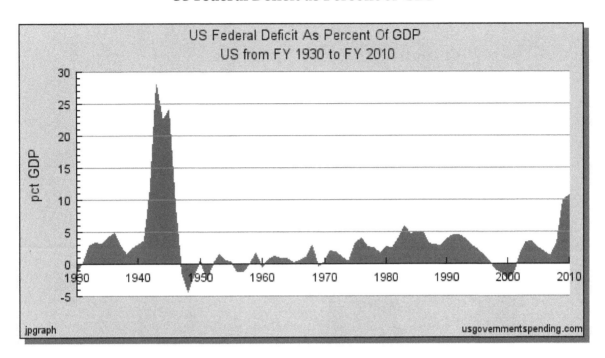

US Federal Debt as Percent of GDP

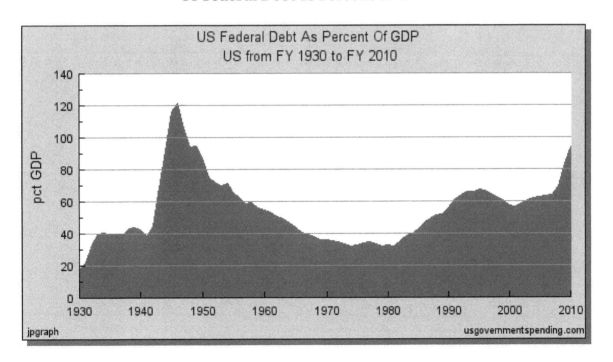

Federal Government Spending
Expenditure GDP—Charts—Deficit Debt

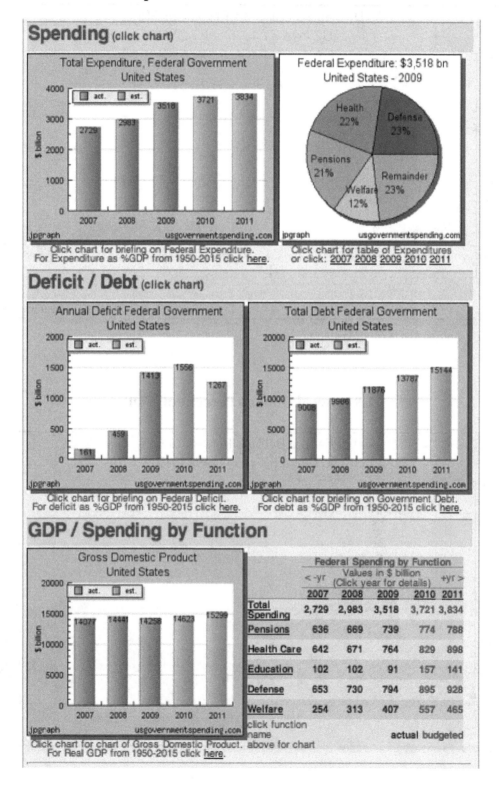

State Guesstimated* Government Revenue
Revenue GDP—Charts—Defict Debt

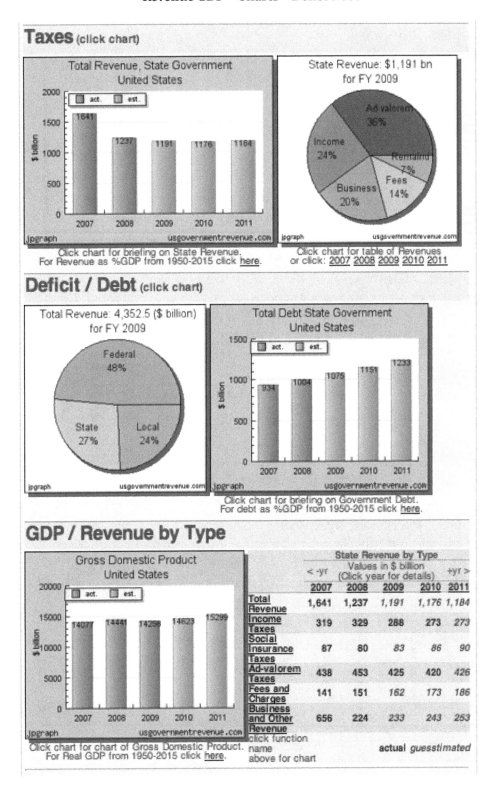

Federal Government Revenue
Revenue GDP—Charts—Defict Debt

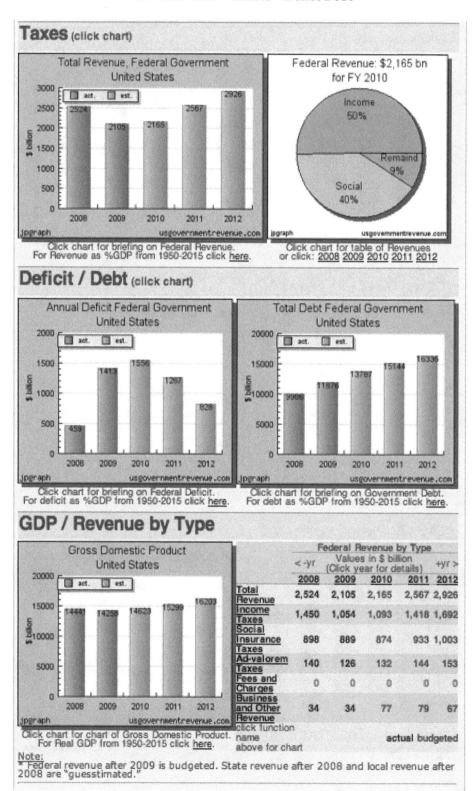

Total Government Revenue
Revenue GDP—Charts—Defict Debt

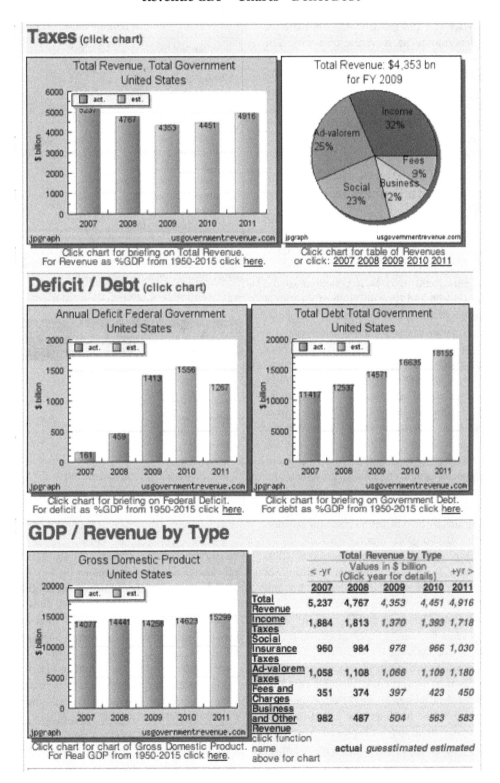

that require an exchange of money (anything with which you can purchase goods and services). You pay taxes which infuses the governmental part of the economy. You buy services and goods which stimulate the business and corporate parts of the economy. The framework within which each of us functions economically is the **political economy,** those facets of economic activity that are affected by public policy, public institutions and public interests that are greater than the individual or household interests in day to day survival and reproduction.

The Economic Engines of Business, Corporations, and Enterprises

Obviously, those entities that convert land, labor, and capital, historically—or today and tomorrow that convert information, communication, technology and service—into the marketing, production, distribution, delivery, and sales of goods and services are essential to the development, growth, and diversification of a national economy. Corporations and other forms of business—proprietorships, partnerships, professional associations, and individual inventors and entrepreneurs—clearly provide comprehensive, competitive, and complementary sources of goods and services. Businesses, unlike households, governments, and nonprofit organizations are uniquely designed to generate profits, their central reason for existence. Whether business functions in the mode of demand economics or "supply side" economics, its main purpose is profit making—and that is generally positive for the investors, employees, suppliers, and government that collect taxes and redistributes national wealth, as well as communities and households that directly and indirectly benefit from successful business enterprises who are also good corporate citizens.

Traditional economics is demand-economics—"You want it? You got it!" Supply-side economics is a creature of modern complex economies in which market research and promotion can contribute to demand. "You do not sell steak. You sell sizzle" "We make it! YOU take it!" Both approaches to economic development have been implemented in the United States and elsewhere in highly developed economies where marketing and promotion are more pervasive and financial resources more plentiful, especially for the higher risk demand creating supply-side economics.

Participation in the funding, profits and losses of American business is more widely distributed than in any country in the world. Average citizens own stock, bonds,

Employment by industry (in thousands and percentages)		
	Employment	**Percentage (%)**
Total Employment	129,558	100
Agriculture	3,399	2.6
Mining	634	0.48
Construction	8,302	6.40
Manufacturing	20,835	16.08
Transportation Communications and other public utilities	9,182	7.08
Wholesale/Retail Trade	26,777	20.6
Finance & Insurance	8,297	6.40
Services*	46,393	35.8
Public Administration	5,738	4.4

* Services include business and repair services, advertising, personnel support services, entertainment and recreation, hotels, hospitals, health services, schools, colleges and universities.

Gross Domestic Product by Industry (Percentages)	
Agriculture, forestry and fishing	1.6
Mining	1.4
Construction	3.7
Manufacturing	16.4
Transportation and utilities	7.5
Wholesale trade	7.3
Retail trade	9.2
Finance, insurance and real estate	18.9
Services	21
Government	13

real estate investment trusts (REITs) shares, mutual funds, and other financial instruments by which business is funded, and a successful business pays off bonds with interest, stock dividends, REIT interest rates and so forth. Nearly 50% of American households participate in some financial aspect of corporations and business directly or through retirement plans—in addition to being consumers. Business and corporations are clearly engines for national political economies and beyond. And they deliver economic payoffs to individuals and households when they operate effectively and profitably in addition to paying corporate taxes and observing pertinent health, safety, environmental, and fiscal operations laws.

Government—Regulator, Originator, and Generator of Wealth

The checks and balances within each of the three principal levels of government in the American federal democratic republic provide many assurances, safeguards and complexities in the operation of the national economy and its relationships to households, business, and the global community. To some the intricacies of government appear cumbersome, time consuming, and expensive. To others these intricacies provide stability, equity, due process, and the expenditure of overhead time and money that is worthwhile for fair, predictable, and timely treatment of legal, ethical, and human dimensions of economic transactions. Individuals, corporations (profit and nonprofit), and governments can initiate, influence, and feel the impact of new, renewed, or obsolete laws, legal enforcements/judgments and interpretations of government codes to change, maintain, or eliminate rules, regulations, functional relationships, purchasing, or other aspects of economic activities in their interest, the public interest, or other reasons.

The Federal Government

The Federal Government is composed of the Congress (House of Representatives and Senate), the Chief Executive/President/Commander-in-Chief, and the Judiciary. The Congress originates diverse laws, appropriation bills, treaty approvals, and a variety of enumerated powers that affect the economy. The President of the United States implements the laws through executive directive and Cabinet agencies and his role as commander in chief of the Armed Forces. The Judiciary (Supreme Court and lower federal jurisdictions) interpret Federal law, rules, and practices to ascertain and find judgment pertinent to that application of Constitutional law and the intent of Federal legislation. Within its three principal levels of checks and balances the Federal Government influences and regulates the national economy by public priorities and policy through three areas of its prerogatives:

Fiscal and budgetary policies refer to the setting of spending priorities, limits, and actual appropriations numbers, and allocations for each of the fiscal years within the purview of specific and general legislation. The expenditure of funds within the budget and specific detailed applications of funds has general impacts within different sectors of the national economy as well as in the specific geographic regions and constituencies that will benefit from actual purchases, jobs, and related benefits of government expenditures. The location of military bases, federal government facilities, funded projects—all with employment, local taxes, and economic growth implications are important budgetary issues for many local and state political jurisdictions. The Congress of the United States is most responsible for fiscal policies. In general, higher government spending within limits and lower taxes stimulate economic activity. The opposite policies slow down economic growth.

Setting priorities for rules, regulations, and operational procedures by which laws are implemented impacts the actual cost of doing business as an individual, business, and government. Less "red tape" (rules and regulations) usually means less expensive, professional paperwork, record keeping, tracking expenses. Most citizens feel they benefit from uniform rules, regulations, and procedures at the Federal Aviation Administration, Federal Drug Administration, and Consumer Product Safety Commission. Some people argue about the expense of health and safety rules at the workplace, or sexual harassment rules, or disability protection, or equal employment opportunity, and affirmative action rules—unless they benefit.

Monetary Policy is the increase or decrease in the country's money supply, a transaction by which the U.S. Treasury Department influences one aspect of inflation. The Federal Reserve Board determines the interest rate by which the nation's private banks can borrow money from the federal government. This impacts the rate of mortgages, car loans, consumer loans, and other investment opportunities. Lowering interest rates will encourage more consumer purchases with cheaper borrowed money or more industrial development with lower rates for industrial and commercial loans. Monetary policy clearly shapes major aspects of the American economy, the political economy.

Moralsuasion is the engaging in jawboning, bully pulpit, activist political leadership to encourage individual households, business, and government units and their leadership to behave in a specific manner with economic implications. This is often engaged in by political leaders (and sometimes by citizen/consumer advocates, and business and labor leaders) for the purpose of generating positive behaviors (savings account increases, increased purchases, decreased purchase of energy, wider investment in American enterprises, empathy for foreign funding or investment, or bailouts) with economic consequences. Moralsuasion is most often successful in democratic, open, participatory, educated, and freely communicating societies where transparency (facts are facts and situations are most clear and documentable) is feasible and recognizable. While not operating like a plebiscite, this transaction or relationship directly between leaders and constituents often ameliorates and expedites urgent needs for changes in consumption patterns in times of emergency or opportunity.

State Government

State governments enjoy the prerogative of influencing state economic activity in two areas of initiative including legislation, execution, and adjudication that develop upon the states, in matters not considered the prerogative of the federal government: fiscal and budgetary—priorities, budget recommendation, appropriation, allocation, oversight and evaluation, rules, regulations, procedures, enforcement, and penalties; and moralsuasion—leadership or advocacy on specific issues.

Local Government

Local governments enjoy the prerogatives of influencing local (country or municipal) economic activity in three areas of initiative including legislation, execution, and adjudication that devolve upon them in matters not considered the prerogative of the federal or state governments: fiscal and budgetary—priorities, budget recommendation, appropriation, allocation, oversight and evaluation, rules, regulations, procedures, enforcement, and penalties; and moralsuasion—leadership or advocacy on specific issues.

Three Levels of Political Intervention

The political economy of the United States has many avenues for affirmation, advocacy, intervention, and prevention from individual households who vote in political elections, who vote with purchasing power, who vote through stockholder instruments, and who may freely form voluntary lobbying groups on economic and other issues. At the national, state, and local levels of government, individual households, business, and even governments may choose to influence one or more of the three branches of government and its leadership by individual initiative, formal political intervention (e.g., referendum, voter initiatives) and informal, properly registered lobbying or political action committees focussed on candidates or incumbents and their economy policies.

The New American Economy

Americans might be engaging in totally new rules of economic behavior. Under the traditional rules, unemployment levels as low as now were expected to produce a higher inflation rate than 2.4%, since labor shortages were seen to lead to higher wages and to increased prices. Another new trend is the length of the current recovery. Business cycles in the American economy usually occur every five to seven years. We could be entering an era of less virulent business cycles. A third trend is in the source of employment. Since 1970, employment by Fortune 500 corporations has declined by over 5 million. Yet, the country has gained over 52 million jobs. Many of these come from small, newly created corporations.

The causes of the transition to what appears to be a new American economy are varied. The downsizing of American business, which began during the 1970s but accelerated in the 1980s, made business more efficient. Many Americans had to reinvent themselves by learning new skills and by entering new professions and businesses. This downsizing, when combined with the tax cuts, free trade policies, and less government interventions during the 1980s, forced the business sector to become leaner and more efficient. The end of the Cold War brought a "peace dividend" as many resources previously used for military purposes were redirected for personal and commercial economic use.

A major aspect in the transition to the "new" economy is the success in the avoidance of the high inflation of the 1970s. Paul Volcker and Alan Greenspan of the Federal Reserve Board helped defeat inflation by using tough monetary policies. Afterwards, the lowering of interest rates allowed companies to invest in new and more productive equipment. Business has spent more on information technology than in other forms of capital investments since the industrial revolution. This is coupled with access to an unlimited amount of cheap property via the internet.

Unlike Western Europe, where unemployment averages 11%, the new American economy is based on competition and not on consensus with lavish unemployment benefits and over-generous job security. Important in the transition to the new economy is the computer, which in the 1990s got much easier to use and became affordable to the general population. However, having technology is not enough. The key is that U.S. society is open to entrepreneurs who deploy the new technology to make goods and increase productivity, and who are accepting of change. Accounts which deduct money from income automatically for retirement accounts like 401(K) and 403(b) have provided vast amounts of capital for Wall Street, making the stock market rise over the 11,000 point mark, and giving corporations the resources to modernize.

While wages are rising annually, productivity is increasing, too, so that higher labor costs do not lead to inflation. Moreover, low cost imports contribute to lower inflation. Automation and information technology keep production more in line with consumer demand so that business does not overproduce significantly and force the economy into recession until excess supply or inventory is sold. This innovation could widen business cycles whether, transition or transformation, we appear to have a new American economy.

Sources

Bagby, Meredith. (1998) *The Budget of The United States Of America*, annual edition. New York: Forbes Publishers.

Cole, Don, (Ed.). (1997) *Economics*, 97/98, annual editions. Connecticut: Dushkin/McGraw Hill.

Eggert, James. (1997) *What Is Economics?* (Fourth edition). Mountainview: Mayfield Publishing Company.

Heilbroner, Robert; Thurow, Lester. (1994) *Economics Explained, Everything You Need to Know About How the Economy Works and Where It's Going*, revised and updated. New York: Touchstone Book.

Markovich, Denise E.; Pynn, Ronald, E. (1988) *American Political Economy: Using Economics With Politics*. Pacific Grove: Brooks/Cole Publishing Company.

Peretz, Paul (Ed.). (1996) *The Politics of American Economic Policy Making*, second edition. New York: M.E. Sharp.

CHAPTER SEVEN

Systems of Governing

Paul S. George

Government

Informal Government

At different times and in different places, societies, or groups of people of varying sizes living within close proximity of one another, together, have directed their affairs through informal governments. Even today, in some parts of the world, this is the case. Sometimes, in this arrangement, leadership was invested in all of the adult males of the community who were expected, especially in times of crises, to provide direction for their people. In other societies, however, the leader and his family maintained a distinctive place in the community. They may have lived apart or within the group, but often in a habitat notable for its size and quality.

Civilization and the Emergence of Formal Government

With the rise of more densely populated communities, government became a formal process since the challenge to maintain order grew and became sharper, necessitating a larger, more formidable apparatus for this purpose. As certain societies in different parts of the globe embarked upon the stage of development referred to as civilization several thousand years ago, they exhibited certain characteristics absent elsewhere. Among them was intensive agriculture through cooperative effort, a written language, trade and diplomatic relations with other states, attention to the arts and other elements of culture, an increasingly more complex technology, and, as already mentioned, a formal governmental structure.

Such characteristics appeared first in river valleys in Southwest Asia (Mesopotamia), Egypt, India, and China.

Government can be defined as a body of people and institutions that make and enforce laws for a particular society. It differs in several significant ways from all other social institutions or organizations. Government is the most powerful of all social institutions for its rules apply to all members of society while the rules of any other social organization apply only to the members of that organization. The rules of government are usually recognized as authoritative, that is, they are generally considered to be rules more binding upon all members of society than are the rules of any non-governmental organization. Membership in most social organizations or institutions other than government is voluntary.

However, membership in a country is largely involuntary, since most people initially become citizens of a state and subject to its rules without any deliberate choice or conscious act. While most, or perhaps all, social organizations can muster some physical force to enforce their rules, government can marshal, if necessary, vast amounts of force. Governments perform legislative, executive, and judicial functions with decision-making power exercised by a majority (democracy), a small elite group (oligarchy), or a single all-powerful leader (dictatorship). A republican form of government, which includes representative governing bodies but does not possess a hereditary emperor or king, was characteristic of the Roman state that evolved from the fifth century B.C. through the seventh decade of the first century B.C., after which it became an empire.

An imperial government, one that arises from the task of governing an empire, as typified by the Roman Empire, which existed for five centuries until its demise (in the West) in the late fifth century A.D., represents another type of government. In this form of government, an emperor exercises power and authority not only over his native country, but also over other nations and/or colonies usually taken by conquest and incorporated into, administered by, and subjected to authority of the emperor.

Governments generally operate under the constraining element of a constitution. Governments direct both the internal and external affairs of **nations,** defined here as any sizable group of people united by common bonds of geography, religion, language, race, custom, and tradition, as well as through shared experiences and common aspirations. The term nation is often used interchangeably with "*state*," but this is not entirely accurate since not all national groups have attained statehood. A **state** or a country is a unique assemblage of territory, people, and institutions. States possess clearly defined geographic boundaries and, of course, governments to oversee and administer their affairs. Additionally, the nation and state may be essentially the same, as in the case of a nation-state like Ireland, or a state may be multi-national, such as Switzerland, with its different national groups. The term **nation-state** refers to a country with a dominant group within, such as the

French people in the state of France, which includes smaller numbers of other ethnic and racial groups. Finally, **politics** goes hand and hand with government since it is the means by which individuals affect their government. Politics is also a process, an activity by groups or individuals to achieve an objective. Politics entails a quest for a solution to a problem or an answer to an issue. Politics makes the art of governing possible, for it places candidates into office and brings issues to the fore that are often resolved by the leadership either in a deliberative way or by the fiat of one or a small group of leaders.

Viewpoints on Government

Government as a Positive Good

Historically, there are important, divergent viewpoints on the nature of government. The most favorable views government as a positive good. Its proponents argue that government is necessary for the people of a society to share in all of the opportunities provided by that entity. Without government, there would be chaos until the society eventually (sooner, rather than later) disintegrated. Thomas Paine, whose writings helped to stir the movement for colonial independence from England during the American Revolutionary War, believed that government was necessary "to supply the defect of moral virtue." Paine meant here that government helps to place us on the correct moral course while steering us away from a path that might lead to harm for ourselves and others. Typically, progressives or contemporary liberals favor a government actively involved in many aspects of the life of its people, and hold to this viewpoint. In America, this view manifested itself first in the era of Reconstruction, which followed the Civil War (1861–1865), as the Republican-led national government actively involved itself in uplifting the fortunes of four million former slaves who were struggling to adjust to the realities of freedom in the South. This era of wide-spread government intervention on behalf of the Freed People was brief, however, ending in 1877.

In the Progressive Era, which spanned the last decade of the nineteenth century and the first fifteen years of the twentieth century, along with the presidencies of Franklin D. Roosevelt, Harry S. Truman, John F. Kennedy, and Lyndon Johnson, stretching from the 1930s through the 1960s, the federal government assumed an activist role in American life. During this era, the liberal viewpoint, supportive of a strong, activist government, manifested itself in a welter of laws, programs, and new agencies that involved the national government ever more deeply in the lives of the

America's brand of Presidential Democracy was personified by Franklin D. Roosevelt, who served longer as President than anyone else. In the process, he brought the office to new levels of power and prestige. Courtesy of Library of Congress.

American people. This was a redefinition of the word "liberal," which in the 1800s was associated both in America and in Europe with those who distrusted the powers of government and who wanted to keep them small and limited.

Supporters of this new viewpoint believed that it was government's responsibility to rectify not only what was wrong with American life, but to provide, through legislation and programs, avenues to a better life. President Franklin Roosevelt's New Deal (1933–1941) was an example of this approach. Even more ambitious were the Great Society programs of President Lyndon Johnson, which got underway in 1965, following his election to a full four year term. Johnson and his followers believed that there was little that government could not do to rectify past injustices, while providing unlimited opportunities, through relentless spending on a multitude of programs, to upgrade the lot of Americans.

Government as a Necessary Evil

Another viewpoint widely divergent from the above holds that government is a necessary evil. Its supporters believe that government's *raison d'etre* is to serve as a restraining force. That is, government tells us what we can do and what we cannot do. Government's role is characterized here by such terms as "prohibit," "restrain," "regulate," compel," and "coerce." Government assumes this function primarily through its power to pass laws, and to enforce them. One of the most prominent proponents of this viewpoint was Thomas Hobbes, an Englishman who lived from 1588 to 1679. In his most famous work, *Leviathan,* Hobbes explained the necessity for government and in particular for the monarchical form of rule. People created governments, Hobbes wrote, as protection against themselves since life was by definition "poor, nasty, brutish, and short." This condition resulted from the tendency of humans to attempt to maximize their own pleasure and passion at the expense of others.

Moreover, in a state of nature, defined here as humans living together without an organized government of laws, impartial judges, and executives to enforce judicial decisions and rules, the unsatisfactory resolution of disputes could lead to anarchy, which would spell the effective end of that group as a viable entity. Therefore, with the issue of survival their foremost concern, humans abnegated the right to govern themselves and, instead, turned over all power and sovereignty to a ruler by virtue of a "social contract." The ruler's power was considered supreme and absolute. Hobbes noted the extreme nature of this process, but argued

Elements of the Code of Hammurabi

Hammurabi, the great seventeenth century B.C. Babylonian leader, made justice a function of the state. The importance of the Code lay in the fact that the laws of that society were spelled out in written form for anyone to observe, thereby providing the citizenry with a better chance of achieving justice than was usually possible through the oral promises of a leader. Below, an excerpt from his legal code, known as the *Code of Hammurabi.*

1. If a man has accused another of laying a death spell upon him but has not proved it, he shall be put to death.
2. If a man has accused another of laying a spell upon him, but has not proved it, the accused shall go to the sacred river, he shall plunge into the sacred river, and if the sacred river shall conquer him, he that accused him shall take possession of his house. If the sacred river shall show his innocence and he is saved, his accuser shall be put to death. He that plunged into the sacred river shall appropriate the house of him that accused him.
3. If a man has borne false witness in a trial, or has not established the statement he has made, if that case be a capital trial, that man shall be put to death.
4. If he has borne false witness in a civil law case, he shall pay the damages in that suit.
5. If a judge has given a verdict, rendered a decision, granted a written judgement, and afterward has altered his judgement, that judge shall be prosecuted for altering the judgement he gave and shall pay twelvefold the penalty laid down in that judgement. Further, he shall be publicly expelled from his judgement seat and shall not return nor take his seat with the judges at a trial.
6. If a man has stolen goods from a temple, or house, he shall be put to death; and he that has received the stolen property from him shall be put to death.
14. If a man has stolen a child, he shall be put to death.
15. If a man has induced either a male or female slave from the house of a patrician, or plebeian, to leave the city, he shall be put to death.
16. If a man has harbored in his house a male or female slave from a patrician's or plebeian's house, and has not caused the fugitive to leave on the demand of the officer over the slaves condemned to public forced labor, that householder shall be put to death.
22. If a man has committed highway robbery and has been caught, that man shall be put to death.
23. If the highwayman has not been caught, the man that has been robbed shall state on oath what he has lost and the city or district governor in whose territory or district the robbery took place shall restore to him what he has lost.
25. If a fire has broken out in a man's house and one who has come to put it out has coveted the property of the householder and appropriated any of it, that man shall be cast into the selfsame fire.

that only with such power could the leader of a state achieve the twin goals of order and peace among his people.

Others who came after Hobbes and who embraced the idea of government as the necessary agent to protect the social order believed, however, that the people of a country possessed certain inviolable rights and that it was the obligation of government to protect those rights. Most notable of those adhering to this viewpoint was John Locke, who maintained that the citizens of a society created a government through a "social contract" to protect those rights. Government may exercise only the authority that the citizenry has given it. If that government does not fulfill the purpose for which it was created, or if it exceeds the limited powers granted it, it must be replaced by a new government more consonant with the expectations of its creators, the citizens of a state. Locke's ideas on a social contract and the obligations of a government to its creators are found in his *Second Treatise of Government*, one of the most famous documents examining political thought in the West. In words that have inspired revolutionaries since its publication in 1690, Locke wrote that "The only way by which anyone divests himself of his natural liberty and puts on the bonds of civil society is by agreeing with other men to join and unite into a community for their comfortable, safe, and peaceable living one amongst another, in a secure enjoyment of their properties, and a greater enjoyment of any that are not of it." Locke noted the sovereign powers of the citizenry of a state, observing "that which begins and actually constitutes any political society is nothing but the consent of any number of freemen capable of a majority to unite and incorporate into such a society. And this, is that, and that only, which did or could give beginning to any lawful government in the world."

Still another view of government as a necessary evil was held by Thomas Jefferson. While acknowledging the need for government, Jefferson also believed that government could contribute best to public prosperity by allowing individuals and businesses to manage themselves. Liberty, he believed, can be protected most effectively by a strict adherence to the limits placed on governmental power by the Constitution. Jefferson is regarded as a "strict constructionist," or one who believes that the Constitution mandates that the government can do only what it is specifically authorized to do.

Government as an Unnecessary Evil

A third major perspective on government rejects it as an unnecessary evil because of the alleged constraints and harm it imposes on the citizens of a state. This viewpoint is held by anarchists, who also oppose authority because it thwarts human development. Karl Marx also held the view, but for different reasons from anarchists, that government was an unnecessary evil. Karl Marx, a nineteenth century German philosopher and revolutionary, who wrote passionately about class conflict, the exploitative nature of capitalism, and, ultimately, a workers' revolution, which would lead to the overthrow of the Bourgeoisie, or middle class, and usher in a Utopian Communist society where classes would disappear, private property would be eradicated, the economy and all other institutions of society would be in the hands of the people, and each member would produce "according to his ability (and take) according to his need." Marxism influenced a multitude of revolutionary movements in the twentieth century, beginning with the Russian Revolution of 1917, and brought to power numerous regimes that have operated on a socialist basis.

The Marxist rejection of government stems from its belief that government is merely a tool of the Bourgeoisie, which Marx believed worked closely with it to suppress and exploit the working class. Marxist doctrine taught that in the aftermath of the violent overthrow of the capitalist class through a worldwide workers' revolution, the stage would be set for the elimination of government, which would, in Marx's words, "wither away," since private property and exploitation would cease to exist in a classless society, whose members would be equal, and thus the reason for rulers would no longer exist. Marx was, of course, mistaken on a number of points, including the last. For in today's world, many of the most entrenched governments, including the totalitarian regimes governing China, North Korea, and Cuba, are based on Marxist doctrine.

Considerations on the Power of Government

Power in the context of government and governing refers to the influence and control exercised by one country over another or others within it. Power is both the means employed and the goal sought by states in political, military, economic and social competition with each other. The exercise of power can assume many forms, including persuasion, ideological and psychological warfare, economic coercion, moral suasion, cultural imperialism, the threat of war, and, of course, war itself.

In most systems of government, political power emanates from holding a governmental or party office and utilizing the powers of that office for influence and achievement. However, there are many instances of individuals and organizations who do not hold office or a high party position, but exercise power through their employment of money or wealth to secure their objectives. In other instances, organizations that appeal to broad constituencies exercise influence and political power over the policies and direction of government with the intent of seeing their objectives adopted. Such groups almost always support political candidates sympathetic to their interests. At times, a distinction is made between power and influence, with power being an attribute of those who are in government and influence being sometimes possessed by those outside government.

There are numerous opinions on the amount of power government should possess. The varying viewpoints on this topic have given rise to a series of labels. ***Anarchists*** tend to view government, as well as all institutions of society, as evil, because they limit the freedoms and creativity of people. Anarchists regard the state as an instrument used by the propertied classes to dominate and exploit the people. They wish for as little government as possible; ideally, they would like to see no government at all, with humankind returning to a less restrictive state of nature. Replacing government in the new order would be voluntary cooperatives among individuals and groups. Others, known as ***Libertarians,*** desire greater freedom for people, and call for a minimal role for the state. Their goal is to maximize individual liberty in all areas of life, with particular concern for individual freedom of thought and action. Libertarians consider customs, institutions, and even the family, at times, as unnecessary constraints on the individual's vision of the world. ***Reactionaries*** accept some kind of a role for government but they want to see it reduced to a far smaller size, often pegging the proposed size to a much earlier, simpler period in the history of their country. Larger in number than any of the above categories are ***Conservatives,*** who desire smaller government, but not to the extent envisioned by reactionaries. Conservatives today often have views similar to those of liberals of the 1800s who wanted small, limited government and a free economy. In Europe during the 1800s the word reactionary was sometimes associated with those who did not want to extend civil liberties and civil rights to the middle and lower classes. ***Liberals*** of the 1900s are more positive about government than any of the other categories, for they view it as something

U.S. President Dwight Eisenhower and British Prime Minister Winston Churchill were two prominent leaders with a conservative orientation. Courtesy of Library of Congress.

positive, and they wish to imbue it with even more power. Finally, *moderates* are basically content with the present size and scale of government. In a robust democracy such as that of the United States, each of these views has numerous adherents, and they are often debated in public forums, which is healthy for a democracy. One has to be careful about the meanings of these categories because they can vary depending on time and place.

The Most Important Functions of Government

In the last century, the functions of government have broadened as the citizenry of many states have increased their demands for assistance from this institution. The Preamble to the Constitution of the United States, written in 1787, provides interesting insights into the viewpoints of its framers, or creators, toward the functions of government. The Preamble informs that the framers "in Order to form a more perfect Union, establish justice, insure domestic Tranquility, provide for the common defence, promote the general Welfare, and secure the Blessings of Liberty to ourselves and our Posterity, do ordain and establish this Constitution ..." Nowhere is this nonpareil document more prescient than in its Preamble for most of the major functions of contemporary government are mentioned there.

Protection for its People   The first and foremost function of government is its role as the internal guardian of society and its protector from outside aggression. In this activity, government strives to maintain order within a society so that its people can engage in the normal routine of daily activities without undue difficulty or obstruction.

The United States has struggled with internal strife almost from its inception as a country, whether it was the fractiousness that arose over the issue of slavery, the Civil War that was fought partly over that issue, or rampant crime that dictates, to a large degree, the rhythm of life today. We continue to pour great resources, from additional police, new courts and prisons to more restrictive laws, into fighting the crime epidemic. While the problem appears intractable, government activity in this area, at each level, permits life to proceed—but with restrictions. If government was to fail in this function, the future of the republic would be jeopardized.

On the other hand, the United States has succeeded admirably in protecting its people against outside aggressors, although the terrorists' attacks of September 11,

Mao Zedong, chairman of the Chinese Communist Party and leader of China from 1949 until his death in 1976, took Marxism and adapted it to the unique conditions of China, which was overwhelmingly agricultural. Mao led the Communists to power in 1949. Courtesy of Library of Congress.

2001, were a tragic reminder of how the world remains a dangerous place. Still, seldom has a foreign foe set foot on the territory of the United States. Presently, this country is the world's lone superpower; it contains the most powerful military arsenal the world has ever seen, and the prospects of an enemy invasion or takeover in the foreseeable future are minimal.

Dispensing Justice   Another function of government is dispensing justice. Western governments can trace this function directly to the ancient Near East where the government of Babylonia, under the leadership of Hammurabi, assumed the task of dispensing justice in the seventeenth century B.C. Justice remains a major function of government throughout the world. If government lost the ability to administer justice adequately, or the ability to enforce its decisions, anarchy would spread quickly.

One of the most frequently recurring electoral campaign themes in contemporary American politics is the promise by office seekers to pass more stringent laws in the realm of criminal justice, add police and new courts, appoint more "law and order" judges, and build additional prisons. A candidate's stand on the issue of criminal justice will often dictate his/her electoral chances.

Government as a Regulator   In recent times, government has exercised a broad regulatory role. Through law and administrative fiat, government continues to increase its role as a regulatory agent, involving itself here in a myriad of ways. In the past one hundred years, in the great Western democracies, government has assumed the role of regulator of public utilities, restricted various kinds of business practices and activities, and set standards for practitioners of the various professions. In autocratic societies, where rule is in the hands of one or a small number of persons, government has regulated many aspects of society since the dawn of civilization.

Government as a Welfare Agent   Additionally, in relatively recent times, government has assumed the role of a provider of services and assistance to people in need. Such services include health coverage, social security payments for the elderly, public housing, and education at every level. This role continues to expand in response to the wishes of the electorate.

Government as the Protector of Basic Civil Liberties
In democratic societies, government also serves as the protector of the basic liberties of every person. These include freedom of religion, speech, the press, assembly, petition, and the freedom against unreasonable searches and seizures. As we have already noted, John Locke and other political theorists emphasized this function of government. The United States, Great Britain, and other democratic nations consider this responsibility sacrosanct.

Types of Governments

Aristotle, the great Fourth Century B.C. Athenian philosopher, categorized governments according to the number of persons ruling and the objectives of their rule. Aristotle called one man's rule in the interest of all, **monarchy;** he considered one man's rule in the interest of that ruler, **tyranny.** Aristotle categorized rule by a few in the interest of all, **aristocracy,** while a few mens' rule for personal interest was **oligarchy.** Rule by many for the good of all was, for Aristotle, **polity;** majority rule for personal interest or for the interest of only the majority, **democracy.**

While Aristotle's distinctions are interesting, they are not wholly relevant today where basically two types of government exist: democracy, which has many varieties and versions, and autocracy. By the mid-1990s, the world

contained nearly 200 sovereign countries. They were split almost evenly between **democracies** and **autocracies.** However, most governments claim to be democratic. In fact, some of the world's most repressive governments, even include the term "democratic" in their names.

Moreover, the term "democratic" means different things to different people. Until recent times, there was continuing debate between the Soviet Union and the United States over what constituted democracy. While the U.S. insisted that democracy meant the right of the people to select their leaders in free elections and to influence those leaders through the political process, the Soviet Union insisted that democracy meant, more importantly, jobs, health care, and education for all of its citizens. There are, moreover, many "degrees" of democracy. Some Latin American countries, only now realizing democracy after more than a century of independence, are still more restrictive in their approach to democracy than a broad-based democracy such as the United States. India, the world's largest democracy with nearly a billion people, has placed restrictions, from time to time, on the operations of its press, thereby tampering with one of the key elements of a democracy.

Democracy

Democracy: the term and concept come from the Classical Greeks, 2,500 years ago. The Greek word "demos" means the people, while "kratos" means authority. Together, they mean the rule of the people. Democracy is a modern phenomenon. Until the nineteenth century, few countries were democratic. But its ideas and ideals swept the Western world in the nineteenth and twentieth centuries, influenced as they were by the American and French Revolutions near the end of the eighteenth century.

The Elements of Democracy   There are several dimensions to a democracy. First and foremost, the people in a democracy, as John Locke insisted, are sovereign, that is, they are the source of all power; they are the master of any government established by them to serve their interests. This is the doctrine of popular sovereignty. The presumption here is that the people can control their destiny, and that they can make moral judgments and practical decisions affecting their lives. These sovereign people select their leaders in free elections. In democratic countries, a sizable percentage of the residents of a country possess the right to vote, and choose between candidates representing differing viewpoints and or parties. To maintain this control, the people must possess freedom of speech, effective legislative organizations to represent them, and hold free elections to change the government by legal, peaceful methods.

Secondly, in a democracy, the individual is most important. Democratic theory holds that government and society are considered to exist for the individual, so the best form of government is one that enhances the dignity of the individual and provides for the fullest and richest development of personality.

Thirdly, democracy also means the operation of a liberal, constitutional government, one that guarantees, through a written document, a constitution, and subsequent laws, many basic individual rights and freedoms, such as **habeas corpus,** which is a writ or court order requiring authorities to produce prisoners and answer challenges to the legality of their detainment. Other guarantees include trial by jury, freedom of speech, freedom of religion, and assembly, and the existence of a viable political opposition.

Fourth, democracy also means limited government in the sense that the people possess liberties that are safeguarded by law and that cannot be taken away from them. Such limitations on government include the right to periodically elect or reject their government through the electoral process. The right to mobilize public opinion against

Louis XIV of France was known as the Sun King since he believed himself to be the center of his nation just as the sun was the center of the universe. The long reign of this monarch represents an example of authoritarianism. Courtesy of Muse Antoine Lecuyer, Saint-Quentin, France/Bridgeman Art Library.

government and governmental policy through various kinds of protest represents another limitation as does the demand that government operate within the law rather than above it. Another constraint derives from the presence of a **constitution** requiring that political power be exercised within a framework of constitutional government. This document provides for the structures and processes of orderly government that authorize and limit the use of political power. Under a constitution, government officials are required to exercise power under the rule of law by following a set of procedures that define and limit governmental authority. A constitution is not critical for a democracy, but there must be some kinds of documents or fundamental law observed by the government. In the case of Great Britain, the world's oldest democracy, there is no constitution, but several important documents, beginning with the Magna Carta, or great charter (1215), which bound the king to observe all feudal rights and privileges. Additionally, the laws passed by the Parliament, the judicial precedents throughout British history, known as the common law, as well as the country's customs and traditions place this nation firmly in the democratic camp.

Types of Democracies

Direct Democracy.   The first of a large variety of democracies, the form known as *direct democracy,* appeared initially in Athens, the birthplace of democracy, 2500 years ago. In a direct democracy, political decisions are made by the people directly rather than by their elected representatives. Typically, in a direct democracy, citizens gathered periodically to make laws, voted on public issues to determine government policies, and served on juries in a judicial system bereft of judges.

Other examples of direct democracies were pre-Imperial Rome, some Swiss cantons, and New England town meetings in colonial America. Direct democracy is only practicable in small communities and essentially in resolving simple issues.

Representative Democracy   In the contemporary world, it is not direct but representative democracies that are the norm since the size of a typical democratic nation has effectively eliminated the possibility of direct citizen participation in their government. The people in a *representative democracy,* such as that of the United States or France, elect their representatives who act in their behalf. Political theorist Henry B. Mayo described the process succinctly: "A democratic political system is one in which public policies are made, on a majority basis, by representatives subject to effective popular control at periodic elections which are conducted on the principle of political equality and under conditions of political freedom." Specific criteria are present in a representative democracy, including free elections, whereby all citizens are entitled to vote by secret ballot in regularly held elections featuring more than one candidate and party. Additionally, the elected body of representatives has real legislative authority, including the power to enact taxes and budgets and to debate and deliberate government policy.

Other Kinds of Democracy

There are several other varieties of democracy, and some countries, such as the United States, are found in more than one category. The United States is not only a representative democracy, but it is also a *Presidential democracy,* since the President, the nation's chief executive, exercises vast powers separate from the other branches of government. Great Britain and Italy are examples of nations that embrace a *parliamentary democracy,* since power is centered primarily in their parliament or legislative branch. Great Britain is also an example of a *unitary democracy* because power lies within one level of government, the national level. By contrast, the United States is a *federal democracy* because power is shared by the national government and state governments. Finally, democracy can exist in a republic, such as the United States, or in a constitutional monarchy, as in Great Britain. A republic can also be nondemocratic such as the republic of Rome that preceded the onset of empire in the latter stages of the first century B.C., as well as the more recent Soviet Union. Both Rome and the Soviet Union rejected monarchy and utilized representative legislative bodies to help govern. However, election to these bodies was restricted. For Rome, voting was limited to certain classes. The Soviet Union possessed a one-party system of politics; consequently, there was no choice of candidates and issues for voters.

Democracy Under Capitalism and Socialism   Some people are surprised to learn that democracy is found in two antithetical systems. We normally feel that capitalism is the most appropriate system for democracy, but remember, democracy is not an economic system, nor is it a political system, but, instead, it is a view and approach to governing. Two recent examples of democracies that also embraced *socialism,* or a system where the government controls the economy, was France in the 1980s, when it attempted to socialize its economy, but with adverse results, forcing a return to the private sector, and Sweden, whose economy has been under government control for many years. The government of Sweden has also in recent years divested itself of some of the socialist programs. Such countries, which practice democratic socialism, conduct open elections and adhere to democratic political institutions.

Autocracy

The other major form of government in the world today is *autocracy,* or a system of rule in which a single person or a small group of people exercise unlimited power. Individual rights and other freedoms are subordinated here to the power of the state or a ruling party. Until recent centuries, virtually all of the countries of the world were ruled by autocratic governments.

Historically, the most common variety of autocracy has been monarchy, wherein a ruler exercised complete control over the fortunes of his country. Generally, he acquired rule through his family, and passed it on to a son, to ensure the continuation of the family's influence and power. Sometimes, the ruler claimed to be a God— and he was revered by his people as a deity, further ensuring their obedience to his commands. The Egyptian pharaohs and, until recently, the emperor of Japan, are examples of rulers claiming to be deities. In the Medieval West, leaders of emerging nation-states ruled according to the theory of **Divine Right Monarchy,** which taught that they were appointed by God to lead their people.

Twentieth Century Autocracies   While the world has turned increasingly away from monarchy in recent centuries, autocracy has evolved into new forms and has remained a potent form of rule. Twentieth century autocracy falls into two categories: *authoritarianism* and *totalitarianism.*

Lenin on the platform. Courtesy of FPG/Taxi/Getty Images.

Mussolini on Fascism

Italian Fascist leader Benito Mussolini. Il Duce controlled the destiny of his nation for more than twenty years after coming to power in the early 1920s. His totalitarian rule ended in disaster as Italy was defeated soundly in World War II. At right, Mussolini explains Fascism. Courtesy of Library of Congress.

The nation as the State is an ethical reality which exists and lives in so far as it develops. To arrest its development is to kill it. Therefore the State is not only the authority which governs and gives the form of laws and the value of spiritual life to the wills of individuals, but it is also a power that makes its will felt abroad, making it known and respected, in other words, demonstrating the fact of its universality in all the necessary directions of its development ... Thus it can be likened to the human will which knows no limits to its development and realizes itself in testing its own limitlessness.

The Fascist State, the highest and most powerful form of personality, is a force, but a spiritual force, which takes over all the forms of the moral and intellectual life of man. It cannot therefore confine itself simply to the functions of order and supervision as Liberalism desired. It is not simply a mechanism which limits the sphere of the supposed liberties of the individual. It is the form, the inner standard and the discipline of the whole person; it saturates the will as well as the intelligence. Its principle, the central inspiration of the human personality living in the civil community pierces into the depths and makes its home in the heart of the man of action as well as of the scientist: it is the soul of the soul.

Fascism, in short, is not only the giver of laws and the founder of institutions, but the educator and promoter of spiritual life. It wants to remake, not the forms of human life, but its content, man, character, faith. And to this end it requires discipline and authority that can enter into the spirits of men and there govern unopposed. Its sign, therefore, is the Lictor's rods, the symbol of unity, of strength and justice.

Authoritarianism

Authoritarianism is derived from the term "authority," which, put simply, means the command, jurisdiction, or dominion of someone or something over others. Further, authority means that those who possess it are in a position to exert power, influence, or control over an individual, a group, or a nation.

An authoritarian autocracy, or **authoritarianism,** is a system in which the government exerts total political control, but does permit activities that do not threaten its power. In an authoritarian government, the leadership operates within a one-party system, or if there is more than one party, the other(s) is inconsequential. In an authoritarian system, the party or parties exist to consolidate power and allocate privileges among the ruling group. Usually, one person exerts great power in this system. Authoritarian rulers enjoy power because of the great benefits that accrue to

them in terms of money, power, and influence. The government maintains a strong influence over the economy, which is usually capitalistic. Examples of authoritarian rule include the governments of Louis XIV of France and Catherine the Great of Russia and Augusto Pinochet in Chile.

Totalitarianism

Totalitarianism is a system whereby the government controls all aspects of an individual's life, monopolizing power through a one-party system of rule. Totalitarianism is a twentieth century phenomenon because the technology and other means necessary to achieve this degree of domination were not present prior to this era. Most totalitarian states are based on an ideology that calls for a radical break with the past. Simply defined, an *ideology* is an organized system of ideas for reordering society.

Supporters of an ideology often embrace it with fanatic fervor. Ideologies offer people an outlet to vent this feeling by motivating them to join political parties and mass movements. They also provide the rationale for leaders to mobilize their followers. Proponents of an ideology hold that if their belief system is adopted, it will usher in a Utopia, or a perfect society.

In a totalitarian autocracy, the leader seeks to control every aspect of the life of his people so that he may impose that ideology, upon which his party was founded and on which basis it operates, on his country, and change it in accordance with the major tenets of that blueprint. A totalitarian leader also employs this ideology to justify his actions in terms of the goal of creating a better world.

The term "the end justifies the means" was employed to explain or understand Soviet policies and mass killings during the brutal reign of Joseph Stalin (1927–1953) who murdered millions of Russians.

The goal of a totalitarian leader is total domination in order to eradicate the vestiges of the previous society, and to build a new order based on the prevailing ideology. Additionally, as Charles Funderburk and Robert G. Thobaben observed in *Political Ideologies,* the "intent of totalitarianism is not simply to promote obedience and acquiescence but also to require commitment. The objective is to reconstruct the individual and society in accord with an ideological vision. The certainty that derives from absolute truth brooks no compromise and justifies

Nikita Khrushchev, Address to the Twentieth Party Congress

When we analyze the practice of Stalin in regard to the direction of the party and of the country, when we pause to consider everything which Stalin perpetrated, we must be convinced that Lenin's fears were justified. The negative characteristics of Stalin, which, in Lenin's time, were only incipient, transformed themselves during the last years into a grave abuse of power by Stalin, which caused untold harm to our party.

We have to consider seriously and analyze correctly this matter in order that we may preclude any possibility of a repetition in any form whatever of what took place during the life of Stalin, who absolutely did not tolerate collegiality in leadership and in work, and who practiced brutal violence, not only toward everything which opposed him, but also toward that which seemed to his capricious and despotic character, contrary to his concepts.

Stalin acted not through persuasion, explanation, and patient cooperation with people, but by imposing his concepts and demanding absolute submission to his opinion. Whoever opposed this concept or tried to prove his viewpoint, and the correctness of his position—was doomed to removal from the leading collective and to subsequent moral and physical annihilation. This was especially true during the period following the 17th party congress, when many prominent party leaders and rank-and-file party workers, honest and dedicated to the cause of communism, fell victim to Stalin's despotism ...

... Lenin's traits—patient work with people; stubborn and painstaking education of them; the ability to induce people to follow him without using compulsion, but rather through the ideological influence on them of the whole collective—were entirely foreign to Stalin. [Stalin] discarded the Leninist method of convincing and educating; he abandoned the method of ideological struggle for that of administrative violence, mass repressions, and terror. He acted on an increasingly larger scale and more stubbornly through punitive organs, at the same time often violating all existing norms of morality and of Soviet laws ....

During Lenin's life party congresses were convened regularly; always when a radical turn in the development of the party and the country took place Lenin considered it absolutely necessary that the party discuss at length all the basic matters pertaining to internal and foreign policy and to questions bearing on the development of party and government ....

Were our party's holy Leninist principles observed after the death of Vladimir Ilyich?

Whereas during the first few years after Lenin's death party congresses and central committee plenums took place more or less regularly; later, when Stalin began increasingly to abuse his power; these principles were brutally violated. This was especially evident during the last 15 years of his life. Was it a normal situation when 13 years elapsed between the 18th and 19th party congresses, years during which our party and our country had experienced so many important events? These events demanded categorically that the party should have passed resolutions pertaining to the country's defense during the patriotic war and to peacetime construction after the war. Even after the end of the war a congress was not convened for over 7 years ....

In practice Stalin ignored the norms of party life and trampled on the Leninist principle of collective party leadership.

Stalin and State Terror

When I used to read about the French Revolution as a child, I often wondered whether it was possible to survive during a reign of terror. I now know beyond doubt that it is impossible. Anybody who breathes the air of terror is doomed, even if nominally he manages to save his life. Everybody is a victim—not only those who die, but also all the killers, ideologists, accomplices and sycophants who close their eyes and wash their hands—even if they are secretly consumed with remorse at night. Every section of the population has been through the terrible sickness caused by terror, and none has so far recovered, or become fit again for normal civic life. It is an illness that is passed on to the next generation, so that the sons pay for the sins of the fathers and perhaps only the grandchildren begin to get over it—or at least it takes on a different form with them.

The principles and aims of mass terror have nothing in common with ordinary police work or with security. The only purpose of terror is intimidation.

To plunge the whole country into a state of chronic fear, the number of victims must be raised to astronomical levels, and on every floor of every building there must always be several apartments from which the tenants have suddenly been taken away. The remaining inhabitants will be model citizens for the rest of their lives—this will be true for every street and every city through which the broom has swept. The only essential thing for those who rule by terror is not to overlook the new generations growing up without faith in their elders, and to keep on repeating the process in systematic fashion. Stalin ruled for a long time and saw to it that the waves of terror recurred from time to time, always on an even greater scale than before. But the champions of terror invariably leave one thing out of account—namely, that they can't kill everyone, and among their cowed, half-demented subjects there are always witnesses who survive to tell the tale.

ruthless pursuit of ideological goals. An ideology that rejects the limitations of constitutional government in

Lenin and Stalin seated together, 1922. Stalin, the successor to Lenin as leader of the Soviet Union, had been appointed to the powerful post of Secretary of the Central Committee of the Communist Party shortly before this picture was taken. Courtesy of AFP/Getty Images.

combination with a disciplined, centralized party and modern technology permits a degree of mass mobilization inconceivable prior to the twentieth century." These authors also noted the extent of terror involved in a totalitarian regime, contrasting it with that of authoritarian rule: "authoritarian regimes kill, torture, and maim thousands, totalitarian regimes do the same to millions." Stalin's Great Purge of the late 1920s and 1930s resulted in the death of an estimated twenty to thirty million countrymen!

A totalitarian regime demands complete loyalty to the party and to the state. Dissent, opposition factions or parties, and movements for liberalization of rule are crushed swiftly. To fully exert its control over individuals and the society as a whole, the leaders of a totalitarian regime rely heavily on technology, such as wiretapping to monitor conversations, television to disperse propaganda favorable to them, as well as to observe behavior, an intrusive, brutal secret police, a "spy" system ("citizen watch") that reaches down to the neighborhood and block levels, and systematic state terrorism. Even drugs, psychotropic and otherwise, are employed to extract confessions from dissidents or information from recalcitrant subjects, or unwary suspects. History is rewritten frequently to accommodate the aims and objectives of the regime.

Often the leader of a totalitarian country is more interested in the widespread adoption of the ideology that drives him and his party than in amassing great material benefits (although there are notable exceptions here,

Hitler's boldness and the weakness of the western democracies was on display at the Munich Conference in 1938, when the German Fuhrer extracted major concessions from representatives of England and France in the matter of Czechoslovakia. Above, Hitler is greeted by Neville Chamberlain at the Munich Conference. Courtesy of National Archives (College Park).

such as the voracious appetite of Leonid Brezhnev, a former Soviet leader, for expensive foreign cars). Examples of totalitarian dictatorships and societies abound, ranging from the Soviet Union under the brutal rule of Joseph Stalin, North Korea under Kim II Sung, and Fidel Castro's Cuba. The most important totalitarian ideologies of the twentieth century are Communism and Fascism.

Communism and the Soviet Union

Based primarily on the writings of Karl Marx, **Communism** represents a doctrine that passionately rejects—while offering an elaborately developed alternative to—capitalism, which it held to be highly exploitative. Writing essentially in the second half of the nineteenth century, Marx predicted that capitalism would experience insurmountable problems because of its inherent contradictions which has said would lead to overproduction, bankruptcies and unemployment, leading ultimately to a workers' revolution, the overthrow of the bourgeoisie (middle class), and the establishment of a classless society. Before that Utopia could be achieved, the enemies of the revolution would be eliminated, while the people would have to be educated in

the new system. This necessitated the "Dictatorship of the Proletariat (workers)," a reference to a temporary government that would "wither away" when these goals had been achieved. During this transitional period, which represented the socialist stage of the revolution, the economy would come under the control of the government, the reeducation and socialization of people with bourgeois ideas would occur through the school system and the mass media, and the proletariat would establish itself in political power.

The first Marxist revolution occurred in Russia in 1917, bringing to power the Bolsheviks (this term in Russian means majority, a reference to the fact that this faction of the Russian Communist movement, led by Vladimir Lenin, was larger than that of the Menshiviks, or the minority faction of Russian Marxists). In fact, the Bolsheviks were a minority when these terms were coined. The Union of Soviet Socialist Republics (U.S.S.R.), established by the Bolsheviks in 1922, never advanced beyond the stage of socialism. Accordingly, from the time of its creation until its collapse and disappearance in 1991, the Communist Party of the Soviet Union ruled oppressively over that vast state, controlling every element of its life. In the lengthy history of the U.S.S.R., the Communists transformed a country heavily agricultural (it also contained a nascent industrial base) to one that placed great emphasis on heavy industry and a vast military machine. The new order, however, was plagued by grave economic problems, not the least of which was a floundering agricultural sector and severe shortages of food and other consumer goods. These problems contributed significantly to the demise of the Soviet Union.

The Soviet Union embraced many of the characteristics of a totalitarian nation. A brutal secret police, one party rule with no outlet for dissent, along with absolute allegiance to the Communist Party, reeducation of the Soviet "man," tight governmental control over the media, one party rule, and heavy propaganda campaigns in favor of the regime were elements of the Soviet brand of totalitarianism. Additionally, during the length and rule of Soviet dictator, Joseph Stalin, the Communist Party engaged in a practice referred to by Stalin's successor, Nikita Khrushchev, as a "**cult of personality,**" elevating Stalin's image to that of a demigod. Finally, owing to the expansive nature of revolutionary Marxism, there was a continual effort to export the revolution abroad, which led to Soviet support for Marxist regimes governing China, Cuba, Ethiopia, Angola, Nicaragua, and Vietnam, among other countries.

*Adolph Hitler, the German Fuhrer, speaks to adoring members of his Nazi Party.
Courtesy of National Archives (College Park).*

Fascism and Nazi Germany

Fascism, the other great twentieth century totalitarian ideology, made its first impact upon Italy. Under the leadership of Benito Mussolini, from the early 1920s, till the late stages of World War II in the mid-1940s, Fascism defined the government and nation of Italy. Fascism stressed the preeminent position of the state, which contained an organic life of its own; an omniscient, strong-willed leader cast in the mold of a hero; anti-intellectualism, anti-communism, and anti-liberalism; **corporatism,** an economic system, which linked employers and employees together in huge bureaucratic institutions that acted as instruments for the government's control over the economy; extreme nationalism, imperialism, and anti-pacifism, which claimed that war alone brings out the best in a person and in a nation.

Germany came under the ruthless control of the Nazi Party between 1933 and 1945. Although a totalitarian power, it offered a distinctly different ideology from that of the Soviet Union. **Nazism** began in the aftermath of the crushing—and bewildering (to many Germans)—defeat of Germany in World War I. Most important among its early members were several disaffected members of the German military, including **Adolph Hitler,** a former corporal. A spellbinding speaker, Hitler employed his oratorical gifts, as well as organizational and propaganda abilities to take charge of the nascent German Workers' Party in 1919. In the following year, the tiny organization was renamed the Nationalist Socialist Workers' party, which became known as the Nazi Party. Hitler led an abortive *coup d'etat* against the government of Germany in 1923, which led to a brief imprisonment. Hitler came out of that experience more

Mussolini and Hitler, the two Fascist dictators. Courtesy of National Archives (College Park).

popular than ever among his growing legion of followers, and more convinced of his destiny as the leader of a mighty German empire.

Hitler's Nazi Party grew quickly in the tumultuous climate of Germany in the 1920s. By the beginning of the next decade, it was the majority party in the German Reichstag, the most important body in that nation's parliament. Through good fortune in a country suffering from a severe economic depression and government gridlock, Hitler received appointment as chancellor of Germany in January 1933. Within a few months, he had acquired dictatorial powers from the slavish Reichstag. Germany's Third Reich had come into existence. Hitler predicted that it would last one thousand years.

In fact, the Third Reich lasted but twelve years, but during that period, Hitler and the Nazis imposed a powerful government and police state on Germany, controlling every aspect of German life. In the process, they built a formidable military state, which brought the world to war again. Through an awesome series of conquests in the early years of World War II, Germany gained a vast European empire. But Hitler's peerless early leadership soon disappeared, while a great coalition of countries, led by the Soviet Union, United States, and

In Petrograd, circa 1900, people waiting to receive gasoline. Courtesy of Library of Congress.

Great Britain, ultimately brought Germany to its knees. The war had been made possible when in 1939 Hitler and Stalin had made a peace treaty. Yet, in 1941, Hitler invaded Russia (The Soviet Union).

Nazism grew out of Italian fascism, an ideology that defined the government and nation of Italy, under the leadership of Benito Mussolini, from the early 1920s through the end of World War II in 1945.

Nazism embraced many of these characteristics, but differed in other ways, too. The centerpiece of Nazi ideology was its doctrines of Aryan racial superiority. In *Mein Kampf* ("My Struggle," which Hitler wrote while in prison), the German leader outlined Nazi ideology and politics, maintaining that the advancement of humanity depended on racial struggle. The emergence of the superior Aryan culture, of whom Germans were a prominent part, would be possible, he believed, only when that group subdued inferior peoples. Hitler and other Nazi leaders and theorists held that the state, or the national community, is much more important than the individuals that comprise it. To take this doctrine to its political limit would produce extreme nationalism. Indeed, Hitler demanded of his people "fanatical nationalism" in the struggle against democracy and communism, and believed that everything must be subordinated to the welfare of the state. For Hitler, Germans paid homage to two Gods: "A God in Heaven and A God on earth and that is our Fatherland."

Nazism denied the equality of all humans, insisting that Aryans were superior to all people. They insisted that an elite (the Party and government leaders) must prevail over all people. At the head of this elite group was a fuhrer, "the absolute pinnacle of human perfection. "Known as the Fuhrer principle, this doctrine held that such a leader was infallible, one "endowed with mystical insights." According to Walter

Langer in *The Mind of Adolph Hitler,* a great majority of the German people viewed Hitler as super human, a man imbued with unparalleled qualities for leadership, vision, and energy. The fuhrer, Adolph Hitler, naturally surrounded himself with elite groups, such as the SS and the SA, two uniformed military-police organizations.

National Socialism also embraced irrationalism or the rejection of reason and logic in human affairs, and, instead, reached out to feeling, passion, sentiment, and the irrational. War and violence were also major tenets of Nazism. Hitler believed that "If men wish to live, then they are forced to kill others . . . the stronger has the right before God to enforce his will . . . only force rules . . . Only through struggle have states and the world become great . . . In the power of the sword lies the vital strength of a nation."

Through war and other kinds of violence, the Nazis terrorized segments of their population, as well as subject peoples. The doctrine of racial superiority led directly to the death of millions of Jews, Slavs, Gypsies, and other "inferior" peoples. Nazi Germany's militarism brought on the most destructive war in history. Nazism fell with the defeat of Germany in May 1945, which followed by one week the suicidal death of Adolph Hitler.

Lesser Fascist movements existed but suffered setbacks and decline with the demise of Fascism in Germany and Italy. Spain's authoritarian regime died with the demise of Francisco Franco, its leader, in 1975. Other strong Fascist movements in modern times have appeared in Argentina and Japan. Like Communism, Fascism continues to manifest itself in movements and parties in several Western countries, such as England and Germany, and is regarded by many as a growing menace in these places as well as elsewhere.

Selected Bibliography

Hannah Arendt. (1996) *The Origins of Totalitarianism,* Revised Edition, New York: Harcourt Brace and Company.

Alan Bullock. (1964) *Hitler, A Study in Tyranny,* Revised Edition, London: Harper Collins Publisher.

Alan Bullock. (1993) *Hitler and Stalin: Parallell Lives,* New York: Vintage Books.

Charles Funderburk and Robert G. Thobaben. (1989) *Political Ideologies,* New York: Harper and Row.

Thomas Hobbes. (1982) *Leviathan,* Baltimore: Penguin Books.

Richard Hofstadter. (1954) *The American Political Tradition,* New York: Random House.

John Locke. (1960) *Of Civil Government, Second Essay,* Chicago: Henry Regency.

Nicollo Machiavelli. (1984) *The Prince,* New York: Oxford University Press.

John Stuart Mill. (1962) *Consideration on Representative Government,* Chicago: Henry Regency of Gateway.

Karl Marx and Friedrich Engels. (1968) *The Communist Manifesto,* Baltimore: Penguin Books.

Clinton Rossiter. (1962) *Conservatism in America: The Thankless Persuasion,* New York: Vantage.

Alexis de Tocqueville. (1969) *Democracy in America,* Garden City, New York: Doubleday.

Betram Wolfe. (1948) *Three Who Made A Revolution,* New York: Norton.

CHAPTER EIGHT

The American Political System

A Historical View

Paul S. George

The Uniqueness of America's Political System

It was Abraham Lincoln who said that America was humankind's last, best hope. Among the nation's qualities that moved Lincoln to this felicitous conclusion was its unique political system, which allowed for the active participation in the process of governing of a significant percentage of its citizenry. Many years after this enduring pronouncement, the United States maintains, for all of its problems, a unique position in the firmament of nations, for it remains a country associated with vast freedoms—along with great opportunities—for its residents. Accordingly, it continues to attract large numbers of immigrants in pursuit of the coveted "American Dream", primarily of which is economic opportunity and political freedom.

America's democratic government operates according to the dictates of the world's oldest constitution, a brief, enlightened document created by fifty-five of the most farseeing political thinkers in the nation's history, an assemblage that **Thomas Jefferson** characterized as "demigods." Because of its progressive provisions, the Constitution of the United States has inspired imitators throughout the world since its drafting. What makes this achievement even more remarkable is the fact that the country had gained its independence just four years before when this document appeared. The adoption of the Constitution of the United States in 1789 established a framework, a beginning for what became over time the most democratic country in the world.

How could this achievement have come to pass in a country so young, and, at the time, so immersed in a desperate struggle for survival? What were the influences on its development that led to this juncture? How did the adoption of the Constitution change American government and society? What are the major elements of the nation's government under this system? This chapter will address these questions.

America owes its unique democratic system, at least in theory, to an ancient influence, the Greeks, specifically the great city-state of Athens, which, in the fifth century B.C., conceived of and implemented a democratic system of government wherein all adult male citizens were directly involved in the political process. England and its Judeo-Christian culture represents a later, and more important, influence, on the development of American democracy. This island state emerged from the Middle Ages with a fledgling democratic institution in its parliament or lawmaking body. At first, the parliament represented a limited percentage of the people, but a series of monumental nineteenth century reforms led to a vast expansion in the numbers of persons represented by that august institution, as well as those who were enfranchised, or received the right to vote, for the first time.

John Locke was a great English political philosopher. Locke, who lived from 1632 to 1704, was the author of several influential studies, including the Second Treatise on Civil Government, *which asserted that human beings held certain inalienable rights that no government could take away. In fact, governments were created by the people to protect these rights; therefore, it followed that any government abusive of these rights must be removed by the people and replaced by one responsive to their needs. Jefferson was greatly influenced by this work, and that influence is obvious in the Declaration of Independence. Courtesy of Library of Congress.*

British Influences on American Government

Spain was the first European country to colonize the future United States, establishing a beachhead in today's Florida in 1565, but the influence of the Iberian power remained confined to that single colony, which remained a backwater in the scheme of Spain's New World empire. However, it was the British at Jamestown, beginning in 1607, and, later, with other colonies stretching from Georgia to today's Maine, who left the deepest imprint on the future United States. The British brought to their American colonies such unique ideas, concepts, and institutions as suffrage or elections, representative government, personal rights, common law, trial by jury, and habeas corpus. The British also contributed such political institutions as the legislature and the offices of sheriff and justice of the peace.

The most important of the early colonial governmental institutions were the legislatures, which were comprised

of, at least in the case of the lower houses, elected lawmakers who, by representing the interests of their constituents, gave rise to the ideal and reality of representative government (contrasting sharply with Spain and her New World empire, which she ruled in autocratic fashion).

The colonial legislatures consisted of two houses, like that of the British parliament. The more conservative of the two bodies was the upper house, as it was in England, for it usually represented the interests of the Mother Country. Moreover, its members were appointed by the British government. Members of the lower houses were elected by the small percentage of colonists eligible to vote. This electoral constituency generally consisted of freemen with land. What made the lower house so prominent was its power to initiate tax laws and appropriation bills, which remain two of the most powerful elements of our national legislative body, the Congress, especially the House of Representatives.

Colonial America

By the 1700s, England's thirteen colonies were unlike colonies anywhere else in the world for they were prosperous, relatively independent, and imbued with a modicum of self government. England was inconsistent in administering her colonies, at times ruling with a tight fist, while on other occasions exercising a policy known as **Salutary Neglect,** wherein she allowed the colonies wide freedoms within the Empire.

Following the great British victory in the Seven Years' War (1756–1763), a worldwide conflict whose American version was known as the French and Indian War (1754–1763), England initiated a radical change in the manner of administering her American colonies. In the French and Indian War, England and her Indian mercenaries fought against France and her Native American surrogates. England's American colonies did little to assist the Mother Country in this conflict, even trading with France during the course of the war.

Although the victory left England with a great empire in North America, which came to include all of the land west of the Appalachian Mountains, as well as Canada, it also left her mired in deep debt, causing her to adopt a much tougher policy toward her troublesome North American colonies primarily in hopes of reducing her economic liabilities by placing new demands on them. The British introduced this new policy in 1763. It included the infamous **Stamp Act Tax**, which was a tariff on products used by the colonists, the quartering of

British troops in colonial homes, and favored treatment for companies from the Island nation competing with colonial businesses. These policies led to increasingly stormier relations between London and the colonial capitals. Ultimately, the implementation of an increasingly more stringent British policy, especially in terms of heightened economic demands toward the colonies and their resistance to it led to the American Revolutionary War.

The American Revolution

The American Revolutionary War began in April 1775 with an exchange of fire between the colonists and British forces at Lexington and Concord in Massachusetts. In the ensuing months and years the conflict grew and spread. The colonies' chances of success against a superior foe appeared dim. But the Americans possessed certain advantages. They received brilliant leadership from General **George Washington**, who was able to keep his Army together and his men focused on the next engagement, even amid adversity. The familiarity of colonial forces with the native topography upon which the conflict was fought and the ability to turn it to their advantage was of

great help to their cause. Finally, the colonies received invaluable aid from France at a critical juncture in the conflict, allowing the smaller, ill-equipped American forces to defeat the British. Long before the conclusion of the war in 1781, other important events had occurred that would stamp forever America's uniqueness.

The First and Second Continental Congresses

In 1774, as relations between the colonies and the Mother Country grew more strained, the former organized the First Continental Congress, with fifty-six members representing twelve of the original colonies (controlled by pro-British leaders, Georgia, the thirteenth colony, did not send a delegate, nor did the two Floridas, East and West, acquired by Great Britain through treaty with Spain in 1763), to decide on a course of action in light of these circumstances. The colonies asserted certain rights and powers in their relationship with the Mother Country through the Congress, which, before adjourning, agreed to meet again after one year to observe the progress of events.

One of the most celebrated instances of colonial opposition to a more exacting policy by Britain toward her North American colonies was the Boston Tea Party. In 1773, British tea was sold at a price purposely lower than that of colonial merchants, threatening the economic well-being of these entrepreneurs. Angry colonists dressed as Mohawk Indians boarded a British trading company's ship and dumped hundreds of boxes of its tea into Boston harbor. In retaliation for this event, known to history as the Boston Tea Party, the British placed severe restrictions on the city of Boston and the colony of Massachusetts. Courtesy of Library of Congress.

George III of England. George III, whose reign covered the years from 1760 through 1820, was the ruler of England at the time of the American Revolution. Even though the British Parliament played a major role in passing legislation despised by the colonies in the years leading up to the American Revolutionary War, George was singled out by Thomas Jefferson and other revolutionary leaders for the lion's share of condemnation. The Declaration of Independence listed a large number of alleged crimes by George III and his government against the American people as the basis for the colonies' break with the Mother Country. Courtesy of Library of Congress.

A second Continental Congress met in 1775, and quickly took charge of the colonial troops gathered around Boston, giving them a name, the Continental Army, and a leader, **George Washington.** At the outbreak of hostilities, only a few extremists wished complete separation from England. But after one year of fighting, reconciliation between the belligerents seemed impossible. In June 1776, the Second Continental Congress approved a **Resolution of Independence** written and introduced by Richard Henry Lee of Virginia.

Striking Out for Independence

Lee's document declared that "these colonies are, and of right ought to be, free and independent states ... and that all political connection between them and the state of Great Britain is and ought to be totally dissolved." After Lee's Resolution was approved, the leaders of the Congress turned to Thomas Jefferson, a delegate from Virginia, and charged him with writing a rationale for Lee's document, as well as for the colonial pursuit of independence. Both

the Resolution of Independence and the Declaration of Independence were authorized by the Second Continental Congress to establish the "legitimacy" of the new nation in the minds of other nations, as well as in the minds of the colonists themselves.

Just thirty-three years of age at the time, Jefferson was a brilliant thinker, voracious reader, a versatile scholar and achiever, and the possessor of a facile pen. John Adams of Massachusetts, one of the prime movers behind the Declaration, favored Jefferson for the task because of the latter's "peculiar felicity of expression." Adams insisted that Jefferson embrace this task, because, as he told Jefferson, "I am obnoxious, suspected, and unpopular. You are very much otherwise." Additionally, Adams announced, "You can write ten times better than I can." For three days, Jefferson remained ensconced in a house near the Pennsylvania Statehouse in the center of Philadelphia where he created his famed **Declaration of Independence.** Drawing on the writings of the great British political theorist, **John Locke** (1632–1704), especially his *Second Treatise of Civil Government*, as well as the writings of certain Scottish theorists, Jefferson, in stirring, eloquent prose, asserted in the Declaration of Independence, the natural rights of man, including the right to revolution. The Declaration of Independence consists of four parts. Part one outlines a political philosophy, which serves as the underpinnings of American political philosophy. The second section contains the reasons for the separation from England. The third portion is the actual declaration itself and it is contained in the final paragraph. The fourth and final part lists the signatories to the document. The first section of the document contains an eloquent statement by Jefferson and, by inference, his fellow revolutionaries, that describe, in Lockian terms, a government that derived its powers from the people:

> When in the Course of human events, it becomes necessary for one people to dissolve the political bands which have connected them with another, and to assume among the powers of the earth, the separate and equal station to which the Laws of Nature and of Nature's God entitle them, a decent respect to the opinions of mankind requires that they should declare the causes which impel them to the separation.
>
> We hold these truths to be self-evident, that all men are created equal, that they are endowed by their Creator with certain unalienable Rights,

that among these are Life, Liberty and the pursuit of Happiness. That to secure these rights, Governments are instituted among Men, deriving their just powers from the consent of the governed. That whenever any Form of Government becomes destructive of these ends, it is the Right of the People to alter or to abolish it, and to institute new Government, laying its foundation on such principles and organizing its powers in such form, as to them shall seem most likely to effect their Safety and Happiness. Prudence, indeed, will dictate that Governments long established should not be changed for light and transient causes; and accordingly all experience hath shown, that mankind are more disposed to suffer, while evils are sufferable, than to right themselves by abolishing the forms to which they are accustomed. But when a long train of abuses and usurpations, pursuing invariably the same Object evinces a design to reduce them under absolute Despotism, it is their right, it is their duty to throw off such Government and to provide new Guards for their future security. Such has been the patient sufferance of these Colonies; and such is now the necessity which constrains them to alter their former Systems of Government. The history of the present King of Great Britain is a history of repeated injuries and usurpations, all having in direct object the establishment of an absolute Tyranny over these States. To prove this let Facts be submitted to a candid world …

The great ideas embodied in this document, which have influenced untold numbers of revolutionary movements since then, include the following: the people have a right to rise up and overthrow an oppressive government

Just thirty-three years of age at the time that he authored the Declaration of Independence, Thomas Jefferson was selected for the task because of his "felicity for writing." He was also a brilliantly versatile person and a voracious reader. Courtesy of Library of Congress.

The Declaration of Independence went through a few drafts before Jefferson delivered it, at the beginning of July 1776, to the Second Continental Congress for its approval, which came on July 4. Courtesy of Library of Congress.

since the latter was created by the former and exists only to protect the basic rights of the people (Locke's Social Contract between the people and their rulers). All persons are created equal (although Jefferson and a few others owned slaves!), and each possesses certain inalienable rights, such as those of life, liberty, and the pursuit of happiness.

The second part of the document listed numerous alleged crimes perpetrated upon the colonists by George III and his government. The Second Continental Congress adopted Jefferson's Declaration of Independence on July 4, 1776.

Winning the War

It was one thing for the colonies to declare themselves independent of England, but it was another to bring that situation to reality with the odds stacked strongly against the colonies. At the time of the issuance of the Declaration of Independence, the colonists were on the defensive. They had recently lost New York while retreating before the British armies. In the following year, the British captured Philadelphia, the colonial capital. But later in 1777, a colonial army under the leadership of Horatio Gates and Benedict Arnold stunned the British at Saratoga in New York, forcing the British to surrender

their entire army of 5,800 men to the Americans. This unlikely triumph drew France, England's bitter enemy, into the war on the side of the colonists, and marked a turning point in the conflict. French assistance in the way of leadership, men and material helped turn the war in favor of the colonies. Finally, in 1781, the British surrendered to a joint American-French force at Yorktown, Virginia, in the last major battle of the war. Two years later, the Treaty of Paris recognized America's Independence from England, and the birth of a new nation.

The Articles of Confederation Government

America had won the war against insurmountable odds, and in the postwar era it confronted a similar uphill task. In 1777, the Second Continental Congress adopted the **Articles of Confederation,** the work of a special committee charged with creating a government for the colonies when independence was finally attained. A confederation or confederate system meant that the states, as independent entities, were joined together in a permanent union to create a government. In a confederation government, the individual states, though sharing a union, retain significant individual powers. The Articles

John Trumbull's famous painting of the signing of the Declaration of Independence. From left to right, standing, are John Adams, Roger Sherman, Robert R. Livingston, Thomas Jefferson and Benjamin Franklin. The Declaration was not signed by all members of the Second Continental Congress until several weeks after its completion. Courtesy of Bettmann/Corbis Images.

provided for a weak central government largely because of the fear of centralized tyranny, such as that, in the minds of colonists, of the government of George III's England.

In March 1781, the **Articles of Confederation and Perpetual Union,** as they were formally called, were adopted. Under the Articles, the thirteen original colonies became states, establishing a government of the states, called the **Congress of the Confederation.**

The Congress   A unicameral Congress was the lone branch of government, since there was no separate executive or judicial branch. Each state, through its "ambassadors" to the Congress, possessed one vote. The Congress was given complete control over foreign affairs, and some degree of authority over interstate relations. It could also appropriate, borrow, and issue money. However, that deliberative body did not possess the authority to raise troops and levy taxes, two critically important powers. Instead, it was required to make requisitions upon the states for these needs.

The Executive   There was no separate, single executive, such as the office of president in our present scheme of government. Under the Articles of Confederation, the president was merely the presiding officer over a session of Congress. He was selected by his peers for this ceremonial office. In fact, the nation had fourteen presidents under the short-lived Articles government (1781–1789).

Powers of the States   Under the Articles of Confederation, the real power lay with the states. This authority is evident in the document establishing the Articles, which declared that each state retained its "sovereignty, freedoms, and independence." Article III of the Articles merely established a "league of friendship" among the states, giving no indication that a national government was intended. The states possessed all powers of taxation, and they had the right to regulate interstate commerce. As one authority has noted, the Congress, under this scheme, was little more than an assembly of diplomats looking after the common good.

Problems for the New Country

This framework of government was clearly unsuitable to a new nation, which encountered towering problems domestically and in the realm of foreign affairs in the immediate aftermath of independence. Notable among

Small in stature but tall in intelligence, James Madison was the most important single person in the creation of the Constitution. Madison's Virginia Plan called for a strong central government, and served as the basis for the form that the government of the United States ultimately possessed, including its bicameral legislature, single chief executive, supreme court and inferior courts. James Madison, by Thomas Sully, 1809, courtesy of the Corcoran Gallery of Art, Washington, DC. Oil on panel. Gift of Frederic E. Church.

them was the continued presence of British troops in outlying territories within the boundaries of the United States, which now reached as far west as the Mississippi River, troubling border problems with the Spanish in the south, separatist movements on American soil involving Spain and England, and an economic depression brought on by a large trade imbalance and indebtedness accrued during the revolutionary war. Hard times led to large numbers of property foreclosures, and, ultimately, in Massachusetts, to rioting and an armed rebellion on the part of disaffected farmers.

Shays Rebellion and the Urgency for a Change of Government   Daniel Shays was one such disaffected farmer as well as a veteran of the American Revolutionary War who lived in Massachusetts and attempted to resist by arms the efforts of authorities to foreclose on his farm. In the summer of 1786, Shays organized an army of followers, that numbered about 2,000, and moved throughout parts of Massachusetts in armed bands to break up court sittings and sheriff's sales in an effort to prevent the collection of debts and foreclosures. **Shays' Rebellion,** as it was styled, was finally put down in January 1787, by members of the Massachusetts militia financed by wealthy merchants who feared a new revolution. But the rebellion held out important consequences for the future of the United States, because it lent an added urgency to the movement for a new Constitution and a change of government.

The Necessity for a New Government

As 1787 unfolded, the issue was not whether the Confederation should be changed, but how drastic should the changes be. Virtually everyone agreed that the government needed strengthening at its weakest point: its lack of power to tax. One of the foremost champions of a new government was **Alexander Hamilton,** a onetime military aide to George Washington, a New York attorney, and a political and financial genius. Since the early days of the Articles of Confederation, Hamilton had been dissatisfied with that government. In fact, as early as 1780, he argued that the thirteen sovereign states were not fit to govern the country in war or peace. "There is only one remedy," he declared "to call a convention of all the states" and to prepare the people for change by "sensible and popular writings."

The Call for a Constitutional Convention

Accordingly, in 1787, Hamilton urged that a national convention be held to overhaul the entire document. To achieve this aim, Hamilton, took advantage of a movement for interstate cooperation that began in 1785, when a group of Marylanders and Virginians met in Alexandria to settle differences between their two states. One of the Virginians involved here was **James Madison,** who, like Hamilton, was eager to see a stronger government for the new nation. Accordingly, Madison induced the Virginia legislature to invite all the states to send delegates to a larger conference on commercial questions.

The group met at Annapolis in 1786, but representatives from just five states appeared at the meeting. However, the conference adopted a report by Hamilton and sent copies of it to the state legislatures and to the Congress. Hamilton's report recommended that the Congress call a convention of special delegates from all of the states to gather in Philadelphia in 1787, to consider ways to "render the Constitution of the federal government adequate to the exigencies of the union." All but Rhode

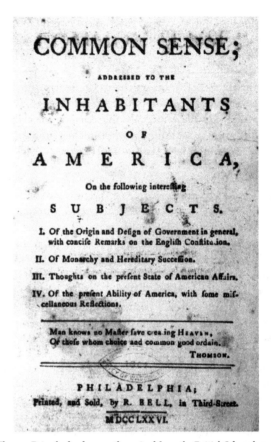

Thomas Paine had only recently arrived from the British Isles when his Common Sense, *which called for a break by the colonies from England, appeared. Published in January 1776, it became an instant bestseller, and an influential molder of colonial thought. Courtesy of Library of Congress.*

Island, whose legislature opposed increased central authority, answered the call and agreed to send delegates to a constitutional conventional in Philadelphia in May 1787, "for the sole and express purpose of revising the Articles."

For the next four months, until the middle of September 1787, fifty-five delegates worked behind closed doors under the leadership of presiding officer, **George Washington,** to create a new government. Not surprisingly, there were wide differences of opinion on several key points, such as the question of how much power should the central government possess, what specific powers should it claim, what structure should it assume. While many championed a government with great power at its core, others, known as **states rights advocates,** favored a system where the states remained strong and influential. There were also differences over the relative influence that the large and the small states (a reference here to their population) should exert in the new government, as well as the method of determining representation in the new congress. A corollary to the latter was the question of whether slaves should be included in the population count, which determined the amount of representation in the House of Representatives. And, of course, there were philosophical differences between free and slave states. Finally, the issue of interstate commerce brought strong opposing viewpoints between the North and South as a fault line began to emerge between two sections with dramatically different characteristics. Over the summer, delegates agreed to a series of compromises relative to the above areas of dispute and discord, paving the way for completion of the Constitution and the creation of a new government.

The Powers of the Congress   Congress retained the powers that it had exercised under the Articles of Confederation, and acquired important, additional powers. Congress was empowered to levy and collect taxes, duties, imports, and excises (a tax on the manufacture, sale and consumption of goods within a country). It could regulate foreign and interstate commerce, pass naturalization and bankruptcy laws, and "make all laws which shall be necessary and proper for carrying into execution the foregoing powers" (this is the famed "elastic clause," which will be discussed later in this chapter). Congress could also call in the militia to execute the laws of the Union, to suppress insurrections, and to repel invasions.

The size of the House delegation for each state was based on population. The Constitution directed that this number "shall not exceed one for every thirty thousand, but each State shall have at least one Representative." The issue of representation was complicated because of the presence of slavery throughout the South. Representatives of these states insisted that their slaves be counted along with the free population for the purpose of representation in the Congress. After a lengthy debate, which was indicative of an incipient cleavage between the sections, an agreement, the famous **"three-fifths compromise,"** was reached. With this agreement, five slaves would be counted as the equal of three freemen in the federal population census.

A candidate for a House seat had to be at least twenty-five years of age and have "been seven years a Citizen of the United States." Representatives were chosen in popular elections for two-year terms.

According to the Constitution, every state would have two senators. A senator had to be at least thirty years of age and a citizen for at least nine years. Initially, United States Senators were chosen by state legislatures for six year terms. The seventeenth amendment to the Constitution, ratified in 1913, changed the method of electing Senators. It called for the direct election of Senators by qualified voters.

The Executive   After considerable debate, the Constitution makers decided on a single executive to be known as the **"President."** Since the framers of the Constitution did not want the Congress to choose the President, nor did they wish to leave such a powerful post directly to the people to fill, they created an electoral college for this purpose. Under this scheme, each state would be entitled to as many electors as it had senators and representatives in the new Congress. The method of choosing electors was left to the states. Electors were directed to vote for two candidates. If any candidate received a majority of the electors' votes, he was declared President. In case no one candidate received a majority, the House of Representatives voted by states to elect a President, with each state casting one vote.

Powers of the President   Under the Constitution, the President would serve as Commander in Chief of the Army and Navy (at first, the lone branches of the armed forces). Additionally, he could make treaties with foreign powers. A two-thirds vote of the Senate was necessary to make the treaty effective. With the consent of the Senate, he could appoint ambassadors, ministers, consuls, and judges for the federal courts. The President could also call Congress into special session, as well as veto bills passed by that deliberative institution. A two-thirds vote by both houses of the Congress was necessary to override a Presidential veto.

The Judiciary   A **Supreme Court,** the highest court in the land, was provided for by the Constitution. The Judiciary Act of 1789 set the size of the Supreme Court at six members. Since then, the Congress has established the size of the Supreme Court through law. The President of the United States selects prospective justices of the Supreme Court, as well as all other federal courts, but the U.S. Senate, by a majority vote, must approve these selections. The Constitution also empowered the Congress to establish inferior courts if it so desired, but it did not mandate their creation. The Judiciary Act also established thirteen federal district courts and three circuit courts of appeal. Nowhere did the Constitution give the

Principal Plans before the Constitutional Convention

	Legislative	Executive	Judicial	Federal-State Relations
Virginia Plan	Bicameral One house popularly elected; second chosen by first from nominees of state legislatures. Voting based on money contributions or free population or both. Powers of Congress broad.	Single executive chosen by Congress for one term only. Authority to execute laws and exercise executive rights invested in Confederation Congress.	Supreme and inferior courts; judges appointed by Congress for life; Council of Revision to exercise a suspensive veto over acts of the national and state legislatures.	Federal government to admit new states and guarantee republican forms of government; federal government to negate state laws incompatible with the Union; also to use force against any state failing to fulfill its duty.
New Jersey Plan	Unicameral Delegates to be chosen by state legislatures. Each state one vote. Powers of Congress enlarged; states to collect taxes but Congress to act if states default.	Plural executive chosen by Congress for one term only. Authority to execute laws, appoint, direct military operations.	Supreme court only; judges appointed by plural executive for life.	Acts of Congress and treaties "supreme law of the respective states"; conflicting state laws forbidden; federal executive to use force against non-cooperative states.
Hamilton's Plan	Bicameral Assembly elected by people on basis of population; terms, 3 years; Senate elected for life terms by electors chosen by people. Congress to have power to pass all laws deemed necessary to common defense and general welfare of Union; Senate alone to declare war, approve treaties and appointments.	President elected for life term by electors chosen by people within each state. Powers included veto, execution of laws, war, treaties, appointments pardons.	Supreme court appointed by President with consent of Senate for life terms; legislature given power to institute courts in each state.	State laws contrary to Constitution are void; governors of states appointed by federal government and have veto over state legislation; a special court provided to hear controversies arising between United States and particular states over territories.

Supreme Court the power to declare laws unconstitutional, but soon after the new government was launched, the Supreme Court, in *Marbury v. Madison* (1803), assumed this power, known as **judicial review,** with great consequences for the development and direction of the nation. Since members of the United States Supreme Court, as well as other federal courts, serve for life, they can exercise as much independence as they wish from the political whirl around them.

Separation of Powers   As this brief survey indicates, the three branches of the national government possess powers exclusive of each other, while their members assume office by different routes. The framers of the Constitution followed this path to prevent tyranny, keeping power diffused among the three branches, so that no one branch exercised an amount of authority out of proportion with the other two. **James Madison,** a delegate from Virginia, who is considered the most important individual behind the creation of the Constitution, explained this theme: "The accumulation of all powers, legislative, executive, and judiciary, in the same hands, whether for one, a few, or many, and whether hereditary, self-appointed, or elective, may justly be pronounced the very definition of tyranny."

Checks and Balances   Separation of powers works closely with another element of the Constitution, namely a **system of checks and balances** to prevent one branch of the federal government from assuming such powers that it essentially eliminates the effectiveness—and even the independence—of the other branches. For example, the Senate can check the President through its power to approve his appointments. For his part, the President can check the Senate and the House by vetoing their bills. The Judiciary acts as a brake on the other two branches of government through its power to declare a Congressional act unconstitutional, or direct a President to comply with a legitimate demand of Congress (both of these powers were assumed after the Constitution went into effect).

Federalism   Federalism is the division of power between the national government and the states. For the framers, the national government possessed only those powers delegated to it, while all others belonged to the states. This arrangement, which infuses the Constitution, ensured a two-tier power structure, that appeared to favor the states. However, the opposite has occurred as the power of the national government has grown rapidly at the expense of

the states, mostly in the 1900s as a result of domestic and international crises.

The Constitution outlined two kinds of powers for the national government: delegated and implied powers. The former were those powers expressly granted the national government by the Constitution, such as the Congress's authority to declare war, to coin money, and to establish a post office; implied powers are those that are not expressly stated in the Constitution, and can only be inferred from it. The exercise of implied powers by the national government, especially in times of crises, but also in response to new challenges and problems arising from the changing nature of America's dynamic society, has served to significantly enhance its strength vis a vis that of the states.

Implied powers are based on the "elastic clause," found in Article I, Section 8, of the Constitution, which instructs the Congress "to make all laws which shall be necessary and proper for carrying into execution the foregoing powers, and all other powers vested by this Constitution in the government of the United States, or in any department or office thereof." Congress has used this clause repeatedly since its beginnings, and in the process has seen its powers grow enormously.

The Supreme Law of the Land   The accrual of additional power to the national government stems from two other sources. The Constitution's Supreme Law of the Land clause, found in Article VI, states, in part, that "This Constitution, and the Laws of the United States which shall be made in Pursuance thereof and all Treaties made, or which shall be made, under the Authority of the United States, shall be the Supreme Law of the Land; and the Judge in every State shall be bound thereby, any Thing in the constitution or Laws of any State to the Contrary notwithstanding." Therefore, when a conflict exists between a state or states and the national government, the former must undertake the necessary changes to conform to national law. The other source of this power is the **interstate commerce clause** of the Constitution. This clause gives the federal government the power to regulate commerce or travel among the states.

Amendment   The Constitution provided a means of amendment, which involves the passage of a law containing the proposed change by a two-thirds vote of each house of Congress, and its ratification by three-quarters of the states. A second method is also available, although it has never been employed. This procedure calls for two-thirds of the states to call for a convention for the purpose of amending the Constitution.

The framers of the Constitution made the process of amendment purposely difficult to prevent the destruction of the major elements of the document, which, as noted, came only after a series of difficult compromises. After the adoption in 1791 of the **Bill of Rights,** which represent the first ten amendments to the Constitution, just seventeen additional amendments have been ratified since then.

Amending the Constitution

Proposal	Ratification
Proposed amendments may be recommended by:	Proposed amendments are adopted if they are approved by:
a national constitutional convention called by Congress upon receipt of petitions from two-thirds of the state legislatures	legislatures in three-fourths of the states
or a two-thirds vote in both houses of Congress	or special ratifying conventions in three-fourths of the states.

Radical Features   From the American point of view, the Constitution was designed to be—and was—a conservative document. But when compared with the other forms of government among the countries of the world at that time, it was very radical. Here was a document that embodied the principle of popular sovereignty, or the power of the people of a state to influence their government through the political process. Throughout the rest of the world, autocracy, or rule by one or, at most, a few persons, was the predominant form of government. Thus, the Constitution was a document without precedent for its time. The United States was born with many imperfections but the Constitution presented a framework through which an evolving nation could address its problems. After the final session of the Constitutional Convention, Benjamin Franklin was confronted by a woman and asked, "What kind of government have you given us, Dr. Franklin?" The sage of Philadelphia replied, "A Republic, Madam, if you can keep it."

Ratification of the Constitution   The final article of the Constitution provided that as soon as nine states called conventions and ratified the document, it would go into effect. There were, of course, opponents of the Constitution, who were called **anti-Federalists.** Their ranks included Patrick Henry, Richard Henry Lee, and Samuel Adams. They and other anti-Federalists disliked the loss of power by the states if the Constitution was implemented. Furthermore, they objected to the absence of written guarantees of the basic rights of citizens.

Their opponents, the **Federalists,** were led by **Alexander Hamilton, James Madison,** and **John Jay,** who argued, under the pen name of Publius, in *The Federalist*, eighty-five masterly and persuasive essays on government which called for the adoption of the Constitution as the only means of saving the nation from further chaos and ultimate collapse. Hamilton informed "The People of the State of New York," in the first of *The Federalist* essays, that "After an unequivocal experience of the inefficiency of the subsisting federal government, you are called upon to deliberate on a new Constitution for the United States of America. The subject speaks of its own importance; comprehending in its consequences nothing less than the existence of the UNION, the safety and welfare of the parts of which it is composed, the fate of an empire in many respects the most interesting in the world." Madison pleaded in a *Federalist* essay that the Constitution should be evaluated "on its own merits solely."

The Federalist essays originally appeared in newspapers, and were important vehicles in organizing public opinion in support of the adoption of the Constitution. Yet both sides waged a fierce struggle before the Federalists prevailed.

The Bill of Rights   Many of the states agreed to ratify the Constitution only after receiving assurances that amendments protecting the basic rights of the citizenry would become a part of the new national government. Again, James Madison was the moving force behind the creation of a bill of rights for he believed that a constitution of procedures for decision making (the U.S. Constitution) was insufficient to guarantee fundamental human rights. In Madison's view, the bill of rights would take the form of amendments to the Constitution requiring the federal government to respect and safeguard certain rights of the citizenry.

As a member of the House of Representatives, Madison circulated a proposed list of forty-two rights, twenty-six of which were actually incorporated into the first ten amendments. The Congress submitted twelve amendments to the states for approval. The ten that were approved included eight that form the basis of individual rights, such as freedom of speech and the right to trial by jury. The ninth and tenth amendments provide for general protection for those rights not enumerated and for states' rights. The Bill of Rights became officially a part of the Constitution on December 15, 1791, following its approval by the requisite number of states.

Two years before, in the spring of 1789, the new government, as provided for by the Constitution, had come into being. In the years and decades that followed, it provided remarkable guidance for the country's political leaders faced with the challenges of rapid growth and change that have characterized the republic throughout its history. While many reasons are offered for the remarkable achievements of the United States, none exceeds in importance its remarkably stable government, which has resulted, in large measure, from the continued guidance, direction, and even the inspiration it derives from the Constitution. Indeed, it remains a document for the ages, an inspiration to those who inhabit this land, and a hallowed roadmap for government to follow.

Other Governments

America's democratic government differs from its counterparts elsewhere owing to the traditions and experiences of the United States. This section will examine two other democratic nations to broaden our perspective of government by the people.

The United Kingdom

The United Kingdom of Great Britain and Northern Ireland possesses a **Parliamentary Democracy** form of government. In a political system such as that of Great Britain, the citizens do not elect a **Prime Minister** or members of the **Cabinet,** which constitute the **Executive Branch** of government in Britain.

Instead of electing the Prime Minister, as we Americans elect our President through voting, the British elect members of the **House of Commons** which, in turn, holds all the power and authority in the British political system. The **House of Lords,** the upper house, is not elected. Membership in the **Lords** is determined by heredity, and, for the most part, it functions as an advisory body to the **"Commons"** or "Lower House."

The political party that secures a majority in the House of Commons becomes the party of the executive branch of government. Its leader then becomes Prime Minister, and forms a government. He or she proceeds to select members of the cabinet. If neither party obtains a majority, the party with a plurality of votes becomes the executive party and its leader becomes Prime Minister.

While the English Parliament has been around since the Middle Ages, the country's current executive branch only began with the accession of **George I of Hanover** to the monarchy of England in 1714. An historical explanation is in order here. Since the Protestant Reformation and the establishment of the Church of England, or the **Anglican Church,** by King Henry VIII in 1534, England had been struggling with the issue of Catholicism and religious dissent versus the acceptance of Anglicanism by all Englishmen. To complicate matters, Queen Elizabeth I, Henry's Protestant daughter, died without an heir. Parliament, therefore, invited James VI of Scotland, Elizabeth's cousin, to become James I of England in 1603.

The arrival of the Stuarts provoked an ongoing conflict with Parliament largely because James and his successors were Catholic and had consistently displayed "absolutist tendencies," or the tendency to rule without heeding the feelings and needs of the citizens of the country. After a bloody Civil War (Parliament vs. Crown), 1642–1649, the restoration of Charles II in 1660 and the brief reign of his brother James II (1685–1688), Parliament provoked the overthrow of the latter, and thereafter awarded the crown to James's daughter Mary, herself a Protestant, and her husband, William of Orange (a Dutchman) who would rule jointly under a constitutional agreement drafted by Parliament. The so-called **Glorious Revolution of 1688** represents a major turning point in the history of England's Parliamentary system and its abandonment of royal absolutism.

The problem of succession arose again when Anne, Mary's sister and successor, died in 1714 without an heir. Anne was the last of the Stuart monarchs, and although she was a Protestant, Parliament did not want to take any chances by calling upon another Catholic prince to ascend the English throne. Instead, they invited George of Hanover, a Protestant great-grandson of James I, to wear the English crown.

George I hardly spoke English and despised the English climate. He spent most of his time in his native

Hanover, and rarely met with members of his cabinet. During his reign, the king's lengthy absences prompted the rise of the office of Prime Minister with Robert Walpole, its first occupant. By the end of the century, the office was firmly entrenched and executive power continued to move from the monarchy to the Prime Minister and his cabinet. By the time of the death of Queen Victoria, in 1901, the power of the executive branch of government rested wholly in the hands of the Prime Minister and the Cabinet. This is what is known as the **Cabinet System.** While the king or queen is the most visible leader in the United Kingdom, he or she is merely the titular head of government and exercises virtually no power. Instead, the Prime Minister is the single most powerful figure in the government.

While the English Parliament has been operating since the Middle Ages, the country's executive branch only came into being with the accession of George I. In Great Britain's Parliamentary System, the cabinet, although selected by the Prime Minister, reports to Parliament. The Prime Minister can serve an unlimited number of terms as long as his or her party retains a majority in Parliament. The Prime Minister can also dissolve Parliament and call for a new election whenever he or she is given a "no confidence" vote by Parliament.

The British monarchy, presently under attack as a result of a succession of royal scandals and divorces, is a rich symbol of British history. Its continuity through centuries of monarchial leadership and political responsibilities is a source of national pride in England. Its present role may be, and in fact has been, revised, but there is nothing to indicate that it will be abolished. Today's dynasty is still the Hanoverian—but the anti-German sentiment of World War I led to a renaming. Since that

Queen Elizabeth bestows knighthood on Sir Francis Chichester in a 1967 ceremony. Courtesy of Library of Congress.

war, it has been called the Windsor Dynasty. Queen Elizabeth II is highly liked and respected by her subjects. It should be noted that in Great Britain, the Prime Minister is the head of the government and the reigning monarch is the head of the state.

In Great Britain there is no separation of powers among the three branches of government. The legislative or law-making function of the state is in the hands of Parliament; the executive is in charge of enforcing the law. Since there is no constitution per se in Britain, all laws passed by Parliament (statutory law), judicial precedents issued throughout British history (common law) and customs and traditions are part of what is known as Britain's "unwritten constitution."

In England, therefore, there is no equivalent of an American Supreme Court to interpret and decide upon the constitutionality of law passed by Congress and signed by the President of the United States. This means that all legislation automatically becomes law since there is no principle of judicial review. Powers in England are clearly fused and there is no system of checks and balances.

The British have developed a unitary system of government; that is to say, that all power is concentrated at the national level. Similarly, political parties are also highly centralized and disciplined. All members of the two principal political parties in Great Britain—Labor and Conservative—are compelled to follow a rigid party-line to the strictest observance. Failure to do so will result in expulsion from the party and, most likely, the end of the individual's political career. Still, there is room for dissent in the British Parliamentary system. Times and political agendas do change, and, as with other democracies, elected officials cannot afford to ignore their constituents' needs and wishes. In Britain, political platforms reflect consensus within the party membership.

Elections in Great Britain take place at flexible intervals within a period of five years. A Prime Minister can dissolve Parliament and call for new elections if he/she believes that it may help his/her majority in a new Parliament, or if, in fact, as noted earlier, Parliament issues a "no-confidence" vote against his or her government.

The Parliamentary System seems to work better in countries with a two-party system, such as Great Britain. In multiparty societies, such as France and Italy, it is difficult, if not impossible, for any political party to win a majority of votes. The multi-party system reflects an electorate deeply divided over issues and objectives, so much so that a coalition of two or more parties is required to ensure the passage of legislation. Despite the complexities of this system, it has served many countries well.

Japan

Between 1600 and 1868, Japan was ruled by the **Tokugawa Shogunate**, a succession of military dictators or shoguns over which the Tokugawa family had a monopoly for 200 years. During this time, the authority of the emperor declined sharply.

The opening of Japan to western ideas and technology began in 1854, when the United States dispatched a fleet of ships to that country under the command of Commodore Matthew Perry. Japan's exposure to Western trade and ideas resulted in the establishment of the imperial **Meiji government** in 1868, whose principal objective was the restoration of imperial authority and the modernization (westernization) of Japanese society and institutions.

The German-influenced Meiji (meaning "enlightened") Constitution of 1889 represents the first major response to Western ideas, although Japan had already begun to restructure its economy according to a Western model. The document stated that the emperor, who was accorded divine status, would exercise supreme power in this scheme of government. The Meiji Constitution also called for a bicameral legislature, known as the **National Diet,** with limited powers. The Meiji Constitution was drafted as "a gift" from the imperial office, and could at any time be removed if the people abused its powers. Although in theory, the emperor held absolute power, in fact he delegated power and authority to other government offices.

In spite of the emperor's lofty status, the military, by 1930, was the dominant authority which had become

His Majesty the Emperor Hirohito reviews the troops in his capacity as Supreme Commander of the Armed Forces. Courtesy of Fox Photos/Getty Images.

a fascist-oriented dictatorship. By 1930, the military virtually controlled both Diet and the imperial throne. In a reckless display of power, the Japanese military mastermined the invasion of the Chinese province of Manchuria in 1931. The civilian authorities had no choice but to support the Manchurian invasion. Meanwhile, the moribund League of Nations simply issued a note of condemnation.

Encouraged by the success of the Manchurian adventure, the Japanese bombed Pearl Harbor in 1941 and brought America into World War II. After Japan's defeat in 1945, the United States selected General Douglas MacArthur to lead the occupying forces of Japan, and charged him with the reconstruction and demilitarization of Japan.

Under the Constitution of 1947, the emperor renounced his divine status, and was stripped of his temporal powers, becoming a figurehead ruler. Written by Americans, the **Japanese Constitution** of 1947 renounced war and guaranteed that the Japanese would not keep an army. The demilitarization of Japanese society since World War II has benefited the nation's budget as there is no need to engage in military or defense expenditures.

The Japanese bicameral legislature, or Diet, as provided by the Constitution of 1947, consists of an upper chamber or House of Councillors composed of 242 members popularly elected for six-year terms. Some councillors are elected from specific geographical districts and others are elected at large. The lower chamber, or House of Representatives, consists of 480 members serving four-year terms. The Japanese House of Representatives holds the greatest power and behaves much like the British House of Commons.

The Japanese Prime Minister is the chief executive officer. He is chosen by the Diet as leader of the majority party, and stays in power as long as he has the support of his party. Members of the Japanese cabinet are selected by the Prime Minister and must be members of the Diet.

For the most part, Japan's Liberal Democratic Party (LDP) controlled the country's political destiny for nearly forty years before splitting into factions in the early 1990s. Thereafter, a coalition government formed by the Social Democratic Party (SDP) and the Liberal Democratic Party exercised power until the Fall of 1996, when the Liberal Democratic Party returned to power. It has remained in power since then. In 2005, the Liberal Democratic Party formed a coalition government with the New Komeito Party.

Selected Bibliography

James Barber. (1995) *The Book of Democracy*, Englewood Cliffs, New Jersey: Prentice Hall.

Barbara A. Bardes, et al. (1996) *American Government and Politics Today: The Essentials*, 1996–1997 Edition, Saint Paul/Minneapolis, West Publishing Company.

Charles A. Beard. (1913) *An Economic Interpretation of the Constitution of the United States*, New York: Macmillan. Reissued in a paperback edition in 1965 by The Free Press.

W.B. Beasley. (1973) *The Modern History of Japan*, New York: Holt, Rinehart & Winston.

Anthony J. Eksterowicz, et al. (1955) *American Democracy*, Englewood Cliffs, New Jersey, Prentice Hall.

Merrill Jensen. (1940) *The Articles of Confederation*, Madison, Wisconsin: University of Wisconsin Press.

Theodore J. Lowi, et al. (1994) *Readings For American Government*, New York: W.W. Norton & Company.

James Madison, Alexander Hamilton, and John Jay. (1937) *The Federalist*, New York: Modern Library.

Robert Middlekauff. (1982) *The Glorious Cause: The American Revolution*, 1763–1789, New York: Oxford University Press.

J.W. Peltason. (1994) *Understanding the Constitution*, New York: Harcourt Brace.

Clinton Rossitor. (1787) *The Grand Convention*, New York: Macmillan, 1966.

Garry Wills. (1978) *Interpreting America: The Federalist*, Macon, Georgia: Mercer University Press.

Gordon S. Wood. (1993) *The Creation of the American Republic* 1776–1787, New York: Norton.

CHAPTER NINE

The American Political Process

Paul S. George

Arthur Schlesinger, Sr., an eminent twentieth century American historian, described the Founding Fathers as "the most remarkable generation of public men in the history of the United States or perhaps any other nation." He characterized them as fearless, high-principled, deeply versed in ancient and modern political thought, astute and pragmatic and "convinced of man's power to improve his condition through the use of intelligence." Many of the Founding Fathers were not only responsible for the creation of our Constitution, but they also guided the young republic in the first years and decades following its adoption.

For all of its vision and substance, the Constitution was essentially a skeletal guide to the government that has evolved since then in the United States. So much of the political process today centers on political parties and interest or pressure groups, as well as the input and involvement of women, African-Americans, Hispanics and other minorities who have struggled to obtain greater recognition of their political rights along with an entree to the political process. Yet none of these groups or organizations was part of the political landscape when the republic was launched.

Political Parties

The word **politics** is derived from an ancient Greek word, polis, which meant political community. (The polis, or Greek city state, was also a distinctive political entity.) **Polis** is also the root word for **political party,** which, succinctly and traditionally defined, is a group of people organized for the purpose of selecting candidates for office and placing them in those offices in order to control policies and conduct the business of government. In today's America, political parties have assumed additional functions. They also seek to educate and help formulate public opinion in issues; recruit and select leaders; represent and integrate group interests; control and direct government. Additionally, in a democratic society, there are many conflicting interest groups competing for control of the government or for favorable legislation. The government cannot provide for all of them, especially when many of these groups stand strongly opposed to one another. Accordingly, it is left to political parties to bring together these opposing positions through compromise and to prepare a legislative "wish list" for Congress to address while in session. Moreover, in a large, diverse country such as ours where unity is essential and frequently challenging, each of the major parties performs the valuable function of bringing together under one roof many groups whose interests vary significant. Finally, in our two-party system, the minority party acts as a check on the majority party.

The first political parties appeared in England in the seventeenth century. Those who supported the monarchy and the Anglican or English Catholic Church were known as **Tories** by their opponents, a pejorative term apparently of Irish origin, which had been applied to royalist outlaws. On the other hand, those who favored a constitutional monarchy under a Protestant king, with toleration for religious dissenters (with the notable exception of Catholics) came to be known as **Whigs** by some of their opponents, a term considered

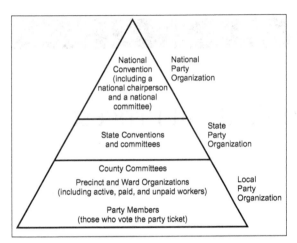

A pyramidal structure of the American political party from top to bottom.

derisive by the latter. The Whigs found their expression in the British Parliament, which was emerging, by the seventeenth century, as a strong rival to the monarchy as the most powerful English governmental institution. The British party system continued to develop in subsequent centuries, assuming additional functions as well. This was especially the case in the nineteenth and early twentieth centuries, a period of great reform in British government and politics.

Political parties were central to the system of government in the United States almost from its beginnings, yet they were not mentioned in the Constitution. Further, many of the nation's early leaders opposed them. **James Madison**, the Virginian who was most responsible for the creation of the Constitution, noted, in one of *The Federalist* essays, that "Among the numerous advantages promised by a well constructed Union (is) its tendency to break and control the violence of faction." Versatile Thomas Jefferson remarked that "If I could not go to heaven but with a party, I would not go at all." Additionally, the nation's first chief executives opposed them. "Let me warn you," intoned **George Washington**, in his famed Farewell Address in 1797, "in the most solemn manner against and baneful effects of the spirit of party generally. This spirit...exists under different shapes in all government, more or less stifled, controlled, or repressed; but in those of the popular form it is seen in its greatest rankness and is truly their worst enemy." As Washington viewed it, political parties "provoke the mischief of associations and combinations." John Adams, who succeeded George Washington as President, maintained that his great dread was the division of the young nation into "two great parties."

Yet the emergence of full-fledged political parties was inevitable with the rise of strong opposing viewpoints in the Congress over taxes and the role of government, the place of manufacturing and agriculture, along with that of cities and rural areas, in the life of the nation, and differences over taxes and foreign policy for the new country, especially with regard to the issue of the **French Revolution**, which found supporters as well as critics when it began in 1789. Such differences led to shifting coalitions in both houses, spirited debates, and divergent voting patterns almost from the beginning of the new government in 1789. **Alexander Hamilton**, Washington's brilliant and controversial Secretary of the Treasury, was the lighting rod for these divergent viewpoints, since it was he who introduced an ambitious economic program, which was, in large measure, adopted. Hamilton's program called for a strong manufacturing base and a flourishing commerce as part of an American economy strong and independent of Europe; it also advocated government assumption of debt, subsidies and a protective tariff for infant industries, and a national bank.

By the time of the elections of 1796, differing factions over the question of the proper course of direction for the

One of the most formidable third party candidates was former Republican President Theodore Roosevelt, who, in 1912, ran on the Progressive Party, popularly known as the Bull Moose Party, ticket after failing to become the Presidential nominee of the Republican Party. Courtesy of Library of Congress.

young nation had acquired labels. Hamilton was instrumental in the creation of the **Federalist Party,** which arose from a voting bloc in the Congress that enacted his economic program. The federalists supported a strong national government, in addition to the aforementioned components of Hamilton's plan for the country's economy. Hamilton's supporters maintained that the name Federalist implied that they stood strongly behind the Constitution and the new government, whereas their opponents were the same old anti-Federalists who had opposed adoption of the constitution. **James Madison** was the single most important figure in organizing the opposition party, which was called the **Democratic-Republican** or **Republican Party** (not to be mistaken for today's Republican Party). Its name implied—or so its supporters claimed—that it was the party of the people as opposed to the Federalists, which represented elite, even monarchical interests.

Adding to the differences between the emerging parties was the unfolding of the French Revolution, a transcendent event that led to a radical change in the government and society of France, and, incidentally, claimed a wide audience in America.

Influenced by the American Revolution, the French Revolution took place between 1789 and the middle years of the following decade. Catalyzed by a severe financial crisis and the growing discontent of talented but powerless elements of the third estate, or the middle class, the revolution led to the toppling of the monarchy and the removal of many of the privileges of the first two estates, the clergy and the nobility. By the outset of 1790s, France had its first constitution and a government dominated by the third estate. Liberal reforms were adopted. The Catholic Church was stripped of its independence and power. A new calendar was adopted. Formerly disenfranchised men were now in power.

By 1792, the revolution had grown increasingly more radical leading to the period of the Terror in 1793–1794, resulting in the execution of King Louis XIV and his wife, Marie Antoinette and numerous other representatives of the *Ancien Regime.* The Thermidorean Reaction, a conservative backlash to the excesses of the revolution, ended the reign of terror in 1794. France now came under the rule of the Directory, five men who ruled France in conservative fashion, undoing many of the reforms of the revolution. Waiting in the wings was Napoleon Bonaparte, a brilliant soldier who would seize power at the end of the 1790s, and soon thereafter establish a dictatorship and an empire incorporating many of the ideals and reforms of the earlier revolution in the country he ruled.

Thomas Jefferson, Madison's friend and ideological soulmate, was a strong Francophile, and a great supporter of the French Revolution, as were most members of the Democratic-Republican Party. The Federalists opposed much of what the Revolution represented. The increasingly more radical cast of the Revolution, and a war that erupted in 1792, between France and a conservative coalition of nations bent on destroying the revolutionary virus before it "contaminated" them, split the American body politic into two camps over the question of support or opposition to France. In fact, as Jefferson noted, it was that war that "kindled and brought forward the two parties with an ardour which our own interests merely, could never excite."

Geographically, the Federalists enjoyed their strongest support in New England because of its vast commercial ties to Great Britain. But farther south the Federalists were weaker, gaining significant support only in South Carolina, with its aristocratic airs stemming from a thriving plantation agriculture and affluent merchants. The strength of the Democratic-Republicans centered in the West, yet the party did possess support in the middle states. The party also appealed to other non-establishment elements, such as the newly rich, who felt excluded by the old monied class with its disproportionate political influence, immigrants, and dissenting religious sects who wanted more acceptance.

During the presidencies of **Washington** and John Adams (1789–1801), a time in which political factions developed into full-fledged parties, the Federalists

American Political Parties Since 1789

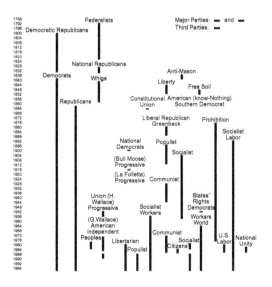

The parties depicted in this chart ran candidates for president sometime during the republic's 200-year history of presidential elections.

dominated the federal government, but Jefferson's election to the Presidency in 1800 heralded the beginning of a new era, one in which the Democratic-Republican Party would dominate American politics for nearly a generation. In fact, the Federalist Party faded from the scene by the beginning of the 1820s, effectively ending the first era in the party system. Replacing it was the **National Republican Party,** organized by **Henry Clay,** a powerful congressman, and John Quincy Adams, the son of the nation's second president.

This second era began to unfold with the Presidential election of 1824, which marked **Andrew Jackson's** first campaign for the country's highest office. This period featured a significantly larger electorate, the selection of presidential electors by popular vote, as opposed to their selection by state legislatures, as had previously been the case, and national campaigning on the part of presidential candidates. The Anti-Masonic Party, a third party, introduced the method of nominating a presidential candidate through the vehicle of a party convention in 1831. This mode of selection replaced the party caucus, which was composed of members of Congress who gathered to nominate presidential candidates, with a method more democratic or broad-based. Additionally, party organization reached downward to local communities, as early versions of political bosses organized party support on the local and state levels for national candidates.

A formidable figure in American history and politics, Andrew Jackson was the presidential candidate of the Democratic Party, the direct predecessor of today's Democratic Party, when he was elected President in 1828 and 1832. Courtesy of National Gallery of Art.

The number of state-sponsored internal improvement projects increased in the 1820s, as did the amount of government jobs employing party workers. Accordingly, politics was moving out of the exclusive province of the wealthy and into the hands of professional politicians and political hacks. In the meantime, the **Democratic-Republicans** had split into factions. After the disputed presidential election of 1824, when Democratic-Republican Party candidate, **Andrew Jackson,** claimed foul, his party began calling itself Democrats. They were followers of Andrew Jackson, the coarse Tennessee frontiersman who, as the dominant political figure of that era, cast a large shadow over American politics.

By the early 1830s, the **National Republicans** had evolved into the **Whig Party,** which arose in opposition to the policies of Jackson and was less a "party of the people", as Jacksonian Democrats claimed, and more a party supportive of the emerging capitalistic economy. The Whigs supported **Henry Clay's** American System, which sought to foster national economic development through a protective tariff, a national bank, and federal aid for internal improvements. This party system held until the 1850s, when the cleavages between sections, which deepened over the issue of states rights, slavery, and widely divergent economic interests, led to a split in the ranks of the Whigs and the consequent destruction of the party.

Thus driven by the fires of sectionalism, many voters changed allegiances and others joined parties for the first time, ensuring the collapse of the two-decade old party system. By the time the process of realignment had been completed, a new party system had appeared. The earliest manifestation of this new political order was the organization of the **Republican Party** in 1854. Composed of many former Whigs, free-soilers who campaigned to keep slavery from spreading into new areas, and supporters of the north's emerging industrial economy, the new party would elect **Abraham Lincoln,** its first president, in 1860.

Republican dominance over national politics continued into the era following the Civil War (1861–1865)—and through the first three decades of the twentieth century. Typically, in every national election in the century's last quarter, the Republicans could count on sixteen states in the North and West to support their candidates, while the Democrats were secure with fourteen, primarily in the South where the Republican Party was an outcast because it was viewed as the party of Lincoln, Emancipation, and Reconstruction.

This was also the period during which the party machine reached its peak of power and influence. Political machines were organizations that controlled a political and party and often the government of a municipality or even of a state. Carefully constructed machines, under the rule of a boss and his top lieutenants, took control of parties, arranged for the election of their candidates through their control of every aspect of the electoral process, and reaped the benefits of rule by awarding lucrative municipal franchises for construction, transportation, energy, and the like to bidders offering munificent sums of money. The machine maintained its power by building a huge cadre of loyal supporters through its ability to provide jobs and take care of their needs in the areas of employment, social welfare, and, on, occasion, the law.

The Great Depression (1929–1939), the gravest economic crisis in the country's history, brought an end to Republican dominance because of that party's association with the unpopular presidency of Herbert Hoover and his failed attempt to lift the country out of the Depression. Further, the growing dominance of urban America, whose problems and needs were better answered by the Democratic Party, and the rise of charismatic Franklin. D. Roosevelt as the Democratic standard bearer, also contributed to the rise of the Democratic party as the dominant political coalition. Roosevelt's New Deal, the massive involvement of the federal government in many areas of American life through a series of social welfare and regulatory programs, brought droves of new supporters to the Democratic Party. **The New Deal** weakened considerably the hold of **political machines** over local and state politics since it assumed many of the social welfare functions formerly provided by boss or machine rule. Since the era of the **Great Depression,** the Democrats have almost always dominated the Congress (with the notable exception of the mid-1990s and early 2000s), while splitting the Presidency with the Republicans.

Today, the country's two major parties exhibit marked differences domestically, but continue to support for the most part of bipartisan foreign policy. The Republican Party remains the organization oriented more toward business and less toward social welfare. The Democratic Party is the more inclusive of the two parties because its broad umbrella provides cover for labor, African-Americans, feminists, and others. Yet the two parties usually do not differ sharply in program or principle. Both parties appeal to a broad constituency. Accordingly, they offer relatively moderate philosophic orientations and programs. They are capable of—and on occasion do—promise virtually everything to everybody, since they are desirous of attracting people from all interests groups.

Modern political parties embrace several important functions or activities. Most importantly, they provide for the selection of candidates for governmental office. This function provides them with the power to shape, in selecting winning candidates, governments and policies. Once party nominees have been chosen, political, parties play important roles in conducting and financing the campaigns to secure their elections. Next, political parties play a major role in organizing government by providing the institutional framework or organization within which party officeholders operate. For example, legislators belonging to a particular party usually join together in a caucus, or group, to select their leaders and to determine who will serve on which legislative committees. Additionally, they consult on matters of legislative policy and strategy. Nowhere is the party structure more important than in the United States Congress, for there the party determines all committee and leadership assignments for its Congressional delegation and it presents members with its wish list of legislative measures to be secured. Other and perhaps less important activities or functions of political parties in our democratic system include socials where the rank and file can mingle with party leaders. Parties also establish youth organizations to organize new voters, and to recruit party workers.

Membership in a political party is easy to achieve. Prospective members merely have to register to vote upon reaching age eighteen. At that time, they can select which of the two major parties they wish to join, or they can choose independent status. Moreover, each of the major parties, and, sometimes, even a minor or third party will mount recruitment drives, assisting eligible voters to register while encouraging them to join their party.

Members of political parties can play as active a role in their party as they desire, from getting out the vote at election time to campaigning for the party's nomination for office. Indeed, the active participation of individual citizens in their party and in the American political process is critical to the survival of our democracy. By voting regularly, expressing one's opinion with strength and clarity on contemporary issues, and holding our elected representatives accountable to their campaign promises as well as to high standards of honesty and compassion for the electorate will surely help maintain our democracy and strengthen it. For the most part, the American electorate is passive in comparison with their counterparts in other democracies. Voter turnouts are typically low, the electorate is often uninformed about the complexities of an issue, and a broad cynicism has replaced the enthusiasm and

THE THIRD-TERM PANIC.

"An Ass, having put on the Lion's skin, roamed about in the Forest, and amused himself by frightening all the foolish Animals he met with in his wanderings."—SHAKESPEARE or BACON.

The Republican and Democratic Parties received their enduring animal caricatures from Thomas Nast in the 1870s. Nast was the foremost political cartoonist of that era. For him the elephant was the symbol of the Republicans while the donkey depicted the Democrats. One-hundred-twenty-years later, these symbols remain affixed to the parties. Courtesy of New York Public Library.

optimism that from time to time proved so healthy to our body politic.

While the two major parties continue to dominate the body politic, America's electorate is more restless than ever, giving rise to the tendency of growing number of voters to register as independents or embrace third parties. Moreover, the pervasiveness of television and the entry of a large cast of political operatives who work to manipulate the image of their candidate as well as that of the opposition party, and the continuing specter of corrupt public officials has led to a growing public cynicism toward the political process.

As opposed to many other democracies, which operate on the basis of a multi-party system, the United States is aligned around a two-party system, meaning two major parties and usually a multitude of small "third" parties. Third parties are common to the American political system. Third parties, sometimes called minor parties, often arise for the following reasons: they are promoting ideologies unpopular with the major parties; they appeal to persons dissatisfied with the positions of one or both of the major parties; they advocate reforms considered too radical by the major parties. Third parties have failed to experience pronounced and prolonged success in our system, as opposed to the experience of many other democracies, for a host of reasons. Yet, many of the reforms advocated by the Third parties, such as the direct election of U.S. senators and the introduction of a federal graduated tax, have been embraced by the two major parties and enacted into law.

As we know, from the beginning, the nation has operated under a system of two major political parties, each of which was broad—and practical—enough to include disparate groups and ideas, thereby negating the need for additional parties. Additionally, the nature of our electoral system discourages third parties. For example, the election laws of most states make it difficult for new or small parties to gain a place on the ballot. Further, the process of electing a president discourages minor parties because the electoral college operates on a winner-takes-all basis for the candidate who receives a plurality of the popular vote in the state.

Interest or Pressure Groups

Organized political activity in the United States is conducted not only through political parties, but also through **interest groups,** sometimes called pressure groups. Such entities are important in shaping public opinion, as well as in influencing legislative and administrative decisions. Defined simply, interest groups are organizations that seek to influence public or governmental policy. Interest or pressure groups are legal entities, and their representatives, or lobbyists, tend to be registered as such although not all interest groups have registered lobbyists. All interest groups—and their numbers stretch into the thousands, representing a vast array of causes and interest—share certain characteristics. They are formally organized; their members tend to agree on the same major points; they act through or upon government institutions to further their objectives and influence public policy. Interest or pressure groups attempt to influence public policy decisions in several ways. They often use their influence to propose new ideas, as well as promote or block new legislation from reaching the floor of the Congress or of a state legislature. Moreover, interest groups sometime ensure that people sympathetic to their interests are placed in administrative positions.

Interest groups represent a vital, though vexsome, part of the political process. Since American society is so variegated with people of many diverse backgrounds and with so many agendas, interest groups become important for the advancement of the many diverse interests of these people. Additionally, since the three branches of government share political authority, and, by virtue of federalism, the government shares power at different levels of our society, interest groups are again considered necessary to assist persons and groups with widely varying agendas and needs, who often will need to approach more than one level or branch of government. A third reason for the importance of interest groups stems from the fact that the strength of political parties vary from place to place in America. Where there is a strong party **political machine,** such as that of Mayor Richard Daly's Democratic Party machine, which dominated Chicago's political life from the 1950s–1970s, interest groups are at a disadvantage since they are forced to deal with the dominant party, which already provides a broad umbrella of services for its constituents, usually on its own terms. By contrast, in regions where parties are weak, **interest groups** will grow and thrive, and play a larger role in policymaking.

An anti-war protest in Madison, Wisconsin. Courtesy of Bettmann/Corbis Images.

Origins

Virtually every era in American history has seen interest groups bidding for governmental favors. During the era of the American Revolution, groups pushing the cause of American independence from England came to the fore. At the time that the Constitution of the United States was being considered for adoption, its prime author, **James Madison,** who disapproved of interest groups, nevertheless wrote in *Federalist 10,* that such entities were "sown in the nature of man" owing to economic and other inequities between people. Therefore, the best that the country can do about interest groups is to ensure that they are many so that no one group can dominate the entire political system.

A vigorous reform wave that swept America in the third and fourth decades of the nineteenth century prompted Alexis de Tocqueville, a shrewd French observer of America, to write that "Americans of all ages, all conditions, and all dispositions constantly form

			PAC	Dem	Rep	Principal
Rank	Contributor	Total	%	%	%	Category
1.	National Association of Realtors	$3,094,228	100%	55%	44%	Real estate
2.	American Medical Association	$2,647,981	100	49	51	Doctors
3.	Teamsters Union	$2,438,184	99+	92	8	Teamsters
4.	National Education Association	$2,334,715	99+	93	7	Teachers unions
5.	United Auto Workers	$1,801,772	99+	99	1	Manufacturing unions
6.	Letter Carriers Union	$1,755,478	99+	86	14	Postal unions
7.	American Federation of State/Country/Municipal Employees	$1,549,720	99+	98	2	Local government unions
8.	National Association of Retired Federal Employees	$1,545,122	100	76	24	Federal worker unions
9.	Association of Trial Lawyers of America	$1,539,550	100	87	13	Lawyers
10.	Carpenters Union	$1,526,534	99+	96	4	Construction unions
11.	National Association of Life Underwriters	$1,487,800	100	51	49	Life Insurance
12.	Machinists/Aerospace Workers Union	$1,487,495	99+	98	1	Manufacturing unions
13.	AT&T	$1,477,200	98	57	43	Long distance
14.	American Bankers Association	$1,473,061	100	55	45	Commercial banks
15.	National Association of Home Builders	$1,362,550	99+	48	52	Residential construction
16.	Laborers Union	$1,359,119	99+	92	8	Construction unions
17.	National Auto Dealers Association	$1,313,900	100	38	62	Auto dealers
18.	International Brotherhood of Electrical Workers	$1,257,920	99+	97	2	Communication unions
19.	Air Line Pilots Association	$1,167,797	100	81	19	Air transport unions
20.	American Institute of CPAs	$1,089,294	99+	56	44	Accountants

The Top Twenty PAC Contributors

PACs, or Political Action Committees, have become formidable fundraisers for aspirants for public office since their inception in the mid-1970s.

associations" to further their interests, whether it be for temperance, women's rights, or for the abolition of slavery cause. Additionally, de Tocqueville observed the wide variety of such groups: "They have not only commercial and manufacturing companies, in which all take part, but associations of a thousand other kinds—religious, moral, serious, futile, extensive or restricted, enormous or diminutive."

Lobbyists, or agents representing the case for these groups before the government, swarmed all over Washington in the immediate post-Civil War era after the mid 1860s, prompting Mark Twain and Charles Dudley Warner to write derisively of them in *The Gilded Age,* a novel whose title was employed as the descriptive phrase for the last quarter century of the nineteenth century, an era marked by a pell mell rush toward industrialization and the accumulation of great wealth by enterprising, sometimes ruthless, entrepreneurs. While farmers and workers organized with some success in the late nineteenth century, the early years of the following century were especially rich, in terms of emergent interest groups, with the organization of the National Association for the Advancement of Colored People, American Farm Bureau, Anti-Defamation League, American Medical Association, the Chamber of Commerce, and a host of other organizations with widely varying agendas. Recent interest groups include many organized and sponsored by consumer crusader Ralph Nader, citizens lobbies, such as Common Cause, and an increasing number of environmentally oriented organizations. In fact, since the 1960s the number of interest groups has spiraled in number. Moreover, since electoral reform legislation was enacted in 1974, limiting the amount of money a person could contribute to the campaign of a candidate, a new approach to the old business of influencing government policy through interest groups has appeared with the rise of **Political Action Committees or PACs.** Such lobbies, which usually center around a single issue or interest, raise and channel campaign contributions to political candidates in amounts greater than that allowed under existing election laws for individuals.

Types of Interest Groups

Interest groups could be classified into three types. One type consists of business and occupational groups which represent the economic interests of the member and their concern about the actions of other groups, the government or the economy in general. They include the National Association of Manufacturers, the National Chamber of Commerce, the Business Round Table, the union confed-eration AFL-CIO, the American Bar Association, and the American Medical Association among others. A second type consists of public interest groups which are a diffuse number of groups, law firms, think-tanks and community organizations which lobby on behalf of consumer and environmental issues, government and tax reforms, and other matters which affect the public in general. They include Common Cause, Public Citizen, Congress Watch, the Heritage Foundation, and others.

Finally, a third type are social interest groups whose more special agenda might not be represented by either economic, occupational, or public interest groups. These include organizations such as the National Association of Colored People, the Spanish American League Against Discrimination, the Native American Rights Fund, the National Organization for Women, the American Jewish Congress, the Catholic League, and the National Rifle Association. The success of all these groups depend on the size and intensity of their membership, financial resources, expertise, organizational leadership, strategic alliances with other groups,

---

The Five Commandments of Successful Lobbying

1. Tell the truth.
2. Never promise more than you can deliver.
3. Know how to listen so that you accurately understand what you are hearing.
4. Staff is there to be worked with and not circumvented.
5. Spring no surprises.

Consumer Crusader Ralph Nader has lobbied, with great efficiency, on a number of consumer-related issues for more than three decades. Courtesy of Keystone/Getty Images.

Selected Lobby Registrations

The following groups, corporations, and individuals were among those registering with the Office of Records and Registration of the House of Representatives during one month in 1994.

Lobby	Type	Interest
Alliance of American Insurers	Trade association	Health Security Act
American Chiropractic Association	Professional association	Health care
American Institute of Certified Public Accountants	Professional association	Modification of liability for accountants
Armour Pharmaceutical Co.	U.S. corporation	New technology in stabilizing blood supplies
Emily's List	Interest group	Campaign finance reform
General Atomics, Inc.	U.S. corporation	Funding of nuclear reactor research
Government of Mexico, Finance Ministry	Foreign government	Ratification of tax treaty
Independent Defense Contractors Association	Trade Association	Small business
International Women's Health Coalition	Interest group	Women's reproductive health and rights issues in foreign aid
Leech Lake Tribal Council	Interest group	Agriculture
Major League Baseball Players Association	Labor organization	Antitrust exemption of major-league baseball
McDonnell Douglas Corp.	U.S. corporation	Defense authorization and appropriations
Pizza Hut, Inc.	U.S. corporation	Taxes and mandated benefits
U.S. Term Limits	Interest group	Limitation on terms of political office

SOURCE: *Congressional Quarterly,* February 12, 1995.

media support, and political conditions in the country at any given time. Interest groups can make financial contributions, propose ideas through position papers, write letters and make phone calls to politicians, demonstrate on the streets, and publish public letters on newspapers to shape public opinion.

The Role the Media

Political opinion is the set of views expressed by the community on the political issues of the day. It can change rapidly, even though people's core attitudes remain basically the same throughout their lives. The mass media—newspapers, magazines, radio, television, cable, satellites, etc. carry massive amounts of information which can shape or influence popular opinion, which then affects political debate and the legislative process. If an issue is not covered by the media, those who care about it might not get sufficient popular support to convince their legislators to address their concerns. The issue then dies. Nothing can be done. Therefore, media coverage is essential to support any attempt to affect the political process.

Unfortunately, the presentation of news by the media can be very biased. News is what the editors of these institutions decide to cover. It is something they

Votes Cast for Minor Parties and Independents Since 1892			
Year	Candidate	Party	Percentage of Vote
1892	John B. Weaver	Populist	8.5
	John Bidwell	Prohibition	2.3
1900	John G. Wooley	Prohibition	1.5
1904	Eugene V. Debs	Socialist	3.0
	Silas C. Swallow	Prohibition	1.9
1908	Eugene V. Debs	Socialist	2.8
	Eugene F. Chafin	Prohibition	1.7
1912	Theodore Roosevelt	Progressive	27.4
	Eugene V. Debs	Socialist	6.0
	Eugene F. Chafin	Prohibition	1.4
1916	Allan L. Benson	Socialist	3.2
	J. Frank Hanley	Prohibition	1.2
1920	Eugene V. Debs	Socialist	3.4
	Parley P. Christensen	Farmer-Labor	1.0
1924	Robert M. La Follette	Progressive	16.6
1932	Norman Thomas	Socialist	2.2
1936	William Lemke	Unionist	2.0
1948	J. Strom Thurmond	States' Rights	2.4
	Henry A. Wallace	Progressive	2.4
1968	George C. Wallace	American Independent	13.5
1972	John Schmitz	American Independent	1.4
1980	John B. Anderson	Independent	6.6
	Ed Clark	Libertarian	1.1
1992	H. Ross Perot	United We Stand	19.0

*Only candidates with more than 1 percent are included.

believe is worth knowing, either because of their ideological preferences or because of their commercial/entertainment objectives. Media editors could very easily suppress information damaging to media allies, summarize issues unfairly, present a glamorous, articulate spokesperson for their one side of the issue, and a harsh, "ugly" one for the other side, use anonymous "high Washington sources" or "experts" who express their opinion, or at worst, deceive. The problem of bias seems to be growing worse as more media outlets are being owned by fewer corporations, and as more cities have only one newspaper.

Increasingly, politicians in local, state and federal legislatures are relying on polls—questioning of persons selected at random to obtain information or opinions to be analyzed—to acquire information on public opinion and to plan their own voting. Unfortunately, these polls, produced by media outlets and other interest groups, might not be objectively identifying popular

opinion because their samples might be unreliable, and the wording of the questions might be biased or manipulative in nature. Consequently, some of these polls instead of responding to public opinion might actually be creating it, as people are influenced by the result of prejudiced polls.

Lobbying

The process by which interest groups seek to influence the government and policy at every level, especially the legislative branch, is known as **lobbying.** The name emanates from the longtime tendency of influence seekers at the state legislature level to congregate in the lobbies near the legislative chambers. Their activity was called "lobbying". Lobbyists are able to affect the fate of a piece of legislation at several levels since the country's political system, is multi-tiered, consisting of national, state, and local levels.

How a Bill Becomes a Law

Bills may be sponsored by any member or members of Congress, often acting on behalf of the Executive branch of government. The lone exception here involves revenue-raising bills (such as taxation proposals), which must be first introduced in the House. Often, the same bill is introduced in each house of the Congress at the same time.

After a bill has been introduced, it will be referred to the appropriate committee, which then assigns it to an appropriate subcommittee of that committee. There testimony is heard on the merits, and even the short comings of the bill. It is also at this stage that the bill can be "marked-up," or altered. Finally, the members of the subcommittee vote on the bill. If it passes, it is sent back to the full committee for hearings, "markup," and vote.

If approved by the full committee, the bill is sent, in the House, to that body's Rules Committee, which determines the rules, or the guidelines, governing consideration of the bill by the whole House. Thereafter, the bill is placed on a calendar that determines the date it will be brought to the floor of the House for debate and vote. In the Senate, a bill approved by committee is placed on a calendar scheduling Senate floor debate and voting.

Bills approved by a majority vote in the House are then introduced in the Senate, or vice versa. If a bill passes both the House and the Senate and it contains identical language in each version, it goes directly to the President of the United States for his approval or veto. However, if a bill approved by one house differs from the version approved by the other house, select members of each body meet to agree upon a compromise version, which must then be reconsidered in each house again for final approval. This stage is known as the conference stage, and the select members are organized into conference committees.

If both the House and the Senate approve identical versions of a bill, it is sent to the President for his approval or disapproval. If he vetoes the bill, it can still become law if both houses approve it in another vote by at least a two-thirds majority. Otherwise, it is dead for that session of the Congress.

Fred Harris, a former United States Senator from Oklahoma, and an astute observer of the American political scene, has explained that such fragmentation of power produces "pressure points," or opportunities to influence the fate of a bill through face to face contact with one or more of the principles involved in the decision-making process. Harris explained that pressure points in the United States Congress—along with legislative bodies at the state and local levels—begin at the level of a subcommittee, where a bill comes under consideration for the first time, at the committee level, where a bill is approved and given shape and meaning, and on the floor of both houses of the Congress where a bill is approved and enacted into law or rejected. Pressure points, or opportunities for lobbyists, are also present when House and Senate conference committees meet to iron out the differences between two versions of the same bill passed in both houses of the Congress, and again when these bodies vote on the bill that comes out of conference committee with its identical language and awaiting passage by the two houses. A final pressure point rests with the White House when the President approves or disapproves (vetoes) the bill.

Since many of the bills that are approved by the Congress are only **"authorization" bills** or bills that call for the creation of a government program, there exists additional prospects for pressure points. Before a program provided for by the authorization bill can become effective, an **appropriation bill,** providing the funding for it, must work its way through the same tedious process as the former. Here again, a lobbyist has the opportunity to influence the fate of legislation through a series of pressure points.

Pressure or **interest groups** attempt to influence public policy decisions in several ways. They use their influence to propose new ideas, promote legislation or block new legislation from reaching the floor of the Congress or of a state legislature. Moreover, they work to ensure that people sympathetic to their interests are placed in administration programs.

Lobbyists tend to be attorneys or employees of interest groups or consulting firms. Many have held office previously at the national level or high-level administrative positions, an accomplishment that often provides them entree to officials otherwise difficult to reach directly.

The Power of the Supreme Court

The American political process is not only affected by the political parties, interest groups, members of Congress, public opinion and the media, but also by the decisions taken by the nine members of the U.S. Supreme Court. For example, the Court's judicial review ended

Shortly before the opening of the 1948 Democratic National Convention in Philadelphia, pickets appeared outside Convention Hall demanding equal rights for Negroes and an anti-Jim Crow plank in the party platform. Courtesy of Bettmann/Corbis Images.

school segregation by law, prayer in public schools, mandated the busing of students from one school to another to achieve racial balance, and permitted the abortion of the unborn. As the courts, district, appellate and Supreme, have exercise greater power influencing the political process, there is concern that they might be overstepping their constitutional role. For example, the 1973 Roe v. Wade Supreme Court decision which stated that women have a constitutional right to privacy that justifies abortion if they so choose, was criticized by conservatives who argue that there is no such right to privacy in the Constitution. Conservatives in general, want a strict interpretation of the Constitution, based on what is exactly written on the document. Liberals respond, however, saying that the Supreme Court can make their interpretations based also on what the Constitution implies so that

they can decide on new issues which the writers of the Constitution had not considered, but which require resolution. This controversy between the conservative and the liberal interpretations of the Constitution applies to many other issues including pornography, immigration, and interstate commerce regulation, among others.

Minorities and the Fight for Inclusion

America is a much better place today than it was earlier in this century because of the greater inclusion of so called minorities in all areas of the country's life. Despite the lofty ideals of the Declaration of Independence, the Constitution, and the Bill of Rights, many Americans, until recent times, were left out of the political process and thereby denied the vast opportunities that this country affords its residents. Whether they were African-Americans, women, Native Americans, Hispanics or other minorities, these Americans did not possess the same opportunities as others in this country.

African-Americans and the Civil Rights Movement

Slavery is an evil that has permeated societies since the dawn of civilization. Typically, slaves in early societies were unfortunates taken prisoner in warfare and then enslaved, or persons placed in bondage for debt. The era of Black enslavement began with the Muslims of North Africa and then at the dawn of exploration in the late Middle Ages following New World conquests by the Spanish and Portuguese. In the race to exploit the mineral wealth in Latin America and develop a plantation agriculture in the Caribbean, these Iberian powers followed by the English and others turned to black slaves to provide the labor for extracting precious minerals from mines, or for working long hours under a broiling sun on sugarcane plantations in the Caribbean.

The first slaves who toiled in the future United States resided in Spanish Florida. In fact, St. Augustine possessed a slave colony by the latter part of the sixteenth century. But a much larger number of black African slaves were utilized by settlers in subsequent centuries in areas north of Florida. By the eve of the American Civil War (1861–1865), four million slaves were living in the South, a region whose entire population numbered nine million.

With the defeat of the Confederacy in 1865, **slavery** was finally banished. The era of **Reconstruction** (1863–1877), which marked an attempt to rebuild the South physically as well as to reorder it socially, culturally, and even economically in the aftermath of the Civil War and the elimination of slavery, represented a heady era for Freed People, who tasted freedom and opportunity for the first time. While African-Americans had gained their freedom by virtue of Lincoln's Emancipation Proclamation, the success of Union armies in the field of battle, and the ratification of the **Thirteenth Amendment** in 1865, they acquired full citizenship rights only with the adoption of the **Fourteenth Amendment** in 1867; further, Freed People won the right to vote with the approval of the **Fifteenth Amendment** to the Constitution in 1870. Assisted by Union soldiers, electoral officials, and Carpetbaggers, who were Northerners who came south after the conflict in quest of new opportunities, Blacks voted in large numbers and held important political offices at each level of government during Reconstruction.

Reconstruction's end followed a deal between Republican and Democratic Party leaders to ensure the inauguration of Republican Rutherford B. Hayes, who gained the Presidency as a result of a disputed election in 1876. Abandoned by the federal government, which removed troops and election officials from the South as part of the agreement, black Southerners were left thereafter to their own devices in an increasingly more hostile climate both in the South, with the return of white rule, and in the country at large. Fifteen years after the end of Reconstruction, the era of **Jim Crow,** or racial **segregation** by law, had overtaken the region. For Blacks Jim Crow (the name came from a black minstrel show that toured the South in the decades before the Civil War) meant second class citizenship, discrimination, disfranchisement, and continuing poverty. The era of racial discrimination by law lasted until the 1960s.

The system of segregation began to unravel slowly as a result of several court rulings that struck down portions of it. Leading the legal assault on Jim Crow or segregation laws, was the National Association for the Advancement of Colored People, founded in 1909 and composed of both Blacks and Whites, which pursued the fight against racial separation in the courts. The most celebrated victory on this front was a unanimous Supreme Court ruling in 1954, in the case of **Brown v. Board of Education,** that held that the equal protection of the laws provision of the Fourteenth Amendment prohibited separate public schools for blacks and whites.

By the 1950s, the legal assault on segregation was joined by a civil rights movement featuring passive resistance and modeled after Mahatma Ghandi, the great Indian resistance leader, toward discrimination. The first major victory for the civil rights movement came with the Montgomery Bus Boycott under the inspirational leadership of **Martin Luther King Jr.,** a young Baptist Minister, and his newly-formed Southern Christian Leadership Conference. The son of a prominent minister, King held a Ph.D. in Philosophy (his dissertation focused on Mahatma Ghandi and the use of passive resistance in breaking the English grip over India). The King-led boycott began in December 1955, after Rosa Parks, a seamstress, refused to give up her seat on a crowded bus to a white passenger, a practice mandated by law, triggering a year-long bus boycott by Montgomery's Black population, which sought to desegregate that city's public conveyances. Finally, Montgomery acquiesced, eliminating the hoary law and practice of segregation on public transportation.

Susan B. Anthony was one of the most prominent feminists and women's suffrage leaders of the nineteenth and early twentieth century. She was one of the founders of the National Suffrage Association which was organized in 1869. Shortly before her death, she organized, the International Women's Suffrage Alliance in Berlin Courtesy of Library of Congress.

The victory in Montgomery was followed by others, as King became a world renowned figure for his great oratorical talents, intelligence, and bravery. Slowly, reluctantly, and after numerous violent confrontations between civil rights demonstrators and federal troops on one side and recalcitrant Southerners on the other, the South began to dismantle its segregation system, but only in the wake of additional incidents of fierce fighting, new Black acts of passive resistance and boycotts, court rulings, and, in some cases, the entry of federal troops to enforce these rulings. Accordingly, public facilities, such as bus stations, universities and other institutions of learning were desegregated in the 1960s.

The centerpiece of the civil rights movement were two pieces of legislation, finally enacted in the mid-1960s, after years of effort. **The Civil Rights Act of 1964** prohibited racial or religious discrimination in such public accommodations as restaurants and theatres. This Act also withheld federal funds from any public institution involved in school segregation, mandated the Attorney General to enforce this provision, created a Civil Rights Commission to investigate the causes of discrimination, and developed the Equal Employment Equal Opportunity Commission to discourage discrimination

in hiring and employment. In the following year, the **Voting Rights Act** became law. This legislation empowered federal examiners to halt deep-seated discriminatory practices in voter registration procedures in the South. In its wake, ambitious voter registration drives brought many Blacks to the polling stations for the first time. The net result of these two laws was a marked improvement in the lot of Black Southerners. Few had voted or held political office before the Voting Rights Act, but in subsequent decades Black officeholders by the hundreds, and even thousands were boldly changing the political landscape of the South.

The federal government intervened in other ways to assist **African-Americans** in their quest for a better life in America. In the 1960s, the implementation of President **Lyndon B. Johnson's Great Society**, featuring a War on Poverty program, led to a vast expansion of social welfare and other federal assistance programs. Black Americans benefited from this ambitious agenda, which provided new and enlarged programs of educational, medical, and legal assistance. For many African-Americans, this era marked their first opportunity to partake of the vast opportunities held out by the country for its citizens. Critics, however, believe that some Great Society programs created a dependency on government programs and undermined the Black family.

Affirmative action, a plan or program designed to remedy the effects of past discrimination in employment, education, or other activities and to prevent its recurrence, was of significant assistance here. Affirmative action usually involves, after careful study of the country's workplace and work-force, the establishment of goals and timetables to increase use of underrepresented classes of persons, and the establishment of administrative responsibility to implement the program. Since the 1960s, affirmative action has been required by law for all governmental agencies as well as for recipients of public funds. However, critics of affirmative action believe that it constitutes reverse discrimination against qualified individuals who now are excluded because of race, ethnicities, etc.

For many **African-Americans,** however, these changes and reforms were not enough. Many Blacks were impatient over the seemingly slow pace of racial progress and embittered at the cost of achieving it. Many remained alienated from American society, and embraced, instead, Black national groups and their strident doctrines. Despair, anger, and deprivation spilled over into ruinous big city rioting the second half of the 1960s. While many Black Americans have realized great progress in terms of education and careers, America remains a society significantly stratified and divided by race. Although it no longer is the America of Swedish sociologist, Gunnar Myrdal, who pronounced, in 1944, the nation's racial divide as "An American Dilemma," in a classic study by that name, it remains a country bedeviled by residential segregation, and disproportionate rates of poverty, crime, and despair among a significant part of its African-American population, whose numbers, by 2006 had reached thirty-three million or twelve percent of the population. Accordingly, race remains one of the nation's most intractable problems.

The civil rights revolution stirred many other minorities, from **gay-rights activists** or **feminists,** to reach for a more elevated status in American life. As the Civil Rights revolution entered one of its climactic phases in the early 1960s, women (not really a minority, since the country contains more women than men), so-long denied equal status in many critical areas of American life, were poised to enter another era of feminist activism.

The Women's Movement

The idea of sexual equity in politics, economics, law, and in other areas of American life reaches back to the beginnings of the country. At the time of the Declaration of Independence, Abigail Adams, the wife of John Adams, reminded the future president, apparently with little effect, that the lofty words and ideals of that great document must apply to women, too.

The great reform era of the 1830s and 1840s included a strong feminist movement because the status of women had changed little since the beginning of the republic. Women not only were denied the vote (suffrage), but those who married were, in the eyes of the law, totally subordinate to their husbands. If a marriage ended in divorce, the husband gained custody of the children. Unmarried women, moreover, were made wards of a male relative.

The highpoint of feminist activism in this era came in 1848 with a women's conference in Seneca Falls, New York, attended by one hundred women. The convention approved resolutions calling for educational and professional opportunities for women, along with greater control of their property, recognition of legal equality, and the right to vote. Yet victories were few in that era, and, on such major issues as the securing of suffrage for women, the day was still far off. Despite the discouraging pace of reform on issues affecting women, many of them were involved in the movement to abolish slav-

ery, which swept the north in the decades leading up to the Civil War.

In the decade following the Civil War, another era in the crusade for women's rights got underway, but it too yielded little in the way of change. In the long run, however, it would set the stage for passage of the **nineteenth amendment,** which, at long last, provided suffrage for women in 1920. In the short term, one of the most striking—and almost comical—manifestations of the movement was the occasion when Victoria Woodhull, the feminist publisher of a weekly magazine, divorced her husband and ran for president in 1872 as the candidate of the Equal Rights Party. In pressing her case for sexual freedom, Mrs. Woodhull announced, "I am a free lover. I have the inalienable, constitutional, and natural right to love whom I may, to love as long or as short a period as I can, to change that love every day if I please!"

At the dawn of the twentieth century, **Progressivism,** a broad based movement for reform, impacted nearly every area of American life. Accordingly, the status of women began to change rapidly. A spirited suffrage movement spread across the nation and led numerous states to grant women the vote in statewide elections by the time of World War I. By the time of the ratification of the nineteenth amendment, sixteen states had already granted the suffrage to women. With the electoral empowerment of women, a great new force of indeterminate power entered American politics. Soon the feminine vote was playing a pivotal role in elections, and women officeholders began to take their place with men in Congress and in other deliberative bodies.

Another major step in the rapidly changing status of women came with their massive involvement in the work force in World War II. The percentage of women employed outside of the home increased markedly in the immediate postwar years, while the number of divorced women and single mothers rose dramatically. In 1963, Betty Friedan published *The Feminine Mystique,* a clarion call for change, which critiqued a culture that "does not permit women to accept or gratify their basic need to grow and fulfill their potentialities as human beings."

The reception accorded this book energized the feminist movement, leading to the **Equal Pay Act** passed in the same year of its publication, as well as the addition of gender to the forms of discrimination outlawed by the Civil Rights Act of 1964. In 1966, a group of women (along with two men) founded the National Organization for Women (NOW) to campaign for women's rights. In 1967, NOW persuaded President Johnson that women should be added to the list of groups, which included

Blacks, Hispanics, and other minorities covered by federal affirmative action programs. In the same year, NOW members agreed to a "Bill of Rights" calling for maternity leave for working mothers, federally supported day-care facilities, childcare tax deductions, and equal education and job training. They were, however, divided over the issue of an **Equal Rights Amendment** (ERA) to the Constitution. But the movement for an amendment that held that "Equality of rights under the law shall not be denied or abridged by the United States or any State on account of sex," grew anyhow.

In 1972, the Congress passed the proposed Equal Rights Amendment. Soon after this action, a large number of states approved it, and its ratification seemed inevitable. But the rise of stong, vocal conservative opposition, both male and female, to the movement, who saw the ERA as either unnecessary or as morally or constitutionally dangerous, as well as a group of women who wished to use the political system itself rather than a constitutional amendment to eliminate the most egregious inequities between the genders, led ultimately to the failure of the amendment to gain ratification.

Despite the failure of the Equal Rights Amendment, women today are better off politically, professionally, legally, and in many other ways than they were just one generation earlier. They are making great inroads into such professions are medicine and law, where just one generation earlier they had little representation. Their movement has made the country more sensitive to the role and place of women in society. No longer are many of the slang terms for women acceptable; moreover, only a foolish man today would exhibit, at least outwardly, a patronizing attitude toward women, an attitude especially commonplace in the workplace, just one generation earlier. Women, however, still suffer from salary discrimination, while corporate America has been notoriously slow to open up to them senior positions. Therefore, much remains to be accomplished.

Native Americans

When the Spanish arrived in the "New World," an estimated ten million native peoples, called "Indians" by Christopher Columbus and by the Europeans who followed, resided in North America. European governments and settlers pursuing opportunity in the New World practiced an unofficial policy of conquest toward the native populations as they moved into and settled their ancestral lands. Armed with superior weaponry, and assisted inadvertently by the spread of diseases for which the Indians possessed no immunity, this campaign succeeded with tragic results for the Indians who saw their ranks decimated and their lands lost in many parts of North America to the Spanish, French, and English, among others.

Since its beginnings as a country, the United States has pursued an inconsistent policy in its relations with the Indians, one that has been consistently deleterious to the latter. Until recent times, government policy toward the Indian nations living within the borders of the United States has treated them, in order, as foreign governments; placed them on reservations; attempted to assimilate them into the mainstream of American society; and relocated them to cities. In the last generation, the United States has pursued a policy of self-determination, or a "hands off" policy toward the Indians, partly because **Native Americans** have developed a new cohesiveness and pride in their heritage.

As a manifestation of this growing pride, a new militancy emerged by the beginning of the 1970s, as seen in the organization of the American Indian Movement (AIM), which has participated in a series of highly visible takeovers of public lands and properties in several parts of the country. The National Congress of American Indians, the National Tribal Chairmen's Association, and Americans for Indian Opportunity are other Native American groups active in helping their people regain control of their land, mineral, and other natural resources.

Today, Native Americans are members of more than 400 tribes, representing nearly 2.5 million Indians. Although the great majority reside in American cities, many continue to reside on the nearly 3,300 tribal reservations in the country. Indians maintain a unique niche because they possess their own tribal governments, which serve as recognized political units of government, thereby providing their subjects with dual citizenship in the United States—citizenship as Americans, as well as in the tribe to which they belong. Further, they are recipients of dual entitlements, meaning that they are entitled not only to the services and privileges that other American citizens enjoy, but they also receive special consideration as to health, education, and other needs owing to their heritage as Indians.

Paralleling the rise in Indian pride and awareness in recent decades has been their remarkable progress in terms of education and professional advancement. Yet Native Americans remain far behind white America in many leading determinants of educational and financial well-being. The time is still in the future when these descendants of the original Americans will have finally overcome centuries of persecution and discrimination by those who came later to America.

Asian-Americans

Asian-Americans represent another rapidly growing segment of the population of the United States. By 2006, more than 12 million Asian and Pacific Islanders lived in the United States. While Asian-Americans come from many areas of the world's largest continent, the majority of them have emigrated from southeast Asia and the Pacific Ocean region. Many have fled political upheaval and repressive regimes. Most live in large cities; many have experienced great success as small businessmen. They are noted for their industriousness and eagerness to succeed in an environment that offers opportunities that were nonexistent in their original homes.

Asian-Americans tend to live together in their own neighborhoods, thus giving rise to Little Seouls, Tokyos, and, of course, Chinatowns. The family remains a strong force among Asian-Americans, and education is the way up for the sons and daughters of immigrants. The education success stories of this group are legion, especially so in California where Asian-Americans comprise a significant percentage of the student enrollment in many universities and colleges. Most notable here have been Koreans, Chinese, Japanese, and Vietnamese.

Hispanic Americans

Hispanic Americans, defined here as those with Spanish-speaking or Spanish-surnamed backgrounds, now number nearly 44 million, including more than three million persons living in Puerto Rico, making the United States the third largest Spanish-speaking nation in the Western Hemisphere. Recent U.S. Census reports indicate that **Hispanics** are the fastest growing component of the population, and will represent, by the year 2050, America's largest minority group. Yet it is far from accurate to group all persons of Spanish speaking heritage together because of the sharp differences between them.

Mexican Americans

The three largest groups nationally are Mexicans, Puerto Ricans, and Cubans. Each is sharply distinctive from the others. Most Mexicans have migrated to the United States for economic reasons, Moving primarily to the border states of California and Texas, which, along with New Mexico and Arizona, represent areas that were once part of Mexico, and, along with Colorado, represent the center of the Mexican-American population. About sixty percent of Hispanic Americans have Mexican backgrounds. Many of today's Mexican-Americans trace their roots to forebears who came to Mexico, the former capital of Spain's New World empire in the sixteenth and seventeenth centuries. Many lived in the territories which the United States took from Mexico in the 1840s. In the early 1900s, the first substantial wave of Mexican immigrants entered the United States. Since the 1950s, a steady wave of Mexicans have migrated to this country. In recent years, increasing numbers of illegal immigrants from Mexico have been pouring over the border in southern California and Texas, leading to a broad-based movement to restrict benefits to Mexican-Americans, and even, in some case, to those who came legally, living in California and elsewhere in the country.

In many ways, Mexican-Americans have struggled economically and educationally, most notably as low-paid itinerant farm workers, but also as increasing numbers of Mexicans crowded in barrios districts of neighborhoods of cities, in Los Angeles and in many other great American cities. Mexican-Americans, or "chicanos," as many of them were calling themselves by the 1960s and 1970s, have attempted, with some success, to rectify this situation through different pressure groups, reflecting the rise, in recent decades, of a more aggressive movement amid enhanced ethnic pride. In the future, Mexican-Americans will be called on to maintain unity and continue to defend themselves in response to a growing national xenophobia, which has targeted them perhaps as much as any other immigrant group.

Puerto Ricans

Puerto Rico, acquired from Spain by the United States as a result of the Spanish-American War, which was fought in 1898 over the issue of Cuban independence, is a commonwealth, or self-governing territory, of this country. Puerto Ricans are citizens of the United States, and they are represented in the United States House of Representatives by a nonvoting resident commissioner. The numbers of Puerto Ricans migrating to the mainland United States, primarily in quest of jobs, has increased dramatically since the 1950s. While New York has traditionally welcomed the largest number of Puerto Ricans, many other large American cities, including Miami, with its mosaic of Spanish-speaking groups, have also become large centers of a Puerto Rican population.

Many Puerto Ricans are living in poverty since they lack the educational and professional skills necessary for success in this complex society. However, it is encouraging to note that increasing numbers of Puerto Ricans are receiving college education, moving into high level jobs, and becoming over more involved at every level of the political process.

Cuban Americans

The greatest success story among Spanish-speaking Americans has been that of Cuban-Americans. Owing to Cuba's political tumult, small groups of Cubans have fled one regime or another for exile in New York City, Key West, Tampa, and Miami in the decades and years preceding the **Fidel Castro** takeover in 1959. The Castro revolution and the transformation of Cuba into a Marxist state has led to an influx of more than one million Cubans, representing nearly ten percent of that Island's present population, to the United States. Nearly 800,000 Cubans live in Miami and in other parts of Miami-Dade County, while significantly smaller numbers reside in nearby Broward County, New Jersey, and New York City. Marked by a powerful work ethic, a strong entrepreneurial background, at least on the part of the early waves of refugees, a shared sense of responsibility, family pride and affection, and the beneficiaries of invaluable assistance from the government of the United States (which, in the first decades of exile, showcased these refugees from Castro's Cuba as shining examples of the failure of Communism and, by contrast, the success of the American way of life), Cuban-Americans have quickly become an important part of the economic, cultural, and political life of their adopted home. Their economic accomplishments in such a relatively brief period of time have set them apart from all other immigrant groups in American history. Still, they have held on to the culture and memories of the Old Country as tightly as anyone before them.

Miami and Miami-Dade County are unlike any other communities in the country owing to their strong Hispanic majorities, consisting primarily of Cubans but also of Nicaraguans, Puerto Ricans, Hondurans, Columbians, Venezuelans, Brazilians and others who have arrived relatively recently, and yet, in the case of the Cubans, already dominate many aspects of community life. Many of American's great cities are in the process of being transformed in a manner somewhat similar to that of Greater Miami. As immigrants pour into these cities from all over the globe in pursuit of the American Dream, they are transforming them into great mosaics of races and nationalities. Like those who have come before, these new arrivals, whether they are Russians, Gambians, Salvadoreans, or Haitians, will eventually take their place in the country's political system. In the process, they will change, broaden, and strengthen that system, which will be the better for it.

Selected Bibliography

Taylor Branch, (1989) *Parting The Waters: America in the Age of Martin Luther King.* New York: Simon and Schuster.

John Hope Franklin, (1974) *From Slavery to Freedom.* New York: Knopf.

J. Freeman, (1975) *The Politics of Women's Liberation.* New York: Longmans.

Betty Friedan, (1996) *The Feminine Mystique,* New York: W. W. Norton and Company.

Richard Hofstadter, (1969) *The Idea of a Party System: The Rise of Legitimate Opposition in the United States,* 1780–1840, Berkeley, CA.; University of California Press.

Roger Nichols, (1986) *The American Indian: Past and Present,* New York: The McGraw-Hill Companies.

James Olsen and Raymond Wilson, (1984) *Native Americans in the Twentieth Century,* Champaign, Ill: University of Illinois Press.

Alejandro Portes and Alex Stepik, (1993) *Miami: City on the Edge,* Berkeley, CA: University of California Press.

James Roger Sharp, (1993) *American Politics in the Early Republic,* New Haven, CT: Yale University Press.

Joel L. Silbey, (1994) *The American Political Nation, 1838–1893,* Stanford, CA: Stanford University Press.

Ronald Taylor, (1975) *Chavez and the Farm Workers.*

Arnulfo Trejo, Ed. (1979), *The Chicanos: As We See Ourselves,* Tucson, AZ: University of Arizona.

C. Vann Woodward, (1994) *The Strange Career of Jim Crow.* New York: Oxford University Press.

CHAPTER TEN

Global Prosperity and Poverty

Germán Muñoz

T he world is politically complex and fragmented. There are 192 countries represented at the **United Nations** and 195 in the world. In addition, many of these have numerous nationalist groups which would like to secede and create their own states. As a result, political conflicts are now taking place in Russia, in the former Yugoslavia, India, Northern Ireland, Somalia, South Africa, Sudan, Ethiopia and in other states. **New countries will surely be created while others disappear. This is an ongoing process in history.** Large, centralized states are created from ethnic diversity only to disintegrate later back to their components. Viewing this complexity and trying to understand it, scholars, journalists and others have tried to classify countries according to some measurable standards.

One popular classification of states is according their economic organization and economic output per person. At the top are the rich, **industrial developed countries** with a large industrial base and income over $20,000 per capita. Sometimes, they are also called the North since most of them, with the exception of Australia, Japan and New Zealand, are in the Northern hemisphere. They include the United States, Germany, Canada, France, Britain and others. Then come the **high-income oil exporting countries** which have significant revenues per capita because of their energy exports but lack a sophisticated industrial base. They include Kuwait and Saudi Arabia, among others. The **tran-** sitional countries are those which used to be communist during the Cold War but which are now trying to develop both democracy and capitalism. These include Hungary, Poland, the Czech Republic, and Slovenia. Next are the **poor, developing countries** which are the majority of states of the world, with a per capita income ranging from $300 to $2,000 per year. These countries can be subdivided into the middle-income and low-income economies. Sometimes they are collectively called the **South,** since most of them are in the Southern hemisphere. Finally, there are the **communist countries,** whose governments have totalitarian control over their economies. China, Cuba, and North Korea are examples.

A second type of classification for the countries of the world was used frequently during the Cold War. Countries were placed either in the First World, or the Second World, or the Third World. The **First World,** included the capitalist, industrial democracies of the West such as Britain, France, and the United States. The **Second World** consisted of such communist countries as Czechoslovakia, Poland and Russia. The **Third World** included the poor countries of the world, and particularly those state coming out of the European empires in Africa and Asia, which were originally seen as a third bloc of countries between the First and Second worlds.

Later, this classification was modified. The Third World was subdivided into Third, Fourth and Fifth Worlds. The

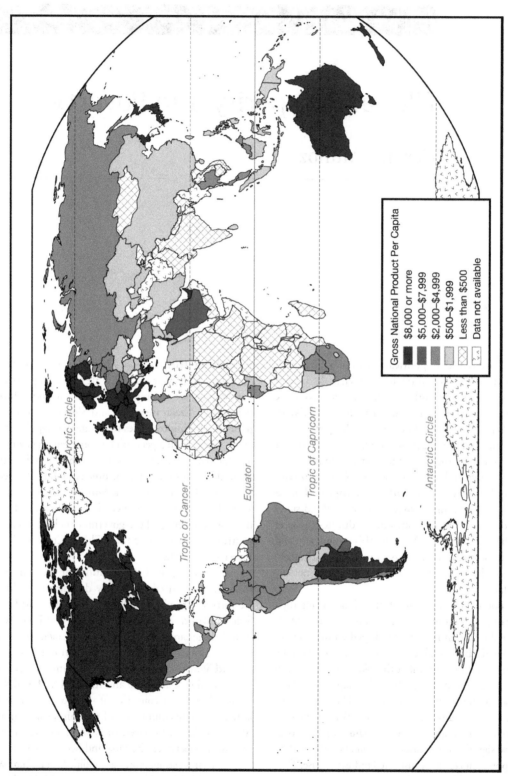

Rich Nations vs Poor Nations

Courtesy of maps.com.

Third World includes those poor countries which have great potential to develop such as Argentina, Brazil, Chile, South Korea, Nigeria, India, and others. These states have developed infrastructures, skilled populations, and other resources to industrialize. Their per capita income could range between $1,000 and $6,000. The Fourth World consists of those countries which have some potential to develop such as Bolivia, Zaire, Egypt, Kenya, and others. Their per capita income ranges from $500 to $1,000. The Fifth World includes those countries which have little or no potential to develop such as Somalia, Niger, Bangladesh, Afghanistan, Haiti, and others. Their per capita incomes are below $500.

In addition to the economic and to the Cold War era models of categorizing countries, there are others. One alternative method is by region: African, Asian, Eastern European, European, Latin American, and North American. Since geographically grouped countries often share a cultural heritage and common physical demographic characteristics, they also often face similar problems. What is important is that no grouping works perfectly. They are all intellectual constructs which simplify what are in reality very complex matters.

The Developed World

The developed rich world, also referred to as the First World usually includes the advanced industrialized democracies: the United States, Germany, Canada, France, Great Britain, Australia, and several other Western countries. These countries are also referred to as the **West** since they are part of Western civilization, or as the **North** since most of them are in Northern Europe or North America. Japan is often included, although it is not actually a Western country. Since 1945, Japan has also developed some democratic institutions, has reached significant industrial growth, and has internalized some Western attitudes. Other countries of Asia such as the Republic of South Korea and Singapore could soon join this category. These countries of the developed world all have a high standard of living.

The states of the First World, Britain, the Netherlands, Belgium, France, other European states, and later the United States, were the first to move from mass poverty to wealth. This was a move away from death, famine, hunger, and diseases. The transition to wealth is also a move towards literacy, education, and a wider variety of experience, and therefore, toward greater possibility of privacy, individual choice, and democracy for the vast majority of people. Other civilizations like China, India, and Persia might have had great wealth in

ancient times, but the developed world is the first region to extend its wealth beyond its leaders and toward the general population. Later, the success of Europe expanded beyond the continent to the United States, Canada, Australia, New Zealand, and other countries.

The Causes of Prosperity

It took Europe centuries to rise form the depths of physical disaster following the tumultuous centuries from the 400s through the 800s. The first thing that had to occur to lift itself for material improvement was political order so that there could be protection of the merchants, a revival of trade, a return of urbanization or city living, and an increase in the number and quality of universities. This political stability began in the 900s, primarily in the areas controlled by the **Anglo-Saxons** of England, by the **Franks** of France, and by Italians in their city-states. **Political stability stimulated the rise of a merchant class grown wealthy from its international trade in profitable luxury goods.**

This merchant class, in turn, helped bring about a cultural change which dramatically transformed Southern and West-central Europe and gave it a material boost. This revolution in attitudes is known as the Renaissance, whose philosophy of Humanism in the 1300s and 1400s promoted such secular values as the pursuit of power, wealth, status, and individualism in the search for temporal rather than other-worldly values. **The merchant class' obsession with finding ways to maximize profits created the foundations of modern capitalism, and the rationale for the European voyages of discovery.** Both would motivate Europeans to travel worldwide in search of higher returns on their investments. Their profits from silver, gold, sugar, tobacco, rum, and the slave trade would be reinvested in Europe and further accelerate its growth. The loss of human lives in wars, plagues, and social conflicts, reduced the European population in the 1400s. This increased the value of each peasant and worker and many began to insist on being paid with money. **The result was a money economy in Europe which also stimulated agriculture, some manufacturing, and commerce. This monetization created even more demand for the goods of the traders.**

All these events, in addition to the growing technical and inventing skills of the Germanic people, the higher literacy promoted by the invention of the printing press, the constant wars in the continent which enhanced the creation of new weapons and more sophisticated tools, led to increases in productivity in all economic areas. One result was what it now called the

European agricultural and industrial revolutions of the 1600s and 1700s, respectively, which began to slowly raise more people above starvation and an early death. The success of the rising merchant class increased their desire for political power and the middle class began in the 1600s to challenge the nobility and the monarchs throughout Europe, but their first successes were in England. Desire for economic and political liberty gave rise to the movement which later in the 1820s became known as **Liberalism.** It began with aristocratic roots, but would gradually spread to the middle and lower classes. Liberalism is a political view that seeks to change the political, economic, or social status quo to foster the development and well-being of the individual. It seeks to restrain the power of any institution which can undermine individual political and economic liberty. The active participation of larger groups of people in the political and economic processes of Europe increased their purchasing power to further stimulate the European economy.

European society created numerous innovations to support business activity, banking and accounting techniques, among others. This also included a **commercial morality** based on the ethics of punctuality, frugality, trust, industry, diligence, and the sanctification of work, that is, the virtue of work. **All of these cultural innovations and attitudes encouraged savings, investments, profit, respect for private property, and experimentation by entrepreneurs in the search for cheaper and better products.** The governments of Great Britain, Holland, France and other enterprising states encouraged the profit-making activities of the merchants. **There was no persecution of the business class as a target group, or confiscation of their property and capital.** Europe became a truly commercial civilization, something which had not been the case during the Roman and the Medieval periods. Some governments were more mercantilistic than others, that is, more involved in regulating economic activity. Yet, with some exceptions, they did stimulate investments.

A second "industrial revolution" occurred in Europe between 1880 and 1914. While much of the earlier economic development of the West had been due to political stability, the growth of trade, technological ingenuity, new forms of social organization, and increasing liberalization, the new industrial expansion was fueled by the application of pure science and industrial technology to economic production. Laboratories were organized to deepen theoretical knowledge and scientific research. Another major innovation was the **corporation** which allowed larger amounts of capital to be obtained and invested with a minimum of risk to the investor's personal property. Corporations of different sizes were developed to meet different needs. These were some of the conditions and events which fueled the expansion of the West.

One could say that Europe became modernized. In fact, this process of modernization is sometimes referred to as Westernization. **Modernization refers to the socio-economic, political, and cultural changes which transform traditional societies into more productive, complex, economically specialized and socially stratified systems.** Modernization includes several changes: the economic system becomes more specialized as individuals concentrate on performing only one or two economic tasks, and the accumulation of profit becomes the major goal of entrepreneurs; societies develop more distinct social classes with clear positions and roles; political power becomes more stratified and hierarchical; science and technology achieve greater significance; public education competes with religious schools; and public administration grows as professional bureaucrats or civil servants become more involved in the day-to-day operation of government. The beginnings of modernization were in Western Europe, but its reach is global and undermines traditional societies.

Several modern theories provide alternative explanations of how the West grew rich. First, that it was due to **science** and innovation. Unfortunately, this does not explain why China and the Hellenistic world, for example, did not profit from their technological and scientific genius. Second, that it was due to the availability of **natural resources** in Europe. However, this does not explain why countries such as Japan, Switzerland, and Holland have grown prosperous without them. Also, if natural resources are so important, why did the natives in America, Asia, and Africa not turn their plentiful natural resources into wealth? Third, that it was due to **economic greed.** This does not explain why all prior civilizations which have also exhibited greed failed to prosper as much as the West. Fourth, that Western prosperity was due to **exploitation** of the workers. Exploitation did take place, but this does not explain why the workers in the capitalist West have the world's highest wages. Besides, exploitation is probably a universal condition, and yet not every region profits from it. Fifth, that it was due to **slavery.** It is true that significant amounts of profits generated from the Atlantic Slave Trade were invested in European industry, but this argument does not explain why other civilizations which also had slavery did not prosper economically. The Muslims of

North Africa were involved in the African slave trade long before the Europeans, but this practice did not generate prosperity for them. Also, in Europe slaves were not active in trade and industry, the two main wealth-creating sectors.

The sixth alternative explanation for the economic success of the First World is that of **colonialism or imperialism,** which argues that the West grew rich by exploiting its colonies. Imperialism is a superior-inferior relationship in which an area and its people have been subordinated to the will of a foreign state or power. This argument was first made popular by John Hobson and by Vladimir Ilyich **Lenin.** The thesis has several difficulties. Colonization benefited only some people in Europe, while the governments had to pay high administrative and military costs for the empire. Interestingly, some of the richest countries presently were once colonies themselves: the United States, Canada, Australia, New Zealand, Hong Kong and Singapore, among others. They did not need to be imperialistic to grow wealthy.

In addition, Portugal and Spain were the first European empires and they never really became prosperous. In fact, it could be argued that their empires actually made them poor instead. On the other hand, Switzerland and the Scandinavian countries had no empire but grew rich. It would seem that for the West to have been able to conquer close to eighty percent of the world's land by 1914, it must have had sufficient power for the conquest beforehand. In turn, the people conquered must have had serious internal deficiencies before they came in contact with the West. **Thus, it could be reasoned that imperialism was not so much a cause of Western prosperity as it was a result of it, even though imperialism did provide economic benefits to those states already productive and able to take advantage of commercial opportunities.**

Characteristics of the More Developed World

When **developed countries** are examined and contrasted with developing ones, they exemplify various common characteristics: high per capita Gross Domestic Product and energy use; emphasis on secondary (industrial) and tertiary (services) occupations rather than on primary occupations (agriculture and mining); longer life expectancy and lower infant mortality rate (deaths per one thousand live births in the first year of life); better and more abundant food supply; low rate of population growth; heavy dependence on minerals; favorable trade balance with the developing world, except in oil; high personal and corporate income which can be invested; materialist commitment to success as measured largely by wealth; a Judeo-Christian ethic (except Japan), although it is declining rapidly as a result of the increasing materialism of Western society; and an educated and mobile urban population which can be receptive to change and to the use of new technologies. **In addition, rich countries have a widespread use of technology which increases industrial and labor productivity and allows improvement in the infrastructure: roads, communications, energy, water supply, sewage disposal, credit institutions, schools, housing and medial services.** Moreover, they attach great importance to education, particularly that geared toward economic advancement: engineering, economics, agronomy, biology and chemistry.

The Transitional Countries (The Second World)

The Second World was originally a term used to describe the Soviet Union, Mongolia, Communist countries in Eastern Europe, and sometimes the pro-Soviet allies in the Third World. Russia became the first Communist state on October 25, 1917. On July 10, 1921, **Mongolia,** with Russian support, freed itself from China and became the world's second Communist state. **Later, in December 1922, the Russian Republic, Byelorussia, Transcaucasia, and the Ukraine formed the Union of Soviet Socialist Republics (USSR), or Soviet Union.** Transcaucasia later split into separate republics: Armenia, Azerbaijan and Georgia. Other territories were later incorporated by the USSR: Estonia, Kazakhstan, Kyrgyzstan, Latvia, Lithuania, Moldavia, Tajikistan, Turkmenistan, and Uzbekistan. **Fifteen republics made up the Soviet Union after the Second World War.** After 1945, the Soviet Union also established political, economic and military control over most of East-Central Europe.

However, the countries of East-Central Europe **(Poland, Czechoslovakia, Albania, Romania, Yugoslavia and Bulgaria) as well as East Germany in Central Europe began to move away from communism in 1989, and to demand that Soviet troops leave their region.** Furthermore, this anti-Communist and anti-Soviet fervor later spread to the Soviet Union itself. **The Soviet Union ceased to exist on December 21, 1991, and the fifteen Republics sought independence.** The Baltic Republics of Lithuania, Estonia and Latvia have become independent republics. The Ukraine voted for independence on December 2, 1991. Moldavia wants to join with Romania but Russia is not allowing it. The Russian Republic itself has rejected communism. In fact, many autonomous regions within the Russian republic itself also want their independence. Georgia refused to participate in Mikhail Gorbachev's Independent Sovereign Republics.

Instead, some eleven of the former republics created a loose federation or **Commonwealth of Independent States.** Communism is in retreat worldwide even though some former communists have been voted back in power as socialists in various states of East-Central Europe. China, North Korea, Vietnam, and Cuba are major states under communist control.

Another crack in the Communist world appeared in Yugoslavia in 1991 when Croatia and Slovenia abandoned the union with communist Serbia. In 1992, Bosnia and Herzegovina, another province of the former Yugoslavia began to seek independence from Serbia. The independence of Bosnia has resulted in a bloody civil war among Croats, Muslims, and Serbians living in Bosnia. The fighting escalated in 1995 into the worst killing in Europe since World War II. Also in 1992, the Slovaks of Czechoslovakia decided to separate themselves from the Czechs and create a separate state. This gave rise to the Czech Republic and to Slovakia. **Nationalism seems to have replaced communism as the major organizing and integrating force in the region.**

Communist-bloc countries of the former "Second" World are making a transition to more open, democratic and capitalist societies. These countries had several common characteristics. The levels of investment and production were decided by the government; prices were set by the state bureaucrats and did not reflect the real interaction between consumer demand and the supply of goods. Capital and natural resources were owned by the government. Currencies could not be converted. Persistent budget deficits were needed to pay the large losses of state enterprises which gave food and housing subsidies. The lack of economic incentives for people to produce goods led to long lines of people waiting to buy consumer items. Government emphasis on military and industrial goods for defense also used many resources which were then not available for consumer use. As a result, governments rationed consumption. Multilateral trade with other countries was difficult because consumers could not convert currencies and get foreign exchange. The **Council for Mutual Economic Assistance (COMECON),** which regulated trade among

Communist countries, prevented them from buying goods from low-cost countries outside the COMECON bloc and isolation led to lack of competition and innovation. Human rights violations were common. Political freedoms were scarce.

All these factors inhibit a smooth transition to a market economy where prices for goods fluctuate freely based on the demand for and supply of goods, and where citizens can own property. **These countries have problems attracting foreign capital because of high inflation, low quality products, and the existence of unstable legal systems to protect foreign investment.** In general, these transitional economies seem to go through certain phases. In Phase One, which may last one to five years, they eliminate state ownership, price controls and subsidies. In Phase Two, which may last three to ten years, there is the creation of modern banking system and privatization of small and mid-size companies. In Phase Three, there is large-scale privatization and the creation of competitive companies and an entrepreneur mentality.

What is needed to make a successful transition from a Communist, command economy to a free-market economy? **Privatization, the converting of government-owned business enterprises into competitive privately owned companies and corporations, is not enough.** Other conditions must be met: austere fiscal policies to restrain inflation and protect people who are dependent on fixed wages and salaries; income subsidies to help those hurt by the transition like the unemployed, state employees, welfare recipients, and farmers; companies able to compete, to be efficient so not to pass their high cost to consumers; reduction in government subsidies so that more resources can go to areas of **comparative advantage;** a market system allowed to work even if it leads to higher unemployment and inflation in the short run; meaningful privatization of old, large monopolistic state enterprises; full currency convertibility so that countries can trade freely in the international market; and increased productivity by shifting resources to high efficient sectors.

Developing Countries (The Third World)

The classification "Third World" became a residual classification for countries which were not in the First World or Second World, or which were neutral in the Cold War. As a result, the concept has always lacked precision.

In 1919, The **League of Nations** became the first general international organization. It urged the self-determination (independence) of the people or nations which were part of the European empires of the 1800s and 1900s, primarily the German, the Austro-Hungarian and the Ottoman empires. The **United Nations,** created in 1945, also promoted this process of decolonization or independence which helped create the countries that today make up the poor world.

The concept of the "Third World" developed after the **Bandung Conference of Colored Peoples** in 1955, a conference greatly influenced by Communist China after it began feuding with Russia (the Sino-Soviet split). **Its main idea was that a third power bloc had to be created that would be distinct from the capitalist, industrial world (First World) and the Communist, industrial world (Second World).** The French economist Alfred Sauvy popularized the term "Third World" to refer to these countries. The Bandung Conference adopted the Chinese-sponsored Five Principles of Coexistence: mutual respect for territorial integrity and sovereignty; non-aggression; non-interference in the internal affairs of other countries; equality and mutual benefit; and peaceful coexistence. The fact that Communist China itself violated some of these same principles did not disturb many of the conference's participants. **"Third World" was also used in the West to refer to countries receiving foreign aid.**

In 1965, the leaders of Indonesia, Egypt and Yugoslavia, Sukarno, Nasser, and Tito, respectively, created the **Non-Aligned Movement,** made up of twenty-five countries which tried to pursue a political line independent of the United States and the Soviet Union. However, gradually some became pro-American and others pro-Soviet. Only a few were truly non-aligned. Today, there are over one hundred countries and organizations in the movement. Their principal ideology is **nationalism.** The Non-Aligned Movement began to crack after 1975 when pro-Soviet countries such as North Korea, North Vietnam, and Cuba began to pressure the movement to take a position more favorable to the Soviet Union. In fact, Cuba itself, a Soviet satellite then, became the head of the non-aligned states for a brief period in the 1980s.

The Group of 77

Many of the poor countries have turned to the General Assembly of the United Nations and to **international governmental organizations** (IGOs), to make their demands for economic assistance. **The Group of 77** (now with over 122 states), is very active in the United Nations. **Important IGOs are the Organization of African Unity, the Association of Southeast Asian Nations, the Arab League, the Caribbean Common Market, the Latin American Integration Association, and the Economic Community of West African States.**

The Group of 77, created in 1964, wanted to create a **New International Economic Order (NIEO).** To accomplish this order, the leaders of these countries urged various policies: increase in the economic assistance of the rich world to the poor world to 0.7% of their GNP; tariff reduction and quota increases for imports from the developing countries; increased Third World role in the financial decisions of international economic organizations; less intrusive First-World demands for financial information from poor countries; massive redistribution of the international credit system in favor of the less-developed states; and technical and financial assistance for processing facilities, transportation, and distribution systems under the control of developing governments, corporations and individuals.

In the 1950s and 1960s, the Group of 77 was concerned with political issues, particularly those involved with sovereignty matters and the Cold War (East-West conflict). However, in the 1970s, this organization was more interested with issues of economic development (North-South conflict). They wanted the rich countries of the North to provide more economic assistance such as foreign aid to the poor countries of the South. **In the 1990s, the Group of 77 became concerned with attracting capital investment from the developed world and with expanding its exports to the rich countries.**

Close to 60% of the world's population has income at or below subsistence. **While they are similar in that they have the majority of their population in poverty, and receive foreign aid, developing countries have many religious, racial, ethnic, linguistic, ideological, political, social, and economic differences.** Moreover, although they are all poor, developing countries have different degrees of poverty, ranging from a per capita income of $100 per year to over $25,000. In addition, poor countries often have in their midst very wealthy communities. On the other hand, developed countries often have pockets of great poverty. **For these reasons, scholars have often divided the Third World into oil-exporting developing countries, advanced countries, middle-income developing countries, and low-income developing countries.**

Characteristics of the Developing World

The countries of the less developed or poor world have several common characteristics: low per capita GDP and energy use; high proportion of the labor force in primary pursuits (agriculture and mining); comparatively short life span; high infant mortality rates; a diet often deficient in quantity and/or quality; a high rate of the population younger than fifteen years of age and not involved in direct economic activities; **exclusion of women from many advanced economic, educational, and political activities;** low literacy rate, depriving many of the chance to be more productive and healthy; a culture generally resistant to change; **multiculturalism,** which often leads to violence among competing and culturally diverse groups; a dual economy with some people organized for the domestic market and others selling for the external market (exports); reliance on flow resources (renewable), principally those of agriculture; reliance on the export of cheaper natural resources (minerals), but dependence on the import of more expensive finished goods made with their resources; high unemployment; and poverty.

The Causes of Poverty

Many explanations have been given for poverty. There does not seem to be just one cause. Perhaps there are several factors which interact to produce economic backwardness. These could actually vary from country to country or even from region to region within a particular state. It is unwise to assume that world poverty can be reduced to just one type of explanation.

Some factors might exist within the poverty-stricken region such as the culture of its people, the geography which involves them, the corruption of their leaders the violence of the population, and the lack of motivation and education of its individuals. Yet, other causes of poverty could be external. Imperialism, military conquest, unstable international market forces and the type of foreign aid which entrenches dictators and their supporters could also have an impact.

The Culture

Those cultures which affirm that the human mind cannot understand reality or that there is no such thing as reality but that it is an illusion tend to fall behind technologically and scientifically. They do not spend significant effort in the development of scientific thinking, experimentation, observation and generalization, all of which are essential ingredients of the West's economic development. **A culture whose major values are introspection, asceticism, detachment from the world and collectivism might not be as economically successful as one which values more worldly pursuits, sensuality, social activism, materialism and individualism.** The first culture might have much that is good in itself but probably will not excel economically as much as the second one. This is the case with some traditional societies found in Asia and in Africa. Thus, the culture or a people, its metaphysical assumptions and beliefs, its religion, literacy and vision of reality can be important factors behind its economic success.

Physical Geography

Physical geography includes a region's climate, topography, vegetation, soils, water resources, and minerals. These are all significant variables in a society's struggle for survival. Tropical climates might be too tough on top-soils, crops, and on human health. The heat, humidity, and illnesses (malaria, yellow fever, etc.) associated with the tropics, might inhibit human enterprise and food production. Tropical soils are often leached of their humus by excessive rainfall. This is the case in the Amazon Basin, West Africa, Equatorial Africa, and in Southeast Asia. As a result, commercial and subsistence agriculture is made difficult. Not enough wheat, corn or barley can be grown to support a large population. Then, scarce revenues have to be used importing food from other regions. Interestingly, most of the economically prosperous nations are in the temperate zones, and most of the poor ones are in or near the tropics.

On the other hand, there are many countries in desert and steppe climates which do not get enough rainfall. This situation is common is Southwest Asia and parts of Africa. However, technological developments, an enterprising people, and a good legal framework could promote some prosperity even in those hard climates, as has happened, for example, in Israel. **Climate is just one factor among many others in the existence of poverty.**

The way mountain landforms are placed can also have significant results on specific regions. In the Southwest of the United States, the north-to-south layout of the Rocky Mountains prevents adequate precipitation from falling on the eastern side of the mountains (the rain shadow effect), creating deserts. The Rocky Mountains block the westerly humid air coming from the Pacific Ocean. However, the east-to-west layout of the mountains of Western Europe allows countries like France, The Netherlands, Belgium, Germany, and others to benefit from a mild and humid climate which permits abundant agriculture. The mountain formations permit the westerly moist and mild air mass coming from the Atlantic Ocean. The same impact of landforms is seen on the "Third World." Much of the dryness of the Sahara comes from the position of the Atlas Mountains of Northwest Africa. They block the moist air coming from the Atlantic Ocean. The Andes Mountains of South America create serious communication and transportation problems which prevent the material exploitation of the region. In addition, some areas benefit from abundant mineral deposits. Others do not. There is a degree of geographical "bad luck" in the poverty of some countries.

Statism and Greed

Developing countries tend to have authoritarian governments which often inhibit economic competition, experimentation, liberty, and market forces. **Statism, or an excessive reliance on government action to solve problems or to regulate the economy, encourages cronysm, paternalism, nepotism, corruption, caudillismo, and other conditions which lead to social unrest and economic decline. Cronyism** is the practice by a high government official of appointing his close friends to governmental posts regardless of their merit or experience. **Paternalism** is the principle or practice of managing the affairs of a country or group of employees as a "father" manages the affairs of children. People might not be allowed to vote, to organize an opposition, or to move about freely in the territory. **Nepotism** is the granting of political favors to relatives, often in the form of appointment to office. **Caudillismo** is the principle of personal or "boss-type" political rule where personal ties among the rulers serve as a substitute for the formal institutions of government from the local to the national level.

Many of the people who control these governments are often able to steal the financial assets of the country. Even more damaging is that the leaders of the country and their government officials often will not allow other residents in their countries to prosper or maximize their wealth if they believe such economic progress could threaten their own political power. **Statism would not be as economically counter-productive if the state would judiciously promote savings, capital investment, private enterprise, and the health and education of the population.**

The arbitrariness and injustices of the powerful frequently lead many of the most educated and productive citizens to flee their countries for a safer and richer place in the developed world. This is why immigration can be so beneficial to the rich countries. This migration constitutes, in some cases a devastating "**brain drain.**" The migration is even worse if in addition to the professional class, the merchants and the business classes also emigrate, creating a "**capital drain,**" for it is the entrepreneurial groups which usually contribute the most to the development of a country. Greed, wanting more than one needs, goes hand-in-hand with statism. Political, military and business leaders of the elite usually take advantage of their power to monopolize the resources of the country.

The Control of the State. In the developing world the government often becomes the big prize sought by competing groups. Once one faction takes over, it seeks to control the state. This is accomplished in various ways: **state monopoly** of major branches of industry and commerce, notably in the important and profitable export trade; numerous **state-owned and operated enterprises** where allies and family members can be employed; **official licensing** of commercial and industrial activities which can discriminate against competing groups; **ethnic quotas** in employment and in the allocation of licenses to undermine the success of other competing groups; comprehensive **control over international transactions** which can lead to payoffs from domestic and foreign investors for the entrenched bureaucrats; and **officially-set prices and wages** which usually benefit economically and politically privileged groups, at the expense of small farmers, traders, and other small entrepreneurs.

Other ways of increasing government control include forced collectivization of agriculture, large-scale state support for cooperative societies which are often extensions of government departments rather than voluntary cooperative societies, confiscation of property, and maltreatment of productive groups unpopular with the rulers. The state can also set restrictions on the external and domestic movement of people, capital, and commodities. If these measures are not enough, **murder** and terrorism are the instruments of choice to finalize the consolidation of power. The immediate result of autocratic state control is that the

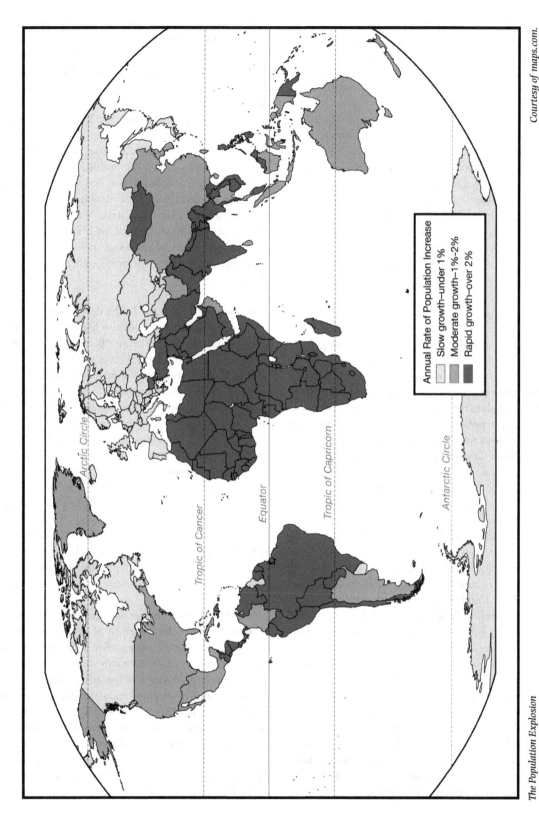

Courtesy of maps.com.

The Population Explosion

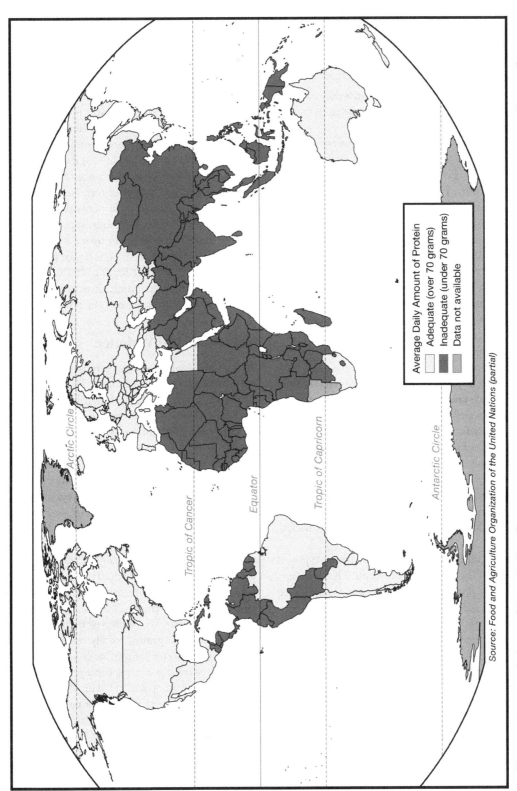

Courtesy of maps.com.

Source: Food and Agriculture Organization of the United Nations (partial)

World Nutrition (Average Daily Amount of Protein Per Capital)

elite increases its hold over the society, creating positions of power, prestige and economic benefits for politicians, technocrats, then the military, and their associates. This also benefits those private interest parties who seek privileged, protected status so that they do not have to compete against other businesses. It also increases political tension as the population rightly resists the government's unpopular policies.

As economic controls by the government decrease private choices, they restrict the range and variety of external contacts and the movement of people and goods within the territory. This limits the spread of new ideas, methods, attitudes and capital. The result is lowered economic incentives and opportunities. **State controls in authoritarian settings politicize economic life by making political considerations and the support of vested interests, the main criterion in economic decisions.** One consequence is an increase in political conflict among religious, ethnic and other groups, many of whom feel discriminated in the allocation of jobs and licenses. This political tension then is used to justify further authoritarianism, which requires additional coercion, corruption and violence.

Government planners of autocratic societies often want large-scale coercion of the population to remake entire societies and their people so that they abandon traditional beliefs, values, attitudes, mores and modes of living, and adopt the ways of the planners themselves. Planning, and the controls which come from it, are frequently supported by academicians, politicians, bureaucrats, and the military, all of which seldom participate directly in the process of wealth-creation. They often lack sympathy for small entrepreneurs, particularly traders.

The Role of Traders.   Historically, traders have played a major role in the generation of wealth. They play several functions: provide and extend markets and widen opportunities for people, both as producers and consumers; bring cheaper goods to people and induce them to improve their economic performance; stimulate agricultural surplus on the part of profit-seeking farmers; link producers and consumers, creating new wants and new production to pay for them; acquaint people with the workings of an exchange economy and the attitudes appropriate to it; force people to question existing habits, and promote the uncoerced erosion of attitudes and customs negative to material progress.

However, many autocratic governments in the **developing countries** often implement policies which inhibit the economically-dynamic role of traders. They create marketing boards to reduce the price fluctuations of commodities which can be so devastating to the revenues of poor states. **This power to monopolize the control of prices, can be used by the government to pay producers and traders less than what they would get in the open market.** An arbitrary lower price for a product is the equivalent of a tax on the producer. This results in lower production and well-being for the peasant and middle-class farmers as they get less for their cash crops.

Additional policies which hurt merchants are the restrictions in the number of traders, which inhibit the development of distribution networks and better efficiency in the allocation of goods; suppression of private traders and their replacement by state-trading organizations which lock people in subsistence production; and large-scale state support for cooperative trading which usually politicizes economic growth by favoring only some traders at the expense of the rest.

Tribalism and Violence

New countries often have numerous ethnic groups which do not get along with each other. The primordial ties or primary bonds based on kinship, tribes, religion, etc., are stronger than the associational or secondary ties among people of different groups. **As countries become more modernized, the mix of people in the cities increases, and groups which were never in contact meet and compete. The competition for jobs and other resources can lead to much distrust, jealousy, envy, unfairness and violence.** Opportunistic and demagogic leaders can use their own ethnic group's fears to intensify their hatred against the other groups and thus gain political power.

This tribal violence usually increases until a central power becomes strong enough to impose order. In approximately forty countries, no one group has more than fifty percent of the population. This usually means much friction unless there are wise leaders who can encourage cooperation among the groups. Ideally, once central authority is established, some form of nationalism might create greater social cohesiveness as people gain a sense of belonging to the same group and of having shared values. However, this is not always the case. One country's nationalism can be used to repress ethnic minorities or to attack neighboring countries. This is what has been happening in the conflict between the Hutus and Tutsis, which began in Rwanda and then spread into Burundi and Congo. One million people have died. **Even democracy itself can be** a source of violence if the majority does not have the restraint, the patience, and the tolerance to compromise with minorities.

Envy

Few scholars mention envy as a possible source of poverty. Envy, discontent or ill-will toward another's good fortune because one wishes to have it, is a universal occurrence. It is an emotion whereby the person or group views another's good as diminishing one's own intrinsic value, and wishes that the other would not have it, even if it means that no one would have it either. **The envious person or group is unable to admire and respect what is nobler and better, and therefore tries to pull down or destroy what is exceptional or successful.**

The spirit of envy is loose in the world and it is particularly damaging in poor countries where it is a major force in some ideologies and government policies. These often urge government confiscation of the private property of wealthy individuals, excessive "progressive" taxation of their incomes, expulsion of economically successful foreign minorities such as Biafrans, Cubans, Chinese, Haitians, Hindus, Jews, and Lebanese, exiling, arresting or murdering upper-class leaders, and inciting class warfare by telling the poor and the politically frustrated that others are responsible for their plight. While envy is an emotion which most often remains secretly hidden in an individual's psyche, in the poor world it is often transformed into "ressentiment" or political action against the groups envied for their success. **As these envied people are killed, exiled, or repressed, the country loses their energy, creativity, talents, and wealth. Poverty is then the result.**

Imperialism

Imperialism is a superior-inferior relationship in which an area and its people have been subordinated to the will of a foreign state or group. Imperialism is as old as the first states which began appearing in the world after the consolidation of Egypt in Africa around 3100 BC. Most regions of the world have had imperialist states which have conquered other groups: Akkadians, Babylonians, Assyrians, Hittites, Persians, Muslims, and Turks in Southwest Asia; Egyptians, Nubians, Axxumites in the North and in the Horn of Africa; Ghanians, Mali and Zimbabweans in Black Africa; Aryans in India; Mongols and Japanese in East Asia; Aztecs, Incas and Americans in the Western Hemisphere; Macedonians, Romans, Russians, Frenchmen, Spaniards, Swedes, British, Germans, Portuguese, Italians and Belgians in Europe; and others. **As the power and pride of a people grow and expand, adjacent peoples have to assimilate, pay homage or flee. Many are killed. Imperialism is a universal temptation.**

Ever since J. A. Hobson's *Imperialism, a Study* (1903), and Vladimir I. Lenin's *Imperialism, the Highest State of Capitalism* (1916), Socialists and other Leftists have argued that European imperialism is responsible for the poverty of the poor world. This is a new idea since Karl Marx and Fredrick Engels, founders of Marxism, the major socialist movement between 1860 and 1914, actually believed that Western civilization and Capitalism were needed to lift up these poor regions. Engels even argued that the bourgeoisie represented and improvement over the feudal lord and the robber because of their civilization, industry, and order.

On the other hand, Lenin's neo-colonialist framework stated that the rich countries exploit the poor, just as in Marxist analysis the capitalist classes are supposed to exploit the proletariat. Both Hobson and Lenin argued that European countries became imperialists as the technology of capitalism became more efficient producing goods, and led to overproduction, unemployment, bankruptcies, and economic recessions and depressions.

As a result, they argued, the Capitalist countries had a production surplus (the income of the people was not enough to buy all the goods made), and this forced them to acquire colonies where they could sell their excess goods. The colonists would be forced to buy these surplus goods which then allowed the capitalist countries to keep up their production and employment levels. **In their view, the Capitalist countries also became imperialist to guarantee sources of raw materials and of foreign investment, both necessary to keep up the level of profits.** For Lenin, imperialism is thus the last stage of capitalism. At one point, the imperialist countries would run out of colonies and would then begin fighting each other to gain new ones.

Yet, Hobson and Lenin's theory can itself be subjected to some criticisms. First, imperialism is older than Capitalism so it seems misleading to say that imperialism is the last stage of capitalism. Second, some of the countries which were imperialist in the 1880s, Italy and Russia, for example, did not have much industrial surplus to dump on colonies. The search for glory, and not profit by itself, might have played a greater role in the case of Italy and of others. Third, most of the investments of the capitalist countries actually were in other capitalist countries and not in the colonies themselves. The French had more investments in Russia and the rest of Europe than outside it. Fourth, most of the colonies did not have sufficient disposable income to buy the excess goods the imperialist countries were supposed to have. Fifth, a country does not need to have colonies for it to have access to raw materials, or to invest, or to sell its products. Much of these things can be obtained through trade, though it is true that this trade can be based on unfair conditions. **The fact is that much of the modern imperialism of the capitalist countries after the 1870s happened accidentally as they tried to protect their sea lanes and resupply stations from their European political, economic and military competitors, which were taking advantage of the collapse of the Ottoman empire in North Africa and of the weakness of native African political institutions.**

This is not to say that imperialism has not had **negative economic consequences in the poor world. Imperialism has had devastating consequences in some regions. It can be argued that foreign goods brought from the West at times destroyed local agriculture and industry, as well as displaced the labor of many skilled natives.** On the other hand, it could also be said that the natives did benefit by getting cheaper products, which then allowed them to buy other goods which in turn stimulated other domestic producers. **Another negative impact of imperialism is that some of the best lands in particular territories were taken by foreigners for cultivating crops for exports rather than for growing food for the local population.** This happened frequently in Sub-Saharan Africa. And yet, it can also be stated that new crops brought into the colonies by the Europeans did serve to improve nutrition and support a larger population. Their exports also brought in revenues to the country, although it is true that not everyone shared them equitably. **Additionally, foreign states often arbitrarily established borders for their colonies which negatively affected ethnic groups, dividing them at times, or placing them with hostile groups within one territory.** This led to much violence and waste of valuable resources. Still, sometimes, as was the case with the British in India, the imperialists pacified a region and prevented competing groups from killing each other. **Imperialists often destroyed a people's traditional lifestyle and their mode of survival.**

Nevertheless, sometimes the introduction of new values, medicines, skills, and modes of social organization improved people's lives. Population increases were signs of such improvement. **The instability of capitalism with its boom and bust cycles and rise and drop of prices for export products was also brought to the poor world. It is a source of much social and economic instability.**

In addition, some of the colonial powers, particularly the Portuguese and the Belgians, excluded the local population from participating in their own governance, which gave rise after independence to a lack of trained personnel to run a state. Imperialists frequently discovered and exploited the best resources of the colonies, without contributing in a significant degree to the social betterment of the local population. One could say, however, that they often brought improvements in hygiene, medicine, literacy and overall education. **They also brought statism to many parts of Africa creating government bureaucracies which destroyed the autonomy of native institutions.** Moreover, they took part in the African slave trade which had been carried on earlier by the Muslims. Millions died. However, it can not be said that slavery is responsible for the poverty of Africa for many of the areas from where the slaves were extracted are more prosperous today than areas where slavery was nonexistent. **Imperialists also brought diseases, which perhaps more than any other factor led to the death of millions of people in the Americas in the 1500s and 1600s.**

European imperialism, in general, made some positive contributions to the non-Western world. It reduced infant mortality and increased life expectancy. It reduced internal fighting in some places by inhibiting tribal warfare, military raids, slavery, and serfdom. It brought a unified system of law conducive to stable expectations, security, and planning. It extended more advanced technologies and systems of organization. It introduced literacy to many areas and opened isolated regions to world-wide contacts which helped increase their creativity and energy. Almost no African community south of the Sahara had managed to harness draft animals to pull plows and wagons until the Europeans came in the 1800s and 1900s, and most were unable to use wind or water power. Literacy was practically unknown outside Ethiopia.

Western technology gave value to the natural resources which often laid dormant in non-Western regions. Oil in Venezuela or in the Arabian Peninsula had no great value until the Europeans and the Americans created the technology which required gasoline. **It could even be argued that the poorest countries today are those like Afghanistan, Ethiopia, Tibet, Nepal, and others which had the least contact with the West.** Furthermore, Western culture brought to the non-Western world some concepts which expanded freedom: individual liberty, political democracy, the rule of law (and not just the arbitrary rule of elders), human rights, cultural freedom, and freedom of inquiry and individual expression. The Western powers often failed to apply in their colonies the high principles of political liberty and democracy which were part of their civilization. Ironically, many of the leaders of the anti-Western, independence movements in Africa and Asia were themselves educated in Western institutions and used these liberating ideas to justify and to inspire their desire for independence. **While Western imperialists committed many atrocities, as have all previous imperialisms in Africa, Asia, and in the Americas, they also brought forward ideologies and institutions for the self-correction of those errors.**

The proof of this self-correction mechanism is that it was the West which pushed the crusade to abolish the slave trade in Africa. It was England which sought the end of suttee (burning alive of widows on their husband's funeral pyres) in India. It was the French who freed Algerian women from the veil, and it is the West which is most responsible for promoting competitive political parties, independent judiciaries, free press, environmental protection, and the rule of law. **Obviously, Western imperialism has had negative as well as positive consequences. This is why it is difficult to demonstrate categorically that it is responsible for the poverty of the poor world.**

Corruption and Militarism

Dishonesty in public affairs, like envy, is a universal condition. It happens in all countries. But it is particularly damaging in poor countries because of their lack of savings necessary for investment, capitalization, and economic production. Sadly, many of the public funds misappropriated in the poor world are used for buying luxury goods and services produced elsewhere. This diminishes the resources available for promoting local industries.

Also, poor countries often collect less than five percent of appropriate taxes because of the many privileges which the powerful manage to include in the tax laws. **Corruption tends to be worse under dictatorships because these regimes lack public scrutiny, checks and balances, and financial accountability.** The dictators usually build support for their rule by letting subordinates redirect portions of the public revenues into their personal expense and bank accounts, the latter usually being outside their countries in Miami, Los Angeles, New York, London, Zurich, Geneva, and other financial centers. Corruption is not just something practiced by the powerful and the wealthy. Often corruption permeates all social sectors as people see it as a normal prerequisite for survival.

Militarism is an attitude which associates a country's success and welfare with excessive accumulation and use of military resources in and outside the country. Overall, poor countries tend to spend more on military hardware than they do on health, housing, and education. These military expenditures are often justified by their leaders as necessary to address ethnic and boundary disputes. However, many resources are actually spent repressing internal dissidents, in wars of conquest, and enhancing the prestige of the state and the personality of its leader.

Natural Resources and Population

A country without sufficient natural resources to generate products will have a difficult time. The same will happen if the country is dependent on one crop or mineral and the demand for these resources is weak or unstable on the international markets. This would make revenues of the country rise and fall unpredictably creating chaos in its budget and future plans. **On the other hand, it is possible for a country to have an abundance of natural resources and still be unable to make use of them because of technological and organizational backwardness and the lack of imagination, creativity and political stability.**

It is possible that a state might be oil and mineral poor, as is the case with Japan, and still compensate for this condition by discipline, organizational capability, a skilled labor force, and a successful export record. As a result, Japan has a higher per capita income and living standards than Mexico, which has more natural resources. Finally, natural resources are relative to the available technology, because a natural resource which might have been worthless, could suddenly become valuable if a new technology can utilize it. Therefore, natural resources are relative to the level of imagination and technological sophistication of the population.

The world population has risen from 250 million in 1 A.D. to 500 million in 1650, 2 billion in 1930, and 4 billion in 1975. It is expected to reach 11 billion in 2100. It took 1649 years for it to double between 1 A.D. and 1650. However, in the 1900s, it took just forty-five years for it to double from 2,000 to 4,000 million. Part of the increase in population has been due to a decrease in the death rate due to better diet, hygiene, medicines, crop rotation techniques, fertilizers, synthetic seeds, new lands and machinery. **Population growth is in part the result of economic success.** There are also socio-cultural reasons for the birth-rate to have increased: a desire for male heirs, machismo, or irresponsible male sexual promiscuity and chauvinism, a need for child labor in rural areas, and the desire of parents for security in one's old age.

By the year 2012, approximately eighty percent of the population will be in the developing world. **This population explosion in poor countries is often seen as a cause of poverty. Yet, not every poor country is over-populated. In addition, not every highly populated country is poor.** For instance, there are more people in Singapore, Britain, and in Hong Kong, than in Ethiopia, but the latter is the poorest. The first three are prosperous. **The hunger of many people around the world is often more the result of corrupt, evil or ignorant government policies than of population size.** The population of Europe was growing rapidly at the same time the economy was booming during the start of the industrial revolution, though it is also true that millions were leaving Europe, allowing those behind to have more opportunities.

Population growth can have an impact on the depletion of energy supplies, minerals, and topsoil, especially in developing countries where the political systems are frequently corrupt and irresponsive to social needs. Nevertheless, population growth can actually lead to more efficient use of available resources, or to the use of previously untouched ones. Recycling, reduction in the commodity content of products, water purification projects, and reforestation, are currently taking place in the United States and other developed countries. **Population is often a factor in poverty in countries with corrupt, unwise, and insensitive governments, which do not let their people make the necessary adjustments to deal with the demographic explosion.** If developing countries would let their women participate more

fully in the education, political and economic systems, increases in population would be moderated for as women become more skilled, educated and prosperous, they tend to have less children. Also what might be over-population in one country might be an economic stimulus in another state, as it uses the increase in people to open new businesses, which can increase employment, raise incomes, and create new technologies and institutions to deal with congestion, pollution, resource depletion, and social conflicts. The end result of economic growth is usually a reduction in the rate of population growth without any government coercion. This is why the rate of growth of global population began to decline in 1966 and why many Western states will actually experience in the 2000s a political and economic crisis caused by a fall in population growth.

The Value System

In addition to all the previously-stated factors frequently associated with poverty, some value systems could be damaging to the kind of motivation which needs to exist for countries to prosper economically. **People must have certain beliefs and convictions to prosper:** that work is good, and that some ambition is acceptable; that there must be a responsibility for the future, and so one must save, invest and conserve; that the contemplative life must be balanced with an active and productive life; that all people, including women, should be allowed to participate with dignity in the economic and political process; that the family is the basic unit of economic welfare; that families should not be too large; that private property, legally and fairly acquired, should be protected; that government should be as limited as possible to avoid corruption and repression; that fatalism is an irresponsible mental state since humans can help create their own future; that violence must be avoided as much as is possible; and that liberty must be pursued with justice so that all persons can develop their talents.

The political society must understand that there are certain economic conditions which seem to lead to prosperity: low tax rates (increases in taxation should not be higher than the increases in the economic production of the society), balanced budgets unless there is a crisis, small debt, some forms of free-trade, limits on the size of government, and a good public education. Many poor countries, as well as poor communities within the developed world, have difficulty in accepting these values. As a result, they do not prosper.

Foreign Aid

Arguments for Foreign Aid

Foreign aid is the transfer of taxpayers' money to distant governments and to official international organizations. The main rationale for it is that without foreign aid countries cannot progress at a reasonable rate. In this view, low economic production in the poor world leads to low savings and investment levels and then to low capital levels. This then is responsible for low production. As a result, a vicious cycle is created. However, this rationale for aid ignores that economic development existed long before foreign aid was invented. **The rich countries of today grew wealthy without the type of foreign aid presently given to large parts of the "developing world."**

Southeast Asia, West Africa and Latin America progressed rapidly before President Harry S. Truman began the foreign aid program in 1949 under his *Point Four Program*. **Those which have not progressed are kept back by other factors which cannot be overcome by aid. These are personal, cultural, social and political variables such as capabilities, motivation, mores, institutions, and the conduct of people and their governments.**

A second rationale for aid is the relief of poverty. Unfortunately, much of government foreign aid does not go to the poor but to governments and rulers whose policies often make the poor worse. Most often the rulers simply look to their own interests. Therefore, a lot of the foreign aid helps these governments deal with crises resulting from their own policies. Actually, the foreign aid ensures that they do not have to make reforms. The irony of this is that much foreign aid is paid by taxpayers who are poorer than many of the recipients.

A third argument on behalf of foreign aid is that it would reduce the interest costs incurred by countries when they borrow from commercial private institutions. However, the saving of this interest cost is not a significant determinant of "Third World" development. Many countries have developed fast without the aid. Foreigners will still provide finances for projects if these projects show merit. Private financial projects have a greater chance to be productive for they are geared to market conditions and usually function with a greater degree of accountability.

Foreign aid has indebted many countries because of ineffectiveness, mismanagement, and government corruption. This has been the case in Brazil, Mexico, Nigeria, Venezuela, and many other countries. Governments and people can always borrow commercially at home and abroad. Therefore, the only benefit of foreign aid is the avoided cost of borrowing and amortization charges which are a small portion of the national income. **Most often the savings gained by not paying commercial interest are not offset by the adverse repercussions of foreign aid.**

A fourth argument often heard in favor of foreign aid to the poor world, is that the West is paying for previous injustices it committed against the developing world. However, it can be argued that all national groups have engaged in injustices, the poor world included, but that it is an empirical fact that contact with the West has been the prime agent of material progress or modernization in the poor world. Those countries which have not been "touched" by it are the most technological backward.

A fifth argument for aid is actually made in the United States and argues that assistances to poor countries will increase their economic growth and purchasing power which will then increase U.S. exports and employment in the West. As a result, the United States and other Western States benefit. This argument is not entirely true. First, these exports are being given away, to the benefit of a few American exporters. The aid could probably have been better invested locally to increase employment in the United States. Second, the aid could actually create tougher competition from abroad against the United States, leading to local decreases in production and employment. And third, foreign aid could lead to balance of payment problems and increased taxation, as well as to the strengthening of anti-American and authoritarian regimes.

Argument Against Foreign Aid

The first criticism of foreign aid is that it helps to politicize economic life by increasing the power of the rulers in the poor world, and by establishing too many vested interests. This creates statism and corruption. The government elite then uses its power to monopolize many branches of agriculture, industry, and trade, favoring its political allies, punishing its enemies, independently of their economic efficiency and technological know-how. The privileged bureaucrats will restrict licensing of economic activities to reap payoffs and support cronies. They will control imports and exports and limit access to foreign exchange. The temptation is to use foreign aid to increase the number of state-owned and operated enterprises which usually are inefficient and serve as place to employ the families and political allies of the ruling class. **Ultimately, the growth of this public bureaucracy—made possible by foreign aid—diverts resources from economics to politics. Resources can go to the least productive.** Meanwhile, the national debt to foreigners rises as the aid fails to generate productive projects to pay for the debt because of inefficiency, mismanagement, and theft. The state then becomes dependent on additional debt to pay for previous debt.

A second criticism of foreign aid is that it allows governments to implement policies which retard growth. These operate negatively on the personal, social, and political factors which are critical determinants of material progress. They increase the power of the government compared to the rest of society by: expropriating the economic assets of political opponents; persecuting and expelling the most productive groups, particularly ethnic minorities; installing arbitrary economic controls over exports, imports, foreign exchange, and investments, all of which reduce external contacts, mobility and the spread of ideas and methods; the involuntary or compulsory purchasing of foreign enterprises, which reduces further capitalization and skills; taking over agriculture and industry; imposing prices which hurt farmers to benefit the urban populations, consequently reducing food production; wasting resources in prestige projects like building expensive new capitals (Brazilia, Islamabad, Lilongwe, and Dodoma among others), or running costly airlines (Burundi, Laos, Zaire, Ghana, and others); spending lavishly on military and police forces to repress their own people; and overvaluing exchange-rates to allow increased import purchases at the expense of exports which can increase revenues.

Improving Foreign Aid

Foreign aid would be more effective if it were given directly to specific projects which have appropriate budgetary controls to evaluate and monitor costs and benefits. Soft loans—which have low interest rates and long repayment schedules—could be replaced by outright grants to avoid problems of measurement and the confusion between gifts and loans. Direct grants should

be made from the donor country to the recipient state rather than through multilateral financial organizations which can further politicize and misdirect the funds. **Aid could be given only to democratic and free-market systems where all sectors of the population have representation and where accounting and political mechanisms exist to minimize corruption. Humanitarian voluntary agencies which are not politicized charities, could be used in poverty relief. Official aid could be limited mostly to meet unforeseeable and exceptional disasters. Aid is much better used in the developing world itself to help lower barriers to imports from the "poor world," for exports might be the most effective engine for economic development in the "poor world." Giving money to governments will not by itself expand the economies of poor countries.**

The Road Out of Poverty

The countries of the West and Japan used to be poor. They are not anymore because these countries were able to increase their production and employment by finding markets for their goods and services. They also increased productivity in their use of natural, labor, capital and managerial resources. Developing countries must do the same. They will have to export what they can. In some cases, all they have are primary products such as crops and minerals. Profits in these areas will have to be invested in secondary industries such as manufacturing. Simultaneously, they have to stimulate both foreign and domestic investments in these areas.

For these investments to occur, foreign and domestic investors must have confidence in the overall political and financial condition of the country. The investor must know that the state will not expropriate (steal) assets without paying their net current value. The investor must know that one's property (liquid savings, farms, businesses, investments, etc.) and its use, will not be subject to the arbitrary actions of the government. The investor must know that the government will not devalue one's savings by the arbitrary manipulation of the money supply, interest rates, inflation, and foreign exchange rates. If the government prints or expands the money supply faster than the supply of goods is rising to give more money to its political allies, it might create inflation by lowering the value of the currency and of people's savings. The end result is a lowering of living standards.

Once individuals (persons and corporations) feel safe to use their savings to invest in the economy, the level of capitalization and consumption will rise. This will in turn raise the level of production and employment. The government can destroy this progress if it starts making several unwise decisions: arbitrarily protecting some inefficient industries through tariffs; creating discriminatory or differential/preferential tariff rates for some products which usually lead to bribes and corruption and to a "crony-type" of capitalism; indebting the country to pay for large and wasteful government investments; subsidizing privileged businesses to promote their exports; and imposing high taxation. All of these conditions can ultimately reduce the competitiveness of local industry and damage exports which are essential to improving the economy.

The government must have a coherent regulatory framework. It must avoid ambiguity. There must be clear and rigorous banking, securities and anti-trust laws. Banks must be discouraged from making risky ventures because bullish lending can bring down the whole financial system. Steps can also be taken by the government to widen the market for its products. Perhaps this can be done by collaborating with other governments in creating free trade areas, common markets, or economic unions. **A crucial step is for governments of poor countries to convince developed countries to open up their markets to the exports of developing states by lowering their tariffs or eliminating their duties.**

Another essential point is the development of policies which improve the technical, educational, and health standards of the local population so that they can work more efficiently, raise their incomes and consumption, enlarge the local market, and increase their savings so that the country will not have to depend excessively on foreign savings and investments. A free-trade system is not helpful if the local population is not fit to compete in the market place or if their standard of living is being forcibly reduced by devaluations which destroy their savings and their investment and consumption. This is why a good public school system is a necessity. It is also essential that government taxation and regulation be simple enough to make it possible for small entrepreneurs to create their own businesses. The society is better off if private entrepreneurs are encouraged to open up businesses, than if the state controls most of the investments. **Large, ambitious capital projects are often less effective than a political and financial sector which encourages the growth of small entrepreneurs.**

The Importance of Order and Capital in Development

Economic development, which is what poor countries need, is the extension of the range of choices of people as consumers and as producers. This is best accomplished by an economic order in which individuals and firms largely determine what is produced and consumed, where they will work and live, how much they will save, and how they will invest their savings. Individuals and families tend to know better than state bureaucrats what they need and how they feel.

Development can happen without the following policies: conscription of people; forced mobilization resources; forced modernization of attitudes and behavior; large-scale, state-sponsored industrialization; national independence; a sense of national identity; enthusiasm for revolution; conscious effort at nation-building; large-scale public spending by an activist government; and a previously developed infrastructure.

What is needed most by poor countries can be summarized by the concepts of order and capital. Order comes indifferent forms. **Physical order** involves the safety of individuals. Development can not occur where people's lives and their property are constantly at risk. **Political order** exists where the laws and government institutions of a country protect individuals from the arbitrary loss of life, liberty and material possessions. **Financial and economic order** occurs where the value of legal savings and investments of individuals and corporations are not threatened by government arbitrary and politicized actions on taxes, monetary policy, litigations, exchange-rate devaluations and others. **Spiritual order** is present when the culture promotes an awareness of and respect for the common good, that is, for those concerns like education, health, human rights, environmental quality, ethical behavior, which impact on every person.

Capital is also another key requirement for development. It also comes indifferent forms. **Physical capital** are buildings and machinery needed to make other goods and services. **Financial capital,** or accumulated savings, is also crucial. Often, state technocrats emphasize too much the importance of large capital projects and neglect the value of the slow but constant accumulation of capital by the small entrepreneur. The increase in capital is not as important to the increase in per capita income, as is improved efficiency in the use of resources, and the movement of resources from less productive to more productive sectors. **As important as capital accumulation,**

Human Development Index 2007 and Its Components

HDI rank	Human development index value	Life expectancy at birth (years)	Adult literacy rate (% aged 15 and above)	Combined gross enrolment ratio in education (%)	GDP per capita (PPP US$)	Life expectancy index	Education index	GDP index	GDP per capita rank minus HDI rank[b]
	2007	2007	1999–2007[a]	2007	2007	2007	2007	2007	2007
VERY HIGH HUMAN DEVELOPMENT									
1 Norway	0.971	80.5	.. [c]	98.6 [d]	53,433 [e]	0.925	0.989	1.000	4
2 Australia	0.970	81.4	.. [c]	114.2 [d,f]	34,923	0.940	0.993	0.977	20
3 Iceland	0.969	81.7	.. [c]	96.0 [d]	35,742	0.946	0.980	0.981	16
4 Canada	0.966	80.6	.. [c]	99.3 [d,g]	35,812	0.927	0.991	0.982	14
5 Ireland	0.965	79.7	.. [c]	97.6 [d]	44,613 [e]	0.911	0.985	1.000	5
6 Netherlands	0.964	79.8	.. [c]	97.5 [d]	38,694	0.914	0.985	0.994	8
7 Sweden	0.963	80.8	.. [c]	94.3 [d]	36,712	0.930	0.974	0.986	9
8 France	0.961	81.0	.. [c]	95.4 [d]	33,674	0.933	0.978	0.971	17
9 Switzerland	0.960	81.7	.. [c]	82.7 [d]	40,658	0.945	0.936	1.000	4
10 Japan	0.960	82.7	.. [c]	86.6 [d]	33,632	0.961	0.949	0.971	16
11 Luxembourg	0.960	79.4	.. [c]	94.4 [h]	79,485 [e]	0.906	0.975	1.000	-9
12 Finland	0.959	79.5	.. [c]	101.4 [d,f]	34,526	0.908	0.993	0.975	11
13 United States	0.956	79.1	.. [c]	92.4 [d]	45,592 [e]	0.902	0.968	1.000	-4
14 Austria	0.955	79.9	.. [c]	90.5 [d]	37,370	0.915	0.962	0.989	1
15 Spain	0.955	80.7	97.9 [i]	96.5 [d]	31,560	0.929	0.975	0.960	12
16 Denmark	0.955	78.2	.. [c]	101.3 [d,f]	36,130	0.887	0.993	0.983	1
17 Belgium	0.953	79.5	.. [c]	94.3 [d]	34,935	0.908	0.974	0.977	4
18 Italy	0.951	81.1	98.9 [i]	91.8 [d]	30,353	0.935	0.965	0.954	11
19 Liechtenstein	0.951	.. [k]	.. [c]	86.8 [d,l]	85,382 [e,m]	0.903	0.949	1.000	-18
20 New Zealand	0.950	80.1	.. [c]	107.5 [d,f]	27,336	0.919	0.993	0.936	12
21 United Kingdom	0.947	79.3	.. [c]	89.2 [d,g]	35,130	0.906	0.957	0.978	-1
22 Germany	0.947	79.8	.. [c]	88.1 [d,g]	34,401	0.913	0.954	0.975	2
23 Singapore	0.944	80.2	94.4 [i]	.. [n]	49,704 [e]	0.920	0.913	1.000	-16
24 Hong Kong, China (SAR)	0.944	82.2	.. [o]	74.4 [d]	42,306	0.953	0.879	1.000	-13
25 Greece	0.942	79.1	97.1 [i]	101.6 [d,f]	28,517	0.902	0.981	0.944	6
26 Korea (Republic of)	0.937	79.2	.. [c]	98.5 [d]	24,801	0.904	0.988	0.920	9
27 Israel	0.935	80.7	97.1 [i]	89.9 [d]	26,315	0.928	0.947	0.930	7
28 Andorra	0.934	.. [k]	.. [c]	65.1 [d,l]	41,235 [e,p]	0.925	0.877	1.000	-16
29 Slovenia	0.929	78.2	99.7 [c,l]	92.8 [d]	26,753	0.886	0.969	0.933	4
30 Brunei Darussalam	0.920	77.0	94.9 [i]	77.7	50,200 [e]	0.867	0.891	1.000	-24
31 Kuwait	0.916	77.5	94.5 [i]	72.6 [d]	47,812 [d,e]	0.875	0.872	1.000	-23
32 Cyprus	0.914	79.6	97.7 [i]	77.6 [d,l]	24,789	0.910	0.910	0.920	4
33 Qatar	0.910	75.5	93.1 [i]	80.4	74,882 [d,e]	0.841	0.888	1.000	-30
34 Portugal	0.909	78.6	94.9 [i]	88.8 [d]	22,765	0.893	0.929	0.906	8
35 United Arab Emirates	0.903	77.3	90.0 [i]	71.4	54,626 [d,e,q]	0.872	0.838	1.000	-31
36 Czech Republic	0.903	76.4	.. [c]	83.4 [d]	24,144	0.856	0.938	0.916	1
37 Barbados	0.903	77.0	.. [c,o]	92.9	17,956 [d,q]	0.867	0.975	0.866	11
38 Malta	0.902	79.6	92.4 [r]	81.3 [d]	23,080	0.910	0.887	0.908	1
HIGH HUMAN DEVELOPMENT									
39 Bahrain	0.895	75.6	88.8 [i]	90.4 [d,g]	29,723 [d]	0.843	0.893	0.950	-9
40 Estonia	0.883	72.9	99.8 [c,i]	91.2 [d]	20,361	0.799	0.964	0.887	3
41 Poland	0.880	75.5	99.3 [c,i]	87.7 [d]	15,987	0.842	0.952	0.847	12
42 Slovakia	0.880	74.6	.. [c]	80.5 [d]	20,076	0.827	0.928	0.885	3
43 Hungary	0.879	73.3	98.9 [i]	90.2 [d]	18,755	0.805	0.960	0.874	3
44 Chile	0.878	78.5	96.5 [i]	82.5 [d]	13,880	0.891	0.919	0.823	15
45 Croatia	0.871	76.0	98.7 [i]	77.2 [d]	16,027	0.850	0.916	0.847	7
46 Lithuania	0.870	71.8	99.7 [c,i]	92.3 [d]	17,575	0.780	0.968	0.863	3
47 Antigua and Barbuda	0.868	.. [k]	99.0 [r]	.. [n]	18,691 [q]	0.786	0.945	0.873	0
48 Latvia	0.866	72.3	99.8 [c,i]	90.2 [d]	16,377	0.788	0.961	0.851	3
49 Argentina	0.866	75.2	97.6 [i]	88.6 [d]	13,238	0.836	0.946	0.815	13
50 Uruguay	0.865	76.1	97.9 [i]	90.9 [d]	11,216	0.852	0.955	0.788	20
51 Cuba	0.863	78.5	99.8 [c,i]	100.8	6,876 [q]	0.891	0.993	0.706	44
52 Bahamas	0.856	73.2	.. [o]	71.8 [d,g]	20,253 [d,s]	0.804	0.878	0.886	-8
53 Mexico	0.854	76.0	92.8 [i]	80.2 [d]	14,104	0.850	0.886	0.826	5
54 Costa Rica	0.854	78.7	95.9 [i]	73.0 [d,g]	10,842 [q]	0.896	0.883	0.782	19
55 Libyan Arab Jamahiriya	0.847	73.8	86.8 [i]	95.8 [d,g]	14,364 [q]	0.814	0.898	0.829	2
56 Oman	0.846	75.5	84.4 [i]	68.2	22,816 [d]	0.841	0.790	0.906	-15
57 Seychelles	0.845	.. [k]	91.8 [r]	82.2 [d,l]	16,394 [q]	0.797	0.886	0.851	-7
58 Venezuela (Bolivarian Republic of)	0.844	73.6	95.2 [i]	85.9 [l]	12,156	0.811	0.921	0.801	7
59 Saudi Arabia	0.843	72.7	85.0 [i]	78.5 [d,l]	22,935	0.794	0.828	0.907	-19

Human Development Report 2009.

Courtesy of Palgrave Macmillan.

HDI rank	Human development index value 2007	Life expectancy at birth (years) 2007	Adult literacy rate (% aged 15 and above) 1999–2007[a]	Combined gross enrolment ratio in education (%) 2007	GDP per capita (PPP US$) 2007	Life expectancy index 2007	Education index 2007	GDP index 2007	GDP per capita rank minus HDI rank[b] 2007
60 Panama	0.840	75.5	93.4 [j]	79.7 [d]	11,391 [q]	0.842	0.888	0.790	7
61 Bulgaria	0.840	73.1	98.3 [j]	82.4 [d]	11,222	0.802	0.930	0.788	8
62 Saint Kitts and Nevis	0.838	.. [k]	97.8 [t]	73.1 [d,q]	14,481 [q]	0.787	0.896	0.830	-6
63 Romania	0.837	72.5	97.6 [j]	79.2 [d]	12,369	0.792	0.915	0.804	1
64 Trinidad and Tobago	0.837	69.2	98.7 [j]	61.1 [d,q]	23,507 [q]	0.737	0.861	0.911	-26
65 Montenegro	0.834	74.0	96.4 [r,u]	74.5 [d,u,v]	11,699	0.817	0.891	0.795	1
66 Malaysia	0.829	74.1	91.9 [l]	71.5 [d]	13,518	0.819	0.851	0.819	-5
67 Serbia	0.826	73.9	96.4 [r,u]	74.5 [d,u,v]	10,248 [w]	0.816	0.891	0.773	8
68 Belarus	0.826	69.0	99.7 [c,j]	90.4	10,841	0.733	0.961	0.782	6
69 Saint Lucia	0.821	73.6	94.8 [x]	77.2	9,786 [q]	0.810	0.889	0.765	8
70 Albania	0.818	76.5	99.0 [c,j]	67.8 [d]	7,041	0.858	0.886	0.710	23
71 Russian Federation	0.817	66.2	99.5 [c,j]	81.9 [d]	14,690	0.686	0.933	0.833	-16
72 Macedonia (the Former Yugoslav Rep. of)	0.817	74.1	97.0 [j]	70.1 [d]	9,096	0.819	0.880	0.753	8
73 Dominica	0.814	.. [k]	88.0 [x]	78.5 [d,q]	7,893 [q]	0.865	0.848	0.729	10
74 Grenada	0.813	75.3	96.0 [x]	73.1 [d,q]	7,344 [q]	0.838	0.884	0.717	18
75 Brazil	0.813	72.2	90.0 [l]	87.2 [d]	9,567	0.787	0.891	0.761	4
76 Bosnia and Herzegovina	0.812	75.1	96.7 [y]	69.0 [d,z]	7,764	0.834	0.874	0.726	11
77 Colombia	0.807	72.7	92.7 [l]	79.0	8,587	0.795	0.881	0.743	4
78 Peru	0.806	73.0	89.6 [l]	88.1 [d,q]	7,836	0.800	0.891	0.728	7
79 Turkey	0.806	71.7	88.7 [l]	71.1 [d,q]	12,955	0.779	0.828	0.812	-16
80 Ecuador	0.806	75.0	91.0 [r]	.. [n]	7,449	0.833	0.866	0.719	11
81 Mauritius	0.804	72.1	87.4 [l]	76.9 [d,q]	11,296	0.785	0.839	0.789	-13
82 Kazakhstan	0.804	64.9	99.6 [c,j]	91.4	10,863	0.666	0.965	0.782	-10
83 Lebanon	0.803	71.9	89.6 [l]	78.0	10,109	0.781	0.857	0.770	-7
MEDIUM HUMAN DEVELOPMENT									
84 Armenia	0.798	73.6	99.5 [c,j]	74.6	5,693	0.810	0.909	0.675	16
85 Ukraine	0.796	68.2	99.7 [c,j]	90.0	6,914	0.720	0.960	0.707	9
86 Azerbaijan	0.787	70.0	99.5 [c,l]	66.2 [d,aa]	7,851	0.751	0.881	0.728	-2
87 Thailand	0.783	68.7	94.1 [l]	78.0 [d,q]	8,135	0.728	0.888	0.734	-5
88 Iran (Islamic Republic of)	0.782	71.2	82.3 [l]	73.2 [d,q]	10,955	0.769	0.793	0.784	-17
89 Georgia	0.778	71.6	100.0 [c,ab]	76.7	4,662	0.777	0.916	0.641	21
90 Dominican Republic	0.777	72.4	89.1 [l]	73.5 [d,q]	6,706 [q]	0.790	0.839	0.702	7
91 Saint Vincent and the Grenadines	0.772	71.4	88.1 [x]	68.9 [d]	7,691 [q]	0.774	0.817	0.725	-2
92 China	0.772	72.9	93.3 [l]	68.7 [d]	5,383	0.799	0.851	0.665	10
93 Belize	0.772	76.0	75.1 [x]	78.3 [d,q]	6,734 [q]	0.851	0.762	0.703	3
94 Samoa	0.771	71.4	98.7 [l]	74.1 [d,q]	4,467 [q]	0.773	0.905	0.634	19
95 Maldives	0.771	71.1	97.0 [l]	71.3 [d,q]	5,196	0.768	0.885	0.659	9
96 Jordan	0.770	72.4	91.1 [l]	78.7 [d]	4,901	0.790	0.870	0.650	11
97 Suriname	0.769	68.8	90.4 [l]	74.3 [d,q]	7,813 [q]	0.729	0.850	0.727	-11
98 Tunisia	0.769	73.8	77.7 [l]	76.2 [d]	7,520	0.813	0.772	0.721	-8
99 Tonga	0.768	71.7	99.2 [c,j]	78.0 [d,q]	3,748 [q]	0.778	0.920	0.605	21
100 Jamaica	0.766	71.7	86.0 [l]	78.1 [d,q]	6,079 [q]	0.778	0.834	0.686	-2
101 Paraguay	0.761	71.7	94.6 [l]	72.1 [d,q]	4,433	0.778	0.871	0.633	13
102 Sri Lanka	0.759	74.0	90.8 [l]	68.7 [d,q]	4,243	0.816	0.834	0.626	14
103 Gabon	0.755	60.1	86.2 [l]	80.7 [d,q]	15,167	0.584	0.843	0.838	-49
104 Algeria	0.754	72.2	75.4 [l]	73.6 [d,q]	7,740 [q]	0.787	0.748	0.726	-16
105 Philippines	0.751	71.6	93.4 [l]	79.6 [d]	3,406	0.777	0.888	0.589	19
106 El Salvador	0.747	71.3	82.0 [r]	74.0	5,804 [q]	0.771	0.794	0.678	-7
107 Syrian Arab Republic	0.742	74.1	83.1 [l]	65.7 [d,q]	4,511	0.818	0.773	0.636	5
108 Fiji	0.741	68.7	.. [o]	71.5 [d,q]	4,304	0.728	0.868	0.628	7
109 Turkmenistan	0.739	64.6	99.5 [c,j]	.. [n]	4,953 [d,q]	0.661	0.906	0.651	-3
110 Occupied Palestinian Territories	0.737	73.3	93.8 [l]	78.3	.. [d,ac]	0.806	0.886	0.519	
111 Indonesia	0.734	70.5	92.0 [l]	68.2 [d]	3,712	0.758	0.840	0.603	10
112 Honduras	0.732	72.0	83.6 [l]	74.8 [d,q]	3,796 [q]	0.783	0.806	0.607	7
113 Bolivia	0.729	65.4	90.7 [l]	86.0 [d,q]	4,206	0.673	0.892	0.624	4
114 Guyana	0.729	66.5	.. [o]	83.9	2,782 [q]	0.691	0.939	0.555	13
115 Mongolia	0.727	66.2	97.3 [l]	79.2	3,236	0.687	0.913	0.580	10
116 Viet Nam	0.725	74.3	90.3 [r]	62.3 [d,q]	2,600	0.821	0.810	0.544	13
117 Moldova	0.720	68.3	99.2 [c,j]	71.6	2,551	0.722	0.899	0.541	14
118 Equatorial Guinea	0.719	49.9	87.0 [y]	62.0 [d,q]	30,627	0.415	0.787	0.955	-90

(continues)

HDI rank	Human development index value 2007	Life expectancy at birth (years) 2007	Adult literacy rate (% aged 15 and above) 1999–2007[a]	Combined gross enrolment ratio in education (%) 2007	GDP per capita (PPP US$) 2007	Life expectancy index 2007	Education index 2007	GDP index 2007	GDP per capita rank minus HDI rank[b] 2007
119 Uzbekistan	0.710	67.6	96.9 [y]	72.7	2,425 [q]	0.711	0.888	0.532	14
120 Kyrgyzstan	0.710	67.6	99.3 [c,j]	77.3	2,006	0.710	0.918	0.500	20
121 Cape Verde	0.708	71.1	83.8 [j]	68.1	3,041	0.769	0.786	0.570	5
122 Guatemala	0.704	70.1	73.2 [j]	70.5	4,562	0.752	0.723	0.638	-11
123 Egypt	0.703	69.9	66.4 [r]	76.4 [d,q]	5,349	0.749	0.697	0.664	-20
124 Nicaragua	0.699	72.7	78.0 [r]	72.1 [d,q]	2,570 [q]	0.795	0.760	0.542	6
125 Botswana	0.694	53.4	82.9 [j]	70.6 [d,q]	13,604	0.473	0.788	0.820	-65
126 Vanuatu	0.693	69.9	78.1 [j]	62.3 [d,q]	3,666 [q]	0.748	0.728	0.601	-4
127 Tajikistan	0.688	66.4	99.6 [c,j]	70.9	1,753	0.691	0.896	0.478	17
128 Namibia	0.686	60.4	88.0 [j]	67.2 [d]	5,155	0.590	0.811	0.658	-23
129 South Africa	0.683	51.5	88.0 [j]	76.8 [d]	9,757	0.442	0.843	0.765	-51
130 Morocco	0.654	71.0	55.6 [j]	61.0	4,108	0.767	0.574	0.620	-12
131 Sao Tome and Principe	0.651	65.4	87.9 [j]	68.1	1,638	0.673	0.813	0.467	17
132 Bhutan	0.619	65.7	52.8 [r]	54.1 [d,q]	4,837	0.678	0.533	0.647	-24
133 Lao People's Democratic Republic	0.619	64.6	72.7 [r]	59.6 [d]	2,165	0.659	0.683	0.513	2
134 India	0.612	63.4	66.0 [j]	61.0 [d]	2,753	0.639	0.643	0.553	-6
135 Solomon Islands	0.610	65.8	76.6 [j]	49.7 [d]	1,725 [q]	0.680	0.676	0.475	10
136 Congo	0.601	53.5	81.1 [j]	58.6 [d,q]	3,511	0.474	0.736	0.594	-13
137 Cambodia	0.593	60.6	76.3 [j]	58.5	1,802	0.593	0.704	0.483	6
138 Myanmar	0.586	61.2	89.9 [y]	56.3 [d,q,aa]	904 [d,q]	0.603	0.787	0.368	29
139 Comoros	0.576	64.9	75.1 [j]	46.4 [d,q]	1,143	0.666	0.655	0.407	20
140 Yemen	0.575	62.5	58.9 [j]	54.4 [d]	2,335	0.624	0.574	0.526	-6
141 Pakistan	0.572	66.2	54.2 [j]	39.3 [d]	2,496	0.687	0.492	0.537	-9
142 Swaziland	0.572	45.3	79.6 [y]	60.1 [d]	4,789	0.339	0.731	0.646	-33
143 Angola	0.564	46.5	67.4 [y]	65.3 [d]	5,385	0.359	0.667	0.665	-42
144 Nepal	0.553	66.3	56.5 [j]	60.8 [d,q]	1,049	0.688	0.579	0.392	21
145 Madagascar	0.543	59.9	70.7 [y]	61.3	932	0.582	0.676	0.373	21
146 Bangladesh	0.543	65.7	53.5 [j]	52.1 [d]	1,241	0.678	0.530	0.420	9
147 Kenya	0.541	53.6	73.6 [y]	59.6 [d,q]	1,542	0.477	0.690	0.457	2
148 Papua New Guinea	0.541	60.7	57.8 [j]	40.7 [d,y]	2,084 [q]	0.594	0.521	0.507	-10
149 Haiti	0.532	61.0	62.1 [j]	.. [n]	1,155 [q]	0.600	0.588	0.408	9
150 Sudan	0.531	57.9	60.9 [y,ad]	39.9 [d,q]	2,086	0.548	0.539	0.507	-13
151 Tanzania (United Republic of)	0.530	55.0	72.3 [j]	57.3	1,208	0.500	0.673	0.416	6
152 Ghana	0.526	56.5	65.0 [j]	56.5	1,334	0.525	0.622	0.432	1
153 Cameroon	0.523	50.9	67.9 [j]	52.3	2,128	0.431	0.627	0.510	-17
154 Mauritania	0.520	56.6	55.8 [j]	50.6 [d,j]	1,927	0.526	0.541	0.494	-12
155 Djibouti	0.520	55.1	.. [o]	25.5 [d]	2,061	0.501	0.554	0.505	-16
156 Lesotho	0.514	44.9	82.2 [j]	61.5 [d,q]	1,541	0.332	0.753	0.457	-6
157 Uganda	0.514	51.9	73.6 [j]	62.3 [d,q]	1,059	0.449	0.698	0.394	6
158 Nigeria	0.511	47.7	72.0 [j]	53.0 [d,q]	1,969	0.378	0.657	0.497	-17
LOW HUMAN DEVELOPMENT									
159 Togo	0.499	62.2	53.2 [y]	53.9	788	0.620	0.534	0.345	11
160 Malawi	0.493	52.4	71.8 [j]	61.9 [d,q]	761	0.456	0.685	0.339	12
161 Benin	0.492	61.0	40.5 [j]	52.4 [d,q]	1,312	0.601	0.445	0.430	-7
162 Timor-Leste	0.489	60.7	50.1 [aa]	63.2 [d,q]	717 [q]	0.595	0.545	0.329	11
163 Côte d'Ivoire	0.484	56.8	48.7 [y]	37.5 [d,q]	1,690	0.531	0.450	0.472	-17
164 Zambia	0.481	44.5	70.6 [j]	63.3 [d,q]	1,358	0.326	0.682	0.435	-12
165 Eritrea	0.472	59.2	64.2 [j]	33.3 [d,q]	626 [q]	0.570	0.539	0.306	12
166 Senegal	0.464	55.4	41.9 [j]	41.2 [d,q]	1,666	0.506	0.417	0.469	-19
167 Rwanda	0.460	49.7	64.9 [y]	52.2 [d,q]	866	0.412	0.607	0.360	1
168 Gambia	0.456	55.7	.. [j]	46.8 [d,q]	1,225	0.511	0.439	0.418	-12
169 Liberia	0.442	57.9	55.5 [j]	57.6 [d]	362	0.548	0.562	0.215	10
170 Guinea	0.435	57.3	29.5 [y]	49.3 [d]	1,140	0.538	0.361	0.406	-10
171 Ethiopia	0.414	54.7	35.9 [j]	49.0	779	0.496	0.403	0.343	0
172 Mozambique	0.402	47.8	44.4 [j]	54.8 [d,q]	802	0.380	0.478	0.348	-3
173 Guinea-Bissau	0.396	47.5	64.6 [j]	36.6 [d,q]	477	0.375	0.552	0.261	5
174 Burundi	0.394	50.1	59.3 [y]	49.0	341	0.418	0.559	0.205	6
175 Chad	0.392	48.6	31.8 [j]	36.5 [d,q]	1,477	0.393	0.334	0.449	-24
176 Congo (Democratic Republic of the)	0.389	47.6	67.2 [y]	48.2	298	0.377	0.608	0.182	5
177 Burkina Faso	0.389	52.7	28.7 [j]	32.8	1,124	0.462	0.301	0.404	-16

HDI rank	Human development index value 2007	Life expectancy at birth (years) 2007	Adult literacy rate (% aged 15 and above) 1999–2007[a]	Combined gross enrolment ratio in education (%) 2007	GDP per capita (PPP US$) 2007	Life expectancy index 2007	Education index 2007	GDP index 2007	GDP per capita rank minus HDI rank[b] 2007
178 Mali	0.371	48.1	26.2 [i]	46.9	1,083	0.385	0.331	0.398	-16
179 Central African Republic	0.369	46.7	48.6 [y]	28.6 [d,q]	713	0.361	0.419	0.328	-5
180 Sierra Leone	0.365	47.3	38.1 [j]	44.6 [d]	679	0.371	0.403	0.320	-5
181 Afghanistan	0.352	43.6	28.0 [y]	50.1 [d,q]	1,054 [d,aq]	0.310	0.354	0.393	-17
182 Niger	0.340	50.8	28.7 [i]	27.2	627	0.431	0.282	0.307	-6
OTHER UN MEMBER STATES									
Iraq	..	67.8	74.1 [y]	60.5 [d,q]	..	0.714	0.695	..	..
Kiribati	..	.. [k]	..	75.8 [d,q]	1,295 [q]	0.699	..	0.427	..
Korea (Democratic People's Rep. of)	..	67.1	..	..	..	0.702	..	..	..
Marshall Islands	..	.. [k]	..	71.1 [d,q]	..	0.758	..	..	..
Micronesia (Federated States of)	..	68.4	..	..	2,802 [q]	0.724	..	0.556	..
Monaco	..	.. [k]	.. [c]	..	..	0.948	..	..	..
Nauru	..	.. [k]	..	55.0 [d,q]	..	0.906	..	..	..
Palau	..	.. [k]	91.9 [d,r]	96.9 [d,q]	..	0.758	0.936	..	..
San Marino	..	.. [k]	.. [c]	..	..	0.940	..	..	..
Somalia	..	49.7	..	..	..	0.412	..	..	..
Tuvalu	..	.. [k]	..	69.2 [d,q]	..	0.683	..	..	..
Zimbabwe	..	43.4	91.2 [j]	54.4 [d,q]	..	0.306	0.789	..	..
Arab States	0.719	68.5	71.2	66.2	8,202	0.726	0.695	0.736	..
Central and Eastern Europe and the CIS	0.821	69.7	97.6	79.5	12,185	0.745	0.916	0.802	..
East Asia and the Pacific	0.770	72.2	92.7	69.3	5,733	0.786	0.849	0.676	..
Latin America and the Caribbean	0.821	73.4	91.2	83.4	10,077	0.806	0.886	0.770	..
South Asia	0.612	64.1	64.2	58.0	2,905	0.651	0.621	0.562	..
Sub-Saharan Africa	0.514	51.5	62.9	53.5	2,031	0.441	0.597	0.503	..
OECD	0.932	79.0	..	89.1	32,647	0.900	..	0.966	..
European Union (EU27)	0.937	79.0	..	91.0	29,956	0.899	..	0.952	..
GCC	0.868	74.0	86.8	77.0	30,415	0.816	0.835	0.954	..
Very high human development	0.955	80.1	..	92.5	37,272	0.918	..	0.988	..
Very high HD: OECD	..	80.1	..	92.9	37,122	0.919	..	0.988	..
Very high HD: non-OECD	..	79.7	..	..	41,887	0.912	..	1.000	..
High human development	0.833	72.4	94.1	82.4	12,569	0.790	0.902	0.807	..
Medium human development	0.686	66.9	80.0	63.3	3,963	0.698	0.744	0.614	..
Low human development	0.423	51.0	47.7	47.6	862	0.434	0.477	0.359	..
World	0.753	67.5 [af]	83.9 [af]	67.5	9,972	0.708	0.784	0.768	..

(continues)

NOTES

a Data refer to national literacy estimates from censuses or surveys conducted between 1999 and 2007, unless otherwise specified. Due to differences in methodology and timeliness of underlying data, comparisons across countries and over time should be made with caution. For more details, see http://www.uis.unesco.org/.

b A positive figure indicates that the HDI rank is higher than the GDP per capita (PPP US$) rank; a negative figure, the opposite.

c For the purposes of calculating the HDI, a value of 99.0% was applied.

d Data refer to a year other than that specified.

e For the purposes of calculating the HDI, a value of 40,000 (PPP US$) was applied.

f For the purposes of calculating the HDI, a value of 100% was applied.

g UNESCO Institute for Statistics estimate.

h Statec (2008). Data refer to nationals enrolled both in the country and abroad and thus differ from the standard definition.

i Data are from a national household survey.

j UNESCO Institute for Statistics estimates based on its Global Age-specific Literacy Projections model, April 2009.

k For the purposes of calculating the HDI unpublished estimates from UN (2009e) were used: Andorra 80.5, Antigua and Barbuda 72.2, Dominica 76.9, Liechtenstein 79.2, Saint Kitts and Nevis 72.2 and the Seychelles 72.8.

l National estimate.

m HDRO estimate based on GDP from UN (2009c) and the PPP exchange rate for Switzerland from World Bank (2009d).

n Because the combined gross enrolment ratio was unavailable, the following HDRO estimates were used: Antigua and Barbuda 85.6, Ecuador 77.8, Haiti 52.1, Singapore 85.0 and Turkmenistan 73.9.

o In the absence of recent data, estimates for 2005 from UNESCO Institute for Statistics (2003), based on outdated census or survey information, were used and should be interpreted with caution: the Bahamas 95.8, Barbados 99.7, Djibouti 70.3, Fiji 94.4, the Gambia 42.5, Guyana 99.0 and Hong Kong, China (SAR) 94.6.

p HDRO estimate based on GDP from UN (2009c).

q World Bank estimate based on regression.

r Data are from a national census of population.

s Heston, Summers and Aten (2006). Data differ from the standard definition.

t Data are from the Secretariat of the Organization of Eastern Caribbean States, based on national sources.

u Data refer to Serbia and Montenegro prior to its separation into two independent states in June 2006. Data exclude Kosovo.

v UNESCO Institute for Statistics (2007).

w Data exclude Kosovo.

x Data are from the Secretariat of the Caribbean Community, based on national sources.

y Data are from UNICEF's Multiple Indicator Cluster Survey.

z UNDP (2007d).

aa UNESCO Institute for Statistics (2008a).

ab UNICEF (2004).

ac In the absence of an estimate of GDP per capita (PPP US$), an HDRO estimate of 2,243 (PPP US$) was used, derived from the value of GDP for 2005 in US$ and the weighted average ratio of PPP US$ to US$ in the Arab States. The value is expressed in 2007 prices.

ad Data refer to North Sudan only.

ae UNDP (2006b).

af Data are aggregates provided by original data source.

ag Calculated on the basis of GDP in PPP US$ for 2006 from World Bank (2009d) and total population for the same year from UN (2009e).

SOURCES

Column 1: calculated based on data in columns 6–8.

Column 2: UN (2009e).

Column 3: UNESCO Institute for Statistics (2009a).

Column 4: UNESCO Institute for Statistics (2009b).

Column 5: World Bank (2009d).

Column 6: calculated based on data in column 2.

Column 7: calculated based on data in columns 3 and 4.

Column 8: calculated based on data in column 5.

Column 9: calculated based on data in columns 1 and 5.

are ambition, skills, energy, and a favorable political condition. **Human capital** is also essential. Humans must be well-fed, educated, healthy, and motivated to perform to their capacity. Many government policies like excessive taxation, laissez-faire, forced conscription and manipulation of the currency to raise consumer prices, are harmful to human capital and become economically counter-productive. **The poor need more money in their hands so that this can motivate them to improve their behavior. Social capital** refers to the ability of people to co-exist in peace. This requires legitimate political institutions, fair government policies and judicial decisions, a moral consensus, and a culture which emphasizes the protection of the common good. The end result of social capital is a high level of trust among people which can then lead to peace and to prosperity.

Sources

Books

Bauer, P. T. (1981) *Equality, the Third World, and Economic Delusion.* Cambridge: Harvard University Press.

Bauer, P. T. (1984) *Reality and Rhetoric. Studies in the Economics of Development.* London: Harvard University Press.

Bruckner, Pascal. (1986) *The Tears of the White Man: Compassion as Contempt.* New York: The Free Press.

Davidson, Basil. (1992) *The Black Man's Burden: Africa and the Curse of the Nation-State.* New York: Times Books.

Fisher, James S. ed. (1992) *Geography and Development: A World Regional Approach.* Fourth Edition. New York: Macmillan Publishing Company.

Fuller, Graham E. (1991) *The Democracy Trap: The Perils of the Post-Cold War World.* New York: Dutton.

Harrison, Lawrence E. (1992) *Who Prospers? How Cultural Values Shape Economic and Political Success.* New York: Basic Books.

Kennedy, Paul. (1993) *Preparing for the Twenty-First Century.* New York: Vintage Books.

Nash, Ronald. (1986) *Poverty and Wealth: The Christian Debate Over Capitalism.* Westchester: Crossway Books.

Papp, Daniel S. (1991) *Contemporary International Relations.* New York: Macmillan Publishing Company.

Rosenberg, Nathan and Birzdell, L. E. (1990) *How the West Grew Rich.* New York: Basic Books, Inc., Publishers.

Stavrianos, L. S. (1995) *A Global History.* Englewood Cliffs: Prentice Hall.

Warshaw, Steven. (1990) *Japan Emerges.* Berkley: Diablo Press.

Weigel, George and Royal, Robert. (1991) *A Century of Catholic Social Thought: Essays on Rerum Novarum and Nine Other Key Documents.* Lanham: Ethics and Public Policy Center.

Wheeler, Jesse H. and Kostbade, J. Trenton. (1990) *World Regional Geography.* Philadelphia: Saunders College Publishing.

Youngguist, Walter. (1990) *Mineral Resources and the Destinies of Nations.* Portland: National Book Company.

CHAPTER ELEVEN

The Global Economy

Germán Muñoz

The global economy consists of all those interactions among people, businesses, governments, and other institutions that cross international borders, whether in the form of goods, services, transfer of funds, or migratory movements. A process of **globalization** has been accelerating since the end of World War II in 1945. It consists of greater economic interdependence and integration among the people of the world. This globalization seems to be fueled by at least four major forces; **trade** which has increased due to declining international trade barriers; **investments** by multinational corporations which generate goods and services in many countries; **technology**, which is traded, promoted through joint ventures and cross-border contacts, and which has created a revolution in communications and transportation; and **international finance** facilitated through international bank lending, and stocks and bonds issued on international markets.

Trade

People trade, that is, they exchange merchandise and services because someone else can make goods better and cheaper. International trade takes place mainly if it makes people better off than they would be without it. It is cheaper, for example, for Kuwait to dig for oil rather than for South Korea to do it. There is abundant oil in Kuwait just below its surface. However, it is more efficient for South Korea to make textiles since it has a plentiful and highly skilled population. Each of these states has an advantage in a particular industry due to the nature of their economic resources. Yet, even if one country were to have an **absolute advantage** over another in the production of all goods because they might be more productive or efficient, trade could still be possible between them. It might be better if the superior country specialized in the production of those goods in which it has a relatively higher efficiency or **comparative advantage**, and for the other country to concentrate in an industry in which it is relatively more productive. Each country would then trade with the other to satisfy their diverse needs.

Comparative advantage is the idea that agents or assets are more efficiently employed in activities in which they perform relatively better than in others. Comparative advantage is the ability to be better suited to the production of one good than to the production of another good. Country A, let's say the United States, might be more productive than country B, Venezuela in the production of aircraft and petroleum. Country A has an absolute advantage in both products. The advantage of A over B is 100% in aircraft manufacturing but only 10% in the production of oil. As a result, it might be advantageous for the United States to specialize in its the production of airplanes where it has a comparative advantage and for Venezuela to specialize in search for oil and its conversion into petrochemical products where it does well. Then country A can trade for petroleum and its derivatives and country B can buy planes from country A. The key is for countries to invest their limited savings in those activities they do best.

If countries were to trade in this manner all would benefit from more goods at lower prices. People and countries could improve their economic well-being if they would specialize in producing the goods and services for which they have a comparative advantage and then trade to acquire other goods for which they do not have such an advantage.

For instance, the United States has a comparative advantage in **capital goods**—machinery and equipment that can be put to work making other goods. It is successful in exporting equipment and aircraft, among others. On the other hand, the United States imports **industrial supplies** such as fuel, metals, non-medicinal chemicals, and **consumer goods** such as household appliances, computers, clothing, vehicles, and parts. These items are purchased from countries which have a comparative advantage in their production.

As countries with few trade barriers trade with each other, consumers benefit by having access to cheaper and better products. This is made possible by the **specialization or division of labor** in which each country, region or group produces what it does most efficiently and buys the rest from cheaper producers abroad. This division of labor results from an international economy which permits free trade among people and countries which follow the principle of comparative advantage.

New customers in other countries increase the size of the market and allow producers to acquire **economies of scale**, as a larger volume of sales reduces their operation costs and permits producers to lower the price of their goods. **Economies of scale are factors which cause the average cost of producing a commodity to fall as output of the commodity rises.** The new customers have the opportunity to share in the special technology or economic conditions which give the producers their comparative advantage. **In addition to consumers and successful producers, trade benefits the economy as a whole. It exposes domestic producers to competition from abroad as natural and human resources shift to where they contribute the most. This forces them to be more innovative and efficient and to lower prices for their products. Consumers get a wider variety of goods at more reasonable prices. The losers are industries which cannot compete in the world economy.**

The major requirement for success in a relatively open world economy is for countries to shift resources to the productive industries where they have a comparative advantage. This advantage could be the result of easier access to natural resources, good climate, low-wage costs, skilled labor, adequate technologies, location, capital resources, and low transportation costs.

A major disadvantage of a highly integrated global economy is the dependency it creates on the goods and services produced elsewhere. If there is an interruption in trade due to wars, natural disasters, or economic dislocations, consumers could experience significant discomfort. Instead of pursuing "free trade," some governments might cheat to undermine the economies of competing countries. On the other hand, greater economic integration might make people more concerned about each other's well being. Countries which trade have a stake in each other's prosperity.

Types of Foreign Transactions

There are four major types of foreign transactions: merchandise, services, investments, and unilateral transfers. **Merchandise trade** is the buying and selling of tangible or visible goods such as cars, computers, cameras, etc. **Services** are intangible, non-transferable economic goods as distinct from physical commodities and include airplane fares, travel services, insurance, royalties earned, entertainment, and tourism, among others. **Investments** abroad refer to real capital formation such as the production or maintenance of machinery or the construction of dwellings that will produce a stream of goods and services for future consumption. **Unilateral transfers** are payments abroad for which nothing was received: foreign aid and grants from the government and money sent by U.S. residents to relatives or friends in other countries.

Accounting Terms for Foreign Transactions

The narrowest measure of a country's trade is the **merchandise trade balance** which includes only visible goods such as cars, recorders, etc. Trade in visible goods is referred to as the trade balance even though it includes only those tangible goods that can be loaded on a ship, plane, or any other transport used in international trade. **The current account is a better measure of trade because it includes a country's exports and imports of services in addition to its visible trade in goods.** Thus the current account is made up of visible trade such as merchandise imports and exports and invisible trade such as income and expenditures for services like banking, insurance, tourism and shipping, together with profits earned overseas and interest payments. Many states make money exporting an "invisible service" such as banking, accounting, and tourism. For example, Japanese tourists visiting Miami buy airplane fares. This is comparable to exporting American services. They buy hotel and restaurant services just like a domestic consumer might buy a house. In the same manner, American tourists in France might buy Guerlain cologne in Paris. From the point of view of the American economy, this is comparable to an import. **A current account deficit means a country spent more abroad that it earned from outside.** The balance on the current account is the difference between the national income and national expenditures for the period.

Trade deficits are balanced by payments that make up the difference. A country with a current account surplus, Japan for instance, can use the extra money to invest abroad, or it can store it up in its foreign currency reserves. These could be used later to buy goods, services or investments. On the other hand, a country running a current account deficit, the United States for example, has to look abroad for loans or foreign investments, or be forced to use its own reserves to pay for its excessive imports. **The deficit in the current account must be balanced.** If the United States, for example, has a $740 billion (2008) deficit in the current account, it must attract $740 billion into the country. These outside funds could be used to purchase American real-estate or U.S. bonds. If Americans want to buy more from the world than they sell to the world, they must allow foreigners to use their resources to buy American property. No country can continue having deficits in the merchandise trade balance and current accounts without attracting foreign money to even out the imbalance.

All these payments and transfer of funds in and out of a country are added up in a state's capital account. The capital account is made up of such items as the inward and outward flow of money for investment and international grants and loans. The widest measure of a country's trade is its **balance of payments.** It includes not only payments abroad but the goods, services, and all transfer of funds that cross international borders. **The balance of payments is a tabulation of the credit and debit transactions of a country with foreign countries and international institutions. It adds up everything in a country's trade, current and**

capital accounts. Since all the trade in goods and services is "balanced" by the international transfer of funds, the balance of payments should add up to zero at the end of the accounting period.

Foreign Investment

One of the basic components of international trade is the freedom to invest abroad. **Foreign investment is the acquisition by governments, institutions or individuals in one country of assets in another.** For a country in which savings are insufficient relative to the potential demand for investment, foreign capital can be a fruitful means of stimulating rapid growth. In addition, direct investment may be a means of financing a balance of payments deficit which might otherwise occur in response to an increase of home demand.

Basically, foreign investment is a result of trade surpluses. When a country exports more than it imports it has more money available to invest in the world markets, to purchase foreign government bonds, real estate, and companies, among other things. In turn, states with trade deficits can often benefit from foreign investments which can create jobs and promote economic efficiency. This foreign contribution can then make domestic industries more efficient on international markets and increase exports to close the trade imbalance. When a country restricts foreign investment, jobs and much needed capital are often lost to other countries with more open and safe economies.

Trade deficits in the United States, for example, mean that foreigners accumulate lots of American dollars to buy foreign goods and services. The other country, let's say Japan, can do three things with those extra dollars. First, they can buy U.S. goods and services, that is, import goods from the United States. Second, they can buy American property, including buildings, corporations, or bonds. Third, the Japanese can change those dollars into another currency if they find people outside the United States who want to buy something from America but who first need to buy dollars to buy those goods or services.

The United States, for instance, needs foreign investments to cover its excess spending on foreign goods and services. The capital account needs to be balanced. Money needs to come into the United States in the same amounts as the deficit. The deficit occurred because foreigners did not want a lot of the goods and services the United States had to sell and yet, they might want other things. So other countries purchase

American farms, publishing companies, manufacturing and service firms, movie studios, stocks and government bonds.

Accumulated foreign trade deficits caused by the American people's willingness to buy more from abroad than they were able to sell abroad made the United States a debtor nation because foreigners were willing to use their surpluses to finance such deficits. **Thus, a foreign trade deficit eventually results in foreign investment in the country that created the deficit. A creditor nation is a country with a balance of payment surplus. A debtor nation is a country with a balance of payment deficit.** The United States went from being a creditor nation to a debtor nation in 1985.

Other conditions aside, investors will select a foreign investment if it is more profitable than a domestic one—consistent with risk. For example, higher interest rates in U.S. government risk-free bonds will draw investment out of Japan as Japanese seek to earn a high return for buying American bonds which the United States sells to pay for its government deficit, that is, for having spent more money than it had in revenues. To make a foreign investment in the United States, the investor must first buy the money the country uses, making the business person also an investor in the foreign currency, in this case dollars. **The main difference between domestic and international trade is the use of foreign currencies to pay for the goods and services crossing international borders.**

Now, if the Japanese investor makes a 7% profit, let's say in U.S. bonds, but the currency needed to buy the bonds—dollars—drops 5% in value, the profit is only 2% when money is changed back from dollars to yen. When one makes an investment in another country, the return is made up of two parts: the local profits received in the foreign country from the investment property, and the change in the value of that country's money when it is converted back to the home money. Therefore, an important consideration when investing abroad is the expected exchange rate.

Foreign investment is less certain because of foreign **exchange-rate risk.** There is the chance that investors in foreign property will lose money because of a change in the exchange rate. A favorable exchange rate can be profitable but losses can also be incurred that would not have happened by investing at home. As a result, businesses often buy insurance coverage to reduce these financial risks.

Money and Exchange Rates

The global economy runs on the **trade** of goods and services. However, without money, trade would be very difficult. It is hard to barter, to exchange one good for another—cheese for strawberries, for example—because one does not really know how both are valued. **Primitive economies rely on barter which is acquiring goods or services by means of exchange for other goods or services, rather than with money.** As economies mature, money, which represents value, is used. **Money is a highly financial asset that is generally accepted in exchange for other goods. Money has three basic purposes. It serves as a medium of exchange, as a unit which can be stored to accumulate value, and as a unit of account.**

Money, as a medium of exchange, makes trade more manageable because it acts as a go-between for all transactions of goods and services that make up the world economy. **Money is something which is widely accepted in payment for goods and services and in settling debts.** For instance, strawberries can be sold for money which can then be used to buy cheese. Money can also be used to store value from a period of plenty to a later period of need. One cannot keep strawberries for too long without their getting spoiled. It is better to sell the strawberries while they are good and use the money to buy cheese later. One can also invest the money from the sale of strawberries to earn interest or gain a profit. In addition, money can be used as a unit of account which allows goods and services to be valued by using a common measure. It can tell how many strawberries a slice of cheese is worth. Money allows for all goods and services to be expressed in terms of a standardized unit so it makes domestic and worldwide trade easier.

International trade takes place whenever someone buys or sells goods and services across national borders. Trade would be more efficient if there were only one world currency. However, actual international trade requires the use of foreign money or currencies. A Mexican importer of American goods must first buy American dollars to purchase them. **The money of another country is called the foreign exchange.** The foreign exchange is thus claims on another country held in the form of the currency of that country or interest-bearing bonds. The market in which transactions are conducted to effect the transfer of the currency of one country into that of another is called the **foreign exchange market. The price of another country's money in terms of one's**

own money is called the **foreign exchange rate or the exchange rate.** In the case of the United States, the exchange rate is the amount of foreign money Americans can buy with each dollar. The exchange rate also influences what foreigners have to pay to get dollars to buy American goods and services.

Therefore, **the exchange rate is the price of foreign currency or the price at which one currency is exchanged for another. This price increases and decreases like any other price based on its supply and demand.** For example, if there is a high demand for Mexican oil, the price of the Mexican peso tends to rise as importers of Mexican oil around the world buy pesos to buy the oil. As the demand for pesos rises so does the value of the peso. This means that the Mexican exchange rate increases in value and the peso can buy more foreign currencies. On the other hand, if the demand for Mexican products drops, so will the demand for pesos by foreigners. This lowers the value of the peso and its exchange rate and pesos will then buy less amounts of foreign currency.

Exchange rates vary daily and are constantly updated in banks and foreign exchange offices around the world. There are hundreds of financial centers where currency trading is going on. These markets are all banked electronically. Banks and "Bureaus de Change" look at the global interbank market to set their daily rates, which are given to foreign travelers when they change their money abroad. The exchange rate is slightly different if the customer is buying or selling any one particular currency. This spread between the "buy" and "sell" rates ensures that banks and exchange bureaus make a small profit every time the currency is traded.

Now, how do foreign exchange markets decide how much a currency is worth? The actual rate at any one time is determined by supply and demand conditions for the relevant currencies in the market. These in turn would depend on the balance of payments, deficits or surpluses of the relevant economies and the demand for the currencies to meet obligations, and expectations about the future movements in the rate. When enough Mexican traders want to buy U.S. dollars to buy American goods, the value of the dollar tends to rise, while the value of the Mexican peso tends to drop. This determination of value is influenced by economic and political events, and sometimes by the speculation of individual traders. For example, if traders believe that the Mexican economy is in trouble and the peso might lose value, they might rush to sell pesos and buy U.S. dollars or euros. As they get rid of pesos, demand for the peso

declines and it loses value. This lowers the Mexican exchange rate but raises the American and the euro exchange rates. During times of turmoil, traders and investors sometimes rush to buy "hard currencies" like the U.S. dollar and the Swiss frank which are expected to preserve their value during crises. These solid currencies are often referred to as **international reserve currencies** which all countries are willing to accept as final payment for obligations owed to it.

Therefore, the country's **exchange rate,** let's say that of the United States, is affected by both trade and investment: dollars are demanded by foreigners who want American goods or property; and dollars are sold by Americans who want to exchange them for foreign currencies to buy (import) goods and services from abroad, or who want to buy property outside the United States. **The foreign exchange market brings together buyers and sellers of a country's money to establish its free market price (exchange rate).**

This exchange rate is the value foreign exchange traders put on money to purchase goods, services, or investments. When exchange rates are allowed to rise and fall according to the demand and the supply for a country's money, they are called **floating exchange rates.** The market value for money will move to a level where the country's supply of money equals the world demand for it. On the other hand, there are some exchange rates which do not float. They are called **pegged rates,** or fixed rates. These are exchange rates in which the relative values of the various currencies are established by agreement between or among countries.

While floating exchange rates have been most common since 1973, central banks often try to intervene and manipulate the exchange rate to raise or lower the value of the currency, or keep it stable. When this government intervention in the global foreign exchange markets takes place, it is called a **managed or dirty float.** A government can buy its own currency to reduce its supply or availability in the international economy and thus raise its value. Or it can increase its supply to lower its value.

If Mexico for example, wants to increase its exports, it might cheapen or lower the value of its currency by printing or creating more money in its domestic economy. When the currency is devalued in this way, other countries can buy more pesos which then they can use to buy more Mexican products. This **devaluation,** however, could have the negative impact of creating inflation in Mexico as the peso now buys less and imports are more expensive. If the inflation rises too much, the Mexican government might then have to intervene by reducing the amount of pesos in the economy. This **appreciation** in the value of the pesos will allow Mexicans to have a stronger purchasing power, reduce inflation, make their imports cheaper, but reduce their exports for the peso now is more expensive for other countries to buy.

Let's use the example of American exports and imports. When the demand for U.S. exports or property goes up so does the cost of the dollars foreigners have to buy to get these exports and assets. The increased value of the dollar raises the exchange rate. After a while, a strong dollar will make imports cheaper because traders can use the dollar to buy more foreign currencies and foreign goods. This in turn tends to reduce domestic inflation by making imports more competitive with American goods, forcing American producers to keep prices down. **However, a strong dollar will gradually make American exports more expensive since foreigners have to spend more of their own currencies to buy each dollar.** This increase in the price of the dollar—originally due to high demand for American goods and services—can make American firms lose export business to other countries. As a result, U.S. firms will compete more to sell their goods in the domestic market, helping to keep inflation low. **On the other hand, if the dollar is too strong and lowers exports dramatically, some American companies might decide to move to another country so they can sell more of their products.**

Thus, a strong currency is not necessarily good for a country's foreign trade. In the case of the United States, it makes American goods and services more expensive for foreigners to buy. Exports decline as soon as foreign buyers find cheaper substitutes for American goods. **A strong dollar is generally bad for American exports but good for foreign producers, since Americans will import more of their goods and services for the dollar can buy more foreign currency.** It is also good for American consumers for they can buy more foreign goods. While the prices of foreign goods do not necessarily change, the favorable exchange rate does make foreign goods cheaper.

However, as American exports decline, the dollar begins to drop in value creating a less favorable exchange rate and the possibility of inflation as the dollar buys less. This can scare foreign investors who might sell their assets in the United States, further declining the demand for dollars and consequently its value. There will however, come a time when a further decline in the price of the dollar will attract foreign investors and buyers of American exports due to the cheapness of the dollar. Exports will then increase and imports decrease. Later, this increased demand for the dollar will again rise in value and the cycle is repeated.

Exports and the Exchange Rate

Approximately 10% of the U.S. Gross Domestic Product comes from exports. **Exports are the goods and services produced by one country which are sold to another in exchange for the second country's own goods and services, for gold and foreign exchange or in settlement of debt.** Exports are vital to some industries. Over 1/3 of all machinery produced in the United States and about 15% of all transportation equipment are exported. These sales then create an **export multiplier** or expansion as money earned from exports is deposited in banks throughout the country to pay for payroll, purchases, financial services, etc. used to make the product exported.

The money that exports bring into an economy create more income than can be measured by the exports themselves as the dollars multiply through the economy. The export multiplier is the ratio of the total increase in a country's national income to the increment in export revenue generating the increase. The size of the multiplier depends on the tendency to save of the recipient of the increase in incomes derived from the increase in export revenue and the country's tendency to import. The more people spend and the less they import at least in the short run, the stronger the export multiplier will be in the economy.

How can a country increase its exports? One way is by designing, producing, and selling innovative products, which consumers want at the lowest possible cost. This requires a substantial degree of investment in research and development (**R&D**) and reducing as much as possible governmental restrictions on savings and investments such as high taxes and regulations. **A second way is by helping trade partners succeed economically.** Exports are primarily determined by income levels in other countries. A country's economic success in the international trade is linked to the prosperity of its trade partners. For example, when the Japanese economy is strong and its citizens have high incomes, its exchange rate is high and they can buy more American dollars and American goods. If Japanese exports perform poorly there will be less demand for the yen, lowering its exchange rate and making it more difficult to buy dollars and American goods.

Clearly, international **trade** is a two-way street; a state cannot sell anything to other countries unless it also buys from them. The reason is that most countries use their own money, and therefore, the money a country receives from selling abroad must be used to buy from abroad. **A state cannot continue to export goods and services without also buying from other states. Unless a country imports, it cannot export.**

However, sometimes governments do not want to wait for the natural cyclical rise and fall in the value of the currency and the exchange rate. They use their **central banks** to promote exports by increasing or lowering the money supply and thus controlling the credit system. The central banks can promote exports by making the currency weak through the selling of newly-created money in the foreign exchange market. Undermining the money by increasing the supply of a country's currency is called a devaluation of the money. **A devaluation is a reduction of the rate at which one currency is exchanged for another.** This reduces the exchange rate making foreign currencies and products harder to buy, inhibiting imports, but promoting exports since foreigners can now buy more of the lower-valued domestic currency.

Yet, a monetary policy of devaluation can have serious consequences. It can increase inflation by reducing a citizen's purchasing power and by lowering living standards. **Thus, a policy of increasing exports could conflict with a policy of reducing inflation.** In addition, when a central bank, or the **Federal Reserve System** in the United States, increases the money supply to devaluate the dollar, domestic interest rates are likely to fall since the price of borrowing money decreases as the supply of available money increases. This discourages foreign investment in the United States because foreigners do not receive as much return on their investments. The increase in the money supply makes it easier in the short run for people and businesses to borrow money and spend it. This could later cause inflation and raise interest rates if the increased economic activity has not led to increased productivity. Devaluation cheats those people who have worked hard and saved their money, for inflation destroys savings. In the long run, it is much better for a country to increase its exports by producing superior products. This can be encouraged through educational and **fiscal policies** (these deal with government taxation and spending) which promote savings, investment, and greater efficiency in the use of human, natural, and capital resources.

Central Banks

Central banks exercise direction over **monetary policy** by adjusting the money supply in the economy which enhances or inhibits economic expansion. Central banks often use the **Bank of International Settlements (BIS)** located in Basel, Switzerland, which often serves as a central bank to the world's central banks. It serves several functions: advises and supervises the international banking community; provides temporary funds **(bridge funds loans)** to help those banks in crisis; transfers funds from one central bank to another; and offers a system of credit and debits without using cash.

Banks and individuals borrow where interest rates are the lowest and money is the cheapest. Funds also move across borders looking for locations where they can get the highest possible interest rates for their investments. **Interest rates regulate economic growth worldwide. They attract or repel capital depending on how high or low interest rates are throughout the world.** However, the great volume and speed behind these transfers can destabilize any one country as capital enters and leaves a country looking for the highest possible rate of return. For this reason, cooperation among central banks is growing in order to resolve the financial crisis.

Budget Deficits and Trade Deficits

Budget deficits tend to lead to trade deficits. A budget deficit is the amount by which the expenditures of a government exceed its revenues. A trade deficit is the amount by which the imports of a country exceed its exports. Most governments pay for their budget deficits by selling government bonds rather than by increasing taxes or cutting spending. Raising taxes and reducing government spending can be politically difficult due to popular opposition. When governments sell bonds they acquire debt; they must pay interest on the money borrowed to pay for the deficit. Sometimes debtor countries have to borrow even more money just to pay the interest. For example, in 2008, the United States spent over $250 billion in interest. This accounts in part for the $10 trillion American debt.

After borrowing to pay for deficits, the amount of money available for other things in the economy declines and this shortage of funds leads to higher interest rates. This occurs because the government's demand for savings (to borrow and pay its deficit and previous debt) is added to the demand of the business or private sector to pay for its desired investments. The supply of funds is limited. Therefore, as the demand for money rises, the price of money (interest rates) increases. Domestic borrowers now have to pay more for money to get loans. This slows down economic activity. However, these higher interest rates attract foreign investors and their money as they try to "cash in" on higher interest, increasing further the demand for dollars so they can buy American bonds. As a result, the value of the dollar rises on the international markets.

This appreciation of the currency and exchange rate makes U.S. exports more expensive because eventually foreigners have to pay more to buy dollars to acquire American products. On the other hand, Americans can import more from abroad because the dollar can buy more foreign currencies. **When imports become less expensive and exports harder to sell on the world markets, countries begin to run trade deficits.** In the short-term, the country with the trade surplus, let's say Japan, might buy bonds in the United States or in any other country with a budget deficit. Yet, if the deficits get out of control, Japan might not trust the capacity of the United States to repay its debt. It might stop buying bonds unless the interest rate is increased to compensate for the risk of an American default.

Capital Markets

Governments often use the world's **capital markets** to borrow money by issuing bonds and other debt instruments. In most cases, this allows them to raise funds at a lower cost than by borrowing directly from a bank. **The capital market is the market for longer-term loanable funds as distinct from the money market which deals in short-term funds.** In principle, capital market loans are used by industry and commerce mainly for fixed investment. The capital market is an increasingly international one and in any country is not one institution but all those institutions that watch the supply and demand for long-term capital and claims of capital, e.g. the stock exchange, banks, and insurance companies.

All advanced countries have highly developed capital markets, but in developing countries, the absence of a capital market is often as much of an obstacle to growth of investment as a shortage of savings. Government and industrialists in these poor countries are obliged to obtain capital in the international capital markets, i.e. that composed of the national capital markets in the advanced countries. There is no one specific center for capital mar-

ket trading but a series of electronically-linked banks and trading floors located in cities all over the world. **They transfer money from those who have it to those who need it and are willing to pay a price to get it.** These debt instruments can be bought and sold just like any other commodity on the international markets.

The price borrowers pay for money is called its **interest rate** which is determined by supply and demand. When money is plentiful, interest rates decline. Capital in this sense is **accumulated wealth**—as distinct from machinery and buildings which is also called capital. Borrowers could be governments, multinational corporations, civic institutions, the International Monetary Fund, the World Bank, or countries. The investors could be pension funds, farmers, and others willing to lend their savings or capital for a price.

While **stocks** represent ownership in a corporation, **bonds** are loan agreements. The borrowers agree to pay the bond holder a certain amount of money at a certain time in the future. Almost anyone can issue a bond. Large institutions such as governments and corporations are the most common borrowers in the international bond markets. Instead of relying on any one bank to lend them money, they issue bonds to raise large sums of funds, often in global issues of securities that are sold to banks and other investors around the world. The issuer must pay back the original amount borrowed called the **principal,** and must pay interest periodically to reward those who buy the bond as an investment.

Essentially bond prices follow interest rates. A bond paying a relatively low rate of interest will be sold at a discount when higher interest bonds are issued, since people abandon the lower-interest paying bond seeking a higher profit. By paying less for a bond, the buyer receives a higher return or yield, on the amount invested. When interest rates fall, the prices of existing bonds rise. In periods of declining interest rates, a relatively high-coupon bond would see its price rise, until its yield is the same as other bonds in the market with similar maturity and risk. The interest rate and the price of a bond are also determined by its risk—the likelihood of the investment being paid. **The riskier the bond, the higher the interest rate a potential borrower has to pay to attract lenders.** Bonds are traded around the world usually in trading rooms of banks and securities houses that are connected by an elaborate system of electronic communications equipment. Here one finds professional "market-makers" who buy and sell bonds for interested parties. Traders make money by buying for less and selling for more. To sell or buy a bond, an investor goes to the trader who makes a "market" with two prices: a bid price and an offer price. The trader makes money by buying bonds at the lower price and selling them at the higher offer price. The difference between the two is called the spread.

Mobility of Resources

Labor and capital mobility refers to any movement of labor, capital, and technology across national boundaries that is motivated by political, socio-economic, or religious reasons. It is an integrating force in the global economy that can substitute or complement trade. Developed countries can import cheap labor products or hire cheap migrant workers to produce them.

Labor Mobility

Migration can be legal as in the case of permanent or temporary guest workers, or it can be illegal as people smuggle themselves into other countries. The developed countries (host states) can either invest in the poor countries (home states) and create jobs to employ the poor there, or be faced with illegal immigration. In the case of labor mobility, it is impossible to determine if immigration itself is always good or bad.

There could be several winners in the case of immigration: immigrants who improve their wages and living standards by moving to the host country; families of immigrants in the home state who get money remittance; workers in the home countries who are now less in number and therefore might get better salaries; producers in the host countries who obtain cheaper labor which can help lower labor costs and improve their profits; the host state receives more tax revenues thus improving their tax base; the welfare system in the home countries realizes a relief because there are less people receiving benefits; and the host countries gain as a whole for they can acquire very educated people without having paid for their education.

However, there could be some losers too as a result of immigration. Home country employers might have to pay higher wages for labor that is now relatively more scarce. Poor workers in the host country have to compete with the immigrants and this can reduce their wages. The tax base in the home country is reduced although this can be offset partly by the reduction in welfare benefits and remittance. The

welfare system and educational institutions in the host country can become stressed by the increased demand for health, housing, and educational needs of the immigrants. The home country can lose some of its best educated people creating a "brain drain" which wastes the countries' previous educational investments. Finally, the social stability in the host countries can suffer due to demographic congestion and ethnic conflict in those large cities which welcome too many immigrants in too short a time.

Capital Mobility

Capital also moves across borders looking for low-wage labor, tax preferences, political and financial stability, better geographical location, and overall higher returns on investment. International capital could be divided into official or private. **Official capital is that which comes from governments or is often channeled through such multilateral agencies as the International Monetary Fund (IMF) and the World Bank. Private capital is that which comes from individuals and business corporations.** One type of private capital consists of **short term exchange-rate movements**, as billions of dollars can suddenly leave a country looking for higher interest rates somewhere else, creating significant financial instability both in the country of origin and of destination.

A second type of **private capital** is **long-term capital movements**. These can be **portfolio investments** like stocks in overseas markets, mutual funds looking for diversification and higher returns, or **direct investments** abroad such as building companies and constructing projects. Direct investments can present important opportunities to exploit a technology, beat a trade barrier imposed by a country, gain control over foreign supplies, and build plants abroad to circumvent trade restrictions.

As with labor mobility, there are potential winners and losers resulting from capital mobility. Possible winners are the owners of capital in the home country since their foreign investments could give them a higher rate of return. The world as whole benefits since capital can flow to work where it is most efficient. This benefits the most productive workers. Potential losers are workers who lose their jobs in the home country because the outflowing capital is not used to expand domestic industry. The transfer of capital can also hurt industries which cannot compete with the incoming investment.

Multinational Corporations

A major part of global capital mobility today is directed by multinational corporations. A multinational corporation (MNC) is an enterprise operating in a number of countries and having production or service facilities outside the country of its origin. A common accepted definition of a MNC is an enterprise producing at least 25% of its world output outside its country of origin. They buy or build a subsidiary to produce goods globally. By doing this, they acquire certain benefits: they protect their proprietary technology or secrets; reduce transportation costs; take advantage of low labor costs and materials; receive favorable tax conditions; help export goods to other countries because of unfavorable exchange rates in the home country; attain economies of scale; fulfill consumer preferences for home products; and take advantage of rationalized production or comparative advantage in design and production.

Multinational corporations account for approximately 20% of global production, and 25% of all trade between subsidiaries. Before 1945, they specialized on primary sectors: oil, mining, and agriculture. Mobil, Alcoa and Anaconda were among the most important names. After 1945, multinational corporations began emphasizing manufacturing and high-tech products such as computers. IBM and Phillips became big names.

Presently, it is difficult at times to determine the nationality of a multinational corporation (MNC). For example, Smith Corona has its headquarters in the United States but manufactures its product in Singapore. Brother, on the other hand, produces typewriters in the United States but its headquarters are in Tokyo. Which is American? Which criteria does one use to decide the nationality of MNC? Where the jobs are? Where management activities are? Or is the main criteria ownership? The problem is that jobs are worldwide, the management might be multi-ethnic and employed globally, and publicly held corporations have stock-holders all over the world. Perhaps the crucial question is not the nationality of a corporation but the well-being which it enhances as a result of its investments and operation.

There are potential winners resulting from MNC activities: the host country receiving the investment can benefit from an inflow of capital, increased production, jobs, income, technology, competition, exports, tax revenues, and business expertise; the MNC can improve its earnings; and the world economy as a whole gains from the effects of specialization of labor and production according to comparative advantage.

However, there are also potential losers: workers can lose their jobs in the home country if a multinational corporation moves its plant abroad simply to gain a few percentages of profit; the home country can lose tax revenues, although this loss can be offset with the inflow of profits from abroad; the home country exports its technology abroad which represents a loss of Research and Development investment; the MNC can lose its investments in the foreign country as a result of terrorism, revolution or natural disasters; and the host country could be destabilized economically and politically by the presence of a very large, corrupt, and manipulative MNC.

Protectionism

Sometimes governments try to restrict imports with protectionist policies. Protectionism is the imposition of restrictions to restrict the inflow of imports. Various reasons are often given for these policies: keeping income high in the country instead of letting it flow outward to pay for imported goods; protecting domestic industries and preserving jobs; protecting strategic industries like aircraft, computers, oil, etc., needed for the preservation of the national security, particularly in times of war when access to foreign resources might not be possible; **helping infant or newly developing industries gain economies of scale until they can compete unprotected;** leveling the playing field against foreign monopolies which are trying to undermine domestic industries by selling their goods at unreasonable and unfair prices; and protecting the national heritage and culture against foreign investments or imports in such industries as movie production, newspapers, and education.

One protectionist instrument is the **tariff,** which is a tax imposed on a commodity import. A tariff may be levied on an ad valorem basis, i.e. as a certain percentage of value, or on a specific basis, i.e. as an amount per unit. A tariff could be imposed to raise revenue or to carry out a specific economic policy such as reducing imports, retaliating against other countries which have high tariffs, or protecting an industry from unfair competition. For example, a 25% ad valorem tariff is equal to 25% of whatever price exporters charge for their products. People can still import products. However, they now have to pay a higher price. The tariff itself protects the domestic producer from the cheaper import.

A second trade barrier is the **import quota** on specific items, which limits the number of products that can be imported. The quota limits the choice of consumers for once a certain amount of a specific good has been imported, consumers cannot buy anymore. It is a more effective protection than the tariff. A third protectionist tool is a **voluntary export restraint (VER)** by which a country "voluntarily" agrees not to exceed its exports beyond a certain amount, though they can increase their price. This often ends up helping the foreign producer for they can raise the price of a good and make a higher profit if consumers are desperate to buy the product. A fourth trade barrier is the **specification of product standards** by which the country can require certain health, environmental, legal, and other requirements which the import must meet to be allowed into the country. Sometimes the requirements cannot be met and the products will not be imported.

A fifth restriction could be **currency controls** which limit the amount of local currency importers are permitted to turn into another currency during a given time to buy imports. Reducing the availability of foreign currencies will reduce imports. A sixth measure is **anti-dumping policies** against countries which charge predatory prices—selling a good outside the country cheaper than in its own country. Often the producer who is dumping sells the product at a price lower than what it cost to make. Governments will compensate such producers with subsidies.

However, these protectionist policies could have several problems. They tend to be expensive. Consumers have to pay higher prices and taxes to protect domestic industries from outside competition. They end up buying less of the desired product. The losses to consumers usually outweigh the gains to the protected industry, its employees, and the government which receives revenues from the tariffs. There is also an efficiency loss in the domestic and international economy because under protectionism, countries do not pursue their comparative advantage. There is a reduction in competitiveness as protected industries are seldom motivated to improve efficiency.

Protectionism encourages lobbying of the government by corporations as they seek special privileges. **This politicizes economic decisions.** In addition, limiting imports often results in retaliation by other countries as they begin to protect their own producers. **It is also difficult to decide which infant industries have a good chance of developing and becoming successful on their own, and which industries are really important to the national security. The decision-making on these matters tends to become too political and discriminatory.** Usually the oldest and more politically established industries will have an unfair advantage over those new industries, which though more efficient, have fewer political friends to protect them.

There are potential winners and losers in protectionism. Foreign consumers benefit from having their domestic producers lower prices to compete in their domestic market since they cannot sell as many goods abroad. Import-competing industries benefit because domestic consumers have no choice but to buy their products. Foreign producers under VER could increase prices and gain higher profits if domestic consumers do not mind paying a higher price for less available products. Potential losers are consumers who have to pay higher prices or have less consumer products available. Domestic producers who need machinery or other resources from abroad to make export goods now have to pay more for their imports. Their exports then become more expensive and less competitive. Most foreign producers are hurt. Moreover, the economy as a whole suffers as natural, labor, and capital resources go to inefficient sectors.

Perhaps one of the best rationales for protectionism is the infant-industry argument. An industry does not operate at an optimum least-cost output until it has reached a sufficient size to obtain significant economies of scale so that the cost of producing a commodity falls. A new industry, particularly in the developing world, therefore, will tend to be in a competitively vulnerable position vis-à-vis an established industry in an advanced country. It follows, according to the argument, that the stage of growth at which the industry (or country) can "take off" industrially will be postponed indefinitely. The argument concludes that protection is necessary until the industry has reached its optimum size. There is much to be said in favor of this argument. However, how does one decide wisely which infant industries deserve such protection? Unfortunately, one protection is extended to an industry, often it is difficult politically to terminate it.

Development Banks

Regional development banks provide development funds for needy countries. They channel funds from the rich countries to the "have-nots." These institutions are not ordinary profit-oriented banks which take traditional deposits. Instead, they are funded by large capital commitments and loans from the developed countries like the United States, Japan, and Switzerland. The funds are loaned at a low rate of interest to needy countries. These usually have a **grace period** of two to seven years before requiring to pay back the original principal. This allows the financed project time to start making money.

Examples of regional development banks are the **Inter-American Development Bank,** the **Asian Development Bank,** the **African Development Bank,** the **European Bank for Reconstruction,** and the **European Investment Bank.**

Also important in the area of development international finance is the **International Bank for Reconstruction and Development (IBRD)** also called the **World Bank.** The World Bank receives funds from its wealthy member countries which provide it credit to borrow cheaply on the world capital markets and then extend cheap development aid to the world's poor countries. **The International Monetary Fund (IMF)** provides temporary funds for countries with severe economic difficulties, particularly balance of trade problems. **However, to extend aid the IMF often requires the receiving country to make difficult political and economic reforms like raising taxes, cutting government spending, depreciating the currency to stimulate exports, and selling government agencies to the private sector to run them more efficiently (privatization).** These measures can reduce the standard of living for the majority of the people and represent a severe political cost to the government. Riots and rebellions are often the consequences of these reforms.

Industrial and Trade Policy

One major question today is whether governments should pick potential winners and losers among business corporations to provide them with assistance. **Industrial policy is an attempt by the government to shift allocation of resources into specific sectors to accelerate their economic growth.** For instance, the government might reduce assistance to the domestic coal industry since it might be cheaper to import coal, and might then increase tax breaks and subsidies to the steel industry. **Trade policy is a particular government industrial policy with a focus on sectors that export. While protectionism concentrates on limiting imports, trade policy concentrates on increasing exports.**

There are several tools of trade policies: **export subsidies** are government funds given to producers for every unit of a good exported, let's say, corn, wheat, etc. Export subsidies, except for agriculture, have been prohibited by the **General Agreement on Tariff and Trade (GATT). Production subsidies** are government funds for every unit of a good produced. **R&D subsidies** are government funds for the research and development of technologies which can generate better products for export. **Interest-free loans** are government subsidies for businesses which borrow money to expand their exports.

The problem with industrial and trade policies is that it is difficult to pick winners. For example, the Japanese government tried to discourage Sony and Honda which are now successful corporations, and picked losers in aluminum, aerospace, ship-building, personal computers and high-definition TV. **The key to trade success is not so much government assistance as it is to follow one's comparative advantage and to increase competition so that producers are motivated to become more efficient.** Also, the costs of government support to industry can lead to high taxes, prices, and inefficiencies. In addition, government aid is often not well spent since it can lead to government corruption, waste, and the politicization of economic decisions as government officials prefer supporting, their political allies in the business world.

Therefore, it might be better for governments to stop interfering with economic production and concentrate instead on creating the preconditions for growth: stable monetary policies which promote low inflation; fiscal policies which increase savings and investments; good legal, health, educational systems, adequate infrastructure of roads, bridges, harbors, power facilities, and research and development funds. As these conditions are addressed, private capital will be free to seek its comparative advantage.

Pollution

Environmental pollution is the addition to the natural environment of any substance or energy form (e.g. heat, sound) at a rate that results in higher than natural concentrations of that substance. Thus defined, pollution includes many naturally occurring substances such as carbon dioxide (CO_2), the natural emission of which by humans and animals has little or no apparent effect on the natural environment—but may be significant in special instances—and other substances such as agricultural fertilizers, which stimulate natural plant growth; therefore, not all forms of pollution are equally destructive. Nor are all the types of pollution irreversible. In addition, natural causes of pollution such as volcanoes, hurricanes and earthquakes can be as serious as pollution by humans who, in the recent literature on the topic of pollution, usually get most of the blame.

Pollution is a failure of the economic system. The full cost of pollution is not being absorbed by the producers and consumers who profit from the productions process creating the pollution. If producers had to pay higher taxes for the pollution they create, and consumers had to pay higher prices for products whose processing causes excessive environmental destruction, then destructive production and pollution would be kept at moderate levels. It is important that the price of a good reflects its full cost, including the expense society incurs by having to clean up the environment, by having to live without a particular resource, or by having to address the physical or health consequences of the pollution.

There are several methods for controlling pollution. One is a **pollution tax** on units produced which created pollution. However, the revenues generated by the tax should only be used for cleaning purposes instead of for general government spending. The tax will also motivate businesses to find cleaner production systems. A second option is **command and control** measures where the government sets production limits. This could be impractical since the government might not know the proper amounts of pollution or have other priorities which do not concern pollution control. In addition, much pollution is across political borders and beyond the control of particular governments. Furthermore, some of the worst environmental destruction occurs in government property or in areas regulated by governments.

A third option is government **subsidies for pollution control equipment** so that business and individuals are able to acquire new technology to produce and consume more cleanly. A fourth option is the **assigning of property rights** which grants private business temporary ownership of particular strips of land, water resources, and other assets, as long as they are also responsible for its maintenance. This could prevent overfishing the oceans, erosion, and other types of waste because at least someone is accountable, responsible for damage in a particular area. Incentives need to be in place so that individuals are motivated to replenish resources at the same time they are generating profits from their use.

There is a point at which incremental costs in fighting pollution are not cost effective and become higher than their incremental benefits. The costs of fighting pollution are easy to identify: pollution taxes, cleanups, scrubbers, more expensive production taxes, etc. On the other hand, the benefits of pollution control such as lower deaths and diseases, more enjoyment of the environment, etc., are harder to identify. So there is a point where the political costs of fighting pollution become very high. Therefore, it might be difficult to eliminate all pollution.

Concern for the environment is related to the level of a country's economic development. Poor countries are usually more concerned with starvation, unemployment, civil wars, and consolidating political power. As they get richer, countries become more concerned with environmental issues. This is a good reason why developed countries should try enlightened assistance on behalf of the economic, social, and political development of the poor world. In fact, some pollution declines as countries prosper. This is the case with water pollution which declines as states install better sanitation and sewer purifying technologies which increase the amount of safe water. Other types of pollution increase as countries develop economically before declining significantly later on. This is the case with dirt particles in the air from burning wood and coal. Urban concentration of sulfur dioxide usually decline. However, some types of pollution seem to increase when countries become richer—such as municipal waste trash and carbon dioxide emissions from the use of fossil fuels. Still, OECD countries have managed to grow while controlling and actually reducing some forms of pollution: nitrogen oxides, sulfur dioxide, lead, and particulars.

Trade Liberalization and Regional Trade Blocs

In 1947, the United States produced 50% of the world's Gross National Product as Europe and Japan had been devastated by World War II. The United States decided to promote trade liberalization, or free trade, to prevent the political instability associated with economic depressions and protectionism, both of which were seen as causes of the war. Free trade is a policy of allowing unrestricted trade among countries. This was done by opening up its markets to foreign goods so that countries would earn much-needed revenues, spending its surplus dollars in foreign investments and supporting the

General Agreement of Tariffs and Trade (GATT). GATT was an international organization with a secretariat in Geneva which came into operation in January 1948, a year after its treaty. The member countries pledge to the expansion of multilateral trade with the minimum of barriers to trade, a reduction of import tariffs and quotas, and the abolition of preferential trade agreements.

The principles of GATT prohibited the following: discrimination against the goods of other countries; barriers against imports except in the case of already declining tariffs; protection of faltering industries from import competition, except temporary measures in emergencies; and export subsidies, except those for agriculture. **A GATT principle is that any new or increase in a tariff has to be compensated by a decrease somewhere else. GATT discouraged most-favored nation clauses which are clauses in an international trade treaty under which the signatories promise to extend to each other any favorable trading terms offered in agreement with third parties.**

There were eight GATT sessions after 1947, using long and drawn-out multilateral negotiations aimed at tariff reductions. There were 116 countries involved in this process at its end. The final agreement came in April 1994. The members agreed to reduce export barriers by an average of 37% to stimulate jobs. Also, farm subsidies were at first to be reduced by an average of 21%. The **World Trade Organization (WTO)** was created to arbitrate disputes and assign responsibility for the violation of the agreement and to replace GATT. The member countries wanted to avoid a collapse of world trade, a worldwide recession, and its resulting political instability. They hoped to increase global output by $6 trillion from 1993 to 2003. There have been significant advances. Average tariff rates in the 1940s were 40% while in 2008 they were only 4%. As a result, trade volume increased over 1,200% during the period.

While tariff barriers have declined globally, there has been an explosion of non-tariff barriers. These include quotas to limit the number of imports, countervailing duties or fees, voluntary export restraints, customs restrictions, product content specifications, and others. **Non-tariff barriers are particularly damaging to the exports of developing countries in areas where they have a comparative advantage.** Developed countries, particularly the United States, have concerns about trade barriers against products in which they have a comparative advantage: trade in services like insurance; trade-related intellectual property (TRIPS) like computer software; and trade-related investments matters (TRIMS) which are outside GATT.

Another threat to the liberalized international trade system, championed by the multilateral GATT approach, has been the growth of regional trade blocs. Countries began to create exclusive trade arrangements as they grew impatient and anxious over the slow and frustrating GATT process. There are four types of economic blocs. **A free-trade area is an association of a number of countries among which all import tariffs and quotas and export subsidies and other similar government measures to influence trade have been removed or diminished.** Each country, however, continues to retain its own international trade measures such as tariffs, quotas, etc., vis-à-vis countries outside the association. An example of a free trade area is the North American Free Trade Area (NAFTA), established in 1993 incorporating Canada, Mexico and the United States.

A customs union is established within two or more countries if all barriers (such as tariffs and quotas) to the free exchange of each other's goods and services are removed and, at the same time, a common external tariff is established against non-members. An example of a customs union is MERCOSUR established in 1991, incorporating Argentina, Brazil, Paraguay and Uruguay and associated states such as Chile and Bolivia.

A **common market** consists of a free movement of labor, capital, technology, among the member countries under a system of lowered tariffs and common trade barriers against outside countries. An example of a common market is the European Common Market, established in 1958 by six European states. An **economic union** is an arrangement in which member countries coordinate fiscal and monetary policies and try to keep external tariffs low.

Regional trade blocs contrast with GATT because there is no global effort to reduce tariffs against all states. Regional trade blocs can provide certain benefits. They enlarge the market where corporations and companies can trade and increase competition among themselves. This can then promote economic innovation, productivity, economies of scale, and comparative advantage. Trade blocs can raise the level of investment and provide consumers with more and better products at a lower price. In addition, they constrain the trade policies of the member countries by reducing the chances of protectionism.

On the other hand, there are potential losses. The governments of the member countries in the trade bloc can lose revenues they used to collect on the tariffs. **There is a possibility of trade diversion or trade loss as the consumers in the trade bloc cannot buy cheaper imports from countries outside the bloc. Trade diversion can eliminate the benefits which come from following comparative advantages.** Also, countries outside the bloc, whose goods are kept out, might retaliate and place import barriers on the goods from the trade bloc. This undermines the multilateral efforts to reduce tariff barriers.

The key issue in the debate between trade liberalization and regional trade blocs is whether in creating a regional trade bloc, trade creation is greater than trade diversion. **Trade-creation**—which benefits the economy as a whole by creating comparative advantages, lower prices, and more products—will be greater than trade diversion the higher the pre-bloc trade barriers were, the lower the bloc's external barriers, the larger the number of countries in the bloc, the more competitive the economies, the closer the geographical proximity of the members, and the greater the level pre-bloc trade.

The Evolving World Economy

There has been a dramatic increase in the flow of goods, services, technology and capital since the end of World War II in 1945. Although it has boosted living standards worldwide, there have been losers and serious human cost. The key to increases in income seems to be through productivity gains, education, trained labor, technology, research and development budgets, savings and investments, open markets and competition, availability of capital resources, and the pursuit of comparative advantage by specialization in what a country can do relatively more effectively.

Comparative advantage is a dynamic thing, but it can change quickly and dramatically. For example, as a product goes from the stage of research and development, innovation, maturation, and standardization, production can go from capital rich/high wage countries, to capital rich/medium wage countries, to capital poor/low wage countries where it can later be mass produced cheaper. This takes advantage of dynamic comparative advantage. The United States, for instance, invented computers and microchips, but now they are mass-produced in Asia which has a comparative advantage in low wage skilled labor.

Manufacturing in developed countries continues to be an important economic sector, but it is now more efficient as excess labor is shed to be employed in now more productive ways and areas. The service area had grown: legal services, business services, health, recreation, hotels, education, retail trade, financial services, and wholesale trade. The developed world has a comparative advantage in these areas. These service sectors jobs are not necessarily low paying/low productive jobs. It is difficult to measure the true value of services, for example, computer software.

Energy Resources

The growth of the world economy is highly dependent on sources of energy. During the early years of the industrial revolution, industry depended on **fuelwood.** However, by 1913 **coal** accounted for 75% of global energy consumption. Technological developments, particularly the **internal combustion** engine, stimulated the shift from coal to **oil,** and to a lesser extent to **natural gas.** The United States led the development of oil-based technologies, especially in the automotive and petrochemical industries. While in 1950 oil was less than 33% of the world energy production, by 1965 it was equal to coal production. Energy derived from oil and natural gas was cleaner and less expensive than from coal. The cost of once-inexpensive coal rose, due to labor demands for higher wages, rules to protect the environment, and more costly safety standards.

The rise of the oil industry was led by eight multinational corporations known as the majors: Exxon, Gulf, Mobil, Standard Oil of California, Texaco, British Petroleum, Royal Dutch Shell, and Compaigne Francoise des Petroles. The first seven are often referred to as the **seven sisters.** In the mid–1920s, the majors controlled close to 66% of the world's oil production, and their operations ranged from exploration to the retailing of petroleum products at their gas stations. The communist countries of the Second World were virtually the only oil-producing states which barred the majors. Since oil was plentiful and cheap, the majors cooperated among themselves to restrict supply and to avoid price competition. This kept prices from dropping too much and allowed them to maintain a profit. This abundant supply of oil at low prices facilitated the recovery of Western Europe and Japan after World War II, and stimulated consumers to use energy-intensive products such as the automobile. However, it also increased worldwide demand for consumption of energy and the need to find and exploit new oil deposits.

The price stability in the oil industry came to an end with the rise of the Organization of Petroleum Exporting Countries (OPEC), an energy cartel. A **cartel** is an association of producers to regulate prices by restructuring output and competition. OPEC was created in 1960 but began to exert great political and economic power in 1973 over the production and price levels of oil. During the 1973 Yom Kippur War between Israel and its Arab neighbors, OPEC—which is made up mostly of Arab states—raised the price of oil 400%, and embargoed oil shipments to the United States and the Netherlands to put pressure on these allies of Israel. These actions created significant financial and political disruption globally as well as poverty in non-oil producing developing countries which now had to spend more for petroleum and oil-based fertilizers.

A second oil "shock" by OPEC occurred in 1979 during the revolution in Iran which brought to power Shiite Muslim fundamentalists. The price of oil rose over 100%. This led to a major debt crisis in the poor world and to a major global economic recession. Iraq's invasion of Kuwait on August 2, 1990, precipitated the third oil shock, with prices rising another 150%. **The price of a barrel of oil (a barrel of oil equals forty-two U.S. gallons) was close to $2 in 1973, $15 in April 1990, and over $40 on September 1990. Now it is close to $145.**

The power of the OPEC commodity cartel was made possible by the absence of energy alternatives in the face of global worldwide demand for oil, the world's growing dependence on cheap Middle-Eastern oil, the ability of OPEC to wrest control of production and pricing policies from the multinational oil companies without retaliation from Western governments, the rise in the number of independent oil companies after the 1950s, which created more competitive markets, and by the willingness of OPEC governments to use their oil as a political weapon against the multinationals, the United States, and Israel. **The United States was hurt by its relatively weaker oil position: while in 1938 the USA produced 66% of the world's oil, by 1973 it produced only 16%, and imported 37% of its oil consumption.**

Oil prices grew fast from 1973, reaching a peak in 1981, before dropping dramatically to $8 a barrel in 1986. The drop in prices had several causes. First of all, Saudi Arabia increased its output to generate revenues and to undermine the American domestic oil industry with very cheap oil which drove many U.S. oil drillers

into bankruptcy. The world recession resulting from the 1979 oil shock created an oil surplus globally which pressured prices downward. Countries began to experiment with alternative energy sources such as coal, nuclear power, natural gas, and gasohol extracted from agricultural products. Developed countries began to generate more fuel-efficient products such as smaller automobiles, air conditioners, heaters, and refrigerators. In 1998, the price of oil fluctuated around $16.00 a barrel.

On the other hand, there are indications that OPEC might be regaining strength and eventually dominate the global oil marketplace. Its share of world oil production is at a high level of 40%. It was only 30% in 1985. Seventy-five percent of the world's proven oil reserves are in OPEC countries, of which 66% are in the Middle East. Also enhancing the importance of OPEC is the expected decline of production among the non-OPEC states. Production is declining in the United States and Mexico. New energy sources being developed in Yemen, Brazil, India, Norway, Angola, Malaysia, and Papua New Guinea might not be enough. Russia's production has declined from the 1980s. **For the United States, which imports more than 50% of its energy consumption, reliance on the Middle East represents a national security issue, a balance of payment problems, and an environmental challenge.**

On the basis of current ratios of production to known reserves, oil will last only until about the year 2035. Long before this, the demand for oil will sky-rocket as the industrializing countries of the Third World, including some OPEC states, compete for available supplies. This rise in demand, faster than the increase in oil supplies, will increase the cost of energy and undermine the global economy. However, it might also stimulate a shift away from the petroleum era as countries experiment with alternative energy sources. In addition, as the price for oil rises producers will probably develop new technologies to extract oil from areas which are not currently included as part of the known reserves. As a result, oil might then become more available.

Based on the current ratios of reserves to production, **coal** will last for more than 200 years. China, the United States and Russia account for more than 60% of world reserves. **Coal is the leading alternative to oil, accounting for 29% of the world's primary energy use, compared with 37% for oil, 22% for natural gas,**

7% for hydropower and 7% for nuclear energy. Unfortunately, coal has a high release of carbon into the atmosphere which could be a cause of global warming and of many physical ailments.

Natural gas is cleaner and more convenient to use than either oil or coal. Natural gas supplies, based on current reserve/production ratio, will last for nearly sixty years. Unlike coal, natural gas is distributed very unevenly on a regional basis which means that its continued development will have to depend on export trade. The Middle East holds nearly 33% of the world's proven reserves. Pipelines are the preferred method of transport, but they are expensive and massive engineering projects which pose serious environmental costs and political resistance. Liquefied natural gas is an alternative but it could be unsafe. In the same way as in the oil industry, as natural gas becomes more scarce its price will rise and it will stimulate conservation, technological innovation and further discovery. This will increase known reserves of natural gas at a lower price.

Hydropower (water-based) accounts for about 7% of world energy use. While it does not pollute the atmosphere hydropower depends on water availability, land management issues, and financial considerations, since building dams and generators can be expensive. North America is the primary consumer of electricity generated by hydropower, followed by Latin America, Europe, and Asia.

Nuclear power accounts for 7% of global energy use. The United States is the single largest consumer of nuclear energy, followed by France, Japan, and Russia. France's use is the most intensive, deriving 30% of its total energy use from nuclear power. Nuclear power is no longer the favorite alternative to oil due to technical and financial problems and a political climate which has turned against it because of safety considerations. Yet, it could once again become attractive as the industry becomes more able to deal with the storage and decontamination of nuclear waste and as the price of oil and energy dependence on hostile countries increase. Other alternative energy sources are **solar power, windpower, gasohol,** and **tidal energy.** Perhaps one day **fusion** (as opposed to fission nuclear power) will generate almost unlimited energy as atoms brought together, release energy.

Sources

Books

Bailey, Ronald, (Ed). (1995) *The True State of the Planet.* New York: The Free Press.

Bannock, Graham; Baxter, R.E.; and Davis, Evan. (1992) *The Penguin Dictionary of Economics.* New York: Penguin Books.

De Rooy, Jacob. (1995) *Economic Literacy. What Everyone Needs to Know About Money & Markets.* New York: Crown Publishers, Inc.

Epping, Randy Charles. (1992) *A Beginner's Guide to the World Economy.* New York: Vintage Books.

Issak, Robert A. (1995) *Managing World Economic Change, International Political Economy.* Englewood Cliffs: Prentice-Hall.

Kegley, Charles W., and Eugene R. Wittkopf (1995) *World Politics. Trend and Transformation.* (Fifth Edition). New York: St. Martin Press.

Pool, John C; and La Roe, Ross M. (1985) *The Instant Economist.* New York: Addison-Wesley Publishing Company.

Russet, Bruce; Starr, Harvey. (1992) *World Politics. The Menu for Choice.* New York: W.H. Freeman and Company.

Vogel, Ezra F. (1991) *The Four Little Dragons. The Spread of Industrialization in East Asia.* Cambridge: Harvard University Press.

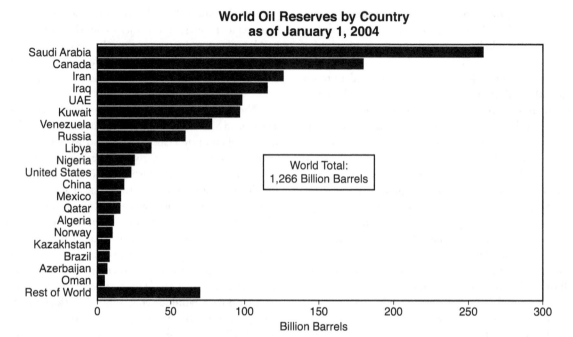

**World Oil Reserves by Country
as of January 1, 2004**

World Total:
1,266 Billion Barrels

Billion Barrels

Source: "Worldwide Look at Reserves and Production." Oil & Gas Journal, *Vol. 100, No. 49 (December 22, 2003), pp. 46–47.*

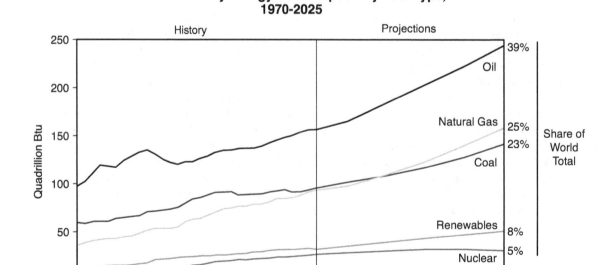

**World Primary Energy Consumption by Fuel Type,
1970-2025**

Source: *EIA,* International Energy Outlook 2004

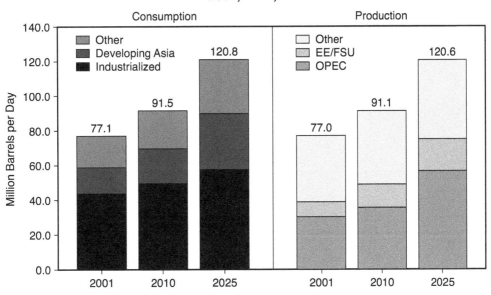

World Oil Consumption and Production, 2001, 2010, and 2025

Source: EIA, International Energy Outlook 2004

CHAPTER TWELVE

War and Peace

Germán Muñoz

W ar consists of hostilities between states, or within a state or territory undertaken by means of armed force. The level of hostility may range from total war with nuclear, chemical, bacteriological, and radiological weapons of mass destruction, to limited war with conventional land, sea and air forces, to coercive diplomacy designed to provoke crises, low-intensity conflict, civil wars and terrorism. In the last 5500 years or so since civilization began, there have been more years of war than of peace. This seems to indicate that perhaps wars are a constant part of the human condition.

History of War

Primitive War

Primitive wars were those during the paleolithic, mesolithic and neolithic periods of the Stone Age, prior to the development of civilization in the 3500s B.C. Humans had speech but lacked writing. They were organized in families, clans, tribes or villages and were armed with stones, clubs, spears, bows and arrows for attack, and animal skins and shields for defense. **The wars then were mostly feuds between families and clans to vindicate group mores and restore honor in controversies dealing with wife-stealing, witch-doctoring and other disagreements**. Economic gain and political conquest were not major motives for war among these hunting and gathering peoples. Later on, as herding, horticultural and agricultural societies developed and humans were able to accumulate goods for surplus storage, wars also took the form of raids on neighboring herds and crops. Also, war served to strengthen the unity of the fighting group and demonstrate its uniqueness and superiority.

"Civilized" War

People built civilizations in the 3500's B.C. by developing a written language, systematic agriculture or herding, a hierarchic political organization controlling a defined territory with economic and political social classes, and commercial centers for a growing population. **At this time, war became an institution conducted by a specialized group to plunder, acquire territory, trade and expand its culture**. Wars were characterized by the use of horses, chariots, disciplined armies, fortified cities, siege engines, etc.

Alliances and power-balancing came to be recognized, leading to a bipolarization of power between groups. This often led to conquest and the creation of civilizations, as under Ahmose I and Thutmose I in Egypt, Hammurabi and Tiglath-Pileser in Mesopotamia, the Ch'in in China, and Julius Caesar in the Mediterranean and in Gaul. This type of "universal state" which included a wide variety of people usually collapsed because of over-centralization, corruption, decay and high taxes, allowing outsider groups and internally-repressed peoples to then seek a new civilization. These bloody struggles united a variety of groups under the winner's culture and commercial and political territory.

Major Wars of Conquest   In the Western and in the Near Eastern worlds, there were eight major wars of conquest during this period of "civilized" wars: **Alexander the Great** (300s B.C.) using the phalanx and siege engines to build an empire from the Indus River to Egypt, and from Iran to Greece; **Rome** and its legions (300s B.C. to 200s A.D.) conquering Greece, the Middle East, Carthage, Spain, and Gaul; **Attila** with an army of Huns and Germans on horseback undermining the Roman Empire (440s); **Mohammed** and his successors (662–1100s) using horsemen and religious enthusiasm to extend into Arabia, Palestine, Iran, India, Eastern Anatolia, Egypt, North Africa and Spain; **Charlemagne** (700s) and his feudal army of knights on horseback and militia, establishing an empire in French, German and Italian lands; **Norsemen** in Viking ships (800s–1000s) invading Northern Europe, Italy, Iceland, Greenland, and America; European Christian **Crusades** (1095–1270) battling against Islam and the Byzantine Empire in the Middle East (1337–1453) and Spain; and **England** unsuccessfully trying to defeat France in the Hundred Years War (1328–1453), with feudal armies, long-bowmen, and naval transport.

The Just War   These eight wars had ideological, economic, psychological, political and juridical underlying causes. During the medieval period, as a result of the Christian theory of the just war, juridical reasons had to be used to justify wars. The *Just-War Doctrine* began with St. Augustine (400s), who argued that not all killing is murder, and that at times, the Christian must fight evil and wickedness. This theory tried to set limits for justifying causes and methods of war, in contrast to the ancient and the modern belief that war is a necessity and a benefit to the state. The doctrine was later elaborated by Thomas Aquinas (1300s) and Francisco de Vitoria (1500s). **The Just War theory called war an evil, but tried to define cases where a war was justified to avoid a worse situation.** There are several justifying conditions: war is permissible as a last resort when all other means of resolution have failed; the decision to go to war must be made by a legitimate authority; war is justified for the right intentions, that is, for the purpose of defense and not revenge; it must be conducted with the proper means; and it must have a good probability that it will succeed under a reasonable loss of life. This emphasis on justice probably reduced some of the worst excesses of medieval warfare in the West.

Modern and Recent Wars

Modern history is often associated with the use of gunpowder, the invention of the printing press, the individualism of Renaissance humanism, the European discovery of the orbits of the planets and of the civilizations of Asia and Africa, the increasing acceptance of sovereign countries, rather than a universal state, as the legitimate actors in international relations, the Protestant rebellion against the Catholic Church, and the use of military power as the basis of political authority. All of these events occurred in the 1400s and 1500s.

The modern period of warfare began with the wars of Turkish expansion against the Byzantine Empire, which ended in 1453 with the Turkish conquest of Christian Constantinople, marking the Turk artillery the first successful use of gun powder in siege strategy. The same underlying causes of war can be found in previous periods. However, from the 1650s to the 1800s, religion was less important, while political and economic imperialism and nationalism became more significant. Legal claims or justification were less important in the modern period than in the medieval period when the idea of a just war was prominent. Political and economic imperialism, and later nationalism become more important motives.

In the modern period, war has been generally regarded as a prerogative of sovereign countries, and "reason of state" was considered as a sufficient justification for war. Raison d'état (reason of state) is a doctrine developed in the 1500s by Nicolo Machiavelli and in the 1600s by Cardinal Richelieu which holds that security and national advantage are paramount consideration in state action. This doctrine of national interests dictates that moral principles and commitments and agreements should be disregarded if they conflict with state security policies or actions.

In modern war, propaganda is considered desirable to cite justifications such as necessary defense, maintenance of the balance of power, correction of historic, strategic, national or economic boundaries, independence from colonial oppression, nationality, or a civilizing mission. Propaganda is useful by both sides in a modern war. Propaganda is communications aimed at influencing the thinking, emotions or actions of a group. It assumes that changes in people's thinking will prompt changes in their actions. Propaganda is not necessarily true or false, but is a strategy based on careful selection and manipulation of data. Propaganda is usually divided into white propaganda, typical of peaceful times when states make truthful statements but leave out selected certain information, grey propaganda, typical of difficult times, when countries begin to distort the truth with inaccurate declarations, and black propaganda, typical of times of war when governments lie outright. The truth is the first victim in times of war.

Recent military history began with the use of atomic weapons and other technologies at the end of World War II, and continued with the development of jet planes, short-range, intermediate-range, and inter-continental ballistic missiles, space satellites and others. However, the recent period has also exhibited some of the previous forms of war.

Types of War

Limited or conventional warfare is any war that is fought without the employment of all major weapons and for objectives other than the complete defeat of the enemy as in total warfare. It involves the use of military forces such as artillery, tanks, infantry, etc., rather than atomic weapons. Examples of a limited or conventional warfare include the Franco-Prussian War of 1870, World War I in 1914, and the Korean War of 1950 to 1953. On the other hand, a case of total warfare was the unconditional surrender policy of the United States and the United Kingdom by which they sought the total defeat and occupation of Germany in World War II.

Guerrilla warfare is irregular warfare fought by small groups of rebels against an invading army or in rebellion against an established government. It is fought mainly in the rural areas by indigenous elements, though perhaps led and assisted by outsiders, who know the territory and are often indistinguishable from the rest of the population. Undermanned and underfinanced, guerillas usually use "hit and run" tactics as they attack superior forces at their periphery before fleeing to avoid frontal retaliation and destruction. This type of war is often one phase of broad political-economic-social and ideological revolution fought against an established order. Examples of guerila warfare include the Spaniards fighting the invading armies of Napoleon in the 1810s, the Americans and the Philippines combatting the Japanese during World War II in the 1940s, and the Afghans struggling against technologically superior Russian forces in Afghanistan in the 1980s.

If the warfare is mostly urban and the killing is directed against civilians or non-combatants in addition to military assets, then it is called **terrorism**. Its objective is to increase the terror and demoralization of the population, and force the government into tactical errors, overreaction, and repression which could be used by assassins to encourage opposition to the regime which they lead until its overthrow. Examples of terrorist warfare include the killing by the Red Bridges, the Red Army, the Palestinian Liberation Organization (PLO), the Tupamaros, and Sendero Luminoso in Italy, Japan, Palestine, Uruguay and Peru, respectively, during the 1980s. Osama bin Laden of the *Global Front Against Jews and Christians* and leader of *al-Qaeda* is a major terrorist of the 1990's and early 2000's.

Preventive war is a military strategy which calls for an attack by a state that enjoys a temporary advantage in striking power. This doctrine calls for a surprise attack against an enemy that is dedicated to the destruction of the attacking state and is developing a superior force for a crushing future blow. An example of a preventive war includes the Israeli attack in 1981 against a nuclear reactor in Baghdad, Iraq, claiming that it could be used to produce nuclear weapons in the future.

On the other hand, **a preemptive war is a military operation undertaken only after state leaders receive intelligence data clearly indicating that a rival country is preparing an immediate attack.** This was the case when Israel in 1967 attacked Egypt, Syria, Lebanon, and Jordan when its intelligence service, the Mossad, detected an imminent attack by these Arab countries. If nuclear weapons are used in this preemptive attack, this would be a case of a first-strike nuclear attack. This first-strike nuclear attack is intended to wipe out the enemy so that it cannot unleash its own missiles. Fortunately, this type of war has never happened.

Massive retaliation is the threat of nuclear attack to restrain the actions of another state. The Eisenhower Administration in the United States had this policy in the 1950s until the Soviets tested their first intercontinental ballistic missile (ICBM) in 1957. It sought to intimidate the Russians so that they would not expand their control throughout Europe. After the Russians developed their own nuclear weapons, both countries enacted a policy of **massive retaliation** with nuclear weapons to threaten the other. This became a **balance of terror** as both countries could destroy each other. It is part of the policy of deterrence: both sides accept the premise that neither could totally destroy the other's retaliatory second-strike capability in a surprise, preemptive or first-strike, and that massive retaliation would follow.

Weapons more compatible with a first-strike capability are heavy land-based ICBMs which can carry many warheads or explosives that can be directed to different targets. Second-strike capability weapons, which can survive a preemptive attack and then launch their missiles, are submarines, and bombers with Cruise missiles. In general, during the Cold War, the Soviet Union had an advantage in land-based missiles, while the United States possessed superiority in submarines and bombers. Other types of weapons are short-range ballistic missiles with a range of 500 miles, intermediate-range ballistic missiles with a range up to 3,500 miles, and intercontinental ballistic missiles with a range of over 3,500 miles. When the Cold War between Russia and the United States ended in 1991, the number of nuclear weapons were reduced and missiles were targeted away from each country.

The Causes of War

There are many causes of war. The causes of one war may be very different from those of another. In fact, for each war there might be a number of interpretations as to what caused it. **Ancient thinkers such as Thucydides and others believed that war is something inevitable, as ineradicable as disease and death, and that people go to war out of personal motives such as honor, fear and interest.**

On the other hand, the modern view tends to see impersonal or structural forces as the causes of war. These might include economic systems, political systems, pressure groups, ideologies and others. Probably, both levels, the human and the impersonal underlying dimension are needed to understand wars. **However, underlying factors such as economic deprivations, political systems, military strength, alliances etc., do not by themselves cause war. For this, human intervention is required.** Individual human decisions are the immediate cause of war.

Human Nature as a Cause of War

The main idea in this type of interpretation is that the causes of war are found in human nature and behavior. Thus all wars, in this view, originate from the decisions of leaders, for the choices they make ultimately determine whether war will occur. For example, biological theories of human aggression argue that wars stem from either human genetic programming or from psychological drives. Humans excel in intra-specific aggression by routinely killing their own kind. Yet, if aggression is an inevitable drive in human nature, why is it that not all individuals and groups exhibit intense aggression, or why are individuals belligerent and non-belligerent at different times?

There is no definite evidence for saying that humans have a violent brain or that war is caused by instinct. Perhaps it is better to say that what seems to be genetically given is the capacity for violence, but not the need for it. The practice of self-sacrifice, of total loyalty to the state, both of which are valuable qualities in a war, are most likely learned beliefs reinforced through socialization.

Neither is there satisfactory evidence for saying that entire nations are predisposed to war or that national character predetermines national aggressions. National character can express itself in different ways and can in fact change, as has occurred with the Swedes and the Swiss since 1809 and 1815, respectively, when they ceased engaging in war. This tends to indicate that war-making is not an inborn national trait. Moreover, many countries have escaped the tragedy of war.

The Seven Deadly Sins Tradition   Augustine believed that it is not nature but human sinfulness which is responsible for wars. The Byzantine, the Catholic, and later the Protestant churches within Christianity, would all develop this idea of sinfulness in a more systematic way developing the tradition of the seven deadly sins which are pride, envy, wrath, greed, sloth, gluttony, and lust.

This view will not so much place human weakness at the genetic, biological or intellectual levels, as on the faculty of the will. For sin, or the violation of God's revelation and of God's natural law, is seen mostly as a bad use of the human faculty for free choice. **In this perspective sin is an evil which, if encouraged, will undermine the faculty of the intellect and color it with selfishness which makes the human person unable to know truth and live in peace with both neighbors and strangers.**

The pride of leaders, and even of entire countries, that is, their feelings of conceit, of self-love, of superiority over others different from themselves explains much of the French expansionism between 1661 and 1815, or the origins of World War I in 1914, and World War II in 1939. Often leaders engage in war because they fear losing prestige in both the international and domestic arenas. Envy, the love of what others have and the desire to take it from them, as the poor were encouraged to eliminate the rich, was frequently an underlying ingredient of international communism fueling its class conflicts and social resentments. Greed, the love of possessing beyond what one needs, is often a silent partner of that type of capitalism which for the sake of profit builds the economic and military strength of militaristic and imperialistic dictators such as Hitler in Germany, Stalin in Russia and Saddam Hussein in Iraq.

The wrath of leaders, that is, their desire to harm others, as they obsessively hate certain groups was exhibited by Napoleon as he invaded Russia in 1812, or Mussolini as he attacked Ethiopia in 1935, or the Serbs as they attacked the Muslims of Bosnia in 1991. Sloth, a state of hopelessness, faintheartedness, self-indulgence, or the unwillingness to pursue virtue in a very imperfect world, has led many leaders and countries to do nothing in the face of aggression by violent and unjust countries. The British refusal to help France stand up to German expansion in the 1930s was probably a major cause of the Second World War. Europe's unwillingness to interfere in the conflict in Bosnia was probably a major factor of its civil war. Gluttony, the love of consuming, can lead to wars of conquest to obtain resources capable of sustaining further consumption. This was the case of Iraq's invasion of Kuwait in 1990. Lust, or love of manipulation of others for self-gratification is typical of the behavior of super powers who support, then abandon less powerful allies once they have fought and fulfilled their national interests.

Psychological Explanations   Another type of explanation of war which places blame on the human condition are the psychological theories. They refer to the mental and emotional states of leaders or to their intellectual mistakes. Leaders often are **reckless** and take dangerous risks as happened when Argentina in 1986 invaded the Falkland Islands which belong to the United Kingdom. Argentina lost the war and its regime collapsed. Sometimes government officials are simply **negligent** and fail to take precautions as when the United States in 1948 withdrew its troops from South Korea. Two

years later in 1950, North Korea invaded South Korea causing a three years war. **Misperception** of the facts can lead to war as occurred in 1990 when Saddam Hussein of Iraq invaded Kuwait thinking the United States would tolerate such action. **Overestimation of one's strength** also convinced Hussein to attack Iran in 1980, an action which led to a horrendous eight-year war. **Boredom** has often been a cause of war as leaders with a chronic need for excitement take actions which lead to war to entertain themselves. Many Medieval wars were carried on by aristocrats and monarchs as sport. **Selfish craving** is, according to Buddhism, a major cause of war, for the selfishness of the leaders and their constant wants meet with the opposition of others, and the resulting frustration is converted into anger, hostility and then war.

Domestic-Structural Causes of War

This second type of explanation about the causes of war argues that not human nature but defects in the internal organization of countries are the key to understanding war and peace, and that perhaps the decision for war is better explained by the nature of the government and by the many domestic or internal pressures which influence the government leaders who, in the end, decide if war will occur.

For example, new states are more likely to start wars than more mature countries. Wars could be used by the regime to create more internal unity. The more warlike states have been poor ones but the frequency of wars depends on their degree of poverty. The most impoverished countries are the least prone to start wars because they cannot afford it. However, as they improve their economies, wars become more frequent. This has been the case with Japan, Russia, Iraq, Iran, etc.

Democracies tend to deal with conflicts against other democracies by methods other than war. When they fight, it is usually against dictatorships. However, it is true that young democracies which are just making the transition from dictatorship tend to be warlike like Russia in the 1990s which has had conflicts with Georgia and Chechnya. **This warlike transition could be related to nationalism, a social and psychological phenomenon that rises from unique social and psychological factors to provide unity and inspiration to a specific people through a sense of belonging together and of sharing values. Nationalism is accompanied in some states by ethnocentrism (the belief in the superiority of one's own group and culture) and by xenophobia**

(an exaggerated fear or distrust of foreigners and of the policies and objectives of other countries). All these forces became more predominant after the French Revolution of 1789.

In addition, new democracies could be made more warlike by the presence of **irredentism** or the desire of the people of a state to annex those contiguous territories of another country that are inhabited largely by linguistic or cultural minorities of the first state. For example, after the creation of the Kingdom of Italy, this country wanted to annex Austrian territories in Trentino and Tyrol. Germany in the early 1930s wanted to annex heavily German-populated territories in Czechoslovakia and Poland. Their annexation was a major cause of World War II.

Other types of wars can be set off by a country's religious and secular ideologies which want to expand their territories: Islam, Fascism, Communism, Nazism, and others. Their exclusivity and the sense of identity and passion which they arouse in people have led to many wars throughout history but especially in the 1900s and 2000s. The religious wars of the 1500s and 1600s—which were about more than simply religious issues—were not as violent as the secular wars of the 1900s.

Financiers, industrialists, media barons and military establishments, all part of a supposed small-group conspiracy, are frequently blamed for starting wars to promote economic gain or to enhance their reputation. In this view, these groups acquire a vested interest in maintaining the country in a constant state of military readiness and engagement. They are seen as continually looking for enemies to fight. The military often overrates its strength and underestimates that of their enemy. It focuses on technology, tactics, strategy, logistics and hardware and not enough on morale, chance, motivation and the unpredictable, devastating consequences of war. This myopia can be a catalyst for war. U.S. President Dwight Eisenhower warned his country in the 1950s about the military-industrial complex, an alliance of politicians, voters, weapons manufacturers and the military to increase military expenditures.

Small groups have occasionally promoted war for private advantage by lending money at high interest to combatants on all sides, by selling weapons and munitions, by sensationalist media circulation, by fixing prices of commodities, and by making themselves indispensable to the political leadership. Yet, not all wars are the result of the conspiracy of the few for material gain. **Often, it is the masses themselves who push for war to fulfill psychological needs for self-importance or who vicariously enjoy killing, conquest and excitement.** The imperialism of the British empire in the 1800s and the many wars it unleashed throughout Africa and other parts were supported by the lower and middle classes which had recently earned the right to vote. Also, while some corporations do benefit significantly from war, most make greater gain from peaceful commercial ventures. Furthermore, diplomatic bureaucracies and political leaders are frequently more willing to go to war than are the military chiefs of some states.

The profit motive of capitalism in general is also mentioned as a possible cause of war. Free traders such as Leonard Hobhouse (1929), and Communists such as Lenin (1924), have argued that capitalist economic systems need colonies to obtain raw materials, to sell surplus goods, and to acquire large returns on foreign investment. The desire for colonies, in this view, leads to war against poor countries and among capitalist states themselves. For Lenin, it is in the nature of the capitalist system itself to become imperialistic in order to keep its rate of growth from slowing down significantly, which could then have serious social and political domestic consequences.

While economic motives are often present in conflicts among individuals and capitalist states, it is also true that capitalist states, especially if they are mature democracies, do not need colonies to acquire raw materials, export goods and achieve high returns on investment. They can achieve all of these through peaceful, though competitive, international trade. In addition, it is also clear that non-capitalist states have throughout history also engaged in empire building, wars, and exploitation of human and natural resources.

Wars have often been fought for issues other than economics. Some wars are claimed to be the result of a conscious decision by the political elite to promote domestic cohesion against sedition, rebellion and civil wars. Other wars are thought to be justified to expand frontiers because of a need for land, wealth and security. This is particularly true in cases of overpopulation and the loss of resources. Wars can also be explained by their economic growth and scientific development. These allow a state to then direct more resources to their military establishment and seek confrontation with other states.

International-Structural Causes of War

This third type of interpretation of the causes of war states that conflicts occur because there is nothing in the international system to prevent them. At the

international level a certain anarchy among states prevails, and this is considered to be the major underlying cause of wars. Where there are numerous states with no system of law enforceable among them, and where each state judges its ambitions according to its own value system, conflict leading to war is a good possibility. Each state pursues its own interest, however defined, in ways it considers best. Force is a means to achieve the external goals of countries because there is no adequate process of reconciling the conflict of interest that arise among states in a condition of anarchy.

In the absence of general common interests among states, there is a constant possibility of war because of the envy, pride, ambition, rapaciousness and vindictiveness which are so often found in humans and because of the power-driven interests of states. **Therefore, the defects of humans and states are worsened by the absence of international institutions to prevent war.** However, the anarchical nature of the international level—its weak legal system, uneven distribution of power, inevitability of unpredictable changes—are all structural characteristics or underlying conditions for war, but they do not in themselves make war inevitable. They are not immediate causes of war.

Some societies have not experienced wars and others have not had them for a long time. In other words, the anarchy by itself does not cause one state to attack another. Whether this happens or not will depend on a number of special circumstances—location, size, type of government, past history, tradition, character of the leaders, political make-up of the society—each of which will influence the actions of a state. These special reasons become the immediate or efficient causes of war. **States are motivated to attack each other and to defend themselves by reason or passion of the few who make policies for the state, and of the many more who influence the few.** Thus the immediate cause of every war must be either the acts of individuals or acts and dynamics of states. The international anarchy is the permissive cause, because it often offers little which can prevent aggression. Both the motivation of the leaders, of the state, and the underlying structure of the international system have to be considered in explaining war.

There are several international approaches towards the explanation of wars: that they result when there is power asymmetry, or an unfavorable tilt in the balance of power which favors one group over others; that wars are caused by an arms race between states; that they are a mode of conflict resolution, that is, wars are a device for challenging and changing unacceptable conditions

between two or more states; and that they are the result of opportunity, the chance for one state to score a cheap victory when a competitor has been weakened by external or internal strife.

Still another perspective is presented by cyclical theories which argue that there are long cycles of war and peace caused by some combination of systemic properties of economic, political and military nature, which produce the major wars that have periodically erupted throughout history. The long-cycle theory perspective is based on the perception that a great power has risen to dominant position at about once every one-hundred years, but that it has not been able to retain its dominion for more than fifty years. There is then a down cycle of power-loss globally or regionally. This decline leads to wars as challengers seek to take advantage of the previous superpower's weakness. As empires lose their vitality and their political hold over their regions and subjects, their former subordinates begin peripheral wars to create and consolidate new states. The fall of such empires as the Austro-Hungarian, the Russian, the German and the Ottoman, led to wars among the new states in each region.

The Causes of Peace

Diplomacy

Peace is the absence of war or other hostilities. History records more years of human conflict than years of peace. Historically, it does not seem to be a natural human condition. Though elusive, it is continuously pursued by many strategies. **One of them is diplomacy which is the total process by which countries carry on political relations with each other.** It is the key technique used in the peaceful settlement of international disputes. Diplomacy actually precedes the state system established by the **Peace of Westphalia** in 1648 which made countries the legitimate actors in the international system. The city-states of ancient Greece had engaged in sophisticated diplomacy in the 400s and 300s B.C. to accommodate the conflicting interests of cities such as Athens, Sparta, Corinth, Thebes, and others. They had diplomatic missions, treaties, negotiations and other concepts of diplomacy. The first professional diplomatic corps began in the **Byzantine Empire** (284 to 1453). It had the world's first department of foreign affairs, strict diplomatic protocols and intelligence gathering.

The machinery of diplomacy includes a policy-making foreign office and diplomatic missions abroad such as an embassy. Official relations between governments are carried on mainly through an exchange of ambassadors. **An ambassador is the top-ranking diplomat sent by the government of a country as its official representative.** Most ambassadors are accredited to foreign countries but the executive might also appoint **ambassadors-at-large** (not assigned to a particular country), **ambassadors extraordinary** (assigned to a specific mission), and **ambassador plenipotentiary** (assigned to negotiate treaties). An **ambassador** typically is the head of an embassy in the capital city of a foreign state.

The ambassador has the support of **attachés** who are technical specialists who function as officials with diplomatic rank and who are attached to an embassy or foreign mission. They specialize in political, military, economic, agricultural, informational, labor, aviation, energy, and cultural fields. They establish good relations with similar officials in the country to which they are accredited.

When a country is seriously displeased with the actions of another government but does not want to take the serious step of severing diplomatic relations, it might withdraw the ambassador, and then the embassy will be run by the **Charge d'Affaires,** a Foreign Service official temporarily placed in charge of the embassy. In this way, a "listening post" in the other country is kept open, as are diplomatic channels. Under international law, ambassadors and other diplomatic officials enjoy special rights and are immune from the jurisdiction of the state to which they are accredited. **Diplomatic privileges and immunities** guarantee, for instance, that the embassy grounds may not be trespassed upon by local officials unless permission is granted by the diplomat or by his or her government. It also ensures that the diplomat and the diplomat's family and official staff are immune from arrest and from civil jurisdiction unless his or her government waives the immunity.

The peaceful adjustment of international disputes can be addressed by several diplomatic techniques. **Conversations are an exchange of views between two or more governments which could increase information by all parties and also lead to more detailed negotiations. Cuba and the United States held conversations in Mexico during the 1980s when there were no formal negotiations between the two. Negotiations is a process in which explicit proposals are put forward ostensibly for the purpose of reaching agreements on an exchange or on the realization of a common interest where conflicting interests are present.** They take

place when each side makes an explicit proposal. Negotiations take place where there are common interests as well as issues of conflict. Negotiations could be **bilateral** if they are between two states or **multilateral** if they are between more than two states, **open** if conducted in public or **secret** if carried on unreportedly.

Good offices are a method of peaceful settlement by which a third country seeks to bring two disputing countries into agreement. The state offering its good offices merely seeks to create favorable conditions under which the countries in conflict can talk over their differences. It does not include participation in the negotiations or the offering of a suggested solution, although the disputing states may request them. Good offices is a useful device in "breaking the ice" between states in conflict by getting them to talk. In recent years, the United Nations has often taken over the role of offering good offices through the Security Council, the General Assembly, or the Secretariat. **Mediation is a diplomatic technique in which a third party or country strives to solve a dispute by establishing the facts and by offering substantive suggestions.** Great skills are required to achieve a solution that does not alienate either side. The Vatican helped mediate in the 1980s a territorial conflict between Argentina and Chile.

Conciliation is a technique in which a group of countries or other agents serves as a third party to help two antagonistic states negotiate their differences. The group determines the facts and makes specific suggestions. The Contact Group of the United States, Britain, France, Germany, Italy and Russia met in 1998 to try to resolve conflicts between Serbians and ethnic Albanians in conflict over Kosovo. Conciliation is often linked with **inquiry which is a formal, impartial determination of the facts involved in an international dispute.** Inquiry procedure involves the establishment of a **factfinding commission** by the parties to the dispute or by some international body. After conducting the investigation, the commission of inquiry issues a report of its finding to the disputants or to the international agency. Unless inquiry is followed by additional peaceful settlement procedures like mediation or conciliation, the parties to the dispute are left free to determine the use to be made of the findings.

Arbitration is a method of settling a dispute between states by judges selected by the partners to the dispute. The judges, who have standing as international jurists, must render a decision or award based on international law, and the parties agree in advance to accept the decision as binding. In arbitration, disputing parties enter into a "compromise" or agreement that specifies the issues to be resolved and procedures to be followed. Generally, states are reluctant to submit disputes involving their primary national interests to an arbitrational tribunal. States that have accepted arbitration have almost always abided by the decision of the tribunal. The International Court of Justice in the 1980s arbitrated, for example, a sovereignty conflict between Nicaragua and the United States dealing with U.S. mining of harbors in Nicaragua.

The success of such techniques as conversation, negotiation, good offices, mediation, conciliation, inquiry, and arbitration depend greatly on the ability of diplomats, who are the accredited agents of a head of state and who serve as the primary medium for the conduct of international relations. They must be realistic in determining whether the objectives pursued by their countries are proportional to their actual power, whether the objectives of other states are also representative of their resources, and how the goals of the states can be compatible. In 1815, at the **Congress of Vienna,** the diplomats of Austria, Prussia, Great Britain, Russia, and France managed to negotiate their differences and as a result Europe enjoyed, from 1815 to 1914, one of the longest periods of peace in its history. Diplomacy was easier then because it could be conducted in secret, there were less countries, diplomats carried more authority, did not have to report to the people of their countries, and were not interfered by **summit conferences** where two or more leaders of state meet directly to resolve differences. Yet, today's more open, multilateral, and public diplomacy still requires the expertise of diplomats.

Diplomats must possess several traits: truthfulness, both in fact and in appearance; intellectual integrity to establish trust; good-tempered personality; patience; modesty; loyalty to the country; and such additional qualities as intelligence, knowledge, discernment, prudence, hospitality, charm, industry, courage, and tact. Even all these qualities are often not enough to maintain peace if the states negotiating have **mutually-exclusive objectives**, that is, goals which cannot be met unless one of the countries is defeated. Political considerations back home could also undermine diplomatic efforts.

Still, diplomats must pursue the major objectives of modern diplomacy: representing their countries and their policies, maximizing points of agreements, minimizing points of disagreements; gathering information and interpreting it; signaling and receiving information on policy changes; negotiating the fine details of important issues while trying to create areas of agreement among two or more countries; managing crises by defusing it while preserving national objectives; and influencing public opinion to win support for their countries.

States come together for a variety of reasons. Diplomats produce and rely on intelligence which is information gathered by a government about other state's capabilities and intentions. Military or strategic intelligence is concerned with uncovering the strength and location of land, sea, and air forces, new weapons and weapon development, troop morale and combat qualities, strategic and tactical plans, secret alliances and agreements, and civilian attitudes and morale. Nonstrategic intelligence efforts are also carried on by most countries to secure pertinent political, diplomatic, economic, and social data to aid governments in pursuit of national interest objectives. Most intelligence is secured openly through careful scrutiny of public documents and private news and data sources, but the more critical strategic information often requires the use of covert, clandestine "cloak-and-dagger" methods. **Meanwhile, counterintelligence units are active in trying to undermine espionage agents carrying on military activities for other countries.** In the United States, for example, the main responsibility for counterintelligence operations falls to the Federal Bureau of Investigation (FBI).

Alliances

Alliances are associations of states to gain security or expansion. They improve military capabilities and permit the defense burden to be shared when countries have a common threat. Alliances can be useful in deterring an attack, creating greater strength if attacked, and preventing an ally from joining another alliance. Alignments might be followed by dealignments at the end of the threat. **Lord Palmerston, who served for more than 30 years as British secretary of war, foreign secretary or prime minister, expressed the role of alliances saying in 1848 that states should have no permanent allies and no permanent enemies but should just follow their interests.** Alliances can be beneficial if states remain flexible and if the international rules support a flexible interpretation of alliance commitments and the rights of neutrals. Alliances tend to function best when they face threats and tend to collapse in their absence.

Alliances also have disadvantages. They reduce a country's capacity to make adjustments when conditions change, limit the number of possible allies, reduce the advantages in bargaining arising from ambiguity which keeps the enemy guessing, provoke fear in adversaries, preserve existing rivalries, entangle states in disputes with their ally's enemies, and create envy and resentment on the part of friends who are outside the alliance and do not benefit from it. Alliances also allow aggressive states to accumulate resources for offensive wars. They threaten enemies and motivate them to form counter-alliances which end up reducing the security of both alliances, and draw otherwise neutral countries into opposing coalitions, requiring each to come to the other's aid. Alliances also force states to try and control the behavior of others in the alliance lest they become too aggressive or try to defect to another alliance. Today's ally might be tomorrow's enemy. Coalition or alliance partners often go to war against each other. Another problem with alliances is that they tend to transform limited conflicts into complex, more global wars. For these reasons U.S. President George Washington in his 1796 Farewell Address warned against permanent military and political alliances for they can lead to major wars. He wanted the United States to remain neutral and to follow a policy of unilateralism.

The Balance of Power

As countries experimented with alliances to maintain their security or to increase their territory with a minimum of cost, they gradually came to appreciate the advantages of shifting alliances at the appropriate time to enhance their survival. **European states created after the 1660s a balance of power, that is, a system of power alignments in which peace and security may be maintained through an equilibrium of power between rival blocs.** During this time, France was the major threat to the stability of Europe, so many countries became allies to stop French aggression. Later Austria, Germany, and Russia became threats. The classical balance of power in Europe consisted of alliances among the following states: Great Britain, France, Spain, Austria, Prussia and Russia. The theory of the balance of power advocates national self-reliance and peace through strength as necessary virtues for a condition of international anarchy, where every state has to fend for itself. Among its essential premises are that defense alliances need to form when one state is upsetting the equilibrium; that weakness invites attack; that countervailing power

must be used to deter potential aggressors; that states must be willing to increase capabilities, negotiate when necessary, fight when the equilibrium is offset, oppose any dominant coalition, permit defeated states to reenter the system, and inhibit states which support supranational organizations, for these states reduce the ability to respond quickly to an international threat.

The balance of power system can work best under certain conditions: a sufficiently large number of relatively equal, independent states within a certain geographic area so that interalignments are possible; a common political culture; the absence of a supranational organization which can interfere with necessary alliance-shifting; similarity in political systems; accurate information about each state's capabilities, and a technology which inhibits preemptive strikes.

The balance of power system might be better at defeating an expansionist power than at keeping international peace. Between 1650 and 1914, when the system was in place, many wars did break out. However, the balance of power equilibrium among states might have prolonged the length of peacetime between wars, and possibly limited the duration and destructiveness of war when it happened.

World War I discredited the theory of balance of power politics. Many blamed arms races, secret treaties and cross-cutting alliances associated with balance of power politics as responsible for the war. However, balance of power proponents argue that World War I resulted from alliances which were too rigid for the balance of power equilibrium to work properly.

Collective Security

After the conclusion of World War I in 1918, the concept of balance of power lost credibility. **President Woodrow Wilson promoted instead the ideal of collective security which is a worldwide security system by which all or most countries agree in advance to take collective action against any state or states that break the peace by committing aggression.** This would replace a system of alliances and counter-alliances. It tries to inhibit war through the threat of collective action instead of accepting war as a legitimate instrument of state policy. Collective security proposes retaliation against any aggression or attempt to establish dominance, action by all states, and creation of an international organization to identify acts of aggression and to defeat them.

The League of Nations, in 1919, was the first general international organization established with headquarters in

Geneva, Switzerland to preserve peace and security and to promote cooperation among states in economic and social fields. Sixty-one states joined the League, though the United States refused membership. When World War II broke out in 1939, collective security was discredited. It did not work because of U.S. refusal to join it, the great powers' fear of League intrusion in their interests, disagreements as to what acts constituted an aggression, the states' unwillingness to act in defense of someone else's security interests, and concern about inequities in the burden to be shared in supporting the system.

Disarmament and Arms Control

Disarmament and arms control follow the Biblical prescription that nations "should beat their swords into plowshares" for those who live by the sword will die by the sword. The buildup of weapons often leads to conflict through preemptive and preventive wars or because of imperialistic desires.

Disarmament refers to the reduction or elimination of weapons with the ultimate end of eradicating war itself, for if there are no weapons there might be no war. Arms control, on the other hand, refers to agreements to regulate arms levels by limiting their growth or restricting how they may be deployed. Both can take place through either bilateral or multilateral agreements. There are few examples of successful multilateral disarmament agreements except those which have been imposed forcefully by conquest or arranged by friendly states which already trust each other.

There are more successes with arms control efforts to limit nuclear weapons. Both disarmament and arms control can be very profitable for they can save resources, reduce tensions and wars, lower health problems, increase the prestige of states, and reduce the chances of desperate preemptive attacks. However, neither disarmament or arms control can eliminate the threat of war altogether. True international security seems to depend not so much on disarmament or arms control, as on reducing as much as possible the sources of conflict in international relations and finding effective non-violent means of resolving the conflicts that remain.

Arms

If disarmament can lead to war perhaps a military buildup can keep the peace. Disarmament by itself does not seem to lead to a more secure world. Arms control can confine the potential destruction in a war, but it does not really eliminate the roots of conflict. **Arms themselves seem to be less a cause of war than the symptoms of political tensions and distrust.** Groups build up their weapons because they do not trust others. Managing political conflicts without violence may be a necessary part of arms control. **Arms buildup is often preferred as a means of preventing wars by deterring potential aggressors.** This quest for national security in an anarchical world springs from states' fear of one another. Unfortunately, a country's security could be another country's source of insecurity. Therefore, both of them will prepare for war to defend themselves. Unless the causes of their fear of each other are addressed, the arms escalation will continue and the possibility of war will also increase. **Arms build up can postpone or deter wars, but other approaches need to be tried lest war erupt by accident, by the personal weaknesses of the leaders, or by the domestic vices of the state.**

International Law and World Order

Another approach to the creation of interstate peace is the development of international law to improve international order. International law is a body of rules and principles that guide the relations among countries and between governments and foreign nationals. Sources of international law include treaties, authority such as the decision of international courts, reason and custom. Treaties and other forms of international agreements are the most important source today, as custom was earlier, in the development of international law. Much of the current international law, particularly that which is called **private international law**, successfully regulates transnational contacts in commerce, communications, travel, mail flows, currency exchange, debt obligations, education and other areas. It has a good record in settling transnational disputes. However, **public international law**, which addresses government-to-government relations, is often unable to reduce tensions even though the body of the Law of Nations is very extensive.

A major principle of public international law is that of **state sovereignty** which means that no authority is legally above the state, except that which the state might voluntarily confer on a supranational organization that it joins. A second principle is that of **non-interference**, by which countries must refrain from uninvited involvement in another's internal affairs. These sovereignty and non-interference principles are seen by some as shaping and reinforcing the current international anarchy.

In this so-called anarchy, states are accountable to no one and abide by only those regulations they voluntarily subscribe to and enforce through self-help measures. The states themselves, not a higher authority, determine the rules and how they should be enforced. A supranational legislative body capable of making and amending norms does not exist. Nor is there an executive body capable of enforcing the rules. However, there are others who see the current situation as one of freedom since there is no one power which can control the entire world.

Another weakness of international law is that the contemporary global order is culturally and ideologically pluralistic and lacks a value-consensus. This makes it very difficult at present for any law to have universal applicability. Much of the international law is not based on justice but on the search for national advantage, which often gives the stronger state an advantage over weaker ones. Frequently, the rules to which the powerful are willing to agree are those which serve their interest. The rules thus tend to preserve the existing power relations, and often become little more than a justification of existing practices, and a codification of customs. The law can also be interpreted widely and be used for propaganda.

With all its deficiencies, public international law does have advantages and most states do spend considerable time trying to abide by it even if they also try to influence it in their favor. International law provides valuable rules for diplomatic recognition, treaties, mediation, good offices, conciliation, arbitration and adjudication. The absence of a centralized authority does not mean that states arbitrarily disobey rules or violate previous commitments. Disobedience is rare. A voluntary compliance system need not be normless. **Countries obey in the majority of the cases because it adds to their economic advantage, reputation and stability, and because compliance avoids retaliation.** Not only is international law obeyed in the majority of cases, it is not violated more often than the laws of other global and domestic systems. This means that domestic law which has clear authorities to make and adjudicate laws also suffers from disobedience and violence particularly by those engaged in organized crime, white-collar crime and street crime.

International Organization and World Order

The creation of an international organization to facilitate peace among nations became a reality with the United Nations created on June 26, 1945, to maintain international peace and security, advance global prosperity, alleviate poverty and unemployment and promote human rights worldwide. **The United Nations accepted publicly the principle of collective security in which each state is asked to share responsibility for another's state security. The United Nations also restored the principle of the balance of power to maintain peace by giving the veto power to each of the five major powers in the U.N. Security Council: China, France, Russia, the United Kingdom, and the United States.** The veto power was a concession to the superpowers' sovereign freedom and security. The veto restricts the capacity of the General Assembly to repel aggressive state actions, and therefore inhibits the power of the United Nations to prevent wars.

The United Nations: A Case Study in International Organization

The Origins of the United Nations

The leaders of the United Kingdom and the British Commonwealth states met in London with representatives of Belgium, Czechoslovakia, France, Greece, Luxembourg, the Netherlands, Norway, Poland, and Yugoslavia, and on June 12, 1941, signed an **Inter-Allied Declaration** pledging to work for a free world where people could work in peace and security. This was followed by the **Atlantic Charter**, a 1941 peace plan designed by U.S. President Franklin D. Roosevelt and British Prime Minister Winston S. Churchill and based on the assurance of a system of security and economic cooperation. On January 1, 1942, twenty-six countries signed the **Declaration of United Nations** in support of the Atlantic Charter. On October 30, 1943, the **Moscow Declaration on General Security** was signed by Britain, China, Russia, the United Kingdom, and the United States, approving the idea of an international organization for preserving world peace.

Other conferences followed, at Teheran in 1943, Dumbarton Oaks in 1944, and at Yalta in 1945, where the final details of the organization were ironed out. The Charter of the United Nations was presented at the **San Francisco Conference** of April 24 to June 26, 1945.

It was accepted on June 26, 1945, by all fifty countries present. The charter went into effect on October 24, 1945. There are now 191 member states.

The United Nations Charter, though broad in objectives and obligations, did not establish a world government. The authority and actions of the United Nations are limited by the acknowledged sovereign equality of all member countries, a prohibition against intervention in matters essentially within the domestic jurisdiction of member states, and the fact that only some decisions of the Security Council are binding on the general membership.

The UN differs from the previous effort at collective security—The League of Nations. The United Nations was assured of universal membership. All the great military powers—except Communist China, were members from the beginning. The United States, unlike with the League of Nations, was an active participant. In addition, the United Nations was born with the belief that it would have the mechanism to enforce its decisions through **Article 43** of the Charter. A military staff made up of representatives from the United States, Russia, China, the United Kingdom, and France was to develop a mobilization plan of UN forces to be ready under the command of the UN Security Council. For the first time in history, collective security was to be institutionalized. Another difference was that the United Nations was also concerned with economic and social problems. **It is the first international organization with a major section devoted to improving the way people live.**

The major idea of the United Nations was its determination to preserve world peace through collective security, that is, through the coming together of the member countries to defeat an aggressor. Collective security is based on several assumptions: that states will identify their own security with the existing world order and will be willing to intervene in situations far from their region and interests; that states will be able to agree if an aggression has been committed; that the aggressor will be intimidated or defeated by the available international force; that states will be willing to punish their closest allies as severely as they would their distant adversaries; that states will be willing to relinquish authority over their own troops in areas in which their national interests are not at stake, and that public debate in international conferences will be more effective than traditional diplomacy with its secret, bilateral, and discreet negotiations between the interested countries alone.

Unfortunately, some of these assumptions often do not hold true in international relations.

Organization of the United Nations

The General Assembly.   The General Assembly is the only major organ of the United Nations where all members are represented. It can discuss any issue and recommend actions by other UN departments. Each country can send five delegates, five alternate delegates, and as many advisers as it wishes, but it has only one vote. Most decisions are by majority vote, except "important questions" (peace and security) which need two-thirds support. The only binding decisions are those regarding the budget. All others are suggestions.

The **General Assembly** elects a president annually, elects the members to the other organs, controls the UN budget, and creates committees. All members are represented on seven main committees: 1st (Disarmament and Related International Security); 2d (Economic and Financial); 3d (Social, Humanitarian and Cultural); 4th (Decolonization); 5th (Administrative and Budgetary); 6th (Legal); and the Special Political Committee, created in 1948 to assist with political issues. Article 12 prohibits recommendations concerning an international dispute or situation that is under consideration by the UN Security Council, without the latter's consent.

However, the "Uniting for Peace" Resolution of November 1950 allows the General Assembly to recommend collective measures, including the use of armed force, to maintain or restore peace in situations in which the Security Council remains dead-locked. This resolution in effect amended the UN Charter and provided a basis for the Assembly's role in peacekeeping activities. **Peacekeeping operations prevent fighting, provide a buffer, police a cease-fire, or help maintain public order. Peacekeeping missions are not enforcement actions to combat aggression.** They do not resolve conflicts, but help foster an atmosphere that is conducive to diplomatic negotiations and peaceful settlement techniques. Peacekeeping operations could be in the form of international observers or military units. The over-all supervision of UN activities is also entrusted to the General Assembly. This includes oversight authority of the Trusteeship Council and the Economic and Social Council, the receipt of reports from the Security Council and other organs, and budgetary matters. The General Assembly has one annual regular session lasting three months, but special emergency sessions can be called.

The Security Council.   The Security Council is where the UN Charter places primary responsibility for the maintenance of international peace and security. Until 1965, it had eleven members, but it was then increased to fifteen, of which five are permanent: China, France, Russia, the United Kingdom, and the United States. The ten non-permanent states are voted by the General Assembly for two-year terms. Each country has one delegate. Some actions can be taken if any nine members agree; others, if the five permanent states plus four others agree. **However, no action can be taken if any of the five permanent members disagree.**

This veto power diluted somewhat the principle of collective security by bringing into the UN the principle of balance of power as it protected the interests of the superpowers from the actions of the General Assembly. The veto, which Russia, for example, used over 100 times from 1945 to 1991, motivated the General Assembly to enact its 1950 Uniting for Peace Resolution. The Security Council's efforts to uphold international peace and security can take two general approaches. One is the peaceful settlement of disputes through such procedures as the interposition of peacekeeping forces. It can investigate any situation to determine if it constitutes a threat to peace. The Council can also mediate a dispute. A second approach involves the use of enforcement measures to protect or restore international peace and security. These could include the severance of diplomatic relations, economic embargoes, and military sanctions ranging from demonstrations of force to actual armed combat. For example, it was the Security Council which declared war on North Korea in 1950 when it invaded South Korea. The Russians were not able to veto this action against a communist ally because they had first walked out of the U.N.

The Secretariat.   The Secretariat has the task of helping the other organs do their job as effectively as possible. It manages the day-to-day business of the United Nations by providing services to the organs. Approximately 15,000 employees from 140 countries work for the Secretariat, one-third at the UN headquarters in New York, and the rest at UN European headquarters in Geneva, Switzerland, or in special UN missions and agencies throughout the world. Each country may fill at least six Secretariat jobs—accountants, mathematicians, translators, typists, writers, etc. Employees are not allowed to take orders from any member country.

The Secretary-General of the United Nations has broader powers than any other UN official. This person is the chief administrator of the UN and reports to the General Assembly each year on its condition. The Secretary General is nominated by the Security Council and appointed by the General Assembly to a five-year term. The five permanent members of the Security Council have to agree. Then, the General Assembly must ratify the selection by majority vote. In addition to the Secretary-General, there are also undersecretaries, clerks, and specialists. In 1977, the General Assembly created the position of Director General for Development and International Cooperation, second only to the Secretary-General.

A tacit agreement exists that the Secretary-General should come from a small and preferably non-aligned country. Only this guarantees that the five permanent members of the Security Council will agree on a selection. **The Secretary-General is the head and chief spokesperson of the UN, is responsible for its administration, performs diplomatic services in the area of pacific settlement, produces the annual report for the General Assembly, and brings to the attention of the Security Council any situation threatening international peace and security. The current Secretary-General is Kofi Annan of Ghana who was selected in 1997.**

The Economic and Social Council.   The Economic and Social Council (ECOSOC) coordinates the social, economic, cultural and humanitarian work of the UN system. It also oversees five regional economic commissions (Africa, Asia, Far East, Europe, and Latin America) and a wide range of committees, expert bodies and functional commissions. **The belief that the development of international economic and social cooperation contributes to the cause of peace led to the creation of ECOSOC.** It has fifty four members elected by the General Assembly for three-year terms. Each year, eighteen members are elected. The permanent members of the Security Council also serve in ECOSOC. In addition to the five regional commissions assisting it, there are six which deal with human rights, narcotics, population, social development, statistics, and women's rights.

The Economic and Social Council makes recommendations to the General Assembly, individual countries, UN specialized agencies, and other agencies like the Red Cross and labor unions. It seeks to promote higher standards of living, better health, cultural and educational cooperation among countries, and observance of human rights. Under the charter, ECOSOC is authorized to make or initiate studies, reports, and recommendations on socioeconomic matters, to promote respect for, and observance of, human rights, to prepare draft conventions on these subjects for submission to the General Assembly, and to call for international conferences. Along with the General Assembly, ECOSOC oversees the operation of such special entities as UNICEF and the World Food Council. It also coordinates the activities of specialized agencies and consults with nongovernmental organizations involved in related matters.

The International Court of Justice/The World Court. The International Court of Justice, also known as the World Court, is the successor to the Permanent Court of International Justice under the League of Nations. Its seat is at The Hague in the Netherlands. The ICJ settles disputes between countries and provides advisory opinions to the other organs of the United Nations. The ICJ consists of fifteen judges who are elected by absolute majorities in both the General Assembly and the Security Council. These judges are supposed to be chosen on the basis of their personal qualifications, not their nationality, though there is an attempt to represent in the court at least the principal legal systems of the world. Two judges cannot be from the same country. Usually, there is a judge from each of the permanent states of the Security Council. Judges serve for nine-year terms and can seek reelection.

Cases can come before the ICJ in two ways. The Security Council and the General Assembly may request from the court an advisory opinion on a legal question. Also, member states may submit a case for adjudication. All parties to a dispute must voluntarily agree to submit it for judgment. Decisions are based on international conventions, accepted customs and practices, recognized principles of international law, previous judicial decisions, and scholarly treatises. All controversies are decided by a majority of the judges present. **Any country bringing a case before the court must abide by its decisions. Then, the Security Council serves as the enforcement agency.** Most countries do not take their disputes to the World Court because they are afraid that if they lose there are no controls over the consequences.

The Trusteeship Council.   The Trusteeship Council was created to watch over and assist a number of small territories which were not self-governing at the end of World War II. The Council was to help them become ready for independence. Many were colonies of Germany,

Italy and Japan, the losing powers of World War II. The Council was responsible for these territories and for any others that countries might entrust to it. The United Nations assigned one or more member states as trustees for each territory, which then governed the territory under the directions of the UN.

There were originally eleven such territories, in Africa, Southeast Asia, and on the Pacific Ocean. Originally, the Trusteeship Council was made up of representatives of the trustee states and of all permanent members of the Security Council that did not govern trust territories. Since in 1990 the last territory achieved independence, the Trusteeship Council is made up only of the permanent members of the Security Council.

In addition to the main organs, the United Nations system includes a group of specialized agencies, each autonomous, with its own charter, budget, and staff. Each specializes in a certain field, studies problems, makes suggestions, and operates projects. They agree to consider recommendations by the United Nations. The Economic and Social Council is responsible for helping the United Nations and the specialized agencies work in cooperation. They include the Food and Agriculture Organization (FAO), the International Bank for Reconstruction and Development (IRBD or World Bank), the International Labor Organization (ILO), the International Monetary Fund (IMF), the UN Educational Scientific and Cultural Organization (UNESCO), and the World Health Organization (WHO).

Successes and Challenges Facing the United Nations

In response to the many deadlocks in the Security Council caused by its veto power, which led to UN inaction during many crises, the Secretariat gradually expanded it activities. It went beyond fact-finding and observer forces and created **peace-keeping operations** where UN troops are placed between clashing armies which voluntarily stopped fighting to allow diplomacy to resolve the conflict. The first peace-keeping effort was during the Suez Crisis of 1956 between Britain, France and Israel against Egypt. Then in the 1980s, the Secretariat began organizing **peace-making operations** in which UN troops enter an on-going war to obtain a truce between states in conflict. The Secretariat also engaged in activities which did not threaten the geopolitical interests of the superpowers: human rights, refugee assistance, technical assistance, decolonization, world trade, drug trafficking, protection of children, disaster relief, and law of the seas, among others.

The UN was instrumental in 1988 in finishing the eight year Iran-Iraq War, in the withdrawal of Russian troops from Afghanistan in 1988–1989, in the independence of Namibia in 1990, in the expulsion of Iraq from Kuwait in 1991, in monitoring of the Nicaraguan elections in 1990, among others. All these successes have led to a recent revival in the concept of **collective security.** It is difficult, however, to determine how much of this progress was due to the efforts of the United Nations itself, and how much was the result of United States bilateral diplomacy and its victory in the Cold War, which temporarily reduced regional conflicts.

One of the earliest disappointments of UN ideals was the demise of Article 43 which would have given the United Nations enforcement powers to implement collective security. As a result of the Cold War tensions between the United States and the Soviet Union and their respective allies, the five generals and eight admirals of the Military Staff Committee could not agree on the appropriate mechanisms for the application of military force. **In addition, the use of the veto in the Security Council inhibited collective security.**

A second problem is that many of the assumptions implicit in the concept of collective security have encountered serious difficulties in the real world of competing states: loyalties built around the state are not easily transferable to any notion of a world community; what is considered aggression for one country might be seen as self-defense or national liberation for others; many small or middle-sized states such as Egypt, Israel, Syria, Iran, and others can inflict serious military damage on an international force of the United Nations fighting aggression; states do not react with equal and objective rigor toward allies and enemies; statesmen will not easily surrender their political authority on such crucial matters as the use of their country's military forces; **traditional diplomacy, with its limited international participation, secrecy, and more humble expectations is often more efficient than public forums like the UN where countries with no crucial interest in a dispute may group together to out-vote and embarrass states whose very survival is at stake.** The United States, for example, is not going to risk its national security simply because other countries in the Security Council do not want to use force against its enemies.

A third problem facing the United Nations in the post-Cold War years is the violence arising from nationalist rivalries, religious fanaticism, unsolved territorial disputes, ancient prejudices and discord, and a sense of exclusion and discrimination afflicting underdeveloped countries whose expectations of a better life after independence have been shattered. These conflicts might require additional peacemaking and peacekeeping forces at a time when budgetary restraints are making them more difficult. **While peacekeeping missions have been relatively successful in Namibia, El Salvador, Cambodia, Mozambique, and maybe Haiti, they have been failures in Somalia and Bosnia because the United Nations sent lightly-armed peacekeepers to areas where there was no peace to keep.**

A fourth problem affecting the UN stems from attacks by many conservatives and isolationists in the United States who believe that its bureaucracy is proliferating, its costs are spiraling and its mission is constantly expanding beyond its original mandate and beyond its capabilities. They see the United Nations as being transformed from an institution of sovereign states into a quasi-sovereign entity which could either threaten U.S. interests or waste American lives and assets fighting in regions far away from vital national concerns.

The Future of the United Nations

If there is no hope for a real collective security system, and if traditional diplomacy might be more effective than public rhetoric, particularly in such issues as peace and security, then what is left for the United Nations to do? **It will probably be more successful in addressing problems whose solution is beyond the capacity of individual states.** There are many issues which seem to be everybody's, and therefore nobody's responsibility: malnutrition, human rights, water-borne diseases, illiteracy, scientific and industrial progress, environmental degradation, drug trafficking, international terrorism, monetary and trades issues, and collapsed—imploding states taken apart by demographic pressures, resource depletion, internal migration, social stress, and corruption. To successfully tackle these common concerns UN reforms might be needed: expanding the Security Council to increase its legitimacy; restricting the veto to only matters of war and peace; revaluating the current operations of ECOSOC to diminish bureaucratic mismanagement and aid to corrupt, violent and dictatorial regimes; and revising the budget practices of the UN which, particularly in the area of assessing payments for peacekeeping, excessively penalize the United States. Also, the United

Nations might have to collaborate closer with regional organizations.

American Withdrawal from the United Nations: An Argument

The **Preamble of the United Nations** is a beautiful ideal to save mankind from the scourge of war, reaffirm fundamental human rights, promote the dignity of the human person, respect the equal rights of men and women, and promote social progress and better standards of living globally. Unfortunately, this dream does not match the actions of an institution which has become a threat to America. The United States should gradually withdraw and collaborate in the creation of a new international entity of free countries to achieve these goals.

First, the United Nations (UN) has become a **threat to American national sovereignty** as it now seeks to become a **world government** with the power to enforce governance in many areas such as refugees and immigration, environmental regulation, gun control, population control, the law of the seas, trade issues, taxation, human rights, and soon even regulation and taxation of the internet. The Secretariat of the UN wants to control access to free information, something which would please the many dictatorships who are members of the organizations. Increasingly, Americans are being conditioned psychologically to accept the laws being generated by the UN as overriding their own laws. The Charter only gives policy power to the Security Council where countries have veto power.

Americans live under a **constitutional republic** where voters elect their representatives to make laws subject to their Constitution and not to foreign laws and institutions. And yet, political pressure from the United Nations and from its supporters, in and outside the United States, is now trying to **undermine the ability of the U.S Congress to declare war.** Many Americans now believe that military force can only be applied under the banner of the United Nations, something which is contrary to the U.S Constitution and to even the original UN Charter of 1945. This could even be considered treason. Recently, some American congressmen even asked the United Nations, one of the most corrupt organizations, to help monitor the 2004 U.S. Presidential elections to avoid cheating.

Another example of the threat to American national sovereignty is the **UN International Criminal Court (ICC)** created by the Rome Statute. It gives a foreign court universal jurisdiction to prosecute anyone, anywhere, allegedly responsible for war crimes and "crimes against humanity" (which could even include actions against the environment). Americans could be accused of any crime and be tried by foreign, un-elected bureaucrats, without trial by jury, full cross-examination, and other protections associated with American due process. Any state or even a non-governmental association could accuse an American of crimes. As anti-Americanism grows globally, and particularly in the United Nations, so will the politicization of "justice" in the ICC and the potential abuse against U.S. citizens.

This unhealthy tendency of allowing foreign laws, bureaucrats, and institutions to affect American political life and to displace the U.S Constitution is now even impacting the decisions of the Supreme Court as in the case of **Ropper v. Simmons.** Justices Ruth Bader Ginsburg, Stephen G. Breyer, Anthony Kennedy, David H. Souter and John Paul Stevens, overturned a capital case decision of the State of Mississippi, and Justice Kennedy rationalized it by citing the legal practices in Congo, Iran, Nigeria, Pakistan, Saudi-Arabia and Yemen, all of them dictatorships! Meanwhile, they overturned more than 200 years of US constitutional history and practices in nineteen American states. Believing the meaning of the Constitution is evolving, they practically rewrote the eighth amendment to the Constitution of the United States. These justices should be making decisions based on the Constitution and not on foreign cases or on their own personal opinions.

Second, the United Nation's Security Council includes three permanent members, China, France and Russia, which are now **using their veto power to undermine any preemptive/preventive policy by the United States against states or groups promoting terrorism or the future use of weapons of mass destruction (WMD).** Preemption requires quick action. The Unites States will not acquire it if it needs to go to the United Nation to ask for permission to act. Five months of debate in the Security Council over Saddam Hussein might have given him time to plan his counter-insurgency, and to either destroy or perhaps move his weapons of mass destruction to Syria, as is claimed by Russia. How many American soldiers have died because of this delay? The goal of China, France and Russia, as stated by French leader Jacques Chirac, is to diminish American power. These countries have the right to pursue their own foreign policies even if they are anti-American, but why should American interests be at their mercy?

Third, the United Nations **includes as members many dictatorships which violate its own Universal Declaration of Human Rights.** Many of these tyrannical regimes also engage in terrorist practices. Moreover, the UN has also includes these countries in its **Human Rights Commission:** China, Cuba, Eritrea, Saudi Arabia, Sudan, as well as Bhutan, Egypt, Mauritania, Pakistan, Qatar, Swaziland, Togo, and Zimbabwe. The United Nations should have used its powers vested in Article Six of the UN Charter to expel these dictatorships. The new Human Rights Council created in 2006 to replace the UN Human Rights Commission includes such dictatorships as Algeria, Azerbaijan, Bangladesh, Cameroon, Communist China, Cuba and Saudi Arabia. The UN Education, Scientific and Cultural Organization (UNESCO) awarded the authoritarian and anti-American leader of Venezuela, Hugo Chavez, the 2000 International Jose Marti Prize for heritage, liberty and values. The award was presented by dictator Fidel Castro.

The United Nations not only allows the presence of tyrannies, but also supports them through the financial allocation of many of its international-related agencies like the IMF, the World Bank and others. The American taxpayer ends up supporting dictators, big banks, and foreign intelligence and military bureaucracies. Many of these agencies support regimes which undermine economic growth with their gigantic bureaucracies, denial of free enterprise, militarism, heavy taxes, controls on prices and profits, and violence. They often act as agents of poverty. Instead of attacking tyrants for the economic backwardness they produce in their countries, the United Nations blames overpopulation and proceeds with programs to kill innocent unborn babies. The guilty escape judgment while the innocent die.

Fourth, the United Nations has **lost the capacity to distinguish between aggressors and victims,** between good and evil people, as defined by its own **Universal Declaration of Human Rights. It has not prevented genocide.** The UN remained "impartial" (frozen might be a better word) when the Khemer Rouge communists killed close to 2 million Cambodians in the 1970's, and then were allowed to participate in the UN led "peace process," when Idi Amin massacred 500,000 in Uganda, when 800,000 Tutsis were exterminated in Rwanda, when 7,000 Bosnian Muslims were killed in Srebrenica (a UN "safe haven"), and when millions were killed in Congo and in Sudan.

In Sudan, both China and France have been desperate to collaborate with the regime to profit from its natural resources, including oil, while Christian Sudanese have been massacred. Could this be why the UN Security Council will not act in Sudan? Kofi Annan wants the US to close the Guantanamo Detention Camp which holds Islamic jihadists because he does not trust American soldiers to be fair, but he wants the same soldiers to go fight in Sudan to protect people being killed by fellow African Muslims. Neither did the UN help the oppressed Iraqi people under Saddam Hussein. Instead, it benefited from millions of dollars which Saddam Hussein sent to the United Nations through the **Oil for Food Program.**

The United Nations actually promoted the man who could have stopped the genocide in Rwanda and the killing in Srebrenica, Kofi Annan, to the position of Secretary General. What did the United Nations do when Syria took over Lebanon or when Cuban troops were involved in terrorist wars throughout the world? Nothing. The United Nations cannot even stabilize Haiti! Instead, UN peacekeepers have made deals with terrorist states and groups, have spread AIDS in Cambodia and East Timor, and engaged in child prostitution rackets in Bosnia, Mozambique, Eritrea and Ethiopia.

Fifth, the **United Nations does not have a clean record in fighting terrorism since many of its members are terrorist states themselves.** Who can forget Syria becoming part of the **Anti-Terrorism Committee,** or Iraq during the Saddam Hussein regime being in the Disarmament Committee? Syria itself, a terrorist state, was in the Security Council. How could this Council be trusted in any war against terrorism? The UN recognizes Hezbollah, one of the most violent, anti-American terrorist groups today. It welcomed Yasir Arafat of the PLO, an organization which has killed Americans, including the torturing and murder of an American ambassador. It has given funds to the UN Relief and Work Agency which has employed terrorists. Neither has the United Nations prevented dictatorships like Iran and North Korea from developing nuclear weapons.

One of the problem is the UN Charter itself, which in Article 2 declares the sovereign equality of all nations. Therefore, today the UN seems to act as if terrorist dictatorships are morally equivalent to free democratic states. Section 7 of this article states that one cannot intervene in matters within the domestic jurisdiction of any state. Does it mean intervention is illegal to aid victims of dictatorship? Is 47 years of Castro dictatorship in Cuba acceptable to the United Nations? When will it dispose of Castro as it did with the apartheid regime in South Africa? Moreover, what would happen if terrorists use the cover of diplomatic UN privileges to enter the United States and detonate a dirty bomb? **The UN has become a base for terrorist groups in what used to be American soil.**

Sixth, the United Nations has a corrupt bureaucracy led mostly by Third World employees who tend to profess deep-seated anti-American feelings. The **Oil for Food Program** might go down as the most corrupt program in history with its misuse of between $20 and $100 billion. The UN has no checks and balances and accountability. Kofi Annan himself received a $500,000 International Prize for the Environment awarded by a jury with people who work for him. The UN Procurement Office has taken millions of dollars in bribes from UN contract seekers. Why should the United States spend $7 billion a year in dues, fees and voluntary contributions and pay 22% of the entire UN regular budget to support an institution which is essentially anti-American? Can anyone forget that recently, the United States was kicked out of the Human Rights Commission and replaced by Sudan, a country guilty of killing close to 2 million Sudanese and of practicing slavery?

These are the main reasons why the United States should leave the United Nations. There are many others. The United States needs to collaborate with other free countries in the creation of a new organization which could promote human rights globally, promote free democracies and markets, and stop the aggression by dictatorships and terrorist organizations. Others need not apply.

Self-Defense Organizations

Regional collective self-defense organizations unite several countries against a common enemy. These are seen at times as good institutions for keeping the peace. They have not been as successful against internal wars as they have been in limiting interstate wars. Major examples are the **North Atlantic Treaty Organization (NATO),** the **Warsaw Pact (WTO),** the **ANZUS Pact,** and the **Southeast Asia Treaty Organization (SEATO).** Other regional organizations are involved in more than just defense: the Organization of American States **(OAS),** the League of Arab States, the Organization of African Unity **(OAU),** the African Union **(AU),** the Nordic Council, the Association of Southeast Asian Nations **(ASEAN),** and the Gulf Cooperation Council. The peace-keeping record of these organizations is mixed. They seem to be able to control or settle problems only when their members are all in agreement.

The North Atlantic Treaty Organization (NATO): A Case Study in Collective Self-Defense

In 1948, the Communist seizure of power in Czechoslovakia and the Soviet blockade of Berlin raised fears that the Russians might use force to gain control of Western Europe. By 1949, all countries of Eastern Europe—Bulgaria, Czechoslovakia, East Germany, Hungary, Poland, and Romania came under Communist rule. This led in April 4, 1949, to the creation of the **North Atlantic Treaty Organization (NATO)** as a unified leadership for the common defense of Western Europe. NATO was established by the North Atlantic Treaty which provided for the collective defense of the members against a possible attack by the Soviet Union or any other aggressor. An armed attack against one or more member countries in Europe and North America would be considered an attack against all members. The founding members were Belgium, the United Kingdom, Canada, Denmark, France, Iceland, Italy, Luxembourg, the Netherlands, Norway, Portugal, and the United States. These twelve states were followed in 1951 by Greece and Turkey, in 1954 by West Germany (East Germany was part of the Communist Warsaw Pact), and in 1982 by Spain. In 1990 when East and West Germany united, the new country of Germany entered NATO.

In 1991, the Warsaw Pact of communist countries dissolved, the Communist Party of Russia lost control of the government, and the Soviet Union itself ended. In response to these dramatic events, NATO formed the **North Atlantic Cooperation Council** which included NATO members as well as former Warsaw Pact countries, and reduced by 80% its supply of nuclear weapons to Europe. NATO expanded its military role in 1992 by making its forces available for peacekeeping assistance to non-NATO European countries. In 1994, NATO began the **"Partnership for Peace"** program under which non-NATO countries were permitted to begin participating in NATO military exercises and planning. More than twenty countries, including Russia and other former communist countries, joined. In 1997, NATO offered complete membership to Hungary, Poland, and the Czech Republic. They became full members of NATO in April 1999.

Political Integration

Political integration seeks to create new political communities and supranational institutions that transcend individual states and can control some of their action. **One proposal is that of World Federalism which recommends that a political union be built at the regional or global level like that of the U.S. federal structure which integrates fifty states.** The different states would have some representation in the world federal congress. This option is criticized by nationalists who see it as a threat to state sovereignty and as a possible totalitarian menace.

A second integration vehicle is that of Functionalism which is a bottom-up approach to promoting integration through transnational organizations which emphasize sharing sovereignty and building cooperative ties among states. Cooperation among countries would first be in technical matters in such social and economic areas as science and medicine which do not give rise to political disputes but bring immediate rewards. States would not give up their national sovereignty. The functionalists argue that poverty and despair cause war.

A third type of integration is **Neo-Functionalism,** a reconstitution of the Functionalist theory. It seeks a federal world system though perhaps beginning with an increase in the size of economic markets and reduction of trade barriers among several countries as in the European Union. This began with six states, then twelve, and now is considering expanding to over thirty. **Perhaps as states integrate economically, they will lose the will to fight each other, and then seek to integrate politically.**

The success of integration seems to depend on geographical proximity, steady economic growth, similar political systems, supportive public opinion, political stability, common historical experiences, shared perception of a common threat, bureaucratic compatibilities, and previous collaborative activities. This might not yet be applicable in the Third World, where states are still struggling to survive and consolidate. In fact, many countries will probably go in the opposite direction and disintegrate or implode as hypernationalism increases.

Peace Showcase: The OECD

The ideal situation is a stable peace. This is an absence of preparation for war or the serious expectation of war in addition to the absence of war. In contrast, an unstable peace is one which can only be enforced by

deterrence or by the fear of violent retribution, in which case one can continually fear for the continuation of peace under the threat of war at anytime. **A stable peace occurs in a security community. This is a group of people with a sense of common ground and who believe that all their social problems must and can be resolved by a process of peaceful change. The use of threat of force to resolve conflict is absent. These conditions of stable peace have been met by the United States, Canada, Japan, Australia, New Zealand and the democratic capitalist countries of the Organization for Economic Cooperation and Development (OECD).**

The **OECD** was created in 1961 to promote economic and social welfare in the member countries and to stimulate and harmonize efforts on behalf of developing countries. The members include Australia, Austria, Belgium, Canada, Denmark, Finland, France, Germany, Greece, New Zealand, Norway, Portugal, Spain, Sweden, Switzerland, Turkey, the United Kingdom, and the United States. **Since 1945, there has been no war among these states which have over 800 million inhabitants and which cover almost half of the land of the northern hemisphere. It is the largest zone of peace that has ever existed.**

Causes of OECD Peace

If the principles which are responsible for this remarkable peace could be reproduced elsewhere, the world would be more prosperous. Analysts do not agree on the causes of this stable peace. **One hypothesis is that the main element was cohesion in the face of an outside military threat, the Soviet Union.** This external enemy motivated the creation of NATO and of the OECD, and led to the deemphasis of the political differences among these countries. The Soviet threat and the presence of nuclear weapons probably helped to bring the peace among these previously competing states, but it probably was not enough to sustain the peace for now the threat of the Soviet Union has disappeared and peace still reigns. Also, this explanation ignores the process of integration, the positive aspects of interdependence, the presence of democracy and a steady economic growth.

A second hypothesis is that the peace is due to the creation of such international institutions as the European Commission, the European Parliament, and the European Court of Justice which exercise legislative, executive and judicial functions, respectively.

These European Union institutions set common standards for the movement of goods, services, workers and capital across national borders. They create a spillover of integration from one area to another and pool sovereignty among countries, excepting in foreign policy and defense. Yet, the area of peace extends beyond the European Union (EU), to countries in the OECD which do not belong to it. Besides, the institutions of the Council of Europe, the OECD, and the EU are not coercive institutions which could force a peace on these states. Most work by negotiations and consensus, not coercion. They facilitate mutual attention and problem-solving among the members. **Therefore, institution-building does contribute to integration whose goal is peace, but by itself is not a major cause of the stable peace. Also, there is peace among those OECD countries with few institutional bonds.**

A third hypothesis is that economic ties and social communications led to peace in the OECD. These links facilitate attention to one another, and identification of one's interest with those of others. They create bonds such as trade, travel, and cultural and educational exchange, and increase the flow of overall information through television, telephone, computer, satellite and fax machines. Interdependence creates a material stake in the economy and well-being of the partners. This type of exchange is mutually advantageous especially if it is done on the basis of relative equality instead of in an exploitative, colonial and involuntary matter. In general, ties between countries that are culturally similar and geographically close are more likely to be favorable.

Total trade and investment among the member states have increased significantly since the 1960s. Yet, peace among the industrialized countries was well established even before the high levels of economic interdependence were achieved in the 1970s. Interdependence deserves some credit for the peace, but other factors were at work.

A fourth hypothesis is that peace in the OECD resulted from economic achievements and continued expectations of mutual economic rewards. Rich and economically growing countries are less likely to have serious disputes with each other. A stable peace can best be maintained under conditions of moderate growth, equity, and a high level of economic activity. Where such conditions do not exist, peace is more likely to be maintained, if at all, only through mutual or one-sided deterrence. Certain common values must also be held in the security community, as well as a mutual responsiveness

among the population. This is made possible by mass communications.

Finally, there is the view that peace in the OECD resulted from the widespread acceptance in all countries of the values and institutions of constitutional democracy. Since the restoration of democracy in Greece, Portugal, and Spain in the early 1970s, all OECD countries have had democratic forms of governments. Mature democratic countries are very unlikely to make war on each other or to have serious military disputes. Perhaps this is so for various reasons: they share a political culture; value individual rights; tolerate dissent; have limited governments which do not tend to abuse their own citizens; respect the right to self-determination; and have institutional constraints such as checks-and-balances and separation of powers, which makes it hard on the leaders to move their countries to war. Their leaders might find that it is harder to mobilize their own people to go to war than it is to negotiate international disputes.

Democracy in the Making

The ability to exercise constitutional democracy has been a major factor in the stable peace of the OECD countries. Can the democratization of the former communist countries and of the developing world provide the element which they need so badly to acquire peace? **Unfortunately, the transition from autocracy to democracy can be very difficult. This can be seen in what is happening in the former Yugoslavia which split into competing states, and what is also occurring in Sub-Saharan Africa. There are reasons why violence increases as countries democratize:** weakening governments prevent autocrats from dictating a consensus which can lead to order, even if it is temporary; young democratic institutions such as political parties are too weak to integrate opposing interests and reduce conflict; highly intense mass politics prevent the growth of coalitions which can bring diverse groups together; previously dominant groups become radicalized as they fear losing their economic and social status; new ambitious groups seek ties with some of the members of the ruling elite to repress other factions; and intense ideological propaganda manipulates and polarizes people in the absence of a free market of ideas to counter false claims with reliable facts.

Increasing popular participation in the election of the chief executive, increasing the competitiveness of political participation, or increasing the constraints on a country's executive, are all related to an increase in the likelihood of war. States making the largest leap from full autocracy to high levels of democracy are on the average more likely to become involved in an interstate war than states that remained autocracies. **Nationalism** and war often go hand in hand with a young democracy.

Mature democracies can integrate some of the new and older political groups through strong party systems and competition for the favor of the average voter. **However, in states making the transition to democracy, political leaders use nationalism, and the primeval emotions it often elicits, to survive politically by getting prestige at home through victories abroad.** Nationalism, democracy, and war are often used to glue together all the competing domestic groups or to disarm threatening internal factions. Thus, states making the transition to democracy tend to be warlike. Yet, the cure for violence might not be less democracy, but more of it.

The average voter might not want war at first. But the elite and their propaganda and military actions presented can arouse mass opinion in favor of war which then can become uncontrollable. What is needed is time for these countries to mature democratically. In the short-term, new democracies will encounter difficulties, but in the long-run they will grow in peace. There is a need for the old elite to find a place in the new system, though with a much weaker political role. This way they will not become too radical and slow down the evolution to democracy. **There is also a need for an independent, aggressive and fair press to disinflate the demagoguery of potential tyrants.** There is a need for neighboring states to create defensive alliances to increase deterrence and discourage demagogues from leading their young democracies to war. There is a need for stable currencies so that the new social groups do not find the new system highly inflationary, creating desperate conditions in food and housing. And, finally, there is a need for the international community to be helpful in matters of trade and technical assistance.

Final Thoughts

War seems as common as peace. **Realists'** reliance on balance of power, defensive alliances, arms buildup and national sovereignty, and **idealists'** affection for democracy, free markets, free trade, open diplomacy collective security, international law, national self-determination, arms control, and good will have not been able to eradicate all wars. Even when a reduction in interstate conflict occurs, sometimes the violence seems to sprout in other forms like civil wars, terrorism, secessionist wars and street violence. **Realists are right to be concerned about war springing up at any time, and about the need to be ready for it at all times. Yet, idealists are right too in their concern for justice, their efforts to address the underlying causes of war, and their attempt to seek international cooperative efforts which can contain ambitious leaders and fearful states.**

However, it might be that at this time, war cannot be completely eradicated, and that the best that can be done is to reduce its frequency and destructiveness through a wide array of mechanisms. Realists are right in pointing out that there are just too many defects in humans themselves, in the composition of states, and in the international system. **Realists are right in that one cannot prevent all wars. Nevertheless, Idealists are correct in saying that many forms of violence have been eradicated and through hard work, planning, sacrifice and wisdom many difficult situations can be defused and wars prevented.** It is impossible to tell at any one time which strategy will be the one to save the peace.

At the personal level it is highly unlikely that political leaders will somehow become free of all those dangerous human inclinations such as pride, envy, anger, greed and fear which make them seek their own selfish interests rather than the common good. These qualities can be inhibited or redirected, but they are difficult to vanquish. Sigmund Freud believed that it was an illusion to suppose that civilization so transforms human nature as to lift it above the impulses of war, and that war is not to be abolished so long as the repulsion between people is so intense.

Thomas Aquinas insisted that those who seek war desire nothing but peace which they deem themselves not to have. For him, man's heart is not at peace so long as he has not what he wants, or if, having what he wants, there remains something for him to want. Peace thus is not just concord, but involves the tranquility of order, which means that all the desires of each individual are being set at rest together and in agreement as to something which they consider mutually beneficial. Unfortunately, often there is no tranquility of order and seldom are human desires at rest.

Yet, even if many leaders were to have interior peace, the domestic conditions of states—the presence of competing factions, the fear of outside threats, the desire for secession or for independence, the greed for the resources of others, the hope of improving the economy, etc.—can unleash the forces of nationalism, militarism and imperialism. **Peaceful, wise and competent leaders might be thrown aside by the demagogues who await in line in every society to fuel the fires of aggression as a means to gaining political power.**

Plato and Aristotle both agreed that war is something rooted in the nature of things, in the nature of humans, and in the nature of cities [states]. Hobbes believed that anarchy and the conditions of war are one and the same. A condition in which each man [or state] is a law unto himself and judge in his own case, must of necessity lead to force if he will impose his will upon, or resist the will of another. This idea that sovereigns are in a continual state of war with one another—because being sovereign they are autonomous, i.e. not subject to any superior government—seems to be accepted by most of the great political thinkers after Hobbes: Locke, Rousseau, Kant and Hegel. States and princes are in this warlike state of nature which leads to a state of war.

Therefore, even if human nature is transformed spiritually, and domestic institutions are reformed to allow greater justice and permit a more peaceful foreign policy, these states can fall prey to less enlightened and more predatory states whose ambitions have less personal and social constraints. It is this perception which has led some idealists to propose world government. In this view, if domestic governments are responsible for domestic peace, then it follows that world government will bring about world peace. This is an inference which only Dante and Kant would make before the 1900s.

Kant is the first major Western thinker to conceive the possibility of a peace that would not only be perpetual but also truly worldwide, even though he felt that this cosmopolitical ideal would not be attainable except by approximation. Only in the 1900s have people begun to argue for world peace as a conclusion because it is necessary. The ancients did speak about world peace and citizenship: Socrates, Epictetus, Marcus Aurelius, Zeno, Alexander, Virgil and Dante. Yet, they all thought of the world coming to a unity of peace by conquest or empire, a type of peace which would probably not be perpetual nor universal.

When, in modern times, the ideal of peace is stated in terms of peaceful methods for achieving it, by law and by consent, something less than the whole world is meant. For example, William Penn and Rousseau were thinking only of Europe. It is Kant who thinks of a universal framework for peace. He believed the world would enter into a Federation of Nations out of necessity. Nevertheless, most proposals for establishing world government can be subject to further questioning. For instance, would the attempt to impose a world order and world peace not lead itself to war against dissident states? And once there is world government, would interstate war simply become civil wars, as regional parts dissent from the central government? Could it be that a world government which enjoys the resources of the whole world, both human and technological, could implant the most totalitarian state ever devised? Who and what will prevent the abuse of power and the manifestation of the seven deadly sins, for instance, once the principles of state sovereignty and of the plurality of state have been ended? Could a world government be created in the absence of one world culture from which global norms would get their support? Clearly, the long conversation over war and peace is not over. Stay tuned.

Sources

Articles

Bremer, Stuart. (June 1992) *"Dangerous Dyads: Conditions Affecting the Likelihood of Interstate War* 1816–1965." Journal of Conflict Resolution 36, 1–15.

Doyle, Michael W. (December 1986), "Liberalism and World Politics." *American Political Science Review* 80, 1151–1169.

Ebban, Abba. (September/October 1995) "The U.N. Idea Revisited." *Foreign Affairs,* 74, 39–55.

Kennedy, Paul and Russett, Bruce. (September/October 1995) "Reforming the United Nations." *Foreign Affairs,* 74, 56–71.

Manfield, Edward D., and Snyder, Jack. (May/June 1995) "Democratization and War." *Foreign Affairs,* 74, 79–97.

Singer, J. David, and Small, Melvin. (September 1974) "Foreign Policy Indicators: Predictors of War in History and in the State of the World Message." *Policy Science,* 5, 271–296.

Walenstein, Peter, and Axell, Karin. (August 1993) "Armed Conflict at the End of the Cold War 1989–1992." *Journal of Peace Research,* 30, 331–346.

Books

Adler, Mortimer J., (1971) (Ed). *The Great Ideas: A Syntopicon of Great Books of the Western World.* Chicago: Encyclopaedia Britannica, Inc.

Ball, Nicole. (1994) *"Demilitarizing the Third World."* World Security. Edited by Michael T. Klare and Daniel C. Thomas. New York: St. Martin Press.

Dougherty, James E., and Pfaltzgraff, Robert L. (1981) *Contending Theories of International Relations: A Comprehensive Survey,* New York: Harper & Row, Publishers.

Dyer, Gwynne. (1985). *War.* London: The Bodley Head.

Haas, Ernest B. (1986). *Why We Still Need the United Nations: The Collective Management of International Conflict 1945–1984.* Berkeley: Institute of International Studies at the University of California.

Holsti, Kalevi. (1992) *International Politics: A Framework for Analysis.* Englewood Cliffs: Prentice Hall.

Joyner, Christopher. (1995). "The Reality and Relevance of International Law in the Post-Cold War Era." *The Global Agenda.* Edited by Charles W. Kegley Jr., and Eugene R. Wittkopf. New York: McGraw-Hill.

Kagan, Donald. (1995) *On the Origins of War.* New York: Doubleday.

Keegan, John. (1993) *A History of Warfare.* New York: Alfred A. Knopf.

Kegley, Charles W., and Wittkopf, Eugene R. (1995) *World Politics Trend and Transformation.* New York: St. Martin Press.

Mendoza, Manuel G., and Napoli, Vince. (1990) *Systems of Society: An Introduction to Social Science.* Lexington: D.C. Health and Company.

Papp, Daniel S. (1994). *Contemporary International Relations* (4th ed). New York: Macmillan College Publishing Company.

Plano, Jack C., and Greenberg, Milton; Olton, Roy; and Riggs, Robert E. (1973). *Political Science Dictionary.* Hinsdale: The Dryden Press.

Plano, Jack C., and Greenberg, Milton. (1993). *The American Political Dictionary* (9th ed). Fort Worth: Harcourt Brace College Publishers.

Riggs, Robert E., and Plano, Jack C. (1994). *The United Nations: International Organization and World Politics.* Belmont: Wordsworth.

Rikhye, Indar Jit. (1989) *The Future of Peacekeeping.* New York: International Peace Academy.

Russett, Bruce, and Starr, Harvey. (1992). *World Politics: The Menu for Choice.* New York: W.H. Freeman and Company.

Singer, J. David. (1991) "Peace in the Global System: Displacement, Interregnum, or Transformation?" *The Long Postwar Peace.* Edited by Charles W. Kegley Jr. New York: Harper Collins.

Sivard, Ruth Leger. (1991) *World Military and Social Expenditures.* Washington D.C.: World Priorities.

Stoessinger, John G. (1990). *The Might of Nations. World Politics in Our Times.* New York: McGraw-Hill Publishing Company.

Suganami, Hidemi. (1991). "The Causes of War: A New Theoretical Framework." *The Theory and Practice of International Relations.* Edited by. William Clinton Olson. Englewood Cliffs: Prentice Hall.

Waltz, Kenneth N. (1993) "Explaining War." *International Relations Theory.* Realism, Pluralism, Globalism. Edited by Paul R. Viotti and Mark V. Kauppi. New York: Macmillan Publishing Company.

CHAPTER THIRTEEN

Current Affairs

A Geopolitical Perspective

Germán Muñoz

The Middle East and North Africa

This region of the world is characterized by a predominantly Muslim population living in a harsh and arid environment with limited islands of ecumene. An Arab heritage dominates the Arabian Peninsula and North Africa, while Turkish and Iranian influences govern the northeastern regions. Three types of life have existed in the area: nomadic herders, peasant dirt farmers, and city-dwellers. Recently, petroleum workers and military personnel have gained in numbers. Despite the high degree of homogeneity among the inhabitants, no common national identity has been created. During the 1800s and early 1900s, much of the area was under Ottoman and European control.

It is useful to classify the region into six distinctive areas: the **Fertile Crescent** of Iraq, Kuwait, Syria, Lebanon, Jordan and Israel; the **Arabian Peninsula** of Saudi Arabia, Bahrain, Qatar, the United Arab Emirates, Oman and Yemen; the **Northeastern Periphery** of Iran and Turkey; **Afghanistan;** the **Nile River States** of Egypt and Sudan; and the **Maghreb** of Morocco, Algeria, Tunisia and Libya. The entire area has a population of approximately 420 million.

Turkey: The Importance of Geographical Location

Turkey possesses great strategic significance because it occupies Asia Minor, stretches into continental Europe, and borders on the Mediterranean and Black seas. It controls the Bosporus Strait by the Black Sea and the Dardanelles Strait by the Aegean Sea. Very few states have such an important location. Turkey has a population of 71 million, of which 66% is urban. Turks account for 80% of the population, while Kurds make up 20%. The official language is Turkish, but Kurdish and Arabic are also used. Muslims comprise 99.8% of the population.

Turkey became a republic in 1923 under Mustafa Kemal, who built his country on the principles of nationalism, secularism and European identity. He included European laws, the Latin alphabet, the Gregorian calendar, personal last names, hats instead of fezzes, monogamy, Sunday as the day of rest, a ban on dervishes, the legal right to drink alcohol, and Turkish as a liturgical language. The Caliphate (or spiritual leadership) of Islam was ended in 1924. Islam was to be only a personal devotion and not a state religion. However, in December

This chapter on current affairs will be updated periodically as it includes information on the most significant recent world events. It allows the reader to apply social science concepts to the analysis of contemporary issues.

1995, parliamentary elections brought into power **Welfare,** Turkey's first self-declared Islamic party. It won 25% of the vote.

Immediately after the election, the big question became whether the rise of the Welfare Party to power would end political secularism in Turkey and polarize secularists and Islamists. Local and regional Islamic groups began to harass women's centers and to pressure secular judges into retirement so that new Islamic ones could be appointed.

On the other hand, there are factions in Turkey which restrain the expansion of Islamism. Islam is very diverse in Turkey, from the left-leaning Alevis to the fundamentalists. Many Turks are devout Muslims who prefer a secular society as long as it satisfies their needs. The very powerful centrist secularist **True Path Party** had the most sensitive posts in the government, such as Defense, the Foreign Ministry, and Internal Security. Moreover, Turkey has an active civil society which serves as a check on any Turkish government, and it also has a relatively free press. The military is an active supporter of democracy and secularism. It has expelled officers for religious activities, refuses to hire religious school graduates, and is heavily represented in the National Security Council, which is important in foreign affairs.

In addition, many Turks support strong ties with Europe and Central Asia. Turkey entered into a customs union arrangement with the European Union in 1996. Turkey is a member of the North Atlantic Treaty Organization (NATO), the most important Western military alliance. The Turks are not as authoritarian as the Arabs, and they tend to trust the electoral system. Since the growth of fundamentalism seems to be associated with the level of social discomfort, the radicalization of the Muslims in Turkey might depend on the degree of corruption, inflation, unemployment, and political repression in the country.

The highest court in 1998 banned, with the encouragement of the military, the Welfare Party for attempting to undermine the country's secular foundations and banned Prime Minister Necmettin Erbakan and five other politicians from participating in politics for five years. They were accused of extending the influence of religious schools, replacing secularist judges with religious ones, encouraging religious apparel in public buildings, filling the military with Islamist supporters, and planning to build a mosque in Istanbul's secular center.

Turkey is increasingly becoming more capitalistic, and this means that it will try to diversify its economic interests. It will seek better relations with Russia to acquire natural gas, with the Ukraine to build an oil pipeline, and with China, Central Asia, and Italy to expand its markets. Turkey has also decided to buy natural gas from Iran. Turkey will benefit from United States' support of private energy development in the Caspian Sea region. The Americans have backed an oil pipeline running from Azerbaijan to Turkey without touching Russian soil. Another oil pipeline is from an offshore Azerbaijan field called Shah Deniz.

Yet, Turkey does have conflicts with its neighbors. It has disputes with Iraq and Syria over water and border issues, and over Syria's support of terrorism. **Turkey has difficulties with many Arab countries because of its military collaboration with Israel.** There are problems with Egypt because Turkey supports the **Muslim Brotherhood** which, among other things, wants an Islamic state in Egypt. Also, it has difficulties with Libya, which wants an independent Kurdish state. The Kurds live in Iraq, Turkey, Iran and Syria. An independent Kurdish state would mean that these countries would have to cede some land to the Kurds. Some of the Kurds in Iraq have mounted terrorist campaigns inside Turkey and Turkey has responded invading Iraq to destroy Kurdish bases there and repressing Kurds inside Turkey itself.

Three recent events are of importance to the future of Turkey. One was the victory of the Islamic-oriented Justice and Development Party (AKP) which won the elections of November 2002, with 34% of the vote. The AKP split from the Welfare Party and seeks to promote on the surface a softer Islamism. There are indications that the leader of AKP, Recep Tayyip Erdogan is seeking to establish an Islamic state in Turkey. Billions of dollars from the Gulf States and Saudi Arabia are financing businesses and organizations which oppose the secularists. There is a penetration of education beginning at four years of age and of the judiciary with the appointment of Koranic school graduates who support the application of sharia, that is, Islamic law.

The AKP is trying to apply the Islamic law by criminalizing adultery and creating alcohol free zones, not to speak of its privileging Islamic courts over secular courts. The AKP has tried to lift the ban on Islamic head scarves in public places and schools. It relies on dirty money and has a bias against religious minorities as well as on the persecution of political opponents. The targets of the Islamists are the Alevi minority, the army, the press, the secular bureaucracy, and working women. However, the secular army is concerned that if it moves against the AKP it might be blamed by Turks for the rejection by the European Union of Turkey's application for membership which requires democratic institutions.

On April 2007, a major crisis developed in Turkey when President Recep Tayyip Erdogan picked Abdullah Güll, a close associate, to run for the Presidency. He failed to get the necessary votes; the Constitutional Court voided the elections and millions of secularists took to the streets fearing the growth of political Islamism. The military hinted of a coup and Erdogan dissolved the Parliament. However, the AKP won on July 22, 2007, a stunning victory in Parliament getting 47% of the vote and a majority of the seats. Perhaps the success came from its ability to double per capita income to $6,000, lowering inflation from 30 to below 7%, and reducing interest rates from 6% to 17%. This vote has made the AKP a mainstream party and weakened the army and the other secularists.

A second key event was the rejection in 2003 by the European Union of Turkey's application to enter this economic bloc. The United States recommended Turkey's application. However, the EU believes that Turkey did not meet the political criteria for entry even though it abolished the death penalty, allowed the Kurds to study and broadcast in their own language, and lifted controls on the press.

The **European Union** is concerned about Turkey's human rights record and its powerful military, which has brought about three coups in the last forty years. Currently, there is tension between the secularist military and the religious **Islamic Justice and Development Party.** Another concern of the EU in regard to Turkey is the unproductive and unstable Turkish economy. Were Turkey to enter the EU, it would be the poorest economy in Europe and could send millions of its poor throughout the European continent. Turkey would be the second country in size and voting power within the union after Germany, but its GNP per capita would be less than 25% that of Germany. In fact, the 70 million Turks would equal the population of the ten new countries which entered the European Union in May, 2004. While its inflation is under 10%, the budget deficit is 10.2% of GDP, way above the 3% limit required of EU members.

There are approximately 12 million Muslims in Europe, five million in France, three million in Germany and one million in the United Kingdom. For many Euro-

peans, these large numbers of hard-to-integrate people tend to promote crime and Islamic militancy. Adding 71 million more Muslims to the European Union is not an attractive proposition for many in Europe. Austria, Denmark and France, for example, do not want the inclusion of Turkey.

Another obstacle to Turkey's entrance into the European Union is the Cyprus problem. Without a deal to resolve Cyprus' thirty-three year division between Greek and Turkish Cypriots, Greece and Cyprus, a new member of the EU and represented only by the island's Greek Cypriots, are likely to veto any talks on Turkish membership. Yet, if the Turks use their strong leverage with the Turkish Cypriot leadership to restart talks along the lines already proposed by the UN maybe a deal is possible. This would help Turkey. Moreover, for many EU leaders, the Turks are simply not European. Turkey also has problems because of police brutality cases, restrictions on property holdings, and interference with the educational activities of religious minorities.

Although the AKP is hoping that the "Accession" talks with the European Union will lead to membership, only approximately 33% of Turks support the effort. Close to 66% of Turks believe that the West (the EU and the United States) wants to divide Turkey. The military is upset with the United States because of what many consider is US support for the Kurds of Iraq, who could create an independent state, and could radicalize Kurds in Turkey, who are 20% of the population. Many Turks believe the United States is unwilling to attack the PKK in Iraq, a violent group of Kurds who often attack Turkey itself. Many Turks also resent the effort by some in the EU and in the United States to force Turkey to acknowledge the genocide Turks committed against the Christian Armenians in 1915, when 1.5 million died. The EU also wants Turkey to extend its Customs Treaty privileges to Cyprus, a rival. Many Turks also resent what they consider the isolation of its allied Turkish Republic of Northern Cyprus. For all these reasons, many in Turkey want the country to move closer to China, India, Iran, and even Russia.

The third event with potential repercussions for Turkey was the Iraqi war which began on March 19, 2003. Some NATO countries such as Belgium and France initially tried to prevent Turkey, a NATO member, from receiving military assets for its defense vis-à-vis Iraq. This disagreement could further weaken an already debilitated NATO. Also, the parliament of Turkey voted not to give access through its territory to

U.S troops trying to create a northern fighting front in Iraq, even when the United States offered Turkey approximately $30 billion in credits and other types of support.

The Turks might have been afraid that Iraqi Kurds could take over Mosul or Kirkuk in Iraq, whose vast oil fields could help them create an independent state which could then radicalize Kurds inside Iraq. Perhaps Turks were also afraid of a negative economic impact from the war, or were unwilling to fight another Muslim country. Turkey has begun a rapprochement with Iran and Syria, two countries which also have a Kurdish problem.

Starting in mid-2004, the Turks began to signal that they might be willing to send 1,500 troops to Afghanistan, and even to Iraq, as part of NATO. However, they would like to see the United Nations take a more active part in Iraq. They also might support an autonomous political jurisdiction for the Kurds in northern Iraq. This would be a major policy shift of their part. The Kurds' region could be a buffer between Turkey and a possible Shiite Islamic state which could radiate violence.

On the other hand, this shift might not take place if Turkey continues attacking in Iraq the Kurdistan Workers Party (PKK), which seeks to create a Kurdish state out of southeast Turkey, northeast Iraq, northeast Syria, and northwest Iran. Naturally, Iran and Syria also oppose the PKK. On October 2007, the Parliament allowed the army to engage in cross-border raids into Northern Iraq. The United States and the European Union oppose Turkey's internationalization of the crisis. They are trying to convince Turkey that the PKK has nothing to do with the dominant Kurdish coalition of the Patriotic Union of Kurdistan and the Kurdistan Democratic Party. Perhaps the real issue is that Turkey does not want the Kurds to control oil-rich Kirkuk, from which they could create an independent state. Many Kurds fear Turkey will fight to prevent a Kurdish state.

One can see from the perspective of 2010 and 2011 that Turkey is moving away from having a secular state. This is taking place gradually as Islamists are filling many positions in government which used to be off limits to them. Saudi Arabia is financing many of the activities and policies which undermine secularism in Turkey. In addition, American diplomacy is actually supporting this change and is backing the Islamic dominant political party in order to win favors elsewhere.

Turkey is also continuing to strengthen its ties with Iran and Syria, while at the same time reducing its traditional closeness with Israel. Many wonder if Turkey will be a reliable ally in the North Atlantic Treaty Organization (NATO).

Afghanistan: The Crossroads of Asia

Afghanistan is a landlocked and mountainous country divided north and south by the **Hindu Kush and Pamir mountain ranges.** It has **Pakistan** on the east and on the south, **Iran** on the west, and **Turkmenistan, Tajikistan,** and **Uzbekistan** on the north. The country's northeast tip touches **China.** Thus, it is at the **crossroads of Asia.** Afghanistan, geographically isolated, used to be a buffer state between the Russian and the British empires. It is now an important area between the people of Central Asia and those of Pakistan and India in South Asia.

Afghanistan has 31 million people. Only 23% of the population is urban. Sunni Muslims make up 90% of the population. The **Pashtun** are 44% of the population and live mostly south of the Hindu Kush (the slaughter of the Hindus by Muslims), where they have strong ties with Pakistan and India. They conquered central Afghanistan in the late 1800s, and were the rulers of Afghanistan until 1979 when Russia invaded Afghanistan. They did not want a centralized government nor openness to the outside world.

North of the Hindu Kush is a zone of conflict between Afghanistan and Central Asia. There are 3 to 4 million Afghan **Tajiks** (25% of the population) in the northeast. They are Persian-speaking, Sunni Muslims who traditionally ran the bureaucracy of Afghanistan. Also north of the Hindu Kush are one million Turkish-speaking **Uzbeks** and **Turkmen** who live in northwest Afghanistan. In West Afghanistan are the Persian-speaking, Shiite Muslim, **Hazara** people (10% of the population), who are closely linked to Iran and controlled the land until the Pashtuns entered Central Afghanistan.

When the Russians invaded Afghanistan in December 1979, they unleashed a war which killed one million Afghans and 15,000 Russians. The United States gave weapons and intelligence to the anti-Soviet forces. Soviet leader Mikhail Gorbachev withdrew the troops in 1989. Afterwards, many of the Afghan factions began fighting each other. Twenty-five thousand died fighting over the capital of Kabul alone. In March 1995, **Taliban,** a Pashtun, Sunni Muslim student movement trained in Pakistan conquered Kabul, killed the Hazara leaders, took the Pashtun provinces of the south, began imposing an extremely authoritarian Islamic state in Afghanistan, and harbored the Muslim terrorist Osama bin Laden. It overran North Afghanistan in 1998.

Pakistan and Saudi Arabia supported the Taliban, while Iran, Russia, India and four Central Asian republics backed the opposition Northern Alliance made up of Tajiks, Uzbeks, Hazaras and Turkmen. Osama bin Laden gave the Taliban an ideological projection beyond Afghanistan which threatens Central Asia, India and Iran. Terrorist camps were created in Somalia, Egypt, Sudan, and Yemen.

In response to the Islamist terrorist attack against the United States on September 11, 2001, the George W. Bush Administration attacked Afghanistan on October 3, 2001. It sought the defeat of Mullah Mohammed Omar, leader of the Taliban, and of Osama bin Laden, head of **al-Qaeda** and of the **World Islamic Front Against Jews and Crusaders**. Following its victory, the United States and its allies began supporting a coalition government led by Amid Karzai. Many of the losing Taliban and al Qaeda forces fled to Iran and to the Afghan-Pakistan border from where they are still conducting attacks against the Karzai regime.

Unfortunately, Afghanistan does not have functioning state institutions. There is no real army, no effective police, no rule of law, and no provincial administration in harmony with the central government.

The central government needs a tax base to pay for these activities, particularly the appropriate type and amounts of international assistance. However, most of the international aid by-passes the central government. If Western troops withdraw, the new government could collapse. In the absence of effective governance, Afghans rely on personalized networks or warlords who have access to political power, weapons, foreign aid, profits from the drug trade, legal taxes and wealth from the ownership of property.

The United States during the war against the Taliban and bin Laden used warlords mostly from the non-Pashtun area, including Tajiks, Uzbeks and, Hazaras who are Shiite, unlike the majority Sunni Pashtans. Now the Pashtuns feel inadequately represented. It is from the Pashtun areas in Southern Afghanistan and Western Pakistan that the Taliban and al-Qaeda are getting their

strongest support. President Karsai and future leaders will have to demilitarize Kabul to make it a credible national capital where no warlord has an advantage. Then the central government can expand an impartial state beyond Kabul. The government needs to prevent Afghanistan from becoming a Narco-state. Opium dominates the economy, being 60% of the gross domestic product. Much of it is being used to finance terrorist activities. Over 90% of the heroin used in Europe comes from Afghanistan.

An issue which has concerned human rights advocates in Europe and in the United States is the lack of religious freedom in Afghanistan, which uses **Islam as the main source for legislation.** The **Rathman case** became an international crisis in 2006 when a Muslim man who converted to Christianity was threatened with death for the "crime" of apostasy. Several Western countries threatened to stop aiding Afghanistan if the sentence was carried out. It was not, because he was sent away from Afghanistan.

The mood among many Afghans is bleak as they believe the Taliban is winning, though this is not factually true. For this reason, the United States began to deploy 3,200 Marines on March 18, 2008. Only the Americans, the Australians, the British, the Canadians and the Dutch have fighting forces there. The North Atlantic Treaty Organization (NATO) assumed leadership of the **International Security Assistance Force** (ISAF) in 2003. Most NATO countries have refused to provide military forces to the battle front, preferring instead reconstruction work. Its level of financing and coordination has been poor.

The international community has not provided the funds needed to expand development beyond the capital. The Taliban is targeting schools and murdering teachers and students. The military of Pakistan is allied with **Jamiat-e-Islam,** which supports the Taliban. The government of Pakistan gave autonomy on September 5, 2006, to the **North Waziristan** region of Pakistan by the Afghan border which hosts Taliban and al-Qaeda terrorists. It is clear that unless the governments of Afghanistan, Pakistan and the United States are able to isolate and extinguish the al-Qaeda and the Taliban bases in the tribal areas of Pakistan, Afghanistan will not be able to win the war. Pakistan allows **Quetta**, the capital of Balochistan, to be used as a base for the Taliban against Afghanistan.

The U.S Obama Administration decided in 2010 to increase by 30,000 the number of American troops in Afghanistan hoping to copy the success of the surge in Iraq which occurred when President George W. Bush increased the number of American troops to defeat the insurgency in that country. The United States also decided to develop a counter-insurgency policy which would concentrate on protecting the Afghan people from the Taliban and winning "the hearts and minds" of the population.

This policy replaced the counter-terrorism strategy whose emphasis was to identify, pursue, and kill the terrorists. Unfortunately, one disadvantage of a counter-terrorism strategy was the high number of civilian deaths and the consequent political cost to the United States. Another difficulty of American policy in Afghanistan is the decision by President Obama to start withdrawing troops by the end of 2011. Critics believe that this deadline undermines the faith of the Afghan people on the United States for they feel the Americans will abandon them in 2011. As a result of this deadline, some Afghans might not want to risk their lives to support a country whose U.S. military support is about to end. And yet, an exit strategy is needed because most of the American people want the troops out of Afghanistan.

A third problem America faces in Afghanistan is the regional balance of power. Iran is involved in undermining the Afghan state and American efforts to consolidate it. Pakistan's security services might be supporting the Taliban both in Afghanistan and in Pakistan. India is increasingly investing resources in Afghanistan, something which Pakistan might not support. And to make it worse, the Afghan regime is too weak and corrupt to exert its authority over the whole territory. If the United States ends its combat mission in Afghanistan, the country might fall apart, might be divided into several parts, or the government might reach a deal with Iran, the Taliban and Pakistan. An American defeat could also motivate the Taliban and other terrorist groups to expand their military activities.

Islamic Theocracy: Iran

Iran is strategically situated between Southwest Asia, South Asia, and Central Asia. Iran has Turkey and Iraq on the west, Armenia, Azerbaijan, and Turkmenistan on the north, and Afghanistan and Pakistan on the east. Its population of 66 million is the largest in Southwest Asia. The urban population is 67%. Iran is 51% Persian, 24% Azerbaijani, and 7% Kurdish. The principal language is Persian (Farsi). Shi'a Muslims make up 89% of the population.

Since 1979, when Ayatollah Ruhollah Khomeini created the first Shiite Islamic theocratic state in history, the government of Iran has increased its centralization of power under an authoritarian religious-political leader, an elected president, and a judiciary under a highly influential judge selected by the religious leader. This top leader is selected by an assembly of experts more for his political acumen and loyalty than for his religious knowledge.

Iranian public policy is based on five main ideas: a return to sharia or Islamic law, which does not allow a non-religious or a free non-Islamic social order; hatred of Western countries and their Arab or Islamic allies; development of nuclear weapons; hatred of Israel; and global leadership of the Muslim World.

Iran and the United States

In response to terrorist activities, the United States began in 1993 a policy of Dual Containment of Iran and Iraq. Also, in 1996, the United States imposed sanctions on foreign companies that invest in Iran. Iran has other problems: a brain drain, as many Iranian professionals seek a better life elsewhere; government corruption; crisis of authority, as more people question the clerics; population growth greater than economic growth; economic stagnation; and difficulties with the Azeri population in the north, a portion of which would like to separate.

Better relations with the United States would bring some advantages to Iran: elimination of the costly U.S. embargo which contributes to its inflation and high unemployment rate; import of modern technology and better products; upgrading of its defense, industrial and oil equipment; unfreezing of $11 billion in frozen assets held by the United States; and increased foreign investments by Europeans who are waiting for the end of the American embargo.

On the other hand, the United States could also benefit from better relations with Iran since this is the only country with long frontages on both the Caspian Sea and the Persian Gulf and a likely pipeline for oil from Central Asia and the Caspian Sea. Also, the American policy of isolating Iran could push the former Soviet states of Central Asia back into the Russian orbit to sell their energy resources. However, Iran follows several policies which places it in conflict with the

United States and with Arab states in the region: it is the largest terrorist nucleus in the Middle East, sheltering al-Qaeda members and supporting such groups as Hezbollah, Hamas and Islamic Jihad; seeks weapons of mass destruction and delivery vehicles for them; considers Syria and Lebanon as a part of Iran; supports separatist movements in Bahrain, Saudi Arabia and Iraq; wants dominance of the oil-rich Persian Gulf; and is trying to undermine American and allied interest in Afghanistan and Iraq.

In 1999 supporters of Iran's "reform" president Mohammed Khatami won in the country's first local elections. They seemed to want better relations with the United States and the West, as well as greater freedom of expression, political participation, and reconciliation between Islam and democracy. In mid-1999, the former Clinton Administration ended blanket sanctions on the export of food and medicines up to $500 million worth of food. It affected various countries including Iran, Libya and Sudan. This was the first change in the policy to Iran since 1995 when the U.S. imposed a total ban on trade. This change in policy did not affect North Korea and Cuba.

In February 2000, the reformists won 70% of the legislature's 290 seats. On June 8, 2001, Muhammed Khatami once again won the presidency of Iran, this time with 76.9% of the vote and the support of young people. Yet, whatever domestic reforms and openness to the world he tried to pursue were restricted by the Supreme Religious Leader, Ayatollah Ali Khamenei, who controls the military and the intelligence services. The Iranian hardliners are threatened by domestic reforms which could diminish their power within the theocratic system.

The February 2004 Parliamentary elections in Iran were pre-arranged. Candidates were handpicked, dissent was not allowed, access to the media was denied, an internal opposition was persecuted, and President Muhammed Khatami, the man often seen as an Islamic reformist, did not put up a fight against the anti-democratic forces. Mahmoud Ahmadinejad won the elections of June 17, 2005, and became the President of Iran. A hard-line supporter of the clerics, he has pledged to destroy Israel and attack the United States. He is also seeking to destroy all internal opposition to the regime. The Iranian leadership is concerned about the democracy promotion program by the United States. In addition, they are concerned about unrest by Iran's large ethnic minorities: Arabs, Azeris, Baluchis, Kurds and Turkmen. Internal repression will continue.

A principal controversy over Iran is the accusation by the United States that the clerics are enriching uranium for the production of nuclear weapons. The Non-Proliferation Treaty (NPT) allows some nuclear development but short of creating nuclear weapons. Iran has been running a 20-year clandestine nuclear program which was missed by U.S intelligence and by the **International Atomic Energy Agency (IAEA).** Iran has manufactured small amounts of highly enriched uranium and plutonium, a violation of the NPT. It could produce nuclear weapons by 2009–2012. Finally on September 24, 2005, the IAEA declared that Iran is in non-compliance with the Non-Proliferation Treaty's Safeguard Agreement. Then in 2006 it submitted the case to the Security Council of the United Nations.

A big debate over the Iranian nuclear weapon program was unleashed on December 3, 2007, when the **U.S. National Intelligence Estimate** (NIE) declared that Iran halted its nuclear program in 2003. This estimate might have derailed American efforts to aggressively deal with Iran over the issue. However, the report has lost much credibility for it mistakenly assumes that weaponization of the warhead—whose work might have stopped in 2003—is the key aspect that constitutes a potential threat, understates the importance of Iran civilian uranium efforts to the development of nuclear weapons, and does not address the military ballistic missile program.

Iran wants nuclear weapons for several reasons. It feels threatened by neighbors such as Afghanistan, Iraq, Israel and Pakistan. Iran also wants to prevent an attack by the United States. It seeks greater prestige, one fitting for a 2,500 year old civilization. Iran hopes to export its revolution, destroy Israel, dominate the Middle East, blackmail Europe, and engage in world domination.

The United States does not want Iran to develop nuclear weapons. It is trying to create a coalition with France, Germany, Russia, and the United Nations to convince Iran to stop its program. If this diplomacies effort fails, will the United States act unilaterally against Iran to destroy twelve to seventy fortified targets? Covert action is a possibility. Another is a naval blockade, but this could increase the world's price of oil and still leave the weapons intact. A third option is a surgical strike with cruise missiles and other weapons. A fourth choice is an all-out-assault, but the United States might not have enough soldiers and coalition allies. Iran could also retaliate with missile strikes against Israel and with terrorism against

Americans. While many young people oppose the Iranian theocratic regime, these people do seem to support their country's nuclear program. Therefore it is possible an attack against Iran might unite the country against the United States. On the other hand, an attack against Iran by the United States could result in a weakening of Iran which the Azeri and others could use to secede from the country.

Multilateral economic sanctions are another option. Unfortunately, many Europeans want more trade with Iran and have invested there over $10.5 billion. Trade with Europe has increased over 300%. France has made a $2 billion deal with Iran, and Russia is building an $800 million reactor which can produce plutonium. It would like also to build up to 100 more reactors and to sell Iran $1 billion in arms, including a Strategic Air Defense Missile System (SAMS). Iran is China's third most important oil supplier. China, France, and Russia are members of the Security Council of the United Nations, and might not want to take a strong diplomatic action against Iran lest it upsets their commercial relations. Iran is also selling oil to Italy, Japan, and South Korea. Germany is a major producer of industrial parts for Iran.

Iranians, if pressured economically by the Europeans and the Americans, or if given sufficient economic incentives by them, might sacrifice nuclear weapons for economic prosperity. Other states have done the same: Australia, Belarus, Egypt, Italy, Kazakhastan, Libya, South Korea, Sweden, and the Ukraine.

Building the Caliphate

Iran hopes to create a Muslim state under its leadership. It would first extend throughout the Middle East, and then beyond. The Revolutionary Guard went to Lebanon in 1982 to arm the Shiites in the Bekka Valley, and created **Hezbollah** to take over Southern Lebanon. They also created **Islamic Jihad,** its Sunni equivalent. Hezbollah taught young Lebanese the cult of martyrdom, kidnapping, bomb-making, intolerance, the social service network, and information warfare. The Iranians infiltrated the city of Badr in Iraq before the US forces reached Baghdad in 2003, and are training the **Badr Corps** which is the militia of the **Supreme Council for Islamic Revolution** in Iraq. If they are successful in southern Iraq, like in Southern Lebanon before, the region would be allied with Iran.

The next step in Iran's strategy is to expand its military and financial ties with Syria, which began in the 1980–1984 Iraq-Iranian war when Syria supported Iran. They now have a Mutual Defense Treaty signed in 2004, and Iran is also willing to share nuclear technology with Syria. **Furthermore, Iran is backing HAMAS, which won the elections of the Palestinian Authority (PA), Hezbollah, Islamic Jihad, the Popular Front for the Liberation of Palestine, as well as the other Palestinian rejectionist groups.** Iran also hopes to aid and control **al-Qaeda** as this group hopes to establish a base in northern Lebanon and in the Gaza Strip. Also, Iran wants to overthrow Israel, Jordan, Kuwait, Saudi-Arabia and the pro-Western Arab monarchies of the Arab/Persian Gulf. The success of Iran will depend on the collaboration of its enemies such as Turkey in the north, Afghanistan on the east, Iraq on the west, as well as Saudi Arabia, Russia and the United States.

So far in the 2010–2011 period, the biggest winner from the American political and military efforts in Afghanistan and Iraq has been Iran. Americans brought down Saddam Hussein and the Baath Party in Iraq, Iran's greatest enemies. The Sunnis were de-empowered and the Shiites, Iran's allies in Iraq were made the dominant force. In addition, al-Qaeda, an enemy of Iran, has been weakened.

Currently, there are some intelligence officers who believe that Iran will have a nuclear weapon by the end of 2011 or beginning of 2012. No amount of public pressure at this time seems to be convincing Iran not to go on with its nuclear project. It is not clear if Israel, who has been threatened with nuclear war by Iran, will be willing to conduct a unilateral military attack against them. Since the United Nations is unwilling to impose damaging sanctions on Iran, the United States is considering unilateral ones. The Obama Administration wanted to first try diplomacy as a means to deal with the nuclear Iranian threat. It has not worked yet. In early 2009, the last Presidential election in Iran led to great civil unrest which was repressed violently by the regime. The winner of the corrupt election was Mahmoud Ahmadinejad.

Iraq

Iraq invaded Kuwait on August 2, 1990. This was followed by an American coalition attack on Iraq in 1991, which forced Saddam Hussein to withdraw his troops from Kuwait. This led to economic sanctions by the United Nations. However, in 1996 the United Nations **Oil for Food Program** allowed Iraq to sell oil to buy food and other special products with the $21 to $52 billion sale of oil. A second war against Saddam Hussein and his Baathist Party began in March 2003. The direct military confrontation ended within a month, but guerilla and terrorist warfare against the United States and its allies continued throughout 2008.

The United States, Great Britain and their allies, including Australia, attacked Iraq on March 19, 2003 for several reasons. One was the belief that Saddam Hussein was developing a program of weapons of mass destruction (WMD). The intelligence services of France, Germany, Israel, Russia, the United Nations and of the United States all agreed on this matter. United Nations Resolution 1441 of 2002 declared that Iraq had failed to account for the biological and chemical weapons they had in 1998. In fact, Iraq had violated over eleven UN resolutions and numerous agreements which were part of the accords that ended the 1991 hostilities. However, UN Security Council members France, and Russia opposed military action against Iraq.

Regarding the weapons of mass destruction (WMD), David Kay of the Iraq Survey Group reported that large stockpiles have not been found in Iraq, though he did find programs and laboratories which could have been used to create these weapons in a short time. Thus, Iraqi Intelligence (IIS), or Mukhabarat, had over two dozen secret laboratories that kept alive Iraq's capabilities to produce both biological and chemical weapons. He also reported that Western intelligence services failed to note that Saddam Hussein tried in 2003 to produce biological weapons using the poison ricin, and sought to revive a nuclear weapons program in 2001–2002, which did not go as far as Libya's or Iran's programs. He was also developing a missile program. Hussein also destroyed some biological and chemical weapons in the mid-1990s, but did not report it to the United Nations.

In David Kay's view, United States President George W. Bush did not "cook" the books to justify the Iraqi war, but was justified to go to war because Iraq was a more dangerous place than was expected. He left open the possibility that the WMD have been buried in the desert or were taken to Syria before the war. This is also the opinion of Gazi George, a former Iraqi nuclear scientist under Saddam Hussein. The other possibility is that Hussein did not have weapons of mass destruction because he had them all destroyed. However, Hussein had used them in previous conflicts against Iran and the Kurds.

The decision of China, France, and Russia, all members of the UN Security Council, not to support military action against Iraq was subjected to much speculation.

China typically dislikes military actions by the United States, especially in Asia. They are not allies. France has a large Muslim population which it does not want to radicalize domestically, and its government actively seeks to reduce American influence globally. Russia's Vladimir Putin resents that the American-led NATO military alliance is encircling Russia.

However, there is also the argument that Saddam Hussein illegally used funds from the **Oil for Food Program** to buy the influence of 270 companies and politicians from 46 countries, especially in France, Russia, and the United Nations (UN) itself. The UN apparently received 2.2% commission on every barrel of oil to pay for overseeing a flow of funds that totaled at least $67 billion by ten UN agencies employing a staff of 1000. There were over $20 billion in bribes and kickbacks, with Hussein pocketing an estimated $5 billion. He sold oil allotments to particular individuals, corporations and political parties at discount prices and they kicked a generous percentage of profits to him. The United Nations collected fees of $1.4 billion to supervise the program and to negotiate with Saddam Hussein, and another $500 million for weapons inspection. Everything was done secretly—prices and quantity of oil, goods for relief, oil buyers, the quality of food and medicines, and financial transactions. Critics of the United Nations argued that the UN had therefore a conflict of interest when dealing with Iraq.

A second justification for the war was the support given by Iraq to terrorists in the Middle East and beyond. This included the funds given by Saddam Hussein to suicide bombers against Israel. Working out of Iraq were Abu Abbas, who attacked the Achilles Lauro, and who was a conduit between Saddam Hussein and Palestinian terrorists and suicide bombers, Abu Nidal, who killed over 407 in twenty countries, Ramzi Yousef and Abdul Rahman Yasin, who were involved in the 1993 World Trade Center attack, and Khala Khadar al Salahat, who is linked to the 1998 destruction of a Pan American plane and the killing of all its passengers. Also present in Iraq before the war was Abu Musab al Zarqawi who had ties to al-Qaeda. There were contacts between Iraq and Osama bin Laden's al-Qaeda since 1995, but there is no proof at this time of close collaboration between the two. In addition, the terrorist organization **Ansar al Islam** was present in Northern Iraq. It is still conducting operations there.

There was a long relationship between Saddam Hussein's regime and Osama bin Laden's second in command, Ayman al Zawahiri. There is speculation about a contact between Iraqi intelligence and several of the 9/11 hijackers in Malaysia in 2000, and about a collaboration of Iraqi and al-Qaeda business interest in Sudan. There was a fear that the oil revenues of Iraq could be used to finance terrorism throughout the Middle East and beyond.

However, critics of the war believe that terrorism in the region actually became worse after the war started. Some accuse President Bush of lying to the American people to attack Iraq. Others believe that the United States is in Iraq to control its oil reserves. Still others think that the United States has no reason to be in Iraq. This is a position which is supported by some elements of both the political Left and the Right, who want the United States out of Iraq, though for different reasons.

A third reason given for the attack was the violent repression of the Iraqi people by the Baathist Party of Saddam Hussein. The mass graves of thousands of political opponents of the regime found after the war have given support to this view. A fourth reason for the war was the establishment of an American military infrastructure in a central location of Southwest Asia from which the United States would project its power, protect allies and promote democracy in the region.

Although major combat was over on May 1, 2003, fighting has continued throughout 2010, in a low-intensity terrorist warfare. Over 4,500 Americans have died and thousands of Iraqis have been killed.

The continuation of fighting in Iraq throughout 2010 could have various reasons. The quick defeat of the Baathist government by the United States and its allies and their original refusal to allow many of the middle echelon of the Sunni controlled Iraqi military and the government bureaucracy to retain their old jobs might have created a power vacuum and violence in the central, Sunni part of Iraq. The Sunni supporters of Hussein kept Iraq together, though at the expense of repression over the Kurds and the Shiites. The lack of sufficient numbers of U.S. and allied military police, intelligence officers, civil affair specialists and special forces, when coupled with the freeing of thousands of Iraqi criminals by Saddam Hussein before the war, created a wave of urban crime and terrorism which undermined American authority and credibility. The US army was short-handed in Iraq. This might have prevented the allies from effectively closing the borders with Syria and Iran, which have been used by Islamic jihadists to enter Iraq to fight Americans, British and other allied troops.

The United States and its allies might have committed two additional errors. One was to fail to understand that the war in Iraq is really a regional war in which Iran, Syria, Saudi Arabia, among other Muslim states, are involved and are often seeking goals which make impossible the stability in Iraq. The second error might have been the effort to create a democracy among people who distrust each other, who have no experience of religious and other liberties, and who are in the middle of a war. Perhaps the need for establishing security should have been more important in the short run than the goal of nation-building and democracy. The lack of sufficient U.S. bipartisanship in foreign policy has been a disaster. In addition, the lack of support from the French and the Russians, in the international sector, has weakened American policy in Iraq.

Much of the success in Iraq will depend on the ability of the three major population groups to co-exist. In a population of 27 million, the Shiite Muslims of the south are the largest group, followed by the Sunni Muslims of Central Iraq, and by the Kurds of the north, who are about 20% of the population. The Sunnis dominated the two other groups during the Saddam Hussein dictatorship. Many Shiites want sharia Islamic government. This will not be accepted by the other two groups. The Kurds, who were forced to merge with Iraq in 1921, do not like Arab culture, do not speak Arabic for the most part, and prefer autonomy and possession of the Kirkuk oilfields. These fields are also desired by Turkomens, Assyrians, Christians, and Arabs.

Saddam Hussein tried to eliminate the Kurds by killing them and by offering booty to his fellow Sunni Arabs to Arabize northern Iraq. So now the Kurds want to return. Some of them would like to turn Kirkuk into the capital of "Kurdistan."

The central government will have to find a federal solution to share not only the oil wealth from the north, but also that from the south. For these reasons, survival of the Iraqi state might depend on a system of government with a weak Presidency, a strong legislature, and a federal system of government where each group retains significant autonomy. Yet this type of federal government might not be strong enough to defeat the violent militias of Sunnis and Shiites who seek to destroy each other.

Iraqi Civil War?

The last hope to prevent the disintegration of Iraq in 2010 and beyond might be the 2007 troop surge of close to 30,000 troops by the United States, which helped the Iraqis target the militias and disarm them.

The goal of this troop increase was to secure Baghdad and end the presence of al-Qaeda in Anbar province. Most important is the protection of the local population, to have a presence in the neighborhoods, and to support the government as it attacks both Sunni and Shia militias. So far the surge has reduced violence significantly, convinced many Baathists to fight al-Qaeda, and encouraged the Shia government to fight Shia militias.

The competing groups, as much as they distrust each other, might not want the end of Iraq. Many Shiites fear that Iran would then control the south. Sunnis fear they will lose the oil in the north and in the south. And the Kurds fear that Turkey will intervene against them.

And yet, Iraq might already be dying. The Iraqi government has no authority in the northern land of the Kurds. Sunnis and Shiites have been removing each other from certain Baghdad neighborhoods. The Mahdi army of Moktada al-Sadr is removing Sunnis and others from Baghdad. The proliferation of militias weakens the central government and encourages the breakup of Iraq. Much of Iraq's human capital has left the country. Iran has great allies in the government and in the militias in the south. They are ready to carve out a piece of Iraq. The Sunnis are waiting for a strong man to unite their forces, probably with American support to offset the presence of Iran in the South. In the end, Americans might just leave united Iraq and create military bases in "Kurdistan" from which it can protect the oil fields in the north and keep the Iranian presence limited to the south.

In August of 2010, the United States withdrew its last combat unit from Iraq, thus ending U.S. military action. It left behind approximately 50,000 troops, which should begin leaving Iraq at the end of 2011. These are engaged in training and supporting the Iraqi military.

Interestingly, the combat troops were withdrawn before the Iraqi political elite could form a new government emanating from the political elections held early in 2010. Critics of the withdrawal believe that the United States is not taking a strong position in the post-war settlement in the region. They are afraid that Iran and Turkey will have significant leverage over the future of Iraq while the United States, which did most of the fighting to bring some form of democracy to the country, would be unable to exert adequate influence. On the other hand, Iraq is now a sovereign country and it should decide what is best for itself.

The United States and the Middle East

The Middle East is at the intersection of three continents—Africa, Asia and Europe—and it is a strategic area which has 70% of the world's petroleum reserves. Therefore, the United States, as the world's major superpower, has several important goals in the region. One is **support of Israel.** In turn, Israel backs several U.S. strategic needs: preventing victories by radical nationalist and terrorist movements in the area; restraining Syria, once a Soviet ally which up to April 2005 had 30,000 troops in Lebanon; battlefield testing American weapons; serving as a conduit for aid to specific states; performing intelligence gathering and covert operations; and researching and developing new jet fighters and anti-missile defense systems.

A second American goal in the Middle East is the protection of pro-U.S. and pro-Western monarchies in the Persian Gulf region. For this purpose, the United States has troops in the region, with naval facilities in Bahrain and ground forces in Qatar. The cost runs to over $70 billion annually. The secret commitments to these oil states are enough to maintain supremacy in the area. These states are particularly vulnerable to Islamic fundamentalist movements, which tend to be radical, violent, anti-Western and misogynist. These radical groups are numerous in areas with physical dislocation of the population as a result of war, uneven economic development, and a lack of democracy and freedom. Successful attacks against the oil fields and waterways in this region would paralyze much of the world economy.

A third goal of the United States is the creation of a free and strong Iraq which could serve as democratic model for other Arab states, and which could also restrain Iran to the east. From a friendly Iraq, the United States could also move troops throughout the region. This requires that the Kurds in the north, the Sunnis in the center and the Shiites in the south learn to live within the confines of one Iraq, without one group repressing the others. It is possible that the United States could use its military position in Iraq to push for regime change in Iran, Syria and Saudi Arabia. This radical transformation of the Middle East has been seen by some as improving the chances for more free institutions in the region, less terrorist safe-havens and training grounds, and more pro-American regimes. Some critics believe that "democracy" in the region will bring to power terrorists.

A fourth goal of the United States is better relations with Syria so that it does not ruin the so-called

peace process between Israel and the Palestinian Arabs. The death in June 2000 of Syrian dictator Hafez Assad, after a thirty-year rule, placed in power Bashar Assad, his son. The saying in the Middle East, that war without Egypt is impossible, and that peace without Syria is improbable, could be true. Syria supports groups such as the pro-Iranian Hezbollah, Islamic Jihad and Hamas. Bashar helped Saddam Hussein circumvent UN sanctions. He allowed Hezbollah Iranian backers to supply it in Lebanon.

Syria's military left Lebanon on April 26, 2005, after being there since 1975. It did not do so because of UN resolution 1559 of September 2004 asking for Syrian withdrawal. The Syrians left because of pressure from France, Saudi Arabia and the United States, following the public indignation over the assassination in Beirut of former Prime Minister Rafik Hariri by, possibly, Syrian intelligence. There is much speculation about the possibility of Syrian intelligence agents remaining in Lebanon where they can maintain their ties with terrorist organizations such as Hezbollah.

Syria has allowed members of Saddam Hussein's regime to escape into its territory, as well as allowed terrorists and other fighters to enter Iraq to fight the Americans in Iraq. Bashar hosted terrorists belonging to the al-Qaeda-connected Abub Musab al-Zarqawi to enter Jordan to conduct terrorist attacks. Syria might have received components of WMD from Iraq. It also controlled Lebanon which serves as a terrorist base for the entire Middle East. For these reasons, the United States passed the **Syria Accountability Act of 2003** which bars American exports to Syria of dual use items with military applications, prohibits new investments by U.S. oil refineries, and bars exports to Syria other than food and medicines. Bilateral trade is currently $300 million.

A fifth objective of the United States is to increase its market for arms exports—over $150 billion since the Gulf War of 1991 against Iraq. The sale of weapons to the region serves various objectives: builds political alliances, particularly with the region's military; provides interoperability benefits, since the U.S. can then use its own weapons if it needs to intervene militarily in the region; **recycles back to the United States much of the money Americans send to the Middle East to buy oil imports;** and it rewards the American weapons industry with ample profits.

Unfortunately, much of the money returning to the United States and to the West from Saudi Arabia is in the form of contributions to build mosques under the control of Wahhabi clerics who preach violent actions against infidels and secular Muslims. Also, money is being given to universities and other institutions of higher learning to promote Wahhabism which is contrary to the Constitution of the United States. Funds are also used to recruit in the prisons and among alienated elements in the country.

The United States hopes to protect Israel and pro-Western Arab states, to dominate the Persian Gulf with its vast oil reserves important for the entire world; and to promote the Palestinian-Israeli peace process, all with a minimum of diplomatic and military cost.

The Israeli-Palestinian Conflict

The Palestinians are Arabs displaced by Israelis during wars with neighboring Arab states in 1948, 1956, 1967, and 1993. Many have developed a distinct ethnic identity from those in Arab countries and are now living in the West Bank of the Jordan and in the Gaza Strip. Most of these territories are controlled by the Palestinian Authority. The "peace" process between Israelis and Palestinians has been sabotaged by a low-intensity warfare among Israelis, Palestinians, Arab and Iranian-backed Muslim forces. Harassed and threatened by all these groups are the Christians, whose numbers are diminishing in the Holy Land. The real goal of Fatah and Hamas which run the Palestinian Authority is not only the creation of a Palestinian state, but also the destruction of Israel. Fueling all this bitterness is the presence of vast numbers of unemployed young people, the undemocratic nature of the Palestinian Authority, the scarcity of water, and the closing of Israel's borders to non-Israeli Arabs.

Palestinians claim that over 360,000 of their people have become refugees as a result of the Israeli occupation in 1967 of the West Bank, the Gaza Strip, and the Golan Heights which Israel won in the Six Day War. They add that this occupation and the many Israeli restrictions on travel, employment, etc., keep Palestinians poor. As a result of this oppression, and their lack of resources, Palestinians believe they had to respond with two violent intifadas against Israel, one from 1987 to 1992, and the second and more violent one, from 2000 to 2005. This last one has been characterized by Palestinian suicide bombers against innocent, Israeli civilians and other non-combatants, including Palestinians themselves, and by violent Israeli retaliation against Palestinians in the West Bank. The suicide bombers are not Christian, but Muslim Palestinians.

Israelis, in general, respond to these arguments saying there is no occupation of Palestine for there has never been an independent political jurisdiction named Palestine ruled by Palestinians, with a distinct Palestinian culture or language. For them, Palestinians are Arabs, indistinguishable from other Arabs, who control 99% of the Middle East, while the Israelis control only 1%. Israelis believe that Arabs could have had an independent state in the region, but they rejected the 1937 **British Peel Commission Plan,** which sought an Arab state in 90% of the land and a Jewish state in 10% of the territory, and refused the 1947 **United Nations Plan** (Resolution 181), which would have created two states, one Arab and one Jewish. Arabs also rejected after the 1967 war a UN plan (Resolution 242) by which Israel would have given up land for peace.

Israelis point out that Arab killings of Jews took place in 1920, 1921, 1929, 1936–1939 (when 2,394 were killed), long before the creation of the State of Israel. The Arab wars against Israel in 1948, 1956 and 1967 took place before the so-called Israel occupation of Gaza, the West Bank and the Golan Heights. The PLO, created in 1964 to destroy Israel, began three years before the occupation of these territories. Israel argues that it captured the West Bank and East Jerusalem in 1967 from Jordan's King Hussein and not from the Palestinians, who only began a serious movement for a homeland after the Jews got the territory which the Jordanians controlled. Gaza was in the hands of the Egyptians, not of the Palestinians. For these reasons, many Israelis see the two intifadas as nothing but a continuation of the Arab war against the Jews. Besides, the land "occupied" by Israel in 1967 was won by preemptive war. Why should it be returned?

There was much optimism in 1993 with the **Oslo Accords** by which Israel supported autonomy for the Palestinians and they, in turn, recognized Israel. There was to be discussions of secondary issues such as weapons, natural resources and population movements. It did not work. Only 10 to 20% of Palestinians accept Israel's right to exist. On May 1, 2003, following his success against Iraq, President George W. Bush presented to Israel and to the Palestinian Authority (PA) a peace plan called the **Road Map** developed by the **"Quartet"** of the European Union, Russia, the United Nations and the United States. **One of its innovations was the creation of a provisional Palestinian state before all issues between Israel and the PA are settled.**

In Phase One, the Palestinian Authority was to stop all violence against Israel, while Israel dismantled settlements and froze new construction in Gaza and in the West Bank. Both were to resume security coordination. Phase One was supposed to have been completed by May 2003. It was not. **In Phase Two, there was the option of a Palestinian state with provisional borders and attributes of sovereignty.** Arab countries would then restore relations with Israel, and Palestinians would create a constitution and conduct elections, which are to be followed by an international conference to oversee international financial assistance.

In Phase Three, an international conference was to oversee final status issues such as borders, Jerusalem, refugees, and Jewish settlements, and lead to a peace treaty by 2005. The deadline was not met because there are many obstacles. While the Palestinian Authority wants the "right of return" for all Palestinians who fled Arab lands conquered by Israel, this position is rejected by Israel as a demographic threat to its national identity. Also, the former President of the Palestinian Authority (PA), Yasser Arafat, might not have wanted a peace process with Israel which might have made his terrorist ways obsolete among his followers. He needed conflict to make him relevant and thus refused to share his political, security, intelligence, budget and media resources with the two prime ministers of the PA, Mahmoud Abbas and Ahmed Qureia. After the death of Arafat in 2004, Mahmoud Abbas replaced him as the head of the PA. Arafat had stolen millions of dollars from the Palestinian Authority while thousands of his followers lived in misery, abandoned and manipulated by Arafat and by the Arab states in their war against Israel. Abbas will have to control the terrorist acts of Hamas, Islamic jihad and others. On the one hand, Abbas needs to negotiate with Israel. On the other hand, he cannot be so friendly with it that terrorist, anti-Israel groups move against him.

Moreover, Syria and Iran encourage terrorism against Israel and the United States to force the Americans out of the Middle East. This they do through their support of groups such as Hamas and Islamic Jihad. The United States supports the territorial integrity of Israel against millions of Arabs who seek its destruction. The United States provides Israel with more than $2 billion annually in aid.

The Israeli government during the leadership of Ariel Sharon gave up hope on the Road Map. Sharon believed Yasser Arafat ended the peace process when he walked out of Camp David and the negotiations with Israeli Prime Minister Ehud Barak and American President Bill Clinton in 2000, and launched the second intifada which killed over 1,000 Israelis. So Sharon got out of Gaza and 21 settlements and removed most of the settlements from the West Bank, except for five major ones. It would still control Gaza, airspace, border crossings, offshore waters and a Southern road bordering Egypt. Israel would still impact on 1.2 million Palestinians. On April 5, 2005, Ariel Sharon ordered the removal of 8,000 Israeli settlers from the Gaza Strip. While some Israelis believed this measure would provide for the security of Israel by providing peace, others claimed the withdrawal would encourage worse violence against Israel. The latter group has been proven right for the presence of Hamas in the Gaza Strip with the collaboration of Iran and Syria has made the area into a base of terrorism against Israel.

Ariel Sharon decided to build a 360-mile, 25-foot high concrete barricade separating Israel from portions of the West Bank to protect its populations from suicide bombers. Many Palestinians object to the location of the fence on what they consider their lands, while Israelis tend to respond that they have suffered over 3,000 deaths in the two intifadas.

The triumph of Hamas in the legislative elections of 2006 for the Palestinian Authority (PA) might make it difficult for a diplomatic solution between Palestinians and Israelis since Hamas seeks the elimination of the latter. Ariel Sharon, before suffering a massive stroke in 2005, created a new party named **Kadima** which seeks almost total separation from the Palestinians. This new organization brings together former members of the Left-wing Labor Party and politicians from the Right-wing Likud Party. **Kadima is not waiting for the Quartet of the Road Map to bring peace to the region. It is unilaterally settling borders and withdrawing from much of the territory it previously held.**

The Fragmentation of "Palestine"

The situation in "Palestine", in areas of the Gaza and of the West Bank, is leading to fragmentation during the 2010–2011 period. Although Mahmoud Abbas of Fatah won the presidency in January 2005, Hamas won the parliamentary elections of January 2006. A Mecca agreement of February 2007 to bring peace between the two groups was derailed in June 2007 as Hamas overwhelmed Fatah forces in Gaza. This Hamas action split the West Bank and Gaza Strip into two separate political bodies. The United States, Israel and the Palestinian Authority (Fatah) are trying to isolate Gaza. Critics of the United States believe it should not be assisting Fatah because of its terrorist activities. Meanwhile Israel is populating parts of the West Bank, what many Jews call Judea and Samaria, with 270,000 people scattered across 140 settlements. These separate Palestinian communities from each other.

New multilateral negotiations began in the summer of 2010 to reach an agreement that would create a Palestinian state and also guarantee the security of the state of Israel. Involved in this process are the United States, Russia, the United Nations, the Palestinian Authority, and Israel, among others. Included among the issues to be negotiated are the Israeli settlements in the West Bank, the status of Jerusalem, the return of Arab refugees to lands controlled by Israel, and the nature of security forces in the new Palestinian state. Some critics believe that the United States should not be wasting its resources dealing with this negotiation effort, but that instead it should be more concerned with regime change in Iran or at least stopping its nuclear project to develop an atomic bomb. While most of the Sunni Muslim Arab states support the creation of a Palestinian state, they do not want to see Iran, a Shiite Muslim state, develop nuclear weapons. Some of these states might support an Israeli strike against Iran.

Lebanon

Lebanon was formed from five Turkish Empire districts. It became an independent state in 1920, but was administered by the French from 1920 to 1941. Many countries and movements have fought in its territory: Syria, the United States, the Palestinian Liberation Organization (PLO), Israel, Iran, and Hezbollah, among others. Today the population is 2.2 million, of which 60% are Muslims and 39% Christians.

Christians and Muslims lived in relative peace until the Palestinian Liberation Organization (PLO) escaped into Lebanon in the 1970s after suffering massive losses in Jordan when they tried to take it over. Iran, Israel, Syria and other countries eventually got involved in the conflict destroying what had been the "jewel" of the Middle East. By 1986, Syria had become the dominant power in Lebanon.

When the Syrians were forced out of Lebanon in 2004, the French, the United Nations and the United

States failed to enforce UN Resolution 1559, which should have forced the Iranian and Syrian-backed **Hezbollah** terrorist organization to disarm before it was allowed to participate in the 2005 Lebanese elections. On July 12, 2006, Hezbollah crossed into Israel, kidnapped two Israeli soldiers and killed several others. Israel retaliated and war ensued until August 14 when a UN-sponsored cease-fire took hold, and French and Italian troops were sent to Southern Lebanon.

There have been several consequences from this war. Hezbollah is admired by Lebanese Shiites but not by the majority of the Lebanese Christians, the Druze, and the Sunnis. The majority of the Lebanese want a settlement with Israel, although not so much the Shiites. Lebanese Christians, Druze and Sunnis fear Israel, Iran, and Syria, while the Shiites only fear Israel. Hezbollah suffered the most damage but it has created an aura of victory over Israel. The Israelis have responded by rebuilding their military and evaluating the wisdom of past unilateral withdrawals from southern Lebanon, the Gaza Strip and the West Bank of the Jordan. Syria could be preparing for war with Israel with the support of Iran and its satellite groups.

In the Spring of 2008, Hezbollah, which is now both a Shiite political organization and an armed military group, began to attack Sunni Muslims in the Islamic neighborhoods of Beirut. This is supported by the Iranian and Syrian backed Shiite population of Lebanon. However, it is opposed by the majority of Sunnis and by the national government which is backed by the United States and other Western countries. In the period 2010–2011, another war between the Hezbollah and Israel could take place.

Russia and the Middle East

Russian President Vladimir Putin is angry at the United States and is aggressively seeking to undermine its policies in the Middle East and in other areas. His visit to Saudi Arabia on February 11, 2007, was the first by a Russian leader. Russia is now again a competitor in this world region. It has several goals. Russia wants to keep the price of energy as high as possible since it is the largest oil producer. Russia wants to sell nuclear reactors, tanks, helicopters, rocket-propelled grenades and anti-aircraft systems, and seeks to attract the countries of the region to its satellite navigation system. It is willing to sell weapons to both sides of the Shia-Sunni divide to establish a military dependence. A third goal is to undermine the American policy of democratizing the Middle East. Instead, Putin is rejecting Western values both in Russia itself and in its foreign policy. This approach is very popular among the Arab dictatorial classes. Putin also seeks to use anti-Americanism, which is popular in the Arab streets, to gain in the region. Finally, Vladimir Putin hopes that by creating ties with the Saudis and the Iranians, they will not support the radicalization of the Muslims within Russia itself.

Sub-Saharan Africa

Sub-Saharan Africa, often called **Black Africa,** is a vast area, four times the size of Europe west of Russia. Yet, it contains approximately the same population since more than 50% of the region consists of rainforests, steppes, or deserts empty of people. There are 53 countries in Africa, of which 48 are in Sub-Saharan Africa. **Each of its states has significant regional groups bearing grievances against some or all of their neighbors. All states but Liberia and Ethiopia experienced decades of Islamic and European colonialism, though few Europeans, except in South Africa beginning in the 1600s, actually settled in the region.**

Most of these territories became independent in the 1950s and 1960s. Virtually all political binding forces of the present states—languages, governmental institutions, infrastructures—are legacies of the colonial period. **Due to the internal ethnic/tribal diversity within states, few countries in Sub-Saharan Africa can claim to have created totally unified states.** Many are actually on the verge of disintegration.

Over 800 languages are spoken in the African continent, including North Africa, but fewer than ten are spoken by more than one million people. Most languages are native to groups of less than 100,000. This creates significant difficulties in forming nations out of different linguistic and tribal groups. Lack of communication among groups leads to political conflicts, isolation, distrust, and economic backwardness. The largest language family is the **Niger-Congo** and Kordofanian, of which the **Bantu** sub-language is the most important. This is the language of the Blacks. The **Sudanic languages** of the Nilo-Saharans are found in a region stretching along the lower Nile and westward through an area known as the Sahel. The Sahel is a region of West Africa extending from Senegal to the Sudan which forms a belt that separates the arid Sahara from tropical West

Africa. The **Afro-Asiatic,** or Hamitic languages, stem from the early Caucasoids who lived primarily in North and Northeast Africa. It includes Semitic, Berber, Cushitic, Chad, and Coptic. The **Khoisan,** or "click," languages are found in southern Africa. In addition, there are the **Indo-European** languages brought by the Europeans: Dutch, English, French, German, Italian, Portuguese, and Spanish.

Causes of Poverty

Most countries of Africa lie between the Tropic of Cancer which is 23 1/2° N of the Equator and the Tropic of Capricorn which is 23 1/2° S of the Equator. The countries of Tropical Africa tend to have some common characteristics: the persistent problem of **droughts;** great **poverty,** as life expectancy averages 48 to 50 years and infant mortality is close to 120 deaths per 1000 live births; **illiteracy;** heavy preponderance of **rural dwellers** (65% to 85% of the population); **unproductive agricultural sectors; declining per capita food production; dependence on the exports of a primary product** such as coffee, cacao, palm products, sugar, vanilla, tea, or minerals such as diamonds, barite, cobalt, and others; **authoritarian military governments or civilian one party states; large foreign debt to Western countries, banks and multinational agencies; tribal conflicts; and poor transportation, among others.**

The population of the Sub-Saharan Africa is approximately 810 million. More than half of it lives in poverty. Since 1990, real income per head has declined .4% annually, although in the last four years the economic growth of the region has been approximately 5%, an outstanding achievement. Over 6.5 million Africans live as refugees, and other millions are displaced within their own countries. Millions are affected by AIDS, particularly in Botswana and South Africa. Despair is a key characteristic in much of Tropical Africa, even though there has been progress in Tanzania, Mozambique, South Africa, Benin, Ghana, Uganda and Botswana. Nigeria, for example, had in 2003 for the first time in 43 years a peaceful, presidential succession. Yet, it is now experiencing religious strife between Christians and Muslims.

According to some of Africa's own elites, the causes of Sub-Saharan Africa's problems are external: Western colonialism which undermined traditional political institutions; exploitation by multinational corporations which produce mostly for export and not for domestic consumption; the injustice of the international economic system which pays too little for African products; too little or, to some, too much foreign aid; too little or, to some, too much Western involvement in Africa.

On the other hand, a new generation of Africans is beginning to place greater emphasis on internal factors as causes for the region's massive poverty: misguided leadership; systemic corruption; economic mismanagement; senseless civil wars; military and civilian dictatorships; violations of human rights; and foreign aid which brings governments to power that then impose dictatorial policies against groups with the best chance to improve the economic standards of Africans.

These governments then prevent the establishment of independent and honest central banks, independent judiciaries to guarantee the rule of law and property rights, an independent press to scrutinize government policies, fair and impartial elections, institutions to monitor public spending, free political parties, protection for the losers in an election, and constitutions which limit the power of the executive. There are then no checks and balances to inhibit abuse of power.

One could argue that the main problems in Africa are political and not economic. And yet, another problem in Sub-Sahara Africa is the geography. There are no major rivers which can permit commercial transportation among the different regions. Since most of the area is above 1000 feet and 50% is above 2,000 feet above sea level, the rivers are just too unstable for transportation as they drop to the sea. This geographical fact also leads to great human isolation and social backwardness. The Atlantic coast has poor harbors.

Yet, both external and internal factors are responsible for the terrible state of many African countries. Interaction between outside conditions and negative conditions for which Africans themselves are responsible is exemplified in the issue of the **territorial borders** delineating the African countries. These borders were mostly imposed by the Europeans after 1885 when they divided most of the African territory among six countries, except for Liberia and Ethiopia. Inside the borders, they often brought together tribes which were traditionally in conflict with each other, or they separated on different sides of the borders people who had belonged to the same tribe.

Europeans often upset the long-term evolution in the power relationship between the tribes living in a particular region. For instance, in southern Rhodesia (Zimbabwe), the British defeated the dominant warrior

Matabele and handed power to their former vassals, the **Mashona;** by Mount Kenya, the Europeans weakened the dominant Nilotic, pastoralist **Masai** masters and then gave power to the humbler, Bantu agriculturalist **Kikuyu; and in the highlands of Rwanda and Burundi, Germans and Belgians supported the aristocratic dominance of the minority Nilotic Tutsis over the majority Hutus.** Then, when the Europeans left the highlands in 1961 and Rwanda and Burundi became independent, the Hutus used the ballot box and the electoral system to repress the Tutsis and massacre them. The Tutsis also engaged in massacres of Hutus. **Thus, the European-imposed territorial borders upset the natural relations among African tribes.**

However, the African leaders who replaced the Europeans after independence have refused to change the borders to accommodate the interests of the many tribes found in most of the African states. These leaders fear that if they start allowing tribes to break away from the current countries, these states will simply shrink and their political power will disappear. As a result, even the **Organization of African Unity** or the new organization, the **African Union** have voted against changing the current territorial borders. Thus the conduct of Africans themselves explains much of the dysfunctional state of government in the region.

Democracy, also brought by the Europeans, is often seen as a potentially destructive force in Africa. Usually, the majority tribe uses the electoral system to gain control of the state and to monopolize its benefits while repressing the losing tribes. This then motivates the losing tribes to secede and create their own states.

Perhaps it could be in the best interest of some of the countries of Sub-Saharan Africa—though not in that of their dictators—to break apart as happened, for example, in the case of Ethiopia, where the region called **Eritrea** separated and became in 1993 the last country created in Africa. The creation of new states out of some of the present countries could allow some tribes to pursue their own needs without fear of extinction by the dominant tribe. **Democracy, in the absence of better drawn-out borders and protection of basic civil liberties, can actually lead to genocide or repression.** Yet, the transition to new states can also be violent. For example, in June 1998 a border war erupted between Eritrea and Ethiopia.

Great damage to Africa by external forces has also come from Arab Muslims who beginning in the 600s began the slave trade in Africa and then proceeded to destroy its Black kingdoms. The slave trade of the Arabs preceded the European one, exceeded it in numbers, and has outlasted it for it is still present today in places like Darfur-Sudan, Senegal, Mauritania and in other regions. The desire of Jihadist Muslims movements to impose Sharia law, Islamic law, in regions of Africa populated by also non-Muslims is creating civil wars in some countries.

African Development

A positive development in Sub-Saharan Africa is the **African Growth and Opportunity Act of 2000,** passed by the United States Congress, which gives duty-free access to nearly all goods produced in 35 countries in the region. This already has led to over 100% increase in trade by Madagascar, Senegal, and a few others. The Act could increase trade, wages, living standards, environmental protection, and political openness.

Perhaps new African leaders realize that foreign aid and a debt relief assistance to Africa are not as effective for increasing national income as are trade and foreign investment, which can increase assets which can then transform societies and sustain economic growth. However, all these improvements require honest and open government and political stability. Government policy must protect those people most likely to engage in entrepreneurship. This means that African governments need to promote the rule of law, property rights, and political and popular participation so people can express legally and non-violently their needs and frustrations, and they also must invest in human capital.

Africa grew by 5.1% in 2004, by 5% in 2005 and by over 5% in 2006 and 2007. These are good numbers. There has been relative stagnation between 2007 and 2010. They are higher rates than those of Latin America. Also 40% of the countries now have elected democracies. Aid from the West is also growing significantly. This is positive if the funds go to **hard infrastructure** projects such as roads and ports and **soft infrastructure** projects which make people more free and productive. Inflation is only 10%. Thirty years of negative economic growth could be over. The future lies in entrepreneurship.

African countries could be classified as follows: **high performers**—Botswana, Ghana, Mauritius, Seychelles, South Africa, and Uganda; **upward bound**—Benin, Madagascar, Mozambique, Senegal and Tanzania; **large—poorly performing**—Ethiopia, Democratic

Republic of Congo, Nigeria, and Sudan; **poor performers**—Burkina Faso, Cameroon, Kenya, Malawi, Republic of Congo, Rwanda and Zambia; **institutionally collapsing**—Central African Republic, Ivory Coast, Guinea, Liberia, Sierra Leone, Somalia and Zimbabwe; **oil producing states**—Angola, Cape Verde, Equatorial Guinea, Gabon and Nigeria.

African Wars

Recently, Sub-Saharan Africa has had a scaled down presence of foreign powers. As this has happened, precolonial ethnic and clan-based political conflicts have reemerged with a vengeance, particularly in Rwanda where up to 800,000 died in 1994, and also in Nigeria, Sudan, Liberia, and Somalia, among others, where millions have died.

During the 1990s, there were nineteen wars in Africa. Many are still continuing. This is tragic because Africa has 30% of the world's mineral resources which could promote economic development, but many of these are used to finance the wars among tribes, private armies, and countries. Many of these struggles are about obtaining mineral resources such as oil and diamonds to enrich competing groups. There are over 300,000 children under 18 fighting in thirty countries. The end result are refugees, abandoned children, landmines, death and famine. Over 38 million are facing famine.

At present, Africa is winding down its biggest war since 1945. Six regional powers have had armies in Congo, formerly Zaire. Eight other states have been involved behind the scenes since August 1998. In the middle were the Congolese forces fighting a rebel movement. This ten-year-long continent-wide war was a continuation of the long feud between Tutsis and the Hutu tribes in Central Africa. During the Rwanda genocide of 1994 to 1997, 200,000 to 800,000 Tutsis were massacred, forcing many Tutsis to flee to Zaire. When the Tutsis regained control of Rwanda, thousands of Hutus also fled to Zaire. The leader of Rwanda, Paul Kagame decided to defeat the Interahamwe, a Hutu militia which was attacking Rwanda from the territory of Zaire, with the approval of dictator Mobutu Sese Seko. Kagame joined forces with Laurent Kabila who wanted to overthrow Mobuto. In 1997, Kabila then the leader of Congo, allowed Rwandan troops to stay in Eastern Congo while they fought and killed Hutus.

However, when in August 1998, Kabila asked Rwandan troops to leave Congo, Paul Kagame began to support an anti-Kabila movement. A desperate Kabila asked Angola, Chad, Zimbabwe and Namibia for help. Rwanda then asked for the support of Uganda and Burundi. It hopes to annex Eastern Congo and recreate the precolonial Tutsi Kingdom. Kabila has also made friends with Sudan and Libya. On the other hand, South Africa provided lethal military aid to Rwanda. These two power blocs are now in conflict all throughout Central Africa. It is possible non-African forces might join in to support their respective African allies.

The peace treaty of 2002 united many of the local factions and led to the exit of eight foreign countries involved in the fighting. It was too late for the four million who died in the war. Kabila was assassinated in 2001. The 2006 elections, the first since 1960, were won by his son Joseph Kabila, who then created a coalition government made up of many of the opposing groups. These now control specific departments of governments. Corruption is massive, and it is made possible by the "international community" which provides $2 billion annually, or 50% of Congo's budget. There are many problems. Fighting is developing in the west. Rwanda and Uganda might be looting timber and minerals from the east. Close to 500,000 have been displaced in this region. One-third of the budget is unaccounted for, and there are few government social services.

Eritrea became independent of Ethiopia in 1993 and in 1998 seized some fertile territory along the 620-mile border, claiming sovereignty under the old colonial-era territory. The war between the two extended throughout 2001 undermining their precarious economies. **Sudan became the first Islamic State in Africa in 1989.** In Sudan over two million have died as the Muslim government of Khartoum has tried to impose Islamic sharia law on the Christian and animist South. This is the world's worst religious persecution and ethnic cleansing. Five million people have been driven from their lands particularly after the discovery of oil in central Sudan.

Sudan seems to have become the center point for Islamic terrorism in Africa. Yet, there are indications that after President George W. Bush declared war on international terrorism, Sudan began to dismantle its terrorist network, many of whose members went to Afghanistan to work with the Taliban. Nevertheless, the war to spread Islam to southern Sudan is continuing, now with the support of oil revenues, though a temporary truce was achieved in 2004. Sudan is also trying to conquer the country of Chad.

And yet, the Sudanese government is now starving its opponents in the area of Western Sudan called **Darfur.** It is using Sudanese troops and Arab militias called **Jingaweit.** They first use air bombardment, and then ground troops, including the Jingaweit, which burn villages, destroy water supplies and food stock. After depopulating the land, they bring their own people to settle it. Hundreds of thousands of Sudanese are starving and over 500,000 have been killed. A great portion of the fighting consists of Arab Muslims with the support of some Islamic states killing Black African Muslims and others. UN Resolution 1706 is supposed to permit 22,000 troops to go to Darfur.

It is possible that Southern Sudan, which won partial autonomy from the Islamist government of Sudan, might begin to mediate the crisis of Darfur. This might also guarantee some autonomy and protection for this region. Another possibility is that the United States might support the secession of both Darfur and Southern Sudan from the country of Sudan. This would not only prevent genocide, but also remove oil resources from the Sudanese and the Chinese.

In 2005, a truce was negotiated to halt the fighting between the Islamic-controlled government of Sudan and the mostly Christian southern part. Included in the truce was a planned referendum election in 2011 to determine if the people from the south prefer to secede from Sudan. The fate of Sudan and of the region of Darfur depends on this election and on the reaction to it by the government of Sudan.

One of the problems with the region of Africa which borders by the Horn of Africa is that it is close to countries involved in conflicts with Islamic Jihadists who desire to destabilize the states they want to conquer. This is the case with Ethiopia, Somalia, Sudan, and others. Yemen, by the southern part of the Arabian Peninsula, has become a major terrorist haven which has an influence in East Africa. Saudi Arabia has also spent resources supporting terrorist groups in this region.

Somalia became a country in 1960 out of Italian territories in Africa. It is an officially Sunni Muslim country of approximately 8 million, and for the last 17 years has been a collapsed state. This condition usually leads to violence as groups fight over security and power. The **Islamists** defeated the US-backed **Alliance for the Restoration of Peace and Counter-Terrorism** by March 2006, and began to apply Sharia law all over the country. When the Islamists began to make an alliance with Eritrea, Ethiopia attacked on December 24, 2006,

and occupied the capital. American soldiers might have given some assistance. The **African Union** sent 1,500 Ugandan troops. Fighting still continues. The main players are US-backed militias, the Council of Islamic Courts in the South, al-Qaeda operatives, Ugandan peace-keepers, Ethiopia, Egypt, criminal gangs, and warlords. Terrorism increased in the 2008–2009 period.

It is clear that many of these African wars involve more than two competing countries or groups. For example, in the war in Darfur which began in 2003, Chad and Eritrea helped the rebels against Sudan. The Ethiopian war against Somalia and in the Ogaden region has Eritrea helping Somalia.

The United States is becoming involved in an area called The **Greater Horn of Africa** which includes Djibouti, Eritrea, Ethiopia, Kenya, Somalia, Tanzania and Uganda. This region has very porous borders, weak states, extremely poor population and Arab minorities which could be recruited by al-Qaeda into Islamic terrorism. For these reasons, the United States has developed a combined **Joint Task Force for the Horn of Africa** with approximately 1,800 soldiers and under US AFRICOM. Eritrea, Ethiopia and Uganda are close allies of the United States in the region. In fact, Africa's importance to the United States led President George W. Bush to announce on February 6, 2007, the creation of a new unified combatant command for Africa (**AFRICOM**) to oversee security, build partnerships, support non-military missions and conduct military operations as necessary. Only Egypt, in Africa, will be outside its jurisdiction.

A new factor in these African wars is the support that China gives to any country which can provide it with oil. China supports the Sudanese dictatorship with military assistance and investments in return for oil, and will block any attempt in the Security Council of the United Nations to undermine Sudan. Currently, China also has 10,000 military personnel and 800 companies in Africa, assisting autocratic regimes which sell it energy resources. China does not promote human rights, the rule of law, property rights or democracy in Africa. It prefers to deal bilaterally with dictatorships. Other Chinese objectives are to find markets for its products, to win support among African states, which make up 25% of the votes in the United Nations General Assembly, against any condemnation of China's violation of human rights, and to isolate Taiwan politically. China is very involved in Angola, Nigeria, Sudan, and South Africa, among other countries. **Another source of instability in Africa is the**

presence of Muslim Jihadists trying to spread their power with the help of Saudi-Arabian money.

These wars have accentuated the problems of famines and disease in Sub-Saharan Africa. Another famine is spreading in the Horn of Africa and 16 million people are at risk in ten countries from Burundi to Eritrea on the Red Sea; but the famine is worse in the Ogaden region of Ethiopia where rebels are fighting the government. Much has been said about the 23.3 million people—out of a world total of 33.6 million—which have contracted HIV/AIDS in Sub-Saharan Africa, particularly in Nigeria, Senegal, South Africa, Swaziland, Tanzania, Uganda and Zimbabwe. Skeptics respond that most people are not actually tested medically and that many diseases of poverty are simply grouped together in the HIV/AIDS category to obtain higher levels of international economic assistance. Global pharmaceutical companies are willing to sell their medicines for AIDS at cost, but these countries cannot afford the other drugs that need to be applied.

Anglo-America

Anglo-America consists of two states, Canada and the United States (and the French possession of St. Pierre et Miquelon). Both are predominantly English-speaking, having been settled by the British. Although both countries are roughly equal in territory, Canada's population is only one-ninth that of the United States, having 80% of its territory virtually uninhabited. Its ecumene is for the most part within 100 miles of its southern border. More than 30% of the United States also is empty, yet its effectively settled territory is the largest of any state in the world.

While both countries have sectional differences, only Canada faces a serious threat of secession in French-speaking Quebec. Adoption of a federal system allowing significant local control of affairs has reduced the chances of regional frustrations in Canada and in the United States. **There is strong national identity in both countries, although Canada has seen two nations emerge divided along linguistic lines. The 4,000-mile mutual unfortified and peaceful border between Canada and the United States is a model for the rest of the world.**

Canada: Will the Federalist, Multicultural State Survive?

The population of Canada is approximately 34 million. It is 77% urban, with the British (40%) and the French

(27%) being the most important national groups. English and French are both official languages. The most important religions are Roman Catholic (46%), United Church (16%), and Anglican (10%). **Canada is the largest country in land size in the Western hemisphere.**

Canada has a federal government at Ottawa, ten provinces and three territories. A new territory called Nanavut was allowed on April 1999 consisting of Amerindians. The provinces are as follows: **The Maritime Provinces** (New Brunswick, Newfoundland, Nova Scotia, and Prince Edward Island), which tend to have below average incomes; **Quebec,** which is French-speaking; **Ontario,** which is the principal economic center with strategic communications links to the United States and to the western Canadian provinces; the **Prairie Region** (Manitoba, Saskatchewan and Alberta), which is minerally and agriculturally rich; and **British Columbia,** whose Vancouver region is a major trade link to the industrializing Pacific Rim countries of Asia.

The federal government of Canada has promoted political multiculturalism since 1971 when the Liberal Party gave financial assistance to cultural groups to retain and foster their separate identity. It created a **Ministry of Multiculturalism** in 1973 and added a clause to the Canadian Constitution requiring the charter to be interpreted in a manner consistent with the multicultural heritage of Canadians. In 1988, the Progressive Conservative government adopted the world's first multicultural law to "assist in the preservation, enhancement and sharing of ethnic cultures, languages and ethnocultural group identity."

These policies seem to have created a society with a multitude of state-supported ethnic identities bearing no common threads. It is significant that these identities are being preserved by government rather than by voluntary, private funds. However, respect for other cultures does not seem to extend to the Catholic Church whose teachings against abortion and on human sexuality are not shared by the powerful, socialist inclined Liberal Party which has controlled the government for decades until it lost power in 2006.

Critics of state-sponsored **multiculturalism** believe that it encourages separate and competing ethnic identities, a mosaic of cultures instead of a melting pot. They are concerned because Canada itself has a fragile identity. It has two official languages and two national holidays (June 24 for French Canada and July 1 for English Canada). Many groups do not even celebrate Thanksgiving Day together, and Canada has no common creed, except perhaps a belief in Socialism as a political binding force, such as is the case with socialized medicine. Only time will tell whether multiculturalism will lead to balkanization, a ghetto mentality, destabilization of Quebec, and a devaluation of the very idea of a common nationality, or whether it will lead to a more vibrant society where every group contributes its essence to the national spirit. Canada's multicultural identity will be truly tested in coming years by the very open or liberal Canadian immigration policies which attract Asians, Hispanics and Muslims.

Quebec's separatists in the 1960s represented only about 15% of its electorate in Quebec, but they have grown since then. **Ottawa has tried to appease Quebec by giving its politicians prominence in the federal government, but what they seem to want is more control over their own lives and the preservation of French culture.** The last time a referendum on sovereignty was held was in October 1995, and it failed by only 50,000 votes out of a population of nearly 5 million. Since then, there has been a significant exodus of English-speakers out of Quebec and into Ontario.

In August 1998, the Supreme Court of Canada stated that Canada may not separate unilaterally without consent from the rest of Canada (the other 9 provinces and the federal government). Also, if the majority of Quebecers vote to secede in a referendum, then the rest of Canada would be obliged to negotiate the terms of secession as it was an amendment to the constitution. Important issues would include Quebec's share of the national debt, joint control of the St. Lawrence Seaway, and the guarantee of minority rights.

Quebec's sovereignty movement is currently supported by only 38% of the population willing to vote for independence. It has been weakened by the 1998 Supreme Court decision, and by the division of the movement into two bickering parties, the **Party Quebecois** and the Action **Democratique du Quebec.** Perhaps the residents of Quebec have other issues of concern: one of the world's highest suicide rates among young people; one of the highest rates of single-parent families; North America's highest abortion rate; and the lowest birthrate. The 2003 Provincial elections in Quebec replaced the separatist Parti Quebecois with the Liberal Party under Jean Charest who wants a strong and united Canada.

The issue of multiculturalism and national identity is also related to the question of whether Mus- **lims in Canada should be allowed to govern themselves by "Sharia" or Islamic law, which is contrary to laws generated by democratically-elected popular assemblies.** Do the very liberal immigration laws and extensive political multiculturalism in Canada strengthen or polarize and radicalize the country? In history, often de-centralizing forces are followed by self-correcting uniformity or centralization movements. This could happen in Canada.

Relations with the United States

Canada has had a fast-growing economy for the last four years. It has a balanced budget and a strong dollar. Quebec is calm. The Liberal Party became the dominant political organization, governing Canada for 70 of the past 103 years, but it lost to the Conservatives in 2006. Unfortunately, its relations with the United States have been tense. In 2003, the United States restricted imports from Canada because of Mad Cow disease.

The refusal of the Canadian government of Prime Minister Jean Chretien to support U.S. President George W. Bush in the war against Iraq, cooled the relations between the two countries. The American President cancelled his official visit to Canada scheduled for May 5, 2003. The Canadians in turn have been unhappy with the American rejection of the **International Criminal Treaty** and of the **Kyoto Global Warming Treaty.**

Yet, both countries have $1.2 billion in traded goods daily and will find ways to continue their many economic and social contacts. Canada sends 85% of its exports to the United States. The rising value of the Canadian dollar in relation to the American dollar has increased American exports to Canada because the American dollar is cheaper to buy to purchase American goods. Also, security and terrorism require close cooperation between the two countries. Canada is helping with the war in Afghanistan and has pledged $300 million for the reconstruction of Iraq and the training of its police. The Canadians, unlike some other NATO countries, are fighting on the frontlines. Moreover, Canada has over 400 troops in Haiti serving with a multinational force to stabilize the country.

On January 2006, Stephen Harper ended the 12-year Liberal Party rule. He is trying to restrict immigration, reform social security, increase defense spending, improve intelligence gathering and security, and collaborate with the United States to expand the Free Trade Area of the Americas. Harper will also work to more fully integrate certain aspects of American, Canadian, and Mexican contacts in the areas of communications, immigrations, security, trade and transportation, among others. Many conservatives in the United States have criticized these talks for fear that the business elite in the three countries are trying to create a **North America Union** which would reduce American sovereignty.

The United States of America: The Dynamic Equilibrium of Checks and Balances

One of the great traits of the government of the United States is the presence of many structural checks and balances which ensures that no institution, party or any other group can control all political power. This dynamic equilibrium is between branches of Congress, among the legislative, executive and judicial branches of government, and between federal and state layers of government. The entire system was created to promote restraint in the use of power, force compromise among competing interests and exercise flexibility. The system of checks and balances often works very well as was the case with the "war" against inflation.

For many years during the 1960s and 1970s, the United States was affected by high inflation. The low inflation growth in the 1980s, 1990s and up to 2010 might have several causes: the process of economic deregulation begun during the Carter Democratic Administration and continued under Republican Ronald Reagan; the emphasis on tax cuts, technological innovation, and free trade of the Reagan Administration, which stimulated economic competition and productivity; a Federal Reserve Board (under Paul Volker in the 1980s and Alan Greenspan in the 1990s and early 2000s), which made sure that monetary policies keep inflation low; Democrat Bill Clinton and his Secretary of the Treasury Bob Rubin, who assured the business community of their commitment to low inflation and free trade by reappointing Republican Greenspan and by fighting protectionist trade policies recommended by their own Democratic party, which could have reduced American competitiveness (they successfully pushed NAFTA and GATT through a Democratic Congress); and a Republican-controlled Congress, the first since 1954, which, after 1994, forced the Clinton Administration to move away from an emphasis on tax hikes, new "stimulus" government spending, socialization/nationalization of the health

industry (14% of the American economy), and increased regulation, toward an emphasis on balanced budgets, tax cuts, and legal, regulatory, welfare, and immigration reforms.

Also important in the fight against inflation were the cost-cutting by business during the 1980s and 1990s which served to reallocate resources to where they were more productive, and the sacrifices of the American labor force in the 1980s which suffered under significant "down-sizing" by business. **Therefore, much of the credit for the present economic success against inflation goes to the combined efforts of former Presidents Carter, Reagan, Clinton, and Bush. Federal Reserve Chairman Paul Volker and Alan Greenspan, and the Republican-controlled Congress, also played a major role.**

For example, when the White House proposed to nationalize the health industry, interest rates for 30-year Treasury bonds—a great political barometer—rose from 5.94% to above 8%, putting a severe strain on the economy. These rates began to decline after the 1994 congressional elections, which brought the Republicans to power promising balanced budgets, tax cuts, and regulatory reforms. Meanwhile, Alan Greenspan's credibility on fighting inflation guaranteed stable money. Interest rates dropped to between 6% and 7%, and the stock market began to take off. The checks and balances of the U.S. Government and American society worked. The United States is still benefitting from this bipartisan dynamic equilibrium.

The American Economy

The American economy went into a terrible recession in December 2007 when the Presidency was held by George W. Bush of the Republican Party and the Congress was controlled by the opposition Democrats. Democrats and Republicans are still arguing about the causes of this dramatic economic meltdown. In reality, many factors, people, and parties were responsible for the recession.

The following conditions were clearly among the most important causes of the recession: the policy by Congress which pressured banks into making risky housing mortgage loans; the decision by the Federal Reserve to expand the money supply to stimulate the economy which redirected money into housing and made possible the bubble in the housing market; the guaranteeing by Freddie Mac and Fannie Mae of the bad loans made by the private banks; the issuing by Wall Street of special financial derivatives,

Left and Right: General Tendencies

The terms "Left" and "Right" have been defined in various ways throughout history. What follows is one interpretation supported by significant historical data. You may send feedback to german.munoz@mdc.edu.

Left	Right
More centralized government	Less decentralized government
More government spending	Less government spending
Higher taxes	Fewer taxes
More regulation of the economy	More economic freedom
More government-regulated environmentalism	More free-market environmentalism
More civil rights	More civil liberties
More gun control	More gun ownership
More internationalism	More nationalism/patriotism
Collective identity & responsibility	Individual identity & responsibility
More ideological uniformity	More ideological variety
More secular society	More Judeo-Christian culture
Pro Abortion/pro-choice	Pro-Life
More willing to reject tradition	More willing to accept tradition
More critical of private property	Supports private property
Emphasis on determinism	Emphasis on free will
Fewer sexual standards	Sexual standards (except libertarians)

The Political Spectrum

Extreme Left Total Government	Authoritarianism	Democratic Socialism	Liberal Democracy	Constitutional Monarchy	Limited Constitutional Republic	Conservatism	Libertarianism	Extreme Right No Government
Totalitarianism								Anarchy
Castroism								
Communism								
Fascism								
Islamism								
Maoism								
Nazism								

based on the risky mortgage loans, which were sold all over the world; the financial panic which resulted when many of these loans began to go bad; and the promise by the Federal Reserve to bail out troubled financial institutions, something which stimulated irresponsible transactions. Obviously, greed played a part in this financial meltdown. It involved both the private and the public sector, and both major political parties.

President George W. Bush tried to deal with the financial collapse by creating the Troubled Assets Relief Program (TARP) which allocated $800 billion to buy the bad loans made by the financial industry. These funds were placed under the Secretary of the Treasury to be managed as he saw fit. The original idea was for the government to buy troubled assets held by the banks for future sale, but eventually the government began to buy ownership in those banks. Conservative critics were upset that the President did not put restrictions on how the money was to be used.

When Barack Hussein Obama became President of the United States in 2009, he continued the TARP program, but he also created a $787 billion stimulus bill and a budget of $1.3 trillion to increase government spending and stimulate the economy. They guaranteed that if this spending increase happened the unemployment rate would stay below 8%.

Unfortunately, unemployment rose to 10% in 2010, government deficits began averaging $1.3 trillion a year and the national debt rose to $14 trillion. This means that the national debt is now higher than the gross domestic product of the United States. The interest on the debt which must be paid to lenders both in and outside the United States is now close to $200 billion. This is one of the largest expenditures in the federal budget. The American economy might experience a decade of high unemployment, very stagnant economic growth, and massive debt.

The combination of incredibly large government spending, which began in the Bush administration and made worse in the Obama administration, the continuation of meager economic growth, and the massive debt which will have to be paid by future generations, has led to the development of a grass root "Tea Party" movement critical of people in both parties who are fiscally irresponsible. It is too early to know if this movement will have a long-lasting impact on American fiscal policies.

The Obama Administration claims that its stimulus bill of February 16, 2009, saved the American economy from total collapse. The opposition believes that such a large stimulus was not needed and that most of the funds went to reward Obama's political allies. They also argue that the American economy got out of the recession in June 2009, just four months after the stimulus bill was passed, so the legislation could not have played a role in the recovery.

American Society

If out-of-control government spending is the Achilles heel of the American economy, family dysfunction might be the point of weakness for American society. The collapse of the American family is one of the main reasons for excessive welfare and overall social spending. The collapse of families places more fiscal burden on the government. The state then has to spend more money assisting children and others. Children raised outside marriage are 700% more likely to be poor. Two-thirds of poor children come from single-parent families. Presently 36.9% of all American children are born out of wedlock. Approximately 70% of Black children are born out of wedlock. In 1941, 80% were born within a marriage. The same trends are found among Hispanic families and among an increasing number of non-Latin white families.

America provides a great amount of freedom for personal relationships. This is a good thing provided it is accompanied by a significant degree of personal discipline and love (commitment to the well-being of others) so that children can grow in stable, mature and happy families. A major difficulty our families have to deal with is the culture of hedonism, permissiveness, selfishness, and violence permeating much of our society. Problems with families can lead to poor educational achievements, crime, promiscuity, sexually-transmitted diseases, depression, and suicide.

American education is also facing difficulties which undermine the vitality of the United States. In fact, the current performance of our elementary and secondary schools guarantees a massive decline in the Americans' standard of living. For instance, Americans' life expectancy has peaked at 78 years of age and has begun to decline among some groups. Over 50% of high school graduates need remedial courses in math and reading when they enter college. They do poorly in cross-national examinations. The job market by-passes American youth in favor of foreigners in the areas of engineering, mathematics and several others. In addition, students are not challenged enough in critical thinking skills in humanities and social sciences courses as faculty across the high schools, colleges, and universities do not have sufficient ideological and political diversity.

For example, at the college level Democrats outnumber Republicans 3 to 1 among economics professors, 28 to 1 in sociology, and 30 to 1 in anthropology, among others. This imbalance towards the Left side of the political spectrum tends to create bias in academia which then results in bias in the media and in the popular culture. The end result is a decline in self-reflection, in critical thinking, in free speech, and in problem-solving. Academic freedom protects teachers so they can speak their mind without retaliation for their views. It is a good thing. But it also should extend to the students who deserve a wide variety of views to be expressed in class. They need this ideological diversity and critical thinking to grow intellectually strong and self-reliant. This lack of intellectual diversity when combined with a dilution in the quality of educational content and the decline in expectations for American children and educators, represents a frontal attack against American society.

Health Care and Retirement

Americans are becoming anxious about the state of health care and social security in the country. **The gap between promised social security and medicare outlays and projected revenues is between $43 and $51 trillion.** This would be $135,000 for every American. This sum is 400% of the country's GDP. For instance, the total household wealth of Americans—including the value of houses, retirement accounts, etc., is only $42 trillion. Structural changes are needed to save the system. Medicare will go bankrupt by 2019. In 2010, Social Security and Medicare are approximately 33% of the federal budget and 7.5% of the Gross Domestic Product. By 2030, they will be 13% of the GDP.

The Medicare Prescription Drug Improvement and Modernization Act of 2003 added to Medicare and signed by the Bush Administration on November 3, 2003, was estimated at $400 billion for ten years, but now it is said to cost $543 billion or one-third more. In 2006, Medicare was 6% of the economy, but by 2059 it will be 9%. Partly, health care is expensive because people in America receive great quality health care, are living longer, and older people have more medical costs.

The Baby Boomer generation, the very large number of people born between 1946 and 1961, will begin retiring in 2008. Life expectancy at 65 is 17 years and it increases 2.5 years per decade. People begin collecting social security benefits at 62 years of age. This is a long period during which people will be collecting benefits. In 1940, there were 42 workers for every retiree, in 2006, there were 3.2 workers, and in 2030, there will be only 2.2 workers for every retiree. The fiscal or tax pressures on every worker to sustain retirees will be high. There could be inter-generational conflict.

In 2018, social security will have more payouts than inflows. Someone born in the 2000s will be promised $24,300 in benefits, but there will be money for only $18,300. Between 2042 and 2052, the system will need to cut benefits 30% so that benefits do not exceed revenues. The country has several options: increase the payroll tax 15%, from 12.4% to 13.9%; increase the ceiling income for the payroll tax from only the first $90,000 in increase to the first $140,000; reduce benefits 13%; reduce the cost of living adjustment; increase the age of eligibility for full benefits which is 67 years of age for those born after 1959; reduce benefits for the "rich"; and invest the current $1.5 trillion surplus in the social security fund in the stock market.

Today the surplus is invested in U.S. Treasury bonds. Currently, the payroll tax is 12.4%, one-half going to present retirees and government programs. Workers born after 1960 will get a return on their investment of only 2%. Amazingly, during the difficult economic years from 1929 to 1948, the average rate of return of the stock market was 3.6%. This observation leads some to suggest that workers should be allowed to invest up to 5% of their payroll taxes in personal retirement accounts which will increase their individual benefits and help increase the economy to afford paying the retirees. Additional options include promoting self-insurance in the private sector, a mandatory savings system, increase in catastrophic insurance so the government system is not strained by extreme costs, and no expansion in entitlements by politicians trying to win votes.

A related issue is the high price of medicinal drugs. One has to pay more for a drug during the seven years that they are under patent protection. This is the price paid for innovation. Socialized countries like Canada which sell drugs at subsidized prices, are seldom involved in creating new advanced drugs and as a result the quality of their health care is not as high, although they might provide cheaper access to medical services. Perhaps competition in the pharmaceutical industry could reduce the price of medicines while also guaranteeing high quality.

Trade Policy

The United States' account deficit for goods and services in 2010 and 2011 could reach over $800 billion. This means that Americans buy billions more in goods and services from the world than they buy from us. This deficit includes over $300 billion in petroleum products, $350 billion in consumer products, and $200 billion in other goods. The only surplus will come in services with a little over $107 billion. This deficit is balanced by foreign capital coming into the United States. As long as other countries are willing to invest in America the surplus acquired by trading with us, then the United States can survive this large deficit. Trade deficits can be associated with an expanding economy as Americans import industrial supplies and capital goods that fuel business expansion and job creation. Thus not all imports are consumer items. Exports began to increase in 2003 and 2004 as Americans increased their productivity, the dollar was devalued, and the tax cuts of 2003 accelerated business and investments. The fastest growing export customers of the United States are now China (39%), Mexico (24%), Japan (15.2%) and Western Europe (12.7%). The United States does have a $150 billion trade deficit with China.

A major controversy in the trade area has become the issue of outsourcing, whereby corporations transfer some of their work overseas. American workers complain about losing their jobs to other countries. Yet, outsourcing is not a new phenomenon. This is part of the process of comparative advantage as people and firms move to where they can receive a higher rate of return on their assets. The truth is that the United States imports more jobs than it exports through outsourcing. It exports low-skill low-paying jobs but imports high-skill and high-paying jobs. Outsourcing of jobs to India is not because of low paying jobs in India, but because India has great productivity in computer programming and engineering. The vast majority of American foreign investment is in high-wage countries which also have high productivity. American firms would outsource less jobs if taxes on corporations were reduced, education improved so that Americans would have better job skills, and litigation against corporations diminished so the cost of doing business decreases.

However, critics of our trade deficit and outsourcing point out why many jobs move overseas. Corporations leave America not only because they hire workers at very low wages, but also because they do not have to pay large employee benefits, and need not worry about many safety and environmental regulations. In addition, corporations which move overseas, for example, to the European Union, do not pay foreign taxes when they export to the United States. This is a tax rebate that attracts companies to move there. At the same time, when Americans sell to these countries they do have to pay all sorts of fees. Critics believe the US Government should retaliate against this discrimination.

Another complaint of US policy is over the H-1B visas which allow US corporations to bring to the country foreign skilled workers, claiming that there are no Americans who can do certain jobs. Critics argue that there are Americans who can do these jobs, but that business simply wants lower-wage employees. Many of these are trained in the United States and are later sent abroad to open foreign branches of the corporations, thus contributing to outsourcing. Jobs which are at risk of being outsourced abroad are accountants, bookkeepers, computer programmers, data entry keyers, financial analysts, graphic designers, and medical transcriptionists, among others.

Americans will probably engage in the near future in an intense **debate over free trade.** While it is true that free trade can stimulate comparative advantage and lead to greater production, lower prices and consumer satisfaction, it can also create havoc with one's economy. In the last seven years, the United States has had over $4 trillion in trade deficits, a loss of 5 million manufacturing jobs, and over $2 billion a day in debt to pay for foreign goods. American industry is increasingly unable to produce the goods Americans buy from abroad. As demand for the American dollar drops, and more dollars are produced domestically to stimulate the economy, its value drops and more foreign interests, many of them hostile to the United States, buy its industrial assets. Profits are then taken out of the United States.

The decline in the value of the dollar does encourage US exports but in the long run makes Americans poorer. Since 2001, the dollar has dropped over 50% versus the Euro, for example. Free trade does make sense with free countries who do not cheat by protecting or by subsidizing their corporations. China is not a free country. It favors its goods by devaluation of its currency. Europe imposes a 15% value added tax on US imports and rebates the VAT on exports to the United States. Japan manipulates the currency and shelters its corporations. The OPEC oil cartel is a "gangster" operation. Many of our former government officials and bureaucrats are now working for foreign business to exploit

America's unwillingness to protect its people from unfair free trade. This is the case of the Pentagon awarding a $35 billion contract to a French company to build a new generation of Air Force tankers. This is a company which received subsidies from several European governments unfriendly to the United States.

The Price of Energy and the Environment

Americans have had to pay from $2.50 to $4.50 for a gallon of gasoline during 2006–2010. The U.S. Federal Trade Commission stated on May 23, 2006, that the rise in gasoline prices has not been caused by manipulation on the part of oil corporations. It is the result of the market forces of supply and demand. Other studies by Congress support this assertion. First, world-wide economic growth has led to higher demand for gasoline, particularly by China and India. Second, the devaluation of the dollar makes all imports, including oil, more expensive. Third, the refining capacity has been curtailed by the impact of hurricanes and by the inability of the country to build new refineries due to environmental and legal restrictions. Fourth, congressional mandates to add ethanol to the gasoline mix have actually made it more costly. Fifth, the world is running out of the more accessible, light, sweet and cheap crude oil, and the abundant reserves available are more costly to extract.

Sixth, the Congress does not allow extensive drilling for oil in the Arctic National Wild Life Refuge (ANWR) or in the Gulf of Mexico or in the Atlantic Ocean. Seventh, legal and environmental restrictions make it difficult to develop nuclear reactors. Eighth, the unwillingness of the automobile industry to invest in cars which can use several types of fuels. Ninth, the speculation in the oil markets which drive up the price at least 20%. The federal tax on gasoline is approximately 17%. The price of oil will decrease only if either demand for energy is lowered or if the supply is increased. Lowered demand could be the result of recessions, conservation, or technological breakthroughs.

There are several options for reducing the use of gasoline or for increasing the supply of energy. The use of **photovoltaic technology** to store solar power is being improved, but it has still limited use at night and in places where sunshine is poor. **Flexible fuel vehicles** (FFVs) are designed to run on 85% ethanol and 15% unleaded gas mix (E-85), and can use all gasoline if E-85 is not available. However, it requires a great deal of energy to produce so its efficiency in the United States is debatable. A combination of 10% **ethanol** and 90% unleaded gas (E10) is already being used in 33% of all gas pumped in the United States. Ethanol from corn is not energy efficient, leads to overuse of land, and tends to increase the price of food. Ethanol from sugar is better. **Bio-diesel** is made from crops like soybeans. It will probably become an important option but can also raise the price of food. This is an important issue now because food is becoming scarce globally and its price is escalating. **Nuclear energy** is generated when uranium, a metal found in rocks is processed in a nuclear reactor, creating thermal energy. It has no green house emissions into the air and water, and produces 20% of the country's electricity. However, there are difficulties with the storage of the waste, the high capital investment to build the plants, and issues of legal liability. Also, it needs an abundant supply of water and some communities do not have it.

Hydrogen can generate power and its only emission is clean water. However, one needs lots of energy to separate hydrogen from hydro-carbons and water. Storage is very difficult. **Natural gas** might be another important replacement for oil. The new Energy Bill passed in 2005 will spend $281 million for clean coal technology research, $150 million for bio-based transportation with agricultural waste products such as wood chips, $148 million for solar energy, $54 million for emission free coal plants, and $44 million for wind energy.

The big energy crisis in America is in the fuels needed to run our transportation vehicles. We import over 12 million barrels of oil daily and we use 20 million per day. So America in the short run must drill for more oil in the United States to replace its imports. Then it must pass a law that every car made in the United States be a **flexible fuel vehicle** able to use gasoline, ethanol and methanol. The increased volume in these fuels will make it profitable for gas stations to diversify their pumps. Meanwhile, the country can proceed on with more public transportation, conservation, and the ultimate energy—nuclear fusion!

Many **environmentalists** seek to replace the use of **fossil fuels** as energy because they fear that increased carbon dioxide emissions are responsible for **global warming.** They fear that dramatically increasing temperatures could lead to the melting of the artic ice, to increases of fresh water in the North Atlantic, to the shutting down of the north-bound and warm Gulf Stream, to the freezing of Europe, and to increased dryness and wind globally. However, not everyone agrees with this assessment. Critics do agree that the temperature has increased one degree in the last 100 years, but they argue that the causes of this trend are not yet clear. More important than the burning of fossil fuels might be water vapor itself, and its accumulation might be caused by cyclical factors such as sun spot activity or deforestation, or the natural changes in the oceans.

The mainstream position is that increases in carbon dioxide since 1978 are leading to global warming. The critics respond that, historically, increases in carbon dioxide usually follow global warming by approximately 400 years, that CO2 increases do not cause global warming, but are actually a result of it. They point out that there have been many warm cycles long before human production of fossil fuels, and also that, for example, there was significant rise in CO2 between 1948 and 1978, but yet world temperatures dropped. There is also evidence that the temperature in some of the planets, like Jupiter, Mars, and Neptune is also increasing, but without man-made fossil fuels. There has been no significant global warming since 1998, and 2007 was one of the coldest years in a decade. Some critics argue that the real threat is global cooling and not global warming. Others argue that both are happening simultaneously. The debate continues.

Environmentalists disagree also on other issues. Some want internationally imposed sanctions to protect the environment. Others prefer grass-root activism and the free market. Some dislike nuclear power because of its potential dangers. Others believe it is the only option to prevent global warming, if it is really taking place as a result of human actions. Some want to reduce economic growth to conserve natural resources. Others believe that economic growth needs to be accelerated to elevate people from poverty and to better educate them so they can protect their environment. Some advocate natural foods. Others promote biotechnology and genetically modified foods. Some believe population is out of control. Others think that a bigger danger today is population decline in the rich world. Some believe that sustainable development implies a static model where the emphasis is on resources preservation. Others believe that sustainable development must be forward-looking and include growth, protection of natural resources and social justice for the poor and powerless, and that new resources and technologies will be created. Some believe that to protect the environment one needs metaphysical, cosmological, religious transformations in the culture. Others think that protection of the environment can occur independently of religion or specific cosmologies.

Immigration

Legal immigration has played a mostly positive impact on American society. Immigrants can bring intellectual and financial contributions to America. But what about illegal immigration? Each year over 350,000 million legal and illegal aliens arrive in the United States. There are 11 to 20 million illegals in the country. The illegals make up 4% of the U.S. population or 1/3 of the foreign born. It is estimated that 56% are from Mexico, 22% from the rest of South America, and 22% from Africa, Asia and Europe. There are 3.1 million US-born children among the illegal population. Approximately 37% of the children and 27% of the illegal adults are poor.

Approximately 80% of the seasonal farm labor is made up of illegals. Many of the illegals perform valuable work in such sectors as construction, home and patient care, restaurants, and many others. However, there are also significant problems with the illegal population. The foreign born are 30% of the federal prison inmates and most gang members are also illegal immigrants. An example is the **Mara Salvatrucha (MS-13)** gang from El Salvador which is found in twelve American states. There is speculation that MS-13 could develop ties with al-Qaeda. Middle-Eastern men have traveled to the **tri-border area** of Argentina, Brazil and Paraguay, learned Spanish and traveled illegally to the United States via Mexico. Gangsters are increasingly found in the business of illegal alien trafficking.

Many Americans believe that out-of-control illegal immigration could dilute the country's culture, intensify social conflict due to political multiculturalism, expose the society to terrorist attacks, hurt those who patiently wait their turn to legally enter the country, and lower the wages of the poorest Americans. No major efforts have been taken to close the border even though public opinion supports it. Over 80% of Americans would like a security fence to be built by the Mexican border, over 75% want illegal aliens to be accused of felony, over 70% do not want illegals to become citizens, and over 85% believe that illegal immigration is a great crisis.

The federal government might not have acted to close the border up to now because most of the costs of illegal immigration are borne by state and local governments, but most of the tax receipts paid by the illegals go to the federal government. Illegal immigration is a good business for the government in Washington. Many Democrats seek to convert the illegals, as well as the legals, into ethnic voters and they support a political multicultural agenda that prevents them from aggressively fighting illegal immigration. Many Republicans, particularly free-market libertarians, enjoy employing illegals in the agribusiness sector for they get low wages.

As the minimum wage rises in the United States, more illegals come and are hired. While those who want more immigration argue that there are many jobs Americans will not do, their opponents respond that if illegal immigration were controlled, the wages for these unattractive jobs would rise and Americans would then take them. Most of the illegal immigrants are poor. In this sense, the United States is importing the world's poverty. The net cost of immigration was over $66 billion in 2009, according to the **Federation for American Immigration Reform.** Approximately 25% of the uninsured are immigrants. Over $6 billion was spent incarcerating illegal aliens between 2007 and 2010. The Federal government repays the states less than 25% of this cost.

On June 7, 2007, the Immigration Reform Bill endorsed by leading Democrats and Republicans, as well as by President George W. Bush, suffered a major defeat. It would have offered, with some exceptions, visa status to illegals who entered the country before January 1, 2007. Starting with Probationary Z visas, then Permanent Z visas, and legal Permanent Residence Status, the illegals could then have applied, upon making certain payments and waiting several years, for American citizenship.

The bill was defeated mostly by conservative Republicans and some Democrats. Many arguments were given, including that the bill was an "amnesty" bill which rewarded law breakers, that current immigration laws should be enforced first, that before any immigration bill is passed, the borders should be secured first, that it did not punish businesses which hired illegals, and that it would lead to even more illegal immigration. A major reason for the defeat of the bill was a report by the Heritage Foundation on the eve of the debate which pointed out that "amnesty" would cost the taxpayers $2.6 trillion during the retirement years of the "illegals", if just 10 million of them received advanced legal status.

It is hard to predict when Congress will have the political courage to tackle this issue again. The political elite probably underestimated the anger at the grassroot levels over the inability of the federal government to control the borders, both the one with Mexico and the one with Canada. Perhaps if this is done, the political Left and the Right will find a compromise which will find some sort of safe, just and efficient way of dealing

with the millions of illegals in the country without increasing their numbers in the future. America needs immigrant labor. Increasing legal immigration could be the solution.

One of the most dramatic political events in 2010 was the decision by the State of Arizona to pass legislation intended to force the United States federal government to enforce its own immigration laws. There is nothing in the Arizona legislation which is not in the federal statutes. In fact, the federal law is much tougher on illegal aliens and actually permits ethnic profiling.

This legislation allows Arizona's police to ask for the identification papers of people who have committed an infraction not related to immigration, but whom they suspect of being in the United States illegally. Other states and political jurisdictions might develop similar legislation. Critics of the Arizona legislation argue that it would lead to unjust ethnic profiling. However, Arizona's law specifically forbids such profiling. Only time will tell whether the law is a just and wise one.

Arizonans who support the immigration law are very upset about the following events. First, the U.S. Attorney General sued Arizona in the federal courts to defeat the immigration law. Second, the President of Mexico publically attacked Arizona during a speech given before the U.S. Congress itself. Third, Hillary Clinton, the U.S. Secretary of State, presented the Arizona legislation before the United Nations Human Rights Council as an example of a law which discriminates. Many Arizonans thus believe that their own federal government has betrayed them.

Presently, the terrorists among the illegals cannot be screened out. The backlog for adjudication is over 4.5 million people. The 3,000 federal immigration agents cannot cope with the 11 to 20 million illegal aliens. One proposal to deal with the problem is the **Homeland Security Enhancement Act** which will try to create cooperation between federal agents and the 650,000 police officers at the state level. Some political jurisdictions have created **sanctuary laws** which prohibit local officers from reporting illegal aliens to federal authorities. These laws are a violation of the 1996 **Illegal Immigration Reform and Immigrant Responsibility Act.**

There are now 400,000 illegals who have deportation orders and are still on the streets. Of these 80,000 are criminals and 3,800 are from countries with known al-Qaeda terrorist presence. Unsecured borders are very dangerous. There are other problems. Currently, about 21,000 pounds of marijuana and cocaine enter the United States daily. In the same way, dangerous explosives could be inserted in the 30,000 trucks, 6,500 trail cars, and 50,000 cargo containers which enter the United States daily. Less than 5% of the containers and less than 10% of the commercial vessels are inspected. A highly enriched uranium (HEU) weapon of 10 kilotons could be exploded in 4 large cities and kill four million Americans, which is a goal of al-Qaeda. There are 130 nuclear reactors and other facilities using HEU in 40 countries. It would not be an impossible task to obtain HEUs and carry them across the Canadian or Mexican borders.

Post 9/11 American Foreign Policy

When on September 11, 2001 Islamic terrorists linked to al-Qaeda crashed four planes into the World Trade Center towers in New York, into the Pentagon in Washington, D.C., and into the Pennsylvania countryside and murdered approximately 3,000 people, domestic and foreign American policies changed dramatically. The Congress authorized President George W. Bush to use all necessary and appropriate force against those responsible. The United States received the support of NATO, Russia, Pakistan, India and others when it attacked on October 7, 2001, the Taliban and al-Qaeda in Afghanistan. President Bush then included Iran, Iraq and North Korea as part of an **"Axis of Evil."**

In September 2002, he stated his **preventive policy of war** with its right to intervene in Iraq and elsewhere "as we did in Kosovo" during the Clinton Administration. His policy actually originated with the Reagan Administration in the 1980s. It rejected article 5 of the United Nations which orders force in self-defense only and not for humanitarian reasons. There was a similarity with President Ronald Reagan's abandonment of the policy of containment for "rollback," making the enemy defend its own land instead of attacking the United States and its allies. President Bush's policies have rejected certain assumptions held by the foreign policy establishment: that North Korea and Iran can be bribed away from nuclear ambitions; that democracy in the Arab world is impossible; that fighting terrorism leads to more terrorism; that Syria poses no threat to U.S. interests; that the United Nations alone gives moral legitimacy; and that supporting Israel explains Islamic hostility to the United States.

The United States also began to change its geopolitical strategies away from just preparing to fight "the next big war" as before the 1990s, and away from preparing to fight two small wars, or China, as during the 1990s. Now it is getting ready to fight simultaneous conflicts, dealing with enemies before they can attack, in areas which are "disconnected" from modernization. It will create strategic bases in places like Afghanistan, Australia, Bulgaria, Guam, Kyrgyzstan and South Korea. Then, there will be foreign operating bases with few troops to maintain equipment in countries like Hungary, Romania, and Turkey, and finally forward operating sites with no permanent US presence in areas like Mali, Kenya and the Horn of Africa. There could be a reduction of troops in Germany, South Korea and Turkey and an increase in Southern Europe, the Middle East and Asia. **This policy will allow quick strikes in the arc of instability which includes Africa, the Caribbean Rim, the Caucasus, Central Asia, the Middle East, North Korea and South Asia.** The American presence in Iraq in March and April 2003 will allow the United States to also place troops in Iraq from which it can move them throughout the Asian Southwest.

President George W. Bush had some significant successes. He overthrew the Saddam Hussein regime which was a major source of instability in the Middle East and vanquished the Taliban/al-Qaeda dictatorship in Afghanistan. Both countries have developed new constitutions although some Americans are very angry at the use of American resources to support regimes whose constitutions are based on Sharia, Islamic law, which discriminate against other religious believers. President Bush convinced the Russians to support the war against Islamic terrorism and to go along with the expansion of NATO along Russia's border, including the placing of US forces in Uzbekistan. Libya is scrapping its nuclear program. India and Pakistan are making serious efforts to combat terrorism and improve bilateral relations. Pakistan stopped its illegal program of trading in nuclear technologies.

Colombia, with American assistance, is making significant advances against communist terrorists in the country. The Saudis seem to be serious in persecuting terrorists inside the kingdom. The United States has very quietly organized a **Proliferation Security Initiative** (PSI) of 16 countries which will cooperate in the interdiction of WMD delivery systems and related materials. The countries so far include Australia, Canada, Denmark, France, Germany, Italy, Japan, Netherland, Norway, Poland, Portugal, Singapore, Spain, Turkey, United Kingdom and the United States. The PSI is outside the control of the United Nations. The United States will sell India nuclear technology and deepen a relationship which will help both countries to combat Islamic terrorism and contain China if it becomes a threat in the South China Seas and in the Indian Ocean.

However, there were some apparent failures: over 4,000 Americans have died in Iraq and the country might disintegrate and allow Iran to gain significant leverage in the south; Afghanistan has not been able to extinguish the Taliban and al-Qaeda because they have established a sanctuary in Pakistan, even after the United States has spent billions of dollars in that country to strengthen the military; China is outworking the United States diplomatically in Southeast Asia and East Asia potentially depriving Americans of access to the largest economic area; Russia, angry about American actions in Kosovo, Georgia, the Ukraine and Central Asia, is now a leader of an anti-American group of countries; and the European Union is increasingly seeking to reduce American influence globally.

Terrorist attacks are increasing in the Arab/Persian Gulf region which sits on two-thirds of the world's proven oil reserves. The increases in the price of oil could choke economic recovery globally. The slow but constant path toward communism in Venezuela could strengthen terrorism and subversion throughout the Andean region. The expanding Leftist alliance of Cuba, Venezuela, the Colombian guerrillas (FARC), and Bolivia could create difficulties in Ecuador, Nicaragua and Mexico, among other places. The North Korean nuclear weapons crisis could worsen. The war on Islamic terrorism seems to have no end.

Moreover, an anti-American bloc of countries made up of China, Germany, Russia and others seem to be undermining American foreign policy in various parts of the world. Russia might be starting another "Cold War" against the United States, and a part of the responsibility for this might fall on the Bush Administration. Also, Brazil is trying to organize a Middle Eastern-South American bloc to "balance" the United States and defeat its globalization policies. Thousands of Muslim Jihadists and sympathizers could be already in the United States as a result of porous immigration policies. The glue that binds these different countries is anti-Americanism.

Homeland Security

Domestically, the United States responded to terrorism by attempting to tighten immigration laws, strengthening the surveillance powers of the Federal Bureau of Investigation (FBI) and of the Central Intelligence Agency (CIA). The Congress and the President created a new bureaucracy called the **Department of Homeland Security** which is divided into four major directorates. **The Border and Transportation Security Administration** brings major border security and transportation operations under one roof including the US Customs Service (Treasury), part of the Immigration and Naturalization Service (Justice), the Federal Protective Service (GSA), Federal Law Enforcement Training Center (Treasury), part of the Animal and Plant Health Inspection Service (Agriculture), and the Office for Domestic Preparedness (Justice).

The Emergency Preparedness and Response Directorate oversees domestic disaster preparedness training and coordinates government disaster response. It brings together the Federal Emergency Management Agency (FEMA), the Strategic National Stockpile and the National Disaster Medical System (HHS), the Nuclear Incident Response Team (Energy), the Domestic Emergency support Teams (Justice), and the National Domestic Preparedness Office (FBI). **The Science and Technology Directorate** seeks to utilize all scientific and technological advantages when securing the homeland. This includes the CBRN Countermeasures Programs (Energy), the Environmental Measurements Laboratory (Defense), and the Plum Island Animal Disease Center (Agriculture).

Finally, there is the **Information Analysis and Infrastructure Protection Directorate** which analyzes intelligence and information from other agencies (including the CIA, FBI, DIA and NSA) involving threats to homeland security and evaluates vulnerabilities in the country's infrastructure. It brings together the Critical Infrastructure Assurance (Commerce), the Federal Computer Incident Response Center (GSA), the National Communications System (Defense), the National Infrastructure Protection Center (FBI), and the Energy Security and Assurance Program (Energy). The Secret Service and the Coast Guard is in the department although remaining intact and reporting directly to the Secretary. The INS Adjudications and Benefits Program reports directly to the Deputy Secretary as the Bureau of Citizenship and Immigration Services.

The Patriot Act of 2001 is a major instrument in the strengthening of homeland security. It gives those investigating terrorists the same tools as those going against mobsters and drug lords. The act expands the government powers to conduct roving wiretaps, secret searches and seizures, and to arrest and detain noncitizens for long periods. It also eliminates the wall of separation between intelligence-gathering professionals and those conducting criminal investigations, so they can share information. The Act was extended in March 2006.

During 2004, a 9/11 Commission was created to analyze the reasons why the terrorist attack on September 11, 2001, occurred. The final report said there was a failure in intelligence. However, maybe there was also a failure in the political culture in Washington which led to the problems in intelligence. The weakening of intelligence gathering began with the anti-military and anti-intelligence movements associated with the Vietnam War and the Watergate crisis. **The Frank Church Senate Select Committee of Intelligence of 1976,** for example, exposed the names of American intelligence assets abroad, and was very critical of covert operations.

The national security functions of the executive began to be regulated by Congress and the courts to protect the civil liberties of Americans. As more people had access to intelligence reports, which often led to leaks to the media, less information was given to American intelligence by foreign agencies. Under the Administration of Gerald Ford, and the accompanying Congress, some of the best CIA covert agents were dismissed. Human intelligence gathering began to be minimized. Reliance on technical, high-tech instruments of intelligence gathering began to be stressed.

President Jimmy Carter and Senator Ted Kennedy, among others, pushed the **Foreign Intelligence Surveillance Act** (FISA) of 1978 which for the first time allowed Congress and the courts to regulate the gathering of intelligence. This act requires intelligence officers to go to a FISA court to approve a surveillance after having proved that the target is an agent of a foreign power. Later, it was added that the request for surveillance needed to pass the "primary purpose" test, that is, that the main objective of the surveillance is counter-intelligence and not criminal prosecution. A significant political controversy developed in 2005 and 2006 when the New York Times revealed that President Bush ordered the National Security Agency to intercept communications between groups abroad connected to terrorism and people in the United States. Critics argue that the President should have gone to a FISA court first to get approval. The President responded that in times of war he has the power by Article II of the Constitution to order such interceptions of communications.

Things got more difficult for intelligence officers when the Clinton Administration in 1995 demanded that a **firewall** had to be placed between national security and domestic criminal prosecutors so they would not be able to communicate with each other. Thus the CIA could not communicate with the FBI, for example, which handles counter-intelligence among other things. It would be the Patriot Act that would end this firewall. The Clinton Administration followed the criminal model of persecution against terrorists, as the government had to present to the criminal defense all evidence and witnesses in the case. This approach made the intelligence services of other countries withhold intelligence from the United States for they did not want to have their information and their sources taken into a trial situation. All these restrictions, plus the directives to avoid contact with so-called human rights violators, criminals, drug lords and murderers, inhibited intelligence gathering and demoralized the CIA and the FBI. Therefore Congress and the Presidency will have to accept a share of the responsibility for the so-called intelligence failure.

The Return of the Democrats

In November 2006, the Democrats regained control of both chambers of the US Congress which they had lost a decade before. The Democrats were able to capitalize on the unpopularity among the American people of the war in Iraq. President George W. Bush's popularity fell to the low 20's. Another factor leading to the defeat of the Republicans was the defection at election time of the conservative base of the party, which blamed President Bush and the Republican elite for excessive government spending, uncontrolled illegal immigration, blunders and political constraints on the military in the conduct of the war in Iraq, inaction in the face of discriminatory trade policies against the United States, and too large an immigration from Muslim countries.

Another concern of the conservative base of the Republicans has been the rumors that the Administration is discussing with Canada and Mexico the idea of a **North American Union.** This is in part a proposal of the Center for Strategic and International Studies and the North American Future 2025 Project which wants to discuss issues of regional integration such as labor mobility, energy, the environment, security, competitiveness, border infrastructure and logistics. The Conservative Right of the party believes this amounts to a loss of American sovereignty. They also criticize the Republican elite for backing the **United Nations Law of the Sea Treaty** which will strengthen international bureaucracies at the expense of American economic interests.

When Barack H. Obama became President in 2009, the Democrats took control of the Congress and of the Executive branch. The most important priority of the Democrats became the passage of a massive health reform package, which passed in 2010. This legislation allows 31 million additional people to receive medical coverage and prevents insurance corporations from discriminating against people with serious illnesses. The money to pay for this reform will come from $500 billion taken from Medicare and from legislation forcing people to pay for medical insurance if they didn't have a policy. Also, money will come from the student loan program which the government took over. In addition, the Democrats passed a large bailout and stimulus legislation to deal with the economic recession, as well as a financial reform to avoid future financial meltdowns.

The President has been opposed by the Republicans in Congress who claim that Obama is making the government too powerful. Close to 50% of the American economy is now owned by the state. They prefer to have solutions to economic problems that involve market incentives more than government direct participation in the economy. Republicans also believe in lowering taxes and simplifying regulations so that the private sector can create jobs. While President Obama accuses the Republicans of being obstacles to his reforms, the Republicans respond that he has enough control of the political system to pass legislation without them. Any obstacles could be coming from the Democrats themselves.

Meanwhile, the unemployment rate is between 9.5% and 10%, and the poverty rate has gone from 12.5% to 15%, the worst in 40 years. Damaging to the Democrats is the loss of the majority of the Independents, most of whom voted for them in 2008.

Asia

Largest of all the continents, Asia covers nearly 33% of the Earth's land surface, and is home to more than half of the planet's population in 47 countries with 3.3 billion people. The continent can be divided into various regions. **Southwest Asia** includes Egypt's Sinai Peninsula and the Middle East. The area tends to be dry and of low population density. Oil is abundant in some regions. The major population groups are the Arabs, Turks, Iranians, and Pashtuns of Afghanistan. The dominant religion is Islam, with small Jewish and Christian groups in Israel and Lebanon. **South Asia** includes Pakistan, India, Sri Lanka, Nepal, Bhutan and Bangladesh.

The Hindus of India are the majority group in this region, followed by the Muslims of Pakistan and Bangladesh. There are also millions of Muslims in India. This area is encircled and isolated by the tallest mountains in the world. It has a high population density.

Southeast Asia includes Myanmar (Burma) on the east, followed by Thailand, Laos, Cambodia, Vietnam, Malaysia, Indonesia, Singapore and the Philippines. The population is mostly Mongoloid, and the main religion is Buddhism on the continental mainland, Islam south of it, and Catholicism in the Philippines. **East Asia** includes China, Taiwan, North and South Korea and Japan. **Central Asia** is often described as including Mongolia, Tibet, Kyrgyzstan, Tajikistan, Kazakhstan, Turkmenistan, Uzbekistan, Azerbaijan, Armenia and Georgia, even though the last two are often considered an extension of Europe. The majority of the population is Muslim. They are Turkic-speakers. Yet, there are also Christians in Armenia and Georgia. **North Asia** is the Russian region east of the Ural Mountains, also called Siberia, and Mongolia.

China: The Inner War between Capitalism and Communism

The People's Republic of China occupies most of the habitable mainland of East Asia. It has a population of 1.3 billion, 92% being Han Chinese. The rest of the population is made up of Tibetans, Mongols, Koreans, Manchus, and other ethnic Chinese groups. Only 38.6% of the population is urban.

China has a totalitarian communist system directed by a **selectorate** made up of 300 members of the Central Committee of the Communist Party, several dozen Communist Party elders, and top officials of the **People's Liberation Army (PLA),** which has 2.3 million soldiers. During the 1980s, following the death of Chairman Mao Zedong on September 9, 1976, his successor, Deng Xiaoping and the new ruling group enacted far-reaching economic reforms, moving China away from rigid central planning and towards a market-oriented socialism with an economic opening to the world markets. **Today the Chinese Model refers to a country whose economic system has some free market attributes, but whose political system is a totalitarian dictatorship.**

As a result of these changes, China had one of the world's fastest growing economies during the 1980s and 1990s and early 2000s, averaging from 6% to 10%

growth per year. China's per capita GDP is approximately $7,000. It is expected that by 2011, China will be double the size of the German economy. Some economists actually believe that China is already the second largest economy. China was the largest recipient of foreign, direct investment (FDI) between 2005 and 2008. **In 2008, China surpassed the United States as the world's largest manufacturing power ($2.717 trillion).** China is an economic superpower which spends 3.8% of its GDP on its military, patiently waiting for the right time to challenge the United States.

However, China's political system inhibits what could be an even more vigorous economic performance. The Communist Party is China's ruling class, overseeing government, industry, courts, parliaments, and the army. This monopoly of power prevents a true rule of law, guarantees in business transactions, security of property, and protection of basic human rights. Religious groups such as Catholics and other Christians are persecuted. Torture is widespread. **There are no checks and balances or government accountability in China because there is no free press, free speech, political opposition, or free elections;** the Party will not tolerate independent political and civic organizations. In addition, the People's Bank of China prints money arbitrarily to support the 100,000 state-owned firms. These enterprises most often consume capital unproductively. The result is inefficiency, economic stagnation, and inflation. State-owned firms consume 60% of all fixed-asset investment in China though they only produce 40% of industrial output.

Another problem in China in addition to dictatorship, inefficient state-owned industries, and inflation, is the great regional inequalities between the coastal cities, where capitalism is growing, and the backward inland provinces. Of the 19 inland provinces, 16 have incomes below the national average. City dwellers on the average earn 300% more than rural dwellers. They do not receive as many housing and welfare benefits as urban Chinese and are more vulnerable to the depredations of village officials who tax them heavily. Cropland has been lost due to soil erosion, desertification, energy projects, and industrial and housing developments. Among the serious problems China will face are its need to import over 1.2 million barrels of oil a day and to attract more capital to sustain the growth rates of 7% to 10% a year necessary to absorb its huge, growing labor force. China does not support small and mid-sized businesses, intellectual property laws, and does not train enough managers.

The United States and other Western countries are promoting a strategy of constructive engagement, hoping that as China becomes more economically interdependent with the rest of the world through capitalism, free trade and open markets, it will become less totalitarian and expansionistic. Business interests in the West also hope to profit significantly by trading with the huge China market. Supporting this policy of engagement is the international financial community. The Chinese obtained a great victory in the Congress of the United States when the Americans voted in June 2000 to normalize relations with China. This means trade relations with China will not be subjected to yearly reviews to see if the Chinese have improved their performance in the area of human rights and democracy. The United States also supported the inclusion of China in the World Trade Organization. Final negotiations between the two ended successfully in June 2001.

However, Chinese communist leaders are aware of the threats which greater economic interdependence pose to their dictatorship. For instance, China can become more dependent on foreign markets for food, energy, capital and technology, and foreigners can then use this dependence to pressure Chinese domestic and foreign policies. China's leaders are also aware that free trade in goods and capital can undermine their inefficient, state-owned firms, drive them to bankruptcy, and increase unemployment in the short term.

For example, now that China is in the 137 member **World Trade Organization (WTO),** it has to eliminate tariffs protecting farmers, urban laborers and bureaucrats. This can create political unrest in China. To avoid difficulties, China will probably try to protect its auto, electronics, and pharmaceutical industries from foreign direct investment (FDI). The Chinese will also probably pressure foreign investors to give them advanced technologies. Since 2004, many Chinese have become alarmed by mergers and acquisitions by foreign companies in China. **Interestingly, more than 50% of Chinese exports are by foreigners. The All-China Federation of Industry and Commerce dislikes the laws which allow foreigners to buy up to 25% of the shares in Chinese banks, and to strip assets from businesses.** It complains of the tax privileges for foreigners who pay only an income tax of 15% instead of the usual 30%.

Another threat to the communist regime from capitalist economic interdependence is the political and economic decentralization usually brought by liberalization. Those pushing for a more open China demand such international liberal practices as rule of law, tax reforms, privatization, free flow of information, computer and Internet networking, intellectual property rights, public financial disclosure, and managerial accountability.

However, these liberal demands would reduce corruption in China and threaten the power of the selectorate because corruption is the glue that binds the elite. It allows them to use the resources of the system to reward supporters and punish dissenters. Thus corruption will probably continue since the three things which most threaten the regime—rule of law, political accountability, and a free press—would challenge the security of the regime.

And yet, there might be some Chinese sectors which could push for greater liberalization: PLA investors in the telecommunications industry, which might increase objective information; rich, coastal provinces whose assets are threatened by the Beijing tax regime; and Chinese investors in foreign firms. Also, China gains significantly from trade relations with the United States. In 2009, it had over $165 billion surplus in trade.

Chinese exports are very competitive due in part to China's low manufacturing costs. Its competitiveness has increased even more after 2008 as a result of the drop in the value of the America dollar, 20% against the euro, for example. This is so because the Chinese yuan is virtually pegged to the U.S. dollar. This Chinese strength hurts the exports from South Korea as well as those from other Asian economies. For instance, the Japanese yen, and the South Korean won have risen in value in relations to the yuan, which makes their exports more expensive vis-à-vis the Chinese. It also hurts the United States which cannot make up the deficit which it has with China.

Democracy in China?

While expansion of democratic participation by the masses in China is not likely to happen soon because the Chinese Communist Party is afraid it would lead to their loss of political control and economic benefits and to social chaos, the selectorate will probably enact cautious reforms which will allow the government to deal with the challenges that come with economic development. They are making new rules to make competition within the party less violent: victors absorb the followers of the losers in a party power struggle; mandatory retirement of party and government officials at age 65; term limits to increase middle-age, college-educated technocrats, to

avoid generational and ideological conflicts, and nepotism. The Chinese have also shifted from mass, bloody repression such as Mao's Great Leap Forward in 1958 and the Cultural Revolution of 1966 to 1976 to more selective repression.

The big challenge in China is how to modernize the economy while restructuring political institutions simultaneously in a country without a tradition of peaceful resolution of conflict among the elite, or norms governing the politics between parts of the government, and without popular political participation and concern for human rights. Will a more capitalistic economy undermine the Communist dictatorship, or will the dictatorship use the material gains from capitalism to strengthen its control?

Chinese Foreign Policy: Regional Hegemony or Peaceful Coexistence?

China's elite might decide to reduce internal dissent and unrest by promoting nationalism internally as it creates foreign policy conflicts externally. This could tend to unite the Chinese population. The military's long-term goals probably include the following: consolidate its control over **Hong Kong and Macao;** take over **Taiwan,** even if it is by force; control the southern approaches to the **Japan-Taiwan Straits** and to the **Luzon Straits;** dominate the mainland of Southeast and East Asia; manipulate a united **Korea** and eliminate American troops from East Asia; and **extend its power into the South China Sea, now divided among Vietnam, Malaysia, Brunei and the Philippines, so that it can pressure the only viable international sea-lanes connecting the Pacific with the Indian Ocean, close to the waters off Singapore and Indonesia. These goals would place China in conflict with the United States, whose major objective is to prevent any country from gaining overwhelming power in Asia.**

In the short term, the Chinese have had to moderate their goals, for the Gulf War of 1991 and the Iraqi War of 2003 proved to them how far behind the United States they are in military technology. This might have led them to increase trade with the United States, to accelerate transfer of technology to China, and to work on reducing anti-Chinese feelings in the U.S. government.

They have also begun an unprecedented arms buildup, spending from $87 to $100 billion a year on defense. They are buying Russian destroyers with cruise missiles, SU-27 fighter bombers, and kilo-class submarines.

The Chinese have built 34 modern warships and developed a fleet of M-9 and M-11 mobile-launched missiles. They have bought previously-banned U.S. missile technology. **They rank as the world's third largest nuclear power in the number of delivery vehicles.**

China is now too weak to upset the balance of power in Asia, but it can intimidate its smaller neighbors and threaten American interests in the region by increasing the cost needed for their defense. For now, it is a status-quo power wisely consolidating existing relations with Russia, North and South Korea, Thailand, Burma, Indochina, Central Asia, and South Asia. **Most countries recognize that China naturally will be dominant in the mainland of East Asia. Yet, they fear that China will also try to be hegemonic in the maritime regions of East and Southeast Asia.**

At present, China cannot dominate the **East China Sea** because its land-based air power (F8-11 and Russian SU-27's) is primitive and no match against U.S. jets and the Japanese F-2 fighter jets. Japan has superior air-to-air missiles, advanced AWACS, and surface ships. On the other hand, China can be a threat to the northern reaches of the South China Sea, which include the waters east of Vietnam and the Paracel Islands contested by China, Vietnam and Taiwan. This area is within the range of Chinese land-based aircraft. **However, the southern reaches of the South China Sea—including Malaysia, Singapore, Indonesia and the Philippines—are presently beyond the reach of China's land-based aircraft.** The Chinese would lose in a conflict with Singapore, Malaysia, and Indonesia, which have U.S. and British aircrafts.

China will need **aircraft carriers** to be a power in the South China Sea, capable of challenging America there and in the strategic sea lanes farther south. Yet, China lacks modern technology (power plant, avionics, etc.), advanced pilot skills, funding, system engineering and managerial skills to deploy a carrier before 2005–2010, and it will not be able to secure the minimum of three carriers necessary to project power until at least 2020.

China already has serious conflicts with its neighbors: with Taiwan, 100 miles off the Chinese coast; with Vietnam over the Paracel Islands and the demarcation of the Gulf of Tonkin; with Malaysia, Brunei, the Philippines, and Vietnam, over the oil-rich Spratly Islands; with Japan over the Diaoyu Islands; with India over territories in Kashmir; and with Tibet, which China forcefully annexed.

China-US Tensions

Relations with the United States have also suffered for the following reasons: the desire of President Bush to create a missile defense to protect the United States could neutralize China's small nuclear force of eighteen long-range missiles; the decision of the United States to allow the visit of Taiwanese President Chen Shui-bian to New York and Houston upset the Chinese; the collision of a US reconnaissance plane and a Chinese jet fighter over the South China Sea on April 11, 2001, increased tensions; allegations of Chinese espionage and illegal campaign donations in the United States; the U.S. bombing of the Chinese embassy in Belgrade in May 1999; the American decision to keep China from obtaining the fastest computers and best weapons; the American willingness to sell high-tech weapons to Taiwan; and the growing Chinese presence in the Western Hemisphere selling weapons and explosives to Cuba in 2001, acquiring ports at both ends of the Panama Canal, and venturing into intelligence, oil-drilling, and satellite business in Cuba, Peru, Venezuela and Brazil. The Chinese also have over 10,000 troops in Africa. They help support oil-rich dictators and guarantee a regular supply of energy.

The Chinese Gross Domestic Product (GDP) is $8.9 trillion. It dedicates 3.8% of its GDP to military expenditures. If China were to double its GDP in the next decade, then it would match the military expenditures of the United States. This parity will come in twenty years. **China hopes to challenge American global dominance by producing high quality goods and technology, and by venturing into areas such as war in cyberspace, the oceans and space, where U.S. superiority presently exists.** China had its first space manned space rocket in 2003 and its second in 2005. They are extracting information technology from the West and developing a submarine force to threaten the American fleet. Their $100 billion trade agreement with Iran by which China will provide it with military goods and manufactures in exchange for oil, provides support for a terrorist state which is on the verge of developing nuclear weapons which can threaten American forces and allies.

Other tensions with China are over the seven-member **Shanghai Co-Operation Organization** which includes China, Russia, and Central Asian states, and which might deny the United States valuable energy resources in the region. China also has 700 short-range ballistic missiles facing Taiwan, which is an American ally. In addition, Chinese General Zhu Chenghu threatened to send missiles to 100 American cities if there is a war over Taiwan. The United States is also very concerned about the sale of Russian strategic bombers to China. Furthermore, there is also an awareness by the United States of China's efforts in Africa to support dictatorships with military assets in return for energy resources. The Chinese are now just miles away from the United States exploring for oil north of Cuba. Interesting enough, there are Chinese companies operating some of the ports in the United States itself.

China in 2005 signed an accord with the **Association of Southeast Asian Nations** (ASEAN) to create the world's largest free trade area (2 billion people) by 2010. This will combine ASEAN's $1 trillion economy with China's $7.7 trillion economy creating $140 billion in trade by 2010. Today ASEAN-US trade and ASEAN-EU trade are $120 billion and $110 billion, respectively. They hope to build an Asian community like the EU by 2020. Australia, Japan, New Zealand and South Korea will also explore trade talks with ASEAN. **The accord between ASEAN and China could diminish American and Japanese influence in Southeast Asia.**

This region has very important sea lanes crucial for the delivery of oil and other vital raw materials to China, the United States and its allies. China will use its vast market as a way to gain influence among ASEAN countries. China has recently begun to use **"soft power":** that is, benign, peaceful diplomacy with the countries of ASEAN to avoid pushing them into closer ties with the United States.

If China ends up dominating the Korean Peninsula and a significant part of continental Southeast Asia, it would still not pose a great danger as long as Europe, the Persian Gulf, Japan, India and Russia remain as independent power centers and the United States retains naval footholds in Southeast Asia, such as in Singapore, the Philippines, and Indonesia. Therefore, China does not present now the same type of threat to the free world that Russia posed during the Cold War.

There are also factors which might prevent serious out-of-control conflicts between China and the United States. China exports to the United States over $270 billion annually, which is 26% of its exports or 12% of its GDP. China is one of the best export markets for the U.S. China buys over 7%, or $350 billion, of America's Treasury Securities. So both countries are becoming economically interdependent. They also have foreign policy objectives in common, at least in the short-term: preservation of **mutually-assured destruction** so that both countries can damage each other in a conflict; stability in the **Taiwan Straits** and a peaceful resolution of the Taiwan issue; **denuclearization and unification of the Korean Peninsula; preservation of the US-Japan alliance,** and the maintenance of Japan's non-nuclear state; peaceful settlement of China's maritime disputes with it neighbors, and the preservation of freedom of commercial navigation in the South China Seas; and the preservation of economic openness in East Asia.

However, for the United States to accept the rise of China in the East, while at the same time creating stability in the area, it must do the following: do not threaten China with a first-strike nuclear capability; do not permit Taiwan to be threatened by China, but do not permit Taiwan to become formally independent; maintain alliances and security arrangements with Australia, Japan, the Philippines, Singapore, South Korea, and Thailand; and maintain US maritime supremacy in East Asia to balance Chinese land supremacy in Asia.

The economy of communist China has been growing at 10% a year for a decade, and in 2010 became the second largest economy in the world. This has great consequences in world geo-politics for it means that China can use its great resources to compete against the United States in many areas: diplomacy; conventional and nuclear weapons to project power in Southeast Asia, Africa, and elsewhere; space technologies; the purchase of American corporations; and the creation of massive trade blocks. China can support dictators who provide her with energy supplies. They also buy American debt which compromises U.S. financial and military and political actions affecting China.

However, much of the economic success of China could be compromised if the United States Congress begins to tax the imports coming from the Chinese. This protectionist trade policy would motivate many American corporations not to move to China to produce cheap goods. Protectionism would create significant changes in the world economy and might lead to trade wars. However, it could also lead to the return of manufacturing development in the United States and higher economic growth.

Hong Kong

When Hong Kong was transferred in 1997 from the United Kingdom to the People's Republic of China (Communist China), there was great optimism about the possibility that this tiny bastion of free enterprise would gradually serve to liberalize a China that seemed to want a greater opening to the world. "One country, two systems" was the mantra repeated by the Communists in Beijing as they promised to respect the democratic system in Hong Kong for fifty years. Now people are worried that Hong Kong's new **anti-subversion laws** might be used to increase authoritarianism and even to prevent the pledge for full democracy after 2007 which is mentioned in the constitution for Hong Kong.

Hong Kong in 2010 is an economy in decline with rising unemployment and inflation. Poverty has risen to 10%. The middle class is squeezed by low-wage Chinese competition. There is a higher need to import food. Political reforms have been shelved. The direct election of the chief executive will not happen before 2017.

Taiwan

Taiwan is an island south of China taken over by the Nationalist Chinese when in 1949 they lost the civil war against the Communist Chinese. From 1950 to 1979, the United States was ready to go to war to protect Taiwan. In June 1979, it broke relations with Taiwan to formally recognize the People's Republic of China (Communist China), but through the **Taiwan Relations Act** of the same year, the United States pledged to provide it with the means to defend itself. The Chinese have said they will attack Taiwan if it rejects the One-China policy of the Communists and seeks independence. Communist China does not let Taiwan play a role in the United Nations, even as an "observer" like the Red Cross or the Palestinian Liberation Organization (PLO). It will not even allow Taiwan to join the World Health Organization. This is even the case though Taiwan is the 17th largest economy and the first Chinese-speaking democracy.

President Chen, whose political constituency is Taiwanese and not Chinese, won again the Presidency of Taiwan on March 20, 2004, by 30,000 votes. Chen has promised not to push for outright independence, but he has said privately that Taiwan is already independent. He believes that Taiwan needs a new constitution. This has made China nervous. In May 22, 2004, President Chen declared that he would be willing to stabilize relations with China and engage in talks. A week before, on May 17, 2004, China threatened Taiwan's twenty-three million people with total destruction if Chen did not moderate his independence rhetoric. **China has 700 missiles directed to Taiwan.** In fact, one day before the Taiwanese election of March 20, 2004, China held joint naval exercises with France's navy, as a means of intimidating the Taiwanese.

China will fight to prevent the independence of Taiwan for it fears that if it does not, independence movements in Inner Mongolia, Tibet and Xinjiang, all parts of China, will gain momentum. China also feels that Taiwan belongs to China since it exercised effective control over it after the 1660s and actually became a Chinese province from 1887 to 1895. China will go along with the status quo in Taiwan but not with Taiwanese independence. On the other hand the United States will defend Taiwan if China attacks it, but it will not support Taiwanese independence at this time.

The United States pursues **"strategic ambiguity,"** by recognizing the principle of one China and two systems and maintaining the status quo while protecting Taiwan. The United States needs peaceful relations with China to keep Asia prosperous, to resolve the North Korean nuclear crisis, to maintain peace between India and Pakistan, to continue the work against terrorism, and to promote its own economic investments in China. Interestingly, one million Taiwanese live in mainland China overseeing $140 billion in investment from Taiwan, mostly in electronics, textiles and semiconductor plants. So there is also hope that out of commercial ties, political moderation can result.

Korea

Communist North Korea invaded South Korea on June 25, 1950, unleashing a devastating war which eventually brought in China on the side of the North and the United Nations and the United States on the side of the South. From the end of the war in 1953 to June 2000, there was no meeting between the leaders of the two countries. In June 2000, South Korean President Kim Dae Jung, architect of the **Sunshine Policy** of dialogue among all Koreans, visited the leader of North Korea Kim Jong Il. The United States and Japan would not provide fuel and investment to famine-stricken North Korea unless the meeting took place. Kim Dae Jung hoped that this remarkable meeting would be followed by conversations and negotiations over North Korea's advanced weapons programs, family reunification, political prisoners and the 37,000 U.S. troops in South Korea.

On June 19, 2000, the United States lifted some economic sanctions against North Korea, and on June 21, 2000, North Korea promised to maintain a moratorium on long-range missile testing. On June 7, 2001, the North

Korean government stated that it would have a two-year moratorium on missile tests if the United States normalized relations with them. They also wanted the United States to build two nuclear reactors in North Korea.

Then, on October 2002 North Korea acknowledged it had secretly been producing highly enriched uranium for developing nuclear weapons. It said this would help North Korea reduce the cost of the one million soldier army it cannot afford. This declaration undermined a long diplomatic effort by the United Nations and the United States. Since the 1980s, North Korea has had a nuclear program producing enough plutonium for two bombs.

Yet, this was a reversal of official North Korean policy. In 1985, it did join the **Nuclear Non-Proliferation Treaty** (NPTP). In 1991, the United States got North Korea to accept inspection under the Nuclear non-Proliferation Treaty, but it could not account for all the plutonium. North Korea signed a verification agreement with the **International Atomic Energy Agency** (IAEC). The IAEC found plutonium discrepancies. In 1993, North Korea withdrew from the NNPT and stated it would begin to separate enough plutonium from its 8,000 used fuel rods at its nuclear reactor in Yong Byon to make nuclear weapons. Negotiations led to the **1994 Agreed Framework** with the United States by which North Korea agreed to stop plutonium production and construction on two larger reactors, while the United States agreed to provide them with light-water reactors for electricity generation as well as oil and humanitarian aid shipments. In December 2002, North Korea once more left the NPT when inspectors from the **International Atomic Energy Agency** sought to inspect possible violations in the program for uranium enrichment.

The decision of North Korea to produce nuclear weapons could be a bluff, **a bargaining chip,** to get non-intervention, security guarantees from the United States, or a means of extracting humanitarian assistance from concerned countries, such as South Korea, Japan, Russia, China and the United States. The GDP per capita is $1,700 in contrast to the $20,400 GDP per capita in capitalist South Korea. There are 23 million North Koreans facing starvation and repression. Two million have starved in the last ten years. No one wants North Korea to collapse and send millions of refugees into South Korea and China.

As of 2010, North Korea could have plutonium for at least 10 nuclear weapons. **In October 2006, North Korea let off a small-yield plutonium bomb, becoming the ninth member of the nuclear-weapons club.**

When the crisis began in 2002, it had enough for two weapons. It has now kicked out inspectors, reprocessed 8,000 spent fuel rods into weapon grade plutonium, and threatened to strike the West Coast of the United States. There is a concern that North Korea might sell nuclear technology to terrorist organizations. It is a gangster nation which makes over $1 billion counterfeiting US green-backs, illicit narcotics, and contraband cigarettes. It cooperates with Chinese gangs, the Japanese Yakuza and the Russian mafia. Its Bureau No. 39 smuggles heroin, methamphetamines, gold, diamonds, weapons, ivory and rhino horns. Nuclear technology could be next.

The **Beijing Agreement** of February 13, 2007, by the Six Party talks led North Korea to agree to shut down its Yong Byon nuclear facility—the fissile material source of the plutonium bomb—in exchange for $300 million in fuel aid and direct talks with Washington to lead to normalization of relations and an armistice to officially end the Korean War. This is a dramatic reversal of previous U.S. foreign policy. Critics argue that this agreement does not address the North Korean uranium-based nuclear weapons program and how to get rid of existing nuclear weapons. There are no details about verification for facilities other than those at Yong Byon. As of 2010, North Korea had not allowed full verification of its nuclear program. Other critics believe that China and North Korea are close allies and are playing games at the Six Party negotiations.

Southeast Asia

Southeast Asian countries used to receive 75% of the foreign direct investment going to Asia. In 2006, they received less than 10% because a large amount has been redirected to China or to India. This economic competition has stimulated greater cooperation among the ten countries of the **Association of Southeast Asian Nations (ASEAN):** Brunei, Burma, Cambodia, Indonesia, Laos, Malaysia, Philippines, Singapore, Vietnam and Cambodia. Presently, they are hoping to increase trade with China to take advantage of its expanding economy. These are countries which have great oil and gas resources, a relatively skilled labor force, but they also have widespread corruption, nepotism, collusion and an increasing presence of terrorists linked with al-Qaeda. The Chinese Accord with ASEAN to create the world's largest free trade area could have significant impact in either moderating China's expansionism or in further expanding its interest in the South China Sea.

Some observations about ASEAN can be made. First, post-9/11 US foreign policy has tried to unite the region against Islamic terrorist groups, particularly those in Indonesia, Malaysia, Philippines and Thailand, but did not develop a strategic policy regarding China. Second, ASEAN countries do not want to become an explicit security alliance led by the United States to encircle China, even though they do want the United States involved **multilaterally** with other states to promote stability. Third, ASEAN countries want institutions for the peaceful settlement of disputes, including those among member states. Fourth, the leadership of these countries tends to reject Western notions of individual and political rights. Fifth, while these countries, attracted by the promise of economic gains, do not want to be part of a containment policy against China, they do not want to be part of a security alliance with China that excludes Australia, Japan and the United States, among others.

India: Emergence of the "New Politics"

India occupies most of the Indian Subcontinent in South Asia. The Himalayan Mountains, highest in the world, stretch across India's northern border, keeping out the cold Siberian winds as well as massive Chinese penetration. Below, the Ganges Plain is a wide, fertile and among the most densely populated region in the world. Toward the west, increasingly drier lands blend into Pakistan, and toward the east wetter lands lead into Bangladesh. The area to the south of the northern plains includes the Deccan Peninsula.

The population of India is a little above 1.1 billion, 72% Indo-Aryan, and 25% Dravidian. Only 28% of the population is urban. The principal religions are Hinduism (83%), Islam (13%), Christianity (2%), and Sikhism (2%). The official language is Hindi, although English is an associate official language. India is a federal republic with 25 states and seven union territories. It is headed by a Prime Minister.

India is a 5,000-year-old civilization and a young country, a great experiment in democracy for sixty-one years while preserving its unity and integrity. **There was a consensus from 1947 to the 1960s that India should be a secular, socialist, democratic republic with a centrally planned economy that emphasized the public sector over the private and heavy industry over agri-**

culture. In addition, the new party would be the **Congress Party** led by Jawaharl Nehru. The political system was controlled by an English-speaking, urban educated elite who were shrewd users of information and capital, a condition which harmonized with the brahminist concept of a power hierarchy and leadership. There was a fusion of professional classes—lawyers, politicians, academicians, bureaucrats—and family-run business houses. Their mastery of the English language gave them a sense of exclusivity which separated the elite from the masses.

The Congress Party kept the colonial administration system. This would be a major contradiction in the political system: Indian democracy in a multicultural state within a British-styled, socialist, centralized colonial administration. The introduction of the centrally-planned economy (license-permit raj) made the elite dependent on the survival of the system. Politicians dictated what could be done, and what people could have. Administrators advised and delayed decisions. Big business houses were happy to be in a noncompetitive economy and pleased the politicians and bureaucrats with cash compensation. The system produced some positive contributions: a democratic framework for elections; freedom of expression and the right to vote for all over the age of twenty-one; a tradition of pluralism in Indian culture; a good British legal and administrative system; multiple veto powers and checks and balances to reflect the diversity of the population; and lack of famines in fifty years thanks to the unrestricted flow of communications and information.

Yet, 40% of the population of a billion people is in abject poverty, with a national literacy rate of only 52%. The rate of economic growth until 1980 had raised per capita income by a mere 1.5% annually. Gradually, the legitimacy of the system and of the Congress Party began to be questioned. **Linguistically defined states (there are seventeen officially recognized languages in India) began to seek more political decentralization.** China defeated India in 1962 and took a portion of Kashmir. Bad weather in 1965 and 1966 led to decline in food production and to hunger. Corruption and centralization reduced economic growth. Then, in 1975 Prime Minister Indira Gandhi suspended democracy and declared a state of emergency.

As a result, the Congress Party began to lose elections in 1967 and, after its major 1989 electoral defeat coalition government began to be typical of national politics. Congress had ruled India for 44 of its past 50 years. The rise of coalition politics reflects the diversity or mosaic of Indian society. The old elite could not cope with the demands of democracy. All parties now are regional parties. There are 40 odd parties based on religion, geographical region, language, and caste.

At present, there is a difficult transition from a centralized economy and a monolithic nationwide political system, run by a privileged, English-speaking elite, into a new era of decentralizing economy and regional, identity-based coalition politics. There is democracy at election times, but between elections there is institutional decay, lack of public accountability, deteriorating infrastructure, decline in educational standards, and problems in sanitation and public health.

India needs to grow economically 8 to 10% per year to lift up the 400 million of its one billion people who live with less than one dollar per day. Perhaps if the Indian states can begin to compete with each other and reduce government regulations, the stagnant Indian North can catch up to the dynamic Indian South. India is Asia's fastest growing economy. It is linking economically with the Association of Southeast Asian Nations (ASEAN).

Hindu Nationalism. The **Bharatya Janata Party (BJP),** whose phrase "one nation, one people, and culture" supports the idea of India as a Hindu nation, and seeks to undermine the old ideal of India as a secularist, pluralistic country. This Hindu nationalism has brought significant tension in a country of over 770 million Hindus and 120 million Muslims. A significant amount of violence has taken place against Christians and Muslims. The BJP made it a crime to convert the "untouchables" to Christianity by so-called "allurements". Conversion by religious priests is forbidden. The BJP is an upper-caste Brahim dominated party that is also pro-business and in favor of a free-market economy. However, it seeks to limit foreign investment to infrastructure projects (power plants, roads, etc.). It wants to protect Indian companies from takeover by multinationals.

The Congress Party won the May 2004 elections with a coalition of communists and regional parties. In fact, the Communists gained 62 seats in the 543-seat lower House. The voters apparently rejected the policies of BJP which stressed intelligence technologies, telecommunication advances, road building projects to unite the territory, pro-business capitalism and freer markets, or perhaps they wanted all these but also more popular, grass-roots policies. The Communists immediately proposed policies to stop foreign investments in the insurance, banking, and retail sectors, to raise taxes on corporations, to stop privatization of the public sector, and to increase subsidies to the rural population.

However, when the Indian stock market lost 20% of its value and money began to flee the country after the election, the Congress Party, to reassure the business community, selected economist Manmohan Singh as Prime Minister. He had been Finance Minister between 1991 and 1996 and had pushed many free-market reforms. Singh as a Sikh, is the first religious minority Prime Minister in Indian history. He needs to attract foreign investment into India. Yet, to do so Singh will have to reduce India's fiscal deficit, overhaul restrictive labor practices, and end the bureaucratic harassing of business (the "inspector raj"), all practices which the Communist Left will oppose. His friendly relationship with the United States might also be unpopular with the Congress Party.

The Rise of Nuclear Weapons in South Asia. The Indian decision on September 10, 1996, to vote against a **United Nations Comprehensive Test Ban Treaty (CTBT)** engendered controversy. This was a reversal of India's traditional position since 1954. The treaty would have suspended all nuclear tests. India has even started developing a nuclear test site in Pokran. The reversal might have been a reaction to the United States' **Brown Amendment** of 1995, which allows military and economic assistance to Pakistan, India's main rival in South Asia. The United States had cut arms and supplies to Pakistan in 1991 because of its belief that Pakistan, with Arab funding and Chinese support, was building an "Islamic" nuclear bomb. India saw the Brown amendment as a renewal of U.S.-Pakistan military ties. India also justified its aggressive nuclear policy by claiming that the Clinton Administration helped China, an enemy, modernize its nuclear sector. **India, together with Pakistan and Israel, has also opposed the Non-Proliferation Treaty to contain the spread of nuclear weapons.**

The BJP tested various nuclear bombs in May 1998, claiming that the Russians have 877 nuclear ICBMs, each with numerous warheads, and 452 submarine-based nuclear weapons, and that China has 17 ICBMs and 38 IRBM (intermediate range ballistic missiles), and that India has to protect its national interests. In response, in May 1998 Pakistan also tested some nuclear bombs. These actions could be evidence that arms control treaties do not by themselves control the spread of modern arms. When states feel threatened, they put national security first. The Pakistani action might convince Iran, its competitor over Afghanistan and Central Asia, to also acquire nuclear weapons. It also motivated North Korea to want to break out of an agreement with the United States which froze its nuclear programs.

Pakistan and Kashmir

When the British left India in 1947, most of the Muslims there separated from the Hindus to create East and West Pakistan. From 500,000 to 3 million people died in the fighting. Yet, many Muslims remained within India, particularly in the territory of Kashmir. Pakistan went into war, first in 1948 and again in 1965, in an effort to seize Kashmir, but succeeded only in dividing the region along the **Line of Control,** leaving a large Muslim population in Indian-occupied Kashmir. Later, in 1977, East Pakistan separated from West Pakistan and created the Muslim country of **Bangladesh.** The current conflict over Kashmir began in 1989, when India intervened directly in the territory, triggering a popular uprising of Kashmiris that was met with force. Then around 1990, Pakistan's military embarked upon a covert war in Kashmir to bleed India and force it to leave the area.

Yet, India's attitude toward Kashmir has hardened, particularly after Pakistan sent in 1999 jihadists and troops across the Line of Control. Then, in October 2001, Islamic terrorists from Pakistan attacked the Kashmir state legislature, on December 13, 2001, Islamic terrorists attacked the Indian Parliament itself, killing various members, and in May 2002, they attacked a Kaluchak army base. Also, in April 2002, Pakistan tested two missiles capable of reaching neighboring India. General Pervez Musharraf, then the military leader of Pakistan, was in a tough spot. He moved against those members of the **Interservices Intelligence (ISI) Agency** who helped create the Taliban in Afghanistan when the United States left that country in 1989.

However, Musharraf did not move decisively against domestic terrorists in Pakistan itself, possibly because they backed his policy of undermining Indian control of Kashmir. While Musharraf supported the Bush policy against the Taliban, al Qaeda and other "foreign" terrorists, it is obvious his military is far from controlling the entire territory of Pakistan, and has not been able to defeat terrorists fleeing Afghanistan. **In fact, two of the four provinces of Pakistan, the Northwest Frontier Province and Western Baluchistan are falling under the control of Islamists.** This Talibanization could spread to the other provinces. The two assassination attempts against Musharraf in December 2003 convinced him to strike against both domestic and foreign terrorists. He even sent in 2004 military troops into the Northwest Frontier Province to pursue the Taliban and defeat al-Qaeda linked terrorists.

Musharaff was swept from power in 2008 by the elections won by the Pakistan People's Party whose leader, Benazir Bhutto, was killed in December 27, 2007. The United States wasted $5.4 billion on Musharaff since 2001, who appeased the terrorists, did not deploy the army efficiently in the Northern territories and Waziristan, and did not purge the Islamists from the army and the intelligence services. He repressed democrats which has now made the United States very unpopular in Pakistan.

Ultimately, peace might come to Kashmir when Pakistan ceases to promote terrorism there, and India decides that it might be best to divide Kashmir, perhaps by the Chenab River, and allow people to move freely between the two new secular and independent regions. Possibly, the United States can mediate this dispute and allow both India's and Pakistan's leaders to "save face" by blaming the Americans for whatever tough decisions both must make. President Pervez Musharraf's visit to India on April 17, 2005, his first visit to India since 2001, and the first peace negotiations since 2004 are a significant first step in the reduction of tension over Kashmir and terrorism.

The Pakistani military has three major strategies: first is to use Islam as a means of unifying the country; second is to engage India as its main rival; and third is to ally itself with the United States to get funding. Pakistan has received more than $10 billion in military and economic aid since 2001. As a poor country of 166 million and a GDP per capita of $2,400, Pakistan can use the help. However, critics argue that US assistance to the Pakistani military is preventing the establishment of a democratic civil society. The big concern for others is the possibility Pakistan could collapse and its nuclear weapons fall into the control of Islamic terrorists.

Of great interest is the $4 billion oil pipeline Pakistan is aiming to build with gas-rich Iran which could also link with India. This might create greater trust between India and Pakistan. Naturally, Iran might be trying to get support from India as it is pressured to abandon its nuclear program by the United States. It might also be trying to undermine Pakistan's support for US anti-terrorist policies.

And yet, this pipeline might not extend to India after all because on March 5, 2006, India and the United States signed an agreement by which the

United States will sell nuclear technology to India, and India will open 14 of its 22 nuclear reactors to international inspectors. This agreement could be followed by Indian-American free trade deals. This will reinvigorate the US nuclear reactor industry, try to make India self-sufficient in energy, and strengthen ties between the two countries. However, on October 12, 2007, Prime Minister Singh of India, pressured by the Communists in his coalition who do not want close relations with the United States, decided to slow down the negotiations over the nuclear deal.

The Congress Party was hostile to the United States during the Cold War when it pursued a non-aligned policy which still inclined more to the Soviet Union than to the United States. Nevertheless, geo-political realities are different today. There might be a strategic convergence of both countries' interests. Both fear Chinese long-term dominance. China is an economic rival of India, and also a country which is developing bases and defense pacts with Bangladesh, Burma and Pakistan, thus encircling India. Both are concerned with terrorism. India is concerned with Kashmir, Nepal and Sri Lanka and with the Indo-Burma and Indo-Bangladesh borders. It sees Pakistan as the main source of terrorism and believes it needs to be democratized.

   The United States, on the other hand, sees India as an ally on the war against Islamic terrorism. The navies of both countries are patrolling the Straits of Malacca where China seeks control. They both want to keep China out of the Indian Ocean. The United States and India might also collaborate in the Persian Gulf where issues dealing with energy security, Islamic terrorism, and regional stability predominate. Yet, India fears that the war against terrorism might destabilize the Persian Gulf. Since it is in the middle of the Islamic world, it hopes for good relations with Muslim states.

   However, it is not only the United States that is courting India. Russia wants to use its ties with India as counter weight to China and the United States. Russia provides India with military hardware, nuclear technology, oil and gas. China also is increasing trade with India hoping to use it as a counter weight to Japan and the United States. As India becomes more successful economically, it hopes to stay away from serious global alliances. It is still a poor country with massive educational, energy, and transportation difficulties. India needs more investments in its financial and manufacturing sectors and greater labor flexibility.

Starting at the end of 2009 and continuing still, al-Qaeda and the Taliban began an offensive from North to Central Pakistan. It is possible that certain elements of the Pakistani security services might be assisting the Taliban's activities not only in Afghanistan but also in Pakistan itself. The fact that Pakistan has nuclear weapons makes the situation very serious. Both the United States and India are concerned about these weapons falling into the wrong hands. The radicalization of Pakistan makes the American relation with India very important. India is also investing economically in Afghanistan. As a result, Afghanistan has Iran, the United States, Pakistan, and India as major foreign players. Diplomacy there is very difficult. A case can be made that unless al-Qaeda and the Taliban are defeated in Pakistan, the war in Afghanistan will not end well for the United States and Afghanistan.

Japan: The Economic Decline of an Asian Tiger

Japan is an archipelago off the east coast of Asia. It has Russia on its north and South Korea on its west. Japan consists of four main islands. The population is 127 million, of which 99.4% is Japanese. The urban population is 52%. The principal language is Japanese. The main religions are Buddhism and Shintoism. Japan has a parliamentary democracy with the Emperor as the head of state and the Prime Minister as the head of government.

   The traditional Japanese development model has been copied throughout Asia. It was based on government nurturing of export industries by providing them with discriminatory credit and favorable taxation levels, and protecting them from import competition in domestic markets by means of import quotas, tariffs, and non-tariff barriers such as unfair custom procedures, restrictions on foreign industries, and bidding on government contracts.

   The model advocated that exports should exceed imports so that there is a surplus in its current account. The Japanese policy triangle made up of bureaucrats, business leaders and politicians coincide in the support of this **exported strategy** which created over $220 billion in foreign reserves. However, it has also led to the production of excess capacity in steel, autos, chemicals, semiconductors, rubber and other exports and to a more expensive lifestyle for the average Japanese for they cannot buy many cheaper imports. It also led to great political corruption.

This economic system grew at an annual rate of 10% in the decade leading to 1973, at 4% between 1973 and 1991, but between 1992 and 1995 at only 0.6%, and has been relatively stagnant ever since. It has averaged 1% growth up to 2007. The Japanese deflation of the past decade followed a period of great speculation. As Japan in the 1980s began to move abroad many of its investments to capitalize on cheaper wages and to circumvent protectionist policies against Japanese goods, Japanese business had less need for bank loans. So many Japanese banks went into real estate lending, stocks, and loans to politicians. As more money went into real estate and stocks, the value of land, real estate, and stocks increased out of control, creating a bubble economy. The government reacted to this financial exuberance by reducing the supply of money. In 1987, the growth in the money supply was 13%, but in 1990 it was only 3%, in 1991 0% growth, and by 1994 there was actually less money in the economy. **This radical contraction in the money supply burst the bubble and threw the Japanese economy into a deflationary recession.**

This situation was made worse by the $630 billion in bad loans made by the Japanese banks to Japanese politicians, business, as well as to business interests in South Korea, Thailand, and Indonesia. The Japanese government made the financial crisis even worse by bailing out some of the bankrupt banks which then continued making irresponsible loans. As a result, the bad loans added up to $800 billion by 2003. Meanwhile the public debt of Japan went over 100% of its GDP. The Japanese economic crisis and its unwillingness to buy more goods from Southeast Asia would be factors behind the **Asian Crisis of 1997 and 1998** since Japan represented approximately 66% of the economy of East Asia. Presently, Japan is pumping money into its economy in the form of public works and tax cuts, restricting the bank system and cutting interest rates. This has led to budget deficits and debt.

What is remarkable in Japan is the gradual and limited abandonment of the traditional protectionist, centralized and over-regulatory model of development. In 1995, part of Japan's pension and foreign exchange markets were opened to foreign investors, and in 1996, under the **Big Bang Plan,** regulations which protected the core of the whole Japanese economy—banks, insurers, brokers, etc.—were abandoned. When after 1990, Japan's stocks and property markets collapsed, banks were crippled by bad loans, and pension funds began running out of money to pay retirees, the Japanese began to see deregulation and foreign investment as solutions. In the short run, they experienced unemployment bankruptcies, asset deflation, weak consumer confidence, but gradually the Japanese are becoming more competitive. Westerners are buying many Japanese assets.

A problem facing Japan is the aging of its population. By 2025, 20% of the population will be over 65 years of age. It will take 1.9 workers between 20 and 64 years old to support each person over 65. The elderly do not want to spend for they are afraid public, medical and nursing care insurance will not pay all their expenses. For this reason, the savings rate is at 10%, which reduces the Gross Domestic Product and increases unemployment. Many young people do not want to pay retirement taxes for they fear they will not receive benefits once they retire. Japanese corporations such as Toyota, Honda, Nissan, and others are not opening up new plants. Manufacturing is moving to China. Homelessness is emerging in once-proud Japan. Productivity could compensate for the decrease in population, but it has been less than 1% for the past ten years. People might not want many children because of the long hours of office work, few day care facilities, and the high cost of children's education. In addition, the Japanese do not like immigration. Foreigners are only 1.4% of the population.

Intra-Asian Trade

In spite of all its recent troubles, Japan is still the third-largest world economy. It is a $5 trillion economy, or 2/5 the size of the American one. China and India combined have 18 times more people, but their combined national economies are less than one-third of Japan's. A 3.4% Japanese expansion matches a 10% growth rate in both China and India. Japan's recovery can be attributed greatly to its booming sales to China. In 2009 for example, Japan exported more to China, Hong Kong and Taiwan than to the United States. This has not happened since 1873. However, oil prices could choke off the recovery. Japan imports 99% of its oil. The East China Sea has oil, but both China and Japan want it, as well as other countries, and will have to compete for it. The countries of Asia have become more integrated, with China's manpower and low costs united with the money and technology of Japan, South Korea, Hong Kong, Taiwan and Singapore. These five countries account for most of the investment in China. There is almost an informal Asian union with the same size as the $12 trillion European Union.

Japanese Foreign Policy and the United States

The United States and Japan had a very special, cooperative diplomatic relationship during the Cold War. Japan's foreign policy was based on the **Yoshida Doctrine** which allowed the United States to protect Japan while it concentrated on economics, science and technology. **One difficulty between the two countries is the American complaint that the over \$5 billion Japan pays to the United States to keep U.S. troops there does not pay for the entire cost of equipment, personnel and research expenses.** It wants increased **burden-sharing** on the part of Japan. The Japanese public might not support this change. The majority oppose U.S. troops in Japan in the first place. This might lead the United States, which is already impatient over its trade deficit with Japan, to remove some of its troops. Then, the more expensive **Japanese Strategic Defense Forces (SDF)** might have to increase in size above the present 240,000 troops.

Presently, defense spending in Japan cannot exceed 1% of the GNP by law, and Article 9 of the Constitution renounces war. If the United States withdraws from the region, will the Japanese push above the spending limits for defense spending? Most Japanese now are against it. Yet, increased **nationalism** on the part of a new generation of Japanese, without guilt about Japan's excesses during World War II, might reduce the political restraints on militarization. The elimination of Article 9 would require increased popular support, two-thirds majority in both chambers of the legislature and at least 51% of the vote in a referendum.

The huge Japanese economic investment in Southeast Asia might affect Japan's national security by pulling the SDF's role and mission farther south. **The Japanese Susuki Sea-Lane Doctrine emphasizes protection of sea routes plus the need to defend 90,000 Japanese nationals and over \$60 billion of foreign direct investment in Southeast Asia.** (A War Contingency Bill passed in 2003 will give Japan more responsibility for its security as new laws increase the central power in times of war to respond to terrorism and to North Korea's nuclear and missile programs.) Much of this change in foreign policy has been the result of the intrusion in May 2004 of a Chinese nuclear submarine into Japanese waters. Also, there was in 2005 intrusion by Chinese military surveillance aircrafts.

A declining American presence could make Japan accelerate the development and deployment of ballistic missile defense systems. The Japanese are concerned about the Chinese arsenal of over 300 warheads which can easily reach Japan. **They are worried about persistent Chinese nuclear testing and exports of nuclear technology.** However, the Japanese and the United States agreed in 2006 to develop a new type of missile interceptor. It is clear that the U.S.-Japanese special relation needs readjustments. Japan does not agree with U.S. aid to Israel and might not support the United States in a war with China over Taiwan—though it would help if communist North Korea attacks capitalist South Korea. The Japanese will insist on prior consultation during crises and will demand limited commitments on its part. The Japanese also tend to be critical of U.S. policy in Iraq, its apparent disdain for the United Nations and, what appears to them, America's unilateral foreign policy.

The United States will have to assure Japan of its support to avoid massive Japanese rearmament and a more independent foreign policy, which could create an arms race and regional instability in Asia. The nuclear testing by India and Pakistan might destabilize the region as China could support both Pakistan and North Korea. On the other hand, the United States, which has 100,000 troops in Asia, needs bases in Japan if it is to defend it. The United States cannot help Japan from faraway bases in Hawaii and Guam. And Japan needs to make commitments to the United States on certain contingencies. Both need to readjust the one-way flow of American military technology to Japan, which gives the United States less leverage, reduces American industrial competitiveness, and results in other inequities.

Although Japan and the United States have serious concerns about future Chinese expansion in the region, other countries in East Asia and Southeast Asia do not want outright confrontation with China. They prefer to trade with it and envelop China in multilayered international organizations to moderate its foreign policy. The ten countries of **ASEAN** would like to create an **ASEAN +3** to allow cooperation with China, Japan and North Korea. The new **Northeast-Asian Security Dialogue** includes China, South Korea and Japan. The United States used to discourage regional arrangements which excluded them, such as the East-Asian Economic Caucus (EAEC), but it might be changing its view.

However, all countries in the area, especially Japan, still want the American presence in the region to deter North Korea and China, if peaceful diplomacy fails. In addition to close relations with United States and

Australia, Japan might be getting closer to a former enemy, Russia, as it might be willing to exchange Japanese investment for Russian oil. This relationship could also prove fruitful if China becomes a threat to Japan.

What seems to be happening in the 2010–2011 period is increased collaboration of Japan with the United States and an assertion of Japanese power globally. The Japanese might revise Article 9 of the Constitution, create a stronger Executive, and establish a Ministry of State for the Self-Defense Agency. They have sent troops to Mozambique in 1993–1995, to Rwanda in 1994, to the Golan Heights in 1995, and East Timor from 2001 to 2004. They are conducting naval operations in the Indian Ocean, and are supportive of Taiwan. Its military spending is the third largest in the world. They are discussing the possibility of developing nuclear weapons and venturing into outer space. They are modernizing the military which is at the level of France's.

Perhaps the most important priority for the Japanese is to strengthen their economy. In 2010, they saw their greatest rival, China, become the second largest economy in the world. This has great consequences for the regional balance of power. The Chinese were able to do this due to the stagnation of the Japanese economy which is negatively impacted by demographic decline, excessive government spending and debt, bureaucratic dysfunction, and inefficient banks.

Europe

Europe can be divided into the following areas: **Western Europe** (France, the United Kingdom, and Ireland), with 125 million people; the **Lotharingean States** (the Netherlands, Belgium, Luxembourg and Switzerland), with 34 million; **Northern Europe** (Denmark, Norway, Sweden, Finland, and Iceland), with 24 million; **Iberia** (Spain, Portugal, Andorra, and Gibraltar), with 51 million; **Middle Europe** (Italy, San Marino, and Germany), with 140 million; **East-Central Europe** (Austria, Liechtenstein, Poland, the Czech Republic, Slovakia and Hungary), with 71 million; and **Southeast Europe** (Yugoslavia, Slovenia, Croatia, Bosnia and Herzegovina, Macedonia, Romania, Bulgaria, Albania and Greece), with 66 million.

The most important events in contemporary Europe—aside from the collapse of communism in "Eastern" Europe in 1989—are the continuous expansion of the European Union, the creation of Euroland, the growth of the North Atlantic Treaty Organization (NATO), and the transformation of Germany from an expansionist and nationalist Central-European power into an economically powerful country promoting the multinational or supranational integration of Europe. An additional issue is the status of Muslims and Islam in Europe. Will Muslims rule Europe within a century, or will Europe either reject them or integrate them?

The European Union (EU): The Case for Integration and Euroland

The European Union (EU) is the name of the organization for the 27 member countries that have decided to cooperate on a number of areas ranging from a single economic market, to foreign security and foreign policy, to the areas of justice and home affair, and a common currency. **The EU is the world's largest trading block with a population of over 484 million and a combined GDP larger than that of the United States.** The European Union, as an umbrella organization hosting many activities, came into existence only in November 1993, after the ratification of the **Maastricht Treaty** and after the **Schongen Agreement** of 1995.

However, the constituent organizations of the EU have a longer history; **The European Coal and Steel Community (ECSC)** established by the Treaty of Paris (1951); the **European Economic Community (EEC),** and the **European Atomic Energy Community (EURATOM)** established by the two treaties of Rome (1957), which created the European Common Market. The European Union itself derives from these two 1957 treaties. In 1967, these three institutions were merged into a single European Commission, and a single **European Parliamentary Assembly** was created, to be elected after 1979 directly by the people of all member states. Later, the **Single European Act of 1987** provided for the implementation of a single European market and promoted coordination in the sphere of foreign policy. **The Maastricht Treaty of 1993 re-examined the scope of the EEC to include provisions for an economic and monetary union with a single European currency from the end of the century onwards, and it changed the name of the EEC to European Community (EC).**

The EU now has 27 member states. The process of integration began in 1952 with the **European Coal and Steel Community:** Belgium, West Germany (Germany in 1991), France, Italy, Luxembourg, and the Netherlands. The **first enlargement in 1972** brought Denmark, Ireland, and the United Kingdom, while Norway again rejected membership. The **second enlargement in 1981** brought in Greece, while the **third** in 1986 brought in Portugal and Spain. The **fourth enlargement** in 1995 included Austria, Finland and Sweden, while Norway again rejected membership. The countries that entered in the **fifth enlargement** on May 1, 2004 are Cyprus, the Czech Republic, Estonia, Hungary, Latvia, Lithuania, Malta, Poland, Slovakia, and Slovenia. The **sixth enlargement** brought in Bulgaria and Romania on January 1, 2007. Iceland, Norway and Switzerland do not want to join.

The European Union is now involved in two of its riskiest projects. The first is the round of enlargement, bringing not as before, more or less prosperous "Western" European countries, but the far poorer former Communist countries of Central and Eastern Europe. The twelve new countries of the EU have increased its population by approximately 30%, but they have raised its GDP only 6%. And this enlargement has come when the economies of the union are struggling with low growth, high taxes and deficits and labor market rigidity.

Supporters of the EU enlargement believe it will promote stability and democracy in the region, is a moral obligation to help the victims of Nazism and Communism, and represents an economic opportunity for the EU in the markets to the East. Yet, there are potential problems. Could an EU of 27 member countries operate efficiently? Might some of the new members relapse into dictatorship and corruption? Would extending the present system of guaranteed prices and direct payments to farmers, if extended to the new states, bankrupt the common agricultural policy (CAP) of the EU and hurt Spain, Portugal and Greece, which presently benefit tremendously from it? Would this enlargement make unstable the former trade partners in the East of the new member states? **The last two enlargements have brought the EU close to unstable regions such as the Ukraine, Moldova, the Western Balkan, and such volatile areas as Chechnya, Georgia and Kosovo.**

There are other developmental problems. Major differences exist over the creation of an EU Constitution which must be approved by every member country. It was voted down by the Dutch and the French in 2005. Farm subsidies make up 80% of the EU budget. New members will get assistance only at the expense of the allocation to old members. The United Kingdom and Poland want NATO to be the main security organization in Europe, but France and Germany want it weakened and have the EU develop defensive capabilities to decrease American influence in Europe.

The new members want to enter the EU to share in its prosperity and to protect themselves from Russia, whenever it recovers its strength, or from Germany if it ever returns to a military expansionistic foreign policy. Yet, many Eastern European states are concerned about the high tariffs of the EU, its centralized planning, and the higher expenses they will have to pay to meet environmental regulations.

The entrance of 12 new countries into the European Union has broadened the area of common shared values: respect for individual freedoms, rule of law, equality before the law, protection of minorities, democracy, separation of government powers, political plurality, private ownership, market economies and a strong civil society.

What will have to be decided is if the European Union will become a homogenous United States of Europe, or a union which supports an inter-governmental approach and where there is a significant national sovereignty retained by each country. Already most of the states of the EU have lost the ability to control their own currency and immigration laws. The bureaucrats in Brussels are doing their best to dilute all notions of nationalism, ethnicity and national sovereignty. They are now reintroducing the previously rejected constitution with a **Lisbon Treaty** of December 2007, whose agenda is the creation of a socialist United States of Europe. These bureaucrats hope to avoid putting it to a referendum in the respective countries. Yet nationalism seems to be gaining ground among the people. The more countries which enter the EU, the more difficult it will be to establish a homogeneous unity. Following the twelve new members are other applicants: Belarus, Croatia, Macedonia, Moldova, Serbia, Turkey, and the Ukraine. Some are too corrupt, inefficient, and bureaucratic. Others are too authoritarian, poor or too large. Still others are not European.

The second risky project of the EU is the European Monetary Union (EMU), which created a single currency for the entire region. Supporters believe the new currency, the **euro**, is a logical extension of the single market, the EU's greatest achievement so far.

Germany is willing to sacrifice its strong D-mark, but in return asked for closer political union, tight rules for joining the single currency, and tough controls on borrowing by member states after entry. The Germans, always afraid of the inflation which can result from an excessive money supply, demanded strict criteria for joining the EMU. The main four criteria to enter the EMU are as follows: **price stability** (a rate of inflation with 1.5% off the three best-performing EU countries); **exchange-rate stability; sustainable government financial position** (budget deficits no higher than 3% of GDP); and a ratio of **public debt to GDP** of no more than 60%. These criteria are referred to as the **sustainable convergence** requirements to join the EMU.

At a European Union meeting at Brussels on May 2, 1998, it was decided that eleven countries would be part of a European Monetary Union which would function under a single currency—**the Euro**—which would gradually replace national currencies: Austria, Belgium, Finland, France, Germany, Ireland, Italy, Luxembourg, Portugal, Spain and the Netherlands. The euro would be controlled by an independent European Central Bank (ECB) based in Frankfurt which was established in June 1998. The central banks of the member countries would go out of business. Sweden, Britain and Denmark refused to participate at this time. Greece did not meet the entry requirement. Electronic and other non-cash transactions in Euros began on January 1, 1999, as well as permanent exchange rates between euros and individual currencies. Also, exchange rates were fixed in perpetuity to eliminate competitive devaluations. Euro notes and coins began on January 1, 2002. **From July 1, 2002, the euro became the only legal tender in member countries.**

The benefits to Europe by participating in **Euroland** directed by a European Central Bank could be significant: eliminates foreign-exchange charges for cross-border trade; maximizes savings for exporters; lowers prices for goods since there would be increased competition among suppliers; improves the single-market base to compete against the United States; encourages investment and growth across Europe; avoids political and military conflicts among members; and encourages additional political cooperation in taxes, defense and foreign policies. These are the reasons why the European political, intellectual and business elites support the European Monetary Union. Other benefits could include lower budget deficits, lower inflation, cheaper capital for business, and more emphasis on shareholding practice of openness and accountability.

Yet, there are potential problems with a monetary system which has the same interest rate for all its members, and that prevents budget deficits from rising above 1% of each country's GDP. For example, if Italy has a recession and Germany has excessive inflationary growth, the interest rate should be lower for Italy, higher for Germany. But, this disparity in monetary policy is no longer allowed. Also, Italy might benefit if its deficit spending, at least in the short-term, goes above 3% of GDP to get out of the recession.

Ironically, presently France and Germany have deficits over 3% of the gross domestic product. The same is true of the Czech Republic, Hungary and Poland. **The stability pact seems to be collapsing.** Euroland has no system for fiscal policy redistributing government moneys to areas under economic difficulties and unemployment. In addition, labor mobility is difficult since there is no single language or employment qualification system. This makes it difficult to reduce Euroland's 11% unemployment rate. **It is very ironic that the fastest growing economic areas in the EU are Britain, Denmark and Sweden which are outside the Euro zone.**

Another problem facing the monetary union is that many people oppose the euro. Critics also fear that the European Union could become one gigantic, centralized, and corrupt socialist bureaucracy which could undermine individual freedoms and innovations. An additional problem for Europe is that all the countries of Europe have fertility rates below replacement levels. Due to abortion, contraception and other factors, the average rate in Europe is only 1.5 children per family. Yet by 2025, 33% of Europeans will be collecting pensions. Who will pay them if the population is decreasing? After 2010, Europe's only demographic growth will be from immigration, and by 2025 their people will undergo the most massive population decline since the **Black Death** of the 1340s. Europeans have a demographic and a marriage crisis.

The major economic crisis in Europe during 2010 and 2011 has been the meltdown in Greece and the serious problems in Spain, Italy, and in other countries. These economies, as well as the entire European Union, are burdened by massive debt which no one knows how to finance and pay for. The crisis in government overspending will be made worse by the demographic decline of the region. Any attempt to curtail a portion of the debt and government spending seems to be opposed by the major unions of the respective countries. Violence has already exploded in Greece and in France when their governments tried to address the fiscal crisis by raising the age of retirement and by reducing other types of spending.

Population and Immigration

Another issue of concern in Europe is the apparent relationship between immigration, particularly from Muslim countries, and crime. The murder of Dutch politician Pym Fortuyn in 2002 and of artist Theo Van Gogh in 2004 by Muslims is gradually turning Europeans from "passive tolerance" to worry about Islamic immigration. Many more Europeans are realizing that terrorism is a European problem and not just a by product of U.S. foreign policy. There is a push by many conservative parties to reduce immigration or to change the source of the immigration. This is the case of Austria, Denmark, Italy, Spain, and even of France and Germany. There are millions of illegal aliens in Europe, one million in the United Kingdom, one million in Greece, 400,000 in France, 300,000 in Italy, 90,000 in Belgium, and 110,000 in the Netherlands.

The dynamics of immigration are rooted on a European birth rate of only 1.5 per woman, much lower than the 2.1 ratio needed to sustain the population. The European population could decline from 375 million in 2004 to 275 million in 2075. So Europe needs 1.6 million immigrants a year to keep the working population even. To sustain the present workers-to-retirees ratio requires 13.5 million immigrants annually. Currently, 5% of the EU is Muslim. It could become 10% by 2020. Many European conservatives and nationalists remember the words in 1974 of former Algerian President Houari Boumedienne when he said that the high procreation rates of their Muslim women would give Islam political and cultural victory in Europe. The 1975 meeting of Islamic countries in Lahore urged demographic preponderance in Europe to Islamize it. Demographic warfare plus the dependence of the Europeans on Arab oil and business have given Islamists a powerful edge. Since 1970, twenty million Muslims have legally entered Europe.

Of great concern to European authorities is the growth of the North African Islamic doctrine of **Takfir wal Hijra** which developed in Egypt and later spread to Algeria and Morocco. The **Takfiris**, who are related to the Algerian-based Salafists, believe that an all-out armed jihad is an obligation and they use petty crime, drug trafficking and credit card fraud to finance their activities. They recruit women for their operations and often lead Western-styled lives to camouflage their terrorist inclinations. They shave their beards and avoid mosques, and even violate Koranic rules to maximize deception. The Takfiris believe that jihad and immigration go together. They target their terrorism also against Muslims who fall outside their sects or who truly believe in peaceful relations with others.

A growing concern for many Europeans is the development of Bosnia as a center for the spread of Islamic terrorism. Many of the terrorists came out of the training camps for Islamists during the Bosnia War of the early 1990s. Iran was involved in supporting them, and the Clinton Administration backed many al-Qaeda operatives in the Balkans and encouraged Muslims in both Bosnia and Kosovo. Millions of dollars came from Saudi Arabia which has just built the King Fahd Mosque, the largest in Europe and a center for Wahhabi Islamism.

The Bosnia Muslims reneged on the power-sharing agreement in Sarajero brokered by the European Union. They did not want to live in a multi-ethnic, liberal and democratic state with Croats and Serbs. Instead, they armed many of the foreign fighters and sent them into Kosovo at the end of 1998 to fight with the Kosovo Liberation Army against the Serbs. The core of Bin-Laden Balkan network came out of the El-Moujahed Brigade of the Muslim Army established in 1992. Now these fighters are sneaking into "Western Europe" and the Americas.

The decision of Kosovo to declare its independence in February 2008 with the support of the United States and other countries has divided the Europeans. Critics believe it will become like Bosnia, a center for terrorism, and that it is a violation of international law and of the **Helsinki Final Act.** They believe it will encourage more break up of countries.

There were terrorist attacks in the United Kingdom in May 2005 and weeks of riots by Muslims and others in France during the Fall of 2005. Islamist organizations want to be intermediaries between the French state and the young Muslims of the "banlieus" or neighborhoods where many Muslims live. This would be the birth of a parallel society and demonstrates the difficulty in assimilating large numbers of Muslims into Western societies. The Union des Organization Islamiques de France (UOIF), an offshoot of the Muslim Brotherhood, has radicalized the Muslim youth and has stated that Islamic values are incompatible with a secular society.

The North Atlantic Treaty Organization (NATO): An Example of Collective Defense

In 1994, the 16 countries of NATO began to study the possibility of enlarging the alliance. This enlargement of

NATO worried Russia. As a result, on May 14, 1997, the **Founding Act on Mutual Relations, Cooperation and Security between NATO and the Russian Federation** was signed, creating a new **NATO-Russia Permanent Council,** by which Russia will be consulted on any new members and other NATO matters, but not given a veto on NATO plans. NATO pledges not to deploy nuclear weapons in the new member countries, and Russia will dismantle nuclear warheads aimed at Europe. NATO also signed a similar, though less sweeping pact with the Ukraine.

On March 12, 1999, Poland, Hungary and the Czech Republic became members of NATO. Bulgaria Estonia, Latvia, Lithuania, Romania, Slovakia and Slovenia entered NATO in 2004, bringing the membership to twenty-six. The supporters of this extension of the alliance cite the following benefits: stabilizes Germany's eastern frontier so that it does not have to defend them by itself, reducing thus German nationalism; protects Central Europe from future Russian expansionism; encourages new and future members to proceed with their democratization; ties the United States, Canada and Europe together encouraging further cooperation in Europe as well as in other trouble spots such as the Persian Gulf and others; and it brings the very pro-American states of Eastern Europe into NATO further cementing an American presence in Europe.

However, there are also criticisms of this extension. The increased costs of adding 15% more European territory and moving 400 miles eastward to the Polish-Belarussian border might cost between $2 to $120 billion. The entrance of Lithuania, Latvia, Estonia, Slovakia, Slovenia, Bulgaria, and Romania means that Russia's heartland would be surrounded by NATO from the Baltic to the Black Sea, a military encirclement like the Germans tried in World War II. This is happening at a time when Russian troops have decreased from four million in 1991 to 1.2 million in 1998. So Russia, which is under economic difficulties, might then emphasize nuclear weapons and cheap chemical and biological warfare to respond to any threat to its borders. It will then use nationalism to neutralize its defenses.

Another criticism of the NATO extension is that by joining the alliance, the Czech Republic, Hungary and Poland have to spend from $27 to $42 billion to modernize and integrate their military forces with NATO, an amount which cannot then be used for modernizing their economies. Finally, one might question whether Americans, Canadians and Western Europeans would be willing to fight and die so far away from home.

It is quite clear that since the war in Kosovo in 1999, the United States has become more detached from NATO as the organization has increased its membership. It might be that the United States finds the need for consensus and "war by committee" as too cumbersome and slow in the war against terrorism. The United States might want NATO involved globally but only after the United States and trustworthy allies such as Australia and the United Kingdom neutralize the enemy.

Criticisms also come from Americans who state that while Europe accounts for 40% of NATO spending, it contributes only 10% of its capability since the Europeans lack the advanced technology of American planes. They keep their defense budgets low to keep their deficits within the limits of the Maastricht Treaty. Meanwhile, the EU provides their people significant welfare benefits. Another complaint from some Americans is that NATO was converted from a defensive military alliance to an offensive military force against Serbia in 1999 without any political debate among the member countries, and it attacked a country which had not invaded another state, or a NATO country.

NATO is evaluating new assignments. One is closer cooperation with the European Union. The March 17, 2003 **Berlin Plus Agreement** tries to resolve compatibility issues between the two organizations. Another is **Operation Active Endeavor** which includes maritime operations against terrorism in the Mediterranean. A third is the **Partnership for Peace** with Azerbaijan and Central Asia. There are bases in Kyrgyzstan and negotiations with Tajikistan are on-going. There is also debate over whether NATO should incorporate as members democratic countries outside Europe, such as Australia, Israel and Japan. **At the Bucharest NATO Summit meeting of April 2–4, 2008, the countries approved a nuclear anti-missile defense system in the Czech Republic and Poland. NATO voted down the incorporation of Georgia and the Ukraine.**

Germany: A Transformation from Imperialism to Peaceful Integration

Following World War II, Germany was divided into East and West Germany. This division ended in 1990 when both sides agreed to unification, and in 1991 Berlin again became the capital of Germany. Support for German unification was given in 1989 in return for German commitment to start in 1990 talks on European economic and monetary union. A united Germany was to be part of an integrated Europe. **The Germans themselves**

decided to relate to Europe through integration and not domination. Germany has supported successive enlargements of the European Union and wants a broad definition of European identity by even bringing in "East" European countries which were formerly communist.

For the Germans, Europe now stands for the institutionalization of human and democratic rights and commitment to human welfare in capitalist markets. The German government is also committed to **Euroland,** the creation of a European-wide currency. **Germany is thoroughly European like no other state. It works through consensus and bargaining within international organizations such as NATO and the EU.**

Germany is comfortable with its role as a medium-sized power which wants neither to be neutral like Switzerland or to gain a wider global reach. The identity of the German state has been internationalized. It is not Germany and Europe but Germany in Europe. However, France was not enthusiastic about the unification of Germany, and is not happy about the possible enlargement of the European Union. First, it believes the Eastern markets will make Germany stronger, and second, France thinks that Eastern European countries, if allowed in, would be pro-American, and France seeks to reduce the American presence in Europe.

Europe and the United States

Certain public disagreements have created some concerns about the relations between the United States and Europe: the desire of President Bush to create a national missile defense; the rejection by the United States of the Kyoto Accords on the environment; the French and German proposal of creating a European Security and Defense Policy within the EU, which could weaken NATO; the hostility against the United States by the French and German governments; and the presence of capital punishment in the United States. Other issues of disagreement are China, Cuba, Iran, Iraq, "Palestine," Taiwan, the International Criminal Court, genetically modified foods, trade issues, EU hostility to the nation-state, group rights over individual rights, and unmanaged competition.

Tensions between the United States and Europe are not new. The Europeans were mostly against the Vietnam War of the 1960s and 1970s. Their people were mostly against the deployment of U.S. Pershing 2 missiles in Germany during the 1980s. The United States supports free markets while the Europeans support democratic socialism. Americans are mostly religious while Europeans are mostly secularists. The United States spends $405 billion in military expenditures while the entire EU spends only $205 billion in defense.

A major source of discord has been the desire of the French and the German governments to check what they believe is the excessive and unilateral use of American power throughout the world. For example, France joined Germany and Russia to try to prevent the United States from getting UN Security Council approval for its war against Iraq in 2003. A major confrontation between the United States and Europe might have been averted when the European Parliament voted 431–85 urging the EU, and particularly France and Germany, not to end the arms embargo against China for its Tiananmen Square repression over a decade ago. The French and the Germans wanted to sell weapons to China, weapons which could be used against Americans and their allies in case of conflict in the Taiwan Straits.

Yet, many of the disagreements across the Atlantic are only between the United States and the French and German governments. Only time will tell about the impact of the May 2007 elections in France which brought a conservative, pro-American leader. Other governments and the European private sectors are enjoying unprecedented collaboration with the United States.

The United States has three major concerns regarding Europe in the 2010–2011 period. The first is the **socialist nature of EU policies** which has led to low growth, rigid labor markets, intrusive regulations, high taxes, and protectionism. Low growth in the EU means fewer imports from the United States and less growth for the world economy. GDP per capita in the USA is 45% higher. The US economy doubles every 25 years, but that of the EU every 140 years. The EU will wait to 2023 to catch up to the US in levels of employment if it grew by 0.5% annually more than America, 50 years to catch up in productivity, 67 years in income per capita, and 118 years in research and development.

The second concern of the US is the intense **anti-Americanism** of European elites and a major portion of the population. The United States supported European integration because it wanted strong partners against Soviet expansionism. And yet, today one could argue that the EU is a rival of the United States. The third issue of concern to the United States is the growth of radical Islam in Europe which could undermine free institutions in Europe and shift significantly the global balance of power.

"Eastern" Europe: A Transition from Communism to Capitalist Democracy

When communism spread throughout East Germany, Poland, Czechoslovakia, Hungary, Yugoslavia, Romania, Bulgaria, and Albania after World War II, these countries mistakenly became known as Eastern Europe to distinguish them from the democratic and capitalist countries of Western Europe. After the Cold War ended, East Germany united with West Germany to form Germany, which is really a **Central European** state with mostly Germanic people. Czechoslovakia split into the Czech Republic and Slovakia, which together with Poland, Austria, and Hungary are **East Central European** states with a majority Catholic and Slavic population. Yugoslavia itself split into Serbia and Montenegro (today both are called Yugoslavia), Slovenia, Croatia, Bosnia and Herzegovina, and Macedonia, and together with Romania, Bulgaria, Albania and Greece are **Southeast European** states. Serbia and Montenegro, Macedonia, Romania, Bulgaria, and Greece are mostly Eastern Orthodox; Slovenia and Croatia are mostly Roman Catholic; and Bosnia and Albania are mostly Muslim.

In the 1980s, the Communist "Eastern" European states were on the verge of economic collapse. The transition away from communism and from participation in the Soviet-led **Council for Mutual Economic Assistance (COMECON)** was difficult, but by 1995, most had positive rates of growth in GDP. **The countries doing the best are the Czech Republic, Poland, and Hungary. They have made a complete transition to a market economy.** Worse off are Romania, Serbia, Bosnia, Slovakia, and Bulgaria, which have not privatized as fast.

A second goal of these countries, in addition to their transition to a market economy, is that of implementing democracy or creating at least some pluralism: depoliticizing the police and the army; imposing civilian control on the secret services; encouraging a free press; creating new laws and institutions; and establishing checks and balances to diminish authoritarianism. The most progress has been made in the Czech Republic, Slovenia, Hungary and Poland. There have been slower advances in Romania and Croatia, and little democratic improvement in Slovakia.

The entrance into the European Union of former East European communist countries such as Bulgaria, the Czech Republic, Hungary, Poland, Romania, Slovakia and Slovenia represents a dramatic event in world history and is one of Europe's greatest successes. The rate of growth in GDP and in attracting foreign investments is higher than in the original EU countries. They have been willing to undertake radical market-oriented reforms such as privatization of state companies, tax cuts, deregulation, liberation of price controls, and openness to foreign trade. Eight countries in Eastern and Central Europe have even followed Estonia in enacting a flat tax. More radical even is the inclusion in NATO, the West's military alliance of Bulgaria, the Czech Republic, Estonia, Hungary, Latvia, Lithuania, Poland, Romania, Slovakia and Slovenia, all of whom used to be under communist control and participated in the Soviet military alliance, the Warsaw Pact.

Russia

The Russian Federation occupies more than 76% of the total area of the former Soviet Union, which lasted from 1922 to 1991. Russia is the largest country in the world. It has a population of 141 million, 82% Russian, and 4% Tatars. The urban population is 73%. The Russian Federation has 21 republics and 49 oblasts or large regions. The principal language is Russian, but Ukranian Byelorussian, Uzbek, Armenian, Azerbaijani, Georgian, and other languages are spoken. The main religions are Atheism, Orthodox Christianity and Islam.

Russia's population is dropping about one million a year due to a lower birth rate, violence, and alcohol among other causes. The population could drop 33% by 2050. For example, Russia's population was 147 million in 2000 and could decline to 114 million by 2050. Thirty-six percent, or 52 million, live below the subsistence level of a dollar a day.

Russia's immediate future probably lies with authoritarian government with some democratic features. The 1991 revolutionary ideals of promoting human rights, a market economy, and western values will be difficult to achieve. **Russia's culture is authoritarian and xenophobic. There is as yet no culture of legality which can consolidate human rights, property rights, and an independent judiciary strong enough to enforce the rule of law.** These weaknesses will inhibit much domestic and foreign investment. The increase in poverty, crime, and taxes, and the drop in life expectancy and national economic income will inhibit democracy. **Perhaps the biggest problems in Russia are disregard for the law, corruption and violent crime at all levels of**

society which accentuates its economic stagnation. The central government in Moscow is increasing its centralization, corruption and repression.

However, Russians could gradually develop a more democratic system. They have a history of resistance to tyranny and many have exercised some democratic practices at the local levels. The population is increasingly urban and literate. Close to 80% of the economy is now in the private sector which has been growing 15% to 150% since 1994. However, the official figures are not as positive since about 40% of the family income is not reported to the tax collector. The economy began to recover in 1998. Russia will probably behave like the typical, middle-income ($9,000 GDP/per capita), semi-capitalist country, comparable to Argentina and Mexico. It is trying to make a transition away from military goods' production, centralized state planning, massive corruption, and serious inequality of income. Russia will have an unstable political life until it can develop the right institutions and political culture. **However, many in the government want to imitate the Chinese model where open semi-capitalist economics is combined with authoritarian politics. This might be where its leader, Vladimir Putin, is taking Russia in 2010–2011.**

Foreign money will be wasted or stolen if Russia does not implement basic reforms: overhaul of the tax system; downsizing of the military; creation of serious banking laws; and legal protection of foreign direct investments and shareholder rights. Since 1993, when the new Russia was created, billions of dollars have fled for banks in the Caribbean, Switzerland, and other places. Entrepreneurs are at the mercy of corrupt bureaucrats and state agencies. Many pay protection money to criminal rackets.

Boris Yeltsin was the only Russian leader who promoted decentralization and self-government instead of control by Moscow, except for Czar Alexander II briefly in the 1860s. It was Boris Yeltsin who ended Communism in Russia. By 1997, for the first time the Russian people were ruled by leaders elected by them. However, Yeltsin resigned on December 31, 1999, and was succeeded by former KGB officer Vladimir Putin who won the March 26, 2000 and the March 14, 2004 elections. Putin seems to be reversing the decentralization process by proposing to the legislature measures to dismiss elected regional governors and dissolving local legislative bodies at the request of the executive. In addition, he has placed military and intelligence officers in charge, began to intimidate the press, plans to eliminate some of Russia's

political parties and regulate the rest, and has redrawn administrative borders, along the lines of Imperial Russia. **Putin has expanded the Federal Security Services, the successor to the KGB.** People do not trust their government or each other. Corrupt ex-communists now run much of Russia. Russians might not yet fear increased repression because the economy has been growing significantly under Putin.

In December 2007 Putin chose Dmitry Medredev to be the next President of Russia and assigned to himself the position of Prime Minister which runs the cabinet. These actions were confirmed by the "elections" of March 2, 2008. They both will pursue increased authoritarianism domestically and a more aggressive foreign policy. **These goals will be made possible by the fact that Russia is making in 2008 approximately $1 billion a day in energy exports.**

Russian Foreign Policy: Neo-Imperialism or Peaceful Coexistence?

The Soviet Union, made up of 15 republics including Russia, came to an end in December 1991. Since then, only Belarus has taken steps to reestablish the union with Russia, signing a Treaty of Union on April 2, 1997. It is already a satellite of Russia. Russia tried in 2004 to steal the presidential elections in the Ukraine to support the pro-Russian candidate and thus keep the Ukraine within what Putin calls **Greater Russia.** His efforts were defeated with the help of some countries of the European Union, the United States, and brave Ukrainians who demonstrated on behalf of an independent Ukraine.

Vladimir Putin sees Russia as being surrounded by democratic geopolitical pluralism. He is afraid Ukrainian democracy might spread into Russia itself. The Russians call the neighboring former Soviet republics the **Near Abroad.** Presently, the Russian military, which has experienced a 50% decrease in forces since its peak in the mid-1980s, is too weak to reinstate the Soviet Union. Every branch of the military is in dire straits. In addition, Russians are generally unwilling to use force to regain control of this Near Abroad.

However, electoral politics in Russia have increased nationalist rhetoric and some politicians have labeled the Near Abroad a "national security zone" of Russian rights and interests. There are calls for strengthening the **Commonwealth of Independent States** (CIS), created by Gorbachev and made up of Russia and 11 former Soviet republics, to protect Russians living in the Near and Far

Abroad and to redraw borders by force. **The Russians are using their political dominance in various ways: supplying or withholding energy or access to Russian-controlled pipelines; creating military-basing agreements with adjacent states; promoting dual citizenship agreements with neighbors; unifying air-defense systems controlled by Moscow; organizing peace-keeping missions; and stationing troops abroad.**

Russian foreign policy is particularly active in the **Transcaucasus,** which it considers as being within its sphere of influence, an area where both Turkey and Iran—enemies of Russia—have had interests. **The three former Soviet states of Armenia, Azerbaijan and Georgia are in this region and at present cannot exist independently.** Russia uses its economic power and its military to keep them under its control. In the war between Armenia and Azerbaijan over **Nagorno-Karabak,** an enclave of mostly Armenians living in Azerbaijan (who have built a 7-mile highway into Armenia), the Russians back Armenia, which is being blockaded by Turkey. The Azeris of Azerbaijan are more likely to pursue independence and ties with Muslim Turkey or Iran.

Russian troops have used the secession movement in Georgia's Abkhazia and South Ossetia regions in the Southern Caucasus to pressure Georgia into closer ties with Russia. The Russians use Georgia to arm and supply Armenia with oil and weapons and through Armenia they control Azerbaijan. The Russians have so far refused to remove their two military bases from Georgia.

In 2009, Russia sent military troops into Georgia's Abkhazia and South Ossetia regions to protect Russians living there. Fighting took place between the two countries. Russian troops still remain in Southern Georgia.

Russia is concerned about Azerbaijani oil in the Caspian Sea. It does not want Azerbaijan to build an oil pipe line through Georgia or Turkey, which will give it greater wealth and independence. It is also concerned over the possibility that radical Islamists will take control of Turkey, or that NATO will use Turkey to expand in this area.

From 1994 to 2006 the Russians fought in the republic of Chechnya to prevent its independence. A new Chechen war began in 1999, sparked by Muslims who infiltrated the Russian Republic of Dagestan from nearby Chechnya. The fighting has created unrest in the north Caucasus republics of Chechnya, Dagestan, Adygea, Karachay-Cherkessia, Kabardino-Balkaria, North Ossetia, and Ingushetia where many nationalities are fighting each other. Much of the unrest is due to Islamic militancy, but part is also due to Russian administrative corruption and inefficiency. All of the seven Caucasus republics, except for North Ossetia, are Islamic. Only Chechnya wants independence from Russia to create an Islamic state. Ingushetia and Kabardino Balkaria are the most likely to explode with violence.

The war in Chechnya has left over 200,000 dead and 350,000 displaced. Vladimir Putin introduced sweeping amnesty to Chechen rebels who laid down their arms during the decade ending on August 1, 2003, but it does not extend to "foreigners" and Russians guilty of murder or of serious crimes. In 2002, Chechen terrorists attacked a Moscow theatre, and in 2004 they took a school in Beslan killing hundreds of children and adults.

The Russians need to resolve this instability in the region to avoid the departure of one million refugees from the North Caucasus into Southern Russia, and to prevent the loss of Dagestan which has Russia's only all-weather port on the Caspian Sea (Makhachkala), and which represents 70% of Russia's Caspian coast. This area also has the oil pipeline from Baku to global markets. Furthermore, the upheaval in the north can spread to the South Caucasus republics of Georgia, Azerbaijan and even Armenia. Russians worry that Turkey and Iran could try to be more active in this region.

Russian-U.S.-European Relations

Following the 9/11 attack on the United States, Putin extended support by permitting American troops in Georgia, Kyrgiztan, Tadjikistan, Uzbekistan, closing Russian military bases in Cuba and Vietnam, and accepting the U.S. decision to quit the **1972 Antiballistic Missile Treaty.** The United States on May 24, 2002, rewarded Putin with a new Arms Treaty, which he had desired. It limits the number of long-range nuclear warheads, as he wanted. Both have to reduce their nuclear warheads by 2/3 so they can reach the top ceiling of 1700 to 2,200 deployed warheads by the last day of the Treaty on December 31, 2012. Presently, Russia has 6,000 and the United States 6,000 to 7,000 warheads. They can deploy as many warheads as they want after the treaty ends, unless there is a new treaty. This Arms Treaty strengthens Putin in relation to his internal opponents, particularly at a time when NATO has accepted new members close to the Russian borders. It allows Russia to scrap aging nuclear weapons that are expensive to keep. On the other hand, the United States gets the minimum number of warheads to protect itself. It can also build a missile defense.

Another American policy in support of Russia is the **NATO-Russia Council,** whose agreement of May 28, 2002, gives Russia a voice, but no veto, in NATO, and allows Russia to participate in discussions dealing with airspace security, terrorism, search and rescue, and missile defense.

In June 2002, the **European Union** and the United States also gave Russia another gift by granting it status as a full-market economy which allows tariff-free sales of many Russian goods, protection against European and American anti-dumping laws, and paves the way to entry into the **World Trade Organization.** However, the Russians are concerned with the European Union expansion into Poland and Lithuania for it would mean that the Russians living in Kalinigrad would have to get visas to cross European Union territory into Russia. The Europeans also want the Russians to liberalize their energy markets for the export prices of gas and electricity are about 600% more expensive than prices in the domestic markets. This forces some corporations to specialize in exports to remain profitable.

The Russians also have complaints about American policies: U.S. anti-dumping restrictions against Russian goods; the Jackson-Vanik amendment, which ties Russian trade status to Jewish emigration; the U.S. farm bill of 2002, which increases subsidies to American farmers; and the tariff of up to 30% on imported steel, which affects over $1.5 billion of Russian exports from 2002 to 2005. They complain that American investment in Russia is only $4 billion. In addition, the Russian government is upset about American support for the 2008 unilateral declaration of independence by Kosovo from Serbia, a Russian ally. It resents NATO conversations with Georgia and the Ukraine to incorporate them eventually, and its decision to create a missile defense system in the Czech Republic and in Poland.

On the other hand, the United States also has concerns: Russian assistance to North Korea to build a nuclear plant; broken non-proliferation promises; selling weapons to Iran and helping it build two nuclear reactors; and Russian oil deals and intelligence sharing with former Iraqi dictator Saddam Hussein; Russian attempts to re-enter the Middle East region and undermine American influence among the oil-rich Arab states; and the efforts to exclude the United States from the oil-rich area of Central Asia.

Vladimir Putin is establishing closer relations with China, and has participated in joint military exercises. The Chinese are investing in Russia and buying energy resources and military assets. Russia has also developed business ties with Iran. Both China and Iran are opponents of the United States which Putin hopes to weaken. He is insecure about the three former Baltic republics of the Soviet Union joining NATO, the Western military alliance, which two other former Soviet republics, Georgia and the Ukraine, also want to enter. Putin is also concerned about the American military presence in Georgia and Kyrgyzstan. **Putin also has other complaints against America:** the effort to build a pipeline to deliver Caspian Sea oil from Azerbaijan through Georgia to Turkey, to bypass Russia; the attempt to make permanent in Central Asia American bases used for the war in Afghanistan; the policy of putting anti-missile systems into Eastern Europe; and American bombing of Serbia, a Russian ally, which wanted to hold on to its rebellious province of Kosovo.

Russia feels isolated. Its only true allies are Armenia, Belarus and Tajikistan. On the other hand, the United States needs Russian cooperation to deal with China, Iran, Iraq, energy, non-proliferation and terrorism. So an alliance between the two countries could occur after serious negotiations.

Biological and Chemical and Nuclear Weapons

There is mounting evidence that Russia is violating international accords on biological and chemical weapons, that **Biopreparat,** one of its agencies, has developed biological agents and missiles filled with plague, anthrax and small pox, and aimed at American cities. These weapons have also been developed for assassination purposes. Over twenty Russian state agencies seem to have transferred critical missile technology to Iran. This is of great concern to the United States, for the sale of Russian nuclear materials to terrorists can threaten American cities. Scientists, research institutes and manufacturing plants with knowledge of ballistic missile design have helped Iran build the Shahab-3 missile which when ready could be a threat to Israel, Turkey and U.S. troops in Saudi Arabia. Russia has invested $800 million in a reactor project in Iran.

Following the 2003 controversy over the possible Iranian development of nuclear weapons, the Russians are revaluating their assistance to Iran's nuclear power programs, and are requesting the Iranians to allow the International Atomic Energy Agency to inspect the nuclear sites. Iran violated the Nuclear Non-Proliferation Treaty (NPT). The Russians have not placed much pressure on Iran or on North Korea to abandon their military nuclear power programs.

Latin America

Latin America is a huge territory extending from the southern border of the United States to Antarctica. Four-fifths of the land consists of mainly uninhabited deserts, tropical lowlands, and mountains. **Racial mixing between white Spaniards and Amerindians has created a very large mestizo population. Yet, people of African descent are characteristic of the islands and periphery of the Caribbean, and individuals of direct European stock are predominant in the states of the Southern Cone. Relatively non-assimilated Amerindians constitute about 20% of the total population of Latin America and are found mainly in the Andes Mountains and northern Central America.** Latin America can be divided into subregions: Mexico, Central America, the Caribbean States, the Northern Andes, the Southern Cone, and Brazil.

Central America is made up of Belize, Costa Rica, El Salvador, Guatemala, Honduras, Nicaragua, and Panama. **The Caribbean region is one of the most densely populated areas on earth.** Its 36 million inhabitants are divided among more than 30 states and dependencies. Five-sixths of the population lives on the four large islands of Cuba, Hispaniola, Puerto Rico and Jamaica. These are often called the **Greater Antilles.** In addition to the Greater Antilles, the following are part of the Caribbean: British Antilla, the Netherland Antilles, the French Antilles, the United States Virgin Islands, French Guinea, Suriname, Guyana, and Trinidad and Tobago.

The Northern Andes represents a third region of Latin America. It is made up of Colombia, Venezuela, Ecuador and Peru. The Southern Cone states of Chile, Argentina, Uruguay, and Paraguay are located in the narrowing triangle of southern Latin America. Brazil merits consideration as a separate Latin American region because of its huge size and population and its distinctive Portuguese language.

Neoliberalism or Left-Wing Latin America?

Starting in the 1980s, many Latin American political elites began promoting certain reforms referred by some as the **Washington Consensus.** The policy recommended limiting fiscal deficits to what can be financed in bond mar-

kets, maintaining an independent central bank and market-determined interest rates, welcoming foreign direct investments and liberating trade. Other ingredients of the Washington Consensus are developing local bond and stock markets, privatizing state companies, particularly those losing money, reforming taxation and making the value-added tax the main source of revenue. It is important in this view to let the market set the exchange rate or dollarize the economy to liberalize capital movement, and to promote democracy so that government elites can be more responsive to civil society.

This program, also called **Neoliberalism,** has had some success. Inflation, which weighs terribly on the poor, dropped from a regional average of 196% in 1991 to below 10% in 2008 although it might be increasing in some areas. Intra-regional trade increased. The benefits of freer trade led Argentina, Brazil, Paraguay and Uruguay to create a customs union called **MERCOSUR.** Cheap imports, together with an increased infusion of foreign credit, has helped consumers. Other positives are that more women are joining the workforce, open economies are gaining credibility, household size is decreasing, consumer spending is growing, urbanization is expanding, and volatile Latin American business cycles are getting shorter. Globalization has led to increased privatization and democratization. Economics growth had been 5% and 4% for 2004 and 2005, respectively, and 5% in 2006 and 2007. This was an impressive amount. The regional economy has been stagnant since 2008. In 1986, there were only six democratic countries, but by 2007, all except Cuba had free elections. An additional trade group is the **Andean Community** of Bolivia, Colombia, Ecuador, and Peru, which was called the Andean Pact until 1996.

Neoliberalism has tried to replace the old Latin America which was for the most part authoritarian, protectionist, state interventionist, mercantilistic and economically isolated from the world markets. The new Latin America has much that is good. However, there are those who criticize Neoliberalism, saying that much of the early growth in Latin America during the early 1990s was the result of a one-time inflow of capital as a result of the recently achieved financial stability (reduced inflation), and that the reforms of the Washington Consensus will actually hurt Latin America. **The percentage of the population in poverty has declined, but population growth has actually increased the number of poor people.** The population will keep increasing from 548 million in 2008 to 700 million in 2025. **Real wages seem to have declined since 1990,**

and unemployment is 10% while underemployment is between 20 and 50%.

Privatization has often been undermined when the sale of government agencies has been to large, private monopolies which prevent business competition and lower prices. The economy needs to grow 6% yearly to absorb the increase in population, but it is only at 4%. The middle class has been hurt by government spending cuts, particularly in utility and energy subsidies. Sixty million more Latin Americans live in poverty now than a decade ago. Two in five Latin Americans—210 million people—are poor, and Latin America has the world's most unequal distribution of wealth. The poverty rate averaged 44% between 1980 and 2008.

Other difficulties include tax evasion by the wealthy, weak property rights, national governments imposing their will over local governments, political candidates elected by leaders and not by the voters, the powerful imposing their will, and too many private monopolies. **Free enterprise capitalism is more than free trade and open markets. It requires property rights, the rule of law, independent judiciaries, low taxation, limited government regulations, and stable currencies.**

There are other signs of serious social problems worsening in Latin America: poverty, a 50% elementary school drop-out rate, crime and violence, drug-trafficking, and unemployment. **The issue of violent crime is becoming crucial in Latin America. Police involvement in crime, kidnappings, smuggling, drug trafficking, all make Latin America the most violent region in the world. There are 27.5 homicides per 100,000 people. In Africa, Eastern Europe and Western Europe, the numbers are 22 and 15, respectively. This has a major economic impact as insurance costs for business rise, the cost of protection escalates, and tourism and foreign investment decline. And yet, of $4.4 billion in international assistance to the region, less than 1% goes for law enforcement. It does not make sense. Governments need to spend at least 6.5% of the GDP in education and retraining but they are spending only 4.4%.** Less than $1,000 per pupil per year is being spent on primary and secondary schools.

The old parties seem to be dying as people lose trust in them and place their faith in demagogues. This situation is made worse by adverse international conditions such as a reversal of capital inflow to Latin America, lowered commodity prices for sugar, bananas, coffee, and aluminum, among others, and emigration of some of the most educated citizens.

Colombia is engaged in a 46-year-old guerilla war against communists and in a 25-year-old war against drug traffickers. These two types of wars are now connected. President Alvaro Uribe was elected in 2002 to defeat these guerrillas who use money earned through drug sales to equip themselves militarily. He was reelected in 2006. The government offensive could be extending the wars beyond the borders into Venezuela, Brazil, Ecuador and Peru.

In fact, on March 1, 2008, Colombia attacked the Revolutionary Armed Forces of Colombia (FARC) narco-terrorists at a camp they had established in Ecuador. The information found in the confiscated computers indicate the following: Venezuela has spent millions of dollars assisting the FARC; Ecuador's President Rafael Correa knew about the Colombian FARC's camps in his territory; and the FARC has been found to have 66 pounds of depleted uranium.

The United States is spending over $2 billion to help train Colombia pilots, mechanics, and to equip them with helicopters and other weapons. However, Colombia needs more security forces, intelligence assets, and more air mobility and maritime patrols to defeat the communist narco-guerrillas. The spraying of herbicides is reducing cultivation of poppy. The United States is now allowing its assistance to go not only to combat drug trafficking but also to fight the guerrillas themselves. Many guerrillas are deserting in response to counter narcotics assistance such as job training, reading classes and $4,000 to start businesses.

Venezuela is in a downward economic slide caused by the political polarization effected by President Hugo Chavez, who continues to push Venezuela toward a military state. He was removed from power in April 2002 for a few hours before being reinstated by the military. It might have been a self-coup. In December 2002 and January 2003, Venezuela was paralyzed by a gigantic strike by business, labor and political opponents of Chavez. They failed. A 2004 referendum to determine if Hugo Chavez should remain in office gave him a majority support, but there is much speculation that there was massive fraud in the voting. On December 2, 2007, he lost a referendum on constitutional changes which would have strengthened his power even more. Approximately 4 million new poor have been created in Venezuela under Chavez even though Venezuela has received over $700 billion in oil revenues.

Meanwhile, Hugo Chavez is trying to strengthen his regime by a policy of price and foreign exchange controls so that he can liquidate the economic opposition.

Only the government will be able to determine who can get foreign currency to buy imports. He intimidates the press with the social responsibility law, which prohibits disrespect of government officials, and has packed the Supreme Court. Hugo Chavez will be able to control the judiciary because the Parliament, which he dominates, appoints the Supreme Court, and this court controls the appointment of judges. There is no independent auditor general. Chavez can also increase his power by subsidizing the military generously and by giving dictator Fidel Castro of Cuba 100,000–530,000 barrels of oil a day free, which is repaid by Castro's sending to Venezuela thousands of his paramilitary forces to support Chavez. Chavez's takeover of one of the most important private television stations in June 2007 sparked demonstrations all over Venezuela, particularly by university students.

There is evidence that Venezuela's intelligence and security service (DISIP) is under the control of Cuba's intelligence service, the DGI, and that the Cubans control the Presidential Guard and the Bolivarian Circles. These last are a 100,000-people reserve militia from the poorest classes which are used by Hugo Chavez to intimidate or injure his opponents. Over 8,000 visas have been given to Cuban "teachers", "doctors" and "sports trainers" to enter Venezuela. These Cuban agents will fight to consolidate their power in Venezuela, the source of free oil for Cuba. Hugo Chavez is also suspected of having close ties to FARC Colombian guerrillas and to Left-wing elements in the Andean countries. His control of Venezuelan oil gives him the power to subsidize political and ideological allies throughout the region, at the rate of $3 billion a year.

Recent events in Venezuela are alarming some of its neighbors. Hugo Chavez is upgrading significantly his military assets. He is buying 50 MIG-29 fighters from Russia plus 100,000 assault rifles and 40 attack and transport helicopters. Venezuela is also purchasing 4 naval frigates and battle tanks from Spain. Chavez is also getting 24 Tucano aircraft with air to ground attack capability from Brazil. Other weapons are coming from China and Cuba. Why so much fire power? After the Cubans, the second largest group of foreigners are Iranians.

There are indications that Latin America is in a Left-wing course. While there are differences of opinion regarding the meaning of Left-wing, it could be stated that the term refers to states or movements which advocate centralization of governmental power, a provider state, ideological uniformity, mass egalitarianism, a collectivist economy, a materialist culture, and political

repression to carry out its "messianic" program. This means that leftist, or Left-of-center presidents or dictators now rule in several Latin American countries: Cristina Fernandez de Kirchner in Argentina, Evo Morales in Bolivia, Luis Inacio Lula de Silva in Brazil, Ricardo Lagos in Chile, Fidel Castro in Cuba, and Hugo Chavez in Venezuela. Communist Daniel Ortega in Nicaragua won the Presidency in 2006. Only the future will tell if his leftist demagoguery applies only to foreign affairs and not to their domestic policies.

Perhaps the Left in Latin America needs to be divided between a group of countries and organizations which use violence, terrorism and support street crime to meet their objectives, and another set of countries like Argentina, Brazil and Chile that accept elections and free institutions as the basis of political legitimacy. They have lowered taxes and promoted stable currencies to attract foreign investments.

Cuba and Venezuela are part of the **Radical Left.** They are using violence and the oil wealth of Venezuela to create a bloc which promotes subversion and intimidation in countries such as Bolivia, Colombia, Ecuador, Nicaragua and Panama. Cuba and Venezuela in addition to seeking an Andean and Central American alliance, also seek greater influence in the Caribbean. Cheap oil sales will help them in this objective. Elements of this violent Left include the Nicaraguan Sandinistas, though at this time they are operating within the electoral mode, the FARC and ELN guerrillas in Colombia, the Patria Libre organization in Paraguay, and the **Maras** criminal gangs which have invaded El Salvador, Guatemala, and Honduras, and could be establishing ties in Nicaragua, Panama, Mexico and the United States. The Maras traffic in weapons and cocaine are an example of how criminal activity, terrorism and political ends can all come together wherever states are too weak to govern effectively.

Certain observations can be made about elections in general. The Left is stronger today in Latin America, even in Colombia and Mexico, where it lost the elections. All of the losing candidates accepted defeat, except in Mexico. The elections seemed to be cleaner, except in Venezuela and in a few isolated cases. Stability in Latin America requires an open and competitive political party system where frustrations can be articulated. This will reduce the influence of radical movements. Those parties which support inclusion and equality tend to attract popular support. Neo-liberalism is still alive in Latin America for many people support free trade, foreign investment, privatization, and balanced budgets. The big challenge for all these democracies is how to balance the need for better equity for the masses of poor people with the discipline needed to protect the creators of wealth from the irrational policies of populist demagogues who gain political power by promising people more than can be delivered.

And yet, there might be indications that the Left-wing trend in Latin American politics is being moderated by successful conservative elections in Argentina, Chile, Colombia, Honduras, Mexico, Panama, and in other places. In Honduras, the political elites removed in 2010 the Left-wing President Manuel Zelaya for constitutional infractions and elected a conservative. Zelaya had been supported by the Left-wing bloc of Cuba, Bolivia, Ecuador, Nicaragua, and Venezuela. He was also backed by Brazil. Perhaps there might be a movement toward the center in many of these countries of South America.

Recently, the violence in Mexico has intensified as President Felipe Calderon began to attack the many drug cartels that exist in the country. He has had to rely on the military because many of the police forces have actually been penetrated by the drug traffickers. Thousands of police officers and other individuals have been kidnapped, tortured, beheaded, or suffered other afflictions as a result of gang warfare. The violence is now spreading into the United States from across the border, particularly into Arizona.

The crisis in Mexico is not only one between the government and the drug traffickers. It could also be fueled by Communist Cuba whose major goals have always included the destabilization of Venezuela, Colombia, and Mexico, among other countries, to enhance its geopolitical interests. Now that oil-rich Venezuela is part of its bloc, it is easier to venture into the Andean region and into Mexico. Iran might also be playing an influential role in creating havoc in the Caribbean Basin.

MERCOSUR

The Southern Cone Common Market (MERCO-SUR), negotiated by the Treaty of Asuncion of 1991, is a customs union established in 1995 joining Brazil, Argentina, Paraguay and Uruguay in a single market of 200 million people and a total GNP of over $800 billion. The main economic power is Brazil, followed by Argentina, which have among themselves 50% of the Latin American GDP, and 97% of MERCO-SUR's. Venezuela has just entered the union, and Bolivia, Chile, Colombia, Ecuador and Peru are associate members.

Most goods flow tariff-free inside MERCOSUR except cars, sugar and some sensitive products. However, there are no agreements on trade in services and on non-tariff trade barriers. **The common external tariff (CET), which is typical of customs unions, ranges from 1% to 20%.** Each country has some exemptions and special arrangements. There is as yet no commitment among the five member countries to create a common market which would allow free movement of capital and labor. MERCOSUR is now more a political body than a free trade advocacy group. Recently, Argentina has imposed some restrictions against cheap Brazilian imports, and Brazil will limit imports of wine, wheat, and rice from Argentina. Paraguay and Uruguay might establish special trade relations with the United States.

MERCOSUR has been more trade-creating than trade-diverting. Most of its exports are agricultural but it has enlarged the market for global manufacturers such as cars, auto parts, chemicals and machinery. It has also attracted investments from outside the region. This is leading to greater competitiveness and awareness of global markets. **However, will MERCOSUR last?** It was created by leaders committed to liberalization, democracy, sound macro-economic policies to reduce inflation, export-based growth rather than import-substitution industrialization, lower tariffs, and privatization.

Free Trade Area of the Americas

One of the most talked-about ideas in the Americas is the desire to create a hemisphere-wide free trade area. **The U.S.-Canadian Free Trade Act** of 1988 eliminated most duties and tariffs on goods traded between the two countries. This was followed in 1992 by the **Enterprise of the Americas Initiative** of President George Bush. In 1993, U.S. President Clinton signed the **North American Free Trade Agreement** (NAFTA) with Mexico and Canada which significantly reduced tariffs. From 1994 to 1998, trade rose 70%, to $160 billion. NAFTA pledged that other Latin American countries would be welcomed into the free trade area. Yet, NAFTA has been criticized by Florida farmers, cattle raisers, American truckers, unions and others who believe they have been subjected to unfair competition from Mexico. Environmentalists have also criticized NAFTA for promoting the destruction or overuse of natural resources.

In 1994, 34 heads of states—only dictator Fidel Castro of Cuba was not invited—agreed in Miami, Florida, to institute a **Free Trade Area of the Americas** (FTAA), by the year 2005. The goal was to develop free-market democracy throughout the hemisphere. **This free market ideology replaced 200 years of mercantilistic statism inherited from Spanish colonialism and 50 years of import substitution industrialization influenced by dependency theory and neo-Marxism.** The new emphasis seemed to be on privatization, deregulation, free trade and capitalism.

At the Belo Horizonte meeting of May 1997, former President Clinton promised to open NAFTA membership to other countries and granted trade parity with NAFTA to key exports from Caribbean Basin states. Also, President Clinton pledged to ask the U.S. Congress for **fast-track authority.** This would allow the President to negotiate an agreement with Latin American countries which Congress can then only approve or reject, without adding changes. This pledge was a response to various countries, particularly Chile, which had expected by then to be part of NAFTA. As a result of Clinton's delay—caused in part by congressional and labor union opposition to NAFTA—Chile, Bolivia and other countries began negotiating their entrance into MERCOSUR, and MERCOSUR itself began negotiating a trade arrangement with the European Union. Late in 1997, the U.S. Congress, and in particular Democrats, refused to grant President Clinton fast-track authority, something it had extended to Presidents Ronald Reagan and George Bush.

The April 1998 Santiago **Summit of the Presidents** supported negotiations to establish a **Free Trade Area of the Americas** by 2005, and agreed to hold regular U.S.-Latin American summits. It pushed the World Bank and the InterAmerican Development Bank to double its funding for education and health. This was to be part of a $45 billion three-year package of education programs, justice reform plans, and anti-corruption initiatives to be financed by international financial institutions by shifting resources from big infrastructure programs. The Summit also proposed the creation of a multilateral anti-drug alliance and evaluation system. At the April 2001 **Quebec City Summit on Free Trade,** the thirty-four countries continued supporting the dream of a $1.3 trillion trade bloc from Alaska to Argentina servicing 784 million consumers.

A more moderate goal became clear during the FTAA-Miami Meeting of October, 2004. The United States and a few of the 34 countries began to engage in bilateral trade agreements which eventually could create momentum for larger agreements. A bilateral free trade area agreement was approved with **Chile** in 2004. Another, the **Dominican Republic-Central American Free Trade Area (DR-CAFTA)** agreement was negotiated in 2005, a bilateral Uruguay-US investment treaty is on the way, and a trade promotion accord with Colombia and Peru is being negotiated. There is also a proposed free trade agreement with Bolivia, Colombia, Ecuador and Panama.

The **Free Trade Area of the Americas** (FTAA) has received much attention lately. Yet, there are competing trade models being developed in Latin America. One is the **Bolivarian Alternative of the Americas** (ALBA) which is promoted by Hugo Chavez of Venezuela and Fidel Castro of Cuba. This economic bloc will not advocate capitalism, free markets, privatization and globalization. Instead, it will have a state-to-state trade system and a collectivist orientation. It could resemble the Communist COMECOM used by the former Soviet Union.

Another project being developed following the meeting of May 9–11, 2005, in Brazil is a free trade area of countries in MERCOSUR and other selected Latin American states, and Muslim-Middle Eastern countries such as Saudi Arabia, the United Arab Emirates, Kuwait, Oman, Bahrain, and Qatar. This bloc is supposed to counterbalance the global American influence and create greater leverage against the economic policies of the rich world. In addition, all these countries are looking for greater investments and markets. China is also willing to be part of the bloc to weaken the United States, to acquire energy resources and to sell its industrial exports. Chavez also hopes to buy nuclear technology from Iran.

The United States and Latin America

Latin America is of great importance to the American economy. **Mexico is the United States' third largest trading partner. It buys more American goods than Germany and Great Britain combined. Latin America buys over 40% of U.S. exports.** The United States exports more to Chile with 14 million people than to India with 940 million. The United States sells $106 billion to Latin America, a 300% increase in ten years. Forty percent of U.S. export revenues come from Latin America and the Caribbean. Latin America has great growth potential because over 50% of its population is under 17 years of age.

The United States thus has a stake in consolidating democratic gains in the area and accelerat-

ing economic integration, trade, and equality in elevating the poor from their materially miserable existence. Prosperous democratic states tend to support the security interests of U.S. allies, obey international law, provide their population with an outlet for political expression, and cooperate to solve regional challenges.

The United States needs to help Latin America by providing more access to its markets, supporting growth in property rights, aiding pro-free market groups, training democratic leaders, improving security forces, providing covert intelligence, expanding the Voice of America radio transmissions, expanding people-to-people contacts, training and assisting police forces, encouraging Peace Corps volunteers, and expanding the National Endowment for Democracy.

An important relationship is with **Mexico**—which is part of **NAFTA.** Most Mexicans are poor. Its economy creates only 200,000 to 500,000 jobs per year, but at the same time one million Mexicans enter the work force. Mexico has monopolies in energy and communications which keep these sectors inefficient. They are not improving access to credit nor curbing corruption. Over 20% of the labor force is in an 80-year-old dysfunctional land tenure system. As a result of these difficulties, millions have fled to the United States.

Mexico is now involved in fighting a "drug cartel civil war" with violent organizations, some of which are groups which have left Colombia and are now operating in Central America, Mexico, and in the border with the United States. The United States is trying to create a **Merida Initiative** to help Mexico deal with narco-terrorism.

Democracy in Central America

Most countries in Latin America, except Cuba and Venezuela, have made significant steps toward building liberal democracy. **El Salvador** ended on January 16, 1992, a 12-year civil war where various governments battled insurgents armed by Cuba and Nicaragua. There were 75,000 deaths. A sweeping amnesty was declared on March 20, 1993. The first elections since 1931 to include all groups from the Left and from the Right took place in 1996, and elections for the National Assembly occurred in 1997. **Presidential elections took place in 2004 and Tony Saca of the National Republican Alliance (ARENA) defeated communist leader Shafik Handal of the Farabundo Marti National Front with**

58% of the vote to 36%. A generation earlier these two groups were killing each other in a civil war. The two major problems confronting Salvadoreans are political polarization and civil violence. Conciliation is difficult. Crime is the number one problem as well-organized gangs—some with roots in Los Angeles, California—are wreaking havoc, particularly in coffee and sugar-cane growing regions at harvest time.

Guatemala negotiated in September 1996, with the help of the United Nations, a peace accord which ended 35 years of conflict, the longest-running guerrilla war in Central America. Over 100,000 people were killed from 1961 to 1996, and 40,000 disappeared. Guatemala faces various problems: corrupt police forces, weak judicial system, criminal violence, drug trafficking, racial discrimination against Indians, and an unequal land distribution where 3% of the people control 70% of the land.

Nicaragua, following decades of conflict and dictatorships, has had five consecutive free elections, one on February 25, 1990, in which Violeta Chamorro defeated Daniel Ortega 51% to 38%, and a second on October 20, 1996, in which Arnaldo Aleman defeated Sandinista leader Daniel Ortega 51% to 38%. The last two elections were monitored by the United Nations, the Organization of American States, and the Carter Center. Chamorro reduced the size of the army, cut inflation from 13,500% to a single digit level, negotiated relief of the bulk of $10 billion debt, but left the army and police in the hands of the Sandinistas. The third election was won in 2002 by Enrique Bolanos. Daniel Ortega lost for the third time. However, in 2006 Daniel Ortega and his Communist Sandista Party won the presidency. Only time will tell if they have become liberal democrats.

Central America made tremendous gains in the 1990s and its successes are continuing in the 2000s. Every country has had free elections. There is civilian rule, constitutional and limited government, and protection of individual rights. These countries are currently participating in free and open markets, lowering tariffs, increasing competition, opening up to the world economy and receiving huge remittances from relatives in the United States. There are problems. Political parties are weak, the rule of law is often arbitrary, the application of justice is often politicized, and crime is awful. For example, El Salvador and Guatemala have the worst crime rate in the world.

An important project approved which affects Central America is the **Dominican Republic-Central American**

Free Trade Agreement (DR-CAFTA). Nearly 80% of CAFTA exports already enter the United States duty free. CAFTA eliminates most tariffs on U.S. exports to the region, which average 11% of many goods. U.S. agriculture will gain, particularly feed, potatoes, pork, grains, corn, milk, oil seed, soybean and meats. Two-way trade with CAFTA is the United States 13th largest market, bigger than to Brazil, Singapore and Australia!

Cuba: A Dictatorship in the Americas

Cuban dictator Fidel Castro has been in power since 1959. **Castro has outlasted the following hostile American presidential administrations: Eisenhower, Kennedy, Johnson, Nixon, Ford, Carter, Reagan, Bush, Clinton, and George W. Bush.** Castro came into power after years of guerrilla warfare in which various middle class organizations, with some support from upper and lower class Cubans, battled the dictatorship of Fulgencio Batista, who himself had overthrown the democratically-elected government of Carlos Prio Socarras in 1952.

When Batista fled on January 1, 1959, Castro was able to outflank his opposition and with massive popular support acquired political dominance. He then began a program of sweeping economic and social changes without, however, restoring promised political liberties. Castro used Cuba's significant accumulated economic assets—high by Latin American standards—to undermine his opponents in the upper and middle classes economically and politically, and to co-opt those groups and individuals traditionally outside the power structure. Also, he began relying on communist elites who had earlier backed the Batista dictatorship. **Cattle and tobacco lands were confiscated. By 1960, all banks and industrial companies had been nationalized, including over $1 billion worth of U.S.-owned properties, mostly without compensation.**

Executions claimed the lives of over 12,000 Cubans, first those close to the Batista regime, then former Castro supporters who opposed the increasing political authoritarianism, economic communization and religious atheism. Some 700,000 Cubans emigrated in the first years after the Castro takeover, mostly to the United States. Over a million and a half would eventually flee the island. Approximately 250,000 Cubans have been sent to prison for political reasons. In April 1961, some 1,400 Cubans, trained and backed by the U.S. Central Intelligence Agency (CIA), unsuccessfully tried to invade and overthrow the regime. Castro then intensified his cooperation with the Soviet Union, which alone could support his life-long anti-American and anti-liberal inclinations.

In the Fall of 1962, the U.S. learned that the Soviet Union had brought nuclear missiles to Cuba. A superpower confrontation resulted, and in the end the missiles were removed. However, the United States promised not to invade Cuba and pledged to keep exiled Cubans from attacking the island. After 1967, the Russians began intensively subsidizing the Cuban economy, and Cuba, in turn, began to support Soviet policies globally, particularly in Africa and in the Middle East. Russian economic assistance allowed Castro to organize anti-American guerrilla and terrorist movements in Central America and Andean Latin America. **He also was able, with the cooperation of the KGB and other communist secret services, to develop a totalitarian system of repression in Cuba which made internal rebellion impossible.**

Castro refused to allow in Cuba the basic instruments of liberal expression: freedom of speech, assembly, organization, press and petition; multi-party elections; an independent judiciary; private schools; free enterprise; and many other human rights advocated by the United Nations Universal Declaration of Human Rights. Periodically, when economic and political conditions in Cuba have become desperate, Castro allows Cubans to flee the island as a way of releasing the internal political pressures. This exodus included 125,000 and 30,000 boat people in 1980 and 1994, respectively. Over 10,000 people are estimated to have drowned while escaping on rafts from Cuba to the United States. A 1987 agreement between Cuba and the United States allows 20,000 Cubans to emigrate to the United States each year, if they can get visas.

The Cuban Embargo. On February 3, 1962, the United States imposed an embargo on U.S. exports to Cuba in reaction to the creation of a totalitarian system in Cuba and the island's alliance with the Soviet Union. By this time, Castro had already nationalized much property in Cuba and had begun promoting violence in Venezuela and the Caribbean Basin as he sought a "continental struggle" against the United States. Later, in July 1964, the American embargo became a hemispheric policy against Cuba as the Organization of American States (OAS) responded to the pleas of Venezuela and the United States. Mexico abstained. Presently, Castro is again using Venezuela to promote his communism throughout Andean Latin

America. He hopes to exploit the fact that 45% of this region's population is poor. They are vulnerable to demagogues promising more than can be delivered.

In July 1975, the OAS voted that its members could, individually, decide whether to trade with Cuba. However, the United States retained its embargo policy. It is not a blockade for Cuba is free to trade with other states. U.S. President Gerald Ford had in 1974 explored the possibility of better relations with Cuba, but the effort failed when Castro sent over 40,000 Cuban troops to Angola. President Carter in 1977 also sought improved relations with Cuba. He established an "Interest Section" of the United States in the Swiss Embassy in Washington. Carter also reduced some travel restrictions on Americans visiting Cuba.

The "friendly" Carter policies ended when Castro sent 15,000 troops to Ethiopia and intervened in other African countries, and united and backed guerrilla groups in Nicaragua, El Salvador, Guatemala, and Honduras. In 1980, Castro unleashed an exodus of 125,000 Cubans from Mariel to the United States, including approximately 2,000 criminals and mental patients. Then, in 1982, President Ronald Reagan began to tighten the embargo again. **The Cuban Democracy Act** became law in October 1992, making the embargo stronger by preventing the foreign subsidiaries of U.S. corporations from selling to Cuba (a $700 million market in 1991), and barring merchant ships that stopped at Cuban ports from the U.S. market for six months. It allowed the regulated entry of medicines and humanitarian help, and promised to end the embargo and to provide economic aid to Cuba following its transition to democracy.

When Cuba, on February 24, 1996, shot down two small, unarmed civilian planes over international waters, killing three American citizens and one Cuban refugee, the United States responded with the Helms-Burton legislation. Helms-Burton allows the State Department to deny entry visas to the top officials and representatives of companies and their families that use or benefit from property in Cuba that was confiscated from Americans after 1959. This would exclude these firms from exporting to, or doing business in, the United States. Also, the legislation gives American citizens and businesses the right to sue foreign companies that use or benefit from confiscated property in Cuba. United States courts may order the assets of foreign companies seized to pay judgments. Former President Clinton suspended the provisions allowing private lawsuits.

The visit to Cuba of Pope John Paul II from January 21st to the 25th of 1998, gave the Catholic Church in the country a significant moral boost and gave hope to many that a revitalized Church could help Cubans gain a degree of political space from which Cuban civil society could grow. Castro released 100 political prisoners and 200 common criminals. Yet, political repression has not decreased.

The former Clinton Administration lifted the ban on direct flights to Cuba from Miami, on direct transfer of cash to relatives of Cuban-Americans (up to $300 every three months) and on food transfer to Cuba; and Clinton streamlined the issuance of license to U.S. pharmaceutical and medical equipment companies to sell their products in Cuba. Also, the Clinton Administration reached an agreement with the **European Union** which waives title IV of the **Helms Burton** law, which requires the President to bar from the United States foreign executives and their families if they invest in property in Cuba claimed by U.S. citizens. In return, European governments cannot grant loans, subsidies or political risk insurance to businesses that invest in countries with an "established record" of expropriation. President George W. Bush continued the Clinton Policy.

In 1999, the United Nations Commission on Human Rights approved a Czech-Polish resolution placing Cuba in the list of human rights abusers. This happened again in the spring of 2000 and also in 2001. Cuba received negative world-wide publicity when it sentenced to 3- to 4-year prison terms four individuals accused of publishing a document criticizing the Communist Party's monopoly of power.

Currently, there is pressure from the U.S. Chamber of Commerce and from various politicians in the U.S. Congress to soften or eliminate the U.S. Embargo on Cuba to promote more commercial and humanitarian contact with the island which could help move Cuba to a more democratic state. However, supporters of the embargo believe such changes will guarantee the continuation of the regime, strengthen Cuban state enterprises which are the vast majority in the island, lead to greater repression of Cubans to control greater U.S. influence in Cuba, delay a transition to democracy, allow Fidel Castro to borrow from international organizations, perpetuate the control the military has over the economy, and undermine U.S. policy for Latin America which emphasize democracy, human rights and market economies.

Recent US-Cuban relations have been strained. On June 8, 2001, an America jury convicted five Cuban spies charged with espionage and association with the shooting down of two civilian planes carrying U.S. citizens. In 2002, the United Nations, with American and Czech support, rebuked Cuba for its human rights abuses. In March 2000, Ana Belen Montes, a senior analyst for U.S. Defense Intelligence Agency, pleaded guilty to espionage for Cuba. On May 12–17, 2002, former President Jimmy Carter visited Cuba and spoke against the Cuban embargo by the United States. However, he also supported the **Varela Project,** a 12,000 signature petition drive by Cubans using the 1996 Cuban Constitution to demand free speech, free elections, amnesty for political prisoners and the right to own and operate private business. The United States has given support to the Cuban opposition. In 2003, Castro executed three Cubans for trying to hijack a ship to leave Cuba and imprisoned for up to 28 years seventy-five dissident journalists, artists and peace activists. In response, the United Nations Rights Commission in 2003 gave Cuba only a bland condemnation, and merely asked Cuba to accept a visit of a United Nations human rights investigator.

On April 2004, another resolution of the UN Human Rights Commission passed asking Cuba to refrain from denying human rights, freedom of expression and due process to its own people. The resolution was submitted by Honduras and was co-sponsored by Australia, the Czech Republic, El Salvador, Nicaragua and Peru. Similar resolutions have been approved yearly since 1992, except for 1998. Still, the United Nations will not act to remedy Cuba's terrible human rights violations, as it has done in Haiti, South Africa, and a few other places. Naturally, Cuba's diplomatic relations with Honduras and the sponsoring countries have worsened. Relations with Mexico, its former ally, have hit a low mark after its President accused Cuba of interfering in Mexico's domestic affairs.

In reaction to Fidel Castro's repression, the European Union, which has 35% of Cuba's trade and 50% of its foreign investment and tourism, threatened economic sanctions. Cuba will not be part of the European Union's Cotonou Agreement which provides preferential trade and an aid pact between the EU and 78 poor countries. The United States also responded on March 25, 2003, with new rules: more Cuban-Americans can visit relatives in Cuba; fewer non-academic educational exchanges will occur; the flow of money Cuban-Americans can take to relatives and opponents of the regime in Cuba is increased from $300 to $3,000 per quarter.

However, in April 2004 the Bush Administration reduced travel to Cuba by Cuban-Americans to one trip every three years to visit only immediate family, and reduced the daily spending allowed from $164.00 to $50.00. It excluded distant relatives and Communist Party members from the list of those who can receive the annual $1200 in remittances. The United States committed $45 million over two years to enforce these restrictions and to support dissidents. Cuba responded to these measures by suspending in May 2004 dollar sales of nonessential items at its Dollar stores. Dollars were legalized in Cuba in 1993 after the collapse of the Soviet Union and the end of the $5 billion per year subsidy from Russia. The dollar stores had a $950 million business in 2003.

During 2006 and 2007, Fidel Castro became physically and mentally incapacitated and power was transferred "temporarily" to his brother Raul Castro, the head of the armed forces of Cuba. Fidel Castro is still governing Cuba in 2010. The biggest success of the Cuban regime in the 2000s has been the transformation of oil-rich Venezuela gradually into a Communist ally which provides Cuba with oil and which supports radicalism in the region.

Haiti

Haiti occupies the western one-third of the Island of Hispaniola in the West Indies. It has a population of eight million, of which 95% are Black. Only 32% of the population is urban. The principal languages are Haitian Creole and French. Life expectancy at birth is 47 years for a male and 51 for a female. The infant mortality rate per 1,000 live births is 104. This is the highest rate in the Americas. Literacy is only 50%. Over 23% of children up to five years of age are malnourished. Only 40% have access to clean water. Measles, malaria and tuberculosis are epidemic. One in twelve Haitians has AIDS. Seventy percent are unemployed or underemployed.

The Duvalier family controlled Haiti from 1957 to 1986. Five different governments and much violence followed the exit of Jean-Claude Duvalier in 1986. Then, in December 1990, Jean-Bertrand Aristide was elected President of Haiti. In September 1991, he was arrested and expelled by the military. He was accused of urging violence against his opponents, including the practice of necklacing in which people are burned alive. Waves of refugees (35,000) began leaving Haiti, though most returned, to be followed by more departures in 1993.

The United Nations imposed a worldwide oil, arms, and financial embargo on Haiti on June 23, 1993. The embargo and a planned military invasion of Haiti were suspended on July 31, 1994, when the Haitian military agreed to step down and allow Aristide to return to office. As part of the agreement, American troops began arriving in Haiti on September 19. Aristide was restored to office on October 15, and a United Nations peacekeeping force took over responsibility for Haiti on March 31, 1995. Aristide transferred power to his elected successor, Rene Preval on February 7, 1996. Although the last combat troops left Haiti on April 17, 1996, a small UN peacekeeping force of 1,200 remained until January 1998. U.S. troops left Haiti in January 2000. The total cost to the United States has exceeded $5 billion.

From June 1997 to 2003, the government of Haiti and its opposition almost paralyzed the state over electoral disagreements. Meanwhile, Haiti continued hurting with decrepit roads, dams, electric and telephone utilities and ports. Farmers cannot afford to plant. Crime is out of control. Local industry is going broke because of contraband. Smuggling of refugees is increasing as they leave Port-de-Paix, to the Bahamas, and then to the United States. Although 66% of Haitians live in the countryside and depend on the land, only 7% of international aid has gone into agriculture. There is a need for rural policy to reduce immigration.

Haiti is ranked 153rd in the quality of life index out of 174 countries, and the poorest country in the Western Hemisphere, with a low annual per capita income. Haiti has become a transhipment point for 14% of all the cocaine brought into the United States, gradually converting the country into a narco-state. This undermines the valiant efforts of those who are trying to build democratic institutions. From 1997 to 1999, Haiti lost from $500 to $800 million in foreign aid due to the absence of a functioning parliament. This was due to a conflict between the Lavalas Family group associated with Bertrand Aristide and Rene Preval and their opponents. Rising oil prices and growing inflation have lowered economic production. The general elections of May 21, 2000 were so flawed that the head of Haiti's Provisional Electoral Counsel refused to validate the count and fled to the United States seeking relief from political intimidation. He claimed only five seats were won outright while the Lavalas Family group claimed 17 seats won.

Aristide was accused of corruption, becoming a multimillionaire on a salary of $10,000 a month. When he had been in exile between 1990 and 1994, both Presidents George Bush and Bill Clinton allowed Aristide unrestricted access to the millions of dollars Haiti had in the US Federal Reserve Bank. Upon his return to Haiti, many of his opponents accused him of profiteering out of the national phone company. As a result of violent opposition to his rule, President Bertrand Aristide resigned on February 29, 2004, leaving the country with a $100 million budget

deficit, an energy crunch, devastated armies, and $350,000 in cash at his villa. Over $1 billion in public funds were stolen in the last three weeks of his Presidency. Pro-Aristide forces looted businesses and residences.

The UN Security Council deployed up to 6,700 military peace keepers, 1,622 police officers to replace the 2,000 American marines and 1,500 troops from Canada, Chile and France who rushed to Haiti after Aristide's resignation to stop the violence. Gerard Latortue was selected by a group of influential Haitians to be Prime Minister and Boniface Alexandre was appointed as President. Rene Preval won the presidential election of February 7, 2006. Haitians, and foreign governments assisting it, will have to establish security in the country, repress the gangs, secure property rights, provide electricity, and reinvent the police, court and educational establishments with a maximum of political inclusiveness.

The Caribbean

Leaders from twenty-one Caribbean Basin states held the **Association of Caribbean States Summit** of April 17, 1999, and agreed to pursue a regional tariff system to prepare for a hemispheric-wide trade area. They sought closer cooperation promoting tourism, responding to natural disasters, and upgrading air and sea transportation links.

The countries of the Caribbean, particularly the English-speaking ones, complain that the United States views the region only in the context of narcotics. They are upset about the reduction of U.S. assistance to the area, the failure of the U.S. Congress to upgrade trade incentives, especially on apparel, the repatriation of Caribbean criminals from the United States back to their homelands, and the U.S. complaint to the **World Trade Organization** (WTO) over preferential access of Caribbean bananas to the European Union. President Bill Clinton signed on May 18, 2000, a bill to increase incentives for apparel imports from Caribbean Basin countries.

On the 30th anniversary of the Caribbean Community (CARICOM), its leaders met in July 2003 to seek the creation of a European Union-like economic bloc that could erase trade restrictions, create a regional stock market, and allow the free flow of capital among island countries. A separate commission will oversee the market. CARICOM wants special access to foreign markets and to be able to compete with the larger countries such as Brazil, Canada and others. The 15-member Caribbean Community trades the most with the United States, but the European Union is its second most important trade partner. In 2004, Caribbean trade ministers met with European Union officials to create a new trade pact which could increase commerce by $12 billion a year. However, the **Economic Partnership Agreement** is conditioned upon significant reduction of tariffs among the fifteen countries.

Terrorism

Globalization is a reality which applies not only to trade, investments, and communications, but also to terrorism, as terrorist groups travel and communicate globally and even establish networks of cooperation across borders. **Terrorism is warfare against civilians.** The most virulent form of this type of warfare today is **Islamic terrorism.** Governments which respond to terrorists by killing innocent civilians indiscriminately are also engaging in terrorism. Fidel Castro of Cuba pioneered in global terrorism when he invited in 1966 many terrorist groups to Cuba to train and to establish ties among each other.

While terrorists might have ideological differences among themselves, they tend to have common enemies and traits. They usually oppose such liberal institutions as a free press, market economies, separation of church and state, political parties, emancipation of women, ideological diversity, and other practices associated with modern, westernized societies. Terrorists are willing to murder innocent civilians since they do not distinguish civilians from combatants. In this, they express a totalitarian mentality which does not accept legitimate opposition to its agenda, which typically consists of the takeover of the government and the imposition of absolute power. Terrorists frequently recruit members and raise funding in the same free societies that they seek to destroy. The most important target of the terrorists is the United States of America and its allies worldwide.

One of the most active terrorists are those linked to Osama bin Laden's **Al Qaeda** or the **World Islamic Front Against Jews and Crusaders (Christians).** While these umbrella groups are mostly Arab, and many are Saudi Arabian, they do have links with groups outside the Middle East. Examples are **al-Ittihaad al Islamiya,** active in Africa, **Jemaah Islamiyah** in Indonesia and throughout Southeast Asia, **the Moro Islamic Liberation Front** in the southern Philippines, **Ansar al Islam** in northern Iraq, and the **Salafit Group for Call and Combat** in Algeria, among others.

These groups would not be able to function without the assistance of supporters in the free world and of dictatorships like Cuba, Iran, Libya, Saudi Arabia and Syria. Closely allied with Iran is **Hezbollah** which is active in Lebanon, Gaza, the West Bank and even in Colombia and Brazil. Active in "Palestine" are also **Hamas, Islamic Jihad, and the Palestinian Liberation Organization (PLO),** a majority of whose members want the creation of a Palestinian state and the destruction of Israel. In Latin America, the most active terrorist groups are the Colombian **FARC,** and the **ELN,** which, by the way, receive the cooperation of the **Irish Republican Army** (IRA) and of Fidel Castro of Cuba.

Terrorism feeds upon the insecurities and alienation that globalization and modernization generate among the least able to adapt to the changes of the modern world. It also appeals to those of the highly educated classes whose pride fuels a desire to gain absolute power to impose their totalitarian dreams upon others, using as cannon fodder those most desperate and uneducated. It also appeals to those who fear lives lived in utter insignificance and who feel powerful and meaningful by joining such terrorist groups.

The reason most terrorists attacking Western countries are classified as Islamic terrorists is that the people doing the killing claim to be Muslim and justify their war as a violent Jihad against the infidels and the apostates on verses found in the Koran. The theoretical basis of the Jihadists was provided by Sayyid Qutb (1906–1966), the ideologue of the Egyptian **Muslim Brotherhood,** who in turn influenced Osama bin Laden. Infidels are to be killed wherever they are found (Koran 2:191, 2:244, 4:89, 5:36, 9:5, 9:29). They are to be slaughtered (Koran 8:68). Allah will instill terror in the unbelievers and Jihadists are to cut off their heads and finger tips (Koran 8:12). They are to plunder those they have slain (Koran 8:41, 8:69). Muslims are justified in committing genocide (Koran 17:16, 21:11). Jews and Christians are to be fought and humiliated (Koran 9:29). Friendships with Christians are not allowed (Koran 3:28, 5:51, 9:23). There must be no mercy with infidels (Koran 5:36–38, 48:29). The Jihad cannot end until the entire world worships Allah (Koran 2:193, 8:39, 61:9). The Jihadists believe that all the peace verses in the Koran were abrogated or replaced by the Verse of the Sword (Koran 9:5) and others which seek the killing of the infidels everywhere. Fighting is obligatory (Koran 2:216). While some verses imply that suicide killing is not allowed, others like (Koran 9:111), are used by the Jihadists to support it. There are approximately 109 war verses in the Koran used by the Jihadists to justify their violence. Those Muslims who disagree with this point of view are considered apostates by al-Qaeda and its allies and can be killed.

Map of Freedom 2009

FREEDOM HOUSE

Africa

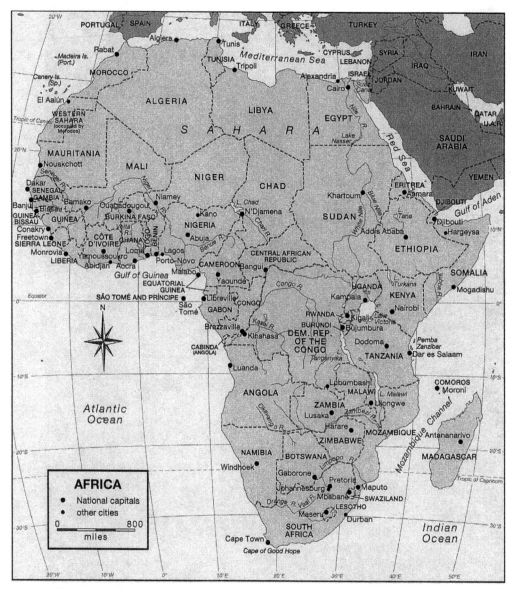

Courtesy of maps.com.

North America

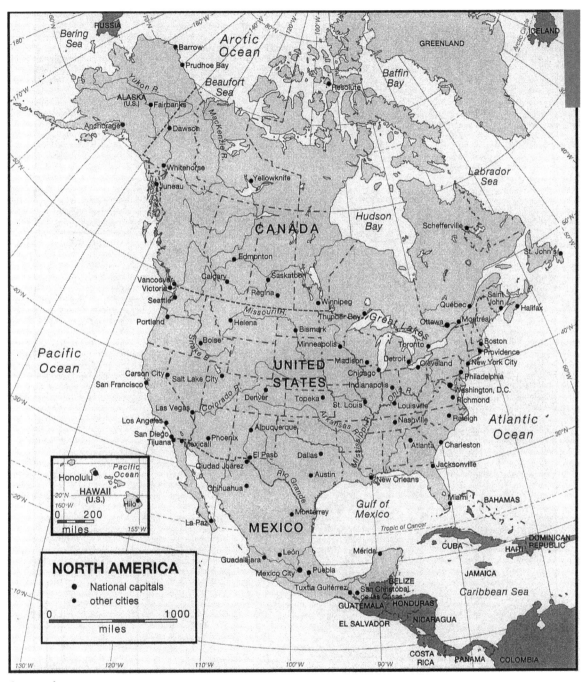

Courtesy of maps.com.

Asia (Pacific)

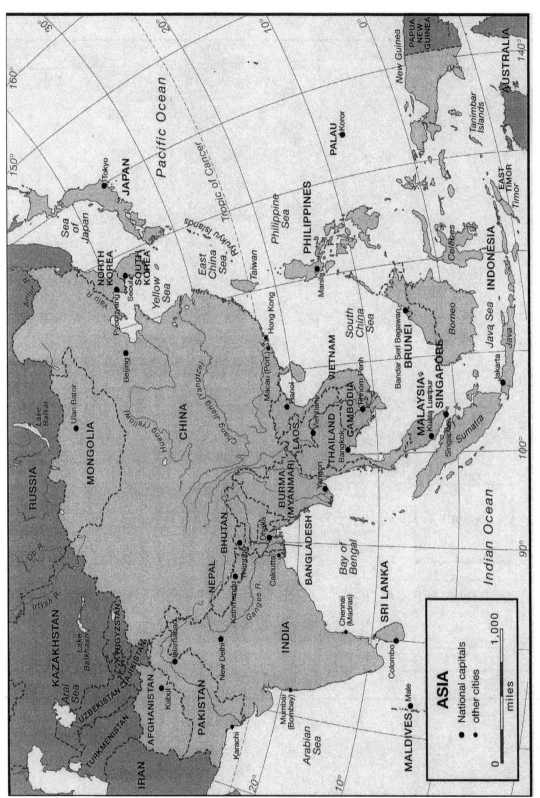

ASIA
• National capitals
• other cities

Courtesy of maps.com.

Europe

Courtesy of maps.com.

Russia and Eurasia

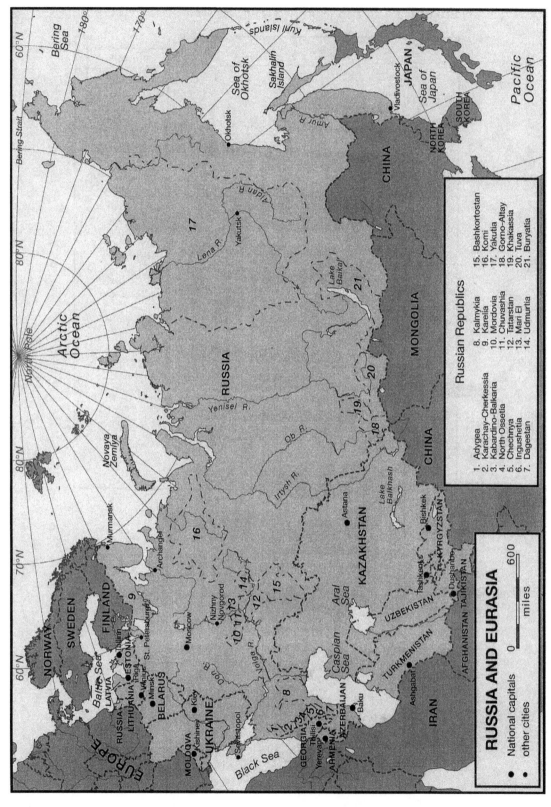

Russian Republics

1. Adygea	8. Kalmykia	15. Bashkortostan
2. Karachay-Cherkessia	9. Karelia	16. Komi
3. Kabardino-Balkaria	10. Mordovia	17. Yakutia
4. North Ossetia	11. Chuvashia	18. Gorno-Altay
5. Chechnya	12. Tatarstan	19. Khakassia
6. Ingushetia	13. Mari El	20. Tuva
7. Dagestan	14. Udmurtia	21. Buryatia

RUSSIA AND EURASIA

● National capitals
· other cities

0   600
miles

Courtesy of maps.com.

Latin America

Courtesy of maps.com.

Magna Carta (1215)

The most important political document in English history, King John (1199–1216) granted this charter of liberties for English freemen under the threat of civil war from this barons.

John, by the grace of God, king of England, lord of Ireland, duke of Normandy and Aquitaine, count of Anjou, to the archbishops, bishops, abbots, earls, barons, justiciars, foresters, sheriffs, reeves, servants, and all bailiffs and his faithful people greeting. Know that by the suggestion of God and for the good of our soul and those of all our predecessors and of our heirs, to the honor of God and the exaltation of holy church, and the improvement of our kingdom, by the advice of our venerable fathers Stephen, archbishop of Canterbury, primate of all England and Cardinal of the Holy Roman Church, Henry, archbishop of Dublin, William of London, Peter of Winchester, Joscelyn of Bath and Glastonbury, Hugh of Lincoln, Walter of Worcester, William of Coventry, and Benedict of Rochester, bishops; of Master Pandulf, subdeacon and member of the household of the lord Pope, of Brother Aymeric, master of the Knights of the Temple in England; and of the noblemen William Marshall, earl of Pembroke, William, earl of Salisbury, William, earl Warren, William, earl of Arendel, Alan of Galloway, constable of Scotland, Warren Fitz-Gerald, Peter Fitz-Herbert, Hubert de Burgh, seneschal of Poitou, Hugh de Nevil, Matthew Fitz-Herbert, Thomas Bassett, Alan Bassett, Philip d'Albini, Robert de Ropesle, John Marshall, John Fitz-Hugh, and others of our faithful.

1. In the first place we have granted to God, and by this our present charter confirmed, for us and our heirs forever, that the English church shall be free, and shall hold its right entire and its liberties uninjured; and we will that it thus be observed; which is shown by this, that the freedom of elections, which is considered to be most important and especially necessary to the English church, we, of our pure and spontaneous will, granted, and by our charter confirmed, before the contest between us and our barons had arisen; and obtained a confirmation of it by the lord Pope Innocent III; which we will observe and which we will shall be observed in good faith by our heirs forever.

   We have granted moroever to all free men of our kingdom for us and our heirs forever all the liberties written below, to be had and holden by themselves and their heirs from us and our heirs.

2. If any of our earls or barons, or others holding from us in chief by military service shall have died, and when he has died his heir shall be of full age and owe relief, he shall have his inheritance by the ancient relief; that is to say, the heir or heirs of an earl for the whole barony of an earl a hundred pounds; the heir of heirs of a baron for a whole barony a hundred pounds; the heir or heirs of a knight, for a whole knight's fee, a hundred shillings at most; and who owes less let him give less according to the ancient custom of fiefs.

3. If moreover the heir of any one of such shall be under age, and shall be in wardship, when he comes of age he shall have his inheritance without relief and without a fine.

4. The custodian of the land of such a minor heir shall not take from the land of heir any except reasonable products, reasonable customary payments, and reasonable services, and this without destruction or waste of men or of property; and if we shall have committed the custody of the land of any such a one to the sheriff or to any other who is to be responsible

to us for its proceeds, and that man shall have caused destruction or waste from his custody we will recover damages from him, and the land shall be committed to two legal and discreet men of that fief, who shall be responsible for its proceeds to us or to him to whom we have assigned them; and if we shall have given or sold to any one the custody of any such land, and he has caused destruction or waste there, he shall lose that custody, and it shall be handed over to two legal and discreet men of that fief who shall be in like manner responsible to us as is said above.

5. The custodian moreover, so long as he shall have the custody of the land, must keep up the houses, parks, warrens, fish ponds, mills, and other things pertaining to the land, from the proceeds of the land itself; and he must return to the heir, when he has come to full age, all his land, furnished with ploughs and implements of husbandry according as the time of wainage requires and as the proceeds of the land are able reasonably to sustain.

6. Heirs shall be married without disparity, so nevertheless that before the marriage is contracted, it shall be announced to the relatives by blood of the heir himself.

7. A widow, after the death of her husband, shall have her marriage portion and her inheritance immediately and without obstruction, nor shall she give anything for her dowry or for her marriage portion, or for her inheritance which inheritance her husband and she held on the day of the death of her husband; and she may remain in the house of her husband for forty days after his death, within which time her dowry shall be assigned to her.

8. No widow shall be compelled to marry so long as she prefers to live without a husband, provided she gives security that she will not marry without our consent, if she holds from us, or without the consent of her lord from whom she holds, if she holds from another.

9. Neither we nor our bailiffs will seize any lane or rent, for any debt, so long as the chattels of the debtor are sufficient for the payment of the debt; not shall the pledges of a debtor be distrained so long as the principal debtor himself has enough for the payment of the debt; and if the principal debtor fails in the payment of the debt, not having the wherewithal to pay it, the pledges shall be responsible for the debt; and if they wish, they shall have the lands and the rents of the debtor until they shall have been satisfied for the debt which they have before paid for him, unless the principal debtor shall have shown himself to be quit in that respect towards those pledges.

10. If any one has taken anything from the Jews, by way of a loan, more or less, and dies before that debt is paid, the debt shall not draw interest so long as the heir is under age, from whomsoever he holds; and if that debt falls into our hands, we will take nothing expect the chattel contained in the agreement.

11. And if any one dies leaving a debt owing to the Jews, his wife shall have her dowry, and shall pay nothing of that debt; and if there remain minor children of the dead man, necessaries shall be provided for them corresponding to the holding of the dead man; and from the remainder shall be paid the debt, saving the service of the lords. In the same way debts are to be treated which are owed to others than the Jews.

12. No scutage or aid shall be imposed in our kingdom except by the common council of our kingdom, except for the ransoming of our body, for the making of our oldest son a knight, and for once marrying our oldest daughter, and for these purposes it shall be only a reasonable aid; in the same way it shall be done concerning the aids of the city of London.

13. And the city of London shall have all its ancient liberties and free customs, as well by land as by water. Moreover, we will and grant that all other cities and boroughs and villages and ports shall have all their liberties and free customs.

14. And for holding a common council of the kingdom concerning the assessment of an aid otherwise than in the three cases mentioned above, or concerning the assessment of a scutage we shall cause to be summoned the archbishops, bishops, abbots, earls, and greater barons by our letters individually; and besides we shall cause to be summoned generally, by our sheriffs and bailiffs all those who hold from us in chief, for a certain day, that is at the end of forty days at least, and for a certain place; and in all the letters of that summons, we will express the cause of the summons, and when the summons has thus been given the business shall proceed on the appointed day, on the advice of those who shall be present, even if not all of those who were summoned have come.

15. We will not grant to any one, moreover, that he shall take an aid from his free men, except for ransoming his body, for making his oldest son a knight, and for once marrying his oldest daughter; and for these purposes only a reasonable aid shall be taken.

16. No one shall be compelled to perform any greater service for a knight's fee, or for any other free tenement than is owed from it.

17. The common pleas shall not follow our court, but shall be held in some certain place.

18. The recognition of *novel disseisin, mort d'ancestor,* and *darrein presentment* shall be held only in their own counties and in this manner: we, or if we are outside of the kingdom our principal justiciar, will send two justiciars through each county four times a year, who with four Knights of each county, elected by the county, shall hold in the county, and on the day and in the place of the county court, the aforesaid assizes of the county.

19. And if the aforesaid assizes cannot be held within the day of the county court, a sufficient number of knights and free-holders shall remain from those who were present at the county court on that day to give the judgements, according as the business is more or less.

20. A free man shall not be fined for a small offence, except in proportion to the measure of the offence; and for a great offence he shall be fined in proportion to the magnitude of the offence, saving his freehold; and a merchant in the same way, saving his merchandise; and the villain shall be fined in the same way, saving his wainage, if he shall be at our mercy; and none of the above fines shall be imposed except by the oaths of honest men of the neighborhood.

21. Earls and barons shall only be fined by their peers, and only in proportion to their offence.

22. A clergyman shall be fined, like those before mentioned, only in proportion to his lay holding, and not according to the extent of his ecclesiastical benefice.

23. No vill or man shall be compelled to make bridges over the rivers except those which ought to do it of old and rightfully.

24. No sheriff, constable, coroners, or other bailiffs of ours shall hold pleas of our crown.

25. All counties, hundreds, wapentakes, and trithings shall be at the ancient rents and without any increase, excepting our demesne manors.

26. If any person holding a lay fief from us shall die, and our sheriff or bailiff shall show our letters-patent of our summons concerning a debt which the deceased owed to us, it shall be lawful for our sheriff or bailiff to attach and levy on the chattels of the deceased found on his lay fief, to the value of that debt, in the view of legal men, so nevertheless that nothing be removed thence until the clear debt to us shall be paid; and the remainder shall be left to the executors for the fulfilment of the will of the deceased; and if nothing is owed to us by him, all the chattels shall go to the deceased, saving to his wife and children their reasonable shares.

27. If any free man dies intestate, his chattels shall be distributed by the hands of his near relatives and friends, under the oversight of the church, saving to each one the debts which the deceased owed to him.

28. No constable or other bailiff of ours shall take any one's grain or other chattels, without immediately paying for them in money, unless he is able to obtain a postponement at the goodwill of the seller.

29. No constable shall require any knight to give money in place of his ward of a castle if he is willing to furnish that ward in his own person or through another honest man, if he himself is not able to do it for a reasonable cause; and if we shall lead or send him into the army he shall be free from ward in proportion to the amount of time during which he has been in the army through us.

30. No sheriff or bailiff of ours or any one else shall take horses or wagons of any free man for carrying purposes except on the permission of that free man.

31. Neither we nor our bailiffs will take the wood of another man of castles, or for anything else which we are doing, except by the permission of him to whom the wood belongs.

32. We will not hold the lands of those convicted of a felony for more than a year and a day, after which the lands shall be returned to the lords of the fiefs.

33. All the fish-weirs in the Thames and the Medway, and throughout all England shall be done away with, except those on the coast.

34. The writ which is called *praecipe* shall not be given for the future to any one concerning any tenement by which a free man can lose his court.

35. There shall be one measure of wine throughout our whole kingdom, and one measure of ale, and one measure of grain, that is the London quarter, and one width of dyed cloth and of russets and of halbergets, that is two ells within the selvages; of weights, moreover it shall be as of measures.

36. Nothing shall henceforth be given or taken for a writ of inquisition concerning life or limbs, but it shall be given freely and not denied.

37. If any one holds from us by fee farm or by socage or by burgage, and from another he holds land by military service, we will not have the guardianship of the heir or of his land which is of the fief of another, on account of that fee farm, or socage, or burgage; nor will we have the custody of that fee farm, or socage, or burgage, unless that fee farm itself owes military service. We will not have the guardianship of the heir or of the land of any one, which he holds from another by military service on account of any petty serjeanty which he holds from us by the service of paying to us knives or arrows, or things of that kind.

38. No bailiff for the future shall put any one to his law on his simple affirmation, without credible witnesses brought for this purpose.

39. No free man shall be taken or imprisoned or dispossessed, or outlawed, or banished, or in any way destroyed, nor will we go upon him, nor send upon him, except by the legal judgment of his peers or by the law of the land.

40. To no one will we sell, to no one will we deny, or delay right or justice.

41. All merchants shall be safe and secure in going out from England and coming into England and in remaining and going through England, as well by land as by water, for buying and selling, free from all evil tolls, by the ancient and rightful customs, except in time of war, and if they are of a land at war with us; and if such are found in our land at the beginning of war, they shall be attached without injury to their bodies or goods, until it shall be known from us or from our principal justiciar in what way the merchants of our land are treated who shall be then found in the country which is at war with us; and if ours are safe there, the others shall be safe in our land.

42. It is allowed henceforth to any one to go out from our kingdom, and to return, safely and securely, by land and by water, saving their fidelity to us, except in time of war for some short time, for the common good of the kingdom; excepting persons imprisoned and outlawed according to the law of the realm, and people of a land at war with us, and merchants, of whom it shall be done as is before said.

43. If any one holds from any escheat, as from the honor of Wallingford, or Nottingham, or Boulogne, or Lancaster, or from other escheats which are in our hands and are baronies, and he dies, his heir shall not give any other relief, nor do to us any other service than he would do to the baron, if that barony was in the hands of the baron; and we will hold it in the same way as the baron held it.

44. Men who dwell outside the forest shall not henceforth come before our justiciars of the forest, on common summons, unless they are in a plea of, or pledges for any person or persons who are arrested on account of the forest.

45. We will not make justiciars, constables, sheriffs or bailiffs except of such as know the law of the realm and are well inclined to observe it.

46. All barons who haved founded abbeys for which they have charters of kings of England, or ancient tenure, shall have their custody when they have become vacant, as they ought to have.

47. All forests which have been afforested in our time shall be disafforested immediately; and so it shall be concerning river banks which in our time have been fenced in.

48. All the bad customs concerning forests and warrens and concerning foresters and warreners, sheriffs and their servants, river banks and their guardians shall be inquired into immediately in each county by twelve sworn knights of the same county, who shall be elected by the honest men of the same county, and within forty days after the inquisition has been made, they shall be entirely destroyed by them, never to be restored, provided that we be first informed of it, or our justician, if we are not in England.

49. We will give back immediately all hostages and charters which have been liberated to us by Englishmen as security for peace or for faithful service.

50. We will remove absolutely from their bailiwicks the relatives of Gerard de Athyes, so that for the future they shall have no bailiwick in England; Engelard de Cygony, Andrew, Peter and Gyon de Chancelles, Gyon de Cygony, Geoffrey de Martin and his brothers, Philip Mark and his brothers, and Geoffrey his nephew and their whole retinue.

51. And immediately after the reëstablishment of peace we will remove from the kingdom all foreign-born soldiers, crossbow men, serjeants, and mercenaries who have come with horses and arms for the injury of the realm.

52. If any one shall have been dispossessed or removed by us without legal judgement of his peers, from his lands, castles, franchises, or his right we will restore them to him immediately; and if contention arises

about this, then it shall be done according to the judgment of the twenty-five barons, of whom mention is made below concerning the security of the peace. Concerning all those things, however, from which any one has been removed or of which he has been deprived without legal judgement of his peers by King Henry our father, or by King Richard our brother, which we have in our hand, or which others hold, and which it is our duty to guarantee, we shall have respite till the usual term of crusaders; excepting those things about which the suit has been begun or the inquisition made by our writ before our assumption of the cross; when, however, we shall return from our journey or if by chance we desist from the journey, we will immediately show full justice in regard to them.

53. We shall, moreover, have the same respite and in the same manner about showing justice in regard to the forests which are to be disafforested or to remain forests, which Henry our father or Richard our brother made into forests; and concerning the custody of lands which are in the fief of another, custody of which we have until now had on account of a fief which any one has held from us by military service; and concerning the abbeys which have been founded in fiefs of others than ourselves, in which the lord of the fee has asserted for himself a right; and when we return or if we should desist from our journey we will immediately show full justice to those complaining in regard to them.

54. No one shall be seised nor imprisoned on the appeal of a woman concerning the death of any one except her husband.

55. All fines which have been imposed unjustly and against the law of the land, and all penalties imposed unjustly and against the law of the land are altogether excused, or will be on the judgement of the twenty-five barons of whom mention is made below in connection with the security of the peace, or on the judgement of the majority of them, along with the aforesaid Stephen, archbishop of Canterbury, if he is able to be present, and others whom he may wish to call for this purpose along with him. And if he should not be able to be present, nevertheless the business shall go on without him, provided that if any one or more of the aforesaid twenty-five barons are in a similar suit they should be removed as far as this particular judgment goes, and others who shall be chosen and put upon oath, by the remainder of

the twenty-five shall be substituted for them for this purpose.

56. If we have dispossessed or removed any Welshmen from their lands, or franchises, or other things, without legal judgment of their peers, in England, or in Wales, they shall be immediately returned to them; and if a dispute shall have arisen over this, then it shall be settled in the borderland by judgment of their peers, concerning holdings of Wales according to the law of Wales, and concerning holdings of the borderland according to the law of the borderland. The Welsh shall do the same to us and ours.

57. Concerning all those things, however, from which any one of the Welsh shall have been removed or dispossessed without legal judgment of his peers, by King Henry our father, or King Richard our brother, which we hold in our hands, or which others hold, and we are bound to warrant to them, we shall have respite till the usual period of crusaders, those being excepted about which suit was begun or inquisition made by our command before our assumption of the cross. When, however, we shall return or if by chance we shall desist from our journey, we will show full justice to them immediately, according to the laws of the Welsh and the aforesaid parts.

58. We will give back the son of Llewellyn immediately, and all the hostages from Wales and the charters which had been liberated to us as a security for peace.

59. We will act toward Alexander, king of the Scots, concerning the return of his sisters and his hostages, and concerning his franchises and his right, according to the manner in which we shall act toward our other barons of England, unless it ought to be otherwise by the charters which we hold from William his father, formerly king of the Scots, and this shall be by the judgement of his peers in our court.

60. Moreover, all those customs and franchises mentioned above which we have conceded in our kingdom, and which are to be fulfilled, as far as pertains to us, in respect to our men; all men of our kingdom as well clergy as laymen, shall observe as far as pertains to them, in respect to their men.

61. Since, moreover, for the sake of God, and for the improvement of our kingdom, and for the better quieting of the hostility sprung up lately between us and our barons, we have made all these concessions; wishing them to enjoy these in a complete and firm stability forever, we make and concede to them the security described below; that is to say, that they shall

elect twenty-five barons of the kingdom, whom they will, who ought with all their power to observe, hold, and cause to be observed, the peace and liberties which we have conceded to them, and by this our present charter confirmed to them; in this manner, that if we or our justiciar, or our bailiffs, or any one of our servants shall have done wrong in any way toward any one, or shall have transgressed any of the articles of peace or security; and the wrong shall have been shown to four barons of the aforesaid twenty-five barons, let those four barons come to us or to our justiciar, if we are out of the kingdom, laying before us the transgression, and let them ask that we cause that transgression to be corrected without delay. And if we shall not have corrected the transgression or, if we shall be out of the kingdom if our justiciar shall not have corrected it within a period of forty days, counting from the time in which it has been shown to us or to our justiciar, if we are out of the kingdom; the aforesaid four barons shall refer the matter to the remainder of the twenty-five barons, and let these twenty-five barons with the whole community of the country distress and injure us in every way they can; that is to say by the seizure of our castles, lands, possessions, and in such other ways as they can until it shall have been corrected according to their judgment, saving our person and that of our queen, and those of our children; and when the correction has been made, let them devote themselves to us as they did before. And let whoever in the country wishes take an oath that in all the above-mentioned measures he will obey the orders of the aforesaid twenty-five barons, and that he will injure us as far as he is able with them, and we give permission to swear publicly and freely to each one who wishes to swear, and no one will we ever forbid to swear. All those, moreover, in the country who of themselves and their own will are unwilling to take an oath to the twenty-five barons as to distressing and injuring us along with them, we will compel to take the oath by our mandate, as before said. And if any one of the twenty-five barons shall have died or departed from the land or shall in any other way be prevented from taking the above-mentioned action, let the remainder of the aforesaid twenty-five barons choose another in his place, according to their judgment, who shall take an oath in the same way

as the others. In all those things, moreover, which are committed to those five and twenty barons to carry out, if perhaps the twenty-five are present, and some disagreement arises among them about something, or if any of them when they have been summoned are not willing or are not able to be present, let that be considered valid and firm which the greater part of those who are present arrange or command, just as if the whole twenty-five had agreed in this; and let the aforesaid twenty-five swear that they will observe faithfully all the things which are said above, and with all their ability cause them to be observed. And we will obtain nothing from any one, either by ourselves or by another by which any of these concessions and liberties shall be revoked or diminished; and if any such thing shall have been obtained, let it be invalid and void, and we will never use it by ourselves or by another.

62. And all ill-will, grudges, and anger sprung up between us and our men, clergy and laymen, from the time of the dispute, we have fully renounced and pardoned to all. Moreover, all transgressions committed on account of this dispute, from Easter in the sixteenth year of our reign till the restoration of peace, we have fully remitted to all, clergy and laymen, and as far as pertains to us, fully pardoned. And moreover we have caused to be made for them testimonial letters-patent of lord Stephen, archbishop of Canterbury, lord Henry, archbishop of Dublin, and of the aforesaid bishops and of Master Pandulf, in respect to that security and the concessions named above.

63. Wherefore we will and firmly command that the Church of England shall be free, and that the men in our kingdom shall have and hold all the aforesaid liberties, rights and concessions, well and peacefully, freely and quietly, fully and completely, for themselves and their heirs, from us and our heirs, in all things and places, forever, as before said. It has been sworn, moreover, as well on our part as on the part of the barons, that all these things spoken of above shall be observed in good faith and without any evil intent. Witness the above named and many others. Given by our hand in the meadow which is called Runnymede, between Windsor and Staines, on the fifteenth day of June, in the seventeenth year of our reign.

The Declaration of Independence

Stimulated by Paine's persuasive arguments, the sentiment for independence grew steadily throughout the colonies in 1776. In early June, Richard Henry Lee, a Virginian, rose in the Second Continental Congress and moved that "these United Colonies are, and of right ought to be, Free and Independent States." To satisfy a reluctant minority, the Congress agreed to postpone for three weeks a final vote on Lee's resolution. Meanwhile, the delegates appointed a five-man committee headed by Thomas Jefferson to prepare a statement of independence.

Jefferson was a surprising choice for this momentous assignment. At thirty-three, he was one of the youngest members of the Congress and relatively unknown. In the Virginia House of Burgesses, he had been a leader in the struggle against British oppression. A shy man in public, he had seldom spoken out in the congressional debates, but he quietly earned the respect of his colleagues as a legislative draftsman. John Adams, a far more prominent colonial leader at that time, developed a genuine admiration for Jefferson's skill as a writer; and when the Virginian asked him to draft the declaration, Adams demurred, saying, "You can write ten times better than I can." In early June, Jefferson retired to his quarters in a Philadelphia boarding house and completed the first draft of the declaration. Adams and Benjamin Franklin, another member of the committee, made a few slight changes; Jefferson gave the document a through revision, and the committee approved it without further alteration and sent it on to Congress on June 28. A week later on July 2, the delegates approved Lee's motion for independence and then spent two-and-a-half days debating the declaration. In the process, they made extensive changes in the text, removing extraneous sections and generally tightening up the arguments. Finally on the evening of July 4, 1776, the Continental Congress formally adopted the Declaration of Independence.

Jefferson's role as author was not widely known for several years, and he always was careful not to claim that the ideas were original with him. He gave expression to the prevailing liberalism of his age, stating the concepts of natural rights in arresting and extremely felicitous language. "I did not consider it any part of my charge to invent new ideas," Jefferson later explained, "but to place before mankind the common sense of the subject, in terms so plain and firm as to command their assent. … It was intended to be an expression of the American mind."

In Congress, July 4th, 1776
The Unanimous Declaration of the Thirteen United States of America

When in the Course of human events, it becomes necessary for one people to dissolve the political bands which have connected them with another, and to assume among the powers of the earth, the separate and equal station to which the Laws of Nature and of Nature's God entitle them, a decent respect to the opinions of mankind requires that they should declare the causes which impel them to the separation.

We hold these truths to be self-evident, that all men are created equal, that they are endowed by their Creator with certain unalienable Rights, that among these are Life, Liberty and the pursuit of Happiness.

That to secure these rights, Governments are instituted among Men, deriving their just powers from the consent of the governed,

That whenever any Form of Government becomes destructive of these ends, it is the Right of the People to alter or to abolish it, and to institute new Government, laying its foundation on such principles and organizing its powers in such form, as to them shall seem most likely to effect their Safety and Happiness. Prudence, indeed, will dictate that Governments long established should not be changed for light and transient causes; and accordingly all experience hath shown, that mankind are more disposed to suffer, while evils are sufferable, than to right themselves by abolishing the forms to which they are accustomed. But when a long train of abuses and usurpations, pursuing invariably the same Object evinces a design to reduce them under absolute Despotism, it is their right, it is this their duty, to throw off such Government, and to provide new Guards for their future security.

Such has been the patient sufferance of these Colonies; and such is now the necessity which constrains them to alter their former Systems of Government. The history of the present King of Great Britain is a history of repeated injuries and usurpations, all having in direct object the establishment of an absolute Tyranny over these States. To prove this, let Facts be submitted to a candid world.

He has refused his Assent to Laws, the most wholesome and necessary for the public good.

He has forbidden his Governors to pass Laws of immediate and pressing importance, unless suspended in their operation till his Assent should be obtained; and when so suspended, he has utterly neglected to attend to them.

He has refused to pass other Laws for the accommodation of large districts of people, unless those people would relinquish the right of Representation in the Legislature, a right inestimable to them and formidable to tyrants only.

He has called together legislative bodies at places unusual, uncomfortable, and distant from the depository of their public Records, for the sole purpose of fatiguing them into compliance with his measures.

He has dissolved Representative Houses repeatedly, for opposing with manly firmness his invasions on the rights of the people.

He has refused for a long time, after such dissolutions, to cause others to be elected; whereby the Legislative powers, incapable of Annihilation, have returned to the People at large for their exercise; the State remaining in the mean time exposed to all the dangers of invasion from without, and convulsions within.

He has endeavored to prevent the population of these States; for that purpose obstructing the Laws of Naturalization of Foreigners; refusing to pass others to encourage their migration hither, and raising the conditions of new Appropriations of Lands.

He has obstructed the Administration of Justice, by refusing his Assent to Laws for establishing Judiciary powers.

He has made Judges dependent on his Will alone, for the tenure of their offices, and the amount and payment of their salaries.

He has erected a multitude of New Offices, and sent hither swarms of Officers to harass our people, and eat out their substance.

He has kept among us, in times of peace, Standing Armies without the Consent of our legislatures.

He has affected to render the Military independent of and superior to the Civil power.

He has combined with others to subject us to a jurisdiction foreign to our constitution, and unacknowledged by our laws; giving his Assent to their Acts of pretended Legislation. For quartering large bodies of armed troops among us: For protecting them, by a mock Trial, from punishment for any Murders which they should commit on the Inhabitants of these States: For cutting off our Trade with all parts of the world: For imposing Taxes on us without our Consent: For depriving us in many cases, of the benefits of Trial by Jury: For transporting us beyond Seas to be tried for pretended offenses: For abolishing the free System of English Laws in a neighbouring Province, establishing therein an Arbitrary government, and enlarging its Boundaries so as to render it at once an example and fir instrument for introducing the same absolute rule into these Colonies: For taking away our Charters, abolishing our most valuable Laws, and altering fundamentally the Forms of our Governments: For suspending our own Legislatures, and declaring themselves invested with power to legislate for us in all cases whatsoever.

He has abdicated Government here, by declaring us out of his Protection and waging War against us. He has plundered our seas, ravaged our Coasts, burnt our towns, and destroyed the lives of our people. He is at this time transporting large armies of foreign Mercenaries to complete the works of death, desolation and tyranny, already begun with circumstances of Cruelty & perfidy, scarcely paralleled in the most barbarous ages, and totally unworthy the Head of a civilized nation. He has constrained our fellow Citizens taken Captive on the High Seas to bear Arms against their Country, to become the executioners of their friends and Brethren, or to fall themselves by their hands. He has excited domestic insurrections among us, and has endeavored to bring on the inhabitants of our frontiers, the merciless Indian Savages, whose known rule of warfare, is an undistinguished destruction of all ages, sexes and conditions.

In every stage these Oppressions We have Petitioned for Redress in the most humble terms: Our repeated Petitions have been answered only by repeated injury. A Prince whose character is thus marked by every act which may define a Tyrant, is unfit to be the ruler of a free people. Nor have We been wanting in attention to our British brethren. We have warned them from time to time of attempts by their legislature to extend an unwarrantable jurisdiction over us. We have reminded them of the circumstances of our emigration and settlement here. We have appealed to their native justice and magnanimity, and we have conjured them by the ties of our common kindred to disavow these usurpations, which would inevitably interrupt our connections and correspondence. They too have been deaf to the voice of justice and of consanguinity. We must, therefore, acquiesce in the necessity, which denounces our Separation, and hold them, as we hold the rest of mankind, Enemies in War, in Peace Friends.

We, therefore, the Representatives of the United States of America, in General Congress, Assembled, appealing to the Supreme Judge of the world for the rectitude of our intentions do, in the Name, and by Authority of the good People of these Colonies, solemnly publish and declare, that these United Colonies are, and of Right ought to be Free and Independent States, that they are Absolved from all Allegiance to the British Crown, and that all political connection between them and the State of Great Britain, is and ought to be totally dissolved; and that as Free and Independent States, they have full Power to levy War, conclude Peace, contract Alliances, establish Commerce, and to do all other Acts and Things which Independent States may of right do. And for the support of this Declaration, with a firm reliance on the protection of divine Providence, we mutually pledge to each other our Lives, our Fortunes and our sacred Honor.

—*July 4, 1776*

The Constitution of the United States

We the people of the United States, in Order to form a more perfect Union, establish justice, insure domestic Tranquility, provide for the common defence, promote the general Welfare, and secure the Blessings of Liberty to ourselves and our Posterity, do ordain and establish this Constitution for the United States of America.

Article I

Section 1 All legislative Powers herein granted shall be vested in a Congress of the United States, which shall consist of a Senate and House of Representatives.

Section 2 The House of Representatives shall be composed of Members chosen every second Year by the People of the several States, and the Electors in each State shall have the Qualifications requisite for Electors of the most numerous Branch of the State Legislature.

No Person shall be a Representative who shall not have attained to the Age of twenty five Years, and been seven Years a Citizen of the United States, and who shall not, when elected, be an Inhabitant of that State in which he shall be chosen.

Representatives and direct Taxes shall be apportioned among the several States which may be included within this Union, according to their respective Numbers, which shall be determined by adding to the whole Number of free Persons, including those bound to Service for a Term of Years, and excluding Indians not taxed, three fifths of all other Persons. The actual Enumeration shall be made within three Years after the first Meeting of the Congress of the United States, and within every subsequent Term of ten Years, in such Manner as they shall by Law direct. The Number of Representatives shall not exceed one for every thirty Thousand, but each State shall have at Least one Representative; and until such enumeration shall

be made, the State of New Hampshire shall be entitled to chuse three, Massachusetts eight, Rhode-Island and Providence Plantations one, Connecticut five, New-York six, New Jersey four, Pennsylvania eight, Delaware one, Maryland six, Virginia ten, North Carolina five, South Carolina five, and Georgia three.

When vacancies happen in the Representation from any State, the Executive Authority thereof shall issue Writs of Election to fill such Vacancies.

The House of Representatives shall chuse their Speaker and other Officers; and shall have the sole Power of Impeachment.

Section 3 The Senate of the United States shall be composed of two Senators from each State, chosen by the Legislature thereof, for six Years; and each Senator shall have one Vote.

Immediately after they shall be assembled in Consequence of the first Election, they shall be divided as equally as may be into three Classes. The Seats of the Senators of the first Class shall be vacated at the Expiration of the second Year, of the second Class at the Expiration of the fourth Year, and of the third Class at the Expiration of the sixth Year, so that one third may be chosen every second Year; and if Vacancies happen by Resignation, or otherwise, during the Recess of the Legislature of any State, the Executive thereof may make temporary Appointments until the next Meeting of the Legislature, which shall then fill such Vacancies.

No Person shall be a Senator who shall not have a attained to the Age of thirty Years, and been nine Years a Citizen of the United States, and who shall not, when elected, be an Inhabitant of that State for which he shall be chosen.

The Vice-President of the United States shall be President of the Senate, but shall have no Vote, unless they be equally divided.

The Senate shall chuse their other, Officers, and also a President pro tempore, in the Absence of the Vice-President, or when he shall exercise the Office of President of the United States.

The Senate shall have the sole of Power to try all Impeachments. When sitting for that Purpose, they shall be on Oath or Affirmation. When the President of the United States is tried, the Chief justice shall preside: And no Person shall be convicted without the Concurrence of two thirds of the Members present.

Judgment in Cases of Impeachment shall not extend further than to removal from Office, and disqualification to hold and enjoy any Office of honor, Trust or Profit under the United States: but the Party convicted shall nevertheless be liable and subject to Indictment, Trial, Judgment and Punishment, according to Law.

Section 4 The Times, Places and Manner of holding Elections for Senators and Representatives, shall be prescribed in each State by the Legislature thereof; but the Congress may at any time by Law make or alter such Regulations, except as to the Places of chusing Senators.

The Congress shall assemble at least once in every Year, and such Meeting shall be on the first Monday in December, unless they shall by Law appoint a different Day.

Section 5 Each House shall be the Judge of the Elections, Returns and Qualifications of its own Members, and a Majority of each shall constitute a Quorum to do Business; but a smaller Number may adjourn from day to day, and may be authorized to compel the Attendance of absent Members, in such Manner, and under such Penalties as each House may provide.

Each House may determine the Rules of its Proceedings, punish its Members for disorderly Behaviour, and, with the Concurrence of two thirds, expel a Member.

Each House shall keep a Journal of its Proceedings, and from time to time publish the same, excepting such Parts as may in their Judgment require Secrecy; and the Yeas and Nays of the Members of either House on any question shall, at the Desire of one fifth of those Present, be entered on the Journal.

Neither House, during the Session of Congress, shall, without the Consent of the other, adjourn for more than three days, nor to any other Place than that in which the two Houses shall be sitting.

Section 6 The Senators and Representatives shall receive a Compensation for their Services, to be ascertained by Law, and paid out of the Treasury of the United States. They shall in all Cases, except Treason, Felony and Breach of the Peace, be privileged from Arrest during their Attendance at the Session of their respective Houses, and in going to and returning from the same; and for any Speech or Debate in either House, they shall not be questioned in any other Place.

No Senator or Representative shall, during the Time for which he was elected, be appointed to any civil Office under the Authority of the United States which shall have been created, or the Emoluments whereof shall have been encreased during such time; and no Person holding any Office under the United States, shall be a Member of either House during his Continuance in Office.

Section 7 All Bills for raising Revenue shall originate in the House of Representatives; but the Senate may propose or concur with Amendments as on other Bills.

Every Bill which shall have passed the House of Representatives and the Senate, shall, before it become a Law, be presented to the President of the United States; If he approve he shall sign it, but if not he shall return it, with his Objections to that House in which it shall have originated, who shall enter the Objections at large on their Journal, and proceed to reconsider it. If after such Reconsideration two thirds of that House shall agree to pass the Bill, it shall be sent, together with the Objections, to the other House, by which it shall likewise be reconsidered, and if approved by two thirds of that House, it shall become a Law. But in all such Cases the Votes of both Houses shall be determined by Yeas and Nays, and the Names of the Persons voting for and against the Bill shall be entered on the journal of each House respectively. If any Bill shall not be returned by the President within ten Days (Sundays excepted) after it shall have been presented to him, the Same shall be a Law, in like Manner as if he had signed it, unless the Congress by their Adjournment prevent its Return, in which Case it shall not be a Law.

Every Order, Resolution, or Vote to which the Concurrence of the Senate and House of Representatives may be necessary (except on a question of Adjournment) shall be presented to the President of the United States; and before the Same shall take Effect, shall be approved by him, or being disapproved by him, shall be repassed by two thirds of the Senate and House of Representatives, according to the Rules and Limitations prescribed in the Case of a Bill.

Section 8 The Congress shall have Power To lay and collect Taxes, Duties, Imposts and Excises, to pay the Debts and provide for the common Defence and general Welfare of the United States; but all Duties, Imposts and Excises shall be uniform throughout the United States;

To borrow Money on the credit of the United States;

To regulate Commerce with foreign Nations, and among the several States, and with the Indian Tribes;

To establish an uniform Rule of Naturalization, and uniform Laws on the subject of Bankruptcies throughout the United States;

To coin Money, regulate the Value thereof, and of foreign Coin, and fix the Standard of Weights and Measures;

To provide for the Punishment of counterfeiting the Securities and current Coin of the United States;

To establish Post Offices and post Roads;

To promote the Progress of Science and useful Arts, by securing for limited Times to Authors and Inventors the exclusive Right to their respective Writings and Discoveries;

To constitute Tribunals inferior to the supreme Court;

To define and punish Piracies and Felonies committed on the high Seas, and offences against the Law of Nations;

To declare War, grant Letters of Marque and Reprisal, and make Rules concerning Captures on Land and Water;

To raise and support Armies, but no Appropriation of Money to that Use shall be for a longer Term than two years;

To provide and maintain a Navy;

To make Rules for the Government and Regulation of the land and naval Forces;

To provide for calling forth the Militia to execute the Laws of the Union, suppress Insurrections and repel Invasions;

To provide for organizing, arming, and disciplining the Militia, and for governing such Part of them as may be employed in the Service of the United States, reserving to the States respectively, the Appointment of the Officers, and the Authority of training the Militia according to the discipline prescribed by Congress;

To exercise exclusive Legislation in all Cases whatsoever, over such District (not exceeding ten Miles square) as may, be Cession of particular States, and the Acceptance of Congress, become the seat of the Government of the United States, and to exercise like Authority over all Places purchased by the Consent of the Legislature of the State in which the Same shall be, for the Erection of Forts, Magazines, Arsenals, dock-Yards, and other needful Buildings;—And

To make all Laws which shall be necessary and proper for carrying into Execution the foregoing Powers, and all other Powers vested by this Constitution in the Government of the United States, or in any Department or Officer thereof.

Section 9 The Migration or Importation of such Persons as any of the States now existing shall think proper to admit, shall not be prohibited by the Congress prior to the Year one thousand eight hundred and eight, but a Tax or duty may be imposed on such Importation, not exceeding ten dollars for each Person.

The Privilege of the Writ of Habeas Corpus shall not be suspended, unless when in Cases of Rebellion or Invasion the public: Safety may require it.

No Bill of Attainder or ex post facto Law shall be passed.

No Capitation, or other direct, Tax shall be laid, unless in Proportion to the Census or Enumeration herein before directed to be taken.

No Tax or Duty shall be laid on Articles exported from any State.

No Preference shall be given by any Regulation of Commerce or Revenue to the Ports of one State over those of another: nor shall Vessels bound to, or from, one State, be obliged to enter, clear, or pay Duties in another.

No Money shall be drawn from the Treasury, but in Consequence of Appropriations made by Law; and a regular Statement and Account of the Receipts and Expenditures of all public Money shall be published from time to time.

No Title of Nobility shall be granted by the United States: And no Person holding any Office of Profit or Trust under them, shall, without the Consent of the Congress, accept of any present, Emolument office, or title of any kind whatever, from any King, Prince or foreign State.

Section 10 No State shall enter into any Treaty, Alliance, or Confederation; grant Letters of Marque and Reprisal; coin Money; emit Bills of Credit; make any Thing but gold and silver Coin a Tender in Payment of Debts; pass any Bill of Attainder, ex post facto Law, or Law impairing the Obligation of Contracts, or grant any Title of Nobility.

No State shall, without the Consent of the Congress, lay any Imports or Duties on Imports or Exports, except what may be absolutely necessary for executing it's inspection Laws: and the net Produce of all Duties and Imposts, laid by any State on Imports or Exports, shall be for the Use of the Treasury of the United States; and all such Laws shall be subject to the Revision and Controul of the Congress.

No State shall, without the Consent of Congress, lay any Duty of Tonnage, keep Troops, or Ships of War in time of Peace, enter into any Agreement or Compact with another State, or with a foreign Power, or engage in War, unless actually invaded, or in such imminent Danger as will not admit of delay.

Article II

Section 1 The executive Power shall be vested in a President of the United States of America. He shall hold his Office during the Term of four Years, and, together with the Vice President, chosen for the same Term, be elected as follows:

Each State shall appoint, in such Manner as the Legislature thereof may direct, a Number of Electors, equal to the whole Number of Senators and Representatives to which the State may be entitled in the Congress: but no Senator or Representative, or Person holding an Office of Trust or Profit under the United States, shall be appointed an Elector.

The Electors shall meet in their respective States, and vote by Ballot for two Persons, of whom one at least shall not be an Inhabitant of the same State with themselves. And they shall make a List of all the Persons voted for, and of the Number of Votes for each; which List they shall sign and certify, and transmit sealed to the Seat of the Government of the United States, directed to the President of the Senate. The President of the Senate shall, in the Presence of the Senate and House of Representatives, open all the Certificates, and the Votes shall then be counted. The Person having the greatest Number of Votes shall be the President, if such Number be a Majority of the whole Number of Electors appointed; and if there be more than one who have such Majority, and have an equal Number of Votes, then the House of Representatives shall immediately chuse by Ballot one of them for President, and if no person have a Majority, then from the five highest on the List the said House shall in like Manner chuse the President. But in chusing the President, the Votes shall be taken by States, the Representation from each State having one Vote; A quorum for this Purpose shall consist of a Member or Members from two thirds of the States, and a Majority of all the States shall be necessary to a Choice. In every Case, after the Choice of the President, the Person having the greatest Number of Votes of the Electors shall be the Vice-President. But if there should remain two or more who have equal Votes, the Senate shall chuse from them by Ballot the Vice-President.

The Congress may determine the Time of chusing the Electors, and the Day on which they shall give their Votes; which Day shall be the same throughout the United States.

No Person except a natural born Citizen, or a Citizen of the United States, at the time of the Adoption of this Constitution, shall be eligible to the Office of President; neither shall any Person be eligible to that Office who shall not have attained to the Age of thirty five Years, and been fourteen Years a Resident within the United States.

In Case of the Removal of the President from Office, or of his Death, Resignation, or Inability to discharge the Powers and Duties of the said Office, the Same shall devolve on the Vice President, and the Congress may by Law provide for the Case of Removal, Death, Resignation or Inability, both of the President and Vice President, declaring what Officer shall then act as President, and such Officer shall act accordingly, until the Disability be removed, or a President shall be elected.

The President shall, at stated Times, receive for his Services, a Compensation, which shall neither be encreased nor diminished during the Period for which he shall have been elected, and he shall not receive within that Period any other Emolument from the United States, or any of them.

Before he enter on the Execution of his Office, he shall take the following Oath or Affirmation:—"I do solemnly swear (or affirm) that I will faithfully execute the Office of President of the United States, and will to the best of my Ability, preserve, protect and defend the Constitution of the United States."

Section 2 The President shall be Commander in Chief of the Army and Navy of the United States, and of the Militia of the several States, when called into the actual Service of the United States; he may require the Opinion, in writing, of the principal Officer in each of the executive Departments, upon any Subject relating to the Duties of their respective Offices, and he shall have Power to grant Reprieves and Pardons for Offences against the United States, except in Cases of Impeachment.

He shall have Power, by and with the Advice and Consent of the Senate, to make Treaties, provided two thirds of the Senators present concur; and he shall nominate, and by and with the Advice and Consent of the Senate, shall appoint Ambassadors, other public Ministers and Consuls, Judges of the supreme Court, and all other Officers of the United States, whose Appointments are not herein otherwise provided for, and which shall be established by Law: but the Congress may by Law vest the Appointment of such inferior Officers, as they think proper, in the President alone, in the Courts of Law, or in the Heads of Departments.

The President shall have Power to fill up all Vacancies that may happen during the Recess of the Senate, by granting Commissions which shall expire at the End of their next Session.

Section 3   He shall from time to time give to the Congress Information of the State of the Union, and recommend to their Consideration such Measures as he shall judge necessary and expedient; he may, on extraordinary Occasions, convene both Houses, or either of them, and in Case of Disagreement between them, with Respect to the Time of Adjournment, he may adjourn them to such Time as he shall think proper; he shall receive Ambassadors and other public Ministers; he shall take Care that the Laws be faithfully executed, and shall Commission all the Officers of the United States.

Section 4   The President, Vice-President and all civil Officers of the United States, shall be removed from Office on Impeachment for, and Conviction of, Treason, Bribery, or other high Crimes and Misdemeanors.

Article III

Section 1   The judicial Power of the United States, shall be vested in one supreme Court, and in such inferior Courts as the Congress may from time to time ordain and establish. The judges, both of the supreme and inferior Courts, shall hold their Offices during good Behaviour, and shall, at stated Times, receive for their Services, a Compensation, which shall not be diminished during their Continuance in Office.

Section 2   The judicial Power shall extend to all Cases, in law and Equity, arising under this Constitution, the Laws of the United States, and Treaties made, or which shall be made, under their Authority;—to all Cases affecting Ambassadors, other public Ministers and Consuls;—to all Cases of admiralty and maritime jurisdiction;—to Controversies to which the United states shall be a Party;—to Controversies between two or more States;—between a State and Citizens of another State;—between Citizens of different States,—between Citizens of the State claiming Lands under Grants of different States and between a State, or the Citizens thereof, and foreign States, Citizens or Subjects.

In all Cases affecting Ambassadors, other public Ministers and Consuls, and those in which a State shall be Party, the supreme Court shall have original jurisdiction.

In all the other cases before mentioned, the supreme Court shall have appellate jurisdiction, both as to Law and Fact, with such Exceptions, and under such Regulations as the Congress shall make.

The Trial of all Crimes, except in Cases of Impeachment, shall be by jury; and such Trial shall be held in the State where the said Crimes shall have been committed; but when not committed within any State, the Trial shall be at such Place or Places as the Congress may by Law have directed.

Section 3   Treason against the United States, shall consist only in levying War against them, or in adhering to their Enemies, giving them Aid and Comfort. No Person shall be convicted of Treason unless on the Testimony of two Witnesses to the same overt Act, or on Confession in open Court.

The Congress shall have Power to declare the Punishment of Treason, but no Attainder of Treason shall work Corruption of Blood, or Forfeiture except during the Life of the Person attained.

Article IV

Section 1   Full Faith and Credit shall be given in each State to the Public Acts, Records, and judicial Proceedings of every other State. And the Congress may by general Laws prescribe the Manner in which such Acts, Records and Proceedings shall be proved, and the Effect thereof.

Section 2   The Citizens of each State shall be entitled to all Privileges and Immunities of Citizens in the Several States.

A Person charged in any State with Treason, Felony, or other Crime, who shall flee from justice, and be found in another State, shall on Demand of the executive Authority of the State from which he fled, be delivered up, to be removed to the State having jurisdiction of the Crime.

No person held to Service or Labour in one State, under the Laws thereof, escaping into another, shall, in Consequence of any Law or Regulation therein, be discharged from such Service or Labour, but shall be delivered up on Claim of the Party to whom such Service or Labour may be due.

Section 3   New States may be admitted by the Congress into this Union; but no new States shall be formed or erected within the jurisdiction of any other State; nor any State be formed by the junction of two or more States, or Parts of States, without the Consent of the Legislatures of the States concerned as well as of the Congress.

The Congress shall have Power to dispose of and make all needful Rules and Regulations respecting the Territory or other Property belonging to the United States; and nothing in this Constitution shall be so construed as to Prejudice any Claims of the United States, or of any particular State.

Section 4   The United States shall guarantee to every State in this Union a Republican Form of Government, and shall protect each of them against Invasion; and on Application of the Legislature, or of the Executive (when the Legislature cannot be convened) against domestic Violence.

Article V

The Congress, whenever two thirds of both Houses shall deem it necessary, shall propose Amendments to this Constitution, or, on the Application of the Legislatures of two thirds of the several States, shall call a Convention for proposing Amendments, which, in either Case, shall be valid to all Intents and Purposes, as Part of this Constitution, when ratified by the Legislatures of three fourths of the several States, or by Conventions in three fourths thereof, as the one or the other Mode of Ratification may be proposed by the Congress; Provided that no Amendment which may be made prior to the Year One thousand eight hundred and eight shall in any Manner affect the first and fourth Clauses in the Ninth Section of the first Article; and that no State, without its Consent, shall be deprived of it's equal Suffrage in the Senate.

Article VI

All Debts contracted and Engagements entered into, before the Adoption of this Constitution, shall be as valid against the United States under this Constitution, as under the Confederation.

This Constitution, and the Laws of the United States which shall be made in Pursuance thereof; and all Treaties made, or which shall be made, under the Authority of the United States, shall be the supreme Law of the Land; and the judges in every State shall be found thereby, any Thing in the Constitution or Laws of any State to the Contrary notwithstanding.

The Senators and Representatives before mentioned, and the Members of the several State Legislatures, and all the executive and judicial Officers, both of the United States and of the several States, shall be bound by Oath or Affirmation, to support this Constitution, but no religious Test shall ever be required as a Qualification to any Office or public Trust under the United States.

Article VII

The Ratification of the Conventions of nine States, shall be sufficient for the Establishment of this Constitution between the States so ratifying the Same.

Done in Convention by the Unanimous Consent of the States present the Seventeenth Day of September in the year of our Lord one thousand seven hundred and Eighty seven and of the Independance of the United States of America the Twelfth. In witness whereof We have here unto subscribed our Names.

Attest William Jackson Secretary

Go: Washington—Presidt.
and Deputy from Virginia

Delaware
Geo Read
Gunning Bedfor Junr
John Dickinson
Richard Bassett
Jaco Broom

Maryland
James McHenry
Dan of St. Thos. Jenifer
Danl Carroll

Virginia
John Blair—
James Madison Jr.

North Carolina
Wm. Blount
Richd. Dobbs Spaight
Hu Williamson

South Carolina
J. Rutledge
Charles Cotesworth Pinckney
Charles Pinckney
Pierce Butler

Georgia
William Few
Abr Baldwin

New Hampshire
John Langdon
Nicholas Gilman

Massachusetts

Nathaniel Gorham
Rufus King
Connecticut
Wm. Saml. Johnson
Roger Sherman
New York
Alexander Hamilton
New Jersey
Wil. Livingston
David Brearley
Wm. Paterson
Jona. Dayton
Pensylvania
B. Franklin
Thomas Mifflin
Robt Morris
Geo. Clymer
Thos. FitzSimons
Jared Ingersoll
James Wilson
Gouv Morris

Amendments to the Constitution

ARTICLES in Addition to, and Amendment of, the Constitution of the United States of America, proposed by Congress, and ratified by the Legislatures of the several States, pursuant to the fifth Article of the original Constitution.

Amendment I

Congress shall make no law respecting an establishment of religion, or prohibiting the free exercise thereof; or abridging the freedom of speech, or of the press; or the right of the people peaceably to assemble, and to petition the government for a redress of grievances.

Amendment II

A well regulated Militia, being necessary to the Security of a free State, the right of the people to keep and bear Arms, shall not be infringed.

Amendment III

No Soldier shall, in time of peace be quartered in any house, without the consent of the Owner, nor in time of war, but in a manner to be prescribed by law.

Amendment IV

The right of the people to be secure in their persons, houses, papers, and effects, against unreasonable searches and seizures, shall not be violated, and no Warrants shall issue, but upon probable cause, supported by Oath or affirmation, and particularly describing the place to be searched, and the persons or things to be seized.

Amendment V

No person shall be held to answer for a capital, or otherwise infamous crime, unless on a presentment or indictment of a Grand Jury, except in cases arising in the land or naval forces, or in the Militia, when in actual service in time of War or public danger; nor shall any person be subject for the same offence to be twice put in jeopardy of life or limb; nor shall be compelled in any criminal case to be a witness against himself, nor be deprived of life, liberty, or property, without due process of law; nor shall private property be taken for public use, without just compensation.

Amendment VI

In all criminal prosecutions, the accused shall enjoy the right to a speedy and public trial, by an impartial jury of the State and district wherein the crime shall have been committed, which district shall have been previously ascertained by law, and to be informed of the nature and cause of the accusation; to be confronted with the witnesses against him; to have compulsory process for obtaining witnesses in his favor, and to have the Assistance of Counsel for his defence.

Amendment VII

In Suits at common law, where the value in controversy shall exceed twenty dollars, the right of trial by jury shall be preserved, and no fact tried by a jury, shall be otherwise re-examined in any Court of the United States, than according to the rules of the common law.

Amendment VIII

Excessive bail shall not be required, nor excessive fines imposed, nor cruel and unusual punishments inflicted.

Amendment IX

The enumeration in the Constitution, of certain rights, shall not be construed to deny or disparage others retained by the people.

Amendment X

The powers not delegated to the United States by the Constitution, nor prohibited by it to the States, are preserved to the States respectively, or to the people.

Articles I.–X. proposed to the states by Congress, September 25, 1789

Ratification completed, December 15, 1791
Ratification declared, March 1, 1792

Amendment XI

The Judicial power of the United States shall not be construed to extend to any suit in law or equity, commenced or prosecuted against one of the United States by Citizens of another State, or by Citizens or Subjects of any Foreign State.

Proposed to the states by Congress, March 4, 1794
Ratification completed, February 7, 1795
Ratification declared, January 8, 1798

Amendment XII

The Electors shall meet in their respective states, and vote by ballot for President and Vice-President, one of whom, at least, shall not be an inhabitant of the same state with themselves; they shall name in their ballots the person voted for as President, and in distinct ballots the person voted for as Vice-President, and they shall make distinct lists of all persons voted for as President, and of all persons voted for as Vice-President, and of the number of votes for each, which lists they shall sign and certify, and transmit sealed to the seat of the government of the United States, directed to the President of the Senate;— The President of the Senate shall, in the presence of the Senate and House of Representatives, open all the certificates and the votes shall then be counted;—The person having the greatest number of votes for President, shall be the President, if such number be a majority of the whole number of Electors appointed; and if no person have such majority, then from the persons having the highest numbers not exceeding three on the list of those voted for as President, the House of Representatives shall choose immediately, by ballot, the President. But in choosing the President, the votes shall be taken by states, the representation from each state having one vote; a quorum for this purpose shall consist of a member or members from two-thirds of the states, and a majority of all the states shall be necessary to a choice. And if the House of Representatives shall not choose a President

whenever the right of choice shall devolve upon them, before the fourth day of March next following, then the Vice-President shall act as President, as in the case of the death or other constitutional disability of the President.— The person having the greatest number of votes as Vice-President, shall be the Vice-President, if such number be a majority of the whole number of Electors appointed, and if no person have a majority, then from the two highest numbers on the list the Senate shall choose the Vice-President; a quorum for the purpose shall consist of two-thirds of the whole number of Senators, and a majority of the whole number shall be necessary to a choice. But no person constitutionally ineligible to the office of President shall be eligible to that of Vice-President of the United States.

Proposed to the states by Congress, December 9, 1803
Ratification completed, June 15, 1804
Ratification declared, September 25, 1804

Amendment XIII

Section 1.   Neither slavery nor involuntary servitude, except as a punishment for crime whereof the party shall have been duly convicted, shall exist within the United States, or any place subject to their jurisdiction.

Section 2.   Congress shall have power to enforce this article by appropriate legislation.

Proposed to the states by Congress, January 31, 1865
Ratification completed, December 6, 1865
Ratification declared, December 18,1865

Amendment XIV

Section 1   All persons born or naturalized in the United States, and subject to the jurisdiction thereof, are citizens of the United States and of the State wherein they reside. No state shall make or enforce any law which shall abridge the privileges or immunities of citizens of the United States; nor shall any State deprive any person of life, liberty, or property, without due process of law; nor deny to any person within its jurisdiction the equal protection of the laws.

Section 2   Representatives shall be apportioned among the several States according to their respective numbers, counting the whole number of persons in each State, excluding Indians not taxed. But when the right to vote at any election for the choice of electors for President and Vice-President of the United States, Representatives in Congress, the Executive and Judicial officers of a State, or the members of the Legislature thereof, is denied to any of the male inhabitants of such State, being twenty-one years of age, and citizens of the United States, or in any way abridged, except for participation in rebellion, or other crime, the basis of representation therein shall be reduced in the proportion which the number of such male citizens shall bear to the whole number of male citizens twenty-one years of age in such State.

Section 3   No person shall be a Senator or Representative in Congress, or elector of President and Vice-President, or hold any office, civil or military, under the United States, or under any State, who, having previously taken an oath, as a member of Congress, or as an officer of the United States, or as a member of any State legislature, or as an executive or judicial officer or any State, to support the Constitution of the United States, shall have engaged in insurrection or rebellion against the same, or given aid or comfort to the enemies thereof. But Congress may by a vote of two-thirds of each House, remove such disability.

Section 4   The validity of the public debt of the United States, authorized by law, including debts incurred for payment of pensions and bounties for services in suppressing insurrection or rebellion, shall not be questioned. But neither the United States nor any State shall assume or pay any debt or obligation incurred in aid of insurrection or rebellion against the United States, or any claim for the loss or emancipation of any slave; but all such debts, obligations and claims shall be held illegal and void.

Section 5   The Congress shall have power to enforce, by appropriate legislation, the provisions of this article.

> Proposed to the states by Congress, June 13, 1866
> Ratification completed, July 9, 1868
> Ratification declared, July 28, 1868

Amendment XV

Section 1   The right of citizens of the United States to vote shall not be denied or abridged by the United States or by any State on account of race, color, or previous condition of servitude.

Section 2   The Congress shall have power to enforce this article by appropriate legislation.

> Proposed to the states by Congress, February 26, 1869
> Ratification completed, February 3, 1870
> Ratification declared, March 30, 1870

Amendment XVI

The Congress shall have power to lay and collect taxes on incomes, from whatever source derived, without apportionment among the several States, and without regard to any census or enumeration.

> Proposed to the states by Congress, July 12, 1909
> Ratification completed, February 3, 1913
> Ratification declared, February 25, 1913

Amendment XVII

The Senate of the United States shall be composed of two Senators from each State, elected by the people thereof, for six years; and each Senator shall have one vote. The electors in each State shall have the qualifications requisite for electors of the most numerous branch of the State legislatures.

When vacancies happen in the representation of any State in the Senate, the executive authority of such State shall issue writs of election to fill such vacancies: *Provided,* That the legislature of any State may empower the executive thereof the make temporary appointments until the people fill the vacancies by election as the legislature may direct.

This amendment shall not be so construed as to affect the election or term of any Senator chosen before it becomes valid as part of the Constitution.

> Proposed to the states by Congress, May 13, 1912
> Ratification completed, April 8, 1913
> Ratification declared, May 31, 1913

Amendment XVIII

Section 1   After one year from the ratification of this article the manufacture, sale, or transportation of intoxicating liquors within, the importation thereof into, or the exportation thereof from the United States and all territory subject to the jurisdiction thereof for beverage purposes is hereby prohibited.

Section 2   The Congress and the several States shall have concurrent power to enforce this article by appropriate legislation.

Section 3   This article shall be inoperative unless it shall have been ratified as an amendment to the Constitution by the legislatures of the several States, as provided in the Constitution, within seven years from the date of the submission hereof to the States by the Congress.

> Proposed to the states by Congress, December 18, 1917
> Ratification completed, January 16, 1919
> Ratification declared, January 29, 1919

Amendment XIX

The right of citizens of the United States to vote shall not be denied or abridged by the United States or by any State on account of sex.

Congress shall have power to enforce this article by appropriate legislation.

Proposed to the states by Congress, June 4, 1919
Ratification completed, August 18, 1920
Ratification declared, August 26, 1920

Amendment XX

Section 1   The terms of the President and Vice President shall end at noon on the 20th day of January, and the terms of Senators and Representatives at noon on the 3d day of January, of the years in which such terms would have ended if this article had not been ratified; and the terms of their successors shall then begin.

Section 2   The Congress shall assemble at least once in every year, and such meeting shall begin at noon on the 3d day of January, unless they shall by law appoint a different day.

Section 3   If, at the time fixed for the beginning of the term of the President, the President elect shall have died, the Vice President elect shall become President. If a President shall not have been chosen before the time fixed for the beginning of his term, or if the President elect shall have failed to qualify, then the Vice President elect shall act as President until a President shall have qualified; and the Congress may by law provide for the case wherein neither a President elect nor a Vice President elect shall have qualified, declaring who shall then act as President, or the manner in which one who is to act shall be selected, and such person shall act accordingly until a President or Vice President shall have qualified.

Section 4   The Congress may by law provide for the case of the death of any of the persons from whom the House of Representatives may choose a President whenever the right of choice shall have devolved upon them, and for the case of the death of any of the persons from whom the Senate may choose a Vice President whenever the right of choice shall have devolved upon them.

Section 5   Sections 1 and 2 shall take effect on the 15th day of October following the ratification of this article.

Section 6   This article shall be inoperative unless it shall have been ratified as an amendment to the Constitution by the legislatures of three-fourths of the several States within seven years from the date of its submission.

Proposed to the states by Congress, March 2, 1932

Ratification completed, January 23, 1933
Ratification declared, February 6, 1933

Amendment XXI

Section 1   The eighteenth article of amendment to the Constitution of the United States is hereby repealed.

Section 2   The transportation or importation into any State, Territory, or possession of the United States for delivery or use therein of intoxicating liquors, in violation of the laws thereof, is hereby prohibited.

Section 3   This article shall be inoperative unless it shall have been ratified as an amendment to the Constitution by conventions in the several States, as provided in the Constitution, within seven years from the date of the submission hereof to the States by the Congress.

Proposed to the states by Congress, February 20, 1933
Ratification completed, December 5, 1933
Ratification declared, December 5, 1933

Amendment XXII

Section 1   No person shall be elected to the office of the President more than twice, and no person who has held the office of President, or acted as President, for more than two years of a term to which some other person was elected President shall be elected to the office of the President more than once. But this Article shall not apply to any person holding the office of President when this Article was proposed by the Congress, and shall not prevent any person who may be holding the office of President, or acting as President, during the term within which this Article becomes operative from holding the office of President or acting as President during the remainder of such term.

Section 2   This article shall be inoperative unless it shall have been ratified as an amendment to the Constitution by the legislatures of three-fourths of the several States within seven years from the date of its submission to the States by the Congress.

Proposed to the states by Congress, March 21, 1947
Ratification completed, February 27, 1951
Ratification declared, March 1, 1951

Amendment XXIII

Section 1   The District constituting the seat of Government of the United States shall appoint in such manner as the Congress may direct:

A number of electors of President and Vice-President equal to the whole number of Senators and Representatives in Congress to which the District would be entitled if it were a State, but in no event more than the least populous State; they shall be in addition to those appointed by the States, but they shall be considered, for the purposes of the election of President and Vice President, to be electors appointed by a State; and they shall meet in the District and perform such duties as provided by the twelfth article of amendment.

Section 2   The Congress shall have power to enforce this article by appropriate legislation.

Proposed to the states by Congress, March 21, 1947
Ratification completed, February 27, 1951
Ratification declared, March 1, 1951

Amendment XXIV

Section 1   The right of citizens of the United States to vote in any primary or other election for President or Vice President, for electors for President or Vice President, or for Senator or Representative in Congress, shall not be denied or abridged by the United States or any State by reason of failure to pay any poll tax or other tax.

Section 2   The Congress shall have power to enforce this article by appropriate legislation.

Proposed to the states by Congress, August 27, 1962
Ratification completed, January 23, 1964
Ratification declared, February 4, 1964

Amendment XXV

Section 1   In case of the removal of the President from office or of his death or resignation, the Vice President shall become President.

Section 2   Whenever there is a vacancy in the office of the Vice President, the President shall nominate a Vice President who shall take office upon confirmation by a majority vote of both Houses of Congress.

Section 3   Whenever the President transmits to the President pro tempore of the Senate and the Speaker of the House of Representatives his written declaration that he is unable to discharge the powers and duties of his office, and until he transmits to them a written declaration to the contrary, such powers and duties shall be discharged by the Vice President as Acting President.

Section 4   Whenever the Vice President and a majority of either the principal officers of the executive departments or of such other body as Congress may by law provide, transmit to the President pro tempore of the Senate and the Speaker of the House of Representatives

their written declaration that the President is unable to discharge the powers and duties of his office, the Vice President shall immediately assume the powers and duties of the office as Acting President.

Thereafter, when the President transmits to the President pro tempore of the Senate and the Speaker of the House of Representatives his written declaration that no inability exists, he shall resume the powers and duties of his office unless the Vice President and a majority of either the principal officers of the executive department or of such other body as Congress may by law provide, transmit within four days to the President pro tempore of the Senate and the Speaker of the House of Representatives their written declaration that the President is unable to discharge the powers and duties of his office. Thereupon Congress shall decide the issue, assembling within forty-eight hours for that purpose if not in session. If the Congress, within twenty-one days after receipt of the latter written declaration, or, if Congress is not in session, within twenty-one days after Congress is required to assemble, determines by two-thirds vote of both Houses that the President is unable to discharge the powers and duties of his office, the Vice-President shall continue to discharge the same as Acting President; otherwise, the President shall resume the powers and duties of his office.

Proposed to the states by Congress, July 6, 1965
Ratification completed, February 10, 1967
Ratification declared, February 23, 1967

Amendment XXVI

Section 1   The right of citizens of the United States, who are eighteen years of age or older, to vote shall not be denied or abridged by the United States or by any State on account of age.

Section 2   The Congress shall have power to enforce this article by appropriate legislation.

Proposed to the states by Congress, March 23, 1971
Ratification completed, July 1, 1971
Ratification declared, July 5, 1971

Amendment XXVII

No law, varying the compensation for the services of the Senators and Representatives, shall take effect, until an election of Representatives shall have intervened.

Proposed to the states by Congress, September 25, 1789
Ratification completed, May 7, 1992
Ratification declared, May 18, 1992

The Universal Declaration of Human Rights

Whereas recognition of the inherent dignity and of the equal and inalienable rights of all members of the human family is the foundation of freedom, justice and peace in the world,

Whereas disregard and contempt for human rights have resulted in barbarous acts which have outraged the conscience of mankind, and the advent of a world in which human beings shall enjoy freedom of speech and belief and freedom from fear and want has been proclaimed as the highest aspiration of the common people,

Whereas it is essential, if man is not to be compelled to have recourse, as a last resort, to rebellion against tyranny and oppression, that human rights should be protected by the rule of law,

Whereas it is essential to promote the development of friendly relations between nations,

Whereas the peoples of the United Nations have in the Charter reaffirmed their faith in fundamental human rights, in the dignity and worth of the human person and in the equal rights of men and women and have determined to promote social progress and better standards of life in larger freedom,

Whereas Member States have pledged themselves to achieve, in cooperation with the United Nations, the promotion of universal respect for and observance of human rights and fundamental freedoms,

Whereas a common understanding of these rights and freedoms is of the greatest importance for the full realization of this pledge,

Now, Therefore,

THE GENERAL ASSEMBLY

proclaims

Article 1   All human beings are born free and equal in dignity and rights. They are endowed with reason and conscience and should act towards one another in a spirit of brotherhood.

Article 2   Everyone is entitled to all the rights and freedoms set forth in this Declaration, without distinction of any kind, such as race, colour, sex, language, religion, political or other opinion, national or social origin, property, birth or other status.

Article 3   Everyone has the right to life, liberty and security of person.

Article 4   No one shall be held in slavery or servitude; slavery and the slave trade shall be prohibited in all their forms.

Article 5   No one shall be subjected to torture or to cruel, inhuman or degrading treatment or punishment.

Article 6   Every one has the right to recognition everywhere as a person before the law.

Article 7   All are equal before the law and are entitled without an discrimination to equal protection of the law. All are entitled to equal protection against any discrimination in violation of this Declaration and against any incitement to such discrimination.

Article 8   Everyone has the right to an effective remedy by the competent national tribunals for acts violating the fundamental rights granted him by the constitution or by law.

Article 9   No one shall be subjected to arbitrary arrest detention or exile.

Article 10   Everyone is entitled in full equality to a fair and public hearing by an independent and impartial tribunal, in the determination of his rights and obligations and of any criminal charge against him.

Article 11   (1) Everyone charged with a penal offence has the right to be presumed innocent until proved guilty according to law in a public trial at which he has had all the guarantees necessary for his defence....

Article 13   (1) Everyone has the right to freedom of movement and residence within the borders of each state.

(2) Everyone has the right to leave any country, including his own, and to return to his country.

Article 14   (1) Everyone has the right to seek and to enjoy in other countries asylum from persecution....

Article 15

... (2) No one shall be arbitrarily deprived of his nationality nor denied the right to change his nationality.

Article 16   (1) Men and women of full age, without any limitation due to race, nationality or religion, have the right to marry and to found a family. They are entitled to equal rights as to marriage, during marriage and at its dissolution....

(3) The family is the natural and fundamental group unit of society and is entitled to protection by society and the State.

Article 17   (1) Everyone has the right to own property alone as well as in association with others.

(2) No one shall be arbitrarily deprived of his property.

Article 18   Everyone has the right to freedom of thought, conscience and religion; this right includes freedom to change his religion or belief and freedom, either alone or in community with others and in public or private, to manifest his religion or belief in teaching, practice, worship and observance.

Article 19   Everyone has the right to freedom of opinion and expression this right includes freedom to hold opinions without interference and to seek, receive and impart information and ideas through any media and regardless of frontiers.

Article 20   (1) Everyone has the right to freedom of peaceful assembly and association....

Article 21   (1) Everyone has the right to take part in the government of a country, directly or through freely chosen representatives....

(3) The will of the people shall be the basis of the authority of government; this will shall be expressed in periodic and genuine elections which shall be by universal and equal suffrage and shall be held by secret vote or by equivalent free voting procedures.

Article 22   Everyone, as a member of society, has the right to social security and is entitled to realization, through national effort and international co-operation and in accordance with the organization and resources of each state, of the economic, social and cultural rights indispensable for his dignity and the free development of a personality.

Article 23   (1) Everyone has the right to work, to free choice of employment, to just and favourable conditions of work and *to* protection against unemployment.

(2) Everyone, without any discrimination, has the right to equal pay for equal work.

Article 24   Everyone has the right to rest and leisure, including reasonable limitation of working hours and periodic holidays with pay.

Article 25   (1) Everyone has the right to a standard of living adequate for the health and well-being of himself and of his family, including food, clothing, housing and medical care and necessary social services, and the right to security in the event of unemployment, sickness, disability, widowhood, old age or other lack of livelihood in circumstances beyond his control.

(2) Motherhood and childhood are entitled to special care and assistance. All children, whether born in or out of wedlock, shall enjoy the same social protection.

Article 26   (1) Everyone has the right to education. Education shall be free, at least in the elementary and fundamental stages....

(2) Education shall be directed to the full development of the human personality and to the strengthening of respect for human rights and fundamental freedoms....

(3) Parents have a prior right to choose the kind of education that shall be given to their children.

Article 27

... (2) Everyone has the right to the protection of the moral and material interests resulting from any scientific, literary or artistic production of which he is the author.

Article 29   (1) Everyone has duties to the community in which alone the free and full development of his personality is possible....

Absolutism: unrestrained powers exercised by government. Absolutism is the opposite of constitutionalism, which provides for government limited by law.

Adaptation: genetic changes which occur within populations in response to environmental pressures.

Adjudication: a legal technique for settling international disputes by submitting them to determination by an established court. Adjudication differs from arbitration in that the former involves an institutionalized process carried on by a permanent court whereas the latter is an ad hoc procedure.

Alien: an individual who is neither a citizen nor a national of the state in which he or she is living.

Alliance: a multilateral agreement by states to improve their power position by joining together in defense of their common interest.

Ambassador: the top ranking diplomat sent by the government of a country as its official representative.

Amendment: changes in, or additions to a constitution.

Anarchism: the doctrine that government is an unnecessary evil and should be replaced by voluntary cooperation among individuals and groups.

Anthropology: the scientific study of the origin and of the physical, social, and cultural development and behavior of humans.

Appeasement: a term used to describe concession made to warlike potential enemies in the hope that these will satiate their appetite for expansion, and that peace will be secure.

Appropriation: a legislative grant of money for a specific purpose.

Arbitration: a method of settling a dispute between states by judges selected by the parties to the dispute.

Armistice: a temporary cessation of hostilities agreed to by belligerents.

Attachés: technical specialists who function as officials with diplomatic rank and who are attached to an embassy or foreign mission.

Autarky: national economic self-sufficiency.

Authoritarianism: concentration of political authority in one man/woman or in a small group.

Authority: influence derived from willing acceptance by others of one's right to make rules or issue commands and to expect compliance with them.

Authorization: a legislative action that establishes a substantive program, specifies its general purpose and the means for achieving it, and indicates the approximate amount of money needed to implement the program.

Autocracy: any system of government in which political power and authority are focused in a single individual.

Balance of payments account: a measure of a country's total economic interaction with other countries. It contains the current and the capital account.

Balance of Power: a system of power alignments in which peace and security may be maintained through an equilibrium of power between the rival blocs.

Balance of terror: the equilibrium of power among nuclear states stemming from common fear of annihilation in a nuclear war.

Balance of trade: the monetary value of exported goods minus the monetary value of imported goods.

Barter: the exchange of goods and services directly for one another, without the use of money.

Bill: a proposed law.

Bill of Rights: the first ten amendments to the United States Constitution.

Budget: an estimate of the receipts and expenditures needed by government to carry out its programs in some future period, usually a fiscal year.

Bureaucracy: an administrative system, especially of governmental agencies, that carries out policy on a day-to-day basis, that uses standardized procedures, and that is based on a specialization of duties.

Capital: assets which are capable of generating income and which have themselves been produced.

Capitalism: an economic system based upon private property and the market, in which individuals decide how, what, and for whom to produce.

Capital account: records such items as the inward and outward flow of money for investment and international grants and loans.

Capital markets: markets in which financial assets having a maturity of more than one year are bought and sold.

Cartel: an agreement among independent business or countries to restrict competition.

Caudillismo: the principle of personal or "boss-type" political rule in Latin American politics.

Charge d'Affaires: a Foreign Service official temporarily placed in charge of the embassy.

Checks and balances: a major principle of the American governmental system whereby each department or branch of the government restraints the actions of the others.

Citizen: an individual who is a native or naturalized member of a state, and is entitled to the protection and privilege of its laws.

Civil liberties: those liberties usually spelled out in a bill of rights or a constitution that guarantee the protection of persons, opinions, and property from the arbitrary interference of governmental officials.

Civil rights: positive acts of government designed to protect persons against arbitrary or discriminatory treatment by governments or individuals.

Civil war: a war fought between different geographical areas, political divisions, or ideological factions within the same country.

Cold War: the extreme state of tension and hostility between the Western powers and the Communist countries between 1945 and 1991.

Collective security: a worldwide security system by which all or most countries agree in advance to take collective action against any state or state that break the peace by committing aggression.

Collectivism: a generic term that describes various theories and social movements calling for the ownership and control of all lands and means of production by the government or groups rather than by individuals.

Colonialism: the rule of an area and its people by an external sovereignty, that results from a policy of imperialism.

Command economy: one in which the government exercises absolute or significant control over the means and ways of production, distribution and allocation of goods and services.

Communism: a political, economic, and social theory based on a collectivistic society in which all land and capital are socially owned and political power is exercised by the masses. In practice, communism has been a political system in which total power is exercised by the Communist Party.

Comparative Advantage: the idea that economic agents are most efficiently employed in activities in which they performed *relatively* better than in others.

Concept: a mental image or construct formed by generalizing from the characteristics of a class of things.

Conciliation: a technique in which a group of countries or other agents serve as a third party to help two antagonistic states negotiate their differences.

Conservatism: defense of the status quo against major changes in the political, economic, or social institutions of a society.

Constitution: a fundamental or "organic" law that establishes the framework of government of a state, assigns the powers and duties of governmental agencies, and establishes the relationship between the people and their government.

Consumer goods: commodities bought by households for final consumption.

Control experiment: an experiment in which the variable factors are controlled so that the effects of changing one at a time can be observed.

Conversations: an exchange of views between two or more governments which could increase information by all parties and also lead to more detailed negotiations.

Corporation: a type of firm that is a legal entity separate from the people who own, manage, and otherwise direct its affairs.

Cronyism: granting of political favors to friends, often in the form of appointments to office.

Cultural anthropology: the study of human culture.

Cultural relativism: the position that cultural systems must be evaluated in their own terms and not according to any other culture.

Culture: the integrated sum total of learned behavioral traits characteristic of the members of a society.

Culture configuration: the distinctive form and characteristic quality of a culture according to how different parts are interrelated.

Current account: made up of visible trade such as merchandise imports and exports and invisible trade such as income and expenditures for services like banking, insurance, tourism and shipping, together with profits earned overseas and interest payments.

Decentralization: an administrative concept applied by large organizations or departments in assigning decision-making responsibility to subunits on a geographical or subject matter basis.

Deflation: an economic condition in which the price level is decreased and the value of money in terms of purchasing power is increased.

Democracy: a system of government in which ultimate political authority is vested in the people.

Depreciation: a decrease in the value of capital, such as from capital wearing out or becoming technologically obsolete; also a decline in the purchasing power of a currency when it is exchanged for other currencies.

Depression: a period of drastic decline in the national economy, characterized by decreasing business activity, falling prices, and unemployment.

Deterrence: retaliatory capability of a country's military forces to discourage a potential enemy from launching an attack.

Devaluation: a policy undertaken by a country to reduce the value of its monetary unit in terms of gold, or its exchange ratio with other national currencies.

Developing economy: an economy which has a low level of GDP per capita and a relatively undeveloped market structure, and has not recently had an alternative, developed economic system.

Dictatorship: arbitrary rule by an individual or junta not constitutionally responsible to the people or their elected representatives.

Diplomacy: the total process by which countries carry on political relations with each other.

Dumping: the selling of a good for less than its cost of production.

Economics: the science that deals with the production, distribution and consumption of commodities.

Embargo: a government edict prohibiting citizens from trading with one or several countries.

Ethnicity: the attribution of characteristics to groups of people who share a common cultural (including religious) heritage.

Ethnocentrism: the attitude that one's culture and people are inherently superior to others.

Ethnology: the comparative study of two or more cultures.

Ethos: the soul, spirit or core of a cultural group which organizes the cultural elements, complexes and institutions in a consistent manner.

Evolution: the process that occurs when natural selection acts upon genetic variations to produce differential reproduction.

Exchange rate: the price of one currency in terms of another.

Existential postulates: consists of those assumption that a culture has concerning the external world, the nature of man, his relation with nature and super-nature.

Experiment: a test made to demonstrate a known truth, to examine the validity of a hypothesis, or to determine the efficacy of something previously untried.

Exports: goods produced in the home country but sold in foreign countries.

Extended families: social groups consisting of one or more parents, children, and other kin, often spanning several generations.

Family: a group of people who identify themselves as being related to one another, usually by blood, marriage, or adoption, and who share intimate relationships and dependency.

Fascism: a political system which incorporates the principles of the dictator, a one-party state, totalitarian regimentation of economic and social activity, and the arbitrary exercise of absolute power by the regime.

Fast-track authority: power given to the President of the United States to negotiate a commercial treaty in its totality before sending it for debate before the Senate.

Federal Reserve System: the private-public banking regulatory system in the United States which establishes banking policies and influence the amount of credit available and the currency in circulation.

Federalism: a system of government in which power is divided by a written constitution between a central government and regional or subdivisional governments.

Fiscal Policy: a government tax and spending policy.

Fixed exchange rates: rates set by governments, at which a currency can be freely exchanged among individuals.

Flexible exchange rates: the exchange rate is set by market forces (supply and demand for a country's currency).

Foreign Aid: the granting of economic or military assistance to foreign countries.

Foreign-exchange: the money of another country.

Foreign-exchange market: market in which one country's currency can be exchanged for another country's.

Foreign investment: the acquisition by governments, institutions or individuals in one country of assets in another.

Foreign Policy: a strategy developed by the decision makers of a state vis-a-vis other states or international entities aimed at achieving specific goals defined in terms of national interest.

Free markets: the collective decisions of individual buyers and sellers that, taken together, determine what outputs are produced, how those outputs are produced, and who receives the outputs; free markets depend on private property and free choice.

Free trade: a policy of allowing unrestricted trade among countries.

Gene: a portion of the DNA molecule which specifies the chemical manufacture of a protein that will assist on the production of one or many physical traits.

Gene flow: changes of gene frequencies in populations caused by migration and by intermating with members of different populations.

Genetic drift: the filial or descendant population differs from the parental pertaining to the frequency of some genes, which occurs when there is a difference in fertility rates among groups of a population, or when some segments of it (boat load effect) migrate.

Genocide: the destruction of groups of human beings because of their race, religion, nationality, or ethnic background.

Genotype: the hereditary endowment that an organism gets at the time of conception from both parents.

Geography: the study of the earth and its features and of the distribution on the earth of life, including human life and the effects of human activity.

Globalization: the processes by which the lives of all people around the planet become increasingly interconnected in economic, political, cultural, and environmental terms, along with an awareness of such interconnections.

Good Offices: method of peaceful settlement by which a third country seeks to bring two disputing countries into agreement.

Government: the political and administrative hierarchy of an organized state.

Gross domestic product (GDP): the market value of the final goods and services produced in the economy within some time period, usually one quarter or one year.

Gross National Product (GNP): the same as gross domestic product, except that the value added to production by U.S.-owned resources located outside the United States is counted in GNP, and the value added to production by foreign-owned resources within the United States is excluded.

Group of Five: group of countries that meets to promote negotiations and coordinate economic relations among states. The five are Britain, France, Germany, Japan and the United States.

Group of Seven: the group of five plus Canada and Italy.

Guerrilla War: irregular warfare fought by small bands against an invading army or in rebellion against an established order.

History: the branch of knowledge that records and analyzes past events.

Holistic: attempts to describe phenomena, cultural systems, social systems, etc., as whole systems rather than piecemeal.

Human rights: protection for individuals from arbitrary interference with or curtailment of life, liberty, and the equal protection of the laws by government or private individuals and groups.

Humanities: those branches of knowledge, such as philosophy, literature and art, that are concerned with human culture, as distinguished from the sciences.

Hypothesis: a statement of an expected relationship between variables that may be tested empirically to determine its validity.

Impeachment: a formal accusation, rendered by the lower house of a legislative body, that commits an accused civil official for trial in the upper house.

Imperialism: a superior-inferior relationship in which an area and its people have been subordinate to the will of a foreign state.

Individualism: the political, economic, and social concept that places primary emphasis on the worth, freedom, and well-being of the individual rather than those of the group, society or nation.

Industrial policy: involves the government promoting certain industries.

Infant industries: start-up industries that might be unable to survive the rigors of competition in their formative years.

Inflation: an abnormal increase in available currency and credit beyond the proportion of available goods, resulting in a sharp and continuing rise in price levels.

Inquiry: a formal, impartial determination of the facts involved in an international dispute.

Institution: an established pattern of human behavior consisting of structured social interaction within a framework of relevant values.

Intellectual Knowledge: the kind of knowledge made possible by the intellect's powers of generating ideas or concepts, of reasoning, and of making judgments as to whether something is or is not what it seems.

Intelligence: information gathered by a government about other states' capabilities and intentions.

Interest rate: represents the cost of borrowing and the reward for saving or lending.

Internationalism: the theory and practice of national involvement in cooperative interstate efforts to solve common security, political, economic, and social problems.

Investment: spending now in order to increase output or productivity later.

Irredentism: the desire of the people of a state to annex those contiguous territories of another country that are inhabited largely by linguistic or cultural minorities of the first state.

Isolationism: the theory and practice of non-involvement in the affairs of other countries.

Judicial review: the power of the courts to declare acts of the legislative and executive branches unconstitutional.

Judiciary: a collective term for courts and judges.

Labor: the individual and collective efforts of humans, including the services performed by workers for wages, a distinguished from those rendered by entrepreneurs or investors for profit.

Laissez-faire: the economic theory, propounded by the French physiocrats and popularized by Adam Smith, that calls for a hands-off policy by government toward the economy.

Land: all natural resources, in their natural state.

Language: a uniquely human form of communicating experiences, ideas, and emotion by means of a system of oral symbols.

Leftist: an individual or a political group advocating liberal, radical or revolutionary political or economic programs, an expanded role by government, or empowering the masses, usually advocating egalitarianism.

Liberalism: a political view that seeks to change the political, economic, or social status quo to foster the development and well-being of the individual.

Limited war: a war that is fought without the employment of all major weapons and for objectives other than the complete defeat of the enemy.

Lobbyist: a person, usually acting as an agent for a pressure group, who seeks to bring about the passage or defeat of legislative bills or to influence their content.

Market: a coming together of buyers and sellers that expedites the voluntary exchange of resources, goods, or services.

Marriage: a culturally approved relationship, usually between two individuals, that provides for a degree of economic cooperation, intimacy, and sexual activity.

Massive retaliation: the threat of a nuclear response to restrain the actions of another state.

Mediation: a diplomatic technique in which a third party or country strives to solve a dispute by establishing the facts and by offering substantive suggestions.

Mercantilism: the economic philosophy and practice of government regulation of a nation's economic life to increase state power and security.

Merchandise trade account: records the value of import and export goods.

Military-industrial complex: an informal alliance among key military, governmental and corporate decision makers involved in the highly profitable weapon procurement and military support system.

Mixed economies: the mixture of free market and command and control methods of resource allocation that characterize modern economies.

Monarchy: any form of government in which the supreme powers of the state are exercised, or ceremoniously held, by a king, queen, emperor or other regal potentate.

Monetary policy: government policy that aims at affecting the amount of currency in circulation and availability of credit.

Money: a medium of exchange that removes the need for barter. It is also a measure of value and a way to store value over time.

Monogamy: a form of marriage in which a person may have only one spouse at a time.

Mutations: consist of a change or alteration in the genetic material and are the starting point or source of evolutionary change, caused by radiation, heat, chemical or other factors.

Nation: any sizable group of people united by common bonds of geography, religion, language, race, custom, and tradition, and through shared experience and common aspiration.

National income: the total income earned by individuals and corporations which is arrived at by subtracting indirect taxes from net national product.

National self-determination: the doctrine that postulates the right of a group of people who consider themselves separate and distinct from others to determine for themselves the state in which they will live and the form of government it will have.

Nationalism: social and psychological forces that spring from unique cultural and historical factors to provide unity and inspiration to a given people through a sense of belonging together and of shared values.

Natural selection: environmental pressures which cause changes in the frequency of genes of a species' genetic pool due to differences in reproductive success.

Naturalistic observation: the watching of the behavior of humans and animals in their natural environment.

Near Abroad: term used by Russians to refer to those former republics of the Soviet Union which are now independent.

Negotiations: a process in which explicit proposals are put forward ostensibly for the purpose of reaching agreements on an exchange or on the realization of a common interest where conflicting interests are present.

Neoliberalism: name given to reforms in Latin America which include privatization of government enterprises, liberalization of commercial and financial transactions, trade reforms to lower tariffs, and democracy. Neoliberalism is also referred to as the Washington Consensus.

Nepotism: granting of political favors to relatives, often in the form of appointment to office.

Net domestic product (NDP): gross domestic product minus depreciation.

Net National Product (NNP): net national product minus depreciation.

Norm: a rule or value that provides a generally accepted standard of behavior within a group.

Normative postulates: the values that a culture has concerning judgment of things or acts as good or meritorious or bad and punishable.

Nuclear family: a social group consisting of one or two parents and their dependent children.

Observation: the purposeful gathering of information by direct sensory contact with the persons or objects being studied.

Oligarchy: any system of government in which a small group holds the ruling power.

Parliamentary government: a system in which legislative and executive powers are fused. Parliamentary government does not require the separate elections of the head of the government, as in the American system, where powers are separated. The leadership of the majority in the legislature forms the Cabinet, which exercises executive power.

Participant observation: a research method by which the investigators become members, or pose as members, of a group they are studying.

Perception: the act of becoming aware of things by means of the senses.

Phenotype: the observable or measurable characteristic of an organism.

Philosophy: the attempt to think clearly and methodically about the causes and laws underlying reality and about the nature of things, as well as the activity of engaging in the critique and analysis of fundamental beliefs.

Physicalism: the doctrine that everything is physical or material and that whatever exists or occurs can be completely described in the vocabulary of physics.

Pluralism: the existence in modern society of heterogenous institutions and organizations that have diversified religion, economic, ethnic and cultural interests.

Political Science: the study of the processes, principles, and structure of government and of political institutions.

Politics: the making of decisions by public rather than private or personal means.

Polygamy: a form of marriage in which a person may have more than one spouse.

Power: the capacity to affect the behaviors of others in some desired way.

Preemptive War: a military operation undertaken after a country learns that it is to be attacked by another.

Pressure group: an organized interest group in which members share common views and objectives and carry on programs to influence government officials and policies.

Preventive War: a military strategy that calls for an attack by a country that enjoys a temporary advantage in striking power.

Primary sources: documents in archives, eyewitness reports and collections, diaries and letters, newspapers, and other publications that historians classify and question to create the historical narrative.

Privatization: transferring property rights from government to individuals or firms.

Profit: total revenue minus total cost.

Propaganda: communication aimed at influencing the thinking, emotions, or actions of a group or public.

Protectionism: the imposition of restrictions to restrict the inflow of imports.

Psychology: the science of mental processes and behavior.

Purchasing power parity (PPP): a method of calculating exchange rates that attempts to value currencies at rate such that each currency will buy an equal basket of goods.

Quota: quantity limit on imports.

Racism: a belief that differences among people are rooted in racial stock.

Radical: an advocate of sudden and substantial political, social, and economic changes.

Radicalism: advocacy of substantial political, social, and economic changes.

Raison d'état: a doctrine which holds that security and national advantage are the most important considerations in a country's actions.

Reactionary: a person who advocates substantial political, social or economic changes favoring a return to an earlier, more traditional system.

Recession: a moderate and temporary decline in economic activity that occurs during a period of otherwise increasing prosperity, often in a recovery period following a depression.

Reductionism: a method of explanation in which the attributes or behavior of the whole are reduced to or explained by reference to, the attributes or behavior of its constituent parts.

Refugee: a person who is expelled, deported, or flees from his country of nationality or residence.

Representative government: any democratic system of government in which the people elect representatives to act as their agents in making and enforcing laws and decisions.

Republic: a form of government in which sovereign power resides in the electorate and is exercised by elected representatives who are responsible to the people.

Revolution: a basic transformation of the political economic, or social principles and institutions of a state, resulting from the overthrow of an established government, or dominant culture.

Scarcity: a situation in which there are too few resources to meet all human needs.

Science: the observation, identification, description, experimental investigation, and theoretical explanation of phenomena.

Scientific method: the totality of principles and processes regarded as characteristic of or necessary for scientific investigation, generally taken to include rules for concept formation, conduct of observations and experiments, and validation of hypotheses by observation and experiments.

Scientism: the attitude of holding that science constitutes the only valid knowledge and is alone capable of solving human problems.

Secondary sources: articles, monographs or specialized books used in the production of textbooks, encyclopedia articles or popularized accounts. (tertiary sources)

Sense knowledge: the kind of knowledge in whose production bodily organs (external sense organs, brain) are immediately involved. External senses produce the first sensations from received impressions, and internal senses further "interpret" the sensation material.

Separation of powers: a major principle of American government whereby power is distributed among three branches of government: the legislative, the executive and the judicial.

Services: intangible, non-transferable economic goods as distinct from physical commodities.

Social anthropology: the study of social relationships in human groups.

Social Sciences: academic disciplines involved in the study of human society and of individual relationships in and to society, and which include such areas as sociology, psychology, anthropology, economics, political science, and history.

Socialism: a doctrine that advocates economic collectivism through governmental or industrial group ownership of the means of production and distribution of goods.

Society: an aggregation of people who have certain common attributes that distinguish them as a group and who interact with one another in some characteristic way.

Sociology: the study of human social behavior, especially the study of the origins, organization, institutions, and development of human society.

State: a political community occupying a definite territory, having an organized government and possessing internal and external sovereignty.

State sovereignty: independence of a state from external control.

Statism: the basic concept that sovereignty is vested not in the people but in the state, and that all individuals and association exist only to enhance the power, prestige and the well-being of the state.

Subsidies: payments from government that are intended to promote certain activities.

Summit conference: a meeting of two or more leaders of state to directly resolve differences.

Supranationalism: power exercised by international institutions to make majority-vote decisions that are binding upon all member states or their citizens.

Survey research: the investigation of social phenomena by means of interviews and questionnaires administered to a number of respondents.

Tariff: tax on imports.

Terms of trade: the relationship between the prices a country receives for its exports and the prices it pays for its imports.

Terrorism: a type of mostly urban warfare directed primarily against civilians or non-combatants in addition to military assets.

Total war: a modern war fought for unrestrictive objectives with all means available for marshaling national power.

Totalitarianism: a modern form of authoritarianism in which the state controls nearly every aspect of the individual's life.

Trade deficit: a negative balance on the merchandise trade account, given when the dollar value of imported goods exceeds the dollar value of exported goods.

Transitional economy: an economy that has had an alternative developed, socialist economic system, but is in the process of changing from that system to a market system.

Treaty: a formal agreement entered into between two or more sovereign states for the purpose of creating or restricting mutual rights and mutual responsibilities.

Unilateralism: a policy whereby a state depends completely on its own resources for security and the advancement of its national interest.

Unitary state: a centralized government in which local or subdivisional governments exercise only those powers given to them by the central government.

Variations: the inherited differences between individuals which constitute the basic of evolutionary chance. There are four causes of variations: meiosis, mutations, genetic drift, and gene flow.

War: hostilities between states, or within a state or territory undertaken by means of armed force.

World Bank: a multinational international financial institution that works with developing countries to secure low-interest loans.

World Trade Organization (WTO): an organization committed to getting countries to agree not to impose new tariffs or other trade restrictions.

Xenophobia: an undue fear or distrust of foreigners and of the policies and objectives of other states.

THE SOCIAL ENVIRONMENT
A PRIMER ON WORLD CIVICS

TWELFTH EDITION

WORKBOOK BY

MAGDALENA RIVERA-LAMARRE

TABLE OF CONTENTS

To the Students and General Readers

This study guide and workbook is designed to help you understand better the text **The Social Environment** Eleventh Edition, written by Phyllis Baker, Paul George, Victor Vazquez-Hernandez, David Shaheen, Michael Lenaghan, and Germán Muñoz. It is not meant to replace the textbook itself. Regular use of the study guide, faithful class attendance, and the daily reading of the text, almost guarantees good results. This study guide consists of twelve chapters, each corresponding to the first twelve chapters of the book.

The **Chapter Outline** is a summary outline of the key points of each chapter. We recommend that you read it before listening to the professor's presentation on the topic and before you read the corresponding chapter in the textbook. Following this strategy, you will be more prepared for the lecture and for your text. **The Learning Objectives** section introduces you to questions whose answers require you to think deeply about the content presented by your teacher in class and in the textbook. These short answer questions will help you to perceive the relationships among the various concepts you have learned and to respond in a comprehensive and articulate manner. The **Chapter Outline** saved you some work by organizing the material for you. However, the Objectives section is designed to make you work.

The **Key Terms** section lists some of the most important concepts presented in the textbook and asks you to define each. You may use the **Glossary** section at the end of your textbook, **The Social Environment,** to identify each term, you can use the text itself, or you can use a dictionary. The **Multiple Choice, True and False Statements, Matching, and Essay** sections of the study guide are challenging opportunities for you to work through after you have read each chapter. An **Answer Key** has been provided at the end of the study guide.

This Study Guide is dedicated to all my students—past, present and future.

As you inspire me to teach, I hope this book inspires you to learn.

It is also dedicated to my husband, Pierre Lamarre,
Who supports me in all of my efforts, and who inspires me.

Chapter 1—Core Principles

Thinking Critically, Multiculturally, and Globally

CHAPTER OUTLINE

I   The Revolution in Information and Communications

    A. Could be as important as the previous agricultural and industrial revolutions.

    B. Brings greater awareness of both human diversity and homogeneity.

    C. Allows us to know more about both human cruelty and goodness.

II   Critical Thinking

    A. Ability to conceptualize and synthesize information in the most careful, exact, logical, and analytical manner.

    B. Includes various mental modalities:
        1. Recall
        2. Similarity
        3. Differences
        4. Cause and Effect
        5. Generalization
        6. Substantiation
        7. Synthesis

    C. Involves various mental operations performed by the mind when engaged in critical thinking:
        1. Analyzing
        2. Comparing
        3. Contrasting
        4. Criticizing
        5. Defining
        6. Describing
        7. Discussing
        8. Enumerating
        9. Evaluating
        10. Illustrating
        11. Interpreting
        12. Outlining
        13. Proving
        14. Stating
        15. Summarizing
        16. Tracing

    D. Critical thinking implies a deep level of thought, evaluation, reasoning and decision-making.

III   Multiculturalism

A. Defined in this textbook as an intellectual method of understanding reality by studying one's subject matter from a wide range of points of view.

B. Intellectual Multiculturalism.

    1. Promotes an awareness and understanding of various cultures to better comprehend any subject matter under study.

C. Academic Multiculturalism.

    1. Educational movement beginning in the 1970s.

    2. Seeks to include information in the American curriculum about the experiences, achievements, and imperfections of non-Western individuals and groups.

D. Political Multiculturalism.

    1. Desires a society in which different racial and ethnic groups maintain their distinctive cultures.

    2. Believes that society should highlight the cultural differences of its diverse members to enrich itself.

    3. Critics of this form of multiculturalism respond that society should stress the common cultural elements to avoid conflicts and divisiveness.

IV   Globalization

A. Defined as a worldwide process by which people, markets, corporations and countries are being integrated to an unprecedented degree in a way that is enabling them to reach around the world farther, faster, deeper, and cheaper.

B. It is made possible by the rise in international trade, investments, and banking, and by improvements in transportation and communication.

C. Critics are concerned about inequities in benefits and the potential for exploitation.

D. Supporters point out the opportunities made available, believing that this process will force societies to be more productive.

Review Section

Learning Objectives

After reading **Chapter One**, you should be able to:

1. Define critical thinking, multiculturalism, and globalization.

2. Analyze the mental operations involved in critical thinking.

3. Discuss the controversy about political multiculturalism.

4. Illustrate examples of globalization, and discuss the positive and negative consequences of globalization.

Key Terms

Define the following glossary terms to test your knowledge:

1. Critical thinking
2. Multiculturalism
3. Globalization
4. Academic multiculturalism
5. Intellectual multiculturalism
6. Political multiculturalism
7. Analysis
8. Comparison
9. Contrast
10. Criticism
11. Discussion

12. Evaluation

13. Illustration

14. Interpretation

15. Proving

16. Stating

17. Summarizing

18. Cause and effect

19. Synthesis

20. Generalization

Multiple Choice

1. Which one of the following seeks the inclusion of non-Western books in the curriculum?
   a. Academic multiculturalism
   b. Intellectual multiculturalism
   c. Political multiculturalism

2. Which of the following best describes Critical Thinking?
   a. Judge correctness of an issue
   b. Conceptualize and synthesize information
   c. Explain clearly by using comparisons or examples
   d. Present opinions without the need to support them

3. Critics of globalization are concerned that:
   a. The rich will get richer while the poor get poorer
   b. Less affluent societies will focus their local economies on producing for the global economy
   c. Less developed societies will be encouraged to use up their vital natural resources
   d. All of the above

4. Supporters of globalization argue that:
   a. Less developed countries must be brought into the global market in order to complete their industrial transformations
   b. In the long run countries can only benefit from globalization
   c. It will force societies to be more productive to compete in the global market place
   d. It will ensure environmental preservation as resources are used more selectively

5. Critics of political multiculturalism argue against it because they contend that:
   a. Society should highlight the differences of its diverse members to enrich itself
   b. Society should stress the common cultural elements in order to avoid conflicts and divisiveness
   c. People should be encouraged to maintain their distinctive cultures
   d. An educational program recognizing past and present cultural diversity will promote understanding and equality

True and False Statements

Indicate if the following statements are True (T), or False (F).

_____ **1.** Globalization is a regional process only affecting Western, modern countries.

_____ **2.** Intellectual multiculturalism enables one to get as complete a picture as possible of whatever topic is under study.

_____ **3.** All forms of multiculturalism are part of a political agenda to undermine Western culture.

_____ **4.** Synthesis has to do with breaking the object of study into its separate parts.

_____ **5.** Defining has to do with giving the meaning of whatever is being studied.

Matching Terms

_____ **1.** Analyze   **A.** Narrowing down, isolating and predicting possible outcomes of an event or situation

_____ **2.** Compare   **B.** Memorization of what was said, done, read, or experienced

_____ **3.** Discuss   **C.** Break into separate parts and discus

_____ **4.** Evaluate   **D.** Examine two or more things, and identify similarities and differences

_____ **5.** Generalization   **E.** Give your opinion or cite the opinion of an expert

_____ **6.** Illustrate   **F.** Give concrete examples

_____ **7.** Interpret   **G.** Blend and evaluate the best information available at the time

_____ **8.** Prove   **H.** Support with facts

_____ **9.** Recall   **I.** Consider and debate or argue the pros and cons of an issue

_____ **10.** Synthesize   **J.** Comment upon, give examples, describe Relationships

Chapter 2—The Human Struggle for Knowledge, Understanding and Wisdom

The Humanities, the Natural Sciences, and the Social Sciences

CHAPTER OUTLINE

I   Knowledge

A. Human beings constantly seek knowledge:
1. May be practical or theoretical.
2. Serves a purpose when it leads to comprehension, application, analysis, and synthesis.
3. The acquisition of knowledge is made possible through the senses and intellect.
4. All human knowledge has its starting point in the senses.
   a. External senses
   b. Internal senses
   c. Sense knowledge
5. Human knowledge is not completed until it engages the intellect. Intellectual knowing includes the powers of:
   a. Conception
   b. Judgment
   c. Reasoning
6. These intellectual mental operations help distinguish humans from the higher animals, which lack the power of abstract reasoning.

B. In their attempts to acquire knowledge, to seek explanations about nature and beyond, and to explore their humanity, humans developed **Fields of knowledge**:
1. Philosophy
2. Humanities
3. Science

C. **Philosophy** originated in religious questions. The ancient Greek philosophers sought answers by thinking and by studying nature.

D. As philosophy evolved it branched out into different schools of thought, and was led by great thinkers:
1. The pre-Socratic philosophers
2. The Sophists
3. Socrates
4. Plato
5. Aristotle

E. During the middle Ages, human knowledge was separated into:
1. Theology
2. Philosophy

F. Until the 1700s, no distinction was made between science and philosophy; then it ceased to include all human knowledge.
   1. Mathematics developed as a distinct discipline.
   2. **Natural Philosophy** evolved into the Natural Sciences, which later divided into:
      a. Life Sciences
      b. Physical Sciences
   3. Social Philosophy subdivided into separate disciplines known as the **Social Sciences**.
   4. **Philosophy** emerged as a separate discipline, containing specific areas of knowledge:
      a. Metaphysics
      b. Epistemology
      c. Logic
      d. Ethics
      e. Aesthetics
      f. Philosophy of Language
      g. Philosophical Psychology
      h. Philosophy of Religion

G. The **Humanities** emerged as a distinct field of study concerned primarily with human values and expressions of the human spirit.
   1. Some areas of study include literature, music, art, religion and philosophy.
   2. Since the 1800s the humanities have been commonly contrasted to the natural sciences; do not attempt to reach general laws

H. **Science** refers to a broad field of knowledge that deals with observed facts and the relationships among facts:
   1. The ancient Greeks were the first to begin a systematic separation of scientific ideas from superstition and mere opinions, and sought rational explanations for natural phenomena.
   2. It is a method for obtaining information and a body of systematically arranged knowledge.
   3. Attempts to discover and explain relationships among observable natural phenomena.
   4. Goes beyond common sense by reflecting on one's knowledge and discovering why it is so.
   5. Great scientific thinkers who contributed to its development and expansion include:
      a. Roger Bacon
      b. Nicolas Copernicus
      c. Johannes Kepler
      d. Galileo Galilei
      e. Isaac Newton
   6. Four major areas have developed within the area of Science:
      a. Mathematics and logic
      b. Physical Sciences
      c. Biological Sciences
      d. Social Sciences

II   The Social Sciences

A. **The Social Sciences** attempt to systematically study humans and society, by studying the various aspects of human relationships and the institutions which mold it.

B. They emerged partially as an attempt to understand the social consequences brought about by three major events of the 18th century:
   1. The Enlightenment (1680s)
   2. Industrial Revolution (1760s)
   3. French Revolution (1789)

    C. Content focused on new themes that emerged in the 1800s:
- **1.** Increase in population
- **2.** Difficult conditions of urban labor
- **3.** Transformation of property.
- **4.** Urbanization
- **5.** Technological innovation
- **6.** Politicization of the masses

    D. Above themes became tied in to new political ideologies:
- **1.** Liberalism
- **2.** Conservatism
- **3.** Radicalism

    E. Social Sciences were also influenced by powerful intellectual tendencies:
- **1.** Positivism
- **2.** Humanitarianism
- **3.** Evolution

III The Social Science Disciplines

    A. Anthropology—the scientific study of humanity and of human culture:
- **1.** Is separated into two major divisions:
  - **a.** Social Anthropology
  - **b.** Cultural Anthropology
- **2.** Cultural Anthropology includes three subfields:
  - **a.** Ethnography
  - **b.** Ethnology
  - **c.** Archaeology
- **3.** Physical Anthropology (not a social science) studies biological characteristics of human beings.

    B. Economics—study of how society meets its needs for goods and services and how they are distributed.
- **1.** Concerned with issues of:
  - **a.** Utilization and allocation of available resources
  - **b.** Production and distribution of goods and services
  - **c.** Scarcity
- **2.** Divided into two subfields:
  - **a. Macroeconomics**
  - **b. Microeconomics**

    C. Geography—study of the location and distribution of living things and of the earth features among which they live.
- **1.** Major divisions of the field are:
  - **a. Physical Geography** (not a social science)
  - **b. Human Geography**

    D. History—the memory of the past experience of humankind as it has been preserved, largely in written records.
- **1.** Is a branch of both Humanities and Social Sciences.
- **2.** Historians seldom develop general laws; use social science theory to help explain the conditions or events of a particular time.
- **3.** Historical research begins with **primary source records**, which results in production of **secondary sources**, and may also be reworked into tertiary resources.
- **4.** Evaluation of work could include **internal criticism** and **external criticism**.

    E. Political Science—the systematic study of political life including politics and government.
       1. Politics is the making of decisions by public rather than private or personal means.
       2. Government refers to the institutions through which public decisions are made and carried out.
       3. Traditionally divided into various fields of study which include:
          a. Political Theory and Philosophy
          b. Comparative Government
          c. International Relations
          d. Political Behavior

    F. Psychology—the scientific study of mental processes and behavior.
       1. Psychologists rely on three basic methods to gather data:
          a. Naturalistic observation
          b. Systematic assessment
          c. Experimentation

    G. Sociology—the study of individuals, groups and institutions that make up human society.
       1. Places attention on the collective aspects of human behavior.
       2. Sociologists have certain major interests:
          a. Population characteristics
          b. Social behavior
          c. Social institutions
          d. Cultural influences
          e. Social change
       3. Modern sociology is divided into several branches including:
          a. Criminology
          b. Demography
          c. Deviance
          d. Human Ecology
          d. Political Sociology
          e. Urban Sociology
       4. Shares with psychology the sub-field of social psychology, and is close to social anthropology.
       5. Methods utilized for research include field observation, surveys or public opinion polls, and controlled experiments to test hypothesis.

IV   The Scientific Method

    A. Although several non-Western groups developed an impressive body of knowledge, it was based on practicality, and not on theoretical knowledge or science.
       1. Several philosophical premises (**scientific attitudes**) would set the groundwork for the emergence of the **Scientific Method**:
          a. The physical world runs according to specific natural laws.
          b. Rationalism
          c. Moderate skepticism
          d. Amorality
          e. Mathematical expression
          f. Rejection of traditional appeals to the supernatural and to human authority.
          g. Rejection of one's own knowledge and expertise if they are based on mere opinion.

    2. A scientific attitude is also associated with three goals:
       a. Verifiability
       b. Systematic inquiry
       c. Generality

B. The ultimate aims of science are:
    1. Description and explanation through the formation of explanatory laws
    2. To obtain precise qualitative data in order to achieve accuracy and predictability

C. The **Scientific Method** is a flexible set of rules developed over the last few centuries to ensure that empirical research will lead to valid theories. Scientific research requires that specific steps be followed, though not necessarily in this sequence:
    1. Selection of an area of study
    2. Observation and measurement
    3. Formulation of a specific researchable hypothesis
    4. Construction of a research design
    5. Data collection
    6. Classification and organization of the data after it is gathered.
    7. Conclusion which consists of an evaluation of the hypothesis based on the data and an attempt to generalize from the result of the study.

D. Empirical methods for gathering data include:
    1. Controlled experimentation:
       a. Involves a deliberate disturbance of the normal course of events.
       b. Seeks to specify **cause-effect relationships** between two variables—**the dependent and independent variable**, under carefully controlled conditions.
       c. Utilizes an **experimental** and a **control group**.
    2. Sample surveys:
       a. Ask people questions to systematically gather standardized information about the behavior, opinions, attitude's, values, beliefs, and other characteristics.
       b. Is possible to identify relationships—correlations, between many different variables for large populations.
       c. Utilizes a **questionnaire** or **interview method**.
    3. Observational studies:
       a. Intensive examination of one unit, first-hand in a natural setting.
       b. Called detached observation if researchers watch without getting involved.
       c. Called participant observation when they participate in the group.

E. Limitations of Science.
    1. Although social science research methods have reduced the incidence of prejudice, superstition and error, they are not always reliable:
       a. Regarding experimentation, not everyone or every situation can be tested, or there may be ethical or methodological restraints.
       b. Sample surveys are often designed unscientifically, and people do not often respond truthfully.
       c. Results of observational studies are often difficult to generalize.
    2. Scientists often fall prey to two common biases:
       a. Physicalism or Materialism
       b. Scientism

Review Section

Learning Objectives

After reading **Chapter Two**, you should be able to respond to the following questions:

1. Describe the elements or steps of the Scientific Method.

2. Describe the major differences between the Humanities, the Natural Sciences, and the Social Sciences.

3. Identify the major social sciences, and explain their objectives.

4. Describe the role of philosophy in the development of the sciences.

5. Identify the sense and intellectual powers of human beings.

Key Terms

Define the following glossary terms to test your knowledge:

1. Philosophy

2. Humanities

3. Science

4. Physical Sciences

5. Biological Sciences

6. Social Sciences

7. Cultural Anthropology

8. Archaeology

9. Government

10. Primary sources

11. Secondary sources

12. Psychology

13. Experimental group

14. Control group

15. Rationalism

16. Skepticism

17. Openness

18. Amorality

19. Experimentation

20. Independent variables

21. Dependent variables

22. Sample surveys

23. Observational studies

24. Hypothesis

25. Correlation

Matching Terms

_____ 1.   Anthropology   **A.** The study of how goods and services are produced.

_____ 2.   Economics   **B.** The systematic study of government and power.

_____ 3.   Geography   **C.** The study of individuals, groups and institutions that make up society.

_____ 4.   History   **D.** The scientific study of humanity and of human culture.

_____ 5.   Humanities   **E.** The memory of the past experiences of humanity.

_____ 6.   Social Science   **F.** The scientific study of mental processes and behavior.

_____ 7.   Sociology   **G.** The study of the location and distribution of living
                                     things, and of the earth features among which they live.

_____ 8.   Philosophy   **H.** Branches of learning that deal with human thought
                                     and culture, excluding the sciences.

_____ **9.**   Political Science   **I.** Attempts a systematic study of the various aspects of the
                                     social relationship of humans.

_____ **10.**   Psychology   **J.** A form of inquiry that involves rational, critical thinking about the world,
                                     oneself, and others.

Multiple Choice

1. Perceptions, memories, and images are all part of:
   a. Intellectual Knowledge
   b. Sense Knowledge
   c. Practical Knowledge
   d. Theoretical Knowledge

2. Concepts, judgments, and reasoning are part of:
   a. Intellectual Knowledge
   b. Sense Knowledge
   c. Practical Knowledge
   d. Theoretical Knowledge

3. According to Plato, philosophy is:
   a. Mere opinion
   b. Rational Knowledge
   c. Socratic Allegory
   d. Love of Wisdom

4. Which of the following **does not** constitute one of the major fields of human knowledge?
   a. Natural Science
   b. Humanities
   c. Biological Science
   d. Social Science

5. Science, according to Aristotle, is an understanding of:
   a. Causes
   b. Effects
   c. Matter
   d. Form

6. This is an example of a Physical Science:
   a. Sociology
   b. Biology
   c. Chemistry
   d. Mathematics

7. This is an example of a Life Science:
   a. Anthropology
   b. Anatomy
   c. Physics
   d. Logic

8. This social science is also considered to be a branch of the humanities.
   a. Anthropology
   b. Sociology
   c. Political Science
   d. History

9. Which of the following deals with large aggregates such as national output, national income, national savings, and national investment?
   a. Political Economics
   b. Economic Geography
   c. Macroeconomics
   d. Urban Sociology

10. This step of the Scientific Method proposes an anticipated explanation that will assist the researchers in determining if there is a cause-effect relationship between two variables.
    a. Selection of an area of study
    b. Formulation of a specific research hypothesis
    c. Construction of a research design
    d. Data collection

True and False Statements

Indicate if the statement is True (T) or False (F).

_____ **1.**   In controlled experimentation, the social scientist merely observes how the human or the animal behaves in the natural habitat.

_____ **2.**   An ultimate aim of science is the description of facts.

_____ **3.**   Physicalism is the doctrine that everything is material and can be described in the vocabulary of physics.

_____ **4.**   In an experiment, the group that is not exposed to the independent variable in order to determine if the treatment may be causing the expected result is called the experimental group.

_____ **5.**   When social scientists want to systematically gather standardized information regarding behavior, opinions, or beliefs, they use sample surveys.

Matching People

_____ **1.**   Aristotle   **A.** Proposed the Theory of Evolution.

_____ **2.**   Socrates   **B.** Used intricate calculations to show that the heliocentric theory could explain the movements of the planets.

_____ **3.**   Plato   **C.** Formulated a law of universal gravitation.

_____ **4.**   Nicolas Copernicus   **D.** Sought definitions of abstract concepts through a question and answer method (dialectic).

_____ **5.**   Galileo Galilei   **E.** Was the first to speak of experimental science, and the understanding of the scientific method.

_____ **6.**   Roger Bacon   **F.** Distinguished a mere opinion—doxa, from a justified opinion—episteme.

_____ **7.**   Johannes Kepler   **G.** Proposed the idea of the scientific treatment of social behavior.

_____ **8.**   Isaac Newton   **H.** He was responsible for the first effective use of the telescope and developed the law of falling bodies, and the hydrostatic balance.

_____ **9.**   August Comte   **I.** Defined philosophy as the totality of human understanding acquired by rational inquiry.

_____ **10.**   Charles Darwin   **J.** In 1543 he challenged Ptolemy's view that the earth was the center of the universe.

Essay Questions

1.   Describe the major differences between the humanities, the natural sciences, and the social sciences. Expand on your discussion of the social sciences by identifying the major disciplines and their focus of study.

2.   Discuss the aims of science, and demonstrate how the Scientific Method achieves them, including in your discussion a description of the steps of the Scientific Method.

Chapter 3—Tribes, Empires, States and Nations: A Brief Introduction to World History

CHAPTER OUTLINE

I   Human Groupings

A. International states are the basic building blocs of political organization and functioning, but each is a unique assemblage of territory, people, and institutions.

   1. A **state** is a political community defined by:

      a. Units of political organization which are internally and externally sovereign.

      b. Permanent borders

      c. Stable populations

   2. States can be organized on a **federal** principle:

      a. Function as a collection of self-governing units.

      b. Central governments have direct responsibility for a limited number of activities.

      c. Examples include Canada and United States.

   3. The majority are organized as **unitary** states:

      a. A highly centralized government tightly controls all parts of the country.

      b. Local or subdivisional governments exercise only those powers that are granted by the central government.

      c. Examples include The United Kingdom and France

B. Modern identities also include:

   1. **Nations** made up of sizeable groups of people:

      a. United by common bonds of geography, religion, language, race custom and tradition

      b. Seek to create own country

      c. Advocate some form of nationalism

      d. Common after French Revolution 1789

   2. **Ethnic groups** that consists of people within a state who share common values and cultural norms and do not seek independence.

   3. **Nation-states** that are countries which contain one major national majority, such as Japan and Greece.

II   Evolution of Nations

A. Ancient Identities.

   1. People have not always had a sense of nationhood; they tended to identify themselves by:

      a. Families, clans, or tribes

      b. City-states, empires or countries

      c. Religion, social classes, race or gender

2. As individuals lost traditional attachments, **nationalism** began to grow:
   a. It can be used to unite people to create a larger group, or to break up a larger state into smaller units and states.
   b. **Liberal nationalism** stressed freedom for national groups.
   c. **Integral nationalism** is based on the belief that a certain nationality is superior to others.

B. The Agricultural Revolution
   1. The emergence of what is termed civilization was preceded by socio-economic changes which occurred during the **Agricultural Revolution,** and which led to:
      a. Domestication of plants and animals.
      b. Agriculture
      c. Population growth
      d. Technological innovation
      e. Laws
      f. Creation of the first villages and cites
      g. Development of urban life and culture

III   Civilization

A. The **Mesopotamian Civilizations** are considered among the first. The **Sumerians** (3500 B.C.) settled in the Mesopotamian Valley, between the Tigris and the Euphrates rivers.
   1. Their contributions include:
      a. Writing
      b. Metallurgy
      c. Mathematics
      d. Wheel, plow, sailing ships
      e. Legal system
   2. The **Semites**, nomads, originally from the Arabian Peninsula, came into the Mesopotamian Valley and captured the region. Important contributions include:
      a. The alphabet
      b. Monotheism
      c. Three major religions: Judaism, Christianity and Islam
   3. **Semitic languages** are generally divided into:
      a. Akkadian
      b. Hebrew, Aramaic and Eblaite
      c. Arabic, South Arabian, Ethiopic
      d. Only Arabic and Hebrew are spoken widely today
   4. The largest language family belongs to the **Indo-Europeans** whose descendants today make up 50% of the world's population
      a. Had a common original language
      b. Original speakers came from area north of the Black Sea
      c. The earliest languages of record are Hittite, Greek, and Sanskrit

B. The **Africans**
   1. Africa was probably the home of the first humans.
   2. As they spread throughout the continent, there was an evolution that created distinct characteristics among groups, who have interacted among themselves.
   3. Major groups include:
      a. Negroes of West Africa
      b. Nilo-Saharans of East Africa

    c. Pygmies of the rainforest

    d. San (Bushmen) of eastern and southern Africa.

  4. White races predominate north of the Sahara, (linguistically grouped as Hamites) related to the Semites of Arabia and Caucasian groups from the Mediterranean.

  5. The **Hamites** are subdivided into three groups:

    a. Berbers of Morocco, Algeria and Tunisia

    b. Egyptians of Northeast Africa

    c. Cushitic

C. The **Egyptians** (3100 B.C. to 1200 B.C.) produced one of the oldest civilizations, which was centered on the Nile River, in north east Africa.

  1. They are credited with organizing the first state in history under the leadership of King Menes (3100 B.C.)

  2. Their historical development is divided into periods:

    a. Old Kingdom

    b. Middle Kingdom

    c. New Kingdom (Age of Empire)

  3. Their accomplishments and contributions include:

    a. The first solar calendar.

    b. Complex irrigation systems to regulate the floodwaters of the Nile.

    c. Ethical religions and monotheism.

  4. They extended their civilization to the south into sub-Saharan Africa, and they conquered the Phoenicians, Assyrians, Syrians, and Hittites.

  5. Their imperial hegemony ended, and they were in turn conquered by various groups, including the Arab Muslims in the 660s A.D.

D. The Negro kingdoms of Africa

  1. Impressive major Negro kingdoms also developed in west, central and south Africa.

  2. The collapse of the greatest Negro Empires of the Sudan-Ghana, Mali, and Songhai, can in part be attributed to the Muslim invasions.

E. The **Indus Valley Civilization** (2500–1500 B.C.) centered in south Asia, in present day Pakistan/India, is considered to be the third world civilization to emerge.

  1. Two archaeological sites have been excavated at the cities of Mohenho Daro, and Harappa:

    a. They equaled Sumer and Egypt in size and complexity.

    b. Had elaborate sewers, sanitation techniques, and drainage.

    c. Language spoken was Dravidian.

    d. May have been influenced by Mesopotamia.

  2. Between 2000 and 15000 B.C., they were conquered by an **Indo-European** group called **Aryans,** who crossed into this region through the Khyber Pass.

  3. The Aryans established many kingdoms and a new civilization in Northern India. Their descendants continue to govern India.

    a. They introduced a new language-**Sanskrit.**

    b. Established new cultural and religious forms which developed into **Hinduism.**

    c. Developed a **caste** social system that segregated the people.

  4. Invaded by numerous groups throughout their history, the Muslim legacy would eventually split the country into Muslim Pakistan and Hindu India.

F. The **Chinese Civilization** (1800 B.C.), established by the Yellow River of northern China, is the fourth oldest civilization.

  1. Chinese history "begins" with the **Shang Dynasty** (1750–1027 B.C.)

    a. Their society was dominated by a warrior aristocracy, who used bronze weapons, and horse-drawn chariots.

    b. Possessed a written language, and the earliest written records date from this era.

2. The **Zhou Dynasty (Chou)** would succeed to rule China from 1122 B.C. to 221 B.C.
   a. To justify their rule they established the **Mandate of Heaven,** which would be used by later dynasties as their legal mandate to seize power.
   b. The **Confucian** tradition would be formulated from the philosophical writings of Kongzi (551–479 B.C.).
3. The **Qin Dynasty (Ch'in)** established the first empire in 221 B.C.
   a. Developed an effective central political apparatus that helped create a unified Chinese civilization.
   b. The Imperial system they established would be used to govern for over 2,000 years.
   c. Built thousands of miles of road to connect the empire and to move their armies quickly, and canals to connect the river systems.
4. The **Mongols** conquered China in 1260, and established the **Yuan Dynasty.**
   a. First time that the Chinese would be conquered by foreigners.
   b. Integrated into the Mongol Empire, they were part of a territory that extended from the Pacific Ocean to Russia.
5. Taking advantage of the declining Ming Dynasty, the Manchus, nomadic peoples from the northeast, invaded in 1644 and established the **Qing (Ching) Dynasty.**
   a. In power until 1911, they would be the last dynasty to rule China.
   b. Constituting a small portion of the population in China, the Qing adopted Chinese institutions and policies
   c. Although contact and trade with Europe was increasing, it was tightly controlled by the Qing under the "Canton System".
   d. Increasing pressure from Europe and America for trade rights, and Qing resistance to modernization led to continued decline.
6. Despite a long history of dynastic changes and internal strife, China has been able to maintain long-term cohesiveness for several reasons:
   a. Powerful and effective central political apparatus
   b. A common written language
   c. Confucian religious tradition

G. **The Americas:** The most impressive civilizations developed in Mesoamerica and the mountainous Andean region of South America. The two earliest civilizations were the originating civilizations of theses two regions.
   1. The **Olmec** (1200–400 B.C.) are considered to have been the most influential civilization in the region.
      a. The center of their civilization was located in what are now the Mexican states of Veracruz and Tabasco.
      b. The cultural core of the civilization was located at San Lorenzo, but included smaller centers.
      c. Large artificial platforms and mounds of packed earth dominated Olmec urban centers.
      d. Their cities were laid out in alignment with the paths of certain stars.
      e. Giant heads sculpted from basalt are a widely recognized part of their legacy.
      f. Developed a form of writing that may have influenced the Maya.
      g. There is little evidence that they created an empire.
   2. The **Chavín** (900–250 B.C.) established the most impressive of South America's early urban civilizations in a region that included large areas of the Peruvian coastal plain and Andean foothills.
      a. Their civilization coincided somewhat with the Olmec.
      b. Its capital Chavín de Huantar was located at 10,300 feet in the eastern range of the Andes.
      c. They used llamas, the only domesticated beasts of burden in the Americas, to move goods from one zone to another.

3. The **Maya** (250–900 A.D.) developed an impressive civilization in a region that today includes Guatemala, Honduras, Belize, and southern Mexico.
   a. Although they shared a single culture they were never unified politically.
   b. Rival kingdoms led by hereditary rulers struggled with each other for regional dominance.
   c. Maya living near the major urban centers drained swamps and built elevated fields, used irrigation, and terraced hillsides.
   d. Their political and ceremonial centers were dominated by large pyramids, built without the aid of wheels or metal tools.
   e. These monumental structures were commonly aligned with the movements of the sun and Venus.
   f. Made important contributions to the development of the Mesoamerican calendar.
   g. Their system of mathematics incorporated the concept of zero and place value.
   h. Their writing system was a form of hieroglyphic inscription that signified whole words or concepts as well as phonetic syllables.
4. The **Toltecs** people established their capital at Tula in 968 A.D.
   a. Little is known about them, and many of the contributions that were attributed to them by the Aztecs were in place long before they gained control of Central Mexico.
   b. They created the first conquest state based mainly on military power, and extended their political influence from the area north of Mexico City to Central America.
   c. Two chieftains ruled the Toltec state together and this may have led to a power struggle that caused the destruction of Tula about 1000 A.D.
5. The **Aztecs,** or Mexica as they called themselves, were northern peoples who pushed into central Mexico in after the collapse of Tula.
   a. At first they served their more powerful neighbors as serfs and mercenaries.
   b. They adopted the political and social practices they encountered, and as they grew in strength they began a military conquest of the area.
   c. Around 1325 A.D. they began the construction of their twin capitals, Tenochtitlan and Tlatelolco—the foundation for modern Mexico City.
   d. Aztec kings and aristocrats legitimized their rule by creating elaborate rituals and ceremonies.
   e. By 1428 A.D. their power extended from Mexico City downward to the Maya areas in Yucatan
   f. They created an empire based on a tribute system, forced labor and large-scale human sacrifice.
   g. They were the last group to rule this area before Spanish conquest in 1521, and their destruction was in part facilitated by spread of smallpox to the population.
6. The **Inca** were the last major civilization to dominate the Andean region of South America.
   a. By 1525 the empire stretched from Chile to northern Ecuador, from the Pacific coast across the Andes to the upper Amazon, and to the south into Argentina.
   b. Their capital city at Cuzco in present day Peru was the center of their empire.
   c. Highly skilled stone craftsmen, the Inca buildings were constructed of carefully cut stones fitted without mortar.
   d. Their empire was based on highly productive agriculture, and rich gold and silver mines.
   f. The empire lasted until 1533, when they were conquered by the Spanish through disease and treachery.

IV   The Birth of Western People

A. The **Hellenes** (ancient Greeks) are often considered the founders of Western civilization:
   1. They were nomadic Indo-Europeans tribes who migrated throughout the Mediterranean and Aegean areas in 600s B.C.
   2. Influenced by the Egyptians, Minoans and Hittites.
   3. Unable to create a politically unified state, they instead organized as **city-states.**
   4. In 478 B.C. they defeated the Persians, the greatest military power of that period.

5. Continued in-fighting led to the **Peloponnesian Wars,** fought between Athens and Sparta.

6. Practiced **balance of power politics** as city-states entered into security alliances with each other between 431 and 338 B.C.

7. Defeated by the Phillip II of **Macedonia** in 338 B.C.

8. Made great contributions to Western Civilization:
   a. Rationalism and primitive science
   b. Philosophy
   c. Democracy
   d. Humanism
   e. Secularization and individualism

B. The **Macedonians**, led by Phillip II, and Alexander "the Great", subdued the Greek city-states and developed a centralized monarchy.

1. Conquered the Persians in 331 B.C. in Babylonia and absorbed their empire.

2. The entire Near East from Greece to Turkey to North Africa to Persia became a unified civilization under Greek-like culture.

3. After Alexander's death the empire was divided into:
   a. Seleucid Empire
   b. Ptolemaic Empire
   c. Kingdom of Macedonia

C. The **Romans/Latins** (Italics) were an Indo-European group which entered the Italian Peninsula circa 1,500 B.C.

1. They were influenced by the Greek city-states, and by the Etruscans in the northern part of the peninsula.

2. In 509 B.C they expelled the Etruscan kings and created an **oligarchy,** which they called a **republic.**

3. After conquering the peninsula by 264 B.C. they would expand their power:
   a. They became the dominant group in the Mediterranean.
   b. They extended their empire to England, the Danube River, North Africa, and Syria.
   c. In 284 A.D. the empire was split into Western and Eastern parts.

4. The Western Roman Empire began a gradual decline and eventual collapse between 190s and 476 A.D. due to:
   a. Military overextension
   b. Overtaxation
   c. Agricultural decline
   d. Technological stagnation
   e. Moral decline

5. The Romans also made important contributions to Western civilization, which included:
   a. Law and Government.
   b. Engineering/Architecture.
   c. Language.

D. The **Germans** were barbaric tribes which originated along the Baltic coast of northeastern Europe, and eventually contributed to the end of the Western Roman Empire.

1. Their highest political organization was the tribe.

2. They migrated widely from the Rhine River to the Vistula River before the Christian era.

3. The **Huns** from Asia pushed them west and by the 400s several Germanic tribes had penetrated the Western Roman Empire:
   a. Franks by lower Rhine (France and Germany)
   b. Alemanni by Upper Rhine (the Low Countries)
   c. Jutes, Angles, Saxons into England

      d. Burgundians by the Main

      e. Vandals into Spain and North Africa

      f. Visigoths into Northern Spain

      g. Ostrogoths into Rome

    4. They did not destroy Roman civilization:

      a. But did contribute to the end of the Western Empire as an independent political reality.

      b. Prepared the coming of European medieval civilization.

      c. After its official collapse, the Roman Catholic Church became the dominant cultural and material institution of the medieval world.

E. The **Christians of Jerusalem** would come into conflict with other Jewish groups and establish a separate identity.

    1. Missionary work of Peter and Paul would spread the teachings of Christ throughout the Mediterranean world of the Roman Empire.

    2. Periodically persecuted, Christianity would eventually become the official religion of the empire.

    3. During the Dark Ages the Roman Catholic Church made several major contributions:

      a. Negotiated truces and developed rules of order

      b. Transmitted technical knowledge and information on many subjects

      c. Preserved part of the classical legacy of Greece and Rome

      d. Founded universities and hospitals in Europe

      e. Performed engineering feats that included roads and bridges

      f. Passed along the Bible to future generations of Christians and non-Christians

    4. The Catholic Church experienced several crises that would end in major divisions:

      a. In 1054 the Orthodox Church in Constantinople split from the Church in Rome.

      b. In 1517 Martin Luther would reject its authority and initiate the **Protestant Reformation.**

      c. In 1530s King Henry VIII of England would break away from Rome and establish the Anglican Church.

V The Expansion of Eastern Peoples and the Slavs

A. The **Arabs** are a Semitic group whose settlement in the Arabian Peninsula can be traced back to 3,000 B.C.

    1. Were originally organized as clans or tribes, mostly nomadic Bedouins, who lacked a government.

    2. Their religion was a mixture of animism and polytheism, and their cultural center was Mecca.

    3. In 624 A.D. Mohammed became the religious, political and military leader of the religion of Islam, and gradually established his power over the entire region:

      a. Preached and established a monotheistic religion.

      b. There was no separation of church and state like in Christianity

      c. United Arabs and later Turks, Iranians and North Africans

      d. Practices holy war against unbelievers

      e. Islamic empire spread from northern Spain to the Indus River

      f. Defeat by Franks in 732 at Battle of Tours halted expansion into Western Europe

B. The **Turks** are Turkic speaking people out of Central Asia, related to the Huns.

    1. The Seljuk Turks, the first of two prominent dynasties conquered Persia, Iraq, and later Asia Minor.

    2. The Ottoman Turks appear in Asia Minor (Turkey) in 1200s:

      a. Defeated the Arabs, but converted to Islam

      b. Conquered the Byzantine Empire (Eastern Roman Empire) in 1453

      c. Established the Ottoman Empire, which at its height encompassed North Africa, Middle East and southeastern Europe, and lasted until World War I.

      d. Defeated at the Siege of Vienna in 1687, their expansion into western Europe was halted and the empire began to decline.

C. The **Mongols** were nomadic tribes of east-central Asia, who were united by Genghis Khan in 1206.
   1. Conquered virtually all of Asia and Russia, and established the greatest land empire in history.
   2. Conquest of Europe ended with their withdrawal in 1241.
   3. Their conquests resulted in:
      a. The unification of China, Inner Asia, much of Southwest Asia and Russia.
      b. Expansion of trade.
      c. Introduction of ideas and commodities such as, gunpowder, paper money, printing, and medical knowledge.
   4. Also transmitted plagues and diseases which decimated European populations.

D. The **Slavs** originated around 3,000 B.C. in the northwestern Ukraine and Southeastern Poland.
   1. Migrated around 200 to 500 A.D. to other parts of Europe, in part due to the western migration of the Huns.
      a. Russians are eastern Slavs
      b. Western Slavs include Belarussians (White Russians), Czechs, Slovaks, Poles and Wends
      c. Southern Slavs include Bulgarians, Croats, Macedonians, Serbs, and Slovenes
   2. The **Russians** are Great Slavs who originated north of the Black Sea in central Russia and spread to the Baltic Sea, the Ural Mountains and the Black Sea:
      a. Conquered by the Mongols (Tatars) in 1237.
      b. The creation of the Russian empire was commenced by Ivan the Great (1462 to 1502) who defeated the Mongols and started Russian expansion.
      c. Ivan the Terrible (1533 to 1584) gained complete control over Russia by 1547 and moved into western Siberia and the Caspian Sea.

VI   European World Dominance

A. In the 1500s Europeans started to outstrip other regions in economic and military success due to certain factors:
   1. Political stability
   2. Competitive interstate system
   3. International trade
   4. Literacy
   5. Capitalist system
   6. Modernization
   7. Liberalization
   8. Technological breakthroughs

B. Until the 1700s international relations in Europe were controlled by families:
   1. Hapsburgs of Austria, Spain and the Netherlands
   2. French House of Valois
   3. Tudors and Stuarts of England
   4. Braganzas of Portugal

C. Europe was engulfed in numerous politico-religious wars between the 1520s and 1640s:
   1. Catholics, Lutherans and Calvinists fought each other
   2. Political, economic and nationalist motives were mixed with religious ones.
   3. Increasing conflict led to **The Thirty Years War** (1618 to 1648), the first continental war in modern history, which combined religious and political issues.
   4. The war ended with the **Peace of Westphalia** (1648):
      a. Switzerland and Holland gained full independence
      b. Reduced powers of the Holy Roman Emperor

    c. Spain lost control of the Low Countries.

    d. France became the major power in Europe.

    e. Recognized the independent states of Europe as the major actors in international relations.

VII The European Inter-State System

A. The countries of Europe entered into alliances and conflicts to protect long-term interests.

B. Portugal began European voyages of discovery in the 1440s:

    1. Explored West Africa.

    2. Reached India and China by sea, and established trade routes.

    3. Colonized Brazil.

    4. Sought to protect its overseas empire and to gain freedom from Spain

C. Spain was the major power in the 1500s:

    1. Defeated the Muslims in 1490s.

    2. Acquired an extensive empire spanning the Americas, Asia and parts of Europe.

    3. Massive accumulation of gold and silver from its colonies inhibited development of its industry because of inflation.

    4. Sought to maintain its possessions in the New World and in the Spanish Netherlands.

    5. Promoted Catholicism.

D. Holland was a great commercial empire in the 1600s, including the East Indies:

    1. Commercial success in shipping and trade led to banking and industry.

    2. Fought wars with England/Great Britain and France over mercantile and territorial disputes.

    3. Long term objective was to deny any major power control of the Low Countries (Belgium, Holland and Luxembourg).

E. France was the major continental power from 1661 to 1815.

    1. Revolutionized the conduct of diplomacy by introducing two new ideas:

        a. Raison d' etat

        b. Balance of power

    2. Under Louis XIV the control of international diplomacy passed from families to the monarchs.

    3. Sought to expand to the Rhine River, the Low Countries and the Pyrenees.

    4. Fought England/Great Britain on three continents.

    5. Wanted to prevent the unification of Germany.

    6. Attempted to conquer the entire European continent.

F. England/Great Britain absorbed Scotland and Wales in the 1700s, and politically integrated Northern Ireland in the 1900s:

    1. Engaged in a long-world wide struggle with France from 1661 to 1815 in an attempt to check France's expansion.

    2. Had personal interest in keeping the Low Countries independent of the Hapsburgs, France and Germany.

    3. Wanted to keep its navy the world's largest.

    4. Sought to prevent Russia from controlling the Mediterranean and Central Asia.

    5. Created an empire which spread British institutions around the world.

G. Russia's main interest lay in ridding itself of outside control and carrying out territorial expansion:

    1. Defeated the Tatars (Mongols), Poland, Lithuania and Sweden.

    2. Sought to acquire warm water ports in the Baltic.

    3. Wanted to gain access to the Black Sea and the Mediterranean.

    4. Expanded to the Pacific, Central Asia and the Balkans.

H. Austria's location in Central Europe, surrounded by enemies, was its major weakness.
  1. First major goal was to defeat France, the Protestants, and the Turks.
  2. Wanted to unite all Germans of the Holy Roman Empire into a Hapsburg state.
  3. At the **Congress of Vienna in 1815,** after Napoleon's defeat, sought to contain France by redrawing the balance of power.
  4. Creation of the Austro-Hungarian Empire by the Germans of Austria and the Magyars of Hungary affected politics in the Balkans.

I. Germany was united in 1871 by Otto Von Bismarck, making Prussia the major German state, and absorbing the German Confederation:
  1. Defeated France and took Alsace-Lorraine, and became the most powerful state in continental Europe.
  2. Sought to keep Austria and Russia from aligning with France.
  3. Upset the balance of power in the region, and planted seeds for World War I.

VIII   Western Revolutions

A. Numerous revolutions have enhanced the material development of Western Civilization:
  1. The **Enlightenment** was a cultural transformation whose supporters believed that the rational order that the scientific revolution had discovered in the physical world should also exist in human societies
  2. **Liberalism,** in its many forms, has focused on the same issues:
      a. Hostility to concentration of power in cultural, economic and political institutions that threaten the freedom of the individual.
      b. A willingness to examine institutions in the light of new needs.
      c. A dislike of sudden changes.
      d. Question how much power should be given to the government.
      e. Liberal principles influenced the American Revolution and the French Revolution.
  3. The **Industrial Revolution** stimulated population growth, urbanization, prosperity, consumerism, military technology, wars and imperialism.
  4. **Socialism,** which advocates economic collectivism through government of ownership of the means of production and distribution of goods, emerged mostly in reaction to the unregulated capitalism of the late 1700s and 1800s.

IX   The New Western Imperialism

A. By 1914 Europeans controlled over 85% of world's land:
  1. A new imperialism began in the 1870s.
  2. Six European states divided Africa among themselves, only Liberia and Ethiopia remained independent.
  3. Most of Asia came under European control, only Japan and Thailand were relatively untouched.

B. Causes of Imperialism:
  1. Decline of Ottoman Empire brought many political changes in North Africa which threatened British interests.
  2. French took most of West Africa in order to maintain balance of power.
  3. Explorers described the great beauty and wealth in the continent.
  4. Christian missionaries propagated the faith.
  5. Private entrepreneurs manipulated their governments into supporting their exploitation of minerals.
  6. Commercial competitors for raw materials.

X   World War I

A. The most important global event of the 1900s had various causes:
1. Conflict between Serbia and Austria over the latter's annexation of Bosnia-Herzegovina.
2. Conflict between Great Britain and Germany over the latter's naval expansion, incursion into British trade routes and commercial competition.
3. Nationalist aspirations of almost all the European groups.
4. Inflexible alliances between the Triple Entente-France, Russia, Great Britain against the German-Austrian Alliance- Germany, Austria, and Ottoman Empire.
5. The immediate cause was the assassination of the heir to the Austro-Hungarian Empire, Francis Ferdinand, Archduke of Austria.
6. War began on August 14, 1914.

B. Results:
1. Tremendous death toll-19 million killed.
2. End of German, Austrian-Hungarian, Ottoman and Russian empires.
3. Rise of Communism in Russia.
4. Recreation of Poland.
5. Creation of Yugoslavia.
6. Undermined Europe's global political and economic leadership.
7. Rise of Japan and the United States as major powers.

C. Until its involvement in World War I the United States had followed a policy of isolationism, avoiding alliances with Europeans.
1. Had concentrated on territorial expansion, political consolidation and economic development.
2. After their victorious experience in WWI, the Americans took on a prominent role in the Paris Peace Conference and proposed the formation of the League of Nations.
3. Became source of financial credit for European reconstruction after the war.

D. Japan's long history of isolationism ended in1853, when the United States forced the country to open its ports to the west.
1. Focused on modernization in order to prevent western penetration.
2. By 1914 was the only industrialized non-European country.
3. From 1875 to 1905 engaged in territorial expansion.
4. Became the leading Asian power.

XI   World War II

A. In addition to other factors, the causes of World War II are linked to the failure to resolve the causes of World War I:
1. Harsh treatment of Germany by the victors of WWI.
2. Italy failed to receive territories promised by the Allies.
3. Japan did not feel that concessions received were worthy of her military involvement.

B. Other major contributing factors:
1. Economic depression of 1930s.
2. Rise of totalitarian dictators in Germany, Italy and Japan, and their imperialistic acts.
3. Alliance between Russia and Germany to absorb Poland and the Baltic states.
4. Rise of imperialistic and racial theories.
5. United Kingdom's unwillingness to defend France.
6. United States' failure to be an active participant in the international system during the post World War I years.

7. The immediate causes included:
    a. Germany's takeover of Austria, Czechoslovakia, and Poland
    b. Italy's invasion of Ethiopia
    c. Japan's expansion into Manchuria, China and Southeast Asia
    d. Japanese bombing of Pearl Harbor

C. Results:
    1. Death toll greater than WWI-55 million killed.
    2. End of European world dominance.
    3. Commencement of the Cold War.
    4. Accelerated the independence movements of colonial territories in Africa and Asia.
    5. Led to the rise of a bipolar international system with only two superpowers: the United States and the Soviet Union.

XII   The Cold War

A. Name given to the bipolar conflict between the United States and the Soviet Union, and their respective allies, whose origins are found in:
    1. Dispute among the winning allies in WWII-Soviet Union, United States and the United Kingdom (Great Britain) over the partition of Germany.
    2. The "**communization**" of Eastern European states.
    3. West's fear of communist subversion in Europe, Turkey, Greece and China.
    4. Development of an active anti-communist philosophy and policy in the United States and the West.
    5. The struggle between the industrial capitalist states of the First World against the communist states of the Second World, while the newly independent states of the third world remained neutral or picked sides.
    6. Tensions heightened by the presence of nuclear weapons.
    7. Soviets and Americans fought only through proxies—their respective allies.

B. In an effort to impede Soviet expansion the United States devised a "**containment**" plan:
    1. Truman Doctrine
    2. Marshall Plan.
    3. North Atlantic Treaty Organization (NATO)

C. The Korean War of 1950 globalized the Cold War:
    1. United States increased its defense budget, established over fifty military alliances, and organized covert operations in numerous places.
    2. Also became directly involved in fighting communists in Korea and in Vietnam.

D. The Soviet Union began to support political movements and countries outside Europe:
    1. Attempted to penetrate developing countries to deny capitalist countries valuable raw materials, markets and investments.
    2. Sought to encircle the capitalists with communist countries.
    3. Became directly involved in fighting in Afghanistan.

E. Ended as an American victory in December 21, 1991 with the collapse of the Soviet Union, reunification of Germany, and dismantling of communist governments in most East European countries.

XIII   The Post-Cold War International System

A. To date the post-Cold War global system has manifested, among others, the following characteristics:
1. One military superpower-the United States.
2. Formation of economic markets and unions.
   a. NAFTA
   b. MERCOSUR
   c. EUROLAND
3. Rise of violent nationalist movements.
4. Growth of terrorist movements.
5. Rise of China as a regional superpower.
6. Political and economic disintegration of countries.
7. Potentially devastating deterioration of ecological resources.
8. Increasing use of the United Nations as a peacemaking or peacekeeping institution.

Review Section

Learning Objectives

After reading **Chapter Three** you should be able to:

1. Contrast a nation and a state.

2. Describe the causes and consequences of World War I, World War II and the Cold War.

3. Enumerate the characteristics of the post-Cold War international system.

Key Terms

Define the following glossary terms to test your knowledge.

1. States
2. Nations
3. Nation States
4. Ethnic Groups
5. The Africans
6. The Aryans
7. The Chinese
8. Indo-Europeans
9. Semites
10. The Hellenes
11. The Macedonians
12. The Latins
13. The Germans
14. The Arabs
15. The Turks

16. The Mongols

17. The Slavs

18. World War I

19. World War II

20. The Cold War

21. Containment

22. Balance of power

23. Nationalism

24. The Enlightenment

25. Socialism

Multiple Choice

1. This religion which originated in Arabia, spread into North Africa, Southwest Asia and Europe:
   a. Christianity
   b. Buddhism
   c. Islam
   d. Judaism

2. This empire spread from England, to North Africa, to the territories of the Germans, to Mesopotamia, but collapsed in the 400s A.D.
   a. Byzantine Empire
   b. Roman Empire
   c. Persian Empire
   d. Mongol Empire

3. Which of the following groups is considered to be responsible for the collapse of the Western Roman Empire?
   a. Huns
   b. Mongols
   c. Germans
   d. Turks

4. This small, poor country began the European voyages of discovery in the 1400s:
   a. Portugal
   b. Spain
   c. Italy
   d. Holland

5. This country has always wanted access to the Baltic Sea:
   a. Russia
   b. England
   c. Germany
   d. France

6. This group of people resides in what was probably the home of the first humans.
   a. Arabs
   b. Africans
   c. Mongols
   d. Turks

7. This civilization has been greatly influenced by the Aryans, an Indo-European group who invaded and dominated the original inhabitants:
   a. Chinese
   b. Mesopotamian
   c. Egyptian
   d. India

8. Which of the following languages is not an Indo-European Language?
   a. Spanish
   b. Slavic
   c. Hebrew
   d. Hindi

9. The States of Pakistan and India were created as a result of:
   a. The Muslim legacy which created conflict and eventually led to splitting the territory.
   b. Alexander the Great's early death, which left his empire without a leader and was divided among his generals.
   c. The Turks invasion and conquest, which made the Indus Valley Civilization part of the Ottoman Empire.
   d. The Aryan invasion which introduced Hinduism and the caste system.

10. The greatest continental power in Europe between 1871 and 1914.
    a. England
    b. France
    c. Germany
    d. Russia

11. Only two states remained independent in Africa in the late 1800s and early 1900s.
    a. Rwanda and Burundi
    b. Liberia and Ethiopia
    c. South Africa and Namibia
    d. Egypt and Sudan

12. The immediate cause of World War I was:
    a. The invasion of Belgium
    b. The formation of the Triple Entente
    c. The assassination of the Archduke of Austria by a Serbian national
    d. The invasion of Poland

13. During the Cold War, the Soviet Union sought to expand its influence outside of Europe by:
    a. Supporting political movements in Egypt, Cuba and Vietnam
    b. Denying capitalist countries valuable raw materials available in developing countries.
    c. Encircling capitalists countries with communists countries
    d. all of the above

14. Which of the following was the only industrialized non-European country in the 19th century?
   a. China
   b. Korea
   c. Japan
   d. India

15. Which of the following groups did not establish an advanced civilization in Mesoamerica?
   a. Olmec
   b. Maya
   c. Teotihuacan
   d. Chavín

True and False Statements

Indicate if the following statements are True (T) or False (F).

_____ **1.** Nations are political jurisdictions which have defined geographic borders, permanent populations and governments.

_____ **2.** Austria was able to halt the spread of Islam into Europe by defeating the Ottoman Empire at the Battle of Vienna in 1683.

_____ **3.** The Cold War was a bipolar conflict between the United States and Communist China.

_____ **4.** The immediate cause of WWII was the division of Poland between Germany and the Soviet Union.

_____ **5.** Among the reasons that explain why the Europeans lost most of their colonial holdings after WWII were the growth of democratic, anti-imperialistic sentiments within the European powers.

_____ **6.** The Fascist dictators who rose to power during the period just preceding WWII did so partly because of promises made to their populations of achieving prosperity through imperialism.

_____ **7.** Concerned with the take over of the Low Countries by one of the major European powers, Holland joined several alliances to fight Britain.

_____ **8.** The earliest civilization to develop in Mesoamerica, whose political and architectural achievements influenced the later peoples of Central America and Mexico was the Toltec.

_____ **9.** The Congress of Vienna of 1815 met to redraw the maps of Europe so that France could not continue expanding its territory.

_____ **10.** The unity of the Christian world that developed in Europe during the period of the Dark Ages was shattered, when Martin Luther rejected the authority of the Roman Catholic Church.

Matching Terms

_____ **1.** Slavs   **A.** Credited with establishing the first state in history.

_____ **2.**   Arabs

B. Established the last dynasty in China which ruled until 1911

_____ **3.**   Hellenes

C. Totally dedicated to war, they are identified as the best fighting machine ever assembled in the Near East

_____ **4.**   The Sumerians

D. Peoples who settled in Russia, eastern and central Europe, and the Balkans

_____ **5.**   The Manchus

E. Considered to be the founders of Western civilization.

_____ **6.**   The Chinese

F. Originally organized mostly as nomadic Bedouins, they were united under the religious, political and military leadership of Mohammed

_____ **7.**   The Egyptians

G. People who came out of central Asia, conquered the Islamic empires of Persia and Iraq, and established the Ottoman Empire

_____ **8.**   The Assyrians

H. Conquered the Greeks and the Persians, and established a unified civilization that also included the entire near east and North Africa

_____ **9.**   The Macedonians

I.   Considered to be the forth oldest civilization, it has maintained control over essentially the same territory for over 2000 years.

_____ **10.**   The Turks

J.   Established what is considered to be the first of the world's civilizations in the Mesopotamian Valley between the Tigris and Euphrates Rivers.

Chapter 4—Conceptualizations of the Family: Race, Ethnicity and Immigration

CHAPTER OUTLINE

I The Family

    A. Sociologists and anthropologists define a family as a group of people who identify themselves as being related to one another, usually by blood, marriage, or adoption, and who share intimate relationships and dependency.

        1. Is the most important social institution.

        2. Serves as agent of **socialization**-lifelong process through which people learn the values, norms, beliefs, attitudes and rules of their culture.

        3. Helps in the development of a sense of identity.

    B. **Marriage** is defined as a culturally approved relationship, usually between two individuals, that provides for a degree of economic cooperation, intimacy, and sexual activity.

II Types of Families

    A. The typical family of modern industrialized societies is the **nuclear family.**

        1. Culture, religious values, and socioeconomic status of the family largely determine the number of children.

        2. Includes only two generations, and normally disintegrates when children leave the household, or the parents die.

        3. Most Northern European and North American families are nuclear.

    B. In many societies and some **subcultures,** people live in **extended families.**

        1. Social groups consisting of one or more parents, children, and other kin, often spanning several generations.

        2. Family will include the basic nuclear family unit, but might also include grandparents, aunts, uncles, cousins, or other close relatives.

        3. This family unit is more likely to preserve traditional family values.

        4. In Eastern and Southern Europe, Africa, Asia, and Latin America extended families are common.

    C. There are cultural variations in who takes responsibility for child-rearing:

        1. Traditionally, the biological parents assume the role of parent in Western European societies.

        2. In the native cultures of French Polynesia, the task of raising children is largely the responsibility of the total commun of families.

    D. Families also vary according to the number of wives or husbands a person may have.

        1. Monogamy.

        2. Polygamy which is manifested in two forms:

            a. Polygyny

            b. Polyandry

    E. **Line of descent** or lineage of the family is very important because it promotes membership in a particular kinship group, allocates power and authority within family, and gives legitimacy to its siblings.

        1. **Lineage** can be traced in various ways.

            a. Patrilineal

      b. Matrilineal

      c. Bilateral

   2. Lines of descent sometimes are associated with how **power and authority** are allocated in the family structure.

      a. Patriarchal

      b. Matriarchal

      c. Egalitarian

   3. Classification of families can also be based on **location.**

      a. Patrilocal

      b. Matrilocal

      c. Neolocal

III   Types of Marriages

   A. Mate selection can take on various forms:

      1. Arranged marriages

      2. Personal choice marriages

      3. Exogamous marriages

      4. Endogamous marriages

   B. All societies impose restrictions on marriages among their members; **incest** is considered a universal **taboo.**

IV   Non-Traditional Families

   A. Some parts of the industrialized world have seen **new family arrangements.**

      1. Family of friends

      2. Rise of **single parenthood** for both men and women

      3. Single-sex families

      4. Single-family households

V   Fundamental Functions of the Family in Society

   A. Functionalist sociologists look at the family in terms of the functions that they perform for the larger society and contribution to social stability.

      1. Biological function needed by society to perpetuate itself.

      2. Nurturance and socialization of children.

      3. Support for the virtually helpless: children, the infirm and the elderly.

      4. Emotional support.

   B. Conflict theorist sociologists argue that families serve to reproduce societal inequality among its members, particularly between men and women:

      1. Family serves to reproduce the relations of authority that exist in the wider society.

      2. Perpetuates division that exists in the wider society.

   C. The American family as a historical and cultural entity has been a major contributing factor to the social, political and economic evolution of the American people.

      1. The family became the center of gravity of colonial society.

      2. In Puritan colonies, the family was empowered with political identity; voting qualifications only recognized the head of the property-owning household.

    3. Slaves were not permitted to legitimize their relationships and establish contracted marriages, and members of the same family could be sold.

    4. Settlement of the American frontier was also a family enterprise.

D. The American family in crisis.

    1. Current crisis facing the American family today has its roots in the Industrial Revolution and rapid process of urbanization after the Civil War.

    2. Several factors have had a disruptive impact (have currently contributed to its fragmentation):

        a. Recent rapid integration of women into the professional and working sectors of the society.

        b. Decline in religious values

        c. Destructive forces of the "drug culture."

        d. Alarming rate of divorce and changing attitudes toward institutionalized marriage and the family.

    3. Resulting characteristics include:

        a. Increasing crime rates

        b. Illegitimate births

        c. Teenage suicide

        d. Increase number of children living in single-parent homes

E. The Conservative interpretation of the current crisis asserts that America's cultural and social decline is directly related to the deterioration of family life.

    1. Contributing factors include:

        a. Cultural shifts

        b. Attitudinal changes regarding value of marriage and fidelity

        c. New philosophy of sexual liberation

        d. Government programs

        e. The media and the entertainment industry

F. The alternative view interprets these changes as an indication that American social life is evolving in new directions, which provide greater individual freedom.

VI   Race, Ethnicity and the American Family

A. Traditionally much of the social and other behavioral sciences research has centered on the white family, however, current scholarly research is focusing on the differences and similarities in American families of various ethnic and racial origins.

    1. Race is a term used to define a group of individuals sharing the same or similar genetic, biological and physical characteristics.

    2. An **ethnic group** is a group of individuals who share a common cultural heritage.

    3. Hispanics are people who share cultural, historical and linguistic ties to Spain, but who represent distinct ethnic groups.

    4. The three largest Hispanic groups in the United States are Mexicans, Puerto Ricans and Cubans.

VII   Ethnic Family Variations: The Hispanic-American Family

A. Mexican-Americans were a dominant group throughout California and the Southwest until U.S. expansion to the west took one-third of Mexico's territory after the Mexican-American War in the 1840s.:

    1. The largest of all Hispanic groups, most came as wage laborers after 1900.

    2. Driven by economic necessity, many young Mexican-Americans drop out of school.

    3. An important aspect is **familism.**

4. Some individuals maintain strong ties to their communities of origin through family ties and institutions such as the **compadrazgo.**

5. Although the extended family is still preferred, the nuclear family model is growing among second and third generation Mexicans in the U.S.

6. Rapid entrance of women into the labor and professional markets is impacting sex roles, and division of labor in the urban, middle class family structure, in this as well as in all other Hispanic groups.

7. Mexican male continues to play a major role in the decision-making process.

B. Puerto Ricans represent the second largest Hispanic group, distinguished by the fact that they are United States citizens.

1. Migration began in the early 1900s when American takeover of Puerto Rico created high unemployment.

2. Most immigrants went to New York, and the term "Newyorrican" is sometimes used to distinguish them from island Puerto Ricans (those who did not migrate).

3. With low skills, and little to no education upon their arrival, they continue to be the most socio-economically disadvantaged Hispanic group.

4. Extended family concept, even when families are separated from the household, is still prevalent.

5. Poverty and an increasing number of single parent (mother) households are major problems affecting the stability of the family.

6. Religion has played an important role in their survival and adaptation, as with all other Hispanics.

C. The national character of Cubans' values and attitudes has been greatly influenced by both Spain, West Africa, and the United States.

1. Labor demands created by the sugar plantations led to the massive importation of African slaves.

2. Primarily indentured servants from China, who after blacks, came to constitute Cuba's most important ethnic minority, met the demand for cheap labor in the late 1880s.

3. Three major immigration patterns have impacted the traditional family structure:

   a. The massive immigration that occurred after the Communist revolution in 1959, left many families fragmented, as parents left in an effort to secure freedom for their children.

   b. The 1980 "Mariel Boatlift" once again caused profound changes, with over 125,000 refugees forced to leave their families behind.

   c. The latest migration of *balseros* (raft people) has left thousands of individuals without a family base in the U.S.

4. With the integration of the Cuban woman into the labor market, her power to make decisions increased, impacting the traditional patriarchal family structure.

D. Other Hispanics originating from Central and South America and the Caribbean, also form part of the Hispanic community in the United States.

1. Today Hispanics make up almost 13 percent of the U.S. population, and are expected to represent close to 20 percent by 2050.

2. Despite strong cultural values emphasizing the importance of family ties, divorce and violence are also affecting them, two conditions affecting many American families.

VIII   Ethnic Family Variations: The Black-American Family

A. Representing the United States' second largest visible minority, the family life of the black community has been of particular concern and subject of study because of their unique history.

1. Four cultural traits distinguish them from other immigrant groups.

    a. Blacks came from societies with norms and values that were dissimilar to the American way of life.

    b. They were from many different tribes in Africa, each with its own language, culture, and traditions.

    c. In the beginning they came without women.

    d. They came in bondage.

2. There are several historical periods of interest in the evaluation of the black family life in the U.S.

    a. Pre-slavery

    b. The **slave family**

    c. After **emancipation**

3. During the nineteenth century, the strong role of women emerged as it became necessary for them to work outside the home in order to provide for the family survival.

4. The past 30 years have culminated in the gradual disintegration of much of the black nuclear family.

5. Women have become economically and psychologically independent of men, have achieved higher educational levels, and have become more competitive in the labor market.

6. Two distinctive patterns have emerged in the black community:

    a. A majority of black children live in one-parent households and the median income available to those families is well below the poverty level.

    b. The Black community has also seen a steady growth of a black middle class, growing involvement in the political system, and an increasing numbers of black youths are availing themselves of educational opportunities.

IX   Ethnic Family Variations: The Haitian Family

A. Haiti is regarded as the world's first independent "black" republic and the second independent nation in this hemisphere.

    1. Colonized by France, who called the island Saint Dominge, it shares the island of Hispañola with its Spanish neighbor, The Dominican Republic.

    2. After the native population who included Tainos, Arawaks and Caribs was decimated, African slaves were brought to work on the plantations.

    3. The Haitian slaves gained their freedom and independence in 1803.

B. The native languages and religious rituals brought by the slaves in Haiti from their native West African nations can be seen today in aspects of the Haitian culture.

    1. The Creole language, largely regarded as the national language, and spoken in most homes, consists of African words and concepts, as well as French words.

    2. Most Haitians are Catholic, but some also practice "voodoo," similar to the Afro-Cuban religion Santeria, which is based on African "animism" and ancestor worship.

    3. One type of Haitian art, the "primitive" style painting in bright colors, is world-renowned.

C. Decades of authoritarian dictatorships have contributed to the abject poverty of the country and political repression has forced many to escape the island in search of political asylum.

    1. Except for those who lived in Port-au-Prince, most came from a rural, agrarian, almost feudalistic society.

    2. Many have died in the Florida straits as they attempt to migrate to the U.S., or have been returned to Haiti.

    3. Compared to refugees from around the world they have been among the least welcomed in the U.S.

        a. Proportionately fewer are granted political asylum.

        b. Until recently they have been subjected to more strenuous application and screening procedures.

    4. Lack of a strong middle class and stable government in Haiti has meant that many Haitian-Americans lack previous experience that might make their assimilation easier.

    5. There has been some family separation due to exile; very seldom do entire families migrate together.

    6. Haitian families place a high value and priority on their children's education.

7. While many unskilled Haitians work for hourly wages, a Haitian-American middle class has emerged in the U.S., advancing into professions such as law, medicine, education and business.
8. Significant numbers of Haitian-Americans can be found in South Florida, New York, Boston, and Montreal, Canada.

X   Ethnic family Variations: Asian-American Families

A. Chinese and Filipino-Americans constitute the largest group of Asian-Americans, but this category also includes representatives from other Asian countries with highly diverse cultures.
1. In general, families emphasize male authority and traditional gender roles.
2. There is a strong sense of respect for cultural heritage and commitment to family loyalty.

XI   Ethnic Family Variations: Native American Families

A. Families tend to be extended, but with the migration from reservations to urban areas, families often resemble those of the dominant culture.
1. Child rearing tends to be permissive, with children stimulated to be internally self-sufficient instead of externally motivated.
2. The group is emphasized over the individual.

Review Section

Learning Objectives

After reading **Chapter Four,** you should be able to:

1. Understand the concepts of family and marriage in the context of culture.

2. Describe the various types of families and marriages.

3. Contrast the functionalist and the conflict-theory interpretation of the family.

Key Terms

Define the following glossary terms to test your knowledge.

1. Family
2. Socialization
3. Marriage
4. Nuclear family
5. Extended family
6. Monogamy
7. Polygamy
8. Polygyny
9. Polyandry
10. Patrilineal lineage
11. Matrilineal lineage
12. Patriarchal family
13. Matriarchal family
14. Egalitarian family

15. Patrilocal family

16. Matrilocal family

17. Neolocal family

18. Incest

19. Taboo

20. Arranged marriages

21. Personal-choice marriages

22. Exogamous marriages

23. Endogamous marriages

24. "family" of friends

25. Single parenthood

26. Single-sex families

27. Functionalism

28. Conflict theory

29. Race

30. Ethnic group

31. Hispanics

32. Familism

33. Compadrazgo

Multiple Choice

1. The foundation of the individual's social environment and the principal agent of socialization is:
   a. The School
   b. The Church
   c. Society
   d. The Family

2. In most primitive societies of pre-historic times, the union of a man and woman was done to satisfy:
   a. Reproductive needs
   b. Emotional needs
   c. Economic needs
   d. Political needs

3. A socially approved sexual and economic union between a man and a woman best defines:
   a. A common bondage
   b. A marriage
   c. A sexual union
   d. A contracted arrangement

4. The family is:
    a. A universal institution
    b. An instrument of cultural change
    c. Affected by social, political and economic changes in society
    d. All of the above

5. Extended families:
    a. Share in the responsibilities of childrearing
    b. Provide for adequate emotional and economic support in a hostile environment
    c. Include three generations or more under the same roof
    d. All of the above

6. The most common form of marriage in the world today is:
    a. Monogamy
    b. Cenogamy
    c. Polygamy
    d. Polyandry

7. The union of one man with several women is a form of polygamy called:
    a. Polyandry
    b. Cenogamy
    c. Polygyny
    d. None of the above

8. Which describes the union of one woman with several men?
    a. Polyandry
    b. Cenogamy
    c. Polygyny
    d. None of the above

9. In America, which of the following religious groups accepted polygamy?
    a. The Puritans
    b. The Catholics
    c. The Mormons
    d. The Methodist

10. A form of family control in which the father is head of the family is called:
    a. Matriarchal
    b. Patriarchal
    c. Matrilineal
    d. Patrilineal

11. In virtually every modern society, incest is:
    a. Taboo
    b. Acceptable
    c. Acceptable under certain circumstances
    d. Desirable

12. Among African-Americans:
    a. The Plantation system succeeded in destroying the traditional African family structure.
    b. Slaves were not allowed to legitimize their relationships.
    c. Slaves were not permitted to establish contracted marriages like everybody else.
    d. All of the above

13. In the traditional Cuban family:
   a. The extended family unit played a very important role.
   b. Afro-Cuban culture was pivotal in the shaping of the Cuban family value system and structure.
   c. The Communist Revolution of 1959 had a tremendous impact.
   d. All of the above.

14. All of the following statements can be applied to the Haitian population in the United States **except**:
   a. They come to escape from decades of authoritarian dictatorships that have contributed to the abject conditions of mass poverty in their country.
   b. Arriving as political exiles, they have been readily welcomed as political refugees.
   c. Although they speak French, Creole is regarded as the national language, widely spoken in most homes.
   d. Their country is regarded as the world's first "black" republic.

15. Which of the following **is not** a Functionalist analysis of the family?
   a. The purpose of the family is to provide for the nurturance and socialization of children.
   b. Families serve to reproduce societal inequalities among its members.
   c. A function of the family is to provide support for the virtually helpless: children, the infirm and the elderly.
   d. The family assures that the biological function which a society needs to perpetuate itself is met.

True and False Statements

Indicate if the following statements are True (T) or False (F).

_____ 1.   In a monogamous marriage, people are allowed to have more than one husband or wife.

_____ 2.   A family that traces descent through the male is patrilineal.

_____ 3.   In a matriarchal family the husband-father exercises total control.

_____ 4.   In the absence of parents, a mate or children, a circle of friends fulfill the functions of a traditional family structure.

_____ 5.   Familism is very rare among Hispanics.

Essays

1. Discuss the fundamental functions of the family from the perspective of functionalist and conflict theory sociologists.

2. Describe the various types of families and marriages, and the restrictions that are culturally mandated regarding marriages among members, in some societies.

3. Briefly discuss the ethnic family variations outlined in your text, and identify some of the most distinguishing characteristics of the main groups.

Chapter 5—The Economy

CHAPTER OUTLINE

I Types of Economic Systems

A. Introduction: **Economics** is a social science discipline that deals with decisions that human beings make in regard to how they allocate and manage resources that are scarce.
   1. Scarcity—goods and services that have attained a certain value based on demand for them in relation to their supply.
   2. Guides decisions made by societies and individuals, regarding how resources are distributed, which ones are produced, and what quantity is produced
   3. Economists classify resources into different types:
      a. Natural Resources
      b. Human Resources
      c. Capital Resources

B. Throughout history, people have used different economic systems.
   1. Traditional Economies
      a. Societies that did not use money as a medium of exchange depended on the **barter system**—the trading of goods and services
   2. Market Economies
      a. Use money to exchange goods and services
      b. There is little to no government intervention
   3. Command Economies
      a. Government makes decisions to plan production and consumption
      b. Private economic choices are minimized
   4. Mixed Economies
      a. Governments makes some decisions that directly impact the economy
      b. Most economic decisions are made by private groups and individuals
   5. Market and command systems are rarely pure in practice.
      a. The U.S. government provides social security and mandates minimum wage laws
      b. Illicit private markets functioned in the former Soviet Union

II History of Economic Systems and the Growth of Capitalism

A. Pre-Industrial Revolution Society
   1. Most people lived in agricultural communities.
   2. Ownership of land indicated wealth and social status, and owners of largest estates dominated economic, political and social structures.
   3. Subsistence agriculture dominated.
   4. Poverty, hunger and famine were commonplace.

B. The **Agricultural Revolution**: Produced technological and agricultural change.
   1. Population growth created a demand for food

2. New techniques—crop rotation methods, scientific breeding of animals, and use of fertilizer, increased production

3. The **enclosure** of common public lands and sale of lands to private holders increased amount of land under cultivation

C. Economic changes in agriculture helped facilitate industrialization.

1. Some English farmers amassed vast fortunes which were later used as **financial capital**.

    a. Investment capital financed new ideas and innovations.

    b. Built roads and canals which developed efficient internal markets.

    c. Improved transportation helped to lower the costs for goods.

    d. Promoted development of new inventions like the steam engine and the railroad.

2. People who used their money to finance these new ideas and innovations were called **capitalists**.

III   Mercantilism and its Critics

A. Newly emerging national states in the late middle ages and early modern era manifested specific characteristics:

1. Administrative centralization.

2. Intent on developing cultural and linguistic uniformity.

3. Government control over economic policy—**mercantilism**.

B. Under **mercantilism**, monarchies used government laws to set and profit from national economic policy.

1. Goal was to create a **favorable balance of trade**:

    a. Emphasized exports should exceed imports.

    b. Gold and silver would remain in the home country.

    c. National wealth and royal tax revenues would increase.

2. Mercantilists favored certain practices:

    a. High **tariffs**.

    b. Power of the state to grant **monopolies**.

3. Believed these policies would promote investment; investors would be protected by removing the risk of competition.

C. During the 18th century mercantile policies were challenged by some, especially those groups that were inspired by **Enlightenment** ideas.

1. Accepted standards of social organization were questioned

2. Reevaluation of preexisting knowledge was encouraged

D. Led by François Quesnay, the French **Physiocrats** challenged the economic policies of the French monarchy.

1. Favored replacing tariffs with a single tax on land.

2. Suggested that government intervention should be replaced by a system of **laissez-faire**.

E. Laissez-faire ideas were most clearly articulated by **Adam Smith**—considered by many to be the father of economics.

1. His work titled *Inquiry into the Nature and Causes of the Wealth of Nations* (1776), outlines the reasons why government should not involve itself with economic activity:

    a. Believed that monopolies and tariffs stunted economic development.

    b. Saw human self interest as the guiding force for economic development.

    c. Argued that freedom of the markets would allow **supply and demand relationships** to freely work.

2. Called the price setting mechanism for products and labor the **invisible hand**.

3. Reasoned that new inventors would be stimulated by rational self interest to create products for the market.

   4. Believed that free-trade policies should replace tariffs.

   5. Argued that competition in the marketplace would force companies to be more efficient and innovative.

F. Formation of business monopolies resulted from laissez-faire policies.

   1. Competitive environment of 19th century industrialization in Europe and the United States led to frequent business failures.

   2. Companies with large cash reserves survived, often buying out or merging with competitors

IV Marxian Critique of Laissez-Faire Capitalism

A. Free market capitalism also contained inherent contradictions, such as monopoly development.

   1. Market capitalism allowed **economic concentration—a situation in which the government allows large businesses to dominate their economic sector**.

   2. Karl Marx critiqued this development in his work, *The Communist Manifesto*, in which he assessed capitalism as an economic system.

      a. Believed that Smith's ideas on the ability to sustain competitive markets in a laissez-faire system was fantasy.

      b. Destruction of small companies created **maldistribution of wealth**.

      c. Predicted that successive economic cycles would create armies of unemployed and underemployed proletariats, who would form a **class consciousness**.

      d. In time this group would lead a revolution that would bring down the market system.

      e. He believed this process was necessary to historical development.

      f. He also contended that capitalism created problems that would eventually lead to its destruction.

      g. Called a future stage in historical development **socialism**.

B. The failure of capitalism would result from **overproduction**.

   1. Oversupply would cause small companies to fail.

   2. Laying off workers would lead to social and political unrest.

   3. Failed to explain what would occur when capitalism collapsed.

C. While capitalism continues to operate in most nations of the world, Adam Smith's laissez-faire version did not endure.

   1. The governments of most industrialized nations intervened in their national economies to address the worst abuses of capitalism.

      a. Enacted child labor laws.

      b. Enacted legislation to break up monopolies.

      c. Levied taxes on corporate wealth.

   2. As a result of government intervention and incorporation of social welfare legislation, nearly all industrialized nations now have mixed economies.

   3. The current system in the United States is called **regulated capitalism**.

V Keynesian Economics and the Great Depression

A. Specific events of the 20th century raised questions regarding the durability of free market systems.

   1. The Russian Revolution of October 1917 and institution of state economic planning in the Soviet Union.

   2. The **Great Depression** of the 1930s, and unemployment rates as high as 25% alarmed many.

   3. **Communism** was viewed by many on the left as the best system for governments to solve economic problems.

   4. **Fascism** instituted in Italy and Germany also became an attractive alternative.

B. Factors contributing to the Great Depression:
   1. Decline in international trade
   2. High tariff policies
   3. Underconsumption by consumers
   4. Increasing maldistribution of wealth
   5. Unsold factory inventories
   6. Tightening of the availability of credit to banks
   7. Private investors refused to pump money into an economy where consumer demand had declined

C. Faced with these conditions, the United States government adopted the policy recommendations of **John Maynard Keynes**.
   1. He believed that government should use their power over **fiscal policy** to shape the economic conditions of a nation.
   2. Policies and programs instituted by President Roosevelt were collectively called the **New Deal**.
   3. This government intervention in the market economy was opposed by **classical economists**.
      a. They viewed economic downturns as natural and necessary occurrences.
      b. Held that governments should maintain **balanced budgets**.

D. Keynes believed that governments should intervene when an economy goes into a recession.
   1. Government should increase spending and lower tax rates.
   2. To offset the resulting **budget deficits** and increasing **national debt,** he believed that government should raise taxes and cut spending during an economic **recovery.**

E. New Deal policies had mixed results and created tremendous controversy.
   1. Critics note that Depression was only ended by America's entry into the Second World War.
   2. Argued that **full employment** was reached by the economic demands created by the war effort.
   3. Supporters of classical economic thinking believed that these policies were bringing the nation toward socialism.
   4. New Deal planners noted that they were able to cut unemployment from 25% in 1933 to 14% early in the President's second term in 1936.
   5. Members of the political left believed that the New Deal reforms had saved capitalism.

VI   The Command Economy Alternative to Market-Based Approaches

A. Market based economies based on classical theories faced significant challenges from different areas:
   1. From Marxians and Keynesian economists.
   2. Most directly from the establishment of a state-controlled approach to economic management in the Soviet Union under Joseph Stalin.
      a. He instituted a planned economy to foster Soviet industrialization.
      b. This system was viewed as the optimal solution to problems of unemployment and economic crisis.
      c. In its pure form government manipulation of economic life requires **central planning.**
      d. Economic life of individuals and organizations are organized to meet the needs of the state.
   3. Planned economies function in direct opposition to market systems.
      a. Planning agencies decide what consumer goods are produced.
      b. Decide the quantities for distribution and prices of goods and services.
      c. In market systems production, consumption, and market price are determined by **laws of supply and demand.**

B. The Soviet Union represents the best historical example of the command economy model.
   1. After Lenin's death in 1924, Stalin consolidated his control of the Communist Party.
   2. Under his regime the Party controlled economic planning to promote rapid industrialization.

3. Since the Soviet state was largely unindustrialized the Soviet planners were forced to use a **rationing** system to distribute goods.

    a. Conservation of food was rigorously enforced in order to reserve most of the harvests for international export.

    b. Cash received for food shipments was invested in heavy industry; agriculture was used to finance rapid industrialization.

    c. Individuals who protested against these practices became victims of the totalitarian communist regime

    d. To speedup the industrialization process Stalin forced **agricultural collectivization** of peasant land.

    e. Historical records indicate that the human cost of agricultural collectivization was the deaths of millions of Soviet citizens.

    f. Significant rates of economic growth were achieved.

4. Production targets known as **five-year plans** were set by **Gosplan**.

    a. Emphasized development of heavy industry at the expense of consumer items.

    b. While high rates of economic growth occurred during the 1930s, growth rates slowed down significantly by the 1970s.

5. A drop in Soviet economic expansion can be explained by economic principle of **diminishing marginal product**.

6. Effectiveness of a command system is impeded by the necessity of coercion.

    a. Command systems rely on the use of fear to gain cooperation.

    b. System had few positive incentives beyond social recognition.

    c. Lack of incentives led to problems with quality control and production stagnation.

    d. Economic rewards were perceived as being antiethical to communism because they fostered wealth inequalities.

C. As the Soviet Union moved toward collapse in the 1980s, the **Peoples Republic of China**, under the leadership of Deng Xiaoping, began to liberalize its economy.

    1. The nation began to transition from a rigid command economy to a new hybrid mixed economy.

        a. Private production, open markets, and foreign investment were encouraged.

    2. The fall of the Soviet Union indicates the failure of command systems to sustain economic growth.

    3. Can be concluded that command systems failed to provide a legitimate economic alternative to market economies.

D. The Soviet Union ceased to exist after 1991.

    1. Each Soviet Republic became sovereign.

    2. Some joined the temporary Confederation of Independent States.

    3. Many factors contributed to its collapse:

        a. Mikhail Gorbachev attempted to reform the Soviet system by introducing changes called **Glasnost** and **Perestroika**.

        b. Nationalists demanded freedom for various Soviet Republics.

        c. Demand for more consumer goods pushed for government to reduce concentration of armaments and heavy industry.

        d. Some called for religious freedom.

        e. Also called for and end to Communist Party domination.

    4. Uneasy with the rapid pace set by Gorbachev's reforms, the Red Army leaders attempted a military coup.

    5. Unable to hold the Soviet Union together without resorting to violence, the Soviet Union disintegrated .

    6. Fall of the Soviet Union was seen as the end of ideological confrontation in world politics between capitalism and communism.

VI   Monetary Policy and the U.S. Federal Reserve System

A. Instead of promoting aggressive **fiscal policies**, some economists believe that **monetary policy** is more effective in stimulating economic growth.

1. Government central banks can affect economic growth by either slowing or accelerating the supply of money available to lending institutions.
2. The **Federal Reserve System (Fed)** has fulfilled this function in the United States since 1913.
   a. It effectively controls the national money supply by determining the **discount rate**.
   b. Increasing that rate helps to combat **inflation**.
   c. Can also be used to combat **deflation** by decreasing the rate.
   d. Supply of money can also be increased or decreased by determining the **reserve requirement**.
   e. The Fed is also involved in **open market operations**.

B. Economists who believe that central banking policies are the most effective tool that can be used to shape the health of a market system are called **monetarists**.

1. Acknowledged leader of this school of thought is Milton Friedman.
2. He blamed the severity of the Great Depression on the Federal Reserve System's contraction of the nation's money supply.
3. Friedman and the monetarists believe that implementing Keynesian policy is largely irrelevant to the creation of economic growth.
4. They argue instead that the supply of money and interests rates play a more significant role in economic expansion and contraction.

VII   Factors Shaping Economic Growth

A. Debate between different groups regarding what factors allow market economies to sustain economic growth continues.

1. Marxian economists **Paul Baran and Paul Sweezy** believed that industrial capitalism would stagnate due to economic concentration.
2. The 20th century economist **Joseph Schumpeter** argued that capitalism would continue to recreate itself with new products and processes.
   a. Innovations would continue to foster new demand for products and services.
   b. Predicted that **creative destruction** would cause economic suffering.

B. The late 19th century economist **Thorstein Veblen** developed the concept of **conspicuous consumption**.

1. This theory states that consumers spend money on goods and services to display their social status.
   a. The spending of financial elites would influence consumers.
   b. Products and services are demanded because of their social value.
   c. His theory demonstrated how the social world drove economic choice.
2. Idea on consumption being dictated by social forces also makes it difficult for economists to gauge living standards.
   a. Economists instead attempt to use quantifiable numbers to determine the poverty line.
   b. However, these definitions do not really indicate how people actually use the money they receive.
   c. Social pressures are significant in determining how individuals spend their money and gauge their own economic success.
   d. An individual may earn more money in a particular year, yet experience **relative deprivation**.

VIII Economic Indicators

A. Economists measure the effects of increasing maldistribution of wealth on the national economy by using other methods to indirectly study economic growth.

   1. Economists examine different indicators to determine the strengths and weaknesses of national, global, and regional economies.

   2. These indicators help economists measure the outlook for economic growth or recession.

B. Indicators include:

   1. The **Consumer Price Index** (CPI).

      a. Measures the prices of a group of goods and services purchased by people living in urban areas.

      b. Used by economists to determine the health of an economy.

   2. **Inflation** levels.

      a. **Inflation** is an increase in prices and money wages.

      b. Hurts people with fixed incomes and creditors.

   3. **Unemployment** levels.

      a. A high level of unemployment is an important indicator of an economy's strength and weakness.

      b. Can have a ripple effect throughout the economy, as demand and production decrease.

   4. **Per capita income.**

      a. This statistic is figured by dividing a nation's total national income by the sum of the national population.

      b. Used by economists to determine the wealth of countries in comparison with other nations.

      c. Is also used to measure national income growth from year to year.

   5. **Gross Domestic Product** (GDP).

      a. Used by the U.S. government to measure the market value of all goods and services produced in a country in a specific year.

      b. Tells the actual size of an economy, and can monitor economic activity that takes place in a single nation.

      c. Can also be used to compare different nations to each other.

   6. **Rate of Economic Growth.**

      a. This statistic measures the rate of increase of GDP factoring in inflation rates in a defined period.

   7. **Overproduction.**

      a. Occurs when factories produce more goods than are consumed in the market.

      b. As demand and prices fall, factories limit future production and layoff workers.

      c. Unemployed people limit consumer spending.

      d. Creates a domino effect as other parts of the economy are impacted.

   8. **Underproduction.**

      a. Limits economic growth by lessening potential sales.

      b. Also creates price inflation since demand now exceeds supply.

   9. **Disposable income.**

      a. Price inflation in one area can affect spending patterns by limiting the amount of personal income people have to spend on other items.

      b. If there is no middle class because the distribution of wealth in a society is unbalanced, economic stagnation can result.

  10. **Life expectancy.**

      a. Used as an indirect economic indicator.

      b. High life expectancy rates indicate that a population has access to health care, which in turn can be used to measure national economic conditions.

IX   Factors Contributing to Economic Development in Market Economies

A. Economists generally agree that certain dynamics are crucial in facilitating economic growth. Among those factors are:

1. Availability of investment capital.
2. Plentiful human and natural resources.
3. Entrepreneurship.
4. Innovation.
5. Growth oriented government policies.
6. Development of stable economic and political institutions.

B. Human Capital is essential to the productivity and success of industries.

1. Employee training and work experiences make them valuable assets to their firms.
   a. Companies often train workers, or provide higher wages to obtain trained workers.
   b. Once trained, they contribute to the value of the organization.
2. A literate and skilled workforce also fosters economic development.
   a. The United States has traditionally benefited from plentiful skilled labor.
   b. Literacy was stressed in colonial New England.
   c. Under the Ordinance of 1785, public schools were encouraged and supported by the sale of western lands.
   d. Under the Morrill Act of 1862 public lands were given to state governments, to finance the creation of colleges and universities.
   e. During the Cold War the federal government increased support for math and science education.
3. A plentiful labor supply is also important to economic development.
   a. Scarcity of workers can impact wages, investment, and profits.
   b. Immigration has consistently supplied the United States' labor market with both skilled and unskilled labor.

C. Natural Resources are essential in promoting economic growth.

1. They are economic goods that are provided by nature:
   a. Can be unfinished goods that are processed into **exploitable resources**.
   b. Can also be unprocessed resources.
2. The most important function of food industries is to provide agricultural self-sufficiency.
3. Scarcity of natural resources can have detrimental effects on a national economy:
   a. Shortages can lead to price inflation.
   b. Depletion of renewable resources can cause environmental degradation.

D. Potential for economic growth can be associated with the amount of **financial capital** available in an economy.

1. Consists of **assets** that can be utilized to create more income.
2. **Physical capital** generates income by providing goods or services.
3. Financial capital is valuable because of its **liquidity**; readily available as monies it provides funding for new ideas and innovations
4. Market economies also require the existence of a **class of financiers**, who provide financial backing for new ventures.

E. Entrepreneurs also play an essential role in an economy:

1. They identify the needs of a particular market and figure out how to satisfy that need for a cost.
2. They are risk takers who exploit opportunities.
3. Are often supported by the investment assistance of capitalists.

F. A **stable government** is essential in order for an economy to function efficiently.

1. Unstable political situations limit financial investment.

    a. Direct foreign investment is likely to occur, when the **rule of law** is present.

    b. Building legitimate political institutions can also promote economic growth.

  2. Policies that governments introduce can also facilitate or hinder economic growth.

    a. Central banks that control a country's money supply can provide financial stability.

G. During its industrial take-off period of the late 19th century the United States followed a **laissez-faire approach** to encourage economic growth, with resulting negative consequences.

  1. This approach encouraged **monopoly formation**.

  2. Experienced social problems that were indirect results of the government's **hands-off-policies**.

  3. Producers were protected at the expense of consumers by the **theory of freedom to contract**.

  4. The law courts were seen as indirectly subsidizing the costs of economic expansion of corporations and businesses through their decisions

  5. **Limited liability** rulings encouraged investment.

  6. Development of **corporations** as distinct entities in the eyes of the law gave them and their investors' legal protection in the federal courts.

H. The U. S. government has encouraged innovation and invention by extending legal protection called a **patent.**

  1. The U.S. Patent Office has regulated this process since 1790.

  2. Patents serve several purposes:

    a. It rewards inventors whose innovations have social benefits.

    b. Encourage new inventions by securing for individuals exclusive rights to a new idea and its potential for profit.

I. Although the U.S. government in the 19th century limited its involvement in the domestic economy, its policy toward international trade tended toward protectionism.

  1. **Tariffs** are rates of taxes on goods imported into a country.

    a. Proposed during the early period of the American republic to encourage Americans to buy American made goods.

    b. Can be used to stimulate domestic production.

    c. Are continued to be used by countries to protect domestic markets.

    d. Are also used to protect "infant industries" from international competitors.

Review Section

Learning Objectives

When you finish reading **Chapter Five**, you should be able to:

1. Describe the two main economic models.

2. Identify major economic indicators and concepts that measure the strengths and weaknesses of modern economies.

3. Contrast the market, command and mixed economic systems.

4. Identify the strengths and weakness of market and command economies.

5. Identify the factors that promote economic development.

6. Describe the main economic theories of Smith, Marx and Keynes.

7. Understand the impact of monetary policy.

Key Terms

Define the following glossary terms to test your knowledge.

1. Economics

2. Scarcity

3. Resources

4. Barter

5. Market Economy

6. Command Economy

7. Mixed Economy

8. Subsistence agriculture

9. financial capital

10. Capitalists

11. Mercantilism

12. Tariffs

13. Monopolies

14. Invisible hand

15. Free trade policies

16. Maldistribution of wealth

17. Overproduction

18. Regulated capitalism

19. Recession

20. Deficits

21. Full employment

22. Law of Supply and Demand

23. Rationing

24. Agricultural collectivization

25. *Glasnost*

26. *Perestroika*

27. Discount rate

28. Deflation

29. Reserve requirements

30. Open market operations

31. Relative deprivation

32. Per capita income

33. Entrepreneurs

34. Corporation

35. patent

Matching Terms

_____**1.**   Natural Resources

A. An economic structure in which some functions to support growth are facilitated by government while others are left to market forces.

_____**2.**   Human Resources

B. Measures all items produced in a country by domestic or foreign companies.

_____**3.**   Capital Resources

C. The total amount of money available to consumers for spending after government taxes have been subtracted.

_____**4.**   Inflation

D. Situation in which the government allows large businesses to dominate their economic sector.

_____**5.**   Consumer Price Index

E. Assumes that consumers and workers are free agents, and that all wage structures and product prices are negotiated in market relationships

_____**6.**   Gross Domestic Product

F. Economic goods in the form of raw materials that are processed into exploitable resources

_____**7.**   Disposable Income

G. Laborers and the labor they provide as a commodity with real value

_____**8.**   Freedom to contract

H. Measures the prices of a group of goods and services purchased by people living in urban areas

_____**9.**   Regulated Capitalism

I. An increase in prices and money wages.

_____**10.**   Economic concentration

J. Real or financial possessions held by companies, investors, or governments such as land, machines, and credit

Multiple Choice

1. The two most distinctive economic systems are:
   a. Mercantilist and Capitalist systems
   b. Market and Command systems
   c. Market and Mixed systems
   d. Capitalist and Command

2. The type of economy in which the government exercises control over the production, distribution and allocation of goods and services is called.
   a. A capitalist economy
   b. A market economy
   c. A mercantilist economy
   d. A command economy

3. Which of the following communist countries has moved from a rigid command system to incorporate some features of a market economy?
   a. Soviet Union
   b. North Korea
   c. China
   d. All of the above

4. Which of the following best describes mercantilism?
   a. Accumulation of national wealth
   b. State provides guidelines for production
   c. There is room for private enterprise
   d. Dependency on imports

5. Which of the following would argue that government involvement in the economy stunted economic development?
   a. Monetarists
   b. Mercantilist
   c. Communist
   d. Laissez-faire economics

6. An example of a natural resource:
   a. Automobiles
   b. Petroleum
   c. Hotels
   d. Entrepreneurs

7. In a mixed economy, the government:
   a. Does not intervene in the economy.
   b. Makes decisions to plans productions and consumption.
   c. Makes some decisions that directly impact the economy.
   d. Private choices are minimized.

8. Fiscal policy can be used by the government to regulate the economy by:
   a. Controlling taxing and spending.
   b. Controlling interests rates.
   c. Imposing tariffs on foreign goods.
   d. Determining wage levels.

9. The prices setting mechanism for products and labor proposed by Adam Smith is called:
   a. Hands off policy.
   b. Freedom of contract.
   c. The natural price.
   d. The invisible hand.

10. Most industrialized countries today, including the United State employ an economic structure best exemplified by which model?
    a. Market economy.
    b. Mixed economy.
    c. Command economy.
    d. Planned economy.

True and False Statements

Indicate if the following statements are True (T) or False (F).

_____ 1.   In a barter economy banks control the production and distribution of money.

_____ 2.   In is most pure form governments using a command economy decide what goods are produced and control consumer prices

_____ 3.   During inflationary times, the purchasing power of money increases and prices decline.

_____ 4.   Entrepreneurs play a vital role in an economy because they provide the financial backing for new ventures.

_____ 5.   The United States has traditionally benefited from a skilled labor force because since its early history, it has supported public education.

_____ 6.   Court rulings during the nineteenth century tended to protect consumers and laborers, and discourage investments by finance capitalists.

_____ 7.   Policies used by governments today to protect domestic markets are labeled as protectionism.

_____ 8.   Mercantilists opposed the granting of monopolies because they limited competition and discouraged investment.

_____ 9.   High levels of unemployment can lead to price deflation because businesses lower prices when there is a decrease in demand.

_____10.   The Fascist systems established in Italy and Germany in the period just before World War II, promoted a state directed economy based on the command model established by Stalin in the Soviet Union.

Matching People

_____ 1.   Adam Smith   **A.** As leader of the Physiocrats, he favored replacing tariffs with a single tax.

_____ 2.   Karl Marx   **B.** His economic theories proposing use fiscal policy to regulate the economy were used in the New Deal.

_____ 3.   Frederick Engels   **C.** Leader of the monetarist, this economist believes that central banking policies are the most effective tool that can be used to shape the health of an economy.

_____ **4.**   John Maynard Keynes

D. Attempted to reform the Soviet system by introducing changes called Glasnost and Perestroika.

_____ **5.**   Thorstien Veblen

E. Under his regime, the Soviet Union was rapidly industrialized by implementation of the command economy model.

_____ **6.**   François Quesnay

F. Author of *The Communist Manifesto,* his analysis of capitalism stated that problems created by system would eventually lead to its destruction.

_____ **7.**   Joseph Schumpeter

G. He developed the concept of conspicuous consumption that states consumers spend money to display their social status.

_____ **8.**   Milton Friedman

H. Considered to be the father of economics, his work, *The Wealth of Nations,* argued against the mercantile system in favor of laissez-faire economics.

_____ **9.**   Mikhail Gorbachev

I. Collaborated in the writing of *The Communist Manifesto.*

_____**10.**   Joseph Stalin

J. Argued that capitalism would continue to recreate itself with new products and processes.

Essays

1. What were the reasons offered by Adam Smith to support his belief that mercantilism limited economic prosperity?

2. John Maynard Keynes believed that fiscal policy could be used to address economic crises. How would he suggest that fiscal policies be used by governments in recessions and depressions, and what policies should they follow during recessions?

3. Discuss why Karl Marx thought capitalism would fail.

4. What factors allowed the United States to experience an Industrial Revolution in the mid to late nineteenth century?

CHAPTER 6—THE AMERICAN POLITICAL ECONOMY

CHAPTER OUTLINE

I Introduction

A. A basic knowledge of economics and a strong sense of how the political economy functions are essential in order to thrive in a global community.

   1. Economics is the social science discipline by which we examine how individual households and communities persist and evolve using limited or scarce resources.

   2. The **political economy** is the study of the political influence of households, business and government on the economy.

II American Economy

A. The American political economy is best described as a mixed, regulated economy—neither a solely command nor singularly market driven economy.

   1. Command and pure market economies both have shortcomings which most negatively impact the consumer.

   2. They have led to wide consumer abuses, corruption, and inefficiencies.

   3. The United States has evolved a political economy that protects civil and human rights, and in which a national social contract and national interests supersedes property rights and profits.

B. Households-groups of individuals living together and making joint decisions-are at the center of the American economy.

III The Economic Engines of Business, Corporations, and Enterprises

A. All the entities that play a role in the conversion process are essential to the development, growth and diversification of a national economy.

   1. Corporations and other forms of business provide comprehensive, competitive and compliant sources of goods and services.

   2. Businesses are uniquely designed to generate profits, but also contribute to the tax base and participate in the redistribution of national wealth.

   3. Nearly 50% of American households participate in some financial aspect of corporations and business either directly or through retirement plans, in addition to being consumers.

IV Government—Regulator, Originator and Generator of Wealth

A. The Federal Government influences and regulates the national economy by public priorities and policy through three areas of its prerogatives:

   1. Fiscal and budgetary policies influence the overall economic performance through governmental decisions regarding spending and taxation.

    2. Monetary Policy relates to increases or decreases in the money supply:
- **a.** The Federal Reserve Board determines the interest rate by which the nation's private banks can borrow money from the federal government.
- **b.** Changes in the money supply are usually associated with an increase or decrease in interests rates.

    3. Moralsuasion attempts to encourage individual households, business and government units and their leadership to behave in a specific manner with economic implications.

B. State and local (county or municipal) governments also enjoy the prerogative of influencing state and local economic activity respectively through three areas of initiative:
- **1.** Fiscal and budgetary policies.
- **2.** Rules and enforcement.
- **3.** Moralsuasion.

C. Three levels of political intervention represent the many avenues for affirmation, advocacy, intervention and prevention available to sectors of the society.
- **1.** Individual households vote in political elections, with purchasing power or through stockholder instruments, or freely form lobby groups.
- **2.** National, state or local levels of government and its leadership can be influenced by individual initiative, and formal political intervention.
- **3.** Can focus on candidates or incumbents and their economy policies through informal, registered lobbying or political action committees.

V   The New American Economy

A. The American economy experienced nine years of economic expansion from 1990 to 2000, and then experienced a small economic slowdown after 2000.
- **1.** Unemployment at 4.6%.
- **2.** Poverty rate is currently at about 12%

B. Causes of the transition of the new American Economy are varied:
- **1.** Downsizing of American businesses has made them more efficient.
- **2.** Many Americans have learned new skills and entered new professions and businesses.
- **3.** Tax cuts, free trade policies, and less government intervention have also forced the business sector to become more efficient
- **4.** End of the Cold War brought a "peace dividend" as many resources available for military purposes were redirected for personal and commercial economic use
- **5.** Avoidance of high inflation through use of tough monetary policies
- **6.** Companies invested in new and more productive equipment, and more on information technology
- **7.** Access to unlimited amount of cheap property via the internet, and the computer
- **8.** Entrepreneurs who deploy the new technology to make goods and increase productivity
- **9.** Both wages and productivity are rising
- **10.** Low cost imports contribute to lower inflation

Review Section

Learning Objectives

After reading **Chapter Six**, you should be able to:

1. Contrast a command economy with a market economy and mixed economy, and discuss which type of economy the United States has.

2. Define households, and explain the role they play on the economy, exist.

3. Describe the contributions that business, corporations and enterprises make to the American economy.

4. Discuss how fiscal and monetary policies operate.

5. Enumerate the characteristics of the "new" American economy.

Key Terms

Define the following glossary terms to test your knowledge.

1. Political economy

2. Regulated economy

3. Household

4. Fiscal policies

5. Monetary policies

6. Moralsuasion

Multiple Choice

1. A command economy provides:
   a. Central control
   b. Decentralized control
   c. Free enterprise
   d. Libertarianism

2. The American economy is :
   a. Centralized
   b. Mixed
   c. Command
   d. Market

3. Households are:
   a. Groups of families
   b. Group of individuals
   c. House of corporations
   d. All of the above

4. Business corporations in the United States, unlike governments, and households are uniquely designed to generate:
   a. Taxes
   b. Public services
   c. Profit
   d. Services

5. Fiscal policies are the responsibility of
   a. The Federal Reserve system
   b. The Supreme Court
   c. The President
   d. the Congress

6. Monetary policies are the responsibility of
   a. The Federal Reserve System
   b. The Supreme Court
   c. The President
   d. the Congress

7. One of the characteristics of the "new" American economy is
   a. Frequent recessions
   b. Low unemployment
   c. High inflation
   d. Low rate of economic growth

8. Individual households are able to exert influence on the political economy by:
   a. Voting in political elections.
   b. Vote with purchasing power.
   c. Voting through stockholder instruments.
   d. All of the above.

True and False Statements

Indicate if the following statements are True (T) or False (F).

_____ **1.**   The American economy is a regulated economy.

_____ **2.**   Households are groups of individuals living together and making joint decisions.

_____ **3.**   Fiscal policies deal with government spending.

_____ **4.**   The unemployment rate in the United States is over 11%.

_____ **5.**   Foreigners invest more in the United States than Americans invest abroad.

_____ **6.**   Property rights are held in higher regard than individual rights within the U.S. Constitution.

Essays

1. Discuss the difference between fiscal and monetary policy, and explain how each is used by the federal government to control the economy.

2. Define the concept of moralsuasion, and explain how it is used by political leaders, and others, to influence economic activity.

Chapter 7—Systems of Governing

CHAPTER OUTLINE

I Government

    A. While earlier societies directed their affairs through informal relationships, the rise of densely populated communities led to the development of government as a formal process.

    B. Societies which developed in Mesopotamia, Egypt, India and China, exhibited certain characteristics:

        1. Intensive agriculture through cooperative or coercive effort.

        2. Written language.

        3. Trade and diplomatic relations with other states.

        4. Attention to arts and other elements of culture.

        5. Complex technology.

        6. Formal government structure.

    C. **Government** is defined as a body of people and institutions that make and enforce laws for a particular society.

        1. Considered one of society's primary social institutions, as well as its most powerful.

        2. Perform legislative, executive, and judicial functions with decision-making power exercised by different groups:

            a. Democracy-a majority of voters elect officials who govern.

            b. Oligarchy-government led by a few businessmen or landed interests.

            c. Dictatorship-coercive government led by a single all-powerful leader.

        3. Generally constrained by a constitution in modern times.

    D. Government directs both the internal and external affairs of countries, and nation-states.

        1. **Nation** is defined as any sizable group of people united by common bonds of geography, religion, language, race, custom and tradition, as well as by shared experiences and common aspirations.

        2. **State** or country is a political jurisdiction with a permanent population, fixed borders, and a government.

        3. **Nation-state** refers to a country with a dominant group though it may include smaller numbers of other ethnic and racial groups.

    E. **Politics**, an essential part of society, refers to the means by which individuals affect their government.

II Viewpoints on Government

    A. Government as a positive good.

        1. Proponents argue that government is necessary for the people of a society to share in a range of opportunities.

        2. Without government, chaos would reign until society disintegrated.

        3. Thomas Paine, American revolutionary writer, believed that government helps place people on the correct moral course.

        4. Progressives or modern liberals favor a government actively involved in many aspects of peoples' lives.

        5. From 1930s to 1960s, the federal government assumed an activist role in American life.

B. Government as a necessary evil.

   1. Supporters believe that government's role is to serve as a restraining force in society: to prohibit, restrain, regulate, compel and coerce; that government is best when it governs least.

   2. Government assumes this function primarily through its power to pass laws, and to enforce them.

   3. Proponents of this viewpoint included:

   a. Thomas Hobbes who wrote that people created government as protection against themselves.

   b. John Locke who supported the concept of government as a **social contract** to protect peoples' inviolable rights.

   c. Thomas Jefferson who believed that government could contribute best to public prosperity by allowing individuals and businesses to manage themselves.

C. Government as an unnecessary evil.

   1. Influenced by the writings of Karl Marx, this viewpoint saw government as a tool of the Bourgeoisie that serves only to suppress and exploit the working class.

   2. Marxist doctrine taught that in the aftermath of the violent overthrow of the capitalist class through a worldwide workers' revolution, government would "wither away", since exploitation would cease in a classless society.

   3. Anarchists also hold this viewpoint; however, they prefer voluntary associations instead of government.

III   The Power and Function of Government

A. Distinction is often made between power and influence.

   1. Power is an attribute of those in government, who are able to make decisions.

   2. Influence is often held by those outside government and imbues them with the ability to help determine decisions made by those who have power.

B. Varying viewpoints exist regarding the amount of power government should possess.

   1. Anarchists support as little government as possible, ideally no government at all.

   2. Libertarians desire greater freedom for people, and call for a minimal role for the state, particularly in the area of economic regulation.

   3. Reactionaries accept some kind of role for government, but want to see it reduced to a far smaller size, modeled on a much earlier, simpler period in history.

   4. Conservatives also desire smaller government, but not to the degree of reactionaries.

   5. Modern Liberals are more positive about government, and wish to imbue it with even more power.

   6. Moderates are basically content with present size and scale of government.

C. Government fulfills many functions in a society, and varying viewpoints also exist regarding what the role of government should be.

   1. Protection for its people.

   2. Dispensing justice.

   3. Government as a regulator.

   4. Government as a welfare agent.

   5. Government as the protector of basic civil liberties.

IV   Types of Governments

A. Aristotle, the Athenian philosopher, characterized governments according to the number of persons ruling and the objectives of their rule.

   1. Monarchy—one man's rule in the interest of all.

   2. Tyranny—one man's rule in the interest of himself only.

   3. Aristocracy—rule by a few in the interest of all.

4. **Oligarchy**—a few men's rule for personal interest.
5. **Polity**—rule by many for good of all.
6. **Democracy**—majority rule for the interest of the majority only.

B. Basically two types of government exist today, democracies and autocracies.
   1. Most governments claim to be democracies, including some of the world's most repressive regimes.
   2. Until recently the United States and the Soviet Union debated over what constituted a democracy.
      a. According to the U.S. democracy meant the right of the people to select their leaders in free elections.
      b. For the Soviet Union it meant more jobs, healthcare and education for all its citizens.

C. **Democracy** as a term and concept came from the classical Greeks, meaning the rule of the people.
   1. A modern phenomenon, its ideas and ideals were influenced by:
      a. The American and French Revolutions.
      b. The English governmental tradition.
   2. According to **John Locke**, people are **sovereign**; the source of all power.
   3. This doctrine of **popular sovereignty** presumes that people can control their own destiny.
      a. People select their leaders in free elections.
      b. Must possess the right to vote, and choose between candidates representing differing viewpoints or parties.
      c. To maintain control they must possess freedom of speech, and effective legislative organizations to represent them.
   4. The individual is most important; government and society are considered to exist for the benefit of the individual.
   5. The society must posses a liberal **constitutional government** that guarantees many basic individual rights and freedoms.
   6. Also means **limited government** where people possess liberties that are safeguarded by law- a constitution, document or fundamental law observed by government.

D. Types of Democracies.
   1. Democracies come in many forms:
      a. Direct Democracy.
      b. Representative Democracy.
      c. Presidential Democracy
      d. Unitary Democracy
      e. Federal Democracy
   2. Democracy can exist in a **republic** where leaders are elected; or in a **constitutional monarchy**, where leaders inherit their power and title by virtue of birth.
   3. Democracy as a view and approach to governing can also embrace some forms of **socialism**, a system where the government controls most of the economy.
   4. The United States model is a representative, presidential, federal republic.
   5. Great Britain is a representative, parliamentary, unitary, constitutional monarchy.

E. **Autocracy** is a system of rule in which a single person or a small group of people exercises dictatorial power.
   1. Individual rights and other freedoms are subordinated to the power of the state or to a ruling party.
   2. Until recent centuries, autocratic governments ruled virtually all nations; the most common form has been the monarchy.
   3. Some rulers claimed to be a God, or ruled according to the theory of **Divine Right of Monarchs**.

F. While the monarchy is less popular today, twentieth century autocracy has evolved into new forms:
   1. **Authoritarianism** is a government that exerts total political control, but permits activities that do not threaten its power:
      a. One person exerts great power often used to accrue wealth.
      b. Forbid activities that threaten their position, while they ignore those that do not threaten their rule.

     c. Leadership operates within basically a one-party system; party or parties exists to consolidate power and allocate privileges among the ruling group.

     d. Government exerts a great deal of influence over the economy that is usually capitalistic.

     e. Examples include the former government of Saddam Hussein in Iraq, and military juntas.

  2. Totalitarianism is a system whereby the government controls all aspects of an individual's life, monopolizing power through a one-party system of rule:

     a. Technology and other means necessary to achieve this degree of domination make this a twentieth century phenomenon.

     b. Most totalitarian states are based on an **ideology**.

     c. Leader seeks to control every aspect of the life of the people in order to impose the ideology.

     d. Features include brutal secret police, one party rule, and tight governmental economic regulation.

     e. Most important totalitarian ideologies of the twentieth century are Communism and Fascism.

     f. Examples of communist countries include China, Cuba, and North Korea.

G. Communism and the Soviet Union:

  1. Based on the writings of Karl Marx, communism rejects capitalism.

  2. First Marxist revolution occurred in Russia in 1917, and brought to power the Bolsheviks led by Vladimir Lenin.

  3. From the establishment of the Soviet Socialist Republics (USSR) in 1922, to its collapse and disappearance in 1991, the **Communist Party** ruled oppressively.

  4. Communism transformed the primarily agricultural society to one that emphasized heavy industry and a vast military machine.

  5. During the brutal rule of Joseph Stalin, the Communist Party engaged in a practice referred to as the "**cult of personality**", elevating the leader's image to that of a demigod.

  6. Continual effort was made to export revolution abroad, leading to the support for Marxist regimes governing China, Cuba, and other countries.

H. Fascism and Nazi Germany.

  1. Germany under control of the Nazi party was a totalitarian power with an ideology distinctly different from the Soviet Union.

  2. Nazism grew out of Italian **fascism**, an ideology that defined the nation and government of Italy under Benito Mussolini:

     a. Stressed the preeminent position of the state, an omniscient strong-willed leader cast in the mold of a hero.

     b. Promoted anti-intellectualism, anticommunism, and anti-liberalism.

     c. Government controlled the economy via an economic system called corporatism.

     d. Promoted extreme nationalism, imperialism and antipacifism

  3. Nazism embraced many of these characteristics, but its core ideology was its doctrine of Aryan racial superiority.

     a. Held that the state or national community is more important than the individuals that comprise it.

     b. Demanded fanatical nationalism in the struggle against democracy and communism.

     c. Denied the equality of all human beings, insisting Aryans were superior to all people.

     d. Insisted that an elite (the party and government leaders) must prevail over the people.

     e. At the head of the elite was the fuhrer, the absolute pinnacle of human perfection.

     f. Also referred to as National Socialism, the ideology embraced war and violence as major tenets; doctrine of racial superiority led directly to the death of millions of "inferior peoples".

Review Section

Learning Objectives

After reading **Chapter Seven**, you should be able to respond to the following questions:

1. Discuss the different viewpoints on government.

2. Contrast the various positions on the political spectrum such as Anarchism, Libertarianism, Conservatism, Liberalism, as well as the nature of reactionaries and moderates.

3. Analyze the different types of democracies and autocracies.

Key Terms

Define the following glossary terms to test your knowledge.

1. Government
2. Politics
3. Power
4. Influence
5. Nation
6. State
7. Nation-State
8. Libertarians
9. Reactionaries
10. Modern Liberals
11. Moderates

12. Monarchy

13. Oligarchy

14. Democracy

15. Popular sovereignty

16. Direct democracy

17. Representative democracy

18. Presidential democracy

19. Parliamentary democracy

20. Unitary democracy

21. Federal democracy

22. Republic

23. Socialism

24. Autocracy

25. Authoritarianism

26. Totalitarianism

27. Ideology

28. Communism

29. Fascism

30. Nazism

Multiple Choice

1. The world's largest democracy:
   a. U.S.
   b. France
   c. Japan
   d. India

2. Examples of authoritarian autocracies include all **except:**
   a. Hussein's Iraq
   b. Hitler's Germany
   c. Catherine the Great's Russia
   d. The France of Louis XIV

3. _____ see no government as the ideal.
   a. Reactionaries
   b. Anarchist
   c. Liberals
   d. Conservative

4. Marx envisioned the workers overthrowing the _____ in a bloody revolution.
   a. Bourgeoisie
   b. Aristocrats
   c. The Monarchy
   d. Democrats

5. This Italian Fascist was the leader of Italy for more than twenty years in the early and mid-twentieth century:
   a. Grasiani
   b. Garibaldi
   c. Cavor
   d. Mussolini

6. Hitler's world view is contained in this work:
   a. *On Liberty*
   b. *What is to be Done*
   c. *Mein Kampf*
   d. *Man and Superman*

7. The Russian Communist Party that seized power in 1917 was led by:
   a. Nicholas II
   b. Lenin
   c. Molotov
   d. Speransky

8. They view government as a positive good:
   a. Conservative
   b. Libertarians
   c. Modern Liberals
   d. Reactionaries

9. All of the following represent major elements of Nazism **except:**
   a. Strong leader
   b. Multi-party system
   c. Glorification of war and violence
   d. Irrationalism

10. While a constitution is not critical for a democracy, some form of fundamental law observed by the government must exist. The world's oldest democracy, this country does not have a written constitution.
    a. France
    b. Greece
    c. Italy
    d. Great Britain

11. Instituted by _____, the Great Purge led to the death of more than 20 million people in the Soviet Union.
    a. Lenin
    b. Trotsky
    c. Stalin
    d. Breshnev

12. In his classic work, *Leviathan*, _____ argued for an authoritarian government along the monarchial model:
   a. Thomas Jefferson
   b. Thomas Hobbes
   c. John Locke
   d. John Stuart Mill

13. _____ is an example of a unitary democracy since power is centered in the national government.
   a. Great Britain
   b. United States
   c. Canada
   d. Turkey

14. He classified governments according to the number of persons ruling and the objectives of their rule.
   a. Plato
   b. Sophocles
   c. Socrates
   d. Aristotle

15. Which of the following countries practices democratic socialism?
   a. Germany
   b. Sweden
   c. U.S.
   d. Canada

True and False Statements

Indicate if the following statements are True (T) or False (F).

_____   **1.**   In a Unitary democracy, power is divided between a national government and state governments.

_____   **2.**   Many leaders in the emerging nation-states of the Medieval West ruled according to the theory of Divine Right Monarchy, which taught that they were appointed by God to lead their people.

_____   **3.**   Democracy and Socialism are incompatible concepts.

_____   **4.**   A state lacks territorial borders and a permanent population.

_____   **5.**   A difference between an Authoritarian dictator and the leader of a totalitarian country is that the latter is more interested in the widespread adoption of an ideology than in amassing great wealth.

_____   **6.**   Intent on promoting industrial development of the country to support the state apparatus, Fascists governments emphasize pacifism and an anti-war ideology.

_____   **7.**   Believing that the only way to achieve a socialist revolution and to establish a socialist state was by creating a strong central government, Marx saw Government as a positive good.

_____   **8.**   The first and foremost function of a government is to serve as the internal guardian of society and to protect its people from external aggression.

_____ **9.**   All of the world's republics are constitutional democracies.

_____ **10.**   Direct democracies are only practical in small communities.

Matching Terms

_____ **1.**   Presidential democracy

A. An organized system of ideas for reordering society.

_____ **2.**   Federal democracy

B. A system whereby the government controls all aspects of an individual's life, monopolizing power through a one-party system of rule.

_____ **3.**   Government

C. Power is shared by the national government and state governments.

_____ **4.**   Politics

D. Stressed the preeminent position of the state.

_____ **5.**   Unitary democracy

E. The nation's chief executive exercises vast powers separate from the other branches of government.

_____ **6.**   Popular sovereignty

F. A system in which the government exerts total political control, but does permit activities that do not threaten its control.

_____ **7.**   Ideology

G. Means by which individuals affect their Government.

_____ **8.**   Totalitarianism

H. A body of people and institutions that make up and enforce laws for a particular society.

_____ **9.**   Authoritarianism

I. Power lies within one level of government, the national.

_____ **10.**   Fascism

J. Asserts that people are the source of all power, master of any government established to serve them.

Essays

1. Discuss the different viewpoints on government, providing examples and justifications for each one.

2. Compare and contrast the various positions regarding the power of government.

3. Identify and discuss the viewpoints regarding what the role government in a society should be.

Chapter 8—The American Political System

A Historical View

CHAPTER OUTLINE

I   Framework of American Political System

A. America's democratic government operates according to the dictates of the world's oldest constitution.
  1. Because of its progressive provisions, the U.S. Constitutions has inspired imitators throughout the world.
  2. Adoption of the Constitution in 1789 established a framework for what has become over time the most democratic country in the world.

B. Unique democratic principles based on various influences.
  1. Democratic system of government in Greek city-state of Athens.
  2. English parliamentary system, Judeo-Christian culture, and liberal principles.
  3. Early colonial legislatures and experiences.
  4. Writings of English political philosopher John Locke.

C. Struggle between England and American colonies for power.
  1. Colonial America functioned with relative independence and modicum of self-government.
  2. British policies after the French and Indian War sought to establish firm control over the colonies:
     a. Stamp Act Tax.
     b. Quartering of British troops in colonial homes.
     c. Favored treatment for British companies competing with colonial businesses.
  3. Colonial resistance to British mercantilist policies led to The American War of Independence.

D. The American Revolution.
  1. The **First Continental Congress** was organized in the colonies in 1774 in order to address strained relations with Mother Country.
  2. Fighting between colonists and British forces originated at **Lexington and Concord** on April 1775, initiating the American Revolutionary War.
  3. On July 4, 1776, the **Second Continental Congress** adopted the **Declaration of Independence** written by Thomas Jefferson and other colonists:
     a. Drew on the writings of John Locke's *Second Treatise of Civil Government*, and Scottish theorists.
     b. The first section of document asserts the **natural rights** of man, including the **right to revolution**, and the belief that government derives its powers from the people
     c. The second part listed the alleged crimes perpetuated by George III and parliament against the colonists.
  4. Although faced with a superior foe, American colonists possessed certain advantages:
     a. Leadership of General George Washington
     b. Familiarity with native topography
     c. French assistance especially in the form of forces and materials
  5. War ended in 1781 with British surrender at Yorktown, followed by recognition of American independence from England, at the Treaty of Paris.

    E. The Articles of Confederation Government
- **1.** On March 1781 the thirteen original colonies became states, and adopted the **Articles of Confederation and Perpetual Union**.
- **2.** The first government for the newly independent states—**a confederate system**—concentrated power in the individual states, while providing for a weak central government.
- **3.** The newly established government was called the **Congress of the Confederation**, and included the following:
  - **a.** A unicameral congress which lacked power to raise troops or levy taxes.
  - **b.** Congress had complete control over foreign affairs and some degree of authority over interstate commerce.
  - **c.** "Ambassadors" for each state cast one vote.
  - **d.** President had no executive power, serving only in a ceremonial capacity as the presiding officer.
  - **e.** Centralized all power within the states, each retaining their "sovereignty", and sole power to tax and to regulate interstate commerce.

II   Problems Faced by the New Country

A. Framework of the government established under the Articles of Confederation failed to meet the needs of the new nation, which encountered many problems:
- **1.** Continued presence of British troops.
- **2.** Border problems with Spain in the south.
- **3.** Separatist movements within the states.
- **4.** Economic depression caused by large trade imbalance and war debt.
- **5.** Property foreclosures, rioting and armed rebellion.
- **6.** A government lacking power to confront domestic and foreign problems.

B. Shays Rebellion served as catalyst for change.
- **1.** Disaffected farmers, led by Daniel Shay and 2,000 farmers attempted to prevent foreclosures.
- **2.** Rebellion demonstrated need for a new constitution and government.

C. Constitutional Convention was called in Philadelphia in 1787, "for the sole and express purpose of revising the Articles".
- **1.** All states with the exception of Rhode Island sent delegates.
- **2.** George Washington served as presiding officer.
- **3.** Conflict arose from degree of power the central government should possess, specific powers it should claim, and how it should be structured.
  - **a.** Many advocated the creation of a strong central government.
  - **b.** States' rights advocates favored a system where the states remained powerful and influential.
- **4.** Issues of representation and degree of influence in the congress arose between large and small states.
- **5.** Inclusion of slaves in population count to determine amount of representation in House of Representatives was questioned and debated between slave-owning states and free states.
- **6.** Philosophical issues over slavery between free and slave states also emerged.
- **7.** Issues of interstate commerce and the tariff defined lines between north and south.
- **8.** A series of compromises paved way for new constitution and government

III   United States Government Under the New Constitution

A. A federal system was adopted. The national government structure is organized into three branches:
- **1.** Legislature
- **2.** Executive
- **3.** Judiciary

B. The legislative branch consists of two houses of Congress, the House of Representative and the Senate.
  1. Congress retained the powers it held under Articles, and acquired new powers:
      a. The power to levy and collect taxes
      b. To regulate foreign and interstate commerce
      c. "Make all laws which shall be necessary and proper for carrying into execution the foregoing powers", referred to as the **"elastic clause"**
      d. Power to call in the militia to execute laws of the Union, suppress insurrections and to repel invasions
  2. Representation in the House of Representatives was to be determined by population:
      a. Based on a federal population census, each state was allowed one representative for every thirty thousand, and also guaranteed that every state would have at least one representative.
      b. Conflict over inclusion of slaves as part of population led to the **"three-fifths compromise"**
      c. Representatives would be elected by direct popular election and serve for two-year terms
  3. Representation in the Senate provided that every state would have two senators:
      a. Initially chosen by state legislatures for six year terms, the Seventeenth Amendment to the Constitution ratified in 1913, calls for their direct election
      b. Powers delegated to the Senate include approval of presidential appointments, and treaties

C. Executive is titled the "President"
  1. Created an **Electoral College** to elect the president, thus removing power of direct election from the people and Congress.
  2. Constitution delegates specific powers to the President:
      a. Serves as commander in chief of the armed forces
      b. Power to make treaties with foreign powers, requiring a two-thirds vote of Senate for final approval
      c. Appoints ambassadors, ministers, consuls and judges for federal courts, with consent of the Senate
      d. Power to **veto** bills passed by Congress, which a two-thirds vote by both houses of Congress can override

D. The Judiciary consists of the Supreme Court, the highest court in the land empowered to interpret the Constitution:
  1. Court assumed the power of **judicial review**, used to declare legislative or presidential acts unconstitutional, in *Marbury v. Madison*
  2. Supreme Court justices are appointed by the president and serve for life.

E. When compared with other forms of government present at that time, the American constitution contained many radical features:
  1. **Separation of Powers:**
      a. Three branches of the national government possess powers exclusive of each other, and members assume power by different routes
      b. Power was diffused to prevent tyranny; no one branch can exercise more authority than the others
  2. **Checks and Balances:**
      a. Prevents one branch of the federal government from assuming power that cancels out effectiveness or independence of other branches.
      b. Senate can check the President via its power to approve appointments and treaties
      c. President can check the Senate and House by vetoing their bills
      d. Judiciary can check the other two branches via its power to declare a Congressional act unconstitutional, or direct a President to comply with a legitimate demand from Congress
  3. **Federalism** provides for a division of power between the national government and the states. The Constitution outlined two kinds of powers for the national government:
      a. **Delegated powers**—expressly granted to the national government by the Constitution
      b. **Implied powers**—not expressly stated in the Constitution; can only be inferred and are based on the "elastic clause"
      c. All other powers belong to the states (as stated in the Tenth amendment in the Bill of Rights)

4. Constitution grants the national government additional power from two other sources:
   a. The **Supreme Law of the Land** clause which requires states to conform to national law when conflict exists between a state or states and the national government
   b. The Interstate Commerce clause which gives the national government the power to regulate commerce or travel among the states
5. Process for Amendments:
   a. Constitution can be changed by the passage of a law by two-thirds vote containing proposed amendment, and its ratification by three-quarters of the states
   b. Second method which has never been used, calls for a two-thirds of the states to call for a convention for the purpose of amending Constitution

F. Ratification of the Constitution
   1. Main opponents to the Constitution were called **anti-Federalists**:
      a. Disliked the loss of power by the states
      b. Protested lack of written guarantees of the basic rights of citizens
   2. Supporters of the Constitution were called **Federalists**, and wrote a series of essays called *The Federalist Papers*, calling for its adoption.
   3. Many states agreed to ratify the Constitution only after **The Bill of Rights**, the first ten amendments were added.

IV Other Democratic Government Models

A. The United Kingdom of Great Britain and Northern Ireland possesses a **Parliamentary Democracy** form of government. Significant features include:
   1. **Executive Branch** of government consisting of the **Prime Minister** and the **Cabinet**; they are not elected through direct voting.
   2. The **House of Commons** is directly elected, and holds all power and authority in the British political system:
      a. The political party that wins the majority in the "Commons" becomes the party of the executive branch of government
      b. The party leader becomes the Prime Minister and selects the members of cabinet
      c. Prime Minister can serve an unlimited number of terms as long as the party retains a majority in Parliament
      d. Prime Minister can dissolve Parliament and call for a new election whenever he or she is given a "no confidence" vote and has no Parliamentary majority
   3. **House of Lords** is not elected; membership is determined by heredity, and it functions as an advisory body to the "Lower House"—Commons.
   4. Great Britain is a **"constitutional monarchy,"** although it does not have a written constitution. Its "unwritten constitution" is based on:
      a. Statutory laws
      b. Common law
      c. Customs and traditions
   5. The reigning monarch holds no power; serves in a ceremonial capacity and is considered the Head of State, while the Prime Minister is the Head of Government (in the US system the President serves in both capacities).
   6. The British system is **unitary**; all powers are fused at the national level.
   7. Elections take place at flexible intervals within a period of five years.
   8. The two principal political parties are the **Labor** and **Conservative parties**.

B. Japan also possesses a **Parliamentary Democratic** form of government, under a constitution written by Americans in 1947.

    1. For 268 years, Japan was ruled by a series of military dictators called shoguns.

    2. In 1854, the arrival of the United States exposed Japan to western trade and ideas, leading to the establishment of the imperial Meji government:

        a. The government's principal objective was the restoration of imperial authority and modernization of Japanese society

        b. Under the **Meji Constitution**, the emperor was supreme and accorded divine status, while the bicameral legislature—the **National Diet**, had limited power

        c. In reality, the military played an active political role, and by 1930 controlled the Diet and the throne

        d. In 1941 the Japanese bombed Pearl Harbor and brought the United States into World War II

    3. After Japan's defeat in World War II, the United States reconstructed and demilitarized the country:

        a. Although the country is a "constitutional monarchy", under the constitution of 1947, the emperor was stripped of all power and turned into a figurehead

        b. The constitution also renounced war and guaranteed that the Japanese would not keep an army

        c. The Japanese bicameral legislature—the **Diet**, consists of an upper chamber or **House of Councilors**, and a lower chamber, the **House of Representatives**

    4. House of Representatives holds the greatest power.

    5. The Prime minister is the chief executive officer and is chosen by the House as leader of the majority party, staying in power as long as he has the support of his party.

Review Section

Learning Objectives

After reading **Chapter Eight**, you should be able to:

1. Describe the forces that influenced the creation of the American government

2. Identify the problems faced by the Articles of Confederation government.

3. Describe the characteristics of the U.S. Constitution.

Key Terms

Define the following glossary terms to test your knowledge.

1. Articles of Confederation
2. Shay's Rebellion
3. Elastic Clause
4. Three-Fifth Compromise
5. Judicial Review
6. *Marbury v. Madison*
7. Separation of Powers
8. Checks and Balance
9. Federalism
10. Delegated Powers
11. Implied Power
12. Amendments
13. Federalists

14. Anti-Federalists

15. Bill of Rights

16. Electoral College

17. Veto

18. Supreme law of the land

19. Natural rights of man

20. Right to revolution

21. Second Continental Congress (1775)

22. Lexington and Concord

23. State's rights

24. Tenth Amendment

25. Seventeenth Amendment

Matching Terms

_____ **1.** Implied powers

_____ **2.** Separation of Powers

_____ **3.** Three-fifths Compromise

_____ **4.** Electoral College

_____ **5.** Checks and Balances

_____ **6.** Amendments

_____ **7.** Tenth Amendment

_____ **8.** Supreme Law of the Land

_____ **9.** State's rights

_____ **10.** Right of Revolution

A. Requires states to conform to national law when conflict exist between a state or states and the national government.

B. Provides for general protection for those rights not enumerated and for states' rights.

C. Process by which the Constitution can be changed.

D. Based on the elastic clause, they are not expressly stated in the Constitution, and are granted to the legislative branch.

E. Proposed by John Locke, this idea asserts that people have a right to rise up and overthrow an oppressive government.

F. A government system in which the state's remain strong and influential.

G. System by which the branches of the national government possess powers exclusive of each other.

H. Resolved the issue over the inclusion of slaves as part of the population to determine representation in the House.

I. Prevent any one branch of the federal government from assuming power that cancels out the effectiveness of the others.

J. Removes the power of direct of election of the president from the people and the Congress

Multiple Choice

1. The chief European influence on the development the American political system.
   a. England
   b. France
   c. Italy
   d. Spain

2. It was from this deliberative body that the Declaration of Independence emerged.
   a. Virginia Legislature
   b. House of Burgesses
   c. First Continental Congress
   d. Second Continental Congress

3. He authored *The Second Treatise of Civil Government.*
   a. Thomas Hobbes
   b. Jean-Jacques Rousseau
   c. John Locke
   d. Leo Trotsky

4. Under the Articles of Confederation the power of the government was:
   a. Shared by the states and national government.
   b. Concentrated at the state level
   c. Held by the Congress
   d. Was shared by the states, congress and judiciary

5. His rebellion helped catalyze the Constitutional Convention to revise the existing government.
   a. Patterson
   b. Shays
   c. Fremont
   d. Adams

6. The famed "elastic clause" applies to which branch of government?
   a. Legislative
   b. Executive
   c. Judicial
   d. State

7. In the case *Marbury v. Madison*, the Supreme Court assumed the power of :
   a. Passing Legislation
   b. Administrative Review
   c. Judicial Review
   d. Promulgating Doctrine

8. The division of power between the states and the central government is called:
   a. Checks and balances
   b. Federalism
   c. States-rights
   d. Judicial fiat

9. Many states agreed to ratify the Constitution only after they were assured that the basic rights of the citizenry would be protected. This was accomplished by adding the first ten amendments to the Constitution known as:
   a. Judicial Review
   b. Supreme law of the land clause
   c. Elastic Clause
   d. The Bill of Rights

10. Opponents of the new Constitutions were called:
    a. Federalists
    b. Anti-Federalists
    c. Constitutionalists
    d. Anti-Constitutionalists

11. Under the Constitution the _____ is commander in chief of the armed forces.
    a. President
    b. Vice President
    c. Secretary of State
    d. Secretary of Defense

12. The number of members that a state claims in the House of Representatives is based on:
    a. Population
    b. Geography
    c. Wealth
    d. Its industrial base

13. The weakness of the Articles of Confederation government stemmed from the fact that it did not have the power of:
    a. Printing money
    b. Direct taxation
    c. Interstate regulation
    d. Control over foreign affairs

14. In the British Parliamentary System, the Prime Minister is:
    a. The oldest member of the House of Lords
    b. Appointed by the Monarch
    c. The leader of the majority party in power
    d. A member of the English Aristocracy

15. Under Japan's current constitution:
    a. The Emperor is the supreme ruler
    b. The Prime Minister is the Head of the Government
    c. The monarchy has been abolished
    d. Power is shared by the monarchy and the Parliament

True and False Statements

Indicate if the following statements are True (T), or False (F).

_____   1.   The United States was created in 1781 out of fourteen original states.

_____   2.   Judicial review is used to declare legislative and presidential acts unconstitutional

_____   3.   Delegated powers are expressly granted to the national government

_____   4.   The United States has a parliamentary government

_____   5.   Amending the Constitution of the United States is easy.

_____   6.   The Constitutional Convention at Philadelphia in 1787 was called by Congress for the avowed purpose of revising the Articles of Confederation.

_____   7.   The power to veto bills signed by the President is granted to the legislature.

_____   8.   Amendments to the U.S. Constitution require ratification by two-thirds of the states.

_____   9.   Under the British system of government, the Prime Minister can dissolve Parliament and call for a new election.

_____   10.   Under Meji Constitution, the emperor was removed from power and the National Diet had supreme power.

Essays

1. Identify the problems faced by the Articles of Confederation government, and discuss the measures taken to solve them.

2. Describe the structure of the United States national government as outlined in the Constitution, and explain how power is distributed and checked among its three major branches.

3. Discuss the specific features of the form of government which is found in the United Kingdom of Great Britain and Northern Ireland, comparing it to the U.S. model.

Chapter 9—The American Political Process

CHAPTER OUTLINE

I Political Parties

A. The word politics is derived from an ancient Greek word polis, which meant a political community. It is also the root word for political party
   1. A **political party** is traditionally defined as a group of people organized for the purpose of selecting candidates for office, in order to influence policies, and conduct the business of government.
   2. Today they have assumed additional functions:
      a. Educate and help formulate public opinions on issues.
      b. Recruit and select leaders.
      c. Represent and integrate group interests.
      d. Control and direct government.
      e. Bring together opposing positions and convert them into legislation or policy.
      f. Bring together many groups whose interests vary significantly.
   3. In the two-party system that has developed in the United States, the minority party acts as a check on the majority party.

B. First political parties appeared in England in the Seventeenth century.
   1. Those that supported the monarchy and the Anglican Church were known as **Tories**.
   2. Those that favored a constitutional monarchy under a Protestant king were called **Whigs**.
   3. Whigs found their expression in the British Parliament, which was emerging as a strong rival to the monarchy.

C. Political parties were central to the American system of government from the beginning, but they were not mentioned in the constitution.
   1. Were originally opposed by many of the country's early leaders.
   2. Were inevitable with the rise of strong opposing viewpoints in the Congress.

D. By the 1796 election, two opposing voting blocs emerged:
   1. Alexander Hamilton, supporting a strong central government created the **Federalist Party**.
   2. Opposition party organized by James Madison was called the **Democratic-Republican Party**, and was labeled the party of the people.
   3. Federalists dominated the federal government during Washington and John Adams' presidencies (1789–1801).
   4. Jefferson's election in 1800 brought in domination by the Democratic-Republican Party.

E. A new era was begun with the election of Andrew Jackson to the presidency in 1824.
   1. The nation had a significantly larger electorate.
   2. Presidential electors were selected by popular vote.
   3. Presidential candidates campaigned nationally.
   4. The **Democratic-Republican Party** split into two factions after the disputed presidential election of 1824.
      a. Andrew Jackson's faction called itself the **Democrats**.
      b. The other faction took the name National Republicans.
   5. During the 1830s the National Republicans had evolved into the Whig Party which arose in opposition to Jackson's policies.

6. The Whigs supported Henry Clay's American System which sought to foster:
   a. National economic development through a protective tariff.
   b. A national bank.
   c. Federal aid for internal improvements.
   d. In the 1831 the party convention replaced the party caucus system, as the method of nominating the presidential candidate.

F. The forerunner of the present day **Republican Party** emerged in 1854 as conflicts arose regarding state's rights, slavery and widely divergent economic interests.
   1. Abraham Lincoln was elected as its first president.
   2. The party would dominate national politics until the 1930's.
   3. Political machines and party "bosses" would also dominate the political scene.
   4. The Democratic Party emerged dominant again during the Great Depression (1932–1939), under the leadership of Franklin D. Roosevelt and New Deal policies.

G. Today the United States is aligned around a two-party system: the **Democratic** and the **Republican** parties, as compared to other democracies that operate on the basis of a multi-party system.
   1. The two parties usually exhibit marked differences domestically, but usually support a bipartisan foreign policy.
      a. The **Democratic Party** has consistently invoked the help of the federal government to provide a wide array of social welfare programs, and tends to be more "liberal" on social issues.
      b. The **Republican Party** remains the organization oriented more toward business, low inflation and lower taxes, and less toward social welfare, and tends to be more "conservative" on social issues.
   2. **Third parties** have failed to experience pronounced and prolonged success in our system.
      a. The country has operated under a system of two major parties, broad and practical enough to include disparate groups and ideas.
      b. Election laws of most states make it difficult for new or small parties to gain place on the ballot.
      c. Process of electing the president—**the electoral college**—operates on a winner-takes-all basis for the candidate who receives the plurality of the popular vote in the state.

II   Interest or Pressure Groups

A. Organized political activity in the United States is also conducted through **interest groups**.
   1. They shape public opinion, and influence legislative and governmental opinion.
   2. Representing a vast array of causes and interests, they share certain characteristics:
      a. Are formally organized.
      b. Members tend to agree on same major points.
      c. Act through or upon government institutions to further their objectives and influence public policy.
      d. Use influence to propose new ideas, and to promote or block new legislation.
      e. Sometimes ensure that people sympathetic to their interests are placed in administrative or political positions.
   3. They represent a vital part of the political process:
      a. Become important for the advancement of many diverse interest
      b. Considered necessary to assist persons and groups with widely varying agendas and needs, in approaching different levels of government.

B. Origins: Every era in American history has seen interest groups bidding for governmental favors.
   1. During American Revolution groups pushed for independence.
   2. **Lobbyists** representing the case for groups swarmed all over Washington in the immediate post-Civil War era.
   3. Farmers and workers organized in late nineteenth century.

4. Early Twentieth century saw emergence of organizations such as the NAACP, Anti-Defamation League, American Medical Association and others.

5. Recent groups include citizens lobbies such as Common Cause, and environmentally-oriented organizations.

6. Electoral reform legislation enacted in 1974 led to creation of a new way of influencing government policy—**Political Action Committees (PACS)**

C. Interest Groups can be classified into three types.

  1. Business and occupational groups:

    a. Represent the economic interests of its membership.

    b. Include the National Association of Manufacturers, the American Bar Association (ABA), and the American Medical Association (AMA).

  2. Public interest groups:

    a. They focus on matters which affect the public in general and include Common Cause and Public Citizen among others.

  3. Social interest groups whose more special agenda might not be represented by above groups:

    a. Include the National Association for the Advancement of Colored People (NAACP), the National Organization of Women (NOW), and the National Rifle Association (NRA) among others.

  4. Success of all these groups depends on various factors, most significant of which are:

    a. Size and intensity of membership

    b. Financial resources, strategic alliances with other groups

    c. Media support

D. The Role of the Media.

  1. Political opinion is the set of views expressed by the community on the political issues of the day.

    a. The mass media-newspapers, radio, television, etc. can shape or influence popular opinion, thus possibly impacting political opinion.

    b. Media coverage is essential to support any attempt to affect the political process.

    c. Presentation of news by media can also be very biased

    d. Increasing reliance on polls, which instead of objectively identifying popular opinion might actually be creating it.

E. **Lobbying**—process by which interest groups seek to influence the government and its policy.

  1. Name emanates from tendency of influence seekers at the state legislature level to congregate in the "lobbies" near legislative chambers.

  2. Lobbyists are able to affect the fate of a piece of legislation at several "pressure points", as it proceeds through the various levels in the political system.

  3. Pressure or interest groups attempt to influence public policy decisions in several ways:

    a. Propose new ideas.

    b. Promote legislation or block new legislation from reaching the floor.

    c. Work to ensure that people sympathetic to their interest are placed in administrative programs.

    d. Contribute money to political campaigns.

  4. Lobbyists tend to be attorneys or employees of interests groups or consulting firms, or have previously held office.

F. The Power of the Supreme Court

  1. The American political process is also affected by decisions taken by the Supreme Court resulting from implementation of its power of judicial review.

  2. Concern has been raised that the Courts might be overstepping their constitutional role.

    a. Conservatives in general support a strict interpretation of the Constitution.

    b. Liberals support the Supreme Court's interpretations based on what the Constitution implies, in order to respond to rising needs.

III   Minorities and the Fight for Inclusion

A. Until recent times, many categories of Americans, were underrepresented or left out of the political process, and denied opportunities. Included in these groups are:
1. African-Americans.
2. Women.
3. Native Americans
4. Hispanics or other minorities.

B. African-Americans, first brought to the New World as slaves, constitute America's second largest minority group, making up slightly more than 12.3 percent of the population:
1. The defeat of the Confederacy in 1865, ended slavery.
2. Passage of the following amendments changed the legal status of the former slaves:
    a. **Thirteenth Amendment** ended and prohibited slavery
    b. **Fourteenth Amendment** provided full citizenship rights
    c. **Fifteenth Amendment** granted them the right to vote
3. With the help of Union soldiers, electoral officials, and Carpetbaggers, blacks voted in large numbers, and held important political offices at each level of government during Reconstruction until 1877.
4. Fifteen years after the end of Reconstruction, the era of **Jim Crow**, or racial segregation by law took hold in the South.
5. Most celebrated victory against segregation was the Supreme Court ruling in ***Brown v. Board of Education*** **(1954)**.
6. The Civil Rights movement of the 1950s, led by **Martin Luther King Jr**. and others led to the dismantling of the Jim Crow system in the South, and passage of important legislation:
    a. **Civil Rights Act of 1964**
    b. **Voting Rights Act of 1965**
7. In the 1960s through the Great Society's War on Poverty programs, the federal government expanded its social welfare and other federal assistance programs.
8. **Affirmative Action** programs designed to remedy the effects of past discrimination have been required by law for all governmental agencies as well as recipients of public funds.

C. Women, although numerically they are not a minority, nevertheless were long denied equal status in many critical areas of American life, and also benefited greatly from the Civil Rights movement.
1. Feminist activism reached a highpoint with a convention at Seneca Falls, New York in 1848.
2. Ratification of the **Nineteenth Amendment** in 1920 granted the suffrage to all women.
3. Another change in status for women came with their integration into the workforce during WWII, and the percentage increased markedly in the postwar years.
4. **The Equal Pay Act** passed in 1963, and gender was added to forms of discrimination outlawed by Civil Rights Act of 1964.
5. National Organization of Women (NOW) founded in 1966 was successful in having women included in the list of minority groups covered by federal affirmative action programs.
6. Failed to get ratification of the Equal Rights Amendment.
7. Despite legal advances, women still suffer salary discrimination, and are underrepresented in senior positions within corporate America.

D. **Native Americans** originally numbered about ten million when Europeans arrived in the New World.
1. According to the 2000 census, there were over 2 million Native Americans (Indians, Eskimos, and Aleuts), members of 400 tribes, and making up 0.9 percent of the population.
2. European governments and settlers practiced an unofficial policy of conquest towards native populations.

3. Until recent times government policy toward the Indian nations has:
   a. Treated them as foreign governments
   b. Segregated them by placing them on reservations
   c. Attempted to assimilate them into mainstream American society
   d. Relocated them to cities
   e. In the last generation has pursued a policy of self-determination, or "hands off".
4. In the 1970s, a new militancy among Native Americans emerged, led by the **American Indian Movement (AIM)**, which participated in takeovers of public lands and properties.
   a. Several Native American groups have emerged active in helping their people to regain control of their land, mineral, and other natural resources.
   b. Today, they possess their own tribal governments which serve as recognized political units of governments, and hold dual citizenship-American as well as in the tribe to which they belong.
5. Despite recent changes, America's oldest minority remains far behind in health, education and financial well being.

E. Asian-Americans characterized by enormous cultural diversity represent a the fastest growing segment of the US population.
1. According to the 2000 census they represent 3.6 percent of the total U.S. population.
2. The majority has emigrated from Southeast Asia and the Pacific Ocean region, and includes people of Chinese, Filipino, Asian Indian, Korean and Japanese ancestry.
3. Many have fled political upheaval and repressive regimes.
4. Education has been a main source of success for members of this group.

F. Hispanic Americans, defined as those with Spanish—speaking Spanish, or Spanish surnamed background, were predicted to become America's largest minority group in the United States by 2050.
1. According to the 2000 Census, this population is now America's largest minority group, about 13 percent of the population.
2. Although of Spanish speaking heritage, sharp differences exist between the three largest representative ethnic groups that include Mexican Americans, Puerto Ricans, and Cubans.
3. Mexican Americans constitute the largest group of Hispanic Americans, representing about 63 percent of the population.
   a. Migrating for primarily economic reasons, they are concentrated in the border states of California, Texas, New Mexico, Arizona and Colorado.
   b. They have struggled economically and educationally as poorly paid itinerant farm workers
   c. As increasing numbers of illegal immigrants arrive, a broad-based movement to restrict benefits, even legal ones, has developed in California and Texas
3. Puerto Ricans are United States citizens, currently representing almost 10% of the Hispanic population.
   a. They migrated primarily to New York since the 1950s in search of jobs, but have also settled in large urban centers like Miami.
   b. Lacking educational and professional skills, many live in poverty.
   c. The 2000 census data indicates that they are receiving college degrees in increasing numbers, are moving into high level jobs, and are becoming more involved in the political process.
4. Cuban Americans have been living in exile in the United States for decades, the most recent and largest group arriving after the Castro takeover in 1959.
   a. Largest numbers live in Miami
   b. Marked by a powerful work ethic, strong entrepreneurial background, and beneficiaries of invaluable assistance from the US government, their economic accomplishments in such a relatively short period of time, has set them apart from other immigrant groups

Review Section

Learning Objectives

After reading **Chapter Nine**, you should be able to:

1. Describe the role of political parties and of pressure or interest groups.

2. Elaborate on the struggle of African-Americans, women, Hispanics, and Native Americans to win recognition of their political rights.

3. Contrast the conservative and the liberal interpretations of how the Supreme Court should function.

Key Terms

Define the following glossary terms to test your knowledge.

1. Political Party

2. Interest Groups

3. Lobbyists

4. Political Action Committee

5. Thirteenth Amendment

6. Fourteen Amendment

7. Fifteenth Amendment

8. Jim Crow

9. *Brown v. Board of Education (1954)*

10. Martin Luther King Jr.

11. Civil Rights Act of 1964

12. Voting Rights Act of 1965

13. Affirmative Action

14. Nineteenth Amendment (1920)

15. Equal Rights Amendment

Multiple Choice

1. Chief author of the Constitution of the United States.
   a. Thomas Jefferson
   b. Benjamin Franklin
   c. James Madison
   d. James Monroe

2. First American political party was the:
   a. Federalist
   b. Democratic
   c. Republican
   d. Whigs

3. U.S government policy towards Native Americans has included:
   a. Segregation by placing them in reservations.
   b. Attempted to assimilate them into mainstream American society.
   c. A policy of self-determination
   d. all of the above

4. Dominant party in the South from the end of Reconstruction until recent times:
   a. Federalist
   b. Democratic
   c. Republican
   d. Federalist

5. Martin Luther King Jr., the great civil rights leader, gained national attention for the first time during the:
   a. Bombing of a black church in Birmingham
   b. Civil rights march in Selma
   c. March on Washington
   d. Montgomery bus boycott

6. *The Feminine Mystique,* considered to be the opening salvo of the contemporary women's rights movement was written by:
   a. Steinem
   b. Bolton
   c. Freidan
   d. Harris

7. The most successful immigrant group, economically speaking, in modern times in the United States:
   a. Mexicans
   b. Nicaraguans
   c. Nigerians
   d. Cubans

8. One of the highlights of the civil rights movement was the passage of this landmark piece of legislation in 1964:
   a. Civil Rights Act
   b. Voting Rights Act
   c. Open Housing Act
   d. Anti-lynching Law

9. Members of this immigrant group are sometimes called Chicanos:
   a. Nicaraguans
   b. Dominicans
   c. Mexicans
   d. Haitians

10. The **two** historical English political parties were the:
    a. Democrats
    b. Whigs
    c. Labor
    d. Tories

11. This Secretary of Treasury's program and personality was the catalyst for the formation of political factions, which led to the appearance of political parties:
    a. Madison
    b. Jefferson
    c. Hamilton
    d. Paine

12. This American President is closely linked to the New Deal:
    a. Roosevelt
    b. Wilson
    c. Truman
    d. Kennedy

13. Interests groups also known as _____, influence the course of legislation and other elements of public policy.
    a. Lobbying groups
    b. Referendum groups
    c. Political Action Committees
    d. Political Parties

14. This great Indian leader influenced the passive resistance policies of Martin Luther King Jr.:
    a. Nehru
    b. Gandhi
    c. Bhutto
    d. Singh

15. Her refusal to give up her seat on a crowded bus in Montgomery catalyzed that city's boycott:
    a. Parks
    b. Davis
    c. Connors
    d. Abernathy

Matching Terms

_____ 1.	Thirteenth Amendment	**A.** Were created as a result of the Electoral reform legislation enacted in 1974.
_____ 2.	Fourteenth Amendment	**B.** Program designed to remedy the effects of past discrimination.

_____ **3.**   Fifteenth Amendment   **C.** Group of people organized for the purpose of selecting candidates for office in order to influence policies and conduct business of government.

_____ **4.**   Nineteenth Amendment   **D.** Established racial segregation by law.

_____ **5.**   PACS   **E.** Prohibited racial or religious discrimination in public accommodations.

_____ **6.**   Emancipation Proclamation   **F.** Granted former slaves the right to vote

_____ **7.**   Civil Rights Act of 1964   **G.** A Native American based militant group that emerged in the 1970s and participated in the takeovers of public lands and properties.

_____ **8.**   Equal Pay Act 1963   **H.** Granted former slaves their freedom in the states that had joined the Confederacy.

_____ **9.**   Interest Groups   **I.** Granted women the right to vote.

_____ **10.**   Jim Crow Laws   **J.** Ended racial discrimination in Education.

_____ **11.**   AIM   **K.** Organizations that seek to influence public or governmental policy.

_____ **12.**   Affirmative Action   **L.** Organization that emerged in the 1960s to campaign for women's rights

_____ **13.**   Political Party   **M.** Provided full citizenship to former slaves.

_____ **14.**   NOW   **N.** Passed same year _the feminine mystique_ law was published.

_____ **15.**   _Brown v. Board of Education_   **O.** Legally ended and prohibited slavery in the United States.

True and False Statements

Indicate if the statements are True (T) or False (F).

_____ **1.**   Provision for the establishment and protection of political parties were described in the Constitution of the United States.

_____ **2.**   Third parties have historically been very strong in the United States.

_____ **3.**   Lobbying is a process by which interest groups seek to influence the government to enact favorable policies.

_____ **4.**   After the disputed election of 1824, Andrew Jackson and his followers separated from the Democratic-Republican Party to form the Republican Party.

_____ 5.   Unique among other groups in the United States, Native Americans hold dual citizenship, as U.S. citizens as well as in the tribe to which they belong.

_____ 6.   Puerto Ricans constitute the largest group of Hispanics in the United States.

_____ 7.   The mass media plays an important role in shaping or influencing popular opinion.

_____ 8.   Public interests groups focus their lobbying efforts on protecting the economic interests of the member and their concerns about the actions of the government or the economy in general.

_____ 9.   James Madison was among the staunchest supporter of political parties and interests groups, as indicated by his arguments in *Federalist 10*.

_____ 10.   The New Deal was able to weaken the hold of political machines over local and state policies by assuming many of the social welfare functions formerly provided by the boss or machine.

Essays

1. Describe the historical development of political parties and interests groups in the United States, and the current role each one plays in the American society.

2. Discuss the struggle carried out by minority groups in the United States in their fight to win recognition of their political rights.

Chapter 10—Global Prosperity and Poverty

CHAPTER OUTLINE

I Introduction

  A. Countries have been classified according to measurable standards in order to understand their complexity.

    1. The most current classification system is based on economic organization and economic output:

      a. At top are industrial developed countries with a large industrial base.

      b. Next are found the high-income oil exporting countries that have significant revenues per capita because of their energy resources but lack a sophisticated industrial base.

      c. Transitional countries are former communist countries, which are now trying to develop both democracy and capitalism.

      d. Poor, developing countries are the majority of the states of the world.

      e. The governments of communist countries have totalitarian control over their economies.

    2. A second type of classification system was used during the Cold War, focusing on communist vs. non-communist criteria:

      a. The **First World** included the capitalist, industrial democracies.

      b. The **Second World** consisted of communist countries.

      c. The **Third World** included the poor countries which were seen as a bloc between the First and Second worlds.

    3. This classification has been modified:

      a. The **Third World** includes those poor countries that have great potential to develop, with infrastructures and other resources in place.

      b. **Fourth World** countries have some potential to develop.

      c. The **Fifth World** includes countries with little to no potential to develop.

II The Developed World (The First World)

  A. Terms used to define democratic and capitalist states which first moved from mass poverty to wealth.

    1. Usually includes the advanced industrialized democracies of the West.

    2. Japan is currently included in this category and may soon be joined by other Asian countries.

    3. The states of the First World were the first to move form mass poverty to wealth:

      a. Moved away from death, famine, hunger and disease.

      b. Moved towards literacy, education, privacy, individual choice, and democracy

  B. Causes of prosperity include specific conditions:

    1. Political stability.

    2. Free and dynamic merchant class.

    3. Technological and business innovations.

    4. High literacy.

    5. Capitalism or free enterprise.

    6. International trade.

    7. Government support of business.

    8. Commercial morality.

    9. Liberalism.

    10. Imperialism in some cases.

    11. Scientific enterprises.

C. Societies of Western Europe were the first to experience **modernization**.

    1. Their economic systems became more specialized as individuals concentrate on performing specific tasks.

    2. The major goal of entrepreneurs became the accumulation of profit.

    3. Societies develop more distinct social classes with clear positions and roles.

    4. Political power becomes more stratified and hierarchical.

    5. Science and technology achieve greater significance.

    6. Public education competes with private education.

    7. Public administration grows as professional bureaucrats or civil servants become more involved in the day-to-day operations of government.

D. Several modern theories provide alternative explanations of how the West grew rich.

    1. Science and innovation.

    2. Natural Resources.

    3. Economic greed.

    4. Exploitation.

    5. Slavery.

    6. Colonialism or imperialism.

E. Countries classified under the **Developed World** category share distinguishing characteristics:

    1. High GNP and energy use.

    2. Large secondary and tertiary sectors.

    3. Longer life expectancy.

    4. Lower infant mortality.

    5. Abundant food supply

    6. Materialistic pursuits.

III   The Transitional Countries (The Second World)

A. The term **Second World** was originally used to describe the communist countries and pro-Soviet allies:

    1. Soviet Union

    2. Mongolia

    3. China

    4. Eastern Europe and others

B. Since 1989 many of the communist states have abandoned totalitarian communism.

    1. Are moving toward democracy.

    2. Are moving toward free-market or mixed economies.

    3. Some are breaking apart:

        a. The Soviet Union ceased to exist, and the 15 republics are becoming independent states.

        b. Several provinces of the former Yugoslavia have also sought independence, leading to a series of civil wars.

        c. Czechoslovakia split into the Czech Republic and Slovakia.

    4. **Nationalism** seems to have replaced communism as the major organizing and integrating force in the region.

C. These former Second World countries shared several characteristics which are inhibiting their transition to a market economy:

1. Levels of production and investment were decided by the government.

2. Prices were set by state bureaucrats.

3. Capital and natural resources were owned by the government.

4. Currencies could not be converted.

5. Persistent budget deficits.

6. Lack of economic incentives for the population.

7. Government emphasis on military and industrial goods for defense.

8. Isolation led to lack of competition and innovation.

D. These countries are also currently facing problems further hampering the transition.

1. Failure to attract foreign investors because of high inflation.

2. Low quality products.

3. Unstable legal systems to protect foreign investments.

4. Organized crime.

IV Developing Countries (The Third World)

A. **"Third World"** term has always lacked precision.

1. Defined countries that were not in the First or Second World.

2. Also used for countries, which were considered neutral in the Cold War.

3. Was also used in the West to refer to countries receiving foreign aid.

B. While the majority of the population in these countries lives in poverty, and they receive foreign aid, countries under this category also have differences:

1. Differing degrees of poverty.

2. Diverse religious, racial, linguistic, ideological, political, social and economic characteristics.

3. Often also have very wealthy communities.

C. In 1965, the leaders of several countries created the **Non-Aligned Movement**, in order to pursue a political line independent of the United States and Soviet Union.

1. Today there are over one hundred countries and organizations in the movement.

2. Their principal ideology is nationalism.

D. The Group of 77 (now 122) are a bloc of poor countries within the United Nations.

1. In the 1950s and 1960s the group was concerned with political issues, in particular sovereignty issues and the Cold War.

2. In the 1970s their focus shifted to issues of economic development:

a. Seek more favorable trade relations.

b. Want more economic assistance such as foreign aid from the developed world.

3. In the 1990s became concerned with attracting capital investment from the developed world and with expanding its exports to the rich countries.

E. Although all developing countries are poor, they also have degrees of poverty and often have very wealthy communities in their midst. For these reasons scholars have divided the Third World into:

1. Oil exporting developing countries.

2. Advanced countries.

3. Low-income developing countries

F. Characteristics of the **developing world** include:

1. Low GNP and energy use.

2. Large primary sector.

    3. Low life expectancy.
    4. High infant mortality.
    5. Low literacy rate.
    6. Exclusion of women from major economic and political activities.
    7. Reliance on exports of raw materials.
    8. A culture generally resistant to change.
    9. Dependence on the import of more expensive finished goods.
    10. High unemployment and poverty

V   The Causes of Poverty

A. The causes of poverty include internal factors:
    1. A culture opposed to change and to free individual enterprise.
    2. A culture that inhibits free scientific investigations.
    3. A physical geography tough on plants, animals and humans.
    4. Dictatorships and other authoritarian systems which can result in the following:
        a. cronyism
        b. paternalism
        c. corruption
        d. "brain" and "capital" drain
        e. political oppression
        f. discrimination against farmers and small entrepreneurs
    5. Tribalism and violence.
    6. Envy.
    7. Militarism, nationalism and war.
    8. Excessive population in some cases.
    9. Depletion of natural resources.

B. The causes of poverty can include external factors:
    1. Imperialism in some cases.
    2. Unstable international market forces.
    3. Foreign aid in some cases:
        a. Strengthens dictators
        b. Leads to massive foreign debts.
        c. Politicizes economic life

VI   Foreign Aid

A. **Foreign aid** is the transfer of taxpayers' money to distant governments and to official organizations. Arguments for foreign aid include:
    1. Without it countries cannot progress at a reasonable rate.
    2. It relieves poverty.
    3. Would reduce interest costs incurred by countries when they borrow from commercial private institutions.
    4. The West is paying for previous injustices it committed against the developing world.
    5. Assistance to poor countries will increase their economic growth and purchasing power.

B. Arguments against foreign aid state:
    1. It helps to politicize economic life by increasing the power of the rulers in the poor world, and by establishing too many vested interests.
    2. It allows governments to implement policies that retard growth.

C. Recommendations for improving foreign aid include:
   1. Aid should be given directly to specific projects that have appropriate budgetary controls.
   2. Soft loans could be replaced by outright grants.
   3. Direct grants should be made from the donor country to the recipient state, not through multilateral financial organizations.
   4. Should be given only to democratic and free market systems
   5. Use humanitarian voluntary agencies that are not politicized charities for poverty relief.
   6. Limit official aid mostly to meet unforeseeable and exceptional disasters

VII The Road Out of Poverty

A. Developing countries must engage in certain activities and practices in order to progress economically.
   1. Must increase their production and employment by finding markets for their goods and services.
   2. Increase productivity in their use of "all of their resources".
   3. Export what they can and stimulate both foreign and domestic investments.
   4. Investors must have confidence in the overall political and financial conditions of the country.
   5. Improve the technical, educational and health standards of the population.
   6. Encourage private entrepreneurs to open up businesses, and to limit state controls over investments.

B. There is a need for order that comes in many forms:
   1. Physical order.
   2. Political order.
   3. Financial and economic order.
   4. Spiritual order.

C. There is a need to develop and attract capital, which also comes in many forms:
   1. Physical capital.
   2. Financial capital.
   3. Human capital.
   4. Social capital.

Review Section

Learning Objectives

After reading **Chapter Ten**, you should be able to:

1. Explain what is meant by Developed world.

2. Enumerate the causes of the developed world's prosperity.

3. Discuss how the Second World became the "Transitional World"

4. Enumerate the characteristics of developing countries.

5. Identify the causes of the poverty of the poor, developing Third World.

6. List the arguments for and against foreign aid.

7. Discuss how developing countries can move away from poverty.

Key Terms

Define the following glossary terms to test your knowledge.

1. Developed World

2. First World

3. Second World

4. Developing World

5. Third World

6. Imperialism

7. Tribalism

8. Foreign Aid

9. Physical Capital

10. Financial Capital

11. Human Capital

12. Social Capital

13. Physical Order

14. Political Order

15. Modernization

Multiple Choice

1. This category includes the advanced industrialized democracies.
   a. First World
   b. Transitional world
   c. Third World
   d. Fourth World

2. A necessary historical condition needed by Europe to begin its economic growth in the 1200s and 1300s was:
   a. Science
   b. Technology
   c. Political Stability
   d. Merchants

3. The most important group in the economic growth of Europe in the early modern period was the:
   a. Mongols
   b. Military
   c. Scientists
   d. Merchants

4. All of the following characteristics apply to the developing world **except**:
    a. Low Infant Mortality Rate
    b. Short Life Expectancy
    c. High rate of population younger than 15 years of age.
    d. Exclusion of women from many advanced economic, political and educational activities.

5. The Developed world was the first to experience this condition:
    a. Humanism
    b. Imperialism
    c. Modernization
    d. Civilization

6. This was the term used to describe the Communist countries during the Cold War:
    a. First World
    b. Second World
    c. Third World
    d. Fourth World

7. This is a name often used to describe poor or developing countries:
    a. First World
    b. Second World
    c. Third World
    d. Fourth World

8. This group represents the poor countries at the United Nations:
    a. Group of 7
    b. Group of 77
    c. The Group of 122
    d. The group of 45

9. This is loyalty and devotion to a group, exalting it above all others and promoting its political interests.
    a. Ethnocentrism
    b. Imperialism
    c. Nationalism
    d. All of the above

10. Which of the following is a characteristic of the developed world?
    a. High infant mortality Rate
    b. High Energy Use
    c. Low Life Expectancy
    d. Traditional economies

11. This category includes countries with almost no chance to develop economically.
    a. Second World
    b. Third World
    c. Fourth World
    d. Fifth World

12. The poor world in general employs most of its workers in this sector:
   a. Primary
   b. Secondary
   c. Tertiary
   d. Quaternary

13. Developing countries tend to have authoritarian governments which often exhibit:
   a. Paternalism
   b. Nepotism
   c. Cronyism
   d. All of the above

14. Arguments in support of foreign aid include:
   a. It allows governments to implement policies which retard growth.
   b. It will increase the economic growth and purchasing power of poor countries
   c. It helps to politicize economic life by increasing the power of the rulers in the poor world.
   d. Promotes growth of a public bureaucracy.

15. Colonialism and exploitation have been used to explain:
   a. Why developed countries grew rich.
   b. Why the developing world experiences so much poverty
   c. Why the Second World countries became communist
   d. Both a and b.

True and False Statements

Indicate if the following statements are True (T) or False (F).

_____ **1.**   The east-west layout of the mountains of Western Europe has served a positive geographic characteristic because it allows some countries to benefit from a mild and humid climate which permits abundant agriculture.

_____ **2.**   Physical capital refers to machines and buildings needed to make other goods and provide services.

_____ **3.**   Foreign aid has greatly benefited the poor in receiving countries.

_____ **4.**   The Non-Aligned Movement was created in 1965 to help countries break free of their colonial situations.

_____ **5.**   Some supporters of giving foreign aid believe that it should be only given to democratic and free market systems where accounting and political mechanisms exist to minimize corruption.

_____ **6.**   There is no one main reason for the prosperity and poverty of countries.

_____ **7.**   An examination of the development of the world's developed countries demonstrates that foreign aid is necessary for economic development.

_____ 8. One means of combating tribalism may be the establishment of central authority in a nation, which might lead to the formation of nationalism and social cohesiveness.

_____ 9. A review of the poor and rich countries of the world indicates that poverty and overpopulation always go hand in hand.

_____10. Fifteen republics made up the Commonwealth of Independent States after the breakup of the Soviet Union.

Essays

1. Explain what is meant by the terms First, Second, and Third world, and discuss their origins. Include in your discussion the problems related to applying these terms, and the new categories that have emerged.

2. Describe the causes of poverty in the developing Third World, and discuss the arguments for and against foreign aid.

Chapter 11—The Global Economy

CHAPTER OUTLINE

I Trade

A. The world economy encompasses all those interactions that occur among people, businesses, governments and other institutions across international borders.

1. **Globalization** is the process by which the economies of the world become more interdependent and interconnected.

2. Four major forces fuel it:
   a. Trade.
   b. Investments by multinational corporations.
   c. Technology.
   d. International finance.

B. **Trade** is based on the concept that goods can be made better and cheaper by someone else.

1. Countries often have an **absolute advantage** in trade due to the nature of their economic resources.

2. All states should follow their **comparative advantage**, specialize in the production of those goods in which they have a relatively higher efficiency.
   a. Comparative advantage could be based on access to natural resources, good climate, low-wage costs, skilled labor, adequate technologies, location, capital resources, and low transportation costs.
   b. Consumers benefit.
   c. Economy as a whole also benefits by exposing domestic producers to competition.
   d. The United States has a comparative advantage in capital goods, but imports industrial supplies and consumer goods.

3. Consumers benefit by having access to cheaper goods as countries with few trade barriers trade with each other.
   a. Made possible by the **specialization of labor**.
   b. By **economies of scale**.

4. Trade also benefits the economy as a whole.
   a. Exposes domestic producers to competition.
   b. Forces them to be more innovative and efficient, and to lower prices.
   c. Consumers have access to a wider variety of goods at more reasonable prices.

5. A major disadvantage of a highly integrated global economy is dependency on the goods and services produced elsewhere.

C. Four major types of foreign transactions are:

1. **Merchandise trade**—the buying and selling of tangible goods.
2. **Services**—intangible non-transferable economic goods.
3. **Investments**—real capital formation such as the production of machinery.
4. **Unilateral transfers**—payments abroad for which nothing was received such as foreign aid and grants.

D. Accounting Terms for foreign transactions:

1. **Merchandise trade balance** is the narrowest measure of a country's trade and includes only visible goods.
2. **Current account** includes a country's exports and imports of services in addition to its visible trade.

3. **Capital account** is made up of the inward and outward flow of money for investment and international grants and loans.
4. **Balance of payments** is a tabulation of the credit and debit transactions of a country with foreign countries and international institutions.

E. **Foreign Investment** is a basic component of international trade, and is a result of **trade surpluses**.
  1. Countries that **export** more than they **import** have money available to invest in the world markets.
  2. States with **trade deficits** can benefit from foreign investment which creates jobs and promotes economic efficiency.
  3. Foreign competition can make domestic industries more efficient on international markets and stimulate more exports to close the trade imbalance.
  4. A **creditor nation** is a country with a balance of payment surplus, while a debtor nation is a country with a balance of payments deficit.

II   Money and Trade

A. Trade would be very difficult without **money.**
  1. It is a highly liquid financial asset that is generally accepted in exchange for goods and services and settling debts
  2. Represents value and serves as:
    a. A medium of exchange.
    b. Unit which can be stored to accumulate value.
    c. Unit of account.
  3. In the absence of reliable, stable money, international trade would have to rely on **barter**.

B. **Foreign currency** is usually needed to buy goods and services from another country.
  1. The money of another country is called the **foreign exchange**.
  2. Supply and demand conditions usually determine the value of a country's money.
    a. The price of another country's money in terms of one's own is called the **exchange rate**.
    b. A strong currency makes imports cheaper and exports more expensive.
    c. A weak currency makes imports more expensive and exports cheaper.
  3. International reserve currencies—**hard currencies**—are expected to retain their value, and therefore all countries are willing to accept them as final payment.
  4. **Floating exchange** rates are rates which are allowed to rise and fall according to the demand for a country's money.
  5. **Pegged or fixed exchange rates** are currencies for which the relative values are established by agreement.

C. **Exports** are the goods and services produced by one country, which are sold to another.
  1. Exports are vital to some industries.
  2. Sales that result from exports create an **export multiplier**.
  3. To increase exports:
    a. Design, produce and sell innovative products consumers want, at the lowest cost.
    b. Spend on research and development (R&D).
    c. Improve the economies of trade partners.
    d. Lower value of currency

D. Governments use their central banks to control the money supply and the credit system.
  1. Central banks exercise direction over **monetary policy** by adjusting the money supply in the economy.
  2. A **devaluation of money** has occurred when a country increases the supply of its currency.
  3. Devaluation results in a reduction of the rate at which one currency is exchanged for another.
  4. The Bank of International Settlements (BIS) located in Basel, Switzerland often serves as a central bank to the world's central banks.

III Budget Deficits and Trade Deficits

A. Budget deficits usually lead to trade deficits.
  1. A **budget deficit** is the amount by which the expenditures of a government exceed its revenue:
    a. Budget deficits lead to borrowing.
    b. Borrowing tends to raise interest rates.
    c. Higher interest rates attract foreign investors which in turn increases demand for money and the value of money.
    d. Stronger currency makes exports more expensive resulting in foreigners buying less money to pay for exports.
  2. A **trade deficit** is the amount by which a country's imports exceed it exports:
    a. When imports become less expensive and exports harder to sell on the world markets, countries begin to run trade deficits.
    b. It might encourage one country to buy another's bonds
    c. It might discourage buying if they do not trust a nation's capacity to pay their debt.
B. Governments often use the world's **capital markets** to borrow money by issuing bonds and other debt instruments.
  1. Capital markets bring together those with surplus money to invest or lend and those with a desire to borrow:
    a. The price borrowers pay is called its **interest rate**, determined by supply and demand.
    b. Capital in this sense, is **accumulated wealth**—as distinct from machinery and buildings.
    c. Allows them to raise funds at a lower cost than borrowing directly from banks.
  2. Consists of all those institutions that watch the supply and demand for long-term capital and capital gain, e.g. the stock exchange, banks and insurance companies.
  3. In developing countries, the absence of a capital market is an obstacle to growth of investment.

IV Mobility of Resources

A. Labor and capital mobility is the movement of labor, capital, and technology across national boundaries, motivated by political, socio-economic, or religious reasons.
  1. The movement of labor—**human resources** across territorial borders has several potential winners:
    a. Immigrants.
    b. Families of immigrants in home state.
    c. Social security system of host state.
    d. Government in home state.
    e. Businesses in host state.
    f. Welfare system in home state.
    g. Workers in home state.
    h. Host state acquires educated people.
  2. There are also potential losers:
    a. Poor people in host state.
    b. Local taxpayers in host state.
    c. Business in home state.
    d. Welfare and educational institutions in the host state.
    e. Capital and labor base in home state.
    f. Home state experiences a "**brain drain**"—loss of its best educated people.
B. Capital mobility involves the movement of capital across territorial borders:
  1. Official capital comes from governments, or through multilateral agencies as the International Monetary Fund (IMF) or World Bank.

2. **Private capital** comes from individuals and private business corporations in the form of :
   a. Short term exchange-rate movements.
   b. Long-term capital movements such as portfolio investments and direct investments.
3. Potential winners:
   a. Investors.
   b. World productivity/comparative advantage.
   c. Workers employed by incoming investment.
4. Potential losers:
   a. Investors losing capital.
   b. Workers unemployed by outgoing capital and by cheaper imports.
   c. Countries made unstable by fleeing capital.

C. **Multinational Corporations** (MNC) are enterprises operating in a number of countries and having production or service facilities outside the country of origin.
   1. They buy or build a subsidiary to produce goods globally and acquire certain benefits:
      a. Protect their proprietary technology.
      b. Take advantage of low labor costs and materials.
      c. Receive favorable tax conditions.
      d. Take advantage of comparative advantage in design and production.
   2. Before 1945 they specialized on primary sectors: oil, mining, and agriculture; after 1945, they began emphasizing manufacturing and high-tech products such as computers.
   3. Potential winners include:
      a. Host country receiving the investment.
      b. The MNC can improve its earnings.
      c. World economy as a whole gains from the effects of specialization of labor and production according to comparative advantage.
   4. Potential losers include:
      a. Workers in home country if MNC moves plant abroad.
      b. Home country can lose tax revenues.
      c. MNC can lose investments due to unstable conditions or natural disasters.
      d. Host country could be destabilized economically and politically.

V   Protectionism

A. Governments try to restrict imports with protectionist policies:
   1. Tariffs.
   2. Import quotas.
   3. Voluntary export restraints.
   4. Specification of product standards.
   5. Currency controls.
   6. Anti-dumping policies.

B. Reasons given for protectionism:
   1. Keep money in the domestic economy.
   2. Protect infant-industries.
   3. Protect national security industries.
   4. Protect jobs.

C. Problems with protectionism:
   1. Higher prices and taxes.
   2. Diminishes comparative advantage.

      3. Reduction in competitiveness.

      4. Political corruption.

      5. Retaliation (Trade Wars), which reduces exports.

D. There are potential winners and losers in protectionism.

    1. Potential winners include:

      a. Foreign consumers benefit when domestic producers lower prices to compete in their domestic market.

      b. Import-competing industries.

      c. Foreign producers under voluntary export restraint (VER).

    2. Potential losers include:

      a. Consumers.

      b. Domestic producers who need machinery or other resources from abroad.

      c. Most foreign producers.

      d. The economy as a whole since natural, labor and capital resources go to inefficient sectors.

E. The best rationale for protectionism is the **infant-industry** argument.

    1. New industries, particularly those in the developing world, tend to be competitively vulnerable, when compared to an established industry.

    2. Protection is necessary until an industry has reached its optimum size.

VI   Development Banks

A. **Regional development banks** provide development funds for needy countries.

    1. Large capital commitments and loans from the developed countries fund these institutions.

    2. Funds are loaned at a low rate of interest, and usually have a grace period of two to seven years before paying back the original principal.

    3. Examples of regional development banks include:

      a. Inter-American Development Bank

      b. Asian Development Bank

      c. African Development Bank

      d. European Bank for Reconstruction

      e. European Investment Bank

B. The International Bank for Reconstruction and Development (IBRD), also called the **World Bank**.

    1. Receives funds from its wealthy member countries which provide it credit to borrow cheaply on the world's capital markets.

    2. It then extends cheap development aid to the world's poor countries.

C. The **International Monetary Fund (IMF)** provides temporary funds for countries with severe economic difficulties.

    1. Often requires the receiving country to make difficult political and economic reforms.

    2. Measures can reduce the standard of living for the majority of the people, and represent a severe political cost to the government.

VII   Industrial and Trade Policies

A. Question has been raised if governments should pick from among its corporations to provide them with assistance.

    1. **Industrial policy** is an attempt by the government to shift allocation of resources into specific sectors to accelerate economic growth.

    2. **Trade policies** are particular government industrial policies with a focus on sectors that export.

3. Tools of trade policies used by government:
   a. **Export subsidies**—funds given to producers for every unit of a good exported.
   b. **Production subsidies**—funds for every unit of a good produced.
   c. **R& D subsidies**—funds for the research and development of technologies which can generate better products
   d. **Interest-free loans**—subsidies for businesses that borrow money to expand their exports.
   e. Tax breaks.

B. Problems associated with industrial and trade policies:
   1. Difficulty in picking industrial winners.
   2. Can lead to high taxes, prices, and inefficiencies.
   3. Political corruption.
   4. Reduction of comparative advantage.

C. A better solution might be for governments to stop interfering with economic production and concentrate on creating the preconditions for growth:
   1. Stable monetary policies and fiscal policies.
   2. Good legal, health and educational systems.
   3. Adequate infrastructure.
   4. Research and development funds.

VIII Pollution

A. Environmental pollution involves adding to the natural environment any substance or energy form at rates, which result in higher natural concentrations of that substance than normally exist.
   1. Includes many naturally occurring substances, as well as chemicals and substances introduced by humans.
   2. Can result from natural causes such as volcanoes, hurricanes, and earthquakes.
   3. Full cost of pollution is not being absorbed by the producers and consumers who profit from the production process that creates it.

B. Several methods have been proposed for controlling pollution:
   1. **Pollution tax** on units produced that created pollution, with revenues used only for cleaning purposes.
   2. Command and control measures where government sets up limits.
   3. Subsidies for pollution control equipment.
   4. Assigning of property rights granting business temporary ownership of resources, and responsibility for its maintenance.

C. Incremental costs in fighting pollution are not cost effective and become higher than their incremental benefits.
   1. Costs of fighting pollution include pollution taxes, cleanups, and more expensive production taxes.
   2. The benefits of pollution control which include lower death rates and diseases, more enjoyment of the environment, etc. are harder to identify.
   3. Concern for the environment is related to the level of a country's economic development:
      a. Poor countries are usually more concerned with meeting social and political needs.
      b. As countries prosper they become more concerned with environmental issues and some pollution declines.

IX   Trade Liberalization

A. It is an effort to make the economies of the world more interdependent, integrated and open, by promoting **free trade**—a policy of unrestricted trade among countries.

    1. Instruments of liberalization are several:

        a. Reduction of tariffs.

        b. Reduction of export subsides, except in agriculture.

        c. Reduction of protection for declining industries.

        d. Liberalization has been negotiated by the General Agreement of Tariffs and Trade (GATT).

        e. The World trade Organization (WTO) was created to arbitrate disputes and to replace GATT.

B. While tariff barriers have declined, the main threat to liberalization comes from non-tariff barriers which include:

    1. Quotas.

    2. Countervailing duties or fees.

    3. Voluntary export restraints.

    4. Customs restrictions.

    5. Product content specifications.

C. Another threat to the liberalized international trade system has been the growth of **regional trade blocs**—exclusive trade arrangements.

    1. There are different types of blocs:

        a. Free-trade area—NAFTA.

        b. Customs unions—MERCOSUR.

        c. Common Market—European Community.

        d. Economic Union—EUROLAND.

    2. Can provide certain benefits:

        a. Enlarge the market where corporations and companies can trade and increase competition.

        b. Promote economic innovation, productivity, economies of scale and comparative advantage.

        c. Can raise the level of investment and provide consumers with more choices at better prices.

        d. Reduce chances of protectionism among the member countries.

    3. Potential losses include:

        a. Governments of the member countries in the trade bloc lose revenue they collected on the tariffs.

        b. Trade diversion occurs if bloc reduces trade.

        c. Countries outside the bloc might retaliate.

D. In the debate between trade liberalization and regional trade blocs, the key issue is whether the **trade creation**—bloc increases trade—is greater than **trade diversion**.

X   **The Evolving World Economy**

A. There has been a dramatic increase in the flow of goods, services, technology and capital since the end of WWII in 1945.

B. Energy resources are at the core of the growth of the world economy, which is very dependent on them.

    1. Eight multinational corporations known as the majors led rise of the oil industry:

        a. Controlled close to 66% of world's oil production.

        b. Mutual cooperation restricted the supply and prevented price competition.

        c. Abundant supply of low priced oil facilitated the recovery of Western Europe and Japan.

        d. Stimulated consumers to use energy intensive products such as the automobile.

        e. Increased demand made it necessary to find and exploit new oil deposits.

    2. Creation of the **OPEC** (Organization of Petroleum Exporting Countries) cartel ended price stability of oil:

        a. Consists of primarily Arab states.

        b. Price of oil rose over 400%, and an oil embargo was placed on the United States and Netherlands.

        c. Action created a global financial and political disruption, and poverty in non-oil producing developing countries.

3. Second oil "shock" occurred in 1979 when Shiite Muslim fundamentalists came to power in Iran:
   a. Price of oil rose over 100%.
   b. Resulted in a major debt crisis in the poor world, and a major global economic recession.
4. Third oil "shock" occurred when Iraq invaded Kuwait in 1990 and prices rose another 150%.
5. Power of OPEC commodity cartel was made possible by several factors:
   a. Absence of energy alternatives in the face of global demand for oil.
   b. Growing dependence on cheap Middle-Eastern oil.
   c. Control of production and pricing policies was taken from multinational oil companies without retaliation from Western governments.
   d. Increase in competitive markets with the rise of independent oil companies.
   e. Oil cartel's willingness to use their oil as a political weapon.
6. OPEC might eventually dominate the global marketplace.
   a. Its share of world's oil production is up from 30% in 1985 to 40%.
   b. Seventy-five percent of world's proven oil reserves are in OPEC countries.
   c. Sixty percent of these reserves are in the Middle East.
   d. Importance is enhanced by decline of production among the non OPEC states

C. Existing oil reserves are only expected to last until 2035.
   1. Long before known reserves of oil disappear, demand will increase the cost of energy and undermine the global economy.
   2. It might also lead to development of alternative energy sources.
      a. Coal.
      b. Natural gas.
      c. Hydropower (water based).
      d. Nuclear Power.
   3. Other proposed alternatives include solar power, windpower, gasohol, tidal energy and fusion.

Review Section

Learning Objectives

After reading **Chapter Eleven**, you should be able to:

1. Explain why people trade, which are the four major types of foreign transactions, and how they are recorded.

2. Describe the role of money in international transactions.

3. Analyze the potential winners and losers in labor mobility or immigration and in capital mobility, particularly involving multinational corporations.

4. Discuss the advantages and disadvantages associated with protectionism.

Key Terms

Define the following glossary terms to test your knowledge.

1. Globalization

2. Trade

3. Investments

4. Technology

5. Comparative advantage

6. Merchandise trade

7. Money

8. Foreign exchange

9. Exchange rate

10. Floating Exchange rate

11. Fixed Exchange rate

12. Capital Markets

13. Labor Mobility

14. Capital mobility

15. Official capital

16. Private capital

17. Multinational corporations

18. Protectionism

19. Tariffs

20. Quotas

21. Industrial policies

22. Trade policies

23. Trade Liberalization

24. GATT

25. World Trade Organization

Multiple Choice

1. Economic interdependence and integration are processes associated with:
    a. Protectionism
    b. Absolute Advantage
    c. Globalization
    d. None of the above

2. This refers to countries producing what they can do most efficiently.
    a. Absolute Advantage
    b. Comparative Advantage
    c. Protectionism
    d. Industrial policies

3. This measure includes only visible trade goods.
    a. The Current Account
    b. The Capital Account
    c. The Balance of Payments
    d. The Merchandise Trade Balance

4. Foreign investment is a result of:
    a. Trade Deficits
    b. Balance of Payment Deficits
    c. Trade Surpluses
    d. None of the above

5. Exchange of one good for another.
    a. Barter
    b. Money
    c. Investment
    d. Services

6. The money of another country is called:
   a. Exchange Rate
   b. Independent Float
   c. Foreign Exchange
   d. Single-Currency Peg

7. This bank serves as a central bank to the world central banks.
   a. International Monetary Fund
   b. Bank of International Settlements
   c. World Bank
   d. Federal Reserve System

8. Budget deficits tend to lead to:
   a. Trade Surpluses
   b. Trade balances
   c. Trade deficits
   d. Trade blocs

9. They transfer money form those who have it to those who need it and are willing to pay a price to get it.
   a. Federal Reserve Board
   b. Capital Markets
   c. Wall Street
   d. None of the above

10. This is capital which comes from governments.
    a. Private Capital
    b. Portfolio Investments
    c. Official Capital
    d. All of the Above

11. These policies restrict imports.
    a. Protectionism
    b. Export Subsidies
    c. Industrial Policies
    d. All of the above

12. This is a tax on an import.
    a. Quotas
    b. Tariffs
    c. VER
    d. Subsidies

13. This is an attempt by the government to shift allocation of resources into specific sectors to accelerate economic growth.
    a. Industrial Policy
    b. Trade Policy
    c. Protectionism
    d. None of the above

14. This international organization was created to promote trade by limiting trade barriers and reducing import tariffs.
    a. NAFTA
    b. GATT
    c. MERCOSUR
    d. European Union

15. This is an oil cartel.
    a. GATT
    b. NAFTA
    c. OPEC
    d. Pemexl

True and False Statements

Indicate if the following statements are True (T) or False (F).

_____ 1.   In a free trade area, the member countries have common tariffs against the outside world.

_____ 2.   In a common market, the member countries might allow their workers and capital to move across their borders.

_____ 3.   Free-floating exchange rates respond mostly to the supply and the demand for money.

_____ 4.   Insurance, entertainment, tourism and transportation are all examples of merchandise goods.

_____ 5.   The current account measures international services.

_____ 6.   OPEC's members include all of the oil producing countries of the world.

_____ 7.   Protectionist policies tend to be expensive because consumers have to pay higher prices to protect domestic industries.

_____ 8.   The International Monetary Fund provides loans to countries that want to carry out special projects in their country such as to build a dam or irrigation system.

_____ 9.   Host countries always benefit from labor mobility.

_____10.   Having a strong dollar helps the American economy since it gradually increases exports, and guarantees that American companies do not move to another country.

Essays

1. Explain why countries practice protectionism, and discuss the various policies which countries carry out to protect their economies. What are the benefits and problems associated with this practice?

2. Discuss the importance of energy resources in the world's economy, and the growth of the oil industry. Include in your discussion the development of OPEC, and the direction that energy sources might take in the future.

Chapter 12—War and Peace

CHAPTER OUTLINE

I War

A. War consists of hostilities between states or within a state or territory undertaken by means of armed force.

  1. Level of hostility may range from **total war** with nuclear and other weapons of mass destruction, to **limited war** with conventional land, sea and air forces.

  2. Includes coercive diplomacy designed to provoke crises, low-intensity conflict, civil wars, and terrorism.

B. Since civilization began, there have been more years of war than of peace.

  1. Primitive wars were mostly feuds between families and clans; economic gain and political conquest were not major motives for war.

  2. **"Civilized"** war emerged when it became an institution conducted by a specialized group to plunder, acquire territory, trade and expand its culture:

   a. A variety of groups were united under the winner's culture and commercial and political territory.

   b. This type of universal state usually collapsed because of overcentralization, decay and high taxes.

  3. During the medieval period the Christian **Just War Theory** emerged:

   a. Used to justify war, this theory tried to set limits for justifying causes and methods of war.

   b. Contrasted with ancient belief that war is a necessity and a benefit to the state.

  4. In the modern period, **"raison d ètat" (reason of state)** became sufficient justification:

   a. Doctrine holds that security and national advantage are paramount considerations in state action.

   b. Moral principles, commitments and agreements should be disregarded if they conflict with state policies or action.

  5. In modern war, **propaganda**—communications aimed at influencing the thinking and emotions or actions of a group—is used in order to gain popular support.

II Types of War

A. Recent military history began with use of atomic weapons and development of other technologies, while still exhibiting some previous forms of war.

  1. Limited or **conventional warfare:**

   a. Is any war that is fought without the employment of all major weapons and for objectives other than the complete defeat of the enemy—**total warfare.**

   b. Makes use of military forces rather than atomic weapons.

  2. **Guerrilla warfare** is irregular warfare fought by small bands against an invading body, or in rebellion against a dominant government.

   a. Mainly fought in rural areas by indigenous elements.

   b. Is often one phase of broad political-economic-social and ideological revolution fought against an established order.

  3. **Terrorism** is a type of warfare that is mostly urban.

   a. Its objective is to increase the terror.

   b. Demoralize the civilian population.

   c. Force the government into tactical errors.

4. **Preventive war** sets out to defeat an enemy long before it can start a war.
5. **Preemptive war** attacks an enemy which is about to begin a war.
6. **Massive retaliation** uses the threat of nuclear attack to restrain the actions of another state:
   a. Is part of a policy of deterrence where states possess counterstrike capability.
   b. Created a "balance of terror" situation, exemplified by the Cold War period.

III   Causes of War

A. While some ancient thinkers believed war was rooted in personal motives, the modern view tends to see **structural forces** as the causes of war.
   1. **Human Factor Theory** of war considers that causes of war are found in human nature and behavior:
      a. Seven Deadly Sins tradition views sin as an evil that places humans in conflict with each other because of their pride, greed, envy, etc.
      b. Psychological explanations stress irrational human wants.
   2. **Domestic—Structural Theory** argues that defects in the internal organization of states—the many domestic or internal pressures—can lead to war:
      a. New states are more likely to start wars.
      b. **Nationalism**—accompanied by **ethnocentrism** and **xenophobia.**
      c. **Irredentism.**
      d. Religious and secular ideologies such as Islam, Fascism, Nazism and Communism.
      e. The profit motive of aggressive capitalism.
      f. A conscious decision by the political elite to unite the country against sedition, rebellion and civil wars—**scapegoat.**
      g. Justified in order to expand frontiers because of a need for land, wealth, security.
   3. **International-Structural Theory** contends that conflicts occur because of a defect in the international system when international institutions to prevent war do not exist:
      a. Weak legal system.
      b. Uneven distribution of power among countries.
      c. Inevitability of unpredictable changes.
      d. Force is a means to achieve external goals because there is no adequate process of reconciling the conflict of interest that arise.

IV   Causes of Peace

A. Peace is the absence of war or other hostilities, pursued by many strategies
   1. **Diplomacy** is the process by which countries carry on political relations with each other; it is the key technique used in the peaceful settlement of international disputes.
   2. Includes a policy-making foreign office, and an **embassy:**
      a. An ambassador is the top ranking diplomat sent by the government of a country as its official representative.
      b. Attachés are technical experts.
      c. Under international law, diplomatic officials enjoy Diplomatic privileges and immunities.
   3. Peaceful adjustment of international disputes can be addressed by several diplomatic techniques:
      a. **Conversations**—exchange of views by two or more governments
      b. **Negotiations**—a process in which explicit proposals are put forward for the purpose of reaching agreements
      c. **Good offices**—method by which a third party seeks to bring two disputing countries into agreement

    d. Mediation—a third party or country strives to solve a dispute by establishing the facts and by offering substantive suggestions

    e. Conciliation—a group of countries or other agents serves as a third party to help two antagonistic states negotiate their differences

    f. Arbitration—a method of settling a dispute between states by judges selected by the partners to the dispute

B. **Alliances** are associations of states to gain security or expansion, which function best when they face threats, and tend to collapse in their absence.

  1. Advantages include:

    a. Improve military capabilities and permit defense burden to be shared.

    b. Deter attacks.

    c. Created greater strength if attacked.

    d. Prevent an ally from joining another alliance.

  2. Disadvantages include:

    a. Reduce a country's capacity to make adjustments when conditions change.

    b. Limit the number of possible allies.

    c. Provoke fear in adversaries.

    d. Preserve existing rivalries.

    e. Entangle states in disputes with their allies enemies.

    f. Threaten enemies and motivate them to form counter-alliances.

    g. Forces states to control the behavior of others in the alliance lest they become too aggressive or try to defect.

C. **Balance of Power Theory** supports a system of shifting alliances, and contends that peace and security can be maintained when military power is distributed in such a way that no state can dominate others.

  1. Major premises include:

    a. Defense alliances need to form when one state is upsetting the equilibrium.

    b. Weakness invites attack.

    c. Countervailing power must be used to deter potential aggressors.

    d. Oppose any dominant coalition.

    e. Permit defeated Sates to reenter the system.

  2. Balance of power system works best under certain conditions:

    a. A sufficiently large number of relatively equal, independent states within a certain geographic area.

    b. A common political culture.

    c. The absence of a supranational organization which can interfere with necessary alliance shifting.

    d. Similarity in political systems.

    e. Accurate information about each state's capabilities.

    f. Technology which inhibits preemptive strikes.

D. **Collective Security** is an international order in which aggression by any country will be met by a collective response.

  1. Would replace a system of alliances and counter-alliances.

  2. Tries to inhibit war through the threat of collective action against any state or states that break the peace by committing aggression.

  3. **League of Nations** established in 1919.

    a. It was the first general international organization created to preserve peace and security.

    b. The U.S refused to join.

    c. It failed to prevent WWII.

4. The **United Nations** is a current international organization serving this purpose, though it is not entirely a collective security entity.

E. Disarmament and Arms Control

   1. **Disarmament** refers to the reduction or elimination of weapons with the ultimate end of eradicating war itself.
   2. **Arms control** refers to agreements to regulate arms levels by limiting their growth or restricting how they may be deployed.
   3. Both can take place through bilateral or multilateral agreements

F. Arms buildup is often preferred as a means of preventing wars by deterring potential aggressors.

   1. Can postpone or deter wars.
   2. Unless the causes of conflict are addressed the arms escalation will continue as will the possibility of war

G. **International law** is a body of rules and principles that guide the relations among countries and between governments and foreign nationals.

   1. Treaties and other forms of international agreements are the most important source of its development today.
   2. Private international law successfully regulates transnational contacts, and has a good record in settling transnational disputes.
   3. Public international law which addresses government-to-government relations is often unable to reduce tensions because of certain principles:
      a. Major principle of public international law is that of **state sovereignty**—no authority is legally above the state.
      b. Principle of **non-interference** requires that countries must refrain from uninvited involvement in another's internal affairs.
   4. Weaknesses include:
      a. States abide by only those regulations to which they voluntarily subscribe.
      b. States themselves determine rules and how they should be enforced.
      c. A supranational legislative body capable of making and amending norms does not exist.
      d. There is no executive body capable of enforcing the rules.
      e. Contemporary global order is culturally and ideologically pluralistic and lacks value-consensus.

H. International Organization and World Order.

   1. In addition to supporting international law, the creation of international organizations to facilitate peace among nations has been proposed.
   2. The United Nations created in 1945, accepted the principle of collective security, and also restored the principle of the balance of power.

V   The United Nations: A Case Study in International Organization

A. Origins of the United Nations can be traced to the failure of the League of Nations to prevent WWII.

   1. Representatives from various nations laid the groundwork for its creation by signing the **Inter-Allied Declaration** on June 12, 1941.
   2. During the Dumbarton Oaks Conference in Washington D.C. the first blueprint of the UN was prepared.
      a. United Nations Charter went into effect on October 24, 1945.
      b. Major idea behind the organization was to preserve peace through collective security, and to also address economic and social problems.
   3. Though broad in objectives and obligations, the United Nations Charter did not establish a world government.

B. Organization of the United Nations

    1. The **General Assembly** is the only major organ where all members are represented.

        a. Can discuss any issue and recommend actions by other UN departments.

        b. Each member has one vote.

        c. Can only make binding decisions regarding the budget; all others are suggestions.

        d. Plays a role in **peace-keeping operations** which can include the use of armed force, but they are not enforcement actions to combat aggression.

        e. Is responsible for the over-all supervision of UN activities.

    2. The **Security Council** has primary responsibility for the maintenance of international peace and security:

        a. Consists of 15 members: only 5 are permanent: China, France, Russia, United Kingdom and United States.

        b. The remaining ten are non-permanent members, voted by the General Council for two-year terms.

        c. **Veto power** is held by the 5 permanent members.

    3. Efforts to uphold international peace and security can take two general approaches:

        a. Peaceful settlement of disputes.

        b. Use of enforcement measures to protect or restore international peace and security.

        c. These measures include severance of diplomatic relations, economic embargoes, and military sanctions which include use of armed forces

    4. The **Secretariat** manages the day-to-day business of the UN by providing services to the organs:

        a. **Secretary-General** is the chief administrator of the UN, and its head and chief spokesperson.

        b. Is nominated by the Security Council and appointed by the General Assembly to a five-year term.

        c. Is responsible for UN's administration and performs diplomatic services.

        d. The current Secretary-General is Kofi Annan of Ghana, selected in 1997.

    5. **Economic and Social Council** (ECOSOC) coordinates the social, economic, cultural and humanitarian work of the UN.

        a. Its creation stemmed from the belief that international economic and social cooperation contributes to the cause of peace.

        b. Seeks to promote higher standards of living, better health, cultural and educational cooperation among countries and observance of human rights.

    6. **International Court of Justice/World Court**, seated at The Hague in the Netherlands, settles disputes between countries and provides advisory opinions to other organs of the UN.:

        a. Consist of fifteen judges representing different nations, and usually from each of the permanent states of the Security Council.

        b. Security Council and General Assembly may request from the court an advisory opinion on a legal question.

        c. Member states may submit a case for adjudication.

        d. All parties to a dispute must voluntarily agree to submit to it for judgment and must abide by its decision.

    7. **Trusteeship Council** was created to watch over and assist a number of small territories which were not self-governing at the end of WWII, become ready for independence.

        a. There were originally eleven such territories in Africa, Southwest Asia, and South Pacific.

        b. Many were colonies of the losing powers of WWII, Germany, Italy, and Japan.

        c. The last territory achieved independence in 1990.

    8. The United Nations also includes a group of specialized agencies.

        a. They are autonomous, have own charter, budget and staff, and specialize in certain areas.

        b. Includes such groups as the International Monetary Fund, the World Health Organization (WHO), and UNESCO.

B. Successes and Challenges facing the United Nations.

1. Demise of Article 43 prevented the United Nations from having enforcement powers to implement collective security. In response the organization has gradually expanded its activities and achieved many successes:

   a. The Secretariat went beyond fact-finding and observer forces, and created peace-keeping operations.

   b. Has also engaged in activities which did not threaten the geopolitical interests of the super powers such as human rights and refugee assistance .

   c. The UN was instrumental in ending the Iran-Iraq War, the withdrawal of Russian troops from Afghanistan, and the expulsion of Iraq from Kuwait, among others.

2. The organization also confronts serious challenges:

   a. A major problem is the use of the veto power in the Security Council which inhibits collective security.

   b. Many of the assumptions implicit in the concept of collective security have encountered difficulties in real world of competing states.

   c. Conflicts arising in the post-Cold War years require additional peacemaking and peacekeeping forces that budgetary restraints prevent.

   d. Attacks by many conservatives and isolationists in the United States Congress who are threatening to reduce financial support.

   e. Lacks a standing UN army.

C. The Future of the United Nations has been put in question.

1. Traditional diplomacy might be more effective.

2. Its potential role may be in addressing problems which are beyond an individual state's capacity to solve. Among many are included:

   a. Malnutrition.

   b. Human Rights.

   c. Illiteracy.

   d. Environmental degradations.

   e. Drug trafficking.

   f. International terrorism.

3. In order for the UN to tackle these problems reforms might be needed.

   a. Expanding the Security Council to increase its legitimacy.

   b. Restricting veto to only matters of war and peace.

   c. Reevaluating the current operations of ECOSOC.

   d. Revising budget practices.

   e. Closer collaboration with regional organizations.

D. USA out of the UN: It has been proposed that it would be in the best interests of the United States to withdraw from the organization, and collaborate in the creation of a new international entity. Reasons for this recommendation include:

1. The United Nations has become a threat to American national sovereignty as it now seeks to become a world government.

2. The Security Council includes three permanent members which are now using their veto power to undermine any preemptive/preventive policy by the United States.

3. The United Nations recognizes as members many dictatorships which violate its own Universal Declaration of Human Rights.

4. It has lost the capacity to distinguish between aggressors and victims.

5. The organization does not have a clean record in fighting terrorism since may of its members are terrorists states themselves.

6. The United Nations has a corrupt bureaucracy led mostly by Third World employees who tend to profess deep-seated anti-American feelings.

E. Regional collective self-defense organizations unite several countries against a common enemy.
   1. Have been more successful in limiting interstate wars than internal wars.
   2. Major examples include:
      a. NATO
      b. ANZUS Pact
      c. SEATO
      d. OAS
      e. OAU
      f. ASEAN

VI North Atlantic Treaty Organization (NATO): A Case Study in Collective Self-Defense

A. **NATO** was created in 1949 as a unified leadership for the common defense of Western Europe, primarily against Soviet expansion.
   1. Provided for the **collective defense** of the members against possible attack by any aggressor.
   2. The Soviet response was to establish the **Warsaw Pact** in 1955, creating a joint armed forces command in the Communist countries of Eastern Europe.

B. In response to the dissolution of the Soviet Union and the Warsaw Pact, the North Atlantic Cooperation Council was formed:
   1. Includes many former Warsaw Pact countries.
   2. Has reduced its supply of nuclear weapons by 80%.
   3. Has expanded peacekeeping assistance to non-NATO European countries.
   4. Under **Partnership for Peace** program has permitted non-NATO countries to participate in NATO military exercises and planning.

VII Political Integration

A. Proposals for **Political Integration** that seeks to create new political communities and supranational institutions that transcend states and control them include:
   1. **World Federalism** that recommends creation of a political union built at the regional or global level, modeled after the United States federal structure.
   2. **Functionalism** which is a bottom-up approach to promoting integration through transnational organizations
      a. Emphasize sharing sovereignty and building cooperative ties among states.
      b. Cooperation would begin in technical matters in social and economic areas such as medicine and science.
      c. States would not give up their national sovereignty
   3. **Neo-Functionalism** which seeks a federal world system.
      a. Proposes an increase in the size of economic markets.
      b. Calls for a reduction of trade barriers among several countries such as currently exists in the European Union

B. Success of integration depends on certain conditions which are not yet present in the Third World, such as:
   1. Geographical proximity.
   2. Steady economic growth.
   3. Similar political systems.

4. Supportive public opinion.

5. Political stability.

6. Common historical experiences.

7. Shared perception of a common threat.

8. Bureaucratic compatibility.

9. Previous collaborative activities.

VIII   Peace Showcase: OECD

A. The Organization for Economic Cooperation and Development.

    1. Was created in 1961 to promote economic and social welfare in the member countries, and to stimulate and harmonize efforts on behalf of developing countries.

    2. An ideal situation is a stable peace in which there is not only an absence of war, but also an absence of preparation for war or the serious expectation of war.

    3. A stable peace occurs when there is a shared sense that social problems must and can be resolved by a process of peaceful change.

B. Analysts do not agree on the causes of this stable peace, but hypothesis presented for the causes of OECD peace include:

    1. Cohesion in the face of an outside military threat, the Soviet Union, as the main element.

    2. Creation of such international institutions as the European Commission, the European Parliament, and the European Court of Justice which exercise legislative, executive and judicial functions, respectively.

    3. Economic ties and social communications led to peace in the OECD.

    4. Peace resulting from economic achievements and continued expectations of mutual economic rewards.

    5. Widespread acceptance in all countries of the values and institutions of constitutional democracy.

IX   Democracy in the Making

A. The ability to exercise constitutional democracy has been a major factor in the stable peace of the OECD countries, but the transition from autocracy to democracy can be very difficult.

    1. Violence increases as countries democratize for many reasons:

        a. Weakening governments prevent autocrats from dictating a consensus which can lead to order.

        b. Mass politics prevent the growth of coalitions which can bring diverse groups together.

        c. Fear of losing their economic and social status radicalizes previously dominant groups.

        d. Intense ideological propaganda manipulates and polarizes people.

    2. Young democracies have several needs that must be met in order to mature democratically.

        a. Time.

        b. The old elite must find a place in the new system, though in a much weaker political role.

        c. An independent, aggressive and fair press to disinflate the demagoguery of potential tyrants.

        d. Neighboring states need to create defensive alliances to increase deterrence and discourage war.

        e. Stable currencies.

        f. The international community needs to be help in matters of trade and technical assistance.

Review Section

Learning Objectives

After reading **Chapter Twelve,** you should be able to:

1. List the types of wars.

2. Discuss the causes of war.

3. Analyze the causes of peace.

4. Enumerate the peace-seeking techniques of diplomacy.

5. Describe the purpose, structure and activities of the United Nations.

Key Terms

Define the following glossary terms to test your knowledge:

1. War

2. The Just War

3. Raison d'etat

4. Conventional War

5. Guerilla War

6. Terrorism

7. Preventive War

8. Preemptive War

9. Massive Retaliation

10. Irredentism

11. Alliances

12. Diplomacy

13. Embassy

14. Conversations

15. Negotiations

16. Good Offices

17. Mediation

18. Conciliation

19. Arbitration

20. Balance of Power

21. Collective Security

22. Disarmament

23. Arms Control

24. United Nations

25. General Assembly

26. Security Council

27. Political Integration

28. World Federalism

29. Domestic-Structural Theory

30. International Structural Theory

Multiple Choice

1. A medieval theory which argued that not all killing is murder:
   a. The Just War
   b. The Theory of "Civilized" War
   c. The Machiavellian Prince
   d. None of the Above

2. The Seven Deadly Sins Tradition believes that the cause of war is:
   a. Political
   b. Structural
   c. Psychological
   d. Will-related

3. According to this theory, peace will result when military power is distributed in such a way that no state can dominate others.
   a. Collective Security
   b. Balance of Power
   c. International Law
   d. Political Integration

4. Under this international order aggression by any country will be met by a group response.
   a. Balance of Power
   b. Collective Security
   c. Bipolar System
   d. Multipolar System

5. This concept means that no authority is legally above the state, except that which the state might voluntarily confer on a supranational organization that it joins:
   a. Anarchy
   b. The Right to Intervention
   c. State Sovereignty
   d. None of the above

6. Since 1945, there has been no war among the member states of this organization, which have over 800 million inhabitants.
   a. Organization of African States
   b. Organization for Economic Cooperation and Development
   c. Organization of American States
   d. The United Nations

7. In this organ of the United Nations, every country has one vote.
   a. General Assembly
   b. Security Council
   c. Secretariat
   d. Economic and Security Council

8. This organ of the United Nations has five permanent member countries, each of which has veto power:
   a. Security Council
   b. ECOSOC
   c. General Assembly
   d. The Trusteeship Council

9. This organ of the United Nations is involved in providing economic, technical, and humanitarian assistance to poor countries:
   a. Security Council
   b. ECOSOC
   c. General Assembly
   d. The Trusteeship Council

10. This effort seeks to create new political communities and supranational institutions that transcend states and control them.
    a. International Law
    b. Alliances
    c. Political Integration
    d. Disarmament

11. Any type of war fought without the employment of all major weapons and for objectives other than the complete defeat of the enemy.
    a. Conventional war
    b. Preemptive war
    c. Preventive war
    d. None of the above

12. The threat of nuclear attack to restrain the actions of another state is called:
    a. Preemptive War
    b. Massive Retaliation
    c. Guerrilla Warfare
    d. Terrorism

13. This is urban warfare directed primarily against civilians:
    a. Tactical Warfare
    b. Guerilla Warfare
    c. Terrorism
    d. None of the above

14. Irregular warfare fought by small groups against an invading army or in rebellion against an established government is called.
    a. Terrorism
    b. Conventional Warfare
    c. United Warfare
    d. Guerilla Warfare

15. According to those who believe in the international-structural causes of war, the problem is:
    a. Human Wickedness
    b. International Anarchy
    c. International Depression
    d. Imperialism

Matching Terms

_____ 1.   League of Nations   **A.** An exaggerated fear or distrust of foreigners and of the policies and objectives of other countries.

_____ 2.   United Nations   **B.** Desire of the people of a state to annex those contiguous territories of another country that are inhabited largely by linguistic or cultural minorities of the first state.

_____ **3.** NATO   **C.** A body of rules and principles that guide the relations among countries and between governments and foreign nationals.

_____ **4.** OECD   **D.** Created for the purpose of preserving world peace through collective security, and to also address economic and social problems.

_____ **5.** Warsaw Pact   **E.** Process by which countries carry on political relations with one another.

_____ **6.** Alliances   **F.** Created at the end of WWI to preserve peace and security by establishing a collective security system.

_____ **7.** World Federalism   **G.** Agreements to regulate arms levels by limiting their growth or restricting how they may be developed.

_____ **8.** OAS   **H.** Arises from unique social and psychological factors to provide unity and inspiration to a specific people.

_____ **9.** International Law   **I.** Organized by the Soviet Union after WWII in order to create a joint armed forces command in the communist countries of Eastern Europe.

_____**10.** Nationalism   **J.** The reduction or elimination of weapons with the ultimate end of eradicating war itself.

_____**11.** Xenophobia   **K.** Created for the purpose of promoting economic and social welfare in the member countries, and to support developing countries.

_____**12.** Irredentism   **L.** Associations of states in order to gain security or expansion.

_____**13.** Diplomacy   **M.** Created after WWII in order to provide for the collective defense of Western Europe

_____**14.** Disarmament   **N.** Recommends the creation of a political union built at the regional or global level.

_____**15.** Arms Control   **O.** Example of a regional collective self-defense organization, involved in more than defense.

True and False Statements

Indicate if the following statements are True (T) or False (F).

_____ **1.** In negotiations there is an exchange of views between two or more governments which could lead to more complete negotiations.

_____ **2.** In "good offices", a third country seeks to bring two disputing countries into agreement.

_____**3.** In conversations explicit proposals are put forward for the purpose of reaching agreements between two countries.

_____**4.** Mediation is a diplomatic technique in which a third party or country strives to solve a dispute by establishing the facts and offering substantive suggestions.

_____**5.** In arbitration, a group of countries or other agents serve as a third party to help two antagonistic states negotiate their differences.

Essays

1. Describe the origins of the United Nations, and discuss the purpose, structure, and weaknesses of the organization. What solutions have been proposed to resolve the concerns that have been raised?

2. Describe the types of war, and discuss which are more likely to occur today. What is the role of diplomacy and what are the different techniques that are employed in diplomatic relations?

Answer Key

Chapter 1

Multiple Choice

1. a
2. b
3. d
4. c
5. b

True and False Statements

1. False
2. True
3. False
4. False
5. True

Matching Terms

1. c
2. d
3. i
4. e
5. a
6. f
7. j
8. h
9. b
10. g

Chapter 2

Matching Terms

1. d
2. a
3. g
4. e
5. h
6. i
7. c
8. j
9. b
10. f

Multiple Choice

1. b
2. a
3. b
4. c
5. a
6. c
7. b
8. d
9. c
10. b

True and False Statements

1. False
2. False
3. True
4. False
5. True

Matching People

1. i
2. d
3. f
4. j
5. h
6. e
7. b
8. c
9. g
10. a

Chapter 3

Multiple Choice

1. c
2. b
3. c
4. a
5. a
6. b
7. d
8. c
9. a
10. c
11. b
12. c
13. b
14. c
15. d

True and False Statements

1. False
2. True
3. False
4. False
5. True
6. True
7. False
8. False
9. True
10. True

Matching Terms

1. d
2. f
3. e
4. j
5. b
6. i
7. a
8. c
9. h
10. g

Chapter 4

Multiple Choice

1.	d	9.	d
2.	a	10.	b
3.	b	11.	a
4.	d	12.	d
5.	d	13.	d
6.	a	14.	b
7.	c	15.	b
8.	a		

True and False Statements

1. False
2. True
3. False
4. True
5. False

Chapter 5

Matching Terms

1.	f	6.	b
2.	g	7.	c
3.	j	8.	e
4.	i	9.	a
5.	h	10.	d

Multiple Choice

1.	b	6.	b
2.	d	7.	c
3.	c	8.	a
4.	a	9.	d
5.	d	10.	b

True and False Statements

1.	False	6.	False
2.	True	7.	True
3.	False	8.	False
4.	False	9.	True
5.	True	10.	False

Matching People

1.	h	6.	a
2.	f	7.	j
3.	i	8.	c
4.	b	9.	d
5.	g	10.	e

Chapter 6

Multiple Choice

1.	a	5.	d
2.	b	6.	a
3.	b	7.	b
4.	c	8.	d

True and False Statements

1.	True	4.	False
2.	True	5.	True
3.	True	6.	False

Chapter 7

Multiple Choice

1.	d	9.	b
2.	b	10.	d
3.	b	11.	c
4.	a	12.	b
5.	d	13.	a
6.	c	14.	d
7.	b	15.	b
8.	c		

True and False Statements

1.	False	6.	False
2.	True	7.	False
3.	False	8.	False
4.	False	9.	False
5.	True	10.	True

Matching Terms

1.	e	6.	j
2.	c	7.	a
3.	h	8.	b
4.	g	9.	f
5.	i	10.	d

Chapter 8

Matching Terms

1.	d	6.	c
2.	g	7.	b
3.	h	8.	a
4.	j	9.	f
5.	i	10.	e

Multiple Choice

1.	a	**9.**	d
2.	d	**10.**	b
3.	c	**11.**	a
4.	b	**12.**	a
5.	b	**13.**	b
6.	a	**14.**	c
7.	c	**15.**	b
8.	b		

True and False Statements

1.	False	**6.**	True
2.	True	**7.**	False
3.	True	**8.**	False
4.	False	**9.**	True
5.	False	**10.**	False

Chapter 9

Multiple Choice

1.	c	**9.**	c
2.	a	**10.**	b,d
3.	d	**11.**	c
4.	b	**12.**	a
5.	d	**13.**	a
6.	c	**14.**	b
7.	d	**15.**	a
8.	a		

Matching Terms

1.	o	**9.**	k
2.	m	**10.**	d
3.	f	**11.**	g
4.	i	**12.**	b
5.	a	**13.**	c
6.	h	**14.**	l
7.	e	**15.**	j
8.	n		

True and False Statements

1.	False	**6.**	False
2.	False	**7.**	True
3.	True	**8.**	False
4.	False	**9.**	False
5.	True	**10.**	True

Chapter 10

Multiple Choice

1.	a	**9.**	c
2.	c	**10.**	b
3.	d	**11.**	d
4.	a	**12.**	a
5.	c	**13.**	d
6.	b	**14.**	b
7.	c	**15.**	d
8.	b		

True and False Statements

1.	True	**6.**	True
2.	True	**7.**	False
3.	False	**8.**	False
4.	False	**9.**	False
5.	True	**10.**	False

Chapter 11

Multiple Choice

1.	c	**9.**	b
2.	b	**10.**	c
3.	d	**11.**	a
4.	c	**12.**	b
5.	a	**13.**	a
6.	c	**14.**	b
7.	b	**15.**	c
8.	c		

True and False Statements

1.	False	**6.**	False
2.	True	**7.**	True
3.	True	**8.**	False
4.	False	**9.**	False
5.	True	**10.**	False

Chapter 12

Multiple Choice

1.	a	**6.**	b
2.	d	**7.**	a
3.	b	**8.**	a
4.	b	**9.**	b
5.	c	**10.**	c

11. a	**14.** d	**11.** a	**14.** j
12. b	**15.** b	**12.** b	**15.** g
13. c		**13.** e	

Matching Terms

1. f	**6.** l
2. d	**7.** n
3. m	**8.** o
4. k	**9.** c
5. i	**10.** h

True and False Statements

1. False
2. True
3. False
4. True
5. False